BICENTENNIAL
1807
WILEY
2007
BICENTENNIAL

THE WILEY BICENTENNIAL—KNOWLEDGE FOR GENERATIONS

*E*ach generation has its unique needs and aspirations. When Charles Wiley first opened his small printing shop in lower Manhattan in 1807, it was a generation of boundless potential searching for an identity. And we were there, helping to define a new American literary tradition. Over half a century later, in the midst of the Second Industrial Revolution, it was a generation focused on building the future. Once again, we were there, supplying the critical scientific, technical, and engineering knowledge that helped frame the world. Throughout the 20th Century, and into the new millennium, nations began to reach out beyond their own borders and a new international community was born. Wiley was there, expanding its operations around the world to enable a global exchange of ideas, opinions, and know-how.

For 200 years, Wiley has been an integral part of each generation's journey, enabling the flow of information and understanding necessary to meet their needs and fulfill their aspirations. Today, bold new technologies are changing the way we live and learn. Wiley will be there, providing you the must-have knowledge you need to imagine new worlds, new possibilities, and new opportunities.

Generations come and go, but you can always count on Wiley to provide you the knowledge you need, when and where you need it!

WILLIAM J. PESCE
PRESIDENT AND CHIEF EXECUTIVE OFFICER

PETER BOOTH WILEY
CHAIRMAN OF THE BOARD

A Primer on Organizational Behavior

Seventh Edition

JAMES L. BOWDITCH

University of Maine

ANTHONY F. BUONO

Bentley College

MARCUS M. STEWART

Bentley College

John Wiley & Sons, Inc.

Vice President and Executive Publisher	*Donald Fowley*
Acquisitions Editor	*Kimberly Mortimer*
Production Services Manager	*Dorothy Sinclair*
Production Editor	*Janet Foxman*
Marketing Manager	*Amy Scholz*
Creative Director	*Harry Nolan*
Designer	*Kevin Murphy*
Editorial Assistant	*Carissa Marker*
Senior Media Editor	*Allison Morris*
Production Services	*Dennis Free/Aptara, Inc.*
Cover Design	*David Levy*
Cover Photo	© *Corbis Digital Stock*
Bicentennial Logo Design	*Richard J. Pacifico*

This book was set in 10/12 New Caledonia and printed and bound by Courier/Westford.

This book is printed on acid free paper. ∞

To order books or for customer service, please call 1-800-CALL WILEY (225-5945).

Library of Congress Cataloging-in-Publication Data:

Bowditch, James L.
   A primer on organizational behavior / James L. Bowditch, Anthony F. Buono,
Marcus M. Stewart.—7th ed.
     p. cm.
   Includes index.
   ISBN 978-0-470-08695-7 (pbk.)
   1. Organizational behavior.   I. Buono, Anthony F.   II. Stewart, Marcus Maharg.   III. Title.
  HD58.7.B69 2008
  658.4—dc22   2007035570

Printed in the United States of America

10 9 8 7 6 5 4 3 2 1

Preface

We are delighted to welcome a new co-author to the seventh edition of the *Primer*—Marcus M. Stewart, one of our colleagues at Bentley. Marcus brings a wealth of insight into the micro-OB area, including expertise on work teams, leadership and organizational change, diversity, career management, and social justice. The basic objectives for this edition—which is now based on four decades of classroom experience with undergraduate, graduate, and executive education classes—however, have essentially remained constant since the first edition. First, to introduce the reader to the key concepts that provide the basis for understanding the field of organizational behavior (OB). Second, to give students a general survey of a "typical" OB course, especially the central facets of micro (motivation, perception, communication, group dynamics, leadership) and macro (organizational structure, culture, and environment) OB and their application in contemporary organizations. Third, to provide sufficient grounding in the field to enable students to read the OB literature in such practitioner journals and scholarly publications as the *Harvard Business Review, Sloan Management Review,* and the *Academy of Management Journal.*

A *Primer on Organizational Behavior* began its life as a series of chapter drafts that our students read during the first few weeks of our course. This initial reading was supplemented by brief lectures, discussions, experiential exercises, case analyses, research- and application-oriented articles, and so forth. We found that not only did our students seem to benefit from this approach, but they preferred a variety of materials for the course instead of one text that attempted to do everything. Accordingly, we set about the task of writing this primer to give classroom instructors greater flexibility in creating the type of course that they want to teach. This book covers the content of OB in a thoughtful, research-based manner—in a way that does not "talk down" to students. It can be used in conjunction with a reader, sets of journal articles, cases, exercises, experiential texts, or fieldwork to customize the course. Additionally, we found that students who came into our advanced elective courses—from human resource management and industrial psychology to organization development—without the usual background in organizational behavior quickly developed an understanding of OB concepts after reading the volume. Thus, the text also provides a useful overview for those individuals who need the background for related coursework or who have been away from the field, as well as a quick introduction for those in an organizational behavior course or management workshop. Since we have successfully used the first six editions at both the undergraduate and graduate levels, instructors can tailor their courses by selecting appropriate supporting materials.

The book has some features that are unique to many OB texts. First, since many instructors rely heavily on research in the field to make the concepts and data understandable, we decided that an integrated appendix covering research methods, how to interpret common statistics, and how to read a research-oriented journal article would be useful. This material is intended to provide an initial foundation for those interested in pursuing a research-based course. Second, because of the growing interest among both faculty and students toward the usefulness and utility of OB research and theory, we have incorporated organizational applications—diagnostic techniques, participative management approaches, and work-related innovations—throughout the book. In addition, the final chapter focuses on organizational development and managing organizational change. We also have attempted to include sufficient references to "classical" works as well as more recent articles, texts, and research findings as a guide for those individuals interested in further exploration of the field.

In addition to a general updating throughout the volume, the seventh edition places continued attention on diversity and information technology and how they are continuing to reshape organizations and the management practices within them. In-depth discussions have been added on early management thought, workplace incivility, social justice, conformity in groups, virtual teams, team conflict, leader-member relations, and organizational change. This edition also includes further assessment of emotional intelligence, knowledge management, social identity theory, and executive coaching. Building on the text's last revision on the evolution of organizational forms, the chapter on organizational structure and design places additional emphasis on network-based organizations and inter-organizational arrangements.

Our careers have continued to evolve since the last edition was published. Jim is now living in Maine and teaching in the University of Maine system. Tony is still at Bentley, with a joint appointment as Professor of Management and Sociology, and Coordinator of the Bentley Alliance for Ethics and Social Responsibility. Marcus moved back to the Boston area, leaving the University of Georgia and joining the Bentley faculty in the management department. Our friends and colleagues continue to provide a source of inspiration and knowledge for our writings. Many of our colleagues (especially at Bentley College) have directly or indirectly influenced our thinking in writing and revising this book—including Aaron Nurick, Judith Kamm, Joseph Weiss, Joseph Byrnes, Susan Adams, Vicki LaFarge, Duncan Spelman, Alan Hoffman, Marcy Crary, Jeffrey Shuman, Diane Kellogg, Iris Berdrow, Earl Avery, Charlene O'Brien, Amy Kenworthy-U'Ren (Bond University), Thomas Slaughter (Bloomfield College), and Flemming Poulfelt (Copenhagen Business School). Michael Hoffman, Robert Frederick, and their colleagues at the Center for Business Ethics have continued to be extremely helpful in our analysis of ethical considerations in the field. Kenneth Kerber continues to stimulate our thinking about the dynamics of organizational change. We are also very grateful to Bentley College for the ongoing support the institution has provided for over twenty-five years.

This edition is, once again, dedicated to Jim and Tony's wives, Felicity and Mary Alice, and Marcus's parents, Leslie Jr. and Lane Stewart, and his grandmother Hazel Stewart. They continued to be very supportive and understanding through the many hours we spent locked away reading, talking about, e-mailing, and ultimately revising this book. Finally, we would like to thank the faculty and students who used the sixth edition and provided many comments, suggestions, and complaints that were quite useful in creating what we hope continues to be an interesting and readable text.

James L. Bowditch

Anthony F. Buono

Marcus M. Stewart

Contents

CHAPTER ONE

Management and Organizational Behavior

M anagement education and development have traditionally emphasized what might be termed the *content* of managerial work. Indeed, much of management education today continues to focus on upgrading the technical competence of managers and managers-to-be in such areas as accounting, finance, marketing, operations, and information technology–related services. This focus on content has been referred to as the *what* of a manager's job, encompassing such concerns as: developing appropriate procedures for auditing and inventory control; creating new marketing programs; establishing management information systems, just-in-time inventory, and production systems; enhancing global supply chain efficiencies; and other specific aspects of managerial work.[1]

While the technical aspects of management are, of course, quite important for the successful functioning of an organization, understanding the *process* of management or the *how* of a manager's job is also a critical component of management education. Within this process view of management, attention is often given to the roles, behaviors, and skills that are necessary for effective managerial performance. Some of these behavioral skills are communicating with peers, subordinates, and bosses; obtaining and sharing information; running meetings; allocating resources to different groups; and handling conflict within or between teams.[2] This understanding of management processes, often referred to as *organizational behavior* (OB), thus extends managerial education to the study of people, groups, and their interactions in organizations.

Recent analyses of our changing business environment reflect the importance of this dimension of management, and corporations are demanding a much broader range of skills and competencies from their business professionals. As summarized in Table 1-1, while technical expertise in one's area of concentration (e.g., accounting, finance, marketing, operations) is a critical dimension of marketability, companies are interested in applicants with a broader, more complex skill set. Thus, rather than focus solely on perfecting relatively narrow technical capabilities, it is also important for business students to develop broader problem-solving, decision-making, communicative, and interpersonal competencies.

TABLE 1-1 Model of the Business Professional for the 21st Century

- Strong functional expertise: Technical proficiency and cross-functional awareness
- Ability to work in an unstructured, team environment
- Interpersonal competency and diversity-related skills
- Excellent negotiating and influencing skills
- Outstanding information technology skills: PC/computer, Internet, and intranet
- Global/transnational perspective
- Exceptional verbal and written communication skills
- Ethical awareness and legal sensibilities
- Critical thinking and analysis capabilities
- Change agent skills and leadership capabilities

LEARNING ABOUT ORGANIZATIONAL BEHAVIOR

Organizational behavior has, thus, become an increasingly important component of management education, focusing on what people actually do in the workplace. Within this context, there are two different levels of learning: a *cognitive understanding* of behavior in different contexts and an *ability to undertake* those activities. This distinction has led to two different approaches to teaching OB.[3] The traditional approach attempts to develop the student's command of conceptual maps and theoretical frameworks, which facilitates an understanding of human behavior in organizations. The essence of this orientation is to encourage an understanding of essential concepts in the field, which then can be applied to different organizational situations. An alternative approach—often referred to as the *experiential orientation*—takes more of an emergent view of the learning process. Proponents of this method argue that schools of management will be able to significantly influence management practice only when they are capable of developing the various "skills" that are associated with the actual job of managing.[4] Thus, learning by experience, which involves practicing a skill (such as decision making under uncertainty) in a simulated situation (such as the classroom), is thought to improve an individual's ability to perform on the job. Within this context, many OB instructors attempt to develop such key management skills as working in teams, effective listening, problem solving, managing conflict, delegating tasks, giving directions, and motivating and leading others.[5]

Although there are differences of opinion as to which of these approaches is indeed the most effective, it seems that a combination of cognitive learning and skill development is the key to management education. This book provides the foundation for a *cognitive understanding* of OB. Combined with an experience-based text and/or book of cases or readings in OB and management, the book is intended to be part of an *integrative approach* to learning about behavior in organizations.

Within this context, the book has three basic objectives: First, to introduce the terms, concepts, and research that are necessary for a fuller understanding of OB and management; second, to give students an overview of a typical OB course, which encompasses concepts from psychology, sociology, and political science among other disciplines; and third, to provide sufficient background in OB to enable students to read the literature in such trade journals and scholarly publications as the *Harvard Business*

Review, Sloan Management Review, and the *Academy of Management Journal.* To facilitate this goal, an integrated set of research-based appendixes, including one on how to read a research-oriented journal article, is included at the end of the book.

In writing this text, care was taken to provide a broad overview of topics in the field. There are, however, two things to keep in mind as you go through this book or any set of readings in OB. First, the field is expanding and changing. A book revised just a few years ago might have 25 percent new material in its latest edition. While there are some research findings that have been confirmed over time, other findings may have been modified or qualified. In many cases, new ground may have been broken, which can lead to further understanding about a particular problem. Second, it is apparent that no one approach to management is effective under all circumstances. You will find, for example, that in some situations a participative leadership style will tend to be more effective than a more directive approach. In other situations, a different style will be more productive. The same can be said for organizational structure, approaches to motivating people, and other key OB topics. One must *not* conclude, however, that because certain approaches may be more effective under different circumstances, it doesn't matter *what* approach is used. Rather, a *diagnostic orientation* is called for, being careful to specify when and under what conditions one approach might be more effective than another.

ETHICS AND ORGANIZATIONAL BEHAVIOR

Although our society has placed increased emphasis on ethics in organizational life, recent events have, once again, shaken our faith in the business system. It doesn't seem all that long ago when the corporate culprits were Drexel Burnham Lambert, Salomon Brothers, and Lincoln Savings and Loan. More recently, Enron, World-Com, Tyco, Arthur Andersen—the list seemingly goes on and on—have quickly gone from highly admired corporations to infamy. Ivan Boesky and Michael Milken have been replaced by Jeffrey Skilling, Ken Lay, Dennis Kozlowski, and Bernie Ebbers as the latest examples of corporate greed, mismanagement, and deception. On the surface, while it appears that questionable deal making and even more questionable accounting practices lie at the heart of many of our current problems, the problems run much deeper,[6] reflecting concerns about our basic approach to organizational life.

Although you may not initially think about it as you read through this book, one of the most difficult issues in OB deals with questions of organizational ethics. Topics such as motivation, trust in relationships, the psychological contract, influence and persuasion, goal setting, and behavior modification all have strong ethical content. The application of OB concepts in such managerial practices as management by objectives (MBO), performance reviews, assessment centers, and reward and control systems, as well as issues raised by organization design, leadership, power, and organizational politics are also influenced by ethical concerns.[7] The growing sociodemographic diversity in the workplace continues to raise our awareness about discrimination and employee rights, sexual harassment, and the use of psychological examinations. In fact, a study of the "tough choices" managers face in their daily job experiences found that the most frequently cited sources of ethical concern fell in the realm of managing their firms human resources: (1) performance evaluation and resultant hiring, firing, promotion, and demotion decisions; (2) designing and administering personnel policies and systems (e.g., disability policies, reward systems); and (3) managing relationships on the job.[8] Such studies underscore that ethical dilemmas in business are an intricate part of, not separate from, the routine practices of management.

Enron's Peer Review Committee (PRC) provides a good illustration of such "tough choices" in action. The PRC process—referred to internally as the firm's practice of "rank and yank"—ranked all employees on a scale of 1 to 5 every six months. The bottom 15 percent was automatically "redeployed"—in essence, they were given a few weeks to find another job within the company or be let go. The PRC process, combined with a very generous bonus system, created a strong incentive for Enron employees to show high-level performance, even if that meant inflating the value of the contracts they were securing. Supported by a culture that suppressed honesty and openness, the result was a company destined to implode amidst financial irregularities, precipitating Chapter 11 bankruptcy, mass layoffs, and shattered pensions and investments. While some employees jokingly referred to Enron as the "Crooked E," supposedly because of its slanted-E logo, it appears that the sentiment reflected the more nefarious aspects of the company's destructive culture.[9]

Business ethics focuses on management's systematic, value-oriented assessment of the moral significance of personal and organizational actions and their consequences for others and the larger society. Yet, while ethics are based on values, ethics and values are not the same thing.[10] Business ethics constitute a way of translating values into appropriate behaviors that respond to the realities of daily life. In practice, however, many of us have difficulties in determining what actually constitutes ethical and un-ethical behavior. In many instances, the ethical issues we are faced with are not simply about choosing between right and wrong—we must often choose between two things that appear "right."[11] There also seems to be an ethical theory to justify virtually every form of behavior—from teleological ethics that examine the consequences of an act (both from self-interest and public-interest perspectives) to deontological ethics that look at the extent to which a behavior conforms to certain universally accepted guiding principles.[12]

Ethical decisions in organizations are a function of individual and organizational factors.[13] In general, when people need to resolve ethical concerns in their daily lives, they draw on their own values and principles of right or wrong. While we would expect a similar dynamic to take place in an organization, people do not exist in a vacuum. As studies have found, a company's culture and values often have a greater influence on work-related decisions than the personal values of its employees.[14] Many managers approach business problems as if they were amoral in nature. While they are not overtly immoral, many managers lack sufficient ethical perception or awareness; as a result they are not as sensitive to the reality that their day-to-day business decisions may have deleterious effects on others.[15]

On an individual level, as a way of thinking through these issues in an applied framework, the Center for Business Ethics at Bentley College has formulated six simple questions about a behavior or act for the "practical philosopher" that are used in its corporate training programs:

1. **Is it right?** (based on the deontological theory of moral rights)
2. **Is it fair?** (based on the deontological theory of justice)

3. **Who gets hurt?** (based on the utilitarian notion of the greatest good for the greatest number of people)
4. **Would you be comfortable if the details of your decision were reported on the front page of your local newspaper?** (based on the universalist principle of disclosure)
5. **What would you tell your child to do?** (based on the deontological principle of reversibility)
6. **How does it smell?** (based on the "gut principle," that using ethical theory or not, we usually have a sense of whether something feels "good")

These questions are not meant to suggest that a naive eclecticism of different ethical theories will produce "good" decisions. Rather, they underscore a process of ethical thought that can be applied to business decision making. An underlying goal is to develop the ability to recognize ethical issues in organizational life, moving away from the type of "moral blindness" that typifies many business decisions.[16]

While these guidelines can promote ethical decision making at the individual level, it is important to support this process at the organizational level. An organizational culture (see Chapter 10) that stresses the importance of ethical values and a comprehensive ethics program that guides and reinforces the decision-making process are also crucial. Training programs, codes of conduct, ethics officers and related high-level personnel who oversee compliance programs, and creation of systems to monitor, audit, and report misconduct are all part of an effective approach to ensuring ethical decisions and behavior.

As you read through this book, think about the ethical issues posed by the different topics. A fine line often exists between motivation and manipulation, participation and deception, goal setting and coercion, and other central facets of organizational life. While these six questions will not automatically help you resolve such concerns, they can assist you in thinking through your decisions in a responsible and thoughtful manner.

A HISTORICAL FRAMEWORK FOR THE STUDY OF MANAGEMENT AND OB

Although many of the great early civilizations—Egypt, China, India, the Middle East, and Peru, for example—had sophisticated management systems, the systematic study of organizations and their management did not occur until the Industrial Revolution had swept through Europe and the United States. Yet, even within this relatively short time span, students often dismiss the thinking and contributions of early management scholars as being either naive or passé. Today's management theory, however, is part of a logical evolution in management thought.

The development of modern management thought and practice can be analyzed by examining the evolution of society as it has passed from an agrarian through an industrial to a postindustrial structure. The framework that will guide this discussion is presented in Figure 1-1.[17] The rationale underlying this historical perspective emerges from an area of study within sociology referred to as the *sociology of knowledge*. This field of study holds that various theories and explanations of the world are in some

Period	Pre-1800s	1800s	1800–1930	1930–1960	1960s	1970–2010
Nature of society	**Agrarian**		**Industrial**			**Postindustrial**
Locus of work	Farm/home		Factory			Office Cyberspace
Nature of work	Physical: agriculture/crafts		Physical: manufacturing		Social: services	Abstract: computer mediated
Key resource	Land		Machinery			Knowledge
Management and organization theory	**Prescientific**		**Classical** Administrative Theory; Scientific Management; Structuralists	**Neoclassical** Human relations; Behavioral	**Modern** Management Science	Systems Theory; Contingency Theory; Organizational Behavior
Assumptions about human nature		Economic person		Social person	Self-actualizing person	Complex person
Focus of managerial control		Patterns of physical movement and precise ways of performing work		Patterns of social interaction		Patterns of attention; Patterns of connectivity
Role of management	Control employee behavior			Maintain employee social systems	Facilitate employee development	Ensure organization-wide integration; Facilitate inter-organizational collaboration

Figure 1-1 The Evolution of Management Theory

measure social products that are influenced by wider cultural, economic, political, and technological forces. By examining the fundamental transitions that have revolutionized our society, changing it from a rural culture based on agriculture and the family as the basic production unit, to a culture based on technology, industry, and urban settings, we can further understand the development of management theory over time.

Early Management

Problems of administration were of great interest to early societies, and they developed sophisticated systems to handle governmental affairs, religious institutions, and trade and commcerce.[18] What is often viewed as the first management text—*The Duties of the Vizer*—was written in the early sixteenth century B.C. as part of an effort to reform and restore the Egyptian system of central administration. Clear procedures were outlined for appointing and managing scribes, royal clerks, secretaries, and key officials such as foremen and provincial governors. The resultant management systems were highly authoritarian, top-down, and minutely organized. Yet since these systems of authority were based on long-standing institutions that were perceived as legitimate by the populations of these societies, most individuals obeyed the ruling elite in accordance with *traditional* customs.[19]

At the end of the Dark Ages, as commerce began to flourish in the Mediterranean region, many of the managerial tools that we continue to use today began to be developed.[20] The needs of mercantile businessmen in Italy during the late 1400s, for example, led to the creation of double-entry bookkeeping as a means of keeping records on business transactions. Since authority was still largely viewed as resting with traditional institutions and the individuals associated with those institutions, however, there was little attempt to actually formulate theories of management. Moreover, considering that the labor force was largely composed of farmers and craftsmen, and production was part of the social life within the family, there was little real need for specific emphasis on management practices.

As members of society begin to question the existing social order, traditional means of authority are slowly undermined and eventually give way to new authority structures. Thus, rather than tradition being the dominant force that legitimized systems of authority, a *rational-legal* form of legitimation emerged. This set of beliefs held that those in power were granted their authority by general sets of rules created as part of organized hierarchies.[21] In other words, instead of tradition being the dominant reason that people listened to or obeyed others, some individuals have power over others based on the position or role they hold in an organization. Accession to this role is based on widely known and agreed-upon rules and policies, forming a "rational" and "legal" basis for authority.

This gradual shift in the way in which authority is legitimated in society thus laid the foundation for our modern form of capitalism. During the 1700s, the United States began to focus more explicitly on economics and profitability. During the 1800s, technological improvements started to minimize the need for agricultural labor (e.g., the cotton gin) and created the basis for a continuous system of manufacturing (e.g., the concept of interchangeable parts). These changes set the stage for the examination of management practices and ways to improve those activities.

Classical Management

Toward the end of the nineteenth century and into the beginning of the twentieth, the social, economic, political, and technological environment created the necessary conditions for the systematic assessment of management. The Industrial Revolution, initiated by the inventions and technological improvements of the eighteenth century, led to changes not only in the workplace, but in the very nature of our society as well. Conceptually, such industrialization occurs through two basic stages: (1) the development of an industrial infrastructure and (2) the creation of a capital goods sector. Essentially, an *industrial infrastructure* consists of such factors as:[22]

- Nationwide systems of transportation (initially canals and railroads)
- Sources of relatively cheap power (coal and oil)
- Technological innovations (such as the cotton gin and the steam engine)
- Modern communication systems (the telegraph)
- Networks of financial institutions (banks, stock exchange, national currency)
- Preparation of the labor force (through education and technical training)

This infrastructure provides the basis for the development of a *capital goods sector,* which consists of the machinery and plants that allow the mass production of consumer goods and services.

The process of industrialization changed the nature of work from farming and crafts to more complex forms of manufacturing and working with machines. It also led to the urbanization of our society as the industrial process transferred the locus of work from the farm and the rural home to the factory and the city. As plants and factories were built in centralized locations (close to transportation systems), people began to migrate from rural areas to where the "new" jobs were located. Immigrants created urban enclaves in areas near the factories as well. As a result, the business firms and a complex division of labor that evolved from this transition further prompted efforts to seriously study these new forms of organization and their management.

The *Classical* school of management was influenced by the wider social, economic, and technological forces that brought about the transition from an agrarian to an industrial society. The dominant set of assumptions about human nature characterized people as rational, economic beings who would act to maximize their own self-interests. Correspondingly, the emerging focus on management dealt with how these new forms of industrial organization could be structured, how work could be delegated and coordinated, and how people within these organizational structures could be motivated.

Administrative Theory

One of the major orientations within the Classical school is referred to as *Administrative Theory* or the *Universal Principles* school of management. Based on deductive reasoning, this group examined certain forms of organization, such as the church and the military, and concluded that there were basic dimensions of organizational structure and characteristics of management that were common to *all* organizations.

Perhaps the most well-known theorist of this tradition is Henri Fayol, a French industrialist who identified five basic functions of management: planning, organizing, commanding, coordinating, and controlling.[23] Based on these functions, Fayol described how management *should* be carried out in fourteen management principles, which included:

- *Division of work:* Specialization of tasks and control of the number of people under each manager improves effectiveness and efficiency.
- *Authority and responsibility:* The person in authority has the right to give orders and the power to obtain obedience; responsibility emerges directly from authority.
- *Unity of command:* No one should have more than one boss.
- *Remuneration:* Pay should be fair and satisfactory to the employer and employee; no one should be under- or over-rewarded.
- *Esprit de corps:* Morale and good feelings about the organization are enhanced by effective face-to-face communication and group cohesiveness.

Over time, other Universalist theorists concentrated on five basic facets of organization, which were distilled from Fayol's fourteen principles:

- *Structure:* an organization's formal design, as represented by an organization chart
- *Division of labor:* dividing work into components that are capable of being done by individuals or groups
- *Coordination:* integrating the various parts of the organization in order to reach organizational goals and objectives
- *Scalar relationships:* creating a hierarchical chain of command and providing for coordination
- *Functional principle:* differentiating work according to the various functional areas of the organization such as production, marketing, and finance

In conclusion, much of our knowledge about and interest in organizational structure came from the Administrative Theory school. Its focus was on the formal structure of organizations, and their top and middle management. The orientation, however, was highly authoritarian, with one best way to approach all organizational and managerial problems. Employees were basically viewed as extensions of the organization's structure and machinery.

Scientific Management

In contrast to the emphasis on principles of organization, the *Scientific Management* school focused on the measurement and structure of work itself, its classification, quantification, and rationalization.[24] Frederick Taylor, a production expert and industrial consultant, focused on creating the most effective way to carry out work tasks. Since people were viewed as rational, economic beings, it was reasoned that they would act on their own interests (and subsequently the organization's) if they understood "correct" work procedures and were rewarded for following them.

The underlying objectives of Taylor's Scientific Management are the subject of considerable debate. Taylor is frequently criticized as someone who ignored the human element, a symbol of "cruel management power" who treated workers as if they were little more than extensions of the tools and machines they utilized.[25] Others, however, argue that it is important to put his work in the context of typical labor-management practices of the time and the relatively unskilled nature of the labor force.[26] As practiced by Taylor and his followers, Scientific Management focused on improving and standardizing existing work procedures, while concurrently attempting to conserve resources. His emphasis was that the real way to increase output was to "work smarter," not necessarily harder. By understanding the nature of jobs—to be deduced from study and analysis—the process of work could be made more effective. He did, however, appear to have the needs of the individual worker at heart. In fact, he would refuse to take a factory as a client unless the owners agreed to first substantially raise wages, sometimes even tripling them.[27]

The four basic tenets of Taylor's Scientific Management are:

1. Develop the one best way to do each job.
2. Select the best individual for the position.
3. Ensure that work is carried out in prescribed fashion through training and by increasing wages for those workers who followed correct procedures.
4. Divide work efforts among employees so that activities such as planning, organizing, and controlling are the prime responsibilities of managers rather than individual workers.

Although Taylor felt strongly that management rather than workers should choose the methods of carrying out and organizing work tasks, these four tenets were qualified by an *exception principle.* Once output standards and routine work procedures were defined (through the use of the scientific method and careful measurement), management should give its attention only to those situations where standards or procedures fell outside those norms.

In numerous instances, the gains and profits that emerged from his system were impressive; in others, such as the attempt to apply these principles to reform naval manufacturing, his efforts were deemed a failure. In these latter situations, the lack of success has been attributed to basic human reactions—internal political battles, resistance to shifts in power, and a lack of incentives to become more efficient—rather than a rejection of Taylor's principles per se.[28]

Other developments from the Scientific Management tradition include Frank and Lillian Gilbreth's *time and motion studies.*[29] Based on the principles of economy of motion, the Gilbreths analytic approach measured body motions to discover the most efficient way to carry out a particular task. Henry Gantt, who like Taylor was interested in production efficiency, was another contributor to this school. Gantt focused on devising remuneration procedures that would provide fair pay for correctly doing a task and a bonus for completing it in a timely fashion.[30] His main contribution is a production scheduling aid referred to as the *Gantt chart,* a way of plotting work in progress against the calendar, which remains the basis for modern scheduling techniques.

Structuralist School

In contrast to the deductive approach taken by the Universalists, the *Structuralist* school used an inductive approach in its study of organizations. Rather than creating a conceptual model of organizational structure and then generalizing to all organizations, members of this school examined many different organizations to empirically determine the common structural elements that characterized how organizations actually operate.

One of the main founders of the Structuralist approach was Max Weber, a German sociologist, who empirically discovered the basic factors that characterized an ideal organization, or what he referred to as a *bureaucracy*.[31]

- Rules and procedures control organizational functions.
- A high degree of differentiation exists among organizational functions.
- The organization of offices is hierarchically determined; no subunit is allowed to "drift," and each subunit reports directly to one higher-level office.
- An emphasis is placed on prescribed rules that regulate behavior.
- Ownership and administration of an organization are separate—in essence, the president does not own the company.
- An administrator must not be able to control positions or the "trappings" of an office.
- All administrative acts are recorded in writing.

Although Weber acknowledged that not all organizations were pure bureaucracies, it is clear that he thought bureaucracies were preferable to other forms of organization. Obviously, this view is in sharp contrast to today's stereotypes about the inefficiencies of any form of bureaucratic organization. To Weber, bureaucracy was one of the most characteristic and ubiquitous forms of administration. It was efficient, it consisted of needed specialists and experts, and, since it dealt with people on an impersonal basis, it ensured that rules would be consistently applied in all situations.

Although there were differences in the manner in which the Universalists and the Structuralists created their models of organization, there are many aspects common to both. Overall, Classical theory was a significant step forward in our attempt to create a theory of organization and management. Today, while it is generally recognized that this orientation does not include important aspects of human behavior and larger environmental influences, the understanding of formal functions and structures that it provides is still an important part of our understanding of the visible and tangible aspects of organizations.[32] It should be noted, however, as Figure 1-1 indicates, given the transition that society had undergone and the prevalent assumptions about human nature, this theory reflected the salient concerns of the period. Emphasis was placed on organizational structures and processes that could closely monitor and control physical labor and precise ways of performing work. Thus, while Classical management theory provides relevant insights into the nature of organization, the value of the theory is limited by its rather narrow focus on the formal anatomy of the firm.

Neoclassical Management and Organization Theory

As early as the 1920s, a number of social critics began to point out the potentially harmful effects of trying to standardize people as well as jobs. Although many of the basic tenets of Classical management theory (e.g., formal structure, division of labor) were *not* directly challenged, criticism was focused on those individual managers and theorists who appeared to treat employees as little more than mere appendages to machines.[33] In fact, when Taylor proposed his theory of Scientific Management, his work was often met with antagonism and hostility. Taylor defended his principles on the basis of a "mental revolution" that would take place in the attitudes of management and labor. In essence, Taylor felt that both sides would recognize the need for cooperation and the importance of scientific investigation rather than individual judgment as the basis for structuring work assignments.[34] Critics, however, argued that while management might seek to standardize skills and methods, it could not expect perfectly standard, emotionless behavior from its employees.

Studies during this period also began to draw attention to the possibility that co-workers could exert a greater influence on work behavior than the economic incentives offered by management. The recognition that workers had social needs led to a new set of assumptions about human nature. Rather than viewing people solely as rational, economic creatures, social considerations were now seen as the prime motivator of behavior and work performance. Since the increasing mechanization of work was stripping jobs of their intrinsic value, people would seek out meaning in their work through social relationships on the job. Management, it was argued, must therefore help people to satisfy these natural desires. Although these arguments may appear to be somewhat moralistic, they were tied to prescriptions for organizational effectiveness and efficiency. If managers did not respond to these socially oriented needs with greater consideration and warmth, lagging work performance and resistance to authority were viewed as likely outcomes.

Thus, in an attempt to compensate for the neglect of human interaction in the Classical school, *Neoclassical* theory introduced the behavioral sciences into management thought. The underlying rationale was that since management involves getting things done with and through people, the study of management must be centered on understanding interpersonal relations. Within this context, the Neoclassical school of thought can be viewed as a critique of the Classical doctrine:[35]

- Each organization should have a defined *structure;* however, human behavior can disrupt the most carefully planned organizational activities. While the formal structure may represent how things are supposed to occur, the informal organization that emerges in response to people's social needs dictates how things are actually done.

- Although a *division of labor* might make sense from the organization's standpoint, some of the unintended outcomes for workers are feelings of isolation and anonymity due to insignificant jobs.

- While the *scalar and functional principles* might be theoretically valid, they deteriorate in practice due to the way in which these processes are carried out (e.g., insufficient delegation, overlapping authority).
- Finally, a manager's *span of control* is a function of human factors and cannot be reduced to a precise, universally applicable ratio.

There are two main sources of Neoclassical theory: (1) the sociologists and social psychologists who were concerned with interaction and relations within groups, often referred to as the Human Relations school, and (2) the psychologists who focused on individual behavior, or the Behavioral school.

Human Relations School

The basic tenets of the *Human Relations* school (approximately 1930–1950) emerged from a series of studies during the mid-1920s and early 1930s known as the *Hawthorne Experiments.* Emerging from Classical theory, these experiments were conducted in Western Electric's Hawthorne plant to assess the effect of working conditions (e.g., lighting, rest periods, length of the work day) on productivity.[36] Initially, a group of women were selected for the experiments and placed in a specially developed room where their behavior was carefully monitored as their working conditions were altered.

Much to the surprise of the researchers, they found that regardless of what they did to the working conditions—whether for better or worse—the group's productivity (i.e., output per worker) increased. Since the conditions under which these individuals accomplished their tasks did not explain the change in productivity, the researchers were forced to look at other factors. One observation was that members of the work group had developed high morale during the experiments that seemed to positively influence their job performance. Further analysis revealed three basic underlying factors that influenced the group's morale:

- The workers perceived themselves as "special" and important to management because they were singled out for this research role.
- The women developed good interpersonal relationships with each other and their supervisor because they had considerable autonomy to decide their own division of work and their own work pace.
- The social contact and easy relations that emerged in the group created a generally pleasant work environment.

Based on these preliminary findings, the researchers hypothesized that the nature of *social relations* among members of a work group, and between employees and their supervisor, was an influential motivator of work performance. In an effort to test this hypothesis, another group of studies was conducted in which three small groups of men who worked on switchboard equipment were examined to assess the relative effects of a complex wage-incentive plan. The researchers found that production norms—those standards that the group created for itself—were more powerful determinants of production than wage incentives. The workers established an implied norm of a "fair day's work," and those who overproduced ("rate busters") or underproduced ("chiselers") were brought into line by their peers. These studies confirmed the importance of the work group and pointed to the existence of an *informal organization* within a firm's formal structure.

The Hawthorne Studies marked a significant turning point in the evolution of management theory because they introduced a new way of thinking about people in organizations. It is important to point out, however, that the Hawthorne Studies and the Human Relations school were not without their critics. A number of questions concerning research methodology and the way in which the experiment's outcomes were interpreted surfaced early on and linger to this day. Even the basic rationale and intent of the experiments have been viewed with a degree of skepticism.[37] Such criticism, however, became submerged in the overwhelming support that was given to the Human Relations school. The emerging set of beliefs held that management could not treat people as if they were mere extensions of an organization's structure and machinery and became the initial underpinning for the field of organizational behavior.[38]

Behavioral School

Influenced by the Human Relations school, a growing number of theorists began to shift their attention to the individual and the nature of work itself.[39] Beginning with the Neoclassical assumption that work had lost its meaning through the mechanization accompanying the Industrial Revolution, these theorists argued that employees had become alienated from their work because their jobs prevented them from fully using their skills and capabilities. While they agreed that people had needs for acceptance, status, and recognition, they went beyond the human relations perspective and proposed that workers also wanted to gain personal satisfaction from their jobs by developing their abilities (and themselves) in the accomplishment of meaningful work.

The basic assumptions underlying human behavior were now perceived to be oriented to personal growth, accomplishment, and inner development. If managers were to become truly effective, it was argued, they must go beyond simply providing fair pay and treatment and attempt to make organizational members feel important. *In the interest* of effective and efficient organizational performance, managers should create jobs and organizational structures that allowed people an opportunity to develop their abilities and to experience personal growth.

This perspective is referred to as the *Behavioral* school. It was developed during the early 1950s and was based on the work of such theorists as Abraham Maslow, Douglas McGregor, Rensis Likert, Chris Argyris, Frederick Herzberg, and David McClelland. The contributions of these individuals will be discussed throughout this book. There has been a continual development of the behavioral perspective and it remains the basis of much management and supervisory education today. It can be viewed as a bridge between traditional Neoclassical theory and many of our contemporary analyses of management.

In summary, the Neoclassical perspective argues that there is a dimension of organizational reality that is not contained in the formal, structural orientation of the classical school—the behavior of groups and individuals within the organization. Emphasis shifted away from controlling patterns of precise physical movement toward patterns of social interaction, and managers were encouraged to develop supportive social systems and facilitate the personal development of their employees. The insights of the Neoclassical doctrine thus added to our understanding of the complexity of organizations. It has been criticized, however, for not integrating the varied facets of human behavior that occur in organizations and, like the Classical school, for being shortsighted and incomplete.[40] Moreover, while the Neoclassical school began to realize that organizations were affected by a wider range of factors than previously thought, its view of relevant environmental forces is quite narrow by today's standards.

Modern Management and Organization Theory

Contemporary or *modern management* and *organization theory* is different from both the Classical and Neoclassical schools in that it emphasizes conceptualization and analysis, relies heavily on empirical research, and, perhaps most important, attempts to integrate the various elements that contribute to the whole organization.[41] The underlying theme is that organizations are systems composed of mutually interrelated and interdependent variables. This is not to suggest, however, that modern theory is a unified body of thought. Indeed, different theorists and researchers have their own particular emphases on what they consider to be the more influential components of organizational systems. A common thread is the attempt to analyze organizations in their totality. A second, emergent trend is greater attention to interorganizational patterns and processes (e.g., mergers, acquisitions, strategic alliances, global supply chains), because fewer and fewer organizations operate on their own as purely independent, stand-alone entities.

The development of modern management theory has also been influenced by a number of social, political, economic, and technological changes in the larger society. Many social observers, for example, argue that similar to the transitions society had undergone when it evolved from an agrarian to industrial structure, we have undergone another transition from a machine-based industrial society to an information-based *postindustrial society.* In contrast to the agriculturally and industrially based societies of earlier periods, postindustrial society is characterized by:[42]

- A basic shift in the orientation of the labor force from goods-producing to services-rendering and information-processing
- A gradual and steady rise in the influence of professional and technical occupations
- A growing influence and centrality of theoretical knowledge as the source of innovation and policy formulation for society
- An increased need for the planning and control of technology and its growth
- An emergence of mass integrated computer systems that create a new "intellectual technology"

We have undergone a transformation that has essentially rearranged our industrial and economic structure.[43] For example, although routine production-type jobs are still found in both traditional manufacturing and high-tech industries, this type of work is increasingly being robotized, automated, and exported to the point where it currently constitutes roughly 16 percent of the U.S. employment base. At the same time, while many people are employed in higher-level, analytic jobs—for instance, research scientists, design engineers, investment bankers, financial consultants—a significant proportion of the U.S. labor force has been relegated to lower-level, in-person service jobs. These latter jobs involve the direct delivery of person-to-person services, such as retail salespeople, hotel workers, waiters and waitresses, cashiers, home cleaning service staff, taxi drivers, and security guards. Combined with the general "flattening" and "delayering" of organizational structures and the strategic *outsourcing* of many business functions, these shifts have raised significant questions about our approaches to management and organization.

In addition to the rapid and often volatile technological changes envisioned by postindustrialism, organizations are also confronted with myriad pressures that include: (1) hyper-competition in the world arena; (2) shifting government regulation, deregulation, and reregulation; (3) increased labor-force and market diversity; and (4) changing cultural norms. Moreover, the growing influence of a number of activist *stakeholders*—public interest groups, environmentalists, local community advocacy groups, consumer advocates—further emphasizes the expanding demands and expectations that are being placed on business firms today.[44] Modern management theory acknowledges this reality and focuses on the organization within its environment and the extent of congruence or "fit" of organizational subsystems within that larger mosaic.

As we began to realize the complexity of organizational environments, many of our basic assumptions underlying human nature were challenged. The move toward increased empirical research also produced inconsistent support for many of our generalized concepts. The major impact of these trends has been the move toward more complicated models of human nature and the resultant implications for how to manage these individuals. A set of complex assumptions about people began to emerge:[45]

- Human needs fall into many categories and vary according to the individual's stage of development and total life situation.
- Since needs and motives interact to form complex motivation patterns, we must realize that for different people the same object or outcome (e.g., money) can vary in importance and fulfill quite different needs.
- People are capable of learning new motives through organizational experiences.
- The same individual may display different needs in different organizations or in different groups within the same organization.
- Employees can become productively involved with organizations on the basis of many different types of motives.
- Organizational members can respond to different kinds of managerial strategies, depending on their own motives and abilities, and the nature of the task.

As shown in Figure 1-1, this change in our underlying assumptions influenced a similar shift in the ways in which we conceive the focus and role of management. We are witnessing a transition from control to collaboration, from managing physical labor and actions within specific departments to guiding knowledge-based activities driven by advanced information technologies that cut across organizational boundaries—a transition that is challenging much of our thinking about organization and management.

The broad changes discussed previously have influenced a number of developments in management thought: (1) Management Science and Operations Research, which emphasizes the use of computers and mathematical models in organizational decision making; (2) Systems Theory, which looks at the organization and its environment in totality; (3) Contingency Theory, which takes a situational (rather than a one-best-way) view of organizational structure and managerial activity; and (4) the growing influence of organizational behavior (OB), which has, for many, become almost synonymous with management.

Management Science

The basic orientation of the *Management Science* school is to apply quantitative techniques to management and organizational problems, and to merge strategic concerns for planning and forecasting with administrative concerns for organizational effectiveness and goal accomplishment. Although there were some earlier developments in the use of statistical theory and quantitative methods in business, most people identify World War II as the starting point of Management Science. During this period, operations experts used quantitative models and computer simulations to calculate the speeds and patterns followed by enemy ships, and the time and fuel required by their aircraft to cover a given sector. Based on this information, Allied commanders were able to reduce the number of reconnaissance flights while increasing the effectiveness of their surveillance efforts.[46]

The late 1940s and 1950s saw the continued development of mathematical techniques—ranging from queuing theory and mathematical programming to game theory—that have become a basic part of operations management (OM).[47] During the 1960s, the field continued to expand, taking a systems view of the production process. This broadened perspective was further influenced over the following decades by the steadily increasing and widespread application of computers and software applications to operational problems.

The past few years have marked two other significant events in the evolution of Management Science and Operations Research. First, the changing competitive circumstances in our increasingly global business world have continued to pressure manufacturers to improve both their productivity and product quality. These pressures have led OM specialists to become more involved in the application of advanced technologies, such as flexible manufacturing systems and computer-integrated manufacturing, as well as new manufacturing philosophies. Management Science has expanded its focus to include such management practices as just-in-time (JIT) production, continuous improvement (CI), and Total Quality Management (TQM) systems. Second, given the evolution of society to postindustrialism, there has been a concomitant emphasis within OM on *service operations management*, looking at such concerns as customer contact, managing waiting periods, and, in general, enhancing the service experience perceived by customers. Yet, as the adoption and implementation of these new technologies and foci have shown, the problems confronted by managers and their firms are just as much social and organizational as they are scientific and technological.[48]

Systems Theory

As researchers began to focus on the interaction between the structural (mechanistic) and behavioral (organic) dimensions of organizations and the influence of the external environment, the concept of a business firm as a system began to dominate organizational theory. According to this perspective, an organization is conceptualized as a system composed of subunits or *subsystems* that continually interact with and are mutually dependent on each other.[49] Actions that occur within one part of the system not only affect that particular unit (department, section, group, etc.) but can have a "ripple effect" through other organizational subsystems as well. The implication of *Systems Theory*, therefore, is that things do not simply happen, but rather they evolve from multiple pressures and can entail multiple outcomes.

Within this context, organizations are often referred to as sociotechnical systems, composed of four basic components:[50]

- A *task/technological subsystem* that consists of the basic work done by the organization, specific work activities or functions, and the tools or technologies that enable the work to be accomplished

- An *administrative/structural subsystem* (formal organization) that includes such things as task groupings (units, divisions, departments); work rules and policies; authority systems (reporting relationships, power bases, control procedures); and the way in which jobs are designed

- A *subsystem of individuals* that involves the people who perform the various organizational tasks, and the nature and characteristics of these individuals in terms of their knowledge, skills, attitudes, values, expectations, and perceptions

- An *emergent subsystem* (informal organization) that develops over time as people interact within the formal system and includes such implicit and unwritten arrangements as norms (standards of behavior), intraorganizational statuses, competition and cooperation between groups, and other "nonprogrammed" activities and interactions.

These four subsystems are highly interdependent on each other. A change in administrative policies, for example, will not only affect those policies, but can also exert an influence on the task, the people performing the task, and the informal system.

Organizations are also referred to as *open systems*. Conceptually, we often compare open and closed systems. Systems that are completely self-contained and do not involve any interaction with their environment are termed *closed systems*. Systems that interact with their environment and are influenced by external forces, by contrast, are defined as open systems. No system, however, is totally open or totally closed. A thermostat, for example, is often viewed as a closed system because it reacts to only one external factor—change in temperature. A thermostat that is connected to a furnace will turn the furnace on when the air around the thermostat is below a certain temperature and turn the furnace off when the air goes above that temperature. Basically, nothing else matters.

Organizations, in contrast, are open systems that are influenced by a multitude of environmental forces or inputs such as availability of raw materials, changes in technology, and government regulation. In a bank, for example, deposits can be perceived as inputs that are transformed (through record keeping and bank policies) into consumer outputs (loans, mortgages). As recent industry trends have indicated, however, this process is influenced by a number of external factors such as changes in the inflation rate, government deregulation, advanced information technologies (e.g., home banking via the Internet, online loan businesses), and consumer attitudes. Thus, organizations receive inputs from their environment and transform these inputs into usable outputs for their customers within the context of their environment.

There are limits or *boundaries,* however, to the *openness* of organizational systems. These boundaries are based on the input–transformation–output process that links the organization to other systems; behavior not linked with these functions lies outside the system. Although the notion of a boundary is somewhat arbitrary and varies from system to system, it is an important concept since open systems are not affected by every external force or change.

As part of the input–transformation–output process, an organization receives *feedback* or information concerning its performance. The continuous flow of information among a system, its internal components, and the external environment forms a *feedback loop* that enables the organization to adapt to changing environmental conditions. Thus, the capacity to use this information to control the system and make necessary changes is crucial if organizations are to become self-correcting systems.

Another important aspect of systems is that they seek *equilibrium,* a steady state of regularity, consistency, or balance. When something occurs that puts the system out of balance, the system reacts to bring itself back into balance. This does not imply that organizations are, or should be, static and unchanging. Rather, as the feedback process discussed earlier indicates, organizational systems can use the information provided through their feedback loops to make certain adjustments to changing conditions (adaptation), and reach and maintain (for as long as appropriate) a new balance point. This equilibrium point then becomes the steady state until another change indicates the need for further adaptation.

The primary advantage to Systems Theory is that it provides a framework for thinking about organizations in more complex and dynamic terms than earlier organizational theories. The application of a systems perspective is especially useful when assessing the need for major organizational change. The theory can guide managers to think about how change in one part of the organization may affect other aspects of the organization, and the potential effect of the external environment. An underlying problem, however, is a tendency to be evaluative in such analytic efforts, that is, perceiving a particular behavior as being "good" or "bad." Systems analysis is based on the *functionality* of a particular event or behavior, or the extent to which the event contributes to the maintenance of the system.[51] If a given event occurs that dislocates a particular system (or subsystem) and leads to difficulties, the event is *dysfunctional* to that system. If an event reinforces the system, it is *functional* to that system. Caution must be exercised, however, when determining functionality. Certain behaviors that may appear to be dysfunctional for task performance (e.g., game playing, socializing) may be quite functional for individuals and their informal system by fulfilling social needs and reinforcing certain norms and interaction patterns.

Contingency Theory

One of the outgrowths of Systems Theory is *Contingency Theory.* The central thesis of Contingency Theory is that there are *no* universal principles of management that can be applied uncritically in all situations. Management approaches must vary from one situation to the next because they *depend* on the unique environmental conditions and internal factors that are inherent to each organization. Thus, a diagnostic, situational approach to decisions about organizational structure and appropriate managerial behaviors is necessary.

There are three main emphases within the Contingency school:[52]

- *Open systems planning:* There is no one "best" solution for all organizations since each firm has to cope with its own unique set of technical, human, and market inputs. The role and influence of the environment will be analyzed in Chapter 8.
- *Organizational design:* In relatively stable and predictable markets with simple, repetitive technologies, hierarchical organization structures tend to be effective; in more uncertain environments with complex technologies, in contrast, a "flatter" form of organization seems to be more effective. This orientation will be discussed more fully in Chapter 9.
- *Leadership:* Rather than taking one basic approach to leadership in all situations, leadership style should vary according to such factors as the nature of leader–member relations, the degree of task structure, the power (positional and personal) a leader has, and the expertise and willingness of subordinates to assume responsibility. This aspect of Contingency Theory will be examined in Chapter 7.

Although Contingency Theory has been criticized for being more of a classification scheme than a true theoretical formulation, it has greatly contributed to our base of knowledge about organizations and their management. It emerged from Systems Theory, a growing appreciation of the influence of the external environment, and the development of more complex assumptions about human nature.

SOCIETAL CHANGE AND ORGANIZATIONAL BEHAVIOR

As suggested by our assessment of the evolution of management theory, our views of management and organization are both shaped and challenged by sociocultural, economic, and technological changes in the broader society. In addition to the current attention given to business ethics that was discussed earlier, a number of shifts are taking place in our society that have significant implications for the ways in which we think about management and behavior.

OB and Advanced Information and Manufacturing Technologies

We are currently experiencing an unprecedented wave of technological growth and innovation in business. Although the Internet and "dot-com" companies that once dominated the business news seem almost passé, the resulting "e-revolution" is continuing to restructure how business is conducted, managed, and even conceptualized.[53] Most of us are struggling to keep up with the literal explosion of technology in our business as well as personal lives. We are continually wrestling with myriad questions and concerns about the new economy, a system based on knowledge and the development of intellectual capital.[54]

Most assessments of these new technologies point to their potential for enriching our lives, creating more opportunities as well as more challenging and interesting work, and improving the overall efficiency and effectiveness of our work processes. Increasing concern, however, is centering on: (1) our ability to competently manage these technologies and (2) the "dark side" of these technological developments.[55] Historically, there has been ample research documenting the effect of technology on workers and the workforce. The foci of these studies range from the human factors engineering examination of person-machine fit and the effects of automation on worker displacement, to psychological and sociological concerns about the dehumanizing character of mechanized work.[56] While these research efforts exerted a significant influence on the nature of many organizational policies and practices, the magnitude of present changes in workplace technologies is creating new pressures and strains on organizations and their members.

Advanced information and manufacturing technologies—computer networks and the e-commerce revolution, robotics, computer-aided design and manufacturing (CAD/CAM), cellular communication devices—are continuing to revolutionize the ways in which organizations operate and people perform their jobs. As outlined in Figure 1-1, over time the basic focus of managerial control has evolved from overseeing patterns of physical movement and precise ways of performing work, to patterns of social interaction, to managing spans of attention and patterns of connectivity within and across organizational boundaries. As advanced technologies continue to influence the way work is performed, managers will increasingly need to focus on their workers' patterns of attention, learning, and mental engagement to their tasks. People, of course, have always had to "pay attention" to their work if they were to properly complete their tasks. Yet, as most observations of routine work have shown, employees typically daydream, banter with one another, and engage in various games to pass the time.[57] They must pay attention to their work with their eyes, but not necessarily with their brains. The quality of attention required by computer-mediated work assignments, in contrast, is quite different. Workers concentrating on a visual display unit, interacting with a robot or collaborating with a colleague thousands of miles away need to pay much closer attention to what they are doing. Indeed, if they are to understand and properly respond to the information they are dealing with, they must be mentally involved in their work.

Technology and Management Control

The changing nature of work is placing increasing emphasis on what might be termed a commitment or involvement-oriented management paradigm.[58] Traditionally, managers have relied on a *control-oriented*, bureaucratic model to ensure that organizational goals and objectives were fulfilled. As underscored by the earlier discussion of Classical management theory, the basic assumption was that organizations can most effectively get people to perform their tasks through formal reward and punishment systems. Thus, jobs are described in detail, job performance is carefully measured, and rewards are handed out on the basis of specified achievements. Lower-level organizational members are not asked to actively participate in planning, scheduling, coordinating, or controlling operational efforts. Instead, their actions and activities are coordinated through rules, procedures, and close supervisory direction. The *involvement-oriented* approach, by contrast, is based on a very different set of assumptions about what makes organizations effective. It stresses that employees can be intrinsically motivated (Chapter 3), that they have a capacity for self-direction and self-control, and that most employees are capable of providing important ideas on how the firm should be run. This orientation is manifested in such practices as self-managed work teams, quality circles, learning teams, skill-based pay and gainsharing programs, and flat, lean organizational structures.

Most management specialists argue that while the control-oriented approach works well with relatively simple, repetitive tasks, it is far less effective in overseeing complex knowledge work. However, given the mundane nature of many computer-mediated jobs, traditional control orientations are still in ample evidence in today's workplace. Computer monitoring, sometimes referred to as electronic supervision, for example, has become a controversial issue in labor-management relations. By using computers as an efficiency tool, managers can prompt employees to work faster, automatically present them with their next task, and warn them when they fall behind predetermined productivity standards. Computers can readily record when operators turn their video display terminals on and off, time customer service transactions, count keystrokes by the second, and track the number of operator errors made during a specified period of time. Biometric technology is increasingly being used for employee fingerprinting and retina scanning for even menial jobs to prevent "buddy punching" (i.e., when a co-worker "punches in" for another employee on a time clock).[59] Due to escalating competitive pressures, many managers appear to be increasingly rationalizing such work speedups and tightening controls as a way to cut labor costs and enhance needed productivity gains. Yet, while some may applaud the efficiency and effectiveness of such capabilities, computer monitoring is also being linked with heightened stress, lowered job satisfaction and organizational commitment, and ironically, employee efforts that ultimately subvert management's goal of greater productivity. Thus, while computerization is often viewed as a potential tool for liberating workers from menial tasks and drudgery, in many instances it has isolated employees from one another and has literally made them servants to their machines.[60]

Self-Service Technologies

Technology is also dramatically and profoundly changing the ways in which services are both conceptualized and delivered to customers—changes that have significant implications for how service operations are staffed and managed.[61] Advanced information technology has created wide-ranging opportunities for companies to implement systems that essentially allow customers to provide their own service. The idea of full service is rapidly being replaced with a new version of customer self-service, as we increasingly pump our own gasoline, do our own banking, self-scan our purchases, purchase airline tickets online, and even check ourselves in for the flight.

While there are myriad positive outcomes associated with such self-service technologies (e.g., cost reduction, ease of access), this technology also allows customers to complete their transactions without any direct interaction with the company's employees. The result, in a growing number of instances, is a significant loss of human interaction in the workplace. Compounded by fears related to job loss and reduced opportunities, many employees are increasingly reluctant to embrace these new technologies, creating difficulties at the organizational level. From an OB perspective, it is important to remember that such information technology solutions still depend on human actions and relationships, and that there are limits to an appropriate and productive use of these technologies in the workplace.

Mobile Employees, Outsourcing, and Contingent Workers

A related offshoot of the increased use of advanced manufacturing and information technologies in the workplace is a fundamental shift in the way work is done. Basic functions once performed in-house are now being accomplished at home, on the road, or outsourced to specialized firms that, in many instances, may be located in distant countries. Core tasks once performed by people are now routinely delegated to robots and computers. Work once performed by full-time, local workers is increasingly being sent to international locations where even highly skilled labor is a fraction of what it costs in the United States.[62] The result is a radically transformed organization and workforce.

It is estimated, for example, that there were more than twenty-five million telecommuters in 2005. On any given day, as many as one-third of the salaried workforce may be operating from remote locations—working at home, in the client's office, or out of a hotel room hundreds or even thousands of miles away.[63] Human resource experts predict that the number of people involved in telework will continue to grow as workers, as well as organizations, require more flexibility (e.g., ability to deal with work overload, avoid frequent interruptions in the workplace, meet family needs) and as high-speed Internet connections make telecommuting easier.[64] Similarly, while outsourcing strategies started with support-related activities (e.g., payroll, maintenance), critical functions—ranging from product design to manufacturing to distribution—are increasingly being shifted to specialist firms in offshore locations.[65] Over the next fifteen years, for example, Forrester Research predicts that 3.3 million service jobs will move to countries such as India, Russia, China, the Philippines, and Ireland—with the IT sector leading the way.[66]

These trends raise myriad implications for managers who must deal with a host of working arrangements—people still in traditional jobs, full-time employees who are not at the office for a typical working day, and part-time or contingent workers who are linked to the organization on a short-term, project-oriented basis. In fact, it appears that traditional employment schemes offering regular, long-term jobs are increasingly being replaced by more flexible, "contingent" arrangements under which workers are hired on a temporary or sporadic basis—a reality that is frustrating to many workers who still desire regular, permanent jobs.[67]

As the field of OB continues to develop and evolve, the exact nature of these challenges is still being defined. As illustrated in Figure 1-2, the electronic office, consisting of information technologies that link people to people, people to information, and people to facilities, is transforming when and where work is accomplished—across the globe. High-speed fiber-optic cable and rapidly dropping bandwidth prices are enabling companies to transfer increasingly sophisticated tasks overseas. These shifts emphasize the need to develop a capacity for change and to deal with such issues as

Figure 1-2 Information Technology and the Electronic Office

Source: Adapted from Thomas A. Finholt, "The Electronic Office," in C.L. Cooper and D.M. Rousseau (eds.), *Trends in Organizational Behavior,* vol. 4 (New York: John Wiley & Sons, 1997), pp. 31–38.

job displacement, redistribution of responsibility in the workplace, changing demands for worker skills, new, innovative compensation systems, and an increasingly diverse workforce.

Boundaryless Careers

While robotics, telecommuting, outsourcing, and self-service technologies create myriad efficiencies and opportunities, the idea of a "post-job" company, in which the bulk of traditional jobs have been automated and outsourced out of existence,[68] raises significant questions for how we think about careers and career planning. In fact, some observers argue that the concept of a career should no longer be linked with one particular job or organization. People instead are being advised to focus on areas of competence, as many of today's "hot jobs" may not be in existence in the near future.[69] Although there are, of course, a number of practical and psychological impediments to continually shifting one's job or organizational identity, the growing reality is that people are likely to experience several career cycles over their lifetimes. Thus, rather than focusing on continuous upward mobility and managed career progress, we will have to change our expectations about our careers, being prepared to deal with periodic cycles of reskilling, lateral job changes rather than upward movement, and the possibility of phased retirement.[70] While this trend has obvious ramifications for individuals, it also raises significant challenges for managers who will be interacting with a different type of workforce and faced with the challenge of creating an environment that will sustain their firm's performance over the long term.[71]

Protean Careers

Careers have traditionally been defined as the evolving sequence of a person's life-long series of work-related experiences and attitudes.[72] In contrast to the traditional career, which is generally linear and managed significantly by one's employing organization, a *protean career* is self-directed and driven by intrinsic factors (e.g., personal values). In the protean conceptualization of career development, the individual manages important career experiences such as formal education, training, employment, and leisure and family life.[73] Relative to boundaryless careers, protean careers place greater emphasis on individuals' values and quest for self-fulfillment.[74]

The Quality Movement

At the same time that emerging technologies are revamping the workplace, the highly competitive, international business environment has placed significant emphasis on product and service quality. Traditionally, business viewed quality as a relatively minor, after-the-fact production assessment usually assigned to lower-level quality inspectors.[75] As global competitiveness began to erode the U.S. position in the world economy, however, many U.S. businesses were criticized for failing to make sufficient improvement in the quality of their products and services that would allow them to be highly competitive in the global marketplace.

Many critics contend that, to a large degree, quality planning is still heavily influenced by Taylorism and the view that lower-level employees are not qualified to plan and evaluate how work should be done.[76] Indeed, despite claims that many employees are ill-equipped to adequately deal with today's complex work processes, some authorities assert that "managerial arrogance" is largely to blame for our current quality situation. By continuing to rely on a control-oriented, bureaucratic model to meet organizational goals and objectives, managers and executives have essentially separated themselves from their employees, suppliers, and customers, making true quality management impossible.

Total Quality Management (TQM) refers to a different philosophy, one that embraces the company-wide application of principles, practices, and systems designed to ensure complete customer satisfaction. Central to the underlying vision of attaining total quality is a belief in and understanding of the fundamental importance of employee participation. In essence, all organizational members must work together to achieve full customer satisfaction through *continuous improvement* (CI), creating systems and processes to ensure that literally everyone in the organization does the right thing, the right way, the first and every time.[77] Emphasis is placed on building quality into the work process and striving to prevent problems rather than scrambling to correct them after the fact. When problems do occur, the focus is not just on fixing them but on having organizational members discover and eliminate their root cause(s) to ensure that the same problems do not keep recurring.

Closely aligned to the idea of TQM and CI is *business process reengineering* (BPR). Rather than simply attempting to improve existing processes (through, for instance, automation), reengineering attempts to transform the organization by literally starting over, designing core business processes from scratch rather than reanalyzing existing systems.[78] BPR's underlying orientation was to:[79]

- Radically redesign and improve the way work is carried out
- Attack broad, cross-functional processes
- Focus on "stretch" goals that would improve organizational performance
- Use information technology to enable new ways of working

Although many BPR efforts became a code word for downsizing and reductions in force, the underlying intent was to enhance how work was accomplished. Yet Michael Hammer, one of the leading BPR gurus, lamented that the role people play in the process was overlooked: "I wasn't smart enough about that.... I was reflecting my engineering background and was insufficiently appreciative of the human dimension. I've learned that's critical."[80]

From an OB perspective, a true commitment to enhanced work processes and quality means that an organization, its management, and its members must reorient their thinking about how they do business and how they function as a company. Key initiatives include: (1) building a commitment to excellence into the firm's basic business concept and strategic objectives, (2) creating new systems for evaluation and assessment, and (3) building a culture that encourages organizational members to enhance their performance.[81] As studies have shown, successful quality improvement initiatives include: (1) involving employees in formal planning processes that have clear and realistic goals; (2) creating supportive structures that encourage people to get involved in decision-making processes and provide them with the information they need to make effective and timely decisions; (3) emphasizing working as a team, breaking down barriers across different work units; (4) communicating clearly, encouraging constructive criticism and open discussion of conflicts; (5) creating high performance standards and holding people accountable for performance objectives; (6) rewarding superior performance; and (7) creating challenging opportunities and a sense of personal satisfaction.[82]

Discontent, Cynicism, and Fear in the Workplace

While the current influence on quality and IT-based workplaces points to the need for an involved and committed workforce, there are increasing signs that discontent, disillusionment, and disenchantment with work and the workplace are growing among both white- and blue-collar workers. As many surveys indicate, a growing number of managers and business professionals feel less and less secure in their positions, more mistrustful of top-level executives and co-workers, and increasingly convinced that companies will not return their loyalty.[83] As studies point out, many U.S. corporations are (1) still preoccupied with short-term results, (2) continue to rely on outdated strategies that focus on mass production and the domestic market, (3) persist in placing financial machinations above production needs and innovation, and (4) continue to neglect their human resources.[84] In essence, U.S. corporations have been criticized as having profound problems in their underlying cultures and orientations.

Similar to the problems associated with BPR, the notion of corporate restructuring became a euphemism for a wide array of painful actions that typically translate into large-scale reduction-in-force, downsizing, and disinvestment activities.[85] As part of this process, critics contend that corporations further contribute to employee discontent by promising much more than they intended to deliver, hiring overqualified people with the expectation of "getting more work out of them," laying off workers and reassigning tasks to those who remain, and giving vague promises of early salary reviews and new job possibilities that rarely, if ever, materialize.[86] One result is what one of the popular business magazines referred to as the "end of corporate loyalty."[87]

Workplace Incivility

The long-term effects of this loss of loyalty and commitment, of course, are quite ominous for both corporate America and the United States in general in an increasingly competitive global economy. A disillusioned and cynical workforce will obviously be far less cohesive and productive than a committed and trusting one.

A growing lack of civility between organizational members is rapidly becoming one of the main causes of work-related conflict and strife. *Workplace incivility*, which is defined as rude or disrespectful conduct that reflects a lack of regard for others, includes such behaviors as:[88]

- Speaking in a condescending manner
- Demeaning, belittling, or harassing others
- Interrupting others in a rude or unnecessary manner
- Rumor mongering and gossiping
- Not listening when another person is speaking directly or indirectly to you
- Exclusionary behavior, especially shutting out new employees

This general decrease in socially acceptable behaviors, while often subtle in nature, can quickly lead to decreased productivity, problems with staff retention, increased conflict, and a general unwillingness to act in a collaborative and cooperative manner.

From a managerial perspective, it is important to help organizational members understand what constitutes workplace incivility. It is important to encourage the use of good communication (see Chapter 4) and conflict resolution skills (see Chapter 6), both of which require training and continuous enforcement. It is also important to model the type of behavior that you would like to see employees use with each other and with customers—listening and paying attention to what others say, being inclusive and empathetic, giving praise when called for, and being constructive when criticizing others.

Workplace Violence and Vengeance

A related, even more problematic aspect of this change is a general increase in illicit, aberrant, and morally questionable behavior in the workplace.[89] Although workplace deviance—which encompasses such acts as theft, fraud, vandalism, sabotage, sexual harassment, and illicit drug use—is suggested to be on the increase, perhaps the most disturbing dimension of this phenomenon is overt violence and aggression at work, where people are either threatened with or actually harmed or killed by physical force. While such incidents of violence are fortunately the exception rather than the rule, they are beginning to occur all too frequently, and homicide has become the second leading cause of death in the workplace.[90]

Employee vengeance against former employers is also on the rise, especially as access to information technology provides disgruntled ex-employees with the ability to infiltrate an organization's computer system.[91] Irate workers, who in years past might have simply simmered or spread slander about their former employers, are hacking into company computers, deleting data, leaking sensitive information to competitors, and even changing customer orders. The ability to access these systems from remote locations, combined with the feeling that this can be done anonymously, is further contributing to the rise in this type of cyber-revenge and providing a new route for workplace anger.

As deviant acts continue to emerge in the workplace, we need to think much more specifically about both the nature and causes of such behavior. Given the range of interpersonal interactions that occur between people in today's organizations, it is important to realize that while many of these interactions are positive and constructive, others can be quite negative and destructive. Organizations often find it necessary to downsize, lay off employees, or shift positions of power and responsibility. Managers often find themselves in situations where they feel it is necessary to reprimand or discipline employees, offer constructive criticism to subordinates, or even use their formal authority to control or coerce certain behaviors. While such actions may not necessarily be inappropriate or lead to an aggressive or violent response, it is important to reflect on notions of fairness and justice when dealing with other organizational members.[92] As research in this relatively understudied area continues to evolve, questions of leadership, empowerment, group dynamics, and interpersonal relations among other central dimensions of the OB field promise to provide us with further insight into this troubling reality of organizational life.

The Workplace as a Darker Place

For many people, September 11, 2001, marked a drastic change in their perception of the world. Such traumatic events, especially those outside normal human experience, create significant stress and tension in our lives, often overwhelming our ability to cope with our surroundings.[93] While there are no typical response patterns to such events, people can experience physical (headaches, sleep disorders, elevated blood pressure), emotional (shock, anger, guilt, anxiety, depression, fear), and cognitive (inability to concentrate, confusion) problems. Job performance typically suffers in the wake of such tragedies, and while some people can work through these difficulties in a matter of days, others can struggle for weeks or even months.

Some jobs have always been rather dismal because they involve dirty, smelly, or hazardous tasks. However, the emergence of new health risks—from terrorism to new viruses—is turning some formerly good jobs into bad ones and making some formerly bad jobs even worse.[94] Postal work, for example, was often characterized as boring but reliable government employment, until postal workers faced the risk of anthrax spores. Package delivery may have been a mundane line of work, but that was before workers had to start screening parcels for bombs or explosives. Nursing has always carried a certain prestige along with some risk, but a combination of orange alerts and a raft of infectious diseases have added new stress. While the glamour and opportunity to travel the world made up for the relatively low pay for flight attendants, their working lives became quite different due to lingering threats of terrorism and risks associated with such illnesses as severe acute respiratory syndrome (SARS) and avian flu.

Combined with a literal explosion of mergers, acquisitions, downsizings, and outsourced jobs, the workplace has become a less desirable place for a growing number of employees. From an OB perspective, it is important for managers to help their employees reconnect to their work roles, facilitating a process of recovery that can begin to recapture their commitment and reenergize them.[95] Managers, for example, are being encouraged to talk with employees about these events, sharing their own concerns, and showing empathy and compassion for what they are experiencing. While many managers may try to quickly return to "business as usual," focusing their efforts and energies on key business imperatives, it is important to help people recover from the emotional realities and traumatic reactions associated with such events.

Sociodemographic Diversity in the Workplace

It is clear that profound demographic changes are occurring in our society and that our labor force is becoming increasingly diverse in terms of age, gender, race, and ethnicity. During the early 2000s, for example, it is estimated that approximately 15 percent of new hires will be white males, with the remaining 85 percent consisting of women, African Americans, Hispanics, Asians, and Native Americans.[96] Our expanding consideration of diversity or social groups today also includes sexual orientation, age and (dis)ability, and other identity groups not covered by Equal Employment Opportunity (EEO) law such as nationality, personality, and cognitive orientation and ability.[97] These changes have obvious implications for managers interacting with a group of disparate individuals, especially in terms of: (1) communicating effectively with employees from diverse cultural backgrounds; (2) coaching and developing sociodemographically heterogeneous individuals and groups; (3) providing meaningful performance feedback; and (4) creating organizational cultures and climates that both nurture and utilize the fruitful mix of talents and perspectives that diversity can offer.[98] At the same time, the basic skills of managing diversity—active listening, coaching, and providing feedback—are a reflection of what is currently thought of as "good" management.[99]

Recent research has begun to distinguish between the concepts of diversity and inclusion. *Diversity* generally refers to the demographic composition of workgroups or organizations, and also is related to the differences in perspective resulting from membership in various cultural and social identity groups.[100] *Inclusion*, in contrast, is the extent to which workgroup and organization members can access information and resources, are involved in workgroups, and can influence decision making. In other words, the notion of inclusion emphasizes the extent to which individuals feel a part of important organizational processes.

There are a number of advantages associated with increased sociodemographic diversity in the workplace.[101] For instance, a diverse workforce can create advantages in recruiting, marketing, and customer service. A varied set of views and perspectives can provide an organization with greater insight into and understanding of a broad customer base, which can translate into a competitive advantage for culturally diverse firms. In contrast, problems associated with increasing sociodemographic diversity in the labor force include communication misunderstandings, increased training costs, increased factionalism among employees, cultural conflicts, and potential increases in tardiness, absenteeism, and turnover. Some critics contend that the effects of a significantly diverse workforce are so pervasive and subtle, and the concomitant business losses so large, that it is virtually impossible to identify the full impact. A recent review of forty years of diversity further acknowledges that while diversity is a social value in our culture, it can have negative effects on group process and performance.[102] Studies have indicated that, especially under conditions of crisis or rapid change, diversity can hinder group and organizational performance since the advantages provided by multiple perspectives are offset by the problems of generating consensus.[103]

Given these realities, concerted effort is needed to explore how diverse perspectives can be shared more effectively and how heterogeneous individuals and groups can work together more constructively. Recent diversity research, for example, distinguishes among organizational approaches to managing diversity.[104] This work has identified three prevalent approaches or "diversity paradigms" representative of organizational diversity management practice. The *discrimination and fairness* paradigm focuses on creating diversity and fostering equality among organizational members via human resources policies (e.g., affirmative action, sensitivity training, mentoring programs). Organizations operating under this paradigm expect minority members to assimilate, and organizational members are trained and encouraged to take a "color-blind" perspective to establish the principle that demographic differences do not matter. Organizations operating under an *access and legitimacy* paradigm seek to exploit the nature of employees' demographic differences to gain access and legitimacy with diverse markets. This orientation is also commonly referred to as the "business case" for diversity. Organizational structures such as special divisions or business units largely comprised of female or minority employees dedicated to the service of emerging niche/minority markets are typical under this approach.

Finally, organizations operating under the *integration and learning* paradigm seek to incorporate diversity throughout the organization, vertically and horizontally, inclusive of the organization's approach to processes, strategy, and work. In contrast to the "color-blind" perspective, cultural differences among organization members are recognized as sources of skill and insight that can have a direct impact on the organization's core tasks. Importantly, and in contrast to the access and legitimacy paradigm, recognizing that people from different cultural backgrounds may contribute different sets of skills and perspectives to the organization does not warrant a cultural identity–based division of labor.

Thus, even thought blatant discrimination may be waning, managers must become more aware of the subtle forces in organizations that can prevent many organizational members from reaching their full potential.[105] Indeed, one of the major challenges of managing diversity is developing the ability to identify problems that are not readily apparent. Old standards of performance, for instance, tend to promote the status quo and provide mainstream employees with advantages over new entrants. As a result, diversity programs that uncover these tendencies can help managers to master human relations and problem-solving skills. The underlying key is to develop the ability to see things from different perspectives, to work with others to find answers, and to allow others to have input into decisions. There is a growing body of evidence to suggest that if done right, diversity can lead to higher organizational performance and profits.[106] As will be explored in subsequent chapters, the foci of these endeavors and the skills that they attempt to develop emerge directly from an understanding of organizational behavior.

FADS AND FOIBLES IN MANAGEMENT

Drawing on the theoretical and conceptual material discussed throughout the book, the chapters that follow include a range of organizational applications. A brief word of caution, however, is necessary. Management is often dominated by various fads and techniques that are fashionable at a particular time. Managers have been criticized for jumping on and off a succession of behavioral-science bandwagons in their search for organizational effectiveness and efficiency.[107] We have gone from T-groups and sensitivity training during the late 1960s and early 1970s, to Theory Z and our literal fixation with Japanese management techniques in the early 1980s, to corporate culture in the mid-1980s and Total Quality Management (TQM) during the latter part of the decade, to downsizing and reengineering in the 1990s. The fascination with downsizing and reengineering ultimately gave way to "organizational growth," an emphasis on achieving sustainable, profitable growth in our companies.[108] At the turn of the twenty-first century, information systems were regarded as the latest organizational savior, with an increased focus on knowledge management as one of the latest "big ideas."[109] Each one of these techniques, and the mass of writings that accompany them, claim to "revolutionize" our understandings of the management process.

Today, postmodern and critical views of diversity are calling the very notions of diversity and inclusion into question. Critics are asserting that affirmative action and other societal and organizational policies ostensibly created to rectify past injustice essentially create divisive social group boundaries, perpetuating negative associations (e.g., stereotypes) and debilitating supposed beneficiary group members.[110] Others are calling into question the very notions of race and gender in organizations as objective properties of individuals, especially as they are currently treated in mainstream organizational diversity literature.[111] An emerging view this research is bringing into focus emphasizes the subjective social and idiosyncratic organizational meanings of gender and race, bringing to our attention the mindsets, structures, and other features of organizational contexts that serve to reinforce prevailing assumptions about various social groups such as race and gender.[112]

Some observers contend that all too often such management fads do little more than diffuse different administrative technologies that, in and of themselves, have little utility for any organization.[113] Given the complexities that abound in organizational life, however, simple solutions rarely, if ever, succeed. In fact, other critics contend that fads are actually harmful since they prompt managers to literally jump from one innovation to another, without allowing sufficient time or support for the intervention to work.[114] Moreover, although Kurt Lewin's suggestion that "nothing is as practical as a good theory" may be true, as we have recently been reminded the "obverse is also true: nothing is as dangerous as a bad theory." [115] Thus, while these prescriptions may have the *potential* to improve organizational performance, they require critical assessment and thoughtful execution. Only through sustained implementation can managers and their organizations develop the tacit knowledge, understanding, and skills necessary to successfully implement new programs and innovations.

Individual managers and organizations, however, often become infatuated with a specific form of intervention (usually after it has successfully been applied in another context), desire to be seen as "progressive," or develop preconceptions about the cause of a particular problem. When this occurs, a frequent tendency is to turn to a particular technique for "relief." The result is a discouragingly high failure rate of these behavioral-science tools in our corporations. The important point to remember is that the theories and approaches that will be discussed throughout the book are *not* panaceas to all organizational problems. Many of them are based on middle-range theories and research, which means that the practitioner/manager must carefully diagnose the situation and choose an appropriate approach to solving a particular problem. There are advantages and disadvantages as well as benefits and costs associated with any of these interventions. Each of these techniques, however, can be effectively used to deal with specific employee and organizational problems and, if applied carefully and thoughtfully, can enhance employee and organizational competency.

CONCLUSION

It should be clear from this introductory chapter that our models and ways of examining people and organizations have become more dynamic and complex. The focus of attention gradually shifted from an emphasis on physical and structural factors, to human relationships and interactions, to the application of quantitative methods and computer technology in organizational decision making. Currently, management theorists have developed a more integrated approach in the systemic analysis of organizations, their members, and their environments. We have moved from "one-best-way" approaches to a situational or contingency perspective.

Within this context, the study of OB today is a result of the gradual convergence of these various schools of thought. The field itself has evolved from what has been termed a *micro*-orientation (emphasis on the structures and processes within and between individuals, small groups, and their leaders) to include more of a *macro*-perspective (emphasis on the structures and processes within and between major subsystems, organizations, and their environments) as well. There is an attempt to combine the "logic" of the Classical school and the "nonlogical" feelings of the Neoclassical tradition through more systematic, integrated analyses of behavior and structure at the individual, small group, organizational, and interorganizational levels. This book does not purport to provide students with a full understanding of all of the subtleties and intricacies of this growing field. It does, however, attempt to provide a solid foundation for more rigorous study of the behaviors that occur within and between contemporary organizations.

NOTES

1. This discussion is drawn from J.A. Waters, "Managerial Skill Development," *Academy of Management Review* 5, no. 3 (1980): 449–453.

2. H. Mintzberg, *The Nature of Managerial Work* (New York: Harper & Row, 1973); C.M. Pavett and A.W. Lau, "Managerial Roles, Skills and Effective Performance," in K.H. Chung, ed., *Academy of Management Proceedings* 1982 (Loveland, CO: Lithographic Press, 1982), pp. 95–100. For an assessment of the growing popularity of the skills approach, see J.A. Miller, "Experiencing Management: A Comprehensive, 'Hands-On' Model for the Introductory Undergraduate Management Course," *Journal of Management Education* 15, no. 2 (1991): 151–169. For an update on the types of skills employers are looking for, see "What Do Recruiters Want?" *BizEd* 2, no. 1 (2002): 9.

3. W.E. McMullan and A. Cahoon, "Integrating Abstract Conceptualizing with Experimental Learning," *Academy of Management Review* 4, no. 3 (1979): 453–458; and D.C. Kayes, "Experiential Learning and Its Critics: Preserving the Role of Experience in Management Learning and Education," *Academy of Management Learning & Education* 1, no. 2 (2002): 137–149.

4. Mintzberg, op. cit., pp. 188–193; D.T. Hall, D.D. Bowen, R.J. Lewicki, and F.S. Hall, *Experiences in Management and Organizational Behavior* (New York: Wiley, 1982), pp. 1–6.

5. See M.D. Lee, J.A. Waters, N.J. Adler, and J. Hartwick, "Evaluating Managerial Skill Development," *The Organizational Behavior Teaching Review* 12, no. 1 (1987–88): 16–34; and G.M. McEvoy and J.R. Cragum, "Management Skill-Building in an Organizational Behavior Course," *The Organizational Behavior Teaching Review* 11, no. 4 (1986–87): 60–73.

6. See J. Morone, "Our High-Flying Habit," *Boston Globe*, October 6, 2002.

7. J.E. Flemming, "On Business Ethics," *Exchange: The Organizational Behavior Teaching Journal* 8, no. 1 (1983): 3–9; D. Vidaver-Cohen, "Motivational Appeal in Normative Theories of Enterprise," *Business Ethics Quarterly* 8, no. 3 (1998): 385–407; and A.H.J. Nijhof and M.M. Rietdijk, "An ABC-Analysis of Ethical Organizational Behavior," *Journal of Business Ethics* 20, no. 1 (1999): 39–50.

8. B.L. Toffler, *Tough Choices: Managers Talk Ethics* (New York: Wiley, 1986).

9. See B. Cruver, *Anatomy of Greed: The Unshredded Truth from an Enron Insider* (New York: Carroll & Graf, 2002); and W. Bennis, "A Corporate Fear of Too Much Truth," *New York Times*, February 17, 2002.

10. This discussion is based on H.B. Karp and B. Abramms, "Doing the Right Thing," *Training and Development* 46, no. 8 (1992): 36–41.

11. See R.M. Kidder, "Tough Choices: Why It's Getting Harder to Be Ethical," *The Futurist* 29, no. 5 (1995): 29–32.

12. For an in-depth discussion of these ethical theories, see M. Velasquez, *Business Ethics: Concepts and Cases* (Englewood Cliffs, NJ: Prentice Hall, 1992); and A.F. Buono and L.T. Nichols, *Corporate Policy, Values and Social Responsibility* (New York: Praeger, 1985), Chapter 2.

13. The following discussion is drawn from O.C. Ferrell, J. Fraedrich, and L. Ferrell, *Business Ethics*, 6th ed. (Boston: Houghton Mifflin, 2005), see pp. 76–82.

14. See, for example, O.C. Ferrell and L. Ferrell, "Role of Ethical Leadership in Organizational Performance," *Journal of Management Systems* 13 (2001): 64–78; and J. Weber and J.E. Seger, "Influences upon Organizational Ethical Subclimates: A Replication Study of a Single Firm at Two Points in Time," *Journal of Business Ethics* 41 (November 2002): 69–84.

15. A.B. Carroll, "The Pyramid of Corporate Social Responsibility: Toward the Moral Management of Organizational Stakeholders," *Business Horizons* 34, no. 4 (1991): 39–48.

16. W.M. Hoffman and E.S. Petry, Jr., "Business Ethics at Bentley College," *Moral Education Forum* 16 (Fall 1991): 1–8.

17. Figure 1-1 is based on a synthesis of numerous analyses of the changing nature of society and the development of management thought, among them: T. Parsons and N. Smelser, *Economy and Society* (London: Routledge & Kegan Paul, 1956); N. Smelser, *Social Change in the Industrial Revolution* (London: Routledge & Kegan Paul, 1959); Daniel Bell, *The Coming of Post-Industrial Society: A Venture in Social Forecasting* (New York: Basic Books, 1973); R. Miles, *Theories of Management* (New York: McGraw-Hill, 1975), Chapter 3; W.G. Scott, "Organization Theory: An Overview and an Appraisal," *Academy of Management Journal* 4 (1961): 7–26; E. Schein, *Organizational Psychology*, 2nd ed. (Englewood Cliffs, NJ: Prentice Hall, 1980), Chapters 4 and 6; and S. Zuboff, "New Worlds of Computer-Mediated Work," *Harvard Business Review* 60, no. 5 (1982): 142–152.

18.   This discussion is based on M. Witzel, "The Invention of Management," *European Business Forum*. 27 (Winter 2006): 62–63. See also R.S. Jacques, "History, Historiography and Organization Studies: The Challenge and the Potential," *Management & Organizational History*. 1, no. 1 (2006): 31–39.

19.   For a fuller discussion of the development of capitalism and its relationship to the type of authority structure in society, see M. Weber, *The Protestant Ethic and the Spirit of Capitalism*, trans. T. Parsons (New York: Scribner, 1930): and M. Weber, *The Theory of Social and Economic Organization*, trans. A. Henderson and T. Parsons (New York: Free Press, 1947).

20.   This discussion draws from D. Wren, *The Evolution of Management Thought* (New York: Wiley, 1979); and C. George, *The History of Management Thought* (Englewood Cliffs, NJ: Prentice Hall, 1972).

21.   Weber, *Theory of Social and Economic Organization*.

22.   A. Etzioni, "Choose America Must—Between 'Reindustrialization' and 'Quality of Life,'" *Across the Board* 17, no. 10 (1980): 42–49.

23.   H. Fayol, *General and Industrial Management*, trans. C. Storrs (London: Pitman, 1949).

24.   F. Taylor, *The Principles of Scientific Management* (New York: Harper & Brothers, 1911); and R. Kanigel, *The One Best Way: Frederick Winslow Taylor and the Enigma of Efficiency* (New York: Viking, 1997).

25.   See J. Hoopes, *False Prophets: The Gurus Who Created Modern Management and Why Their Ideas Are Bad for Business Today* (Cambridge, MA: Perseus, 2003), Chapter 2.

26.   See P. Drucker, *The New Realities* (New York: Basic Books, 1989), pp. 188–189.

27.   P.B. Peterson, "Fighting for a Better Navy: An Attempt at Scientific Management (1905–1912)," *Journal of Management* 16, no. 1 (1990): 151–166.

28.   Ibid.

29.   F. Gilbreth, *Primer of Scientific Management* (New York: Harper & Brothers, 1912); also George, op. cit., pp. 96–98.

30.   Wren, op. cit., pp. 148–158.

31.   Weber, *Theory of Social and Economic Organization*.

32.   W.G. Scott, "Organization Theory: An Overview and an Appraisal," *Academy of Management Journal* 4, no. 1 (1961): 7–26; and J.T. Ziegenfuss, "Do Your Managers Think in Organizational 3-D? *Sloan Management Review* 24, no. 1 (1982): 55–59.

33.   This discussion is drawn from R.E. Miles, *Theories of Management: Implications for Organizational Behavior and Development* (New York: McGraw-Hill, 1975), pp. 39–40; Scott, op. cit., pp. 13–14; E. Schein, *Organizational Psychology*, 2nd ed. (Englewood Cliffs, NJ: Prentice Hall, 1980), pp. 62–64; and H. Koontz, "The Management Theory Jungle," *Academy of Management Journal* 4 (1961): 174–178.

34.   Taken from the testimony of Frederick Taylor at hearings before the Special Committee of the House of Representatives to Investigate Taylor and Other Systems of Shop Management, January 25, 1912, pp. 1387–1389. This is included as one of the readings in M.T. Matteson and J.M. Ivancevich, eds., *Management Classics*, 2nd ed. (Santa Monica, CA: Goodyear, 1981), pp. 5–8.

35.   Scott, op. cit., pp. 14–17.

36.   For the initial analyses of the Hawthorne Experiments see F.J. Roethlisberger and W.J. Dickson, *Management and the Worker* (Cambridge: Harvard University Press, 1950). The discussion in this section has also been drawn from Schein, op. cit., pp. 56–67; and Miles, op. cit., pp. 39–42.

37. The impact of research methodology on the findings of the Hawthorne Studies and the implications that can be drawn from this research have been the focus of much debate up to the present period. See, for example, M. Argyle, "The Relay Assembly Test Room in Retrospect," *Occupational Psychology* 27 (1953): 98–103; A Carey, "The Hawthorne Studies: A Radical Criticism," *American Sociological Review* 32 (1967): 403–416; R. Sommer, "Hawthorne Dogma," *Psychological Bulletin* 70 (1968): 592–595; A.J.M. Sykes, "Economic Interest and the Hawthorne Researches," *Human Relations* 18 (1965): 253–263; R.H. Franke and J.D. Kaul, "The Hawthorne Experiments: First Statistical Interpretation," *American Sociological Review* 43 (1978): 623–642; and J. Gibson, A.H. Shullman, and R.G. Greenwood, "The Hawthorne Studies: What Are We Teaching? What Should We Be Teaching?" paper presented at the 51st Annual Meeting of the Academy of Management, Miami Beach, Florida, August 1991. See also L. Baritz, *The Servants of Power: A History of the Use of Social Science in American Industry* (Middletown, CT: Wesleyan University Press, 1960), pp. 114–115.

38. Hoopes, *False Prophets*, see pp. 153–159.

39. This section is drawn from Schein, op. cit., pp. 68–72; and Miles, op. cit., pp. 41–44.

40. Scott, op. cit., p. 17.

41. Ibid., pp. 17–18.

42. D. Bell, *The Coming of Post-Industrial Society: A Venture in Social Forecasting* (New York: Basic Books, 1973).

43. See, for example, D. Halberstam, *The Next Century* (New York: William Morrow, 1991); and R.B. Reich, *The Work of Nations: Preparing Ourselves for 21st Century Capitalism* (New York: Knopf, 1991). The discussion of new work categories is based on Reich, pp. 172–180. See also, G. Chapman, "Innovation: Here's the Rub on 'Friction-Free' Idea," *Boston Globe*, January 14, 1996, p. 48.

44. For a good example of the influence of these broader, sociopolitical stakeholders see L.E. Post, L.E. Preston and S. Sachs, *Redefining the Corporation: Stakeholder Management and Organizational Wealth* (Stanford, CA: Stanford University Press, 2002).

45. Schein, op. cit., pp. 93–94.

46. C.W. Churchman, R.L. Ackoff, and E.L. Arnoff, *Introduction to Operations Research* (New York: Wiley, 1957).

47. This discussion is drawn from R.J. Schonberger, "The Rationalization of Production," in D.A. Wren, ed., *Papers Dedicated to the Development of Modern Management* (Academy of Management, 1986), pp. 64–70; and R.B. Chase and E.L. Prentis, "Operations Management: A Field Rediscovered," *Journal of Management* 13, no. 2 (1987): 351–366.

48. See D.D. Davis et al., *Managing Technological Innovation: Organizational Strategies for Implementing Advanced Manufacturing Technologies* (San Francisco: Jossey-Bass, 1986); J.B. Kamm, *An Integrative Approach to Managing Innovation* (Lexington, MA: Lexington Books, 1987); M.M. Davis, N. Aquilano, and R. Chase, *Fundamentals of Operations Management* (New York: Irwin/McGraw-Hill, 1999); and M.M. Davis and J. Heineke, "Customer Satisfaction and Waiting Time: Disconfirmation, Expectation and Actual Waits," *International Journal of Service Industry Management* 9, no. 1 (1999).

49. For a fuller discussion and development of systems theory see L. von Bertalanffy, *General Systems Theory: Foundations, Development, and Applications* (New York: Braziller, 1967); L. von Bertalanffy, "The History and Status of General Systems Theory," *Academy of Management Journal* 15, no. 4 (1972): 411; D. Katz and R.L. Kahn, *The Social Psychology of Organizations* (New York: Wiley, 1966); and C.G. Schoderbek, P.P. Schoderbek, and A.G. Kefalas, *Management Systems: Conceptual Considerations* (Dallas: Business Publications, 1980).

50. H.J. Leavitt, "Applied Organizational Change in Industry: Structural, Technical, and Human Approaches," in W.W. Cooper, H.J. Leavitt, and M.W. Shelly, *New Perspectives in Organizational Research* (New York: Wiley, 1964); and D. Nadler and M. Tushman, "A Model for Diagnosing Organizational Behavior," *Organizational Dynamics* (Autumn 1980): 35–51.

51. For a good overview of the concept of function see A.H. Leighton, "The Functional Point of View," in J. Bartunek and J. Gordon, eds., *Behavior in Organizations: A Diagnostic Approach* (Lexington, MA: Xerox, 1978), pp. 13–15; and A.R. Radcliffe-Brown, "Concept of Function in Social Science," *American Anthropologist* 37 (July–Sept. 1935).

52. See Greiner, op. cit., pp. 10–11; J.A. Seiler, *A Systems Analysis in Organizational Behavior* (Homewood, IL: Irwin, 1967); J. Woodward, *Industrial Organization: Theory and Practice* (London: Oxford University Press, 1965); P.R. Lawrence and J.W. Lorsch, *Organization and Environment: Managing Differentiation and Integration* (Homewood, IL: Irwin, 1969); J. Thompson, *Organizations in Action* (New York: McGraw-Hill, 1967); and F.E. Fiedler, *A Theory of Leadership Effectiveness* (New York: McGraw-Hill, 1967).

53. See, for example, D.B. Yoffie and M.A. Cusumano, "Building a Company on Internet Time: Lessons from Netscape," *California Management Review* 41, no. 3 (1999): 8–28; and J. Champy, *X-Engineering the Corporation: Reinventing Your Business in the Digital Age* (New York: Warner Business Books, 2002).

54. See G.H. Toman, "Technology Trends and You," *Ohio CPA Journal* 55, no. 4 (1996): 57–58; "How Much Is Enough?" *Fast Company* (July/August 1999): 108–116; and M.H. Zack, "Developing a Knowledge Strategy," *California Management Review* 41, no. 3 (1999): 125–145.

55. See R. Jaikumar, "Post-Industrial Manufacturing," *Harvard Business Review* 64 (1986): 69–76; K. Chin, "Life on the Line: Silicon Valley's Anonymous Workers," *Infoworld* 6, no. 2 (1984): 50–56; K. Nussbaum and V. du Rivage, "Computer Monitoring: Mismanagement by Remote Control," *Business and Society Review* no. 56, Winter (1986): 16–20; L.L. Martins and A. Kambil, "Looking Back and Thinking Ahead: Effects of Prior Success on Managers Interpretations of New Information Technologies," *Academy of Management Journal* 42, no. 6 (1999): 652–661; and R.P. Gephart, Jr., "Introduction to the Brave New Workplace: Organizational Behav-ior in the Electronic Age," *Journal of Organizational Behavior* 23, no. 2 (2002): 327–344.

56. See R. Blauner, *Alienation and Freedom: The Factory Worker and His Industry* (Chicago: University of Chicago Press, 1964); C.R. Walker and R.H. Guest, "The Man on the Assembly Line," *Harvard Business Review* 30, no. 3 (1952): 71–83; E.B. Shils, *Automation and Industrial Relations* (New York: Holt, Rinehart & Winston, 1963); and W.A. Faunce, *Problems of an Industrial Society* (New York: McGraw-Hill, 1968).

57. Compare S. Zuboff, "New Worlds of Computer-Mediated Work," *Harvard Business Review* 60, no. 5 (1982): 142–152; with D. Roy, "Efficiency and 'The Fix': Informal Intergroup Relations in a Piecework Machine Shop," in S.M. Lipset and N.J. Smelser, eds., *Sociology: The Progress of a Decade* (Englewood Cliffs, NJ: Prentice Hall, 1961), pp. 378–390; and R. Schrank, *Ten Thousand Working Days* (Cambridge, MA: MIT Press, 1978).

58. This discussion is based on E.E. Lawler, III, "Transformation from Control to Involvement," in R.H. Kilmann, T.J. Covin, and Associates, *Corporate Transformation: Revitalizing Organizations for a Competitive World* (San Francisco: Jossey-Bass, 1988), pp. 46–65; and R.E. Walton, "From Control to Commitment in the Workplace," *Harvard Business Review* 63, no. 2 (1985): 76–84. See also, S. Zamanou and S.R. Glaser, "Moving Toward Participation and Involvement," *Group & Organization Management* 19, no. 4 (1994): 475–502.

59. S. Bailey, "Friendly Fenway," *Boston Globe*, July 26, 2006, p. C1.

60. See "Worker Monitoring and Privacy," *The Futurist* 22, no. 2 (1988): 51; Nussbaum and du Rivage, op. cit.; G.T. Marx and S. Sherizen, "Corporations Spy on Their Employees," *Business and Society Review* no. 60 (Winter 1987): 32–37; and T.E. Deal and A.A. Kennedy, *The New Corporate Cultures: Revitalizing the Workplace After Downsizing, Mergers and Reengineering* (Reading, MA: Persus Books, 1999), Chapter 6.

61. This discussion draws heavily from M.J. Bitner, A.L. Ostrom, and M.L. Meuter, "Implementing Successful Self-Service

Technologies," *Academy of Management Executive* 16, no. 4 (2002): 96–108. See also J.S. Brown and P. Duguid, *The Social Life of Information* (Boston: Harvard Business School Press, 2002).

62. For an excellent illustration of how robots are evolving, see P. Menzel, "Robots: Photo Essay," *Business Week*, December 13, 1999, pp. 178–191. For examples of how sophisticated tasks are being sent overseas, see N.D. Schwartz, "Down and Out in White-Collar America," *Fortune*, June 9, 2003.

63. See S. Greengard, "Making the Virtual Office a Reality," *Personnel Journal* 73, no. 9 (1994): 66–79; H. Ogilvile, "This Old Office," *Journal of Business Strategy* 15, no. 5 (1994): 26–34; T.A. Finholt, "The Electronic Workplace," in C.L. Cooper and D.M. Rousseau (eds.), *Trends in Organizational Behavior*, Vol. 4 (New York: Wiley, 1997), pp. 29–42; and L. Chadderdon, "Remote Workforce, Real Work," *Fast Company* (September/October 1999): 62.

64. See Gephart, "Introduction to the Brave New Workplace"; and "Working from Home Is Working: Employee Desires, Quicker Net Fueling Telecommuting," *Boston Globe*, March 15, 2006, p. E2.

65. J.B. Quinn and F.G. Hilmer, "Strategic Outsourcing," *Sloan Management Review* (Summer 1994): 43–55.

66. Reported in Schwartz, "Down and Out in White-Collar America."

67. G. Koretz, "U.S. Labor Gets Flexible," *Business Week*, January 15, 1996, p. 22.

68. W. Bridges, "The End of the Job," *Fortune*, September 19, 1994, pp. 62–64, 68–74.

69. B. Moses, "Career Intelligence: The 12 New Rules for Success," *Futurist* 33, no. 7 (1999): 28–35.

70. P.H. Mirvis and D.T. Hall, "Psychological Success and the Boundaryless Career," *Journal of Organizational Behavior* 15 (1994): 365–380; M.B. Arthur, P.H. Claman, and R.J. DeFillippi, "Intelligent Enterprise, Intelligent Careers," *Academy of Management Executive* 9, no. 4 (1995): 7–20.

71. See D.M. Rousseau, "Organizational Behavior in the New Organizational Era," *Annual Review of Psychology* 48 (1997): 515–546.

72. See D.T. Hall, *Careers in Organizations* (Pacific Palisades, CA: Goodyear, 1976).

73. D.T. Hall, "The Protean Career: A Quarter Century Journey," *Journal of Vocational Behavior* 65 (2004): 1–13.

74. P. McDonald, K. Brown, and L. Bradley, "Have Traditional Career Paths Given Way to Protean Ones?" *Career Development International* 10 (2005): 109–129; and C. Skromme Granrose and P.A. Baccili, "Do Psychological Contracts Include Boundaryless or Protean Careers?" *Career Development International* 11 (2005): 163–182.

75. See B.L. Wisdom, "If Quality Is So Important, Then Why Don't We Teach It?" *The Organizational Behavior Teaching Review* 13, no. 2 (1988–89): 68–78.

76. This discussion is drawn from J.M. Juran, *Juran on Quality by Design* (New York: Free Press, 1992), pp. 363–366; and B.M. Cook, "Quality: The Pioneers Survey the Landscape," *Industry Week*, October 21, 1991, pp. 68–73.

77. This discussion is based on K. Ishikawa, *What Is Total Quality Control? The Japanese Way* (Englewood Cliffs, NJ: Prentice Hall, 1985); Total Quality Systems, *Total Quality: An Introduction* (Total Quality Systems Company, Inc., 1990); and D.M. Schroeder and A.G. Robinson, "America's Most Successful Export to Japan: Continuous Improvement Programs," *Sloan Management Review* 32, no. 3 (1991): 67–81. See also W.J. Kolarik, *Creating Quality: Process Design for Results* (New York: WCB McGraw-Hill, 1999).

78. See M. Hammer and J. Champy, *Reengineering the Corporation: A Manifesto for Business Revolution* (New York: HarperCollins, 1993); and M. Hammer and S.A. Stanton, *The Reengineering Revolution: A Handbook* (New York: HarperCollins, 1995).

79. T.H. Davenport and L. Prusak, *What's the Big Idea? Creating and Capitalizing on the Best Management Thinking* (Boston: Harvard Business School Press, 2003), pp. 156–158.

80. J.B. White, "Next Big Thing: Re-Engineering Gurus Take Steps to Remodel Their Stalling Vehicles," *Wall Street Journal*, November 26, 1996, p. A1.

81. See Juran, op. cit., Chapter 1.

82. See, for example, K. Fisher and J. Spillane, "Quality and Competitiveness," *Training and Development* (September 1991): 19–24; B. Pfau, D. Detzel, and A. Geller, "Satisfy Your Internal Customers," *The Journal of Business Strategy* (November–December 1991): 9–13; and S.K. Lam and D.N. Izraeli, "Total Quality Management and Performance Appraisal: An Experimental Study of Process Versus Results and Group Versus Individual Approaches," *Journal of Organizational Behavior* 20, no. 4 (1999): 445–458.

83. See D.L. Kanter and P.H. Mirvis, *The Cynical Americans: Living and Working in an Age of Discontent and Disillusion* (San Francisco: Jossey-Bass, 1989); A.E. Reichers, J.P. Wanous, and J.T. Austin, "Understanding and Managing Cynicism about Organizational Change," *Academy of Management Executive* 11, no. 1 (1997): 48–59; and J.P. Wanous, A.E. Reichers, and J.T. Austin, "Cynicism about Organizational Change: Measurement, Antecedents, and Correlates," *Group & Organization Management* 25, no. 2 (2000): 132–153.

84. M.L. Dertouzos, R.K. Lester, R.M. Solow, and the MIT Commission on Industrial Productivity, *Made in America: Regaining the Productive Edge* (Cambridge, MA: MIT Press, 1989); and A.F. Buono, "Moral Corporate Cultures in a Down-Sized, Restructured World," in W.M. Hoffman and R.E. Frederick, eds., *Business Ethics*, 3rd ed. (New York: McGraw-Hill, 1995), pp. 226–233.

85. See P. Hirsch, *Pack Your Own Parachute: How to Survive Mergers, Takeovers, and Other Corporate Disasters* (Reading, MA: Addison-Wesley, 1987); and K.P. DeMeuse and M.L. Marks, *Resizing the Organization: Managing Layoffs, Divestitures, and Closings* (San Francisco: Jossey-Bass, 2003).

86. Kanter and Mirvis, op. cit., see Chapters 5 and 8; and C. Heckscher, *White-Collar Blues: Management Loyalties in an Age of Corporate Restructuring* (New York: Basic Books, 1995).

87. See "The End of Corporate Loyalty?" *Business Week*, August 4, 1986, pp. 42–49. For an updated assessment of this problem, see F.F. Reichheld, *The Loyalty Effect* (Cambridge, MA: Harvard Business School Press, 1996).

88. This section draws heavily from M. Rau-Foster, "Workplace Civility and Staff Retention," *Nephrology Nursing Journal* 31, no. 6 (2004): 702. See also S.J. Grove, R.P. Fisk, and J. John, "Surviving in the Age of Rage," *Marketing Management* 13, no. 2 (2004): 41–46.

89. The following section is based on S.L. Robinson and J. Greenberg, "Employees Behaving Badly: Dimensions, Determinants and Dilemmas in the Study of Workplace Deviance," in C.L. Cooper and D.M. Rousseau (eds.), *Trends in Organizational Behavior*, vol. 5 (New York: John Wiley, 1998), pp. 1–30; and R.W. Griffin, A. O'Leary-Kelly, and J.M. Collins, *Dysfunctional Behavior in Organizations: Violent and Deviant Behavior* (Stamford, CT: JAI Press, 1998).

90. See B. Filipczak, "Armed and Dangerous at Work," *Training* (July 1993): 39–43; and R.W. Griffin, A. O'Leary-Kelly, and J.M. Collins, "Dysfunctional Work Behaviors in Organizations," in Cooper and Rousseau, *Trends in Organizational Behavior*, vol. 5, p. 74.

91. See T. Cambanis, "Worker Vengeance Makes Its Way Online," *Boston Globe*, May 22, 2003, pp. A1, A36.

92. See the section on "Justice and HRM" in G.R. Ferris, W.A. Hochwarter, M.R. Buckley, G. Harrell-Cook, and D.D. Frink, "Human Resources Management: Some New Directions," *Journal of Management* 25, no. 3 (1999): 385–415.

93. This discussion is based on J.A. Clair, "Teaching Through Traumatic Events: Uncovering the Choices of Management Educators as They Respond to September 11th," *Academy of Management Learning & Education* 1, no. 1 (2002): 38–54.

94. The following discussion draws heavily from K. Downey, "New Risks Widen Definition of Dirty, Hazardous Work: From Flight Crews to Mail Carriers, Terror, Disease Causing Fear," *Boston Globe*, June 1, 2003, p. E3.

95. M.L. Marks, *Charging Back Up the Hill: Workplace Recovery After Mergers, Acquisitions, and Downsizings* (San Francisco: Jossey-Bass, 2003).

96. See N.B. Songer, "Work Force Diversity," *Business & Economic Review*

(April–June 1991): pp. 3–6; and J. Kennedy and A. Everest, "Put Diversity in Context," *Personnel Journal* (September 1991): 50–54.

97. S. Nkomo and M.M. Stewart, "Diverse Identities in Organizations," in S. Clegg, C. Hardy, T. Lawrence, and W.R. Nord (eds.), *The Handbook of Organizational Studies* (Thousand Oaks, CA: Sage, 2006), pp. 520–540.

98. M. Loden and J.B. Rosener, *Workforce America: Managing Employee Diversity as a Vital Resource* (Homewood, IL: Business One Irwin, 1991); and Griggs and Louw, *Valuing Diversity*, op. cit.

99. B. Geber, "Managing Diversity," *Training* (July 1990): 23–30.

100. This distinction is drawn from Q.M. Roberson, "Disentangling the Meanings of Diversity and Inclusion in Organizations," *Group and Organization Management* 31 (2006): 212–236.

101. See B. Rosen and K. Lovelace, "Piecing Together the Diversity Puzzle," *HR Magazine* (June 1991): 78–84; J.L. Morrison, "Workforce Diversity: The Changing Workplace and Its Impact on Company Policies and Business," *Journal of Education for Business* 71, no. 1 (1995): 5–7.

102. K.Y. Williams and C.A. O'Reilly III, "Demography and Diversity in Organizations: A Review of 40 Years of Research," *Research in Organizational Behavior* 20, (1998): 77–140.

103. K.L. Bettenhausen, "Five Years of Group Research: What We Have Learned and What Needs to Be Addressed," *Journal of Management* (June 1991): 345–381.

104. See T. Cox, "The Multicultural Organization," *Academy of Management Executive* 5 (1991): 34–47; D.A. Thomas and R.D. Ely, "Making Differences Matter: A New Paradigm for Managing Diversity," *Harvard Business Review* 74, no. 5 (1996): 79–90; and R.J. Ely and D.A. Thomas, "Cultural Diversity at Work: The Effects of Diversity Perspectives of Work Group Processes and Outcomes," *Administrative Science Quarterly* 46 (2001): 229–273.

105. S. Overman, "Managing the Diverse Work Force," *HR Magazine* (April 1991): 32–36; and G. Haight, "Managing Diversity," *Across the Board* (March 1990): 22–29.

106. See S. Kuczynski, "If Diversity, Then Higher Profits?" *HR Magazine* 44, no. 13 (1999): 66–75.

107. This discussion is drawn from D. Sirota and A.D. Wolfson, "Pragmatic Approach to People Problems," *Harvard Business Review* 51, no. 1 (1973): pp. 120–123; E. Abrahamson, "Managerial Fads and Fashions: The Diffusion and Rejection of Innovations," *Academy of Management Review* 16 (1991): 586–612; and C.M. Fiol and E.J. O'Connor, "Waking Up! Mindfulness in the Face of Bandwagons," *Academy of Management Review* 28, no. 1 (2003): 54–70.

108. D.L. Gertz and J. Baptista, *Grow to Be Great: Breaking the Downsizing Cycle* (New York: Free Press, 1995); and Weber, op. cit.

109. See Davenport and Prusak, *What's the Big Idea*.

110. M.J. Cavanaugh, "(In)corporating the Other? Managing the Politics of Workplace Difference," in P. Prasad and A. Mills (eds.), *Managing the Organizational Melting Pot: Dilemmas of Workplace Diversity* (Newbury: Sage, 1997), pp. 31–53; and D.R. Litvin, "The Business Case for Diversity and the 'Iron Cage,'" The 16th EGOS Colloquium, Helsinki, 2000.

111. M. Alvesson and S. Deetz, *Doing Critical Management Research* (London: Sage, 2000); D.L. Collinson and K.J. Hearn, *Men as Managers, Managers as Men: Critical Perspectives on Men, Masculinities, and Managements* (Thousand Oaks, CA: Sage, 1996); and D. Grimes, "Putting Our Own House in Order: Whiteness, Change and Organization Studies," *Journal of Organizational Change Management* 14 (2001): 132–149.

112. See Nkomo and Stewart, "Diverse Identities in Organizations."

113. See O. Atkouf, "Management and Theories of Organizations in the 1990s: Toward a Critical Radical Humanism?" *Academy of Management Review* 17, no. 3 (1992): 407–431; E. Abrahamson, "Managerial Fads and Fashions: The Diffusion and Rejection of Innovations," *Academy of Management Review* 16, no. 3 (1991): 588–589; and B. Venard, "Transforming Consulting Knowledge into Business Fads," in A.F. Buono (Ed.), *Current Trends in Management Consulting*

(Greenwich, CT: Information Age Publishing, 2001), pp. 171–188.

114. See J. Micklethwait and A. Wooldridge, *The Witch Doctors: Making Sense of Management Gurus* (New York: Times Books, 1996); and L. Donaldson and F.G. Hilmer, "Management Redeemed: The Case against Fads That Harm Management," *Organizational Dynamics* (Spring 1998): 7–20.

115. See S. Ghoshal's critical assessment, "Bad Management Theories Are Destroying Good Management Practices," *Academy of Management Learning & Education* 4, no. 1 (2005): 86–87.

CHAPTER TWO

Perception, Attitudes, and Individual Differences

Many of the theories discussed in this book attempt to explain general behavioral tendencies. While these concepts provide us with a broad understanding of such behavior, they do not necessarily give us insight into the behavior of a particular individual. By understanding and building on these general theories, however, we can begin to move closer to an understanding of why a specific person may behave the way she or he does.

One of the major determinants of *how* and *why* an individual initiates and sustains certain behaviors is based on the concepts of sensation and perception. *Sensation* refers to the physical stimulation of the senses—our ability to see, hear, smell, taste, and touch. Although knowledge of these different sensations helps to explain some of the *whys* and *hows* of behavior, we also need to understand how an individual reacts to and organizes these sensations. This process is referred to as *perception* and refers to the way in which we interpret messages from our senses to provide some order and meaning to our environment. The key to this definition is the term *interpret*. Since different people can view the same situation in disparate ways, the interpretation of the meaning of a particular event determines how these individuals will react to it. Thus, perception can be thought of as an *intervening variable* that influences behavior.[1]

This chapter begins with a brief discussion of visual and auditory perception and moves toward social perception. An underlying assumption made by perception theorists is that certain types of mental processes that operate in relatively simple visual and auditory situations similarly occur in more complex interpersonal situations. Thus, the ability to examine more complex forms of perception is based on our understanding of these relatively simple perceptual processes.

There are a number of internal and external factors that influence the way in which we view the world around us. Before proceeding to an examination of these variables, however, it is necessary to identify two basic sources of perceptual variation: *physiological limitations* and *cultural and environmental constraints*. We are surrounded by data that are transmitted through our daily interactions with others, the Internet and media, educational experiences, family life and friendships, work experiences, and our socialization processes in general. The physiological aspect of perception defines the limits of what we can actually see, hear, smell, and so forth of these data. Yet, even given these limitations, the information that is gathered by our senses does not enter our minds as raw or unprocessed data. Rather, people tend to interpret this information in a way that is congruent with their sets of beliefs, values, and attitudes, which are shaped by larger cultural and environmental experiences. Thus, perception is determined by the interaction among these psychological and broader sociocultural factors.

BASIC INTERNAL PERCEPTUAL ORGANIZING PATTERNS

Since people are continually subjected to a barrage of visual and auditory stimulation from the outside world, it is necessary to have an internal process or way in which all these data can be *selected* and *organized* into meaningful information. This type of selective process occurs at two basic levels: (1) those data a person is aware of and can recognize fairly readily after selection, and (2) data that may be below the threshold of awareness.[2] Once people select the data to be "processed" or interpreted, the next phase is to order or classify these data in a meaningful way. As suggested earlier, this does not occur in a random or haphazard manner, but instead in a way that is consistent with our beliefs and values.

Gestalt Psychology

According to one school of thought, instead of providing us with a mirror image of the outside world, data enter our minds in already highly abstracted forms, which are referred to as structures or *gestalts*.[3] Although some information is inevitably lost in the translation of raw data into these gestalts, such structural transformations of real-world, primary data enable us to interpret or understand that world. Thus, when we perceive something, we are essentially attempting to fit that object or event into a preestablished frame of reference or classification scheme.

The basic tenet of *gestalt theory* is that organization of the data around us is part of the perceptual process and *not* something that is added after variables are selected. In visual perception, for example, Gestalt psychology explains why we organize the stimuli shown here to "see" groups of dots (e.g., two groups of three, three groups of two), instead of six individual dots:

$$\begin{matrix} \bullet & \bullet \\ \bullet & \bullet \\ \bullet & \bullet \end{matrix}$$

In terms of auditory phenomena, Morse code is a series of short and longer sounds. To many people this may seem to be nothing more than random noise. To a listener who has been trained to understand these sounds, however, this "noise" is a form of communication.

Figure-Ground Phenomena

Another visual tendency that influences how we organize our perceptions is the *figure-ground* relationship.[4] When we observe various phenomena, we tend to organize these data in such a way as to minimize differences and changes while maintaining unity and wholeness. The basis of this process is our tendency to perceive a figure against its background. Compared to the background, a figure will appear to have shape, object-like dimensions, and substance as well as being nearer and more vivid than it actually may be. This figure-ground phenomenon can influence our tendency to perceive configurations even when the individual elements do not bear any relationship to the composite we "see." When looking at clouds, for example, we often perceive vivid faces, mosaics, or other "pictures" that are, in reality, nothing more than a mass of condensed water vapor.

At times, however, a given pattern may be organized so that more than one figure-ground relationship may be perceived. In Figure 2-1, for example, you may "see" two faces looking at each other or an ornate goblet. In auditory phenomena, a close analogue to the figure-ground relationship is the *signal-to-noise* ratio. If a radio signal is weak and the static is strong, we do not hear the radio signal. In social situations, there may also be a number of signals we do not "hear" (e.g., dissatisfaction and complaints from our subordinates) because of the "noise" around us (e.g., pressure to complete a task to please *our* boss). Even though the signal itself may be quite strong, the noisy background often limits our ability to hear it.

Closure

Closure refers to our tendency to perceive incomplete figures as if they were complete. When looking at Figure 2-2, for example, we usually see a triangle instead of three separate lines; we "close" that part of the figure that is left open. Similarly, we often anticipate the end of a song because music usually follows a fairly standard pattern. Thus, even if the last few notes of a song were left out, we could most likely complete the song based on what would sound "right." In work situations, we can also "close" a conversation with someone when we anticipate what their response is likely to be. As will be discussed in Chapter 4, this tendency can readily lead to breakdowns in communication.

Figure 2-1   Figure-Ground Relationships: Which Is the Figure and Which Is the Ground?

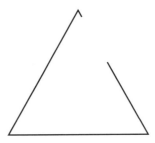

Figure 2-2 Perceptual Closure

In summary, these internal tendencies are some of the factors that influence what we see and hear of the world around us. As indicated earlier, these tendencies are shaped by our cultural and social experiences. Indeed, as research has shown, due to the influence of past experiences and socialization, similar events are perceived quite differently by people from different cultural environments.[5]

EXTERNAL FACTORS IN PERCEPTION

Although what we see and hear is significantly influenced by our internal processes, the way in which various stimuli are presented to us also influences our perception of them. In contrast to the discussion earlier, these factors relate more to the nature of the stimulus itself than to the human mechanisms used to "pick up" the stimulus.

Intensity or relative strength of an object, noise, or occurrence can significantly influence our perception of it. In our brief allusion to the signal-to-noise ratio earlier, we noted that a radio transmission is more likely to be heard only if it is louder than the background noise. Similarly a pungent smell is more likely to be noticed than a subtle one; witness our awareness of the smell of a skunk as opposed to the scent of a rose.

Contrast refers to the extent something stands out in relation to its background. A bright light tends to be more noticeable than a dim one (intensity), but a particularly bright light is less likely to be noticed in a theater district because it is surrounded by other bright lights. Similarly, certain behaviors that tend to be unrecognized in one context will stand out in different social situations. A child's playful behavior, for example, is much more noticeable among adults than among other children.

Size also influences our visual perception. Quite simply, large objects are more noticeable than smaller ones. Since they stand out more fully in relation to their background (contrast), larger objects have a greater probability of being selected into our perception.

Proximity is another factor that can influence what we see. Things that are physically close tend to be viewed as "belonging to" each other more than similar things that are farther away. For instance, in the example shown here, you are likely to see pairs of XOs rather than a number of Xs and Os:

XO XO XO XO XO XO

Similarity of things, however, does tend to influence our perception when objects are in relatively the same proximity to one another. Things that are similar tend to be seen as belonging together more than to other equally close but less similar things. In the example here, there is a tendency to see columns of Xs and Os rather than rows of alternating letters X O X O X O:

```
X O X O X O
X O X O X O
X O X O X O
X O X O X O
```

Repetition or frequency is another external factor that influences what we notice. Things that are repeated or occur frequently are "seen" more readily than those events or objects that are infrequent or not repeated. This is part of the rationale in political and advertising campaigns, where a candidate or product is given repeated exposure.

Motion also influences our ability to select various stimuli, since we tend to notice things that move against a relatively still background. This can also apply to auditory stimulation when we track sounds—such as a police or fire siren—as they move toward or away from us.

Novel and **very familiar** perceptual settings are more readily selected than situations that are neither very novel nor very familiar. For instance, new products that are sufficiently different can attract quite a bit of attention (novelty). At the same time, we seem to take more notice if "our" street is shown in the media (familiarity).

The discussion thus far has focused on some of the relatively simple external factors that influence perception. In summary, we have a tendency to select various external objects, sounds, or events that are more intense, larger in nature, in contrast to their background, close in proximity, repetitive, in motion, and either novel or very familiar.[6] The chapter now turns to an examination of some of the ways in which these influences interact with more complex internal tendencies to affect social and interpersonal perception.

SOCIAL AND INTERPERSONAL PERCEPTION

Just as our perception of different visual and auditory phenomena is influenced by a number of internal and external factors, the perception of other people and social situations is also a dynamic process. To "understand" or make sense of the complex behavior of other people, we often make inferences or assumptions about their motivations, intentions, personalities, emotions, and so forth. Such inferences or impressions subsequently become a significant determinant of our behavior toward and interaction with these individuals.

Schemas and Scripts

People often use *schemas,* cognitive frameworks that systematize our "knowledge" about gender differences, other people, situations, objects, and ideas that we generate through experience, to effectively organize information about these phenomena.[7] These schemas can reflect ourselves, characteristics of others we interact with, the roles we play, and events we experience.

Self-schemas capture generalizations we make about our own behaviors that are shaped by past experience and current situations. Organizational members, for instance, often exhibit self-schemas of competence or decisiveness when confronted with particular tasks they are familiar with.

Person schemas reflect ideal characteristics of others that we sort into different categories. When organizations refer to "role models," for example, they are typically referring to individuals who reflect those qualities (hard work, dedication, innovation, etc.) that the organization is striving for. As will be discussed later, *stereotyping*, which can be both positive and negative, is based on person (and/or group) schemas.

Event schemas, often referred to as *scripts*, capture a mental picture of a series of events that often guides our behavior. In large-scale organizational change efforts, managers often use scripts to try to shape or influence the way in which people react or respond to the changes that are taking place around them.

Role schemas, sometimes referred to as "person-in-situation" schemas, combine self-schemas, person schemas, and event schemas in ways that frame what we expect from people based on the role(s) that we play. Our perception of the student–teacher role set, for example, readily creates expectations about how the individuals in question should act in those roles.

Perceptual Distortion

Similar to our perception of different objects or sounds, our perception of other people is subject to a number of distortions and illusions. We often "see" people in a way that may be quite different from how they are actually or objectively presented to us. Just as we use internal devices to reduce (select) the amount of visual and auditory data around us into manageable portions, we also have a number of devices—*perceptual sets*—that influence how we interpret or "understand" behavior and social interaction. Although some of these perceptual tendencies have greater empirical research support than others, they are all readily observable in everyday situations.[8]

Stereotyping

Stereotyping is the process of using a standardized impression of a group of people to influence our perception of a particular individual. It is a way of forming consistent impressions about other people by assuming that they *all* have certain common characteristics by virtue of their membership (whether ascribed or achieved) in some group or category, such as race, gender, occupation, or social class. There are three basic aspects to stereotyping:[9]

1. Some category of people is identified (e.g., IT technicians, racial or ethnic groups, OB professors).

2. An assumption is made that individuals in this category have certain traits (e.g., nerdy, lazy, sensitive).

3. Finally, the general perception is formed that everyone in the category possesses those traits (e.g., all IT technicians are geeks, all members of a certain ethnic group are lazy, all OB professors are "touchy-feely").

Thus, we create images of people based on characterizations we make about a particular group of people rather than the individual.

To a large extent, people depend on stereotypes to reduce their information-processing demands. Unfortunately, this dependence can create a multitude of problems for organizations and their members. With respect to OB, occupational, gender, race, and age stereotypes are especially relevant. As we will see in Chapter 6, occupational stereotypes (e.g., people in finance are cold and calculating) are often the basis underlying intergroup conflict. Moreover, negative stereotypes, which are resistant to change, can readily contribute to inefficient and uneconomical decisions, and those that focus on a particular gender, race, age, or physical ability can create significant barriers and severely limit the access of minority status individuals to higher-level organizational roles and positions.[10]

Not all stereotypes, however, are necessarily inaccurate or harmful, and they can be useful in helping us to process information fairly quickly. We often use "ideal types" (a form of stereotyping) to make comparisons between extremes—such as capitalism and socialism, or mechanistic and organic environments—as the basis for further investigation. The danger lies in using stereotypes to develop our perceptions about specific people or situations.

Stereotype Content and Out-Groups

The stereotype content model (SCM) recognizes the potential for individuals to hold multiple and mixed stereotypes about out-groups.[11] Perceived *warmth* and *competence* comprise two primary dimensions of group stereotypes. Warmth is associated with beliefs about the out-group's intent toward the in-group. In other words, out-groups tend to be perceived as more (or less) warm to the extent they are perceived to have goals that are consistent (or competitive) with the goals of the in-group. Competence is associated with the extent to which out-groups are perceived as able to successfully pursue their goals. Within this framework, the primary determinant of perceived out-group competence is perceived status, such that high-status groups are construed as having been effective in pursuing key goals, in essence making their status legitimate.

It is important to note that positive stereotypes on one dimension do not necessarily indicate the absence of prejudice. In fact, positive stereotypes on one dimension are often functionally consistent with derogatory stereotypes on the other dimension. For example, socioeconomically successful out-groups, such as Asians, can pose a competitive threat to dominant in-group members, and this success elicits envy. Low-warmth stereotypes justify such attitudes and actions against envied out-groups by casting the groups as being solely concerned with the pursuit of their own goals. Taken together, competent (high-status) but low-warmth (competitive) out-groups may thus be resented and socially excluded. These mixed stereotypes also help to explain the perceived success of the out-group, affirming beliefs that the existing system is just and meritocratic, which serves to maintain the social status quo, benefiting dominant in-groups.

Halo Effect

The halo effect refers to the process of allowing one characteristic of an individual or a group to overshadow all other characteristics of that individual or group.[12] The salient characteristic may be positive or negative, thereby creating a general impression that would correspondingly be positive or negative. We often assume, for example, that simply because an individual may do something very well (e.g., act, play sports) he or she is obviously well informed about other things in life (e.g., cars, deodorants). The advertising community places great faith (and money) in the halo effect on the assumption that if we like a particular individual we will also like the product that person is endorsing.

It is particularly important to be aware of the halo effect when conducting performance appraisals, so that one feature does not influence the overall evaluation. There have been cases where a rater who did not like mustaches or long hair allowed those features to sway an entire appraisal, ignoring the "good" qualities or contributions of the employee. In other instances, if a person performs well on the job but is constantly late, the tardiness may overly influence that person's performance review, causing the rater to devalue the employee's work efforts. Given the increased diversity in the workplace, it is also important to be aware of the *similar-to-me* effect: We tend to be favorably disposed to others whom we perceive to be similar to us and tend to be more guarded with those who we think are different.[13]

Expectancy

Another factor that can readily influence social perception concerns our *expectations* about what we will see (or hear). In many instances, we "see" what we expect to see, rather than what is actually occurring. These expectations subsequently influence our attitudes and behavior toward the person or persons involved and can distort the situation.

Self-Fulfilling Prophecy   If someone expects or perceives that another person will act in a particular way, that other person often lives up to or fulfills that expectation. This tendency is referred to as a *self-fulfilling prophecy.*[14] When we behave toward others according to the way we expect them to respond (e.g., tightly controlling people who we predict will be lazy), they often will react to us as we expected—because of *our* behaviors. In effect, our actions have created the situation we expected, thus reinforcing our initial perceptions.

There is ample evidence that people often behave toward others in ways that produce the very behavior they expected.[15] Moreover, self-fulfilling prophecy dynamics often operate automatically or "entirely nonconsciously," such that the automatic activation of stereotypes encourages individuals to subconsciously act in accordance with their expectations toward others.[16] In essence, their actions influence others to act as expected, with no awareness of the process by either party.

Selective Perception   Another way our expectations can distort a given situation is through *selective perception,* a process of filtering out some messages and paying more attention to others. Two factors that underlie this process are *selective attention* (when we listen to or watch for certain messages and ignore others) and *selective retention* (when we remember certain messages and forget others).[17] For example, when we expect that an individual will behave in a certain way, we tend to concentrate on those (expected) activities and ignore efforts that do not conform to our expectations. We then have a tendency to remember those initially expected behaviors, which influences our attitudes and behaviors and can lead to the type of self-fulfilling prophecy discussed earlier. We often use this mechanism when we draw unjustified conclusions from unclear or ambiguous situations.

Projection   Projection refers to a tendency to place the blame for our own difficulties or problems on others, or to attribute our feelings to other people. In business situations, for example, managers often project power motives to "explain" the behavior of other managers or their subordinates, when the managers who make the observation might be the ones with power-related needs. The same is true of many union-management negotiations, where each party projects its own feelings of mistrust onto the other group. Similarly, an underlying reason why many sexual harassment complaints seem to "fall on deaf ears" is that managers often *blame the victim*, projecting negative attributes and outcomes on the complaining individual (e.g., "she brought it on herself," "she shouldn't have dressed or acted that way").[18]

Perceptual Defense

Once we develop a perception of someone, we have a tendency to cling to that perception by shaping what we see and hear so as to be consistent with our beliefs. Thus, we might refuse to acknowledge a particular stimulus if it does not meet our initial perceptions. We can distort it, deny it, render it meaningless, or even recognize the incongruence, but not allow it to make any real change.[19] In a sense, the various types of perceptual distortions or shortcuts discussed earlier are all kinds of perceptual defenses.

Attribution Theory

Attribution theory is concerned with what people identify as the apparent reason or cause for behavior. Since the way in which we view a situation determines how we will attempt to deal with it, this theory holds important implications for managers. For instance, if one of our subordinates is not doing well on the job and we think that the poor performance is due to laziness, we will come up with a very different solution than if we think the poor performance is due to an unclear job description or to the structure of the job itself. Thus, how we *think* a particular behavior is caused has a direct bearing on the way we approach that situation.

Essentially, attribution theory operates in the following manner:[20] (1) We observe a given behavior and attempt to determine the reason for the behavior (e.g., was accidental or intentional); then (2) if we think the behavior was intentional, we try to assess whether the action was determined by the situation or by the individual (e.g., the person's personality); and finally (3) we attribute a meaning (cause) to that behavior. For instance, if behavior by the same employee on different jobs is similar when other employees' behaviors differ from job to job, we would probably attribute that individual's behavior to personality traits instead of job-related characteristics and react accordingly.

A number of factors help us to determine why a person acted in a particular way. Our methods for making these determinations, however, are not completely rational; they are referred to as *attributional biases*. For instance, while both personal *and* situational factors might have influenced the individual's behavior in the previous example, we often attempt to simplify the judgment-forming process by focusing on *one* set of these factors. Thus, some individuals will tend to perceive internal or personal causes as being responsible for behavior (such as intelligence, motivation, personality), while others will rely more heavily on environmental or situational factors (such as organizational rules, the structure of the job). Some individuals, of course, perceive causation in terms of an additive combination of both internal and external factors. The key to attribution theory, however, is not what actually determines or causes the behavior, but what we *perceive* to be the underlying cause.

A common error individuals engage in when making attributions about their own outcomes is to internally attribute favorable outcomes, and to externally attribute negative outcomes. This is called the *self-serving bias.* Conversely, when drawing attributions about others' outcomes, individuals tend to over attribute favorable outcomes to external factors, discounting possible internal explanations, and to over attribute negative outcomes to internal factors. This tendency is referred to as the *fundamental attribution error.*

While both managers and subordinates often attempt to determine the extent to which a particular behavior varies across different entities, contexts, or people, due to time constraints or insufficient motivation, these same individuals may simply adopt their own assumptions that "explain" the behavior.[21] As suggested above, these patterns of assumptions, referred to as *causal schemes,* are heavily influenced by the attributional biases held by the person, which can vary widely among people. Thus, in many instances, what could be a healthy and productive interaction between a manager and his or her subordinates may be undermined by conflicting attributional biases held by each party.[22] In fact, many theorists argue that much of the conflict that occurs between managers and their subordinates is a result of leaders acting on their own causal schemes (i.e., interpretations of the situation), which are quite different from those of their subordinates. Research also suggests that when individuals perceive ambiguous actions by others as stemming from malicious intentions, they are much more likely to become angry and to retaliate than when they perceive the same actions as stemming from other motives.[23]

As a way of creating more productive employee relations, therefore, researchers suggest attempts to reduce divergent perceptions and perspectives between the parties (e.g., increased interpersonal interaction, open communication channels, workshops devoted to reducing attributional errors) and to place greater attention on the differences that exist among individuals. The popularity of *360-degree feedback*, where individual employees complete the same structured evaluation process that managers, direct reports, team members, peers, and even customers use to evaluate their performance, reflects these concerns.[24]

Locus of Control

A corollary to this discussion is the concept of *locus of control,* the general way in which people view causation in their own lives. Some individuals view their behaviors and outcomes as internally controlled, and thus believe that they are in control of their lives. Others, however, feel that their behaviors and outcomes are externally controlled, believing that their lives are influenced by other circumstances rather than their own efforts. If an individual perceives that he or she is in control of a situation, the outcome is likely to be quite different than if the person feels that external forces are in control. Research has indicated, for example, that employees with a perceived internal locus of control have higher levels of job satisfaction and are more comfortable with a participative style of management than individuals with an external locus of control.[25] These internally oriented employees enjoy participating in work-related decisions as a way of exerting control over their environment. Similarly, an internal locus of control has been found to be related to entrepreneurial activity and a tendency to start new businesses.[26]

Attribution Theory and Motivation

As we will explore in the next chapter, there are different sets of assumptions about why individuals behave the way they do that influence how we attempt to motivate people. A manager who thinks that people are economically oriented might tinker with wage and salary schemes to influence and reinforce good work performance. A manager who thinks that social concerns are more important might concentrate efforts on improving the climate of the work group by making the organization a "happier" place to work. The manager who assumes that people are influenced by opportunities for personal growth and development, in contrast, might try to make jobs as challenging as possible. Finally, the manager who thinks that people are more complex might try to find out "what turns workers on" and develop individually tailored motivational schemes.

In an objective sense, each of these managers might be correct (or incorrect) about what motivates any given person. However, the fact that the manager *perceives* that one thing or another motivates the worker ultimately determines the manager's policies and behavior; and the manager's policies and behavior have a direct influence on the worker's behavior. Since each of these assumptions will tend to influence the individuals involved quite differently, the key is how motivation is *perceived* in terms of what motivates people rather than the accuracy of the motivational model per se. This is an important basis of attribution theory—a person's beliefs about his or her future activities and interpretations of past activities influence that person's actions in the present.[27]

PERCEPTION AND INDIVIDUAL DIFFERENCES

As discussed earlier, there are a number of internal and external factors as well as perceptual tendencies that influence what each of us sees and hears of the world around us. Thus, different individuals organize their perceptions of reality in a distinctive if not unique manner. Within the context of a diverse workplace, these differences can readily moderate the ways in which people respond to a variety of organizational and managerial practices. Different individuals, for example, will vary in terms of how much importance they attach to intrinsic job-related rewards, the style of leadership they prefer, their need for interpersonal contact and interaction, and their tolerance and acceptance of job responsibility.[28]

Within organizational behavior (OB), the concept of individual differences implies that personal characteristics influence the way in which people perform on the job and in the workplace. This section briefly examines how an individual's personality and self-concept can influence perception and work-related behaviors, and the implications for management decision making.

Personality

While many factors influence perception, one of the most influential determinants is an individual's personality. Psychologists use the concept in a neutral, universal sense in terms of what *characterizes* an individual. Although there are a variety of definitions of personality, an underlying theme is *consistency,* the similarity of responses a person makes in different situations. In fact, research evidence is accumulating that suggests virtually all personality measures can be condensed into five key traits, referred to as the "Big Five":[29]

1. **Conscientiousness** is the degree to which a person is dependable, responsible, organized, and a planner (forward looking).

2. **Extroversion** is the degree to which a person is sociable, talkative, assertive, active, and ambitious, and is able and willing to openly express feelings and emotions.

3. **Openness to experience** is the extent to which an individual is imaginative, broad minded, and curious with a tendency to seek new experiences.

4. **Emotional stability (neuroticism)** is the degree to which an individual is anxious, depressed, angry, and generally emotionally insecure.

5. **Agreeableness** is the extent to which a person is courteous, good-natured, flexible, trusting, and liked by others.

Although it is not completely clear how these traits and individuals personalities develop, there appear to be three major influences: (1) our physical traits and biological makeup, which limit the ways we are able to adapt to our environment; (2) our socialization and the culture of our group and society; and (3) the various life events, sensations, and other situational factors we experience.[30] These influences, which both form and interact with our interpretations of these influences, establish the uniqueness of individuals and are responsible for those behaviors and manifestations that we refer to as personality. Research, for example, suggests that various traits interact to form different personality types, such as: (1) the *authoritarian* personality, which is characterized by rigidity, obedience, submission to authority, and a tendency to stereotype; (2) the *Machiavellian* personality, which is oriented toward manipulation and control, with a low sensitivity to the needs of others; and (3) the *existential* personality, which tends to place a high value on choice, attempts to maintain an accurate perception of reality, and tries to understand other people.[31] In essence, our personality acts as a kind of perceptual filter or frame of reference that influences our view of the world.

One personality dichotomy that has enjoyed prominence in the OB literature is the "Type A–Type B" personality. *Type A* personalities are hard-driving, competitive individuals who are prompt but always feel rushed. Characteristic Type A behavior includes a tendency toward impatience, hurriedness, competitiveness, and hostility, especially when the individual is experiencing stress or challenge. *Type B* personalities, in contrast, are reflective, more relaxed, and easier-going individuals who feel more free to express their feelings.[32] Assessments of these two personality types are often associated with stress and health risks (e.g., heart attacks) for Type A individuals. There are also parallels between the needs for achievement and power and Type A personalities, and the need for affiliation and Type B personalities.

Another commonly used personality dimension in work-related research is Jung's extroversion and introversion typology.[33] As noted earlier, the *extroverted* personality is oriented toward the external, objective world, while the *introverted* personality is focused on the inner, subjective world.[34] Beyond these two attitudes or orientations, personality also has implications for our thinking, feeling, sensing, and intuiting.[35] *Thinking* involves our comprehension of the world and our place in it. *Feeling* reflects our subjective affective experiences, such as pleasure or pain, anger, joy, and love. *Sensing* is defined as our perceptual or reality function in that it encompasses concrete facts or representations of the individual's world. Finally, *intuiting* refers to perception through unconscious processes or subliminal means. According to Jung, the intuitive individual goes beyond facts, feelings, and ideas to construct more elaborate models of reality.[36]

One of the currently most popular means of assessing Jungian personality types is the Myers-Briggs Type Indicator. This typology reformulates Jung's model into four dichotomies: (1) extroversion-introversion (EI), (2) sensing-intuiting (SN), (3) thinking-feeling (TF), and (4) judgment-perception (JP). Individuals are "typed" on each of these four dimensions and are given a pattern—for instance, ENFP, ISTJ, or ESTP—which has been found to have some, though limited, predictive validity. Research, for example, has indicated that some people are more open to new information from others (P: high on perception) while others tend to be more closed to new information (J: high on judgment). Individuals high on the high-judgment dimension have a preference to make their own decisions, develop plans, and reach conclusions instead of continuing to collect data or to keep considering alternatives. Those high on the perception dimension, in contrast, tend to be more open and adaptable, and willing to receive new information.[37]

Although some theories suggest that our personalities are largely formed by the time we are six years old, other views of personality development argue that there are critical periods throughout early to late or mature adulthood.[38] Thus, it seems that although our personalities may be initially shaped during our early years, they continue to be altered as we encounter different life experiences. In terms of OB, the implications of such "age-linkages" in personality development are reflected in research indicating that not only do general life experiences affect our adjustment to work, but experiences on the job may actually have a greater impact on our psychological adjustments than the reverse.[39]

In summary, personality develops over the course of an individual's life and influences that person's perception of reality and behavior in organizations. Since organizations can only be as creative and adaptive as the people they employ, these findings reflect some of the main reasons for career development initiatives and employee assistance programs (EAPs).

Organizational Application

Perhaps the most significant illustration of the effect of personality in organizational life is reflected in parallels between common neurotic styles of behavior and typical modes of organizational failure.[40] "Stagnant bureaucracies," for example, are exemplified by organizations that do not have clear goals, lack initiative, react sluggishly to environmental change, and are pervaded by managerial apathy, frustration, and inaction. On an individual level, the depressive personality style exhibits very similar features. This relationship is especially significant in the context of studies indicating that the strategy, culture, and even structure of an organization can be significantly influenced by the personality of the top executive. Since we all possess certain patterns of dealing with our environment, which are deeply embedded, pervasive, and likely to continue, the personality of those at the top of an organization can shape the way in which the firm adapts to its environment.

In organizations where power is broadly distributed, strategy, culture, and structure are typically influenced by many managers, and the relationship between the excessive use of one neurotic style and organizational pathology is more tenuous. In those organizations where power is highly concentrated, in contrast, a neurotic style at the top of the organization can have an impact at all levels. Suspicious top executives, who often expect to find trickery and deception in the behavior of others and seek out "facts" to confirm their worst expectations, gradually create cultures that are permeated with distrust, suspicion, fear, and a preoccupation with "enemies." Employee morale typically suffers a great deal under these conditions, as people at all levels withhold their contributions and focus on protecting themselves from exploitation. In some instances, entire organizations can experience the dysfunctional effects of these dynamics, resulting in what have been referred to as "depressed organizations." These organizations are characterized by (1) a general feeling of lethargy, (2) little creativity or innovation, (3) marginally acceptable productivity, (4) a high rate of absenteeism and tardiness, (5) restricted communication within and between departments, (6) lengthy decision making, and (7) little joy or enthusiasm expressed by employees.[41]

A related area of concern focuses on executives in personal crisis; senior-level managers with problems that go beyond those associated with work overload, stress, and related adjustment difficulties. Such crises can involve alcoholism, drug abuse, depression, and mania—problems that can require hospitalization.[42] While a growing number of organizations are improving their ability to work with lower-level, supervisory, and even mid-level management personnel with such problems through EAPs, there are a number of reasons why these problems often go undetected with higher-level executives: (1) a usual lack of close, day-to-day supervision of senior executives by their superiors; (2) the difficulty in connecting a developing mental health problem with declining performance, especially in the early stages; (3) the desire of subordinates to "cover" for their boss; and (4) a lack of senior colleagues who are aware of the impaired executive's problems and who have sufficient status, knowledge, and desire to confront and work with the individual in question.[43] It has even been suggested that the personality and mental health of top-level managers are related to overall organizational effectiveness and the ability to adapt to change.[44]

Self-Concept

Closely related to the notion of personality is the *self-concept,* the way in which we see ourselves.[45] Whether we realize it or not, each of us has a self-image that influences everything that we say, do, or perceive about the world. This image acts as a filter that screens out certain things and provides an idiosyncratic flavor to our behavior. Much of what was referred to in the discussion of selective perception is influenced by our self-concept.

According to one conceptualization, our self-concept is composed of four interacting factors:[46]

1. *Values* form the foundation of a person's character, reflecting those things that are really important in life and basic to one as an individual.

2. *Beliefs* are ideas people have about the world and how it operates.

3. *Competencies* are the areas of knowledge, ability, and skill that increase an individual's effectiveness in dealing with the world.

4. *Personal goals* are those objects or events in the future that we strive for in order to fulfill our basic needs.

The self-concept reflects each individual's unique way of organizing personal goals, competencies, beliefs, and values. A related construct to the idea of personal competence is *self-efficacy,* the belief that we have in our own capability to perform a specific task. As research has indicated, self-efficacy is strongly related to task performance and openness to new experiences. Those with high self-efficacy expectations tend to be successful in a broad array of mental and physical tasks, while low self-efficacy is related to lower success rates.[47]

Overall, our natural tendency is to maintain our self-concept. In other words, people strive to maintain their images of themselves by engaging in behaviors that are consistent with their values, beliefs, competencies, and goals as *they see them.* While some people might behave in ways that go against personal goals and competencies, most tend to react quite defensively when their beliefs and values are threatened. Such threat often leads to the use of the perceptual defenses discussed earlier. Thus, while we may perceive an individual's behavior as illogical or even self-defeating, it usually makes sense to that particular individual since people generally make choices that are consistent with their self-concepts.

Perception, Individual Differences, and Decision Making

As indicated by the preceding discussion, perception refers to the process by which individuals receive, organize, and interpret information from their environment. In terms of making effective decisions, managers must first obtain information from their organizations (peers, subordinates, their managers) and environments (such as customers, suppliers, and other critical stakeholders), and then accurately interpret those data through the perception process. Although many discussions of managerial decision making suggest that it should be a conscious, rational, and systematic process, with a number of precise steps (including defining and diagnosing the problem, specifying decision objectives, developing and appraising alternative solutions, and then choosing and implementing the best course of action),[48] individuals with different personalities and self-concepts differ in the ways in which they approach such decision making.[49]

In one sense, individuals are constraints in the decision-making process. The decisions that managers make are strongly affected by their values, beliefs, competencies, goals, and personalities. Thus, to understand *why* certain decisions emerge from a group or organization, it is important to examine the premises of the individuals involved in making those decisions. Organizational members, for example, differ in terms of the value they place on the system's goals, their own ideals, their perceptions of the discrepancies between the desired and current state of affairs, the amount of risk they are willing to assume, and so forth. While some of these tendencies are explicit and discussed openly, in many instances they operate on an implicit, unconscious level. Goals are often selected, problems identified, and alternatives framed and chosen on the basis of these implicit values and beliefs, which are not always clear to the decision maker.[50] Therefore, it should not be surprising that recent research suggests that half the decisions made in organizations result in failure.[51]

The models that outline how managers *should* make decisions are largely based on *classical decision theory*, which views the managerial world as certain and stable. The underlying premise is that managers, facing a clearly defined problem, will know all the alternatives for action and their consequences, and be able to select the option providing the best or "optimum" course of action. *Behavioral decision theory*, by contrast, argues that individuals have cognitive limitations and act only in terms of what they perceive about a particular situation. Moreover, due to the complexity of the world, such perceptions are frequently imperfect. Thus, rather than operating in a world of certainty, managers are viewed as acting under uncertainty with limited, ambiguous, and in many instances, irrelevant information.[52]

The main differences between the classical and behavioral decision models are the degrees of certainty and stability surrounding the decision-making process and the presence of cognitive limitations and their influence on our perceptions. People, however, differ in their cognitive structures (i.e., the way they organize their perceptions). Some individuals tend toward complexity, while others have a tendency to be more simplistic in their decision-making process. For instance, people with simple cognitive structures tend to immediately categorize and stereotype, generate few alternatives, and think in "either/or" terms. More complex decision makers, by contrast, spend more time processing information, generating a greater number of interpretations ("and/also"), considering the alternative implications of the information, and thinking through the ethical ramifications of their decisions.[53] Differences in personality also influence the way in which we prefer to approach the decision-making process. Authoritarian personalities, for example, tend to be more directive oriented in their decisions, while more egalitarian personality types tend to prefer to involve others in the process of making decisions.[54]

Decision Making and Knowledge Management

Given the increased complexity of the global marketplace and the explosion of information that is literally available through a keyboard stroke or mouse click, significant attention is being placed on how organizations share and process information and use that information to make decisions. One of the challenges underlying this dynamic focuses on managing the knowledge creation process itself—understanding what it is and how to create, transfer, and use it more effectively.[55] Knowledge can be thought of as information combined with experience, context, interpretation, and reflection.[56]

While *explicit knowledge* can be easily expressed in words and numbers and easily communicated (e.g., hard data, codified procedures, scientific formulae), *tacit knowledge* is much more difficult to formalize, communicate, and share with others. While tacit knowledge involves the expertise ("know-how") an individual has developed over time, it also has an important cognitive dimension consisting of mental models, conceptual maps, beliefs, and perceptions so ingrained that we typically take them for granted. Since tacit knowledge is highly personalized (e.g., intuitions, hunches), it is often described as "fuzzy" and linked closely to the person who holds it. As such, a growing body of research is focusing on how such tacit knowledge can be captured and transferred from the individual to a repository available to the organization.[57]

The concept of knowledge management will be explored more fully in Chapter 4. It is important to note, however, that although intuitive decision making has garnered a bad reputation in the past, we are beginning to place much more emphasis on how our values, beliefs, emotions, and subconscious mental processing shape and influence the decisions we make.[58]

ATTITUDES AND ATTITUDE FORMATION

In the workplace, a person's attitudes are an important determinant of performance-related behaviors—the quantity and quality of output, organizational commitment, absenteeism, turnover, and a host of other important outcomes. On a general level, a person's attitudes influence that individual to act in a particular way.[59] Of course, whether an attitude actually produces a particular behavior depends on a number of factors such as family and peer pressures, past and present work experiences, and group norms (standards of behavior). For instance, people may dislike their jobs or the firm they work for, but may choose to continue working there because alternative positions that pay as well are not available. Similarly, people may like what they are doing but hold back their effort because of a lack of perceived rewards or pressure from co-workers.

Attitudes can be defined as a predisposition to respond to a stimulus (something in a person's environment such as an event, thing, place, or another person) in a positive or negative way.[60] For example, when we speak of a positive job attitude (or job satisfaction) we mean that the people involved tend to have pleasant internal feelings when they think about their jobs. Attitudes have three basic components: cognitive, affective, and behavioral. An attitude's *cognitive component* includes beliefs and knowledge about and evaluations of the stimulus. The *affective component* refers to our feelings, the emotional part of the attitude. Finally, an attitude's *behavioral component* is the inclination to behave in a certain way as a response to one's feelings and cognitions.

Attitudes also have four basic characteristics: direction, intensity, salience, and differentiation.[61] An attitude's *direction* is either favorable, unfavorable, or neutral (no direction). We may like, dislike, or be neutral about certain aspects of our job, the organization we work for, our boss, and so forth. The *intensity* of an attitude refers to the strength of the affective component. Even though we may dislike certain aspects of our job, the force of our dislike may range from weak to strong. In general, the more intense an attitude, the more it will tend to generate consistent behaviors. *Salience* refers to the perceived importance of the attitude. An artist's dislike for computers, for example, might not be perceived to be as important as a similar attitude held by a business student, where familiarity with information technology is increasingly playing a significant role in career success. Finally, attitudes do not exist in a vacuum. They are part of an interrelated mix of beliefs, values, and other attitudes. Attitudes with a large number of supporting beliefs, values, and other attitudes are *high in differentiation;* those based on few beliefs, values, and other attitudes are *low in differentiation.*

Attitude Formation

There are several general processes through which attitudes are learned: (1) the outcomes of our own experiences (trial-and-error); (2) our perceptual tendencies and biases; (3) our observations of another person's responses to a particular situation; (4) our observation of the outcomes of another person's experiences; and (5) verbal instruction about appropriate responses to and characteristics of a particular stimulus.[62] While some attitudes are *adopted* early in life (i.e., learned from our family or cultural environment), most are *developed* gradually over time through life experiences and observations.

Recent models of attitude formation suggest people can hold dual attitudes.[63] One type of attitude is *implicit*, and is similar to an enduring predisposition insofar as we are generally unaware of when or how implicit attitudes are formed. Implicit attitudes are presumably difficult to change because they are automatic and routinized, meaning they are accessed subconsciously when individuals encounter relevant stimuli. Conversely, *explicit* attitudes are the result of conscious, reflective, and motivated cognitive processing, displaying flexibility and responsiveness to context-specific assessments. These are attitudes individuals prefer and espouse when given time to reflect or consider the relevant situation/stimuli.

According to *dual attitude theory*, it is possible for people to hold conflicting or incongruent attitudes toward the same object. For example, a person may hold a *negative* implicit, yet a *positive* explicit, attitude toward the same group of people (e.g., immigrants) or social policy (maternity leave). The difference between them is that less cognitive effort is required to retrieve the negative implicit attitude because it is often activated at a preconscious level. Furthermore, in many instances the negative implicit attitude guides judgment and behavior, especially if the positive explicit attitude is not accessed. In this instance, the implicit attitude overrides the explicit attitude. One of the novel theoretical premises of dual attitude theory is based on the notion that implicit attitudes, once formed, are never completely extinguished or "replaced." Instead, attitudes become compartmentalized as opposed to integrated, such that either implicit or explicit attitudes may be accessed to guide judgments and behavior.

Attitude Change

Managers are often faced with the challenge of changing someone's attitude—a subordinate, boss, supplier, customer, and so forth. While a particular manager's status in the group or organization and leadership capabilities can be influential aspects of this process, the extent to which a specific attitude can be changed is dependent on the attitude's direction, intensity, salience, and degree of differentiation. Those attitudes that are not deeply held and low in differentiation are often relatively easy to change through education, training, and communication efforts. When our attitudes are so deeply ingrained that we are hardly aware of them (a high degree of intensity, salience, and differentiation), however, they are quite difficult to change. In fact, a significant body of social science research indicates that one of the most effective ways of changing deeply held attitudes is to first change corresponding behaviors.[64]

Attitudes and Behavior

Managers attempting to introduce major change in an organization often begin by assessing and then trying to change employee attitudes.[65] This approach is consistent with the conventional wisdom that attitudes influence behavior. In general, beliefs and values precede attitudes, which then influence behavior. The link between attitudes and behavior, however, is tentative. While an attitude may lead to an *intent to behave* in a certain way, the intention may or may not be carried out depending on the situation or circumstances. At the same time, while attitudes do influence behavior, it is important to emphasize that behavior also influences attitudes.

As a significant body of social science research underscores, one of the most effective ways of changing beliefs and values is to begin with changes in related behaviors.[66] Individual values and attitudes, especially those that are deeply held, are notoriously difficult to directly change because people's values tend to be part of an interrelated system in which each value is tied to and reinforced by other values. Thus, managers must realize that it is virtually impossible to change a particular value in isolation from an individual's other values. By focusing on relevant behaviors and interactions, in contrast, managers can begin to shape the outcomes they desire by setting explicit expectations and performance standards, rewarding appropriate behaviors, and providing channels through which people can contribute to goals and objectives. Changes in organizational behaviors in and of themselves, however, do not necessarily translate into attitude change. In fact, changes in a person's attitudes may lag behavioral changes for a considerable period of time or in some instances may never occur. Especially when a firm relies solely on extrinsic motivators (see Chapter 3), organizational members can easily rationalize why they "accepted" the change, leaving present attitudes and orientations intact. If organizational members can see the inherent value of the change, however, they are much more likely to accept and identify with what the organization is attempting to accomplish.

Thus, if attitude change is to take place, managers must support relevant behavioral changes with intrinsic motivators (see Chapter 3) that link the change with other valued attitudes and behaviors.[67] As part of this process, explanations for and justifications of the change must be made to organizational members, reinforcing the behavioral change by articulating and communicating the desired set of beliefs and values.

Cognitive Dissonance

A significant area within the realm of attitude change involves the concept of *cognitive consistency*. Essentially, people strive to achieve a sense of balance between their beliefs, attitudes, and behaviors. If you hold liberal political views, for example, it would be unlikely for you to vote for a highly conservative candidate. There are times, however, when you might be forced into a position or unwittingly do something that does not "fit" with your beliefs and attitudes. This situation creates cognitive inconsistency or imbalance. Since the resulting psychological imbalance is unpleasant or uncomfortable, we try to reduce that imbalance to attain cognitive consistency once again. One of the ways we reduce such imbalance is to modify our attitudes or rationalize our behavior in a way that creates a sense of balance.[68]

The theory of *cognitive dissonance* attempts to explain how people attempt to reduce internal conflicts when they experience a clash between their thoughts and their actions.[69] For instance, if you think it is important to support the American automobile industry but believe that Japanese or German cars are of better quality than U.S. cars, you might experience some dissonance after buying an American car. One of the ways to reduce this imbalance is to alter your beliefs about comparative quality—for example, that U.S. cars are just as good if not better than Japanese cars. If you purchased a Japanese car, you might attempt to reduce the dissonance by thinking that the only way the U.S. automobile industry is going to improve its quality is to lose sales to the Japanese—that the competition will lead to improvements in the quality of U.S.-built cars. In each instance, beliefs and attitudes are modified to support the behavior.

Other sources of cognitive dissonance can be found in situations:

- *Where a choice or decision has negative consequences:* If you vote for a particular candidate who subsequently wins the election but later is perceived to do a poor job in office, you might look for positive aspects of the choice. You might attempt to reduce the dissonance by rationalizing that the candidate was not as bad as he or she could have been, that the opponent would have been much worse, or that conditions had sufficiently changed so that no one would have been able to do a good job.

- *When expectations are unfulfilled or disconfirmed:* Following a merger between two savings banks we studied, a substantial number of organizational members were "let go" due to overlapping job responsibilities. Although the chief executive officer of one of the banks expected that the friendly merger would lead to expanded opportunities for employees rather than the reduction in force, he eventually argued that "due to volatile economic conditions in the industry the bank would have had to fire a number of people even if the merger had not taken place."[70] Thus, when his expectations that the merger would have a favorable impact on the bank's employees were unfulfilled, he rationalized his feelings by arguing that the situation would have been just as bad without the merger.

- *Under forced compliance or insufficient justification:* If we are forced into doing something that is boring, trivial, or difficult without any extrinsic compensation, we often try to think of certain aspects of the task that were interesting in order to rationalize the time spent.[71] Extrinsic rewards, however, can sufficiently reduce dissonance, such as when a task might be boring but we "did it for the money," so that rationalization is unnecessary.

As these brief illustrations indicate, the theory of cognitive dissonance helps to explain why people engage in various behaviors or adopt certain attitudes that would ordinarily be difficult to explain.

EMOTIONAL INTELLIGENCE

Traditionally, our capabilities and potential in the workplace were measured by our expertise in a given area; in essence our training, background, and experience. Given the broad changes that have taken place in the rapidly changing, global business environment, however, we are increasingly being judged by other criteria, especially how well we handle ourselves in different situations and how well we interact with others.[72] As a growing body of work indicates, cognitive abilities in and of themselves are largely irrelevant to these new criteria. Instead, emotional intelligence, often referred to as *EQ* (emotional intelligence quotient), reflects a different way of being smart. Emotional intelligence is "the capacity for recognizing our own feelings and those of others, for motivating ourselves, and for managing emotions well in ourselves and in our relationships."[73] These abilities are distinct from, but complementary to, one's academic intelligence, the cognitive capabilities measured by IQ. As research suggests, EQ is a critical success factor in both careers and organizations in such varied activities as decision making, leadership, developing trusting relationships and teamwork, achieving open and honest communication, capturing creativity and innovation, and developing customer loyalty.

As reflected in Figure 2-3, a recent conceptualization of EQ is based on four basic personal and social competencies:[74]

1. *Self-awareness:* Knowing what we are feeling in the moment, using those preferences to guide our decision making, and having a realistic, well-grounded sense of our own abilities. Specific competencies include emotional awareness, accurate self-assessment, and self-confidence.

2. *Self-management:* Handling our emotions so that they facilitate rather than interfere with the task at hand; being open and honest in one's pursuit of goals; and being flexible in overcoming obstacles or adapting to changing situations. Specific competencies include emotional self-control, transparency (displaying honesty and integrity), adaptability, achievement, initiative, and optimism.

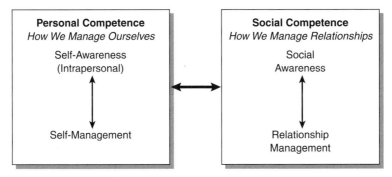

Figure 2-3 Emotional Intelligence Domains

Source: Adapted from D. Goleman, R. Boyatzis, and A. McKee, *Primal Leadership: Realizing the Power of Emotional Intelligence.* Cambridge, MA: Harvard Business School Press, 2002, p. 39.

3. *Social awareness:* Sensing what other people are feeling, being able to take their perspective, and cultivating rapport and attunement with a broad diversity of people. Specific competencies include empathy, organizational awareness (recognizing events, decision networks, and organizational politics), and service (recognizing and meeting follower, client, or customer needs).

4. *Relationship management:* Handling emotions in relationships well and accurately reading social situations and networks; interacting smoothly; using these skills to persuade and lead, to negotiate and lead, and for cooperation and teamwork. Critical skills include inspirational leadership, the ability to exert influence and develop others, conflict management, being a change catalyst, building bonds in terms of cultivating and maintaining a web of relationships, and teamwork and collaboration.

While the concept of emotional intelligence is still relatively new, its importance is reflected in the types of skills and capabilities that companies are looking for in job applicants. Even for entry-level positions, these include: ability to work in an unstructured, team environment; interpersonal competence and diversity-related skills; excellent negotiating and influencing skills; exceptional verbal and written communication skills; ability to consistently deliver high performance, especially under pressure; ethical awareness; and change agent skills and leadership capabilities.[75] As we continue to explore and research the dynamics associated with emotional intelligence, the area promises to enhance our understanding of differences across individuals, including the various roles that leaders play in their organizations (see Chapter 7).

CONCLUSION: THE SOCIAL CONTEXT OF JUDGMENT AND CHOICE

As this chapter has underscored, much of the research on perception and judgment is based on a micro-oriented, psychological view of cognitive processes. Indeed, a large proportion of the work in cognitive psychology is grounded in laboratory studies where strict controls are used to probe a person's thought processes and to examine how perceptions and decisions are made. These studies have made an important contribution to our understanding of cognition and related processes; however, they cannot fully predict judgment or choice behavior outside of the laboratory because of the myriad social realities that can readily influence our decisions. As critics have emphasized, decision making under laboratory conditions differs from actual decision making due to the lack of social pressures that are common in our everyday lives.[76] Thus, concerns have emerged about how to link our understanding of cognitive processes based on laboratory studies to our judgments and behaviors in daily life.

As part of organizational problem-solving and decision-making processes, it is important that managers understand perception, the various perceptual distortions that affect this process, the social context of the decision, and how individual differences influence what we perceive and subsequently use as the basis for making our decisions. Since much of the information managers rely on is gathered through interactions with people inside and outside their organizations, the way in which that information is perceived and processed frames not only the alternatives considered but the decision itself. The key is to actively question and test these perceptions to ensure, as much as possible, both the accuracy and interpretation of information we use in making decisions.

When attempting to explain and predict various phenomena, events, or behaviors, it is important to remember that what is perceived to be true is more important than what actually exists since people's responses are based on their perceptions. While we often assume that individuals perceive reality clearly, research indicates that there are a number of internal and external factors that can create distortions in what we see.

Realistic perceptions of our surroundings are the foundation for effective problem solving, communication, and other managerial activities and working relationships. If, however, behavior is perceived by other individuals differently from the way it was intended, the likelihood of achieving effective working relationships is going to be limited. As research on management perceptions of employee needs has indicated, managers tend to misunderstand what employees actually want from their jobs and why they act in certain ways.[77] Since these perceptions influence the ways in which managers interact with their employees, they are among the underlying reasons why employees are expressing declining levels of job satisfaction and organizational commitment, and a general sense of disenchantment with their organizations. Thus, it is important to be aware of the different ways in which we distort and bias information about people, events, and objects so that we can be more effective in our dealings with others. As the noted sociologist, W.I. Thomas, has argued, situations that are perceived to be real are real in their consequences.

NOTES

1. For an amplification of this point, see B. Berelson and G. Steiner, *Human Behavior* (New York: Harcourt, 1964), p. 87.

2. See J. Kelly, *Organizational Behavior: Its Data, First Principles, and Applications* (Homewood, IL: Irwin, 1980), pp. 139–141; J.S. Bruner, *The Relevance of Education* (New York: Norton, 1971); and J.S. Bruner and C.C. Goodman, "Value and Need as Organizing Factors in Perception," *Journal of Abnormal and Social Psychology* 42 (1947): 33–44.

3. Gestalt theory is based on the work of psychologists from the Berlin school—Max Wertheimer, Kurt Koffka, Wolfgang Kohler, and later Kurt Lewin. For a good synthesis of this work see F.L. Ruch and P.G. Zimbardo, *Psychology and Life* (Glenview, IL: Scott, Foresman, 1971), pp. 283–290.

4. See D. Fisher, *Communication in Organizations* (St. Paul, MN: West, 1981), pp. 74– 78.

5. M.H. Segall, D.T. Campbell, and M.J. Herkovits, *The Influence of Culture on Perception* (New York: Bobbs-Merrill, 1966); F. Lee, "How Culture and Domain Shape Attributions," *Personality and Social Psychology Bulletin* 22, no. 7 (1996): 732–741; and P.C. Earley, *Face, Harmony, and Social Structures: An Analysis of Organizational Behavior Across Cultures* (New York: Oxford University Press, 1997).

6. The discussion in this section was drawn from Ruch and Zimbardo, *Psychology and Life*, pp. 286–290; and D. Coon, *Introduction to Psychology: Exploration and Application* (St. Paul, MN: West, 1977).

7. See R.L. Solso, "Prototypes, Schemata and the Form of Human Knowledge: The Cognition of Abstraction," in C. Izawa, ed., *Current Issues in Cognitive Processes* (Hillsdale, NJ: Erlbaum, 1989), pp. 345–368; R.G. Lord and R.J. Foti, "Schema Theories,

Information Processing, and Organizational Behavior," in H.P. Sims, Jr. and D.A. Gioia, eds., *The Thinking Organization* (San Francisco: Jossey-Bass, 1986), pp. 20–48; J. Bartunek, "The Multiple Cognitions and Conflicts Associated with Second Order Organizational Change," in J.K. Murnighan, ed., *Social Psychology in Organizations: Advances in Theory and Research* (Englewood Cliffs, NJ: Prentice Hall, 1993), pp. 322–349; and E. Barbera, "Gender Schemas: Configuration and Activation Processes," *Canadian Journal of Behavioural Science* 35, no. 3 (2003): 176–184.

8.   This discussion is drawn from Ruch and Zimbardo, op. cit., pp. 303–306; and E.F. Huse and J.L. Bowditch, *Behavior in Organizations: A Systems Approach to Managing* (Reading, MA: Addison-Wesley, 1977), pp. 122–125.

9.   P.F. Secord, C.W. Backman, and D.R. Slavitt, *Understanding Social Life: An Introduction to Social Psychology* (New York: McGraw-Hill, 1976).

10.   L. Falkenberg, "Improving the Accuracy of Stereotypes within the Workplace," *Journal of Management* 16, no. 1 (1990): 107–118; Z. Kunda and K.C. Olsen, "Maintaining Stereotypes in the Face of Disconfirmation: Constructing Grounds for Subtyping Deviants," *Journal of Personality and Social Psychology* 68, no. 4 (1995): 565–579; V. Valian, *Why So Slow?: The Advancement of Women* (Boston: MIT Press, 1998); and J.F. Veiga, K. Fox, J.N. Yanouzas, and K. Eddleston, "Toward Greater Understanding in the Workplace," *Academy of Management Executive* 13, no. 2 (1999): 81–87.

11.   This section is drawn from S.T. Fiske, "Stereotyping, Prejudice, and Discrimination," in D.T. Gilbert, S.T. Fiske, and G. Lindzey (eds.), *Handbook of Social Psychology, Volume 2*, 4th ed. (Boston: McGraw-Hill, 1998), see pp. 357–411; S.T. Fiske, A.J.C. Cuddy, P. Glick, and J. Xu, "A Model of (Often Mixed) Stereotype Content: Competence and Warmth Respectively Follow from Perceived Status and Competition," *Journal of Personality and Social Psychology* 82 (2002); 878–902; and S.T. Fiske, J. Xu, A.J.C. Cuddy, and P. Glick, "(Dis)respecting versus (Dis)liking: Status and Interdependence Predict Ambivalent Stereotypes of Competence and Warmth,"

Journal of Social Issues 55 (1999): 473–491.

12.   See J.M. Feldman, "A Note on the Statistical Correlation of Halo Effect," *Journal of Applied Psychology* 71 (1986): 173–176; and T.H. Feeley, "Comment on Halo Effects in Rating and Evaluation Research," *Human Communication Research* 28, no. 4 (2002): 578–587.

13.   See E.D. Pulakos and K.N. Wexley, "Relationship Among Perceived Similarity, Sex, Performance, and Ratings in Manager-Subordinate Dyads," *Academy of Management Journal* 26, no. 1 (1983): 129–139; and G.P. Erwin, "First Names and Perceptions of Physical Attractiveness," *Journal of Psychology* 127, no. 6 (1993): 625–631.

14.   R. Rosenthal, *Experimenter Effects in Behavioral Research* (New York: Appleton-Century-Crofts, 1966); and R. Rosenthal, "Covert Communication in Classrooms, Clinics, Courtrooms and Cubicles," *American Psychologist* 57, no. 11 (2002): 839–850.

15.   See R. Rosenthal, *On the Psychology of the Self-Fulfilling Prophecy: Further Evidence for Pygmalion Effects and Their Mediating Mechanisms* (New York: MSS Modular Publications, 1974), see Module 53; and D. Eden, "Self-Fulfilling Prophecies in Organizations," in J. Greenberg (ed.), *Organizational Behavior: The State of the Science* (Mahwah, NJ: Lawrence Erlbaum Associates, 2003), pp. 91–124.

16.   J.A. Bargh and T.L. Chartrand, "The Unbearable Automaticity of Being," *American Psychologist* 54 (1999): 462–479.

17.   T.V. Bonoma and G. Zaltman, *Psychology for Management* (Boston: Kent, 1981), p. 307.

18.   S.S. Zalkind and T.W. Costello, "Perception: Some Recent Research and Implications for Administration," *Administration Science Quarterly* 7 (1962): 218–235; and E. Peirce, C.A. Smolinski, and B. Rosen, "Why Sexual Harassment Complaints Fall on Deaf Ears," *Academy of Management Executive* 12, no. 3 (1998): 41–54.

19.   M. Haire and W.F. Grunes, "Perceptual Defenses: Processes Protecting an Organized Perception of Another Personality," *Human Relations* 3 (1950): 403–412.

20. J. Bartunek, "Why Did You Do That? Attribution Theory in Organizations," *Business Horizons* 24, no. 5 (1981): 66–71; K.G. Shaver, *An Introduction to Attribution Processes* (Cambridge, MA: Winthrop, 1975); and H.H. Kelly, *Attribution Theory in Social Interaction* (Morristown, NJ: General Learning Press, 1971).

21. See S.G. Green and T.R. Mitchell, "Attributional Processes of Leader-Member Interactions," *Organizational Behavior and Human Performance* 23 (1979): pp. 429–458; and H.H. Kelley, "Attribution in Social Interaction," in E. Jones, D. Kanouse, H. Kelley, R. Nisbett, S. Valins, and B. Weiner, eds., *Attribution: Perceiving the Causes of Behavior* (Morristown, NJ: General Learning Press, 1972), pp. 1–26.

22. M.J. Martinko and W.L. Gardner, "The Leader-Member Attribution Process," *Academy of Management Review* 12, no. 2 (1987): pp. 235–249; and J.C. McElroy, "A Typology of Attribution Leadership Research," *Academy of Management Review* 7, no. 3 (1982): pp. 413–417. See also M.T. Dasborough and N.M. Ashkanasy, "Emotion and Attribution of Intentionality in Leader-Member Relations," *Leadership Quarterly* 13, no. 5 (2002): 615–634.

23. R.A. Barron, "Interpersonal Relations in Organizations," in K.R. Murphy, ed., *Individual Differences and Behavior in Organizations* (San Francisco: Jossey-Bass, 1996), pp. 334–370.

24. See R. Hoffman, "Ten Reasons Why You Should Be Using 360-Degree Feedback," *HR Magazine* 40, no. 4 (1995): 82–85; E. Van Velsor, J.B. Leslie, and J.W. Fleenor, *Choosing 360: A Guide to Evaluating Multi-Rater Feedback Instruments for Management Development* (Greensboro, NC: Center for Creative Leadership, 1997); A.G. Walker and J.W. Smither, "A Five-Year Study of Upward Feedback: What Managers Do with Their Results," *Personnel Psychology* 52, no. 2 (1999): 393–423.

25. J.B. Rotter, "Generalized Expectancies for Internal vs. External Control of Reinforcement," *Psychological Monographs* 80 (1966): 1–28; Mitchell, C.M. Smysert, and S.E. Weed, "Locus of Control: Supervision and Work Satisfaction," *Academy of Management Journal* 18 (1975): 623–631; and J.B. Rotter, "Internal versus External Control of Reinforcement: A Case History of a Variable," *American Psychologist* 45 (1990): 489–493.

26. See O.C. Hansemark, "Need for Achievement, Locus of Control and the Prediction of Business Start-ups: A Longitudinal Study," *Journal of Economic Psychology* 24, no. 3 (2003): 301–320.

27. T.R. Mitchell, "Matching Motivational Strategies with Organizational Contexts," *Research in Organizational Behavior* 19 (1997): p. 71.

28. See K.R. Murphy, ed., *Individual Differences and Behavior in Organizations* (San Francisco: Jossey-Bass, 1996).

29. See L.R. Goldberg, "An Alternative Description of Personality: The Big Five Factor Structure," *Journal of Personality and Social Psychology* 59 (1990): 1216–1229; R.R. McCrae and P.T. Costa, Jr., "Personality Trait Structure as a Human Universal," *American Psychologist* 52 (1997): 509–516; J.F. Salgado, "The Five Factor Model of Personality and Job Performance in the European Community," *Journal of Applied Psychology* 82 (1997): 30–43; T.A. Judge, C.A. Higgins, C.J. Thoresen, and M.R. Barrick, "The Big Five Personality Traits, Mental Ability, and Career Success Across the Life Span," *Personnel Psychology* 52, no. 3 (1999): 621–652; S. Rocca, L. Sagiv, S.H. Schwartz and A. Knafo, "The Big Five Personality Factors and Personal Values," *Personality and Social Psychology Bulletin* 28, no. 6 (2002): 789–801; and S.V. Pannonen, "Big Five Factors of Personality and Replicated Predictions of Behavior," *Journal of Personality and Social Psychology* 84, no. 2 (2003): 411–426.

30. The following discussion was adapted from D.D. White and H.W. Vroman, *Action in Organizations* (Boston: Allyn & Bacon, 1982), pp. 23–33.

31. For an in-depth discussion of these different personality types and some of the controversy see T.W. Adorno, E. Frenkel-Brunswick, D.J. Levinson, and R.N. Stanford, *The Authoritarian Personality* (New York: Harper, 1950); R. Brown, *Social Psychology* (New York: Free Press, 1965), Chapter 10;

J. Siegel, "Machiavellianism, MBAs and Managers: Leadership Correlates and Socialization Effects," *Academy of Management Journal* 16 (1973): 404–412; G. Gemmill and W. Heisler, "Machiavellianism as a Factor in Managerial Job Strain, Job Satisfaction and Upward Mobility," *Academy of Management Journal* 15 (1972): 5l–64; C.J. Schultz II, "Situational and Dispositional Predictors of Performance: A Test of the Hypothesized Machiavellian X Structure Interaction Among Sales Persons," Journal of Applied Social Psychology 23 (1993): 478–498.

32. See M. Friedman and R. Roseman, *Type A Behavior and Your Heart* (New York: Knopf, 1974); M.T. Matteson and C. Preston, "Occupational Stress, Type A Behavior and Physical Well-being," *Academy of Management Journal* 25, no. 2 (1982): 373–391; J. Schaubroeck, D.C. Ganster, and B.E. Kemmerer, "Job Complexity, 'Type A' Cardiovascular Disorder: A Prospective Study," *Academy of Management Journal* 37, no. 2 (1994): 426–439; and S.M. Jex, *Stress and Job Performance: Theory, Research, Practice and Implications for Management Practice* (Thousand Oaks, CA: Sage, 1998).

33. J.B. Rotter, "Generalized Expectancies for Internal versus External Control of Reinforcement," *Psychological Monographs* 1, no. 609 (1966): 80; J.B. Rotter, "External Control and Internal Control," *Psychology Today* (June 1971): 37; and J.B. Rotter, "Internal versus External Control of Reinforcement: A Case History of a Variable," *American Psychologist* 45 (1990): 489–493.

34. C.G. Jung, *Psychological Types* (New York: Harcourt, 1923).

35. See C.S. Hall and G. Lindzey, *Theories of Personality* (New York: Wiley, 1957), pp. 76–113.

36. Jung, op. cit.

37. I. Briggs Myers and M.H. McCaulley, *Manual: A Guide to the Development and Use of the Myers-Briggs Type Indicator* (Palo Alto, CA: Consulting Psychologists Press, 1985). For an application of the Myers-Briggs, see J. Brownell, "Personality and Career Development: A Study of Gender Differences," *Cornell Hotel and Restaurant Administration Quarterly* 35, no. 2 (1994): 36–46. See also W.L. Gardner and M.J. Martinko, "Using the Myers-Briggs Type Indicator to Study Managers: A Literature Review and Research Agenda," *Journal of Management* 22, no. 1 (1996): 45–83 for an extensive review of this work; C.M. Kaufman, "Know Your Client: The Myers-Briggs Psychology Test Can Help Planners Reduce Communications Frustrations," *Financial Planning* (February 1, 2003): 65–66; and K. Garrety, R. Badham, V. Morrigan, W. Rifkin, and M. Zanko, "The Use of Personality Typing in Organizational Change: Discourse, Emotions and the Reflexive Subject," *Human Relations* 56, no. 2 (2003): 211–235.

38. For a discussion of the different factors that influence personality development, see C. Kluckhohn and H.A. Murray, *Personality in Nature, Society and Culture* (New York: Knopf, 1953), pp. 53–55; L. Rappoport, *Personality Development* (Glenview, IL: Scott, Foresman, 1972), pp. 70–92; E.H. Erikson, *Childhood and Society* (New York: Norton, 1963), pp. 225–274; and R.W. Larson and S. Verma, "How Children and Adolescents Spend Time Across the World: Work, Play, and Developmental Opportunities," *Psychological Bulletin* 125, no. 6 (1999): 701–736.

39. D.J. Levinson, "Periods in the Adult Development of Men: Ages 18 to 45," *The Counseling Psychologist* 6 (1976): 21–25.

40. The following discussion is drawn from M.F.R. Kets De Vries and D. Miller, "Personality, Culture and Organization," *Academy of Management Review* 11, no. 2 (1986): 266–279; D. Miller and P.H. Friesen, *Organizations: A Quantum View* (Englewood Cliffs, NJ: Prentice Hall, 1984); and U. Miller, M.F.R. Kets De Vries, and J.M. Toulouse, "Top Executives Locus of Control and Its Relationship to Strategy-Making, Structure and Environment," *Academy of Management Journal* 25, no. 2 (1982): 237–253.

41. See L.P. Frankel, "Depressed Organizations: Identifying the Symptoms and Overcoming the Causes," *Employee Relations Today* 18, no. 4 (1991–1992): 443–451. See also D.B. McFarlin and P.D. Sweeney, *House of Mirrors: The Untold Truth about Narcissistic Leaders and How to Survive Them* (London: Kogan Page, 2000).

42. This discussion is adapted from J.L. Speller, *Executives in Crisis: Recognizing and Managing the Alcoholic, Drug-Addicted, or Mentally Ill Executive* (San Francisco: Jossey-Bass, 1989).

43. See, for example, M.F.R. Kets de Vries, *Life and Death in the Executive Fast Lane: Essays on Irrational Organizations and Their Leaders* (San Francisco: Jossey-Bass, 1995); and R.W. Griffin, A. O'Leary-Kelly, and J.M. Collins, eds., *Dysfunctional Behavior in Organizations: Non-Violent Dysfunctional Behavior in Organizations* (Stamford, CT: JAI Press, 1998).

44. See, for example, J.C. Quick, J.H. Gavin, G.L. Cooper, and J.D. Quick, "Executive Health: Building Strength, Managing Risks," *Academy of Management Executive* 14, no. 2 (2000): 34–44.

45. P.J. Brouwer, "The Power to See Ourselves," *Harvard Business Review* 42, no. 6 (1964): 156–165; and A.P. Brief and R.J. Aldag, "The Role of Self in Work Organizations: A Conceptual Review," *Academy of Management Review* 6, no. 1 (1981): 75–88.

46. A.R. Cohen, S.L. Fink, H. Gadon, and R.D. Willits, *Effective Behavior in Organizations* (Homewood, IL: Irwin, 1980), Chapter 8.

47. See A. Bandura, "Self-Efficacy: Toward a Unifying Theory of Behavioral Change," *Psychological Review* 84 (1977): 191–215; G.R. Jones, "Socialization Tactics, Self-Efficacy, and Newcomers Adjustments to Organizations," *Academy of Management Journal* 29 (1986): 262–279; S.I. Tannenbaum, J.E. Mathieu, E. Salas, and J.A. Cannon-Bowers, "Meeting Trainees' Expectations: The Influence of Training Fulfillment on the Development of Commitment, Self-Efficacy, and Motivation," *Journal of Applied Psychology* 76, no. 6, (1991): 759–769; K.M. Thomas and J.E. Mathieu, "Role of Causal Attributions in Dynamic Self-Regulation and Goals Processes," *Journal of Applied Psychology* 79 (1994): 812–818; and A.D. Stajkovic and F. Luthans, "Social Cognition Theory and Self-Efficacy: Going Beyond Traditional Motivational and Behavioral Approaches," *Organizational Dynamics* (Spring 1998): 62–74.

48. E.A. Archer, "How to Make a Business Decision: An Analysis of Theory and Practice," *Management Review* 69, no. 2 (1980): 54–61.

49. B.M. Bass, *Organizational Decision Making* (Homewood, IL: Irwin, 1983), Chapter 7. The following discussion is drawn from this work, especially pp. 140–150.

50. See V. Mitchell, "Organizational Risk Perception and Reduction: A Literature Review," *British Journal of Management* 6, no. 2 (1995): 115–133.

51. P.C. Nutt, "Surprising But True: Half the Decisions in Organizations Fail," *Academy of Management Executive* 13, no. 4 (1999): 75–90.

52. See, for example, J.B. Barney, "How a Firm's Capabilities Affect Boundary Decisions," *Sloan Management Review* 40, no. 3 (1999): 137–146; and K.R. Chinander and M.E. Schweitzer, "The Input Bias: The Misuse of Input Information in Judgment of Outcomes," *Organizational Behavior and Human Decision Processes* 91, no. 2 (2003): 243–253.

53. M.J. Driver and S. Streufert, "Integrative Complexity: An Approach to Individuals and Groups as Information-Processing Systems," *Administrative Science Quarterly* 14 (1969): 272–285; P. Suefeld and S. Streufert, "Information Search as a Function of Conceptual and Environmental Complexity," *Psychonomic Science* 4 (1966): 351–352; and C.L. Pennino, "Is Decision Style Related to Moral Development Among Managers in the U.S.?" *Journal of Business Ethics* 41, no. 4 (2002): 337–348.

54. Bass, *Organizational Decision Making*, pp. 145–146.

55. See, for example, I. Nonaka and H. Takeuchi, *The Knowledge-Creating Company: How Japanese Companies Create the Dynamics of Innovation* (New York: Oxford University Press, 1995); W. Halal, ed., *The Infinite Resource: Creating and Leading the Knowledge Enterprise* (San Francisco: Jossey-Bass, 1998); and C. Soo, T. Devinney, D. Midgley, and A. Deering, "Knowledge Management: Philosophy, Processes and Pitfalls," *California Management Review* 44, no. 4 (2002): 129–152.

56. T.H. Davenport, D.W. DeLong, and M.C. Beers, "Successful Knowledge

Management Projects," *Sloan Management Review* 39, no. 2 (1998): 43–57.

57. See S. Newell, L. Edelman, H. Scarbrough, J. Swan, and M. Bresnen, "'Best Practice' Development and Transfer in the NHS: The Importance of Process as Well as Product Knowledge," *Journal of Health Services Management* 16 (2003): 1–12; and A.F. Buono and F. Poulfelt (eds.), *Issues and Challenges in Knowledge Management* (Greenwich, CT: Information Age Publishing, 2005).

58. L.A. Burke and M.K. Miller, "Taking the Mystery out of Intuitive Decision Making," *Academy of Management Executive* 13, no. 4 (1999): 91–99. See also E.N. Brockmann and W.P. Anthony, "Tacit Knowledge and Strategic Decision Making," *Group & Organization Management* 27, no. 4 (2002): 436–455.

59. See J. Cooper and R.T. Croyle, "Attitude and Attitude Change," *Annual Review of Psychology* 35 (1984): 395–426; and J.B. Miner, *Organizational Behavior: Performance and Productivity* (New York: Random House, 1988), p. 224. See also R.E. Kidwell and C. Robie, "Withholding Effort in Organizations: Toward Development and Validation of a Measure," *Journal of Business and Psychology* 17, no. 4 (2003): 537–562.

60. See M. Fishbein and I. Ajzen, *Belief, Attitude, Intention and Behavior: An Introduction to Theory and Research* (Reading, MA: Addison-Wesley, 1975); C.C. Pinder, *Work Motivation: Theory, Issues and Applications* (Glenview, IL: Scott, Foresman, 1984); and S.L. Crites, Jr., L.R. Fabrigar, and R.E. Petty, "Measuring the Affective and Cognitive Properties of Attitudes: Conceptual and Methodological Issues," *Personality and Social Psychology Bulletin* 20 (1994): 619–634.

61. The following discussion is drawn from R.L. Weaver, *Understanding Interpersonal Communication* (Glenview, IL: Scott, Foresman, 1987), pp. 204–206.

62. See D.T. Campbell, "Social Attitudes and Other Acquired Behavioral Dispositions," in S. Koch, ed., *Psychology: A Study of a Science*, vol. 6 (New York: McGraw-Hill, 1963), pp. 94–172; and G.W. Allport, *The Nature of Prejudice* (Reading, MA: Addison-Wesley, 1954).

63. See T.D. Wilson, S. Lindsey, and T.Y. Schooler, "A Model of Dual Attitudes" *Psychological Review* 107 (2000): 101–126. See also A.G. Greenwald and M.R. Banaji, "Implicit Social Cognition: Attitudes, Self-Esteem, and Stereotypes," *Psychological Review* 102 (1995): 4–27; and R.J. Rydell and Allen R. McConnell, "Understanding Implicit and Explicit Attitude Change: A Systems of Reasoning Analysis," *Journal of Personality & Social Psychology* 91 (2006): 995–1008.

64. See D.J. Bem, *Beliefs, Attitudes, and Human Affairs* (Monterey, CA: Brooks/Cole, 1970), Chapter 6; and H.K.S. Laschinger, J.R. Finegan, J. Shamian, and P. Wilk, "A Longitudinal Analysis of the Impact of Workplace Empowerment on Work Satisfaction," *Journal of Organizational Behavior* 25, no. 4 (2004): 527–545.

65. A. Fonvielle, "Behavior versus Attitude: Which Comes First in Organizational Change?" *Management Review* (August 1984): 14; and V. Sathe, *Culture and Related Corporate Realities* (Homewood, IL: Irwin, 1985).

66. See E. Aronson, *The Social Animal* (San Francisco: Freeman, 1976); Bem, op. cit.; and P.G. Zimbardo, E.B. Ebbesen, and C. Maslach, *Influencing Attitudes and Changing Behavior* (Reading, MA: Addison-Wesley, 1977).

67. Sathe, op. cit., pp. 367–369.

68. W.J. McGuire, "The Current State of Cognitive Consistency Theories," in S. Feldman, ed., *Cognitive Consistency: Motivation Antecedents and Behavioral Consequences* (New York: Academic Press, 1966), p. 1; and C.A. Insko, *Theories of Attitude Change* (New York: Appleton-Century-Crofts, 1967) pp. 161–176.

69. L. Festinger, *A Theory of Cognitive Dissonance* (Stanford, CA: Stanford University Press, 1957). For more recent applications of the theory, see R. Harrison and J.G. March, "Decision Making and Post-Decision Surprises," *Administrative Science Quarterly* 29, no. 1 (1984): 26–42; and P. Williams and J.L. Aaker, "Can Mixed Emotions Peacefully Coexist?" *Journal of Consumer Research* 28, no. 4 (2002): 636–650.

70. A.F. Buono and J.L. Bowditch, *The Human Side of Mergers and Acquisitions: Managing Collisions between People, Cultures, and Organizations* (Washington, D.C.: Beard Books, 2003).

71. See L. Festinger and L.M. Carlsmith, "Cognitive Consequences of Forced Compliance," *Journal of Abnormal and Social Psychology* 58 (1950): 203–210.

72. The section on emotional intelligence is based on R.K. Cooper and A. Sawaf, *Executive EQ: Emotional Intelligence in Leadership & Organizations* (New York: Grosset/Putnam, 1996); and D. Goleman, *Working with Emotional Intelligence* (New York: Bantam Books, 1998). See also C.S.P. Fernandez, "Emotional Intelligence in the Workplace," *Journal of Public Health Management & Practice* 13, no. 1 (2007): 80–82.

73. Goleman, *Working with Emotional Intelligence*, p. 317.

74. See D. Goleman, R. Boyatzis, and A. McKee, *Primal Leadership: Realizing the Power of Emotional Intelligence* (Cambridge: Harvard Business School Press, 2002), Chapter 3.

75. A.F. Buono, "Integrating the Business Core: A Learning Community Approach to 21st Century Business Education," in M.H. Abdelsamad & E. Myers (Eds.), *Managing in a World of Change: Learning at Warp Speed. Selected Readings from the 2000 SAM International Management Conference*. Society for Advancement of Management, 2000, pp. 315–326; D. Goleman, "Leadership that Gets Results," *Harvard Business Review* 78, no. 2 (2000): 78–90. See also R. Holiajn; "Management Decision Making, Ethical Issues and 'Emotional' Intelligence," *Management Decision* 44, no. 8 (2006): 1122–1138.

76. See, for example, H. Einborn and R.M. Hogarth, "Behavioral Decision Making," *Annual Review of Psychology* 31 (1981): 53–88.

77. Compare R.L. Kuhn, "Human Reactions on the Shop Floor," in E.M. Hugh-Jones, ed., *Human Relations and Modern Management* (Chicago: Quadrangle Books, 1959); U.M. Gluskinos and B.J. Kestlemen, "Management and Labor Leaders', Perception of Worker Needs as Compared with Self-Reported Needs," *Personnel Psychology* (Summer 1971): 239–246; M. Cooper, B.S. Morgan, P.M. Foley, and L.B. Kaplan, "Changing Employee Values: Deepening Discontent?" *Harvard Business Review* 57, no. 1 (1979): 117–125; D.L. Kanter and P.H. Mirvis, *The Cynical Americans: Living and Working in an Age of Discontent and Disillusion* (San Francisco: Jossey-Bass, 1989); and A.E. Reichers, J.P. Wanous, and J.T. Austin, "Understanding and Managing Cynicism About Organizational Change," *Academy of Management Executive* 11, no. 1 (1997): 48–59.

Motivation

One of the central problems in organizational behavior (OB) concerns *why* people perform and behave the way they do in their jobs and in their organizations. Questions such as "What makes some people work hard while others seem to do as little as possible?" and "How can I influence the performance of those who work for me?" are raised by virtually every manager at one point or another. In fact, the question of how to motivate people remains one of the most fascinating and perplexing areas of managerial concern.

In examining motivation, there are essentially three key questions:[1]

1. What energizes human behavior?
2. What channels or directs that behavior?
3. How can certain behaviors be sustained or maintained over time?

Over the past fifty years, a significant amount of theory building and research has focused on these concerns. Yet, because some researchers take a global view and others take a more specific, situational perspective, it is difficult to develop an all-encompassing framework to simplify the study of motivation. It is not that these questions are unanswerable, but rather that a number of different answers exist.[2] Models that describe the motivational process have been created through inductive and deductive approaches. Motivation itself has been treated as an independent and a dependent variable. Finally, some conceptually appealing models have produced conflicting empirical results, while more simplistic models seem to hold up well under research scrutiny but explain only particular segments of the motivation process.

This chapter will examine these key areas of concern by delving into three broad classifications of motivational theories: (1) *static-content* theories, which look at what energizes human behavior; (2) *process* theories, which look at factors that channel or direct behavior; and finally (3) *environmentally based* theories, which generally focus on sustaining or maintaining behavior over time.

MANAGERIAL ASSUMPTIONS ABOUT HUMAN NATURE

Before proceeding to a discussion of these different theories, it is useful to think about the ways in which our assumptions influence our views about motivation and human behavior. As noted in Chapter 2, managers often have their own "theories" on how to motivate their subordinates. While individual managers may never actually be explicit about why they attempt to motivate people the way they do (or in some instances may not even be aware they are using these "theories"), managers have different sets of beliefs that influence their behavior and their attempts at motivation.[3] Some managers, for example, tend to be quite coercive and assume motivation is nothing more than controlling people's behavior. These individuals often view punishment and threat as the keys to motivation. Other managers may think that money is the prime motivator and subsequently spend their time developing economic incentives to enhance work performance. Still others feel that people are motivated by social considerations and attempt to ensure that workers are happy and work groups are mutually supportive and pleasant to be in. Since some managers think that workers desire responsibility and opportunities to become more knowledgeable and competent in their work, they try to develop ways to keep jobs interesting and challenging. As discussed in Chapter 1 (see Figure 1-1), these basic assumptions greatly influenced the different theories that were used to conceptualize the process of management.

In an attempt to describe some of the basic concepts (or sets of *assumptions*) that managers have about people, Douglas McGregor identified two contrasting perspectives, which he labeled *Theory X* and *Theory Y*.[4] McGregor argued that each of these orientations represents basic underlying beliefs about the nature of human behavior that subsequently influence a manager to adopt one particular motivational approach rather than another. These orientations are *not*, as they are sometimes referred to, managerial strategies as such. Rather, these assumptions are the basic determinant of the ways in which managers *prefer* to control people at work. Moreover, rather than trying to entice managers to choose one approach over the other, McGregor's work was intended to prompt managers to examine the assumptions underlying their behavior and to make them explicit—in essence, to encourage them to realize the importance of theory.[5]

Theory X beliefs lead managers to think in terms of close direction and control of subordinates since people in general are viewed as inherently lazy, lacking in ambition and desire to assume responsibility, self-centered and likely to act contrary to organizational needs, and resistant to change. McGregor argued that the "human side" of business was greatly influenced by such Theory X beliefs and assumptions. In contrast to this rather pessimistic view of human nature, *Theory Y* assumes that people are more growth and development oriented, and *not* necessarily irresponsible and naturally resistant to organizational objectives. Based on this set of assumptions, the central task of management should be to arrange organizational conditions to create opportunities for people, provide guidance, remove barriers, and encourage their growth.

While McGregor argued that a Theory X–oriented authoritarian style of management was becoming increasingly "suspect," he also noted that authority was an appropriate way to influence behavior, albeit under certain circumstances. As he argued, "There is nothing inherently wrong or bad about giving an order or making a unilateral decision. There are many circumstances, however, when the exercise of authority fails to achieve the desired results."[6] Managers with dominant Theory X beliefs, however, may find it difficult to go beyond authority, instead relying on practices based on trust and confidence in their subordinates. At the same time, managers with Theory Y beliefs do not necessarily rely solely on participative techniques. As other research has suggested,[7] managers with dominant Theory Y beliefs are more likely to engage in "reality testing," tending to be more diagnostic in their orientation and more realistic in their appraisal of task requirements, time pressures, and organizational climates.

The influence and importance of such assumptions become even more apparent in our attempts to manage and work with an increasingly diverse workforce. The myriad myths, misperceptions, and stereotypes that exist in organizations often have deleterious effects on opportunities for women and different racial and ethnic groups. While typical advice is that managers should reject simplistic stereotypes and evaluate each individual on his or her own merits, the reality is that our underlying assumptions shape and influence such categorizations.[8] Thus, increased awareness of our underlying biases and orientations, and the influential role they play, are critical first steps in developing the ability to question and modify what may unintentionally be destructive assumptions.[9]

An important conclusion to be drawn from this discussion is that assumptions that we make about people have a significant influence on how we approach motivation. These beliefs will also influence our interpretation of the different motivational theories that follow. From a managerial standpoint, therefore, it seems that using the theories and perspectives discussed in this chapter as part of an ongoing diagnosis of organizational activity—rather than assuming we know all the answers about what motivates people—appears to be the most realistic approach to understanding motivation.

STATIC-CONTENT THEORIES OF MOTIVATION

One of the central issues in understanding motivation focuses on the different variables that energize human behavior—the *content* of what actually motivates people. Content theories are referred to as static because they look at only one (or limited) point(s) in time and are, thus, either past- or present-time oriented. While these theories, therefore, do not necessarily predict motivation or behavior, they can provide a basic understanding as to what energizes (motivates) individuals.[10] Research interest in this area peaked during the 1970s and 1980s, with declining empirical or theoretical work over the past fifteen years. Most of the research that has been done during the 1990s focused on the nature of job attributes that motivate people and an examination of the need for achievement.[11]

Maslow's Hierarchy of Needs

One of the most well-known and appealing motivation models is Abraham Maslow's hierarchy of needs.[12] As depicted in Figure 3-1, Maslow argued that the needs underlying all human motivation could be organized in a hierarchy on five basic levels. The theory further proposes the principle of "prepotency," that an individual's lower-level needs must be satisfied before that person can address higher-level, psychological needs. Essentially, the need to satisfy basic physiological needs, such as the need for air and attempts to quench one's thirst and hunger, are of primary importance. When these basic, survival needs are fulfilled, a person becomes concerned about safety and shelter. Once a feeling of security and order has been satisfied, people then begin to develop desires for affiliation or interpersonal relationships. At this point, people want

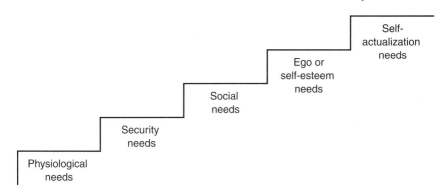

Figure 3-1 Maslow's Hierarchy of Needs

Source: Adapted from A.H. Maslow, "A Theory of Human Motivation," *Psychological Review,* vol. 50, no. 4 (1943): 370–396.

to associate with others and experience such interpersonal attachments as friendship and affection. Since basic survival and safety needs are fulfilled, the opportunity to take part in social interactions and relationships becomes important. As this need is fulfilled, individuals experience the need to feel personal esteem, recognition (especially from those who are significant in their lives), and prestige as well as to satisfy ego needs oriented toward achievement, success, and a certain degree of autonomy or independence. The final stage in the hierarchy focuses on the ultimate fulfillment of one's potential as a person. Once one's ego needs become fully satisfied, the ideal of self-actualization essentially means that the individual focuses more on the needs and well-being of others rather than him- or herself. Although the number is somewhat arbitrary, Maslow suggested that perhaps only 10 percent of our society ever becomes truly self-actualized.

Maslow devised this model through deductive reasoning on the basis of his clinical studies. The model is conceptually simple and has face validity. There is little evidence, however, to support the concept of hierarchical progression. Although cross-sectional empirical research on the model strongly suggests that the levels of the hierarchy are indeed present, progression through the hierarchy from one stage to the next is not clearly supported by longitudinal studies.[13] Moreover, research has raised questions about the extent to which: (1) highly satisfied needs actually cease to be motivators; (2) a highly satisfied need at one level leads to increasingly salient needs at the next level; (3) people can be simultaneously motivated by social, ego, and self-fulfillment needs; and (4) men and women differ with respect to their social and ego needs.[14] A related factor to consider is the idea of *frustration-regression*.[15] This hypothesis suggests that as an individual progresses up the hierarchy, if she or he were unable to satisfactorily meet any given level of needs, that person would become frustrated and regress to a lower level of the hierarchy where satisfaction had been experienced, and proceed to fill that need over and over. Popular examples of this tendency are played out in the media in the form of the forlorn person coming home from a failed attempt at romance (at a party, after a bad date) and eating ice cream and/or chocolate as consolation.

Despite these concerns and limitations, the need hierarchy framework remains a popular model of motivation. It is also important to emphasize that Maslow's formulation was meant as a humanistic perspective on human motivation in general rather than the creation of an empirically testable model for the workplace.[16] The main strength of this approach is the recognition and identification of individual needs for the purpose of motivating behavior. By appealing to an employee's unfulfilled needs, managers can attempt to influence that person's performance. It is clear, of course, that different individuals will be at different places in the hierarchy and that the same person may be at different places at different times. Moreover, many people may wish to fulfill their higher-level needs outside of the workplace. All individuals, therefore, cannot be motivated in the same way. In this sense, Maslow's theory emphasizes a contingency approach to motivation that suggests that managers and organizations should be flexible and able to tailor incentives to individual employees if they desire to maximize employee contributions. This strategy, however, can be quite time consuming and difficult in practice. Moreover, to fully tap motivational potential, managers must be able to relate to the needs of the employees involved and not just their own needs or assumptions.[17]

Alderfer's ERG Theory

One attempt to modify Maslow's hierarchy by reducing the number of need categories was developed by C.P. Alderfer.[18] Based on a review of existing research as well as his own work, Alderfer found evidence for only three levels of needs (ERG): basic *existence* or survival needs, *relatedness* needs dealing with social interaction and the external facets of esteem (recognition and status from others), and *growth* needs focusing on one's desire to achieve and develop one's potential and the internal facets of ego fulfillment (success and autonomy). Although Alderfer found that at times there was a progression from one stage to another, the boundaries overlapped and people could go from one level to another without fully satisfying the first.

Since the ERG model is more fully supported by both cross-sectional and longitudinal research and it is more empirically based than Maslow's hierarchy of needs, it *may* provide a better explanation of the way in which our needs influence our behavior. Studies have found (1) empirical evidence of the three need dimensions, and (2) that individuals tend to characterize their needs in terms of the levels proposed by the framework.[19] Criticisms of Alderfer's model, however, focus on two issues. First, research on ERG theory is limited and, second, its popularity is largely due to its consistency with theories of rational choice.[20] The idea that people shape their actions to satisfy unfulfilled needs provides purpose and direction to individual behavior, an idea that is appealing to many social scientists. Other work, in contrast, has suggested that needs are only *indirectly* related to action.[21] Thus, similar to the concerns about Maslow's hierarchy, questions have been raised as to whether the theory is sufficiently verifiable to be of real value to practitioners.[22] Finally, in an increasingly diverse, multicultural world, questions have been raised about ERG's universality as critics contend that the theory does not help them understand what motivates members of particular groups or organizations.[23]

McClelland's Theory of Socially Acquired Needs

David McClelland identified three basic needs that people develop and acquire from the larger society—the need for *achievement, power,* and *affiliation.*[24] His theory proposes that each of us will be, at different times, influenced by one of these needs, and that the strength of that particular need (and the influence on our behavior) will vary according to the situation. Each of us, however, is likely to have developed a dominant orientation toward *one* of these needs based on our socialization and life experiences. Therefore, some individuals will be more heavily motivated by social needs, while others will be driven by the need to achieve various goals or to gain a certain degree of power and influence over others.

McClelland argued that, in general, the need for achievement influences an individual's orientation to the tasks he or she faces in an organization. For example, is the person motivated by the rewards for a job well done? Do needs for affiliation or power influence an individual's interpersonal relations? Does the person seek friends and act warm and friendly to colleagues, or strive for power and organizational influence?[25]

Although much of the research offered in support of this theory has been produced by McClelland's own research,[26] other studies have tested aspects of this theory with positive results as well. Studies have found that employees with a high need for achievement (referred to as *n Ach*) tend to: (1) experience satisfaction from good performance; (2) set higher goals than those with low achievement needs; (3) be more effective in managing their time; and (4) improve their performance following feedback.[27] Thus, an obvious implication for managers is to draw out those individuals with a high need for achievement. However, a unique aspect of McClelland's work is that people can be taught to increase motivation (need) to achieve.[28] Such training initiatives are also of obvious value when dealing with a diverse, multicultural workforce, modifying and enhancing self-images, and encouraging individuals to seek new job challenges and responsibilities.[29]

McClelland's work thus raises two interesting points. First, the theory suggests that motivation is changeable even in adulthood. Second, rather than treating motivation as an independent variable (as did the previously discussed theories), motivation becomes a dependent variable as the focus is on the antecedent conditions that develop a particular need.

Needs and Goal Orientation

Emerging research related to motivation from a dispositional standpoint has focused on the individual's goal orientation. *Goal orientation* represents a framework for how individuals interpret and respond to task performance situations.[30] Research on goal orientation indicates that people pursue three primary goals to varying degrees in task performance situations: (1) *learning*, wherein individuals focus on development and/or increasing competence; (2) *performance approach*, in which the overriding motivation is to demonstrate competence by meeting or surpassing normative-based standards; and (3) *performance avoidance*, wherein individuals' desire to meet a normative-performance standard is characterized by a desire to avoid unfavorable evaluations or judgment. This latter tendency is in contrast to the desire to attain favorable judgments associated with the performance approach orientation. These orientations are theorized to derive from individuals' implicit beliefs regarding the extent to which ability is either fixed or can be developed.[31] The belief that ability is fixed is associated with a performance approach or avoidance orientation, while the belief that ability is a skill that can be developed or acquired leads to a learning orientation.

Because goal orientation determines the amount of effort that is allocated toward tasks, it is proposed to influence skill acquisition. There is some evidence that compared to low learning-oriented people, those with a high learning orientation are more likely to seek out challenging situations, devote more effort to challenging task activities, maintain the allocation of effort in response to performance feedback, and interpret mistakes as feedback for improvement strategies. In contrast, individuals with relatively high performance orientations are theorized to allocate more resources toward ego maintenance, focus on performance indicators as opposed to task activities, perceive mistakes as threats, withdraw from the task in the face of challenges and setbacks, and employ strategies that minimize the amount of effort required.[32] An important theoretical implication of goal orientation research is that high learning- (or low performance-) oriented people may learn at a faster rate than high performance- (or low learning-) oriented people.

Herzberg's Motivator-Hygiene Theory

Another research-based theory is Frederick Herzberg's *motivator-hygiene* approach.[33] Herzberg's research suggested that motivation is composed of two largely unrelated dimensions: (1) those aspects of the job that can prevent dissatisfaction but do not influence employees to grow and develop (hygiene factors); and (2) those job-related dimensions that actually encourage such growth (motivators). Thus, the factors associated with producing job satisfaction are separate and distinct from those preventing (or precipitating) job dissatisfaction. The main implication of this theory is that a focus on hygiene factors alone could only prevent job dissatisfaction. For employees to be truly satisfied and perform above minimally accepted standards, motivators had to be built into the job. Figure 3-2 illustrates these dimensions and the relative influence the various factors have on job-related satisfaction and dissatisfaction.

Motivator-hygiene theory has led to a significant body of largely contradictory research. While there has been some support for Herzberg's thesis, many empirical studies refute predictions based on his theory. Needs for salary, recognition, and responsibility, for example, have been shown to operate *both* as motivators and as hygiene factors.[34] Similarly, studies have found that while Herzberg's motivator factors were linked with satisfaction rather than dissatisfaction, the same was true for hygiene factors.[35] Such findings contradict Herzberg's conclusion that hygiene factors are sources of dissatisfaction rather than satisfaction. As much of the research on gain-sharing programs suggests, linking employee salaries to organizational productivity and profitability goals is gaining favor as a motivational tool.[36] Studies in non-U.S. environments have also produced conflicting results.[37]

Another criticism of Herzberg's theory is that his results were largely determined by his methodology.[38] Herzberg asked a group of accountants and engineers what they liked and disliked about their jobs. Our society, however, has a cultural bias to attribute one's dissatisfaction to others (or the "system") and one's satisfaction and accomplishments to oneself. Thus, it is not surprising that the research indicated that those aspects that were actually part of job content were linked with satisfaction while those aspects that were more peripheral to the job (context) were linked with job dissatisfaction. When this line of research was repeated with engineers during the 1990s,

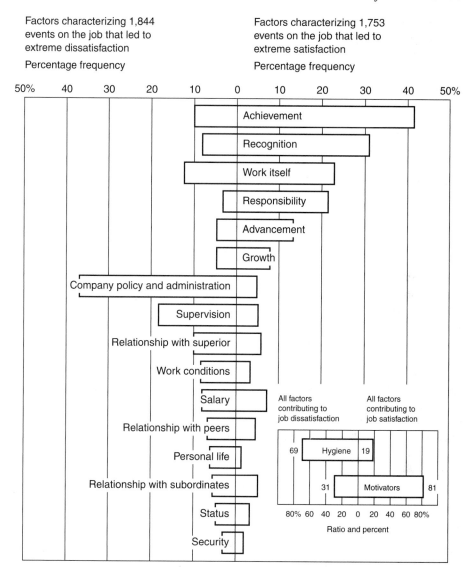

Figure 3-2 Factors Affecting Job Attitudes, As Reported in 12 Investigations

Source: Reprinted by permission of the *Harvard Business Review.* An exhibit from "One More Time: How Do You Motivate Employees?" by Frederick Herzberg (January–February 1968). Copyright © 1968 by the President and Fellows of Harvard College; all rights reserved.

advancement and recognition (important motivators in Herzberg's research) had a higher frequency of *dissatisfaction* than satisfaction.[39] Finally, in his original research only self-reports of performance were used and in most situations the respondents were focusing on job-related activities that had occurred over a long time period.[40] In general, his model equates a willingness to expend effort on the job with job satisfaction. Yet, there is no explanation as to *why* the various intrinsic and extrinsic job factors drawn out in the study affect performance.

Although motivator-hygiene theory has been criticized on this basis, Herzberg is credited with providing the field with a new way of thinking about worker motivation. Prior to his efforts, job satisfaction was largely viewed as a unidimensional concept—job satisfaction was at one end of the continuum and job dissatisfaction at the other. Accordingly, his distinction between hygiene and motivator factors and their implications for motivation have called into question a number of practices that emphasize extrinsic, contextual factors at the expense of the more content-based, intrinsic aspects of the job. As his work suggests, the real keys to motivating people lie in achievement, recognition for that achievement, the work itself, responsibility, and the opportunity for growth or advancement. His framework continues to be an influential factor in attempts to operationalize motivational theory.[41]

Protestant Work Ethic

A question that emerges from Herzberg's work concerns the extent to which work itself is a basic part of a person's need structure. The *Protestant Work Ethic* reflects the degree to which individuals place work at or near the center of their lives.[42] Individuals who score high on this factor tend to be more satisfied with and involved in their jobs, more committed to their organizations, and more likely to stay with the same organization over time. In general, people who have a high work ethic attempt to fulfill their needs within the context of the workplace much more fully than those with a lower Protestant Work Ethic score.[43]

Despite the popular image of declining work dedication, research suggests that there has not been any decline in the work ethic in the United States or the United Kingdom.[44] In fact, as information technology continues to blur the distinction between work and life itself—via pagers, cellular phones, laptop computers, and e-mail— it seems that more and more people are living to work, literally anytime, anywhere.[45] Recent research, for example, indicates that in some industries extreme work demands, known as the "70-hour workweek," are becoming the norm, a reality that virtually necessitates that the job becomes a significant part of the person's self-concept.[46] Among other factors, individuals working in such jobs identify stimulation and challenge, high-quality colleagues, high compensation, recognition, and power and status among their primary motivators.

Figure 3-3 illustrates the relationships between the different static-content theories of motivation. In general, these models continue to provide the foundation for a significant amount of management and organization development and training, including work redesign and career development.

Managerial Application: Work Design and Job Enrichment

Much of the work on job redesign has been influenced by the static-content theorists in general and Herzberg in particular. Instead of simply *rotating* people through different work assignments or *enlarging* jobs by adding activities that are on the same level as the original job, *job enrichment* emphasizes building opportunities for growth and achievement (*motivators*) into the work itself. Job enrichment restructures work to include activities that had previously come before (planning) and after (evaluation) the original job. This can provide a greater sense of job closure, in which the worker has more of an understanding of the entire work process. In essence, a job is often

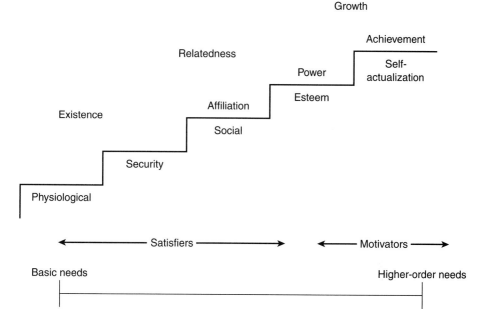

Figure 3-3   Relationship between Static-Content Motivational Models

enriched by assigning workers some of the tasks that were previously performed at the supervisory level.[47]

The most well-known framework for conceptualizing the various aspects of jobs is the *job characteristics model* (see Figure 3-4). This theory identifies five basic job characteristics or core job dimensions that should be considered when attempting to redesign work:[48]

1. **Skill variety** is the degree to which a particular job requires different activities that draw on different skills and talents of the worker.
2. **Task identity** is the degree to which a particular job has a sense of "job closure"—completion of a whole and identifiable piece of work.
3. **Task significance** is the degree to which a job has a perceivable impact on others, whether in the immediate organization or in the external environment.
4. **Autonomy** is the degree to which a job gives individuals independence, freedom, and discretion in work scheduling and work procedures used in carrying out the work.
5. **Feedback** is the degree to which workers are provided with direct and clear information concerning the effectiveness, quality, and quantity of their work performance.

As indicated in Figure 3-4, the core job dimensions are directly related to a set of implementing concepts that enrich jobs and increase their motivational potential.

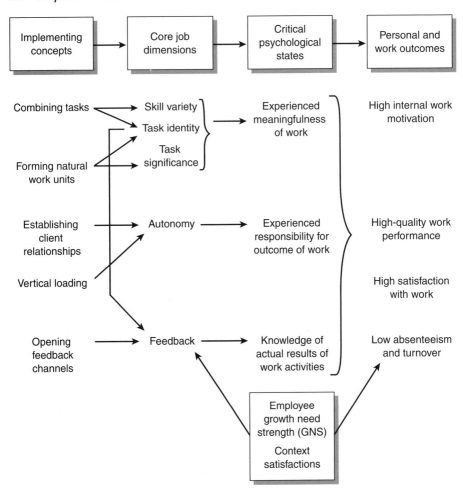

Figure 3-4 Job Characteristics Model

Source: J. R. Hackman, G. Oldham, R. Janson, and K. Purdy, "A New Strategy for Job Enrichment," © 1975 by the Regents of the University of California. Adapted from *California Management Review,* volume XVII, no. 4, p. 62 by permission of the Regents.

As these core dimensions are enhanced, the model posits that they influence three critical psychological states of employees: (1) *experienced meaningfulness of work,* which is affected by the degree of skill variety, task identity, and task significance; (2) *experienced responsibility for work outcomes,* which is influenced by the amount of autonomy in the work; and (3) *knowledge of actual results of work activities,* which is a function of the extent of feedback. In turn, these psychological states are manifested in specific personal and work outcomes. Recent research has supported the proposition that high levels of these critical psychological states lead to such favorable outcomes and work behaviors as high motivation, high-quality work performance, high levels of job satisfaction, and low absenteeism and turnover.[49]

Using the job characteristics model, the motivational potential of a particular job can be calculated as follows:

$$\text{Motivating Potential Score (MPS)} = \left(\frac{\text{Skill variety} + \text{Task identity} + \text{Task significance}}{3} \right) \times \text{Autonomy} \times \text{Feedback}$$

Jobs that have a high motivating potential must be high on at least one of the factors that influence experienced meaningfulness, in addition to high degrees of autonomy and feedback. A low score on one of the major components would have negative consequences for the overall motivating potential of the job. This model can be applied as a diagnostic tool through the Job Diagnostic Survey (JDS), a self-administered questionnaire or job rating form that measures the extent to which a particular job fulfills the dimensions specified by the framework from the perception of the workers themselves. The JDS can be used both to (1) diagnose existing jobs *prior* to planned work restructuring and (2) evaluate the effects of work restructuring interventions.

This approach, however, is moderated by the *growth-need strength* (relative strength of an individual's needs for personal growth and development) of organizational members, a factor that should be considered before redesigning jobs. Employees high on growth-need strength tend to respond more favorably to job enrichment efforts compared with those employees with weak needs for growth.[50] Thus, a diagnostic approach to the redesign of work should be taken.

Most of the recent research on job redesign has focused on advanced manufacturing and information technology.[51] From a theoretical perspective, however, questions have been raised about the extent to which many of the changes that have taken place over the past decade actually constitute job redesign efforts.[52] For example, Total Quality Management (TQM), flexible manufacturing, outsourcing, corporate restructuring, self-managed work teams, and a host of other interventions have all been included as part of work redesign. While these activities do change a lot of aspects of the work process and the ways in which many jobs are carried out, since different dimensions are changed at different times, it is difficult to determine precisely what is going on with respect to the motivational aspects of different jobs. The fundamental advantage of many of these efforts, however, is the movement away from micromanagement and the attempt to make the job itself a motivating experience.

PROCESS THEORIES OF MOTIVATION

While the static-content theories of motivation alert us to the types of factors that can energize human behavior, they have been criticized on a number of levels.[53] Research has indicated, for example, that people vary considerably in the way in which they respond to similar aspects of their jobs, that many different needs may be simultaneously operating, and that other factors rather than unfulfilled needs are influential in motivation. Moreover, since the content models focus on people's needs at a given point rather than on predicting behaviors, other theories were developed to more fully explain the *process* of motivation in terms of the factors that channel or direct behavior.

Expectancy Theory

The basic process model of motivation is referred to as *expectancy* or *VIE theory.*[54] Essentially, the model assumes that motivation is a function of three components: (1) an effort-performance expectation that increased effort will lead to good performance (*expectancy*); (2) a performance-outcome perception that good performance will lead to certain outcomes or rewards (*instrumentality*); and (3) the value or attractiveness of a given reward or outcome to an individual (*valence*). Thus, for an individual to be motivated, the outcome or reward must be valued by the person, and she or he must believe that additional effort will lead to higher performance and that the higher performance will subsequently result in greater rewards or outcomes.

The advantage of expectancy theory is that it provides a framework for understanding *how* motivation operates. Assume, for example, that there is a possibility of a reward (promotion; monetary bonus) for the preparation of a strategic market analysis that must be well done and useful to management. The specified reward is important to the individual (high valence), so he or she is willing to work hard on the analysis. However, if the worker is unclear as to the type of analysis management wants, working hard may be perceived as wasting time. Since the effort involved on the report may require additional work hours, which can cut into household responsibilities, the expectations of potential discord with the person's spouse or significant other could outweigh the potential reward, especially if what constitutes a "useful" report is unclear. Thus, the probability of linking the effort and performance together will be relatively low. Even though it might be acknowledged that the individual worked hard and produced a quality analysis, the report may still not be useful to management (low instrumentality). As a result, receiving the reward (valued outcome) may be perceived as unlikely, undermining the person's motivation to perform (see Figure 3-5). From a diagnostic perspective, each of the model's three components can be analyzed as a way of identifying possible causal factors.

The main implications that can be drawn from expectancy theory are as follows:

- Rewards or other outcomes to motivate people *must* be desired by those individuals. Managers must, therefore, try to *identify* valued outcomes rather than simply *assuming* that they know exactly what their employees want or *attributing* their own needs or desires to others. Increased attention, therefore, should be given to incentive awards and recognition systems that take into account a variety of employee preferences—from the simple fact that some individuals in a diverse workforce might be more appreciative of tickets to the symphony or theater rather than a sporting event as a recognition of their contributions,[55] to more complex subtleties in desired rewards.
- If employees are to be motivated, they must perceive that differences in actual performance will result in differences in (valued) rewards or outcomes. Unless organizational reward systems can provide sufficient flexibility in the ways in which people are rewarded and this is followed through, the link

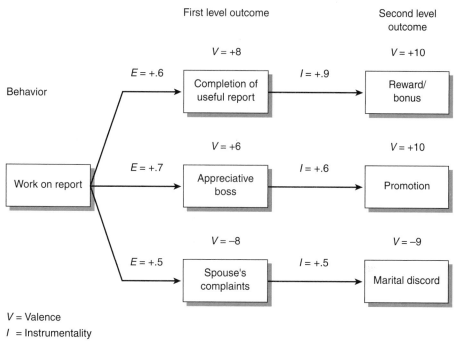

V = Valence
I = Instrumentality
E = Expectancy

Figure 3-5 Expectancy Theory

between high performance and obtaining goals will be undermined (e.g., "merit rating" systems that reward more on seniority than actual merit).

- Employees must also perceive that their effort (behavior) will result in good performance. Properly training employees for their jobs, clarifying managerial expectations concerning "good" performance, and attempting to increase an individual's level of self-confidence or feeling of competency are some of the ways in which this effort-performance link can be strengthened.

Expectancy theory has generated a considerable body of research that examines the extent to which (1) the three basic components (valence, instrumentality, and expectancy) can be reliably and validly measured, and (2) the model actually predicts how people will behave in a given situation. From a research perspective, scholars have criticized the reliability and validity of questionnaires used in early studies of expectancy theory,[56] although subsequent efforts have noted significant improvement in the quality of assessment techniques.[57] A number of measurement and methodological issues, however, remain unresolved—for example, should interviews rather than questionnaires be used to assess the model's components, and how many different outcomes should be studied?[58] From a practitioner perspective, since VIE models have multiple branches, one can begin to diagnose why a certain individual is behaving in a particular way.[59] Managers can therefore focus on those aspects of the work situation that can influence (or hinder) higher performance.

A criticism of expectancy theory is that it assumes that people will act in a rational manner and weigh the various alternatives open to them.[60] Yet, while people may be limited in the amount of information that they can actually process at any given time, recent work suggests that individuals actually process much more information than has been assumed, especially when faced with complex problems and challenges.[61] Moreover, although the interactions between expectancies, instrumentalities, and valences are quite complex, recent meta-analysis points to significant support for VIE theory, particularly when within-subjects designs are used.[62]

Path-Goal Theory of Motivation

A second process theory of motivation, which is derived from expectancy theory, is the *path-goal* model.[63] Although this approach is often referred to in terms of leadership effectiveness, its basic focus is the examination of motivation and the way in which such diagnosis can influence the way people perform. The underlying idea is that people make choices that reflect their preferences in terms of the relative *utility* for them (i.e., a hierarchy of particular outcomes). Thus, as suggested by expectancy theory, individuals will be motivated to produce when they perceive that their efforts will lead to successful performance and the attainment of desired rewards. Management efforts to motivate, therefore, should focus on clarifying a subordinate's "path" to a desired goal or objective.

A basic criticism underlying path-goal theory focuses on the difficulties involved in putting its theoretical constructs—path, goal, and leadership style—into practice.[64] Early empirical studies produced mixed results, with one investigation even finding that subordinates actually saw the path-goal relationship *less* clearly under highly directive leadership compared with less directive styles.[65] When path-goal hypotheses have been tested in specifically designed studies that reflect the conditions outlined in the theory, however, research findings are more promising.[66]

From a practitioner vantage point, this approach suggests that managers can motivate people by increasing the personal benefits of work-goal accomplishment (attempting to increase the valence of a particular goal) while clarifying the path to the reward by reducing ambiguities and organizational barriers. In doing so, the subjective probability that effort (performance) will lead to goal attainment (instrumentality) will be increased. Throughout the process, feedback is important. If, however, the way in which a particular goal can be accomplished is already clear, such additional information may be regarded by subordinates as redundant. The result can be decreased satisfaction and lessened motivation.

Goal-Setting Theory

Closely related to expectancy theory and the path-goal model is the idea that *setting goals*, which is among the most potent of psychological motivators, can *cause* high performance. The basic premise of *goal-setting theory* is that (1) because goals direct our thoughts and actions, (2) a person's conscious intentions (goals) are the primary determinants of task-related motivation.[67] Not every goal, however, necessarily leads to enhanced performance because a particular goal may conflict with other goals a person may have, or be perceived as inappropriate for that particular situation.

There has been a voluminous amount of research on the link between goal setting and behavior that has carried well into the mid- 2000s.[68] As would be suggested by path-goal theory, specific goals appear to result in higher effort than generalized (or no) goals. Furthermore, even when individuals set difficult goals, *if* they are "accepted" as reasonable, performance appears to be better when compared with individuals who set relatively easy goals for themselves (unrealistically difficult goals, however, *could* be worse than no goals at all). The explanation for this goal-difficulty effect is that difficult goals induce greater effort and persistence compared with easy goals (assuming goal acceptance). Difficult goals also make self-satisfaction conditional on a higher level of accomplishment than easy goals.

Assigned versus Participative Goals

The research on participation and goal setting has produced a series of conflicting findings. Most studies of goal setting suggest that goal specificity and difficulty rather than participation per se are the key variables related to higher performance.[69] In fact, some researchers argue that the cognitive benefits of participation are far more powerful than the motivational effects; that telling people which goals to strive for, especially challenging ones, is in itself an indirect means of encouraging self-competence.[70] However, these findings, which contradict many of our contemporary ideas about increased participation and involvement in the workplace, emerged from carefully controlled laboratory settings or field experiments.[71] This situation has thus raised questions about their generalizability.

While the debate over participation, goal setting, and performance continues, it is fairly clear that participation in goal setting enhances the probability of *acceptance* of difficult goals. Thus, the role of participation in setting one's goals seems to be an important part of the motivational process. In terms of goal-setting theory, managers should (1) set clear and specific goals for employees, (2) make goals sufficiently difficult to be perceived as challenging, but not so difficult as to be viewed as impossible, (3) involve employees in goal setting when appropriate to ensure commitment, (4) include subgoals and feedback (either through supervision or the task itself), and (5) link goal accomplishment with valued rewards. It is important that managers facilitate this process by ensuring that organizational members understand how a particular set of goals fits with larger organizational goals and strategies.[72]

Personal (Self-Set) Goals and Self-Efficacy

Much of the research on goal setting over the past decade has focused on the power of self-set goals. In terms of motivation potential, *self-set goals* are typically viewed as more desirable than assigned goals because they engender high commitment.[73] Moreover, individuals who reject assigned goals may set their own personal goals that can exert a powerful influence on their performance. Similarly, *self-efficacy,* what a person believes he or she can do on a particular task, is related to goal commitment and performance. In general, people with high self-efficacy tend to set high personal goals, perform well, and succeed in achieving them.[74]

Managerial Application: Management by Objectives

Management by objectives (MBO) is a process through which managers and their subordinates work together to identify common goals and objectives and to coordinate their efforts in attaining them. Initially developed in the 1950s, MBO was a popular technique in the 1960s and early 1970s, only to fall into disrepute in many organizations. Yet, as most research has indicated, it is the way in which MBO is usually implemented that creates problems rather than the idea of MBO itself.[75]

MBO was initially developed as a synthesis of three processes: goal setting, participation in decision making, and objective feedback. In an MBO program, a supervisor and subordinate attempt to reach consensus on: (1) the goals the subordinate will attempt to accomplish during a specified period of time; (2) the means the subordinate will use to reach those goals; and (3) how progress toward the goals will be measured and evaluated. A key factor underlying this method is the extent to which there is true participation—*mutual involvement and negotiation* in determining objectives and means—during the process.[76] In many instances, however, organizational members are led to believe that they will have a significant say in determining their goals and objectives, only to find that they are forced into accepting their supervisor's goals. In fact, many individuals often feel pressured to accept objectives that they actually feel are unrealistic or undesirable.[77] When this occurs, the outcome is usually characterized by mistrust, lowered commitment, and withdrawal. In fact, many MBO systems degenerate into little more than paperwork rituals that are not supported or taken seriously by the organization and its management.

If MBO is to be successful, the process should be characterized by: (1) an active give-and-take between managers and their subordinates; (2) a high level of face-to-face communication; (3) top management support and involvement; (4) flexibility in setting goals; (5) attention to implementation details (e.g., communication of its importance; MBO-related training; sufficient time frame; monitoring); (6) a high degree of fit with the specific needs of the organization; and (7) an organizational culture and climate that support openness and sharing. Most of the traditional approaches to MBO, however, are insufficient for the demands of today's highly competitive environment. The typical MBO program receives very little top management support and involvement, impacts only a small proportion of an employee's total job, dictates rather than conjointly determines an individual's goals, and is poorly linked with performance appraisal efforts. In fact, far too often MBO is little more than "MBT"—management by terror—rather than a true collaborative approach to setting goals, as managers often report that they are manipulated into agreeing to unrealistic goals and then punished for failing to achieve the goals that they "set for themselves."[78] Accordingly, MBO efforts that look good on paper often detract from overall job performance, to the detriment of both the organization and the individual. As analyses of MBO and goal-setting research have indicated, however, *if* implemented as noted earlier, the process can have a very favorable effect on organizational member performance and productivity.[79]

ENVIRONMENTALLY BASED THEORIES OF MOTIVATION

Thus far, this chapter has examined a number of theories that attempt to depict what energizes and directs human behavior. These different models have largely dealt with motivation as an independent variable; that is, a particular need or goal is the cause of a particular desire that results in certain behaviors. We will now turn to an exploration of some of the ways in which behavior can be sustained or maintained over time. In contrast to the preceding theories, the perspectives discussed in this section view motivation as an intervening and dependent variable. Thus, the focus is on the *antecedents* of those variables to which we commonly attribute motivated behavior.

Operant Conditioning and Reinforcement Theory

The basic assumption underlying B.F. Skinner's theory of *operant conditioning* is that human behavior is determined and maintained by the person's environment. Although behavior may be random at first, as an individual explores the environment and reacts to it, certain behaviors will be *reinforced* and subsequently repeated. Thus, according to Skinnerian theory, an individual's behavior or motivation is a function of the consequences of that behavior.[80] If we are rewarded for behaving in a certain way, we begin to make the connection between the appropriate behavior and the reward, and continue to engage in that behavior. Thus, from a managerial perspective, reinforcement theory suggests that if you desire to maintain a certain behavior in the workplace, you must be able to manipulate the consequences of that behavior.[81] By providing employees with a valued reward for punctuality, for example, a manager should be able to control tardiness. Since this perspective assumes that all behaviors have an operant conditioning basis, motivation is reduced to identifying needs and providing appropriate rewards.

The discussion thus far has focused on *positive reinforcement* (rewards) to encourage the repetition of certain behaviors. Although most reinforcement theorists argue that positive reinforcement is the most effective way of sustaining desired behaviors, *negative reinforcement* (avoidance; the withdrawal of negative consequences) can also increase the likelihood that desired behaviors will be repeated. *Punishment*, in contrast, is not intended to encourage desired (positive) behavior but rather to discourage those behaviors we do not want repeated. It appears, however, that punishment can often have the reverse effect on people. Studies, for example, have indicated that when employees feel that a punishment was inappropriately harsh it led to a *decline* in their performance.[82]

Different *schedules of reinforcement* can also have an effect on resultant behaviors.[83] To quickly solidify a particular behavior, continuous and immediate reinforcement is useful (i.e., every time the behavior occurs rewards should be given without delay). Behavior tends to be persistent, in contrast, when it is learned under conditions of *partial* and *delayed reinforcement* (i.e., reinforcement is given at either fixed or variable intervals after a given period of time has elapsed between the behavior and the reinforcement). For operant conditioning to be successful, however, consequences need to be tied directly and unambiguously to desired behaviors. If there is too much of a time lag between the reinforcement and the behavior, the psychological connection between the behavior and reinforcer may not be formed, or the behavior might even be reinforced by other, unintended consequences.

Some of the criticism aimed at operant conditioning focus on ethical concerns about manipulation. Skinner himself expressed concern that many of these techniques are embedded in our society, especially in marketing campaigns, that attempt to reinforce consumers' "free choice" to purchase their products.[84] Yet other critics argue that while such attempts to control behavior may work well with animals, they are less effective with people, complex beings with multifaceted needs and motives.[85] The existence of conflicting stimuli in the workplace often produces situations where a given behavior might lead to both rewards and penalties. Second, time lags between acts and rewards raise questions about people's expectations, the extent to which they accept deferred gratification, and the level of trust that exists between them and the authority figure (the individual in charge of doling out the rewards). Finally, operant conditioning and reinforcement theory emphasize the environmental conditions that influence individuals to behave in a certain way, virtually to the exclusion of the broader social context surrounding those actions. As underscored by the Hawthorne Studies (see Chapter 1), group and interpersonal relations in the workplace exert a powerful influence on our behavior.

Despite these concerns, Skinner's theory remains very influential[86] and the fact remains that principles of reinforcement and the strategies associated with them can be useful to managers in influencing the behavior of their employees. One only needs to observe behavior in any casino to see operant conditioning in action, not only in terms of the payout schedule of the various games, but in the design of the buildings themselves, their restrooms and their amenities.[87] By linking valued positive reinforcers (e.g., praise, recognition, pay, promotion) to desired behaviors (e.g., task accomplishment, increased effort), managers can increase the probability that those behaviors will be sustained.

Managerial Application: Organizational Behavior Modification

A managerial application of Skinnerian theory is found in organizational behavior modification (OBM), a process focused on acquiring and maintaining certain preferred behaviors while extinguishing those that are undesirable.[88] Often referred to in business settings as *performance management*, OBM attempts to make certain job-related behaviors occur more or less frequently, depending on whether they enhance or hinder organizational objectives, through the systematic manipulation of incentives, the conditions that contribute to a particular set of behaviors (antecedent conditions) and the immediate consequences of those behaviors.

In general, there are three basic characteristics common to most OBM applications:[89]

1. The primary focus is a person's behavior rather than his or her internal states (values, attitudes).

2. OBM's expressed purpose is to make the organization more efficient by increasing worker productivity while enhancing worker satisfaction.

3. The fundamental approach is to link employee behavior to antecedent conditions (sometimes referred to as prompting mechanisms) that appear to evoke the behavior and to the consequences that appear to encourage (or discourage) its recurrence.

From an organizational vantage point, successful applications of OBM programs are related to the extent to which managers are able to: (1) reward people with what they value; (2) explicitly link the reward with the desired behavior; (3) appropriately fit the magnitude of the reward with the magnitude of the behavior; (4) reward better performers more than average performers; and (5) give meaningful feedback and the reward after the performance.[90] By using explicit performance standards (goals) and linking accomplishment of those standards with constructive feedback and valued rewards, managers, in effect, can induce desired behaviors over time.[91]

In general, most studies of OBM have focused on manufacturing rather than higher-level information-processing jobs and relatively simple behaviors (e.g., quantity of output, absenteeism) instead of potentially more complex ones (e.g., quality of performance, customer service).[92] Thus, similar to criticisms of operant conditioning, OBM has been faulted for being less effective in dealing with the types of complex work behaviors required of most working adults. However, recent research, especially studies focused on OBM as part of developing employee problem-solving abilities, suggest that the process can be effective in dealing with complex, higher-level work assignments.[93]

Punishment and Discipline

Although most discussions of performance management emphasize rewards and positive reinforcement, it is important to briefly discuss the role of punishment and organizational sanctions.[94] A distinction can be drawn between the concepts of punishment and discipline. *Punishment* occurs when an aversive consequence follows a behavior. *Discipline* is a deliberate attempt to punish. Thus, it is apparent that not all punishment constitutes discipline, and not all discipline necessarily constitutes punishment. An understanding of the nature of punishment is critical not only as it relates to intentional aversive consequences for undesirable behavior, but also insofar as many constructive behaviors occur less frequently than desired because of unintended aversive consequences (punishment) that follow such behaviors. For example, many managers espouse their desire for employees to give prompt feedback, even—perhaps especially—when the feedback is negative or critical. However, based on the same managers' often less than encouraging reactions to negative information, employees learn quickly not to be the bearer of bad news, regardless of the prevailing rhetoric.

For myriad reasons punishment is considered by many to be the least favored method of motivating or controlling employee behavior. One reason is related to the many variables necessary for punishment to be effective, among them:

- Punishment must be perceived as aversive by the recipient, which can be difficult to determine or evaluate.
- Punishment should be applied before an undesired behavior has time to become ingrained.
- Punishment must happen immediately or soon after the transgression (undesired behavior) so that the employee can make a direct association between the behavior and the consequence.
- Punishment must be quick and relatively intense so that it is experienced as aversive.
- Punishment should focus on a specific behavior rather than the individual.

- Punishment must be consistent across people and time.
- Punishment must have informational value.
- After punishment there must be continued monitoring or surveillance of behavior so that punishment can be administered or removed as appropriate.
- Punishment only temporarily suppresses undesirable behaviors, which often reappear when the threat of punishment is removed.
- Punishment should occur in the context of a trusting, healthy relationship.

In addition to these and other considerations, undesirable side effects can be associated with punishment, such as resentment and hostility, withdrawal or restricting output to "get even," fear that can cause an employee to avoid a manager, and general inhibition due to anxiety, which can stifle positive behaviors such as learning and being truly engaged at work.

Although it is clear that there are a number of compelling reasons to minimize the use of punishment as a method of motivation or control, its use remains widespread. There are several explanations for the frequent use of punishment in organizational settings. First, some behavior engaged in by employees—such as absenteeism, theft, or other egregious violations of organizational policy—may warrant punitive results. Another contributing factor to the prevalence of punishment is related to power. For example, managers at the lower rungs of an organization often have little control over the administration of resources that can serve as rewards (e.g., raises, promotions, job assignments), thus the threat of punishment or discipline may appear to be the most readily available and potent tool for managing the behavior of subordinates. In addition, the act of punishment itself can become a self-reinforcing behavior. In other words, to the extent that a manager utilizes punishment and it yields the immediately desired result (e.g., the abatement of unwanted or dysfunctional behavior), the behavior (punishment) will have been positively reinforced. Drawing on the premises of reinforcement and learning, as a consequence of the positive reinforcement, it becomes more likely that the manager will employ punishment the next time she or he encounters unwanted employee behavior.

Social Comparison Theory

Other theories of motivation focus on the variables that surround the individual who is to be "motivated." One such approach is the process of *social comparison*, which looks at how people view reality based on their own experience.[95] Since people desire to make sense of different situations, individuals are likely to attribute meaning and/or cause–effect relationships to particular experiences.[96] In turn, these experiences allow people to interpret, understand, or even block out certain aspects of their job, organization, or environment. Thus, this theory suggests that attitudes about a particular job are likely to be constructed from both the present job situation and past experiences that are linked to the present job.

Social comparison theory helps to explain how people use external and internal comparisons to determine the appropriateness of a given behavior. Rather than conflicting with the other motivational theories discussed earlier, it can be used to extend our ability to understand levels of employee performance and satisfaction. One model that is based on the social comparison approach is equity theory.

Equity Theory

The basis of *equity theory* is that people compare their efforts (inputs) and rewards (outcomes) with the input-outcome ratios of other comparable individuals.[97] The key is whether an individual perceives equity or inequity in the following relationship:

$$\frac{\text{Individual's outcomes}}{\text{Individual's own inputs}} = \frac{\text{Comparable others' outcomes}}{\text{Comparable others' inputs}}$$

If an individual views this relationship as unequal, an attempt will be made to restore equity either by working more or less effectively or by trying to obtain greater rewards through other means (focus behavior elsewhere, leave the organization, etc.). For instance, experienced employees would probably feel that they were being treated unfairly if a newly hired, recent graduate was being paid a higher salary. The theory suggests that these individuals would then attempt to reduce this inequity. They may complain to their manager, "express" their feelings by being tardy for or absent from work, decrease their level of work effort, search for another job, and so forth. The underlying assumption is that people are aware of each other and are able to make such comparisons in an organization.

Although the theory was originally concerned with discrepancies in pay, it has been generalized to other situations as well. One of the research findings suggests that people who feel that they are overrewarded tend to produce more. These individuals may also attempt to increase the outcomes of others. A question that remains unanswered, however, is whether people who think they are being overrewarded change their self-concept over time (an internal comparison that would make the relationship "equitable"). The research on equity theory is also more definitive on the reactions of people who perceive that they are underrewarded for their efforts. Moreover, drawing on differences across individuals, a recent conceptualization suggests that reactions to equitable and inequitable situations are a function of a particular person's preferences for different outcome–input ratios.[98] Some individuals, for example, may be more benevolent (thinking more in terms of giving than receiving) in their interpretation of what is equitable, while others may feel they deserve greater entitlements than they actually may be due.

Recent work in this area has also related equity theory to perceptions of *organizational justice* and *citizenship behaviors* (i.e., discretionary behaviors that fall outside of the employee's actual job description).[99] Research suggests that people can increase or decrease these activities (e.g., volunteering for certain assignments, helping others outside one's work unit) as a way of adjusting the perceived equity relationship they have with their employer.

An understanding of equity theory provides three potential points of intervention with regard to motivation. Specifically, managers concerned with motivating others can intervene to reframe or reestablish an individual's consideration of his or her meaningful inputs and/or outputs by increasing or changing the factors an individual is including and perceiving as important. A manager can also change or adjust an individual's referent point or comparison person to create a perception (evaluation/comparison) favorable to behavior that is beneficial for the employee and organization. The main implication is that people use external (as well as in-kind) comparisons to determine the appropriateness of their efforts with respect to the rewards that they and comparable others receive. This approach helps us to understand the ways in which our perceptions of what is fair (or unfair) and just (or unjust) are formulated. It does not, however, predict performance as an outcome of those perceptions.[100]

Social Learning Theory

Social learning theory can be conceptualized as an integration of the environmental determinism of operant conditioning and OB modification (where behavior is viewed as a function of external cues and consequences) and the self-deterministic view of traditional motivation theory of Maslow, Alderfer, and McClelland (where behavior is caused by internal needs, satisfaction, and/or expectations). Essentially, social learning theory is characterized by *reciprocal determinism,* where behavior is viewed as a function of internal *and* external cues and consequences *and* cognitive functioning.[101] This approach is based on the premise that we acquire much of our behavior by observing and imitating others within a larger social context. Such modeling, however, is not a one-way process, because our behavior and environment influence each other. For instance, we are expected to comply with unpopular laws until we elect officials who will amend or repeal them (e.g., Prohibition; the military draft), engage in civil disobedience as a way of influencing legislative change (e.g., the Civil Rights movement), and so forth. Similarly, in organizations we may be forced to follow questionable policies until we can convince our bosses—verbally or through our actions—to change them. Thus, while the environment influences our behavior, our behavior can also affect our environment.

Social learning theory also helps us to understand three important processes that are not adequately dealt with by other motivational theories: vicarious learning, the use of symbolism, and the role of self-control. First, managers and executives appear to acquire much of their work-related behaviors by observing and imitating others whom they personally identify with (*vicarious learning*) rather than by trial-and-error shaping (as in operant conditioning where someone is systematically reinforced to produce a particular behavior). Second, instead of simply leaving different things to chance or waiting until we have to react to them, we often attempt to anticipate consequences to various actions or imagine solutions to problems before we experience them firsthand (*mental symbolism*). For instance, considering the stressful and traditionally unhealthy lifestyles of many executives, individual managers as well as their corporations are placing more emphasis on diet (supported by on-site cholesterol screening) and exercise (supported by on-site workout centers) as proactive ways of dealing with health risks. Finally, according to social learning theory, individuals can control their own behavior and actions (*self-control*) if they can manage their environment and cognitive processes. For instance, if we wish to lose weight we can imagine the way we would look after dropping a few pounds (cognitive process) or eliminate high-calorie snack food around the house (alter our environment).

The main attractiveness of social learning theory lies in its ability to balance the two major criticisms of motivation theory. Behaviorists criticize traditional motivation theory because it places too much emphasis on mental processes and emotional states (e.g., perceived needs; expectancies), while humanists criticize behaviorism for its reluctance to consider the role of social processes, modeling, and self-control in learning.[102]

INTRINSIC AND EXTRINSIC REWARDS AND MOTIVATION

One final distinction in types of rewards and motivation is the difference between intrinsic and extrinsic rewards, and how these kinds of motivations are related to performance and satisfaction.[103] *Extrinsic rewards* are outcomes that come to mind when we think about rewards in general—pay, benefits, and tickets to a sporting or cultural event as recognition for performance are common examples. *Intrinsic rewards,* in contrast, are more intangible in nature and include such things as feelings of achievement, growth and challenge on the job, and esteem. Intrinsic rewards are intimately related to the nature of work itself, while extrinsic rewards are related to the context and material aspects of the work being done. In the context of Herzberg's motivator-hygiene theory, motivators are intrinsic in nature while hygiene factors are more extrinsically oriented.

Extrinsic motivation refers to a means–ends relationship; that is, we engage in certain behaviors in order to receive (or avoid) certain incentives (or punishments) that are outside of or external to the task itself. Thus, we are motivated to do the task (means) to receive the desired reward (ends). *Intrinsic motivation,* in contrast, is essentially task motivation in its own right, that is, a desire to work hard solely for the pleasure of task accomplishment. This type of motivation (and behavior) is an end in itself; examples such as the effort people put into sports, personal projects, and volunteer associations often come to mind when discussing intrinsic motivation.

If an organization's goals, values, or particular work assignments are perceived as part of an individual's self-concept, as a means of growth and development, or as a way of asserting and developing personal capabilities, task accomplishment often becomes an end in itself. In this instance, extrinsic incentives become less important as motivators.[104] Social workers and teachers, for example, often complain about their working conditions and level of pay, yet still put in many long hours dealing with clients or working with students because of the fulfillment and satisfaction derived from the work itself. This is *not* to suggest, however, that extrinsic incentives are unimportant. Good pay and benefits, sick leave, pension plans, and so forth are significant aspects of a person's total compensation package.

The interaction between intrinsic and extrinsic rewards and motivation is not entirely clear. On one level, people can be induced to work because they enjoy the work itself and the work environment. On another level, extrinsic rewards can influence people to try new, difficult, or even dangerous jobs. A number of studies, however, suggest that extrinsic rewards can undermine a person's intrinsic motivation.[105] By inducing an individual to engage in a particular task for monetary reasons, a manager may actually weaken that person's intrinsic interest in the task. The internal feeling of accomplishment and achievement *may* be reduced when the task is done primarily for the external reward offered by the manager. Moreover, some research suggests that adding extrinsic rewards to an already intrinsically rewarding job does not necessarily increase an individual's motivation, performance, or satisfaction. Other studies, however, have failed to find such effects.[106] In fact, balancing extrinsic outcomes (such as a sense of economic security or a financial stake in the success of the firm) with intrinsic outcomes (such as greater control, recognition, and a sense of appreciation for one's contributions) are suggested to be important components of effective organizational productivity improvement programs and value-creating knowledge transfers across teams and work units.[107]

Managerial Application: Gainsharing

A growing number of experts argue that the strongest motivation occurs when people have both a psychological (intrinsic) *and* a financial (extrinsic) stake in an organization's success. An application of this idea is referred to as *gainsharing*, an umbrella of pay-for-performance approaches that link financial rewards for employees to improvements in the performance of the entire firm or work unit.[108] Gainsharing generally consists of two fundamental elements: (1) a financial formula that serves as the basis for tying employee bonuses to system-wide productivity, and (2) a formal employee-involvement program.

One of the most well-known organizational gainsharing systems is the *Scanlon Plan*.[109] This system was originally initiated during the Depression of the 1930s by Joseph Scanlon, a local union president who wanted to prevent the shutdown of a financially troubled steel mill. A historical ratio (usually referred to as the Scanlon Ratio) of labor costs to the sales value of production is applied to each month's output and part of the savings (below expected labor costs) is distributed to all workers in proportion to their base pay. The plan also encompasses a Theory Y philosophy of management, explicitly empowering employees to make and review productivity-enhancing suggestions, and implement them as appropriate. This process is accomplished through an interlocking system of joint worker-management committees that are composed of elected representatives from different departments.

Based on a review of the research on gainsharing interventions, a number of underlying factors have been identified that can facilitate its success.[110]

- Clear and tangible payoffs to both employees and management that are perceived to be equitable
- Competent and confident supervisors who are open to employee input and participation
- High degree of employee involvement
- Specialized work teams focused on solving production- and service-related problems
- An organizational history of stable, measurable performance that can be used as an initial baseline for payout
- Effective communication about the program and sufficient levels of trust throughout the organization to facilitate its initiation
- Follow-up efforts to overcome "plateauing" of interests and results over a sufficiently long-term frame to enable the program to fully take effect
- Sufficient workloads and markets to absorb increases in productivity

- Support and commitment from top management and, especially in union environments, an explicit commitment to a participative form of organizational management

While the research on organizational size is somewhat inconclusive, it appears that small- to moderate-sized organizations (those with employee populations of up to 600 employees) have the best chance for success with gainsharing. As organizations get larger, the perceived relationship by employees between their work behaviors and work pay and rewards becomes less clear. In larger organizations, therefore, the plan is sometimes applied to divisions to keep the size manageable. By focusing on both the intrinsic aspects of employee participation and the extrinsic aspects of compensation, however, gainsharing holds significant promise as a strategic tool for motivating organizational members.

MOTIVATION AND THE PSYCHOLOGICAL CONTRACT

As suggested by the environmentally based theories of motivation, the interaction that occurs between people and organizations is based on an ongoing sense of reciprocity and mutual influence. The ways in which organizations treat their members, the kinds of authority and power structures that are utilized, and the kinds of norms and values that operate simultaneously affect employee motives and behaviors. Correspondingly, it has been argued that whether people desire to work effectively, whether they generate enthusiasm for organizational goals, and whether they derive satisfaction from their work are largely dependent on two basic factors:[111]

1. The extent to which *people's expectations* of what the organization will provide them and what they owe the organization in return matches the *organization's expectations* of what it will give and receive

2. Assuming there is agreement between the two sets of expectations, the nature of what is *actually exchanged* (e.g., money in exchange for time at work; social satisfaction and job security in exchange for hard work and loyalty; opportunities for growth and development in exchange for high-quality work and creative effort)

The interaction between an individual and an organization is a dynamic, two-way process of exchange. In a broad sense, both parties participate in this relationship only because of what each expects to receive in return for their involvement. Organizations employ individuals because their services are essential for the organization to successfully achieve its goals. Individuals, in turn, relinquish some of their autonomy to the organization in order to fulfill their personal needs. Thus, this relationship can be viewed as cooperative and fulfilling only when it offers both parties—the individual and the organization—the opportunity to meet their respective needs.[112]

This reciprocal relationship is referred to as the *psychological contract*, the link or bond between the individual and the organization as represented by the expectations of each party. This "contract" is termed psychological because it is largely unwritten and unspoken. Certain material rewards and benefits are explicitly stipulated and agreed upon, but psychological factors such as job satisfaction and expectations of challenging work, fair treatment, and so forth are more implicit in nature. Yet, although unstated, this "psychological income" is perhaps the contract's most critical component.

Organizational Commitment and the Psychological Contract

The fact that a psychological contract exists does not necessarily guarantee effective member and organizational performance. As suggested earlier, the kind of contract that develops depends on a number of factors, including the ways in which organizations treat and communicate with their members, the various values and norms that operate within organizations, and the type of power base and institutional arrangements utilized by an organization. One model, for example, suggests that the individual–organization relationship is shaped by the kind of power and authority structure used to bring about member compliance.[113] Basically, organizations have three main power bases at their disposal: coercive, remunerative, and normative. Organizations that utilize a predominantly coercive power base—that is, control through the use of threats and punishment—tend to elicit a type of *alienative* involvement on the part of their members. Individuals are not truly psychologically involved with the organization and their membership is maintained through force. Many individuals belong to unions, for example, only because union membership is required for employment in certain areas. If the restriction were removed, those individuals would likely drop their membership.

The second type of control system is based on rational-legal authority and uses economic rewards and incentives in exchange for membership and performance. This *remunerative* or *utilitarian* power base tends to evoke a type of *calculative* involvement, an extrinsic relationship that is often characterized by the expression "a fair day's work for a fair day's pay." Finally, organizations that stress a *normative* power base—that is, the use of symbolic rewards and incentives such as prestige, recognition, and respect—elicit more of a *moral commitment* from their members. In this situation, membership is often an end in itself rather than a means to some other ends. Most organizations with such a normative-moral bond would be not-for-profit and voluntary types of organizations.

These three control systems, the levels of involvement they tend to elicit, and the types of psychological contracts that are formulated are summarized in Table 3-1. Although "incongruent" or mixed types of contracts are possible (e.g., a utilitarian-coercive contract as often found in the military under the draft system), the kind of

TABLE 3-1 **Organizational Control Systems, Level of Member Involvement, and Types of Psychological Contract**

Level of Involvement	Type of Control System		
	Coercive	**Remunerative**	**Normative**
Alienative	Forced contract		
Calculative		Extrinsic contract	
Moral			Intrinsic contract

Source: Adapted from Amitai Etzioni, *A Comparative Analysis of Complex Organizations.* Glencoe, IL: Free Press, 1961.

contract formed depends heavily on the *dominant control system* employed by the organization. Thus while this table represents "pure" types of organizational relationships, empirical investigation has indicated the predictive validity of this typology. For example, organizations that primarily use pay incentives and other economic rewards to motivate and involve their members to perform should expect a calculative type of commitment from their employees. If members are expected to display loyalty to the organization, to be intrinsically motivated in their work, or to be psychologically committed to organizational goals, the organization may be asking its members to give more than they are receiving in return. Moreover, research also suggests that the level of trust that exists in an organization's psychological contract is a key determinant of the extent to which its members will engage in systematic absenteeism as opposed to more positive citizenship-related behaviors.[114]

Recent conceptualizations of employee commitment suggest that factors other than the dominant power base utilized by an organization can significantly influence attitudes and behavior. For instance, commitment to top management, to an individual supervisor, or to a work group have been found to be important determinants of job satisfaction, turnover decisions, and "prosocial" organizational citizenship behaviors (e.g., altruism, conscientiousness) over and above commitment to an organization.[115] Similarly, other researchers argue that personal characteristics (e.g., relative desire for an organizational career, degree of self-confidence) and experiences (e.g., familiarity with the organization's core values, past organizational successes or failures) can also shape an individual's *propensity* to commit to an organization.[116]

While most conceptualizations of the psychological contract have focused on the employee view, recent research has begun to reflect broader organizational and managerial perspectives. As information technology continues to reshape the business world, companies are becoming increasingly dependent on the innovativeness of and high-quality performance from their members. Thus, a growing number of organizations are beginning to pay closer attention to establishing clear links with their members, beginning with initial entry-level considerations through day-to-day work expectations and future-oriented, top-down communications.[117] In essence, firms are recognizing the importance of developing and communicating more remunerative-normative types of contracts. In other words, although business firms will still largely rely on a remunerative power structure as the foundation for their employment contracts, many firms are attempting to establish greater commitment and motivation by moving toward control systems with normative overtones.[118]

Many companies are attempting to develop new relationships with their members that shift away from purely remunerative and extrinsic forms of reward to include those that are more normative and intrinsic in nature—even in the context of downsizing and outsourcing. As an example, an exchange often sought by employees and promoted by organizations in the wake of the loss of "job" security is "employment" security (or "employability"). In other words, organizations are attempting to replace the idea of job security with opportunities for employee development, with an emphasis on those skills and experiences that will enhance employees' marketability.

From a contingency or situational perspective, of course, it is important to recognize that people are complex beings and that different things may motivate different people at different times. Especially with respect to a diverse workforce, care must be taken to ensure that the kinds of rewards that managers perceive as intrinsic are viewed similarly by the organization's employees. If we draw on attitude data gathered over the last thirty years, however, it seems that value shifts centering much more fully on personal growth and development are keys to the growing disenchantment in our labor force.[119] Based on these data, it seems that if people are expected to exhibit greater commitment to and motivation toward their work, the organization, and its goals, they must be provided with an opportunity to fulfill valued personal goals such as a sense of autonomy, authority, and influence over organizational decision-making processes.

A critical concern, however, is that the recent movement toward downsized, restructured workplaces and contingent workers radically changed the psychological contract, violating the expectations that people had about their organizations. Recent work, for example, suggests that there is an implicit equation underlying an organizational member's sense of whether the organization has breached its promise:[120]

$$\frac{\text{Benefits provided by the organization}}{\text{Benefits promised by the organization}} \quad \text{Compared to} \quad \frac{\text{Contributions provided by the employee}}{\text{Contributions promised by the employee}}$$

As suggested in the discussion of equity theory, the comparison is between how well the organization has fulfilled its promised obligations and how well the employee has fulfilled his or her role. As such, there has been a drastic increase in "free-agent" behaviors as organizational members are viewing the psychological contract as increasingly extrinsic in nature, in essence adopting more of a "pay as you go" attitude.[121]

CHOOSING AN APPROPRIATE MOTIVATIONAL MODEL

One of the problems involved in presenting an array of motivational models is to sort out which of these conceptual frameworks is most appropriate for a particular situation. Instead of interpreting these theories as universal truths that accurately explain behavior in all cases, motivational models should be considered *middle-range* theories—not as ambitious or as encompassing as universal models but still useful for considering how to motivate people in different ways.[122] As this chapter has hopefully illustrated, it is clear that certain types of models are better suited for particular types of predictions and understandings.

One approach to creating such a middle-range theory of motivation is to consider different types of motivating situations. For instance, expectancy theory is useful for assessing the choices a person is confronted with—the choice a particular person is likely to make depends on the valences, instrumentalities, and expectancies involved. Equity theory and goal-setting models also seem to have utility in predicting choices. However, the amount of effort a person is likely to exert on a task may be better explained by need, reinforcement, and equity theory than by goal or expectancy theory. Similarly, satisfaction with one's work seems best illustrated by need theory and equity theory rather than reinforcement theory, which is primarily focused on behavior instead of feelings. Performance on the job seems well explained by reinforcement, equity, or goal theories, while it is difficult to fully explain inferior performance through expectancy theory or even need theory. Finally, withdrawal behaviors such as turnover and absenteeism can be effectively analyzed through reinforcement, equity, and expectancy theory. If a person quits his or her job, the decision may be explained by inadequate rewards (reinforcement theory), inequitable rewards compared with others doing similar tasks (equity theory), or low probabilities of reaching desired goals or valences (expectancy theory). Need theory and goal-setting theory, by contrast, do not seem to explain withdrawal behaviors as well.

Contrasting Motivation and Learning

An underlying dynamic related to motivation and performance is the fact that performance gains associated with enhanced employee motivation are generally short term. In other words, although employees can be enticed or motivated to contribute increased, above average, or exceptional effort to a given task, this change (increase) in effort and performance tends to be temporary. In fact, studies that have considered the long-term effect of prolonged motivation and increased effort have found adverse consequences including burnout, absenteeism, stress, and anxiety.[123]

When it comes to employee productivity, because motivation effects are generally temporary and often constrained by limited resources, many argue that enhancing learning is preferable to motivation. Though there can be short-term or temporary performance deficits associated with learning (e.g., the learning curve), over the long term learning facilitates performance improvements that are sustainable by the employee without superior or otherwise enhanced motivation and greater effort.

CONCLUSION

The managerial implication of this brief discussion should be clear. Since managers are considered diagnosticians in other aspects of their jobs, they should be diagnosticians in dealing with questions of motivation. A recent formulation, for example, suggests the following diagnostic questions and related actions:[124]

1. Undertake an Initial Diagnosis
   a. *What is the performance problem?* As clearly as possible, describe the discrepancy between the current reality and desired goal or outcome.
   b. *How important is it?* If the situation is perceived to be unimportant, disregard it.
   c. *Is the problem due to situational obstacles?* If so, remove the obstacles.
   d. *Is it due to ability?* If so, focus on training, selection, job assignment, and so forth.

2. Select a Strategy
   a. *What motivational processes are involved?* To what extent are needs unfulfilled, choices unclear, and/or key behaviors not reinforced?
   b. *Do individual tendencies or dispositions explain the problem?* Focus on selection, job assignment, and related actions.
   c. *Which motivational strategy is feasible, given the situation?* List the different approaches that could work.
   d. *Which strategies are affordable?* List those that make economic sense for the company.

e. *Is the target individuals or teams or both?* Make appropriate adjustments to the strategies based on the target.

3. Decide on and Implement a Course of Action

The challenge is to discover which aspects of motivation are missing for a particular situation and work on developing them. Depending on the circumstances, this effort could include such actions as: inspiring people to believe in the importance and worth of their jobs; making jobs more challenging; improving intrinsic *and* extrinsic reward systems; setting more difficult or comprehensive goals; assisting people in reaching their goals; removing barriers that may prevent people from accomplishing their objectives; and reinforcing appropriate behaviors while discouraging others. Perhaps the most useful approach to motivation is to view these different theories as complementary rather than mutually exclusive. Each perspective provides us with some insight into why people behave the way they do. It is also important to realize, of course, that not all aspects of energizing, directing, and maintaining employee behaviors are controlled by managers and their organizations. The challenge is to understand these different theories and to develop a managerial philosophy that allows one to incorporate motivational theory with one's own personal managerial style.

NOTES

1. R.M. Steers and L.W. Porter, eds., *Motivations and Work Behaviors* (New York: McGraw-Hill, 1975); and W.C. Hamner, "Motivation Theories and Work Applications," in S. Kerr, ed., *Organizational Behavior* (Columbus: Grid Publications, 1979), p. 42.
2. See D.E. Terpstra, "Theories of Motivation—Borrowing the Best," *Personnel Journal* (June 1979): 461–466; and B. Dabscheck, "The Motivation to Work," *Journal of Economic Issues* 28, no. 1 (1994): 297–300.
3. See L.G. Bolman and T.E. Deal, *Reframing Organizations: Artistry, Choice, and Leadership*, 3rd ed. (San Francisco: Jossey-Bass, 2003); and G. Morse, "Why We Misread Motives," *Harvard Business Review* 81, no. 1 (2003): 18–19.
4. D. McGregor, *The Human Side of Enterprise* (New York: McGraw-Hill, 1960).
5. See R.S. Jacques, "History, Historiography and Organization Studies: The Challenge and the Potential," *Management & Organizational History* 1, no. 1 (2006): 32–33.
6. McGregor, *Human Side of Enterprise*, p. 31. See also Jacques, "History, Historiography and Organization Studies," p. 33.

7. E. Schein, "In Defense of Theory Y," *Organizational Dynamics* (Summer 1975): 17–30.
8. M. Loden and R.H. Loeser, "Working Diversity: Managing the Differences," *The Bureaucrat: The Journal for Public Managers* (Spring 1991): 25; D. Bilimoria and S.K. Piderit, "Board Committee Membership: Effects of Sex-Based Bias," *Academy of Management Journal* 37, no. 6 (1994): 1453–1477; and V. Valian, *Why So Slow? The Advancement of Women* (Cambridge, MA: MIT Press, 1998).
9. See R.R. Thomas, Jr., "From Affirmative Action to Affirming Diversity," *Harvard Business Review* 68, no. 2 (1990): 114–116; J. Lefkowitz, "Race as a Factor in Job Placement: Serendipitous Findings of Ethnic Drift," *Personnel Psychology* 47, no. 3 (1994): 497–513; and P. Dass and B. Parker, "Strategies for Managing Human Resource Diversity: From Resistance to Learning," *Academy of Management Executive* 13, no. 2 (1999): 68–80.
10. E.F. Huse and J. L. Bowditch, *Behavior in Organizations: A Systems Approach to Managing* (Reading, MA: Addison-Wesley, 1977), p. 100; and Hamner, op. cit., p. 42.

11. M.L. Ambrose and C.T. Kulik, "Old Friends, New Faces: Motivation Research in the 1990s," *Journal of Management* 25, no. 3 (1999): 231–292.

12. A.H. Maslow, "A Theory of Human Motivation," *Psychological Review* 50 (1943): 370–396; and A.H. Maslow, *Motivation and Personality* (New York: Harper & Row, 1954).

13. For an example of this research, see L.M. Porter, "Job Attitudes in Management: Perceived Deficiencies in Need Fulfillment as a Function of Job Level," *Journal of Applied Psychology* 46, no. 6 (1962): 375–387; and C.P. Alderfer, "An Empirical Test of a New Theory of Human Needs," *Organizational Behavior and Human Performance* 4, no. 2 (1969): 142–175.

14. See H.E. Wilkinson, C.D. Orth, and R.C. Benfari, "Motivation Theories: An Integrated Operational Model," *SAM Advanced Management Journal* 51, no. 4 (1986): 24–31; M.A. Wahba and L.G. Bridwell, "Maslow Reconsidered: A Review of the Research on the Need Hierarchy Theory," *Organizational Behavior and Human Performance* 15 (1976): 212–240; E.E. Lawler and J.L. Suttle, "A Causal Correlational Test of the Need Hierarchy Concept," *Organizational Behavior and Human Performance* 7 (1972): 265–287; and V.J. O'Connor, "Women and Men in Senior Management: A 'Different Needs' Hypothesis," *Women in Management Review* 16, no. 7/8 (2001): 400–405.

15. C. Argyris, *Personality and Organization* (New York: Harper, 1957).

16. L. Siegel and I.M. Lane, *Personnel and Organizational Psychology* (Homewood, IL: Irwin, 1987), pp. 376–377.

17. Terpstra, op. cit.; and Hamner, op. cit., p. 44. For an interesting contemporary application of Maslow's hierarchy, see A. Bryant, "Looking for Purpose in a Paycheck," *The New York Times*, June 21, 1998, p. 1 wk; and L.J. Carpenito-Moyet, "Maslow's Hierarchy of Needs Revisited," *Nursing Forum* 38, no. 2 (2003): 3–4. The continued relevance of Maslow's work is further reflected in the republication of a new edition of his classic work: A.H. Maslow with D.C. Stephens and G. Heil, *Maslow on Management* (New York: Wiley, 1998).

18. Alderfer, op. cit.; and C.P. Alderfer, *Existence, Relatedness, and Growth* (New York: Free Press, 1972).

19. J. Rauschenberger, N. Schmitt, and J.E. Hunter, "A Test of the Need Hierarchy Concept by a Markov Model of Change in Need Strength," *Administrative Science Quarterly* 25 (1980): 645–670; C.P. Alderfer and R.A. Guzzo, "Life Expectancies and Adults Enduring Strength of Desires in Organizations," *Administrative Science Quarterly* 9 (1979): 347–361; and J.P. Wanous and A. Zwany, "A Cross-Sectional Test of Need Hierarchy Theory," *Organizational Behavior and Human Performance* 12 (1977): 78–97.

20. G.R. Salancik and J. Pfeffer, "An Examination of Need-Satisfaction Models of Job Attitudes," *Administrative Science Quarterly* 22 (September 1977): 427–456.

21. R. Kanfer, "Motivation Theory and Industrial and Organizational Psychology," in M.D. Dunnette and L.M. Hough, eds., *Handbook of Industrial and Organizational Psychology* (Palo Alto, CA: Consulting Psychologist Press, 1990), pp. 75–170.

22. See B.M. Staw, N.E. Bell, and J.A. Clausen, "The Dispositional Approach to Job Attitudes," *Administrative Science Quarterly* 31 (1986): 56.

23. See F.J. Landy and W.S. Becker, "Motivation Theory Revisited," in L.L. Cummings and B. Staw, eds., *Research in Organizational Behavior*, vol. 9 (Greenwich, CT: JAI Press, 1987), pp. 1–38.

24. D.C. McClelland, *The Achieving Society* (Princeton: Van Nostrand, 1961); and D.C. McClelland, "Business Drive and National Achievement," *Harvard Business Review* 40, no. 4 (1962): 99–112.

25. Wilkinson, et al., op. cit., pp. 28–29.

26. See, for example, D.C. McClelland, "Managing Motivation to Expand Human Freedom," *American Psychologist* 33 (1978): 201–210; D.C. McClelland and D. Burnham, "Power Is the Great Motivator," *Harvard Business Review* 54, no. 2 (1976): 100–111; D.C. McClelland and D.G. Winter, *Motivating Economic Achievement* (New York: Free Press, 1969); and D.C. McClelland and C.E. Franz, "Motivational and Other Sources of Work Accomplishments in Mid-Life: A

Longitudinal Study," *Journal of Personality* 60 (1992): 697–707.

27. R.M. Steers and D.G. Spencer, "The Role of Achievement Motivation in Job Design," *Journal of Applied Psychology* 62 (1977): 472–479; G.A. Yukl and G.P. Latham, "Interrelationships Among Employee Participation, Individual Differences, Goal Difficulty, Goal Acceptance, Instrumentality, and Performance," *Personnel Psychology* 31 (1978): 305–324; T. Matsui, A. Okada, and T. Kakuyama, "Influence of Achievement Need on Goal Setting, Performance, and Feedback Effectiveness," *Journal of Applied Psychology* 67 (1982): 645–648; and J. Barling, E.K. Kelloway, and D. Cheung, "Time Management and Achievement Striving Interact to Predict Car Sales Performance," *Journal of Applied Psychology* 81 (1996): 821–826.

28. D.C. McClelland, "Toward a Theory of Motive Acquisition," *American Psychologist* 20 (1965): 321–333; and D.C. McClelland, *Human Motivation* (Glenview, IL: Scott, Foresman, 1985).

29. See, for example, D.G. Winter, "The Power Motive in Women and Men," *Journal of Personality and Social Psychology* 54 (1988): 510–519; and B. Rosen and K. Lovelace, "Piecing Together the Diversity Puzzle," *HR Magazine* (June 1991): 78–84.

30. B.S. Bell and S.W.J. Kozlowski, "Goal Orientation and Ability: Interactive Effects on Self-Efficacy, Performance, and Knowledge," *Journal of Applied Psychology* 87 (2002): 497–505; J.F. Brett and D. Vanderwalle, "Goal Orientation and Goal Content as Predictors of Performance in a Training Program," *Journal of Applied Psychology* 84 (1999): 863–873; J.A. Colquitt and M.J. Simmering, "Conscientiousness, Goal Orientation, and Motivation to Learn during the Learning Process: A Longitudinal Study," *Journal of Applied Psychology* 83 (1998): 654–665; and D. Zweig and J. Webster, "Validation of a Multidimensional Measure of Goal Orientation," *Canadian Journal of Behavioural Science* 36 (2004): 232–243.

31. E.S. Elliot and C.S. Dweck, "Goals: An Approach to Motivation and Achievement," *Journal of Personality and Social Psychology* 54 (1989): 5–12; and Zweig and Webster, "Validation of a Multidimensional Measure of Goal Orientation."

32. G.B. Yeo and A. Neal, "A Multilevel Analysis of Effort, Practice, and Performance: Effects of Ability, Conscientiousness, and Goal Orientation," *Journal of Applied Psychology* 89 (2004): 231–247.

33. F.W. Herzberg, B. Mauser, and B. Snyderman, *The Motivation to Work* (New York: Wiley, 1959); and F.W. Herzberg, "One More Time: How Do You Motivate Employees?" *Harvard Business Review* 46, no. 1 (1968): 53–62.

34. See T.D. Wall, "Ego Defensiveness as a Determinant of Reported Differences in Sources of Job Satisfaction and Job Dissatisfaction," *Journal of Applied Psychology* 58 (1973): 125–128; M. Dunnette, J. Campbell, and M. Hakel, "Factors Contributing to Job Dissatisfaction in Six Occupational Groups," *Organizational Behavior and Human Performance* 2 (1967): 147; and D. Vinokur-Kaplan, S. Jayarantne, and W.A. Chess, "Job Satisfaction and Retention of Social Workers in Public Agencies, Non-Profit Agencies, and Private Practice: The Impact of Workplace Conditions and Motivators," *Administration in Social Work* 18 (1994): 93–121.

35. See, for example, E.A. Maidani, "Comparative Study of Herzberg's Two-Factor Theory of Job Satisfaction among Public and Private Sectors," *Public Personnel Management* 20, no. 4 (1991): 441–448.

36. For a good overview of the growing popularity and effects of gainsharing programs, see S.C. Hamilton, D.G. Meyer, and R.R. Taylor, "Consequences of Gainsharing," *Group & Organization Management* 19, no. 1 (1994): 87–111; and T.M. Welbourne and L.R. Gomez-Mejia, "Gainsharing: A Critical Review and a Future Research Agenda," *Journal of Management* 21, no. 3 (1995): 559–609.

37. See L.K. Savery and D.L. Wingham, "Coping with the Career Plateau: Motivators for Directors of Child-Care Centers," *Leadership and Organization Development Journal* 12 (1991): 20–23; K.R. Charles and L.H. Marshall, "Motivational Preferences of Caribbean Hotel Workers: An Exploratory Study," *International Journal of Contemporary Hospitality*

4 (1992): 25–29; and U. Leviatan, "Determinants of Work Motivation and Work Satisfaction Among Kibbutz Aged Workers," *Canadian Journal of Community Mental Health* 11 (1992): 49–64.

38. B.L. Hinton, "An Empirical Investigation of the Herzberg Methodology and Two-Factor Theory," *Organizational Behavior and Human Performance* 3, no. 3 (1968): 286–309; and E.A. Locke, "Satisfiers and Dissatisfiers Among White-Collar and Blue-Collar Employees," *Journal of Applied Psychology* 58, no. 1 (1973): 67–76.

39. J. Phillipchuk and J. Whittaker, "An Inquiry into the Continuing Relevance of Herzberg's Motivation Theory," *Engineering Management Journal* 8, no. 1 (1996): 15–20.

40. See E.E. Lawler III, *Motivation in Work Organizations* (Monterey, CA: Brooks/Cole, 1973).

41. For example, see Wilkinson et al., op. cit., pp. 29–31; Terpstra, op. cit; Ambrose and Kulik, "Old Friends, New Faces," pp. 235–236; and J.L. Crompton, "Adapting Herzberg: A Conceptualization of the Effects of Hygiene and Motivator Attributes on Perceptions of Event Quality," *Journal of Travel Research* 41, no. 3 (2003): 305–311.

42. See Ambrose and Kulik, "Old Friends, New Faces," pp. 234–235.

43. A. Furnham, *The Protestant Work Ethic* (London: Routledge, 1990); D.M. Randall and J.A. Cote, "Interrelationships of Work Commitment Constructs," *Work and Occupations* 18 (1991): 194–211; and A.M. Saks, P.E. Mudrack, and B.E. Ashford, "The Relationship Between the Work Ethic, Job Attitudes, Intentions to Quit, and Turnover for Temporary Service Employees," *Canadian Journal of Administrative Science* 13 (1996): 226–236.

44. See, for example, R. Tansey, M.R. Hyman, G.M. Zinkham, and J. Chowdhury, "An Advertising Test of the Work Ethic in the U.K. and the U.S.," *Journal of International Consumer Marketing* 9 (1997): 57–77; C.N. Weaver, "Has the Work Ethic in the USA Declined? Evidence from Nationwide Surveys," *Psychological Reports* 81 (1997): 491–495; C.N. Weaver, "Examining a Work Ethic Myth about Self-Employed People," *Psychological Reports* 81 (1997): 1075–1081; and N.

Ferguson, "Why America Outpaces Europe (Clue: The God Factor)," *New York Times*, June 8, 2003, p. WR4.

45. Bryant, "Looking for Purpose in a Paycheck," p. 1 wk.

46. S.A. Hewlett and C.B. Luce, "Extreme Jobs: The Dangerous Allure of the 70-Hour Workweek," *Harvard Business Review* 84 (2006): 49–59.

47. Job enrichment has received the widest attention of the job redesign strategies in the attempt to improve the quality of people's work lives. For a good overview of the theory and research underlying job enrichment see Herzberg, Mauser, and Snyderman, op. cit.; J.R. Maher, ed., *New Perspectives in Job Enrichment* (New York: Van Nostrand Reinhold, 1971); R.E. Kopelman, "Job Redesign and Productivity: A Review of the Evidence," *National Productivity Review* 4, no. 3 (1985): 237–255; J.E. McCann III and M. Buckner, "Redesigning Work: Motivations, Challenges and Practices in 181 Companies," *Human Resource Planning* 17 (1994): 23–41; and B.P. Niehoff, R.H. Moorman, G. Blakely and J. Fuller, "The Influence of Empowerment and Job Enrichment on Employee Loyalty in a Downsizing Environment," *Group & Organization Management* 26, no. 1 (2001): 93–114.

48. J.R. Hackman and G.R. Oldham, "Developing the Job Diagnostic Survey," *Journal of Applied Psychology* 60 (1975): 159–170. A significant amount of research has been done on the jobs characteristics model; see, for example, J.R. Hackman and G.R. Oldham, "Motivation through the Design of Work: Test of a Theory," *Organizational Behavior and Human Performance* 16 (1976): 250–279; Y. Fried and G.R. Ferris, "The Validity of the Jobs Characteristics Model: A Review and Meta-Analysis," *Personnel Psychology* 40, no. 2 (1987): 287–332; J.E. Champoux, "A Multivariate Test of the Job Characteristics Theory of Work Motivation," *Journal of Organizational Behavior* 2 (1991): 431–446; N.G. Dodd and D.C. Ganster, "The Interactive Effects of Variety, Autonomy, and Feedback on Attitudes and Performance," *Journal of Organizational Behavior* 17 (1996): 329–347; and J. Yoon and S.R. Thye, "A Dual Process Model of Organizational Commitment: Job Satisfaction and Organizational Support," *Work & Occupations* 29, no. 1 (2002): 97–126.

49.   R.W. Renn and R.J. Vandenberg, "The Critical Psychological States: An Underrepresented Component in Job Characteristics Model Research," *Journal of Management* 21, no. 2 (1995): 279–303.

50.   See P.C. Bottger and I. Chew, "The Job Characteristics Model and Growth Satisfaction: Main Effects of Assimilation of Work Experience and Context Satisfaction," *Human Relations* 39 (1986): 575–594; R.B. Tiegs, L.E. Tetrick, and Y. Fried, "Growth Need Strength and Context Satisfactions as Moderators of the Relations of the Jobs Characteristics Model," *Journal of Management* 18, no. 3 (1992): 575–593; and A.L. Patti, S.J. Hartman, L. Fok, and W.M. Fok, "Jobs and People in a Total Quality Management Environment: A Survey of Academicians and Practitioners," *International Journal of Management* 18, no. 3 (2001): 359–368.

51.   See, for example, R.W. Griffin, "Effects of Work Redesign on Employee Perceptions, Attitudes, and Behaviors: A Long-term Investigation," *Academy of Management Journal* 34, no. 2 (1991): 425–435; and S.M. Shafer, B.J. Tepper, J.R. Meredith, and R. Marsh, "Comparing the Effects of Cellular and Functional Manufacturing on Employees' Perceptions and Attitudes," *Journal of Operations Management* 12 (1995): 63–74.

52.   The following discussion is drawn from T.R. Mitchell, "Matching Motivational Strategies with Organizational Contexts," *Research in Organizational Behavior* 19 (1997): 106–109. See also D. O'Doherty and H. Willmott, "The Question of Subjectivity and the Labor Process," *International Studies of Management and Organization* 30, no. 4 (2000/2001): 112–133; and S. De Treville, J. Antonakis, and N.M. Edelson, "Can Standard Operating Procedures Be Motivating? Reconciling Process Variability Issues and Behavioural Outcomes," *Total Quality Management & Business Excellence* 16, no. 2 (2005): 231–241.

53.   For an overview of these criticisms see T.R. Mitchell, "Organizational Behavior," *Annual Review of Psychology* 30 (1979): 243–281. Also see C.L. Hulin and M.R. Blood, "Job Enlargement, Individual Differences,

and Worker Responses," *Psychological Bulletin* 69 (1968): 41–55; and E.M. Elliot and F.P. Williams III, "When You No Longer Need Maslow: Exchange, Professionalism, and Decentralization in the Management of Criminal Justice Agencies," *Public Administration Quarterly* 19, no. 1 (1995): 74–88.

54.   The earliest work to fully articulate this theory was V.H. Vroom, *Work and Motivation* (New York: Wiley, 1964).

55.   The implications for a diverse workforce are formulated from M. Loden and R.H. Loeser, op. cit., pp. 24–26.

56.   P.J. DeLeo and R.D. Pritchard, "An Examination of Some Methodological Problems in Testing Expectancy-Valence Models with Survey Techniques," *Organizational Behavior and Human Performance* 13 (1974): 143–148.

57.   D.R. Ilgen, D.M. Nebeker, and R.D. Pritchard, "Expectancy Theory Measures: An Empirical Comparison in an Experimental Simulation," *Organizational Behavior and Human Performance* 20 (1981): 189–223.

58.   See D. Schwab, J. Olian-Gottlieb, and H. Heneman, "Between Subjects Expectancy Theory Research: A Statistical Review of Studies Predicting Effort and Performance," *Psychological Bulletin* 86 (1979): 139–147; J.P. Wanous, T.L. Keon, and J.C. Latack, "Expectancy Theory and Occupational/Organizational Choices: A Review and Test," *Organizational Behavior and Human Performance* 22 (1983): 66–86; R.E. Allen, M.A. Lucero, and K.L. Van Norman, "An Examination of the Individual's Decision to Participate in an Employee Involvement Program," *Group & Organization Management* 22 (1997): 117–143.

59.   Expectancy theory has been used to predict attitudes and performance in a number of studies. For a review of this research, see R.J. Howe, H.J. Shapiro, and M.A. Wahba, "Expectancy Theory as a Predictor of Work Behavior and Attitudes: A Re-Evaluation of Empirical Evidence," *Decision Sciences* 5 (1974): 481–506; T.R. Mitchell and L.R. Beech, "A Review of Occupational Preference and Choice Research Using Expectancy Theory and Decision Theory," *Journal of Occupational Psychology* 99 (1976): 231–248;

L.E. Miller and J.E. Grush, "Improving Predictions in Expectancy Theory Research: Effects of Personality, Expectancies, and Norms," *Academy of Management Journal* 31, no. 1 (1988): 107–102; R.A. Henry and O.J. Strickland, "Performance Self-Predictions: The Impact of Expectancy Strength and Incentives," *Journal of Applied Social Psychology* 24 (1994): 1056–1069; and P. Steel, "The Nature of Procrastination: A Meta-Analytic and Theoretical Review of Quintessential Self-Regulatory Failure," *Psychological Bulletin* 133, no. 1 (2007): 65–94.

60. M.A. Wahba and R.J. House, "Expectancy Theories in Work and Motivation: Some Logical and Methodological Issues," *Human Relations* 27, no. 2 (1974): 121–147; T.R. Mitchell, "Expectancy Model of Job Satisfaction, Occupational Preference and Effort: A Theoretical, Methodological and Empirical Appraisal," *Psychological Bulletin* 81, no. 12 (1974): 1053–1077; and I. Yamaguchi, "The Relationship Among Individual Differences, Needs, and Equity Sensitivity," *Journal of Managerial Psychology* 18, no. 4 (2003): 324–344.

61. See R.G. Lord, P.J. Hanges and E.G. Godfrey, "Integrating Neural Networks into Decision-Making and Motivational Theory: Rethinking VIE Theory," *Canadian Psychology* 44, no. 1 (2003): 21–39.

62. See W. Van Eerde and H. Thierry, "Vroom's Expectancy Models and Work-Related Criteria: A Meta-Analysis," *Journal of Applied Psychology* 81 (1996): 575–586; and T.A. Judge and R. Ilies, "Relationship of Personality to Performance Motivation; A Meta-Analytic Review," *Journal of Applied Psychology* 87, no. 4 (2002): 797–807.

63. R.J. House, "A Path-Goal Theory of Leadership Effectiveness," *Administrative Science Quarterly* 16, no. 3 (1971): 321–338.

64. Siegel and Lane, *Personnel and Organizational Psychology*, p. 499.

65. See J.F. Schriesheim and C.A. Schriesheim, "A Test of Path-Goal Theory of Leadership and Some Suggested Directions for Future Research," *Personnel Psychology* 33 (1980): 349–370; and T.H. Hammer and H.P. Dachler, "A Test of Some Assumptions Underlying Path-Goal Models of Supervision: Some Suggested Conceptual Modifications," *Organizational Behavior and Human Performance* 14 (1975): 60–75.

66. See J. Indvik, "Path-Goal Theory of Leadership: A Meta-Analysis," in J.A. Pearce and R.B. Robinson, eds., *Academy of Management Best Paper Proceedings 1986* (Academy of Management, 1986), pp. 189–192; R.T. Keller, "A Test of Path-Goal Theory of Leadership with Need for Clarity as a Moderator in R&D Organizations," *Journal of Applied Psychology* 74 (1989): 208–212; A. Sagie and M. Koslowsky, "Organizational Attitudes and Behaviors as a Function of Participation in Strategic and Tactical Change Decisions: An Application of Path-Goal Theory," *Journal of Organizational Behavior* 15, no. 1 (1994): 37–47; and C. Silverthorne, "A Test of Path-Goal Theory in Taiwan," *Leadership and Organization Development Journal* 22, no. 4 (2001): 151–159.

67. E.A. Locke, "Toward a Theory of Task Motivation and Incentives," *Organizational Behavior and Human Performance* 3 (1968): 157–189.

68. For a thorough overview of this research, see E.A. Locke and G.P. Latham, *A Theory of Goal Setting and Task Performance* (Englewood Cliffs, NJ: Prentice Hall, 1990); E.A. Locke, "Motivation Through Conscious Goal Setting," *Applied and Preventive Psychology* 5 (1996): 117–124; E. Emsley, "Multiple Goals and Managers' Job-Related Tension and Performance," *Journal of Managerial Psychology* 18, no. 4 (2003): 345–356; E.A. Locke and G.P. Latham, "Building a Practically Useful Theory of Goal Setting and Task Motivation: A 35-Year Odyssey," *The American Psychologist* 57, no. 9 (2002): 705–717; S.D. Mellalieu, S. Hanton, and M. O'Brien, "The Effects of Goal Setting on Rugby Performance," *Journal of Applied Behavior Analysis* 39, no. 2 (2006): 257–261; and M. Downie, R. Koestner, E. Horberg, and S. Haga, "Exploring the Relation of Independent and Interdependent Self-Construals to Why and How People Pursue Personal Goals," *Journal of Social Psychology* 146, no. 5 (2006): 517–531.

69. G.P. Latham and T.P. Steele, "The Motivational Effects of Participation versus Goal Setting in Performance," *Academy of*

Management Journal 26 (1983): 406–417; and E.A. Locke, L. Shaw, L.M. Saari, and G.P. Latham, "Goal Setting and Task Performance: 1969–1980," *Psychological Bulletin* 90 (1981): 125–152.

70. See Locke and Latham, ibid., pp. 171–172; and B.A. Martin and D.J. Manning, Jr., "Combined Effects of Normative Information and Task Difficulty on the Goal Commitment-Performance Relationship," *Journal of Management* 21 (1995): 65–80.

71. See R.E. Walton, "From Control to Commitment in the Workplace," *Harvard Business Review* 63, no. 2 (1985): 76–84; and E.E. Lawler III, *High Involvement Management* (San Francisco: Jossey-Bass, 1986).

72. J. Humphreys, "The Dysfunctional Evolution of Goal Setting," *Sloan Management Review* 44, no. 4 (2003): 96–106.

73. V.B. Hinsz, L.R. Kalnbach, and N.R. Lorentz, "Using Judgmental Anchors to Establish Challenging Self-Set Goals without Jeopardizing Commitment," *Organizational Behavior and Human Decision Processes* 17 (1997): 287–308; and G. Oettingen, H. Pak, and K. Schnetter, "Self-Regulation of Goal Setting: Turning Free Fantasies into Binding Goals," *Journal of Personality and Social Psychology* 80, no. 5 (2001): 735–753.

74. See, for example, E.A. Locke and P.G. Latham, "Work Motivation and Satisfaction: Light at the End of the Tunnel," *Psychological Science* 1 (1990): 240–246; J.C. Wofford, V.L. Goodwin, and S. Premack, "Meta-Analysis of the Antecedents of Personal Goal Level and of the Antecedents and Consequences of Goal Commitment," *Journal of Management* 18 (1992): 595–615; J.M. Phillips and S.M. Gully, "Role of Goal Orientation, Ability, Need for Achievement, and Locus of Control in the Self-Efficacy and Goal-Setting Process," *Journal of Applied Psychology* 82 (1997): 792–802; and F.K. Lee, K.M. Sheldon, and D.B. Turban, "Personality and the Goal-Striving Process: The Influence of Achievement Goal Patterns, Goal Level and Mental Focus on Performance and Enjoyment," *Journal of Applied Psychology* 88, no. 2 (2003): 256–265.

75. For a good summary of the MBO literature see S.J. Carroll and H.L. Tosi, *Management by Objectives: Applications and Re-search* (New York: Macmillan, 1973); R.C. Ford, F.S. McLaughlin, and J. Nixdorf, "Ten Questions about MBO," *California Management Review* (Winter 1980): 88–94; J.N. Kondrasuk, "Studies in MBO Effectiveness," *Academy of Management Review* 6, no. 3 (1981): 419–430; R. Rodgers and J.E. Hunter, "Impact of Management by Objectives on Organizational Productivity," *Journal of Applied Psychology* 76, no. 2 (1991): 322–336; M. Moravec, R. Juliff, and K. Hesler, "Partnerships Help a Company Manage Performance," *Personnel Journal* 74, no. 1 (1995): 104–107; and R. Moore, "Organizational Alignment: Why It Is So Important," *Plant Engineering* 60, no. 5 (2006): 39–40.

76. See G.S. Odiorne, *M.B.O. II* (Belmont, CA: Pearson, 1979); and G.S. Odiorne, "Management by Objectives for HR Managers," in W.R. Tracey, ed., *Human Resources Management and Development Handbook* (New York: AMACOM, 1985), pp. 101–110.

77. See H. Levinson, "Management by Whose Objectives?" *Harvard Business Review* 48, no. 4 (1970): 125–134; and C.D. Pringle and J.G. Longnecker, "The Ethics of MBO," *Academy of Management Review* 7, no. 2 (1982): 177–186.

78. See L.G. Bolman and T.E. Deal, *Reframing Organizations: Artistry, Choice, and Leadership* (San Francisco: Jossey-Bass, 1991), p. 141.

79. See R.A. Guzzo, R.D. Jeanne, and R.A. Katzall, "The Effects of Psychologically Based Intervention Programs on Worker Productivity: A Meta-Analysis," *Personnel Psychology* 38 (1985): 275–291; Rogers and Hunter, "Impact of Management by Objectives"; and R. Rogers and J.E. Hunter, "The Discard of Study Evidence by Literature Reviewers," *Journal of Applied Behavioral Science* 30 (1994): 329–345.

80. B.F. Skinner, *The Behavior of Organisms: An Experimental Approach* (New York: Appleton, 1938); B.F. Skinner, *Science and Human Behavior* (New York: Free Press, 1953); and B.F. Skinner, *Contingencies of Reinforcement* (New York: Appleton-Century Crofts, 1969). See also J.E.R. Staddon and D.T. Cerutti, "Operant Conditioning," *Annual Review of Psychology* 54 (2003): 115–144.

81. For representative articles that describe the application of operant conditioning to management, see H.W. Babb and D.G. Kopp, "Applications of Behavior Modification in Organizations: A Review and Critique," *Academy of Management Review* 3, no. 2 (1978): 281–292; and W.C. Hamner and E.P. Hamner, "Behavior Modification on the Bottom Line," *Organization Dynamics* (Autumn 1976): 8–21.

82. G.A. Ball, L.K. Trevino, and H.P. Sims, "Just and Unjust Punishment: Influences on Subordinate Performance and Citizenship," *Academy of Management Journal* 37 (1994): 299–322; and K.D. Butterfield, L.K. Trevino, and G.A. Ball, "Punishment from the Manager's Perspective: A Grounded Investigation and Inductive Model," *Academy of Management Journal* 39, no. 4 (1996): 1479–1512.

83. See G.P. Latham and V.L. Huber, "Schedules of Reinforcement: Lessons from the Past and Issues for the Future," *Journal of Organizational Behavior Management* 12 (1992): 125–149; M.E. Kelley, D.C. Lerman, and C.M. Van Camp, "The Effects of Competing Reinforcement Schedules on the Acquisition of Functional Communication," *Journal of Applied Behavior Analysis* 35, no. 1 (2003): 59–64; and V. Dragio, J.E.R. Staddon, R.G. Palmer and C.V. Buhus, "Interval Timing as an Emergent Learning Property," *Psychological Review* 110, no. 1 (2003): 126–144.

84. See Jacques, "History, Historiography and Organization Studies," p. 37.

85. See W.F. Whyte, "Pigeons, Persons and Piece Rates: Skinnerian Theory in Organizations," in J.M. Bartunek and J.R. Gordon, eds., *Behavior in Organizations: A Diagnostic Approach* (Lexington, MA: Xerox, 1978): pp. 49–54; and S. Kerr, "On the Folly of Rewarding A, While Hoping for B," *Academy of Management Journal* 18 (1975): 769–783.

86. See B.F. Skinner, "The Design of Cultures," *Behavior and Social Issues* 11, no. 1 (2001): 4–13; B.A. Thyer, "B.F. Skinner's Contributions to Cultural Design and Social Policy," *Behavior and Social Issues* 11, no. 1 (2001): 8–21; and C.B. Ferster, "Schedules of Reinforcement with Skinner," *Journal of the Experimental Analysis of Behavior* 77, no. 3 (2003): 303–312.

87. See Jacques, "History, Historiography and Organization Studies," p. 35.

88. F. Luthans and R. Kreitner, *Organizational Behavior Modification* (Glenview, IL: Scott, Foresman, 1975); F. Luthans and R. Kreitner, *Organizational Modification and Beyond* (Glenview, IL: Scott, Foresman, 1985); and R. Kreitner, "The Feedforward and Feedback Control of Job Performance through Organizational Behavior Management," *Journal of Organizational Behavior Management* 3, no. 3 (1982): 3–20.

89. See L.W. Frederiksen, *Handbook of Organizational Behavior Management* (New York: Wiley, 1982).

90. W.C. Hamner and E.P. Hamner, "Behavior Modification on the Bottom Line," *Organizational Dynamics* 4 (1976): 8–21.

91. See Locke and Latham, *A Theory of Goal Setting*, pp. 18–19; and A.D. Stajkovic and F. Luthans, "Differential Effects of Incentive Motivators on Work Performance," *Academy of Management Journal* 44, no. 4 (2001): 580–590.

92. A good synthesis of this research can be found in K. O'Hara, C.M. Johnson, and T.A. Beehr, "Organizational Behavior Management in the Private Sector: A Review of Empirical Research and Recommendations for Further Investigation," *Academy of Management Review* 10, no. 4 (1985): 848–864; A.C. Daniels, "Performance Management: The Behavioral Approach to Productivity Improvement," *National Productivity Review* (Summer 1985): 225–236; A.D. Stajkovic and F. Luthans, "A Meta-Analysis of the Effects of Organizational Behavior Modification on Task Performance," *Academy of Management Journal* 40 (1997): 1122–1149; and A.D. Stajkovic and F. Luthans, "Differential Effects of Incentive Motivators on Work Performance," *Academy of Management Journal* 44, no. 3 (2001): 580–590.

93. See R.A. Scott, J.E. Swan, M.E. Wilson, and J.J. Roberts, "Organizational Behavior Modification: A General Motivational Tool for Sales Management," *Journal of Personal Selling & Sales Management* (August 1986): 61–70; F. Luthans, R. Paul, and D. Baker, "An Experimental Analysis of the Impact of Contingent Reinforcement of Salesperson's

Performance Behavior," *Journal of Applied Psychology* 66 (1981): 314–323; H.L. Tosi and L.A. Tosi, "The Decoupling of CEO Pay and Performance: An Agency Perspective," *Administrative Science Quarterly* 34 (1989): 169–189; L.M. Sama, R.E. Kopelman, and R.J. Manning, "In Search of a Ceiling Effect on Work Motivation: Can Kaizen Keep Performance 'Risin'?" *Journal of Social Behavior and Personality* 9 (1994): 231–237. G.P. Latham, "Goal Setting: A Five-Step Approach to Behavior Change," *Organizational Dynamics* 32, no. 3 (2003): 309–409; and J.N. Ricciardi, "Achieving Human Service Outcomes through Competency-Based Training: A Guide for Managers," *Behavior Modification* 29, no. 3 (2005): 488–503.

94. This section is based on R.D. Arvey and A.P. Jones, "The Use of Discipline in Organizational Settings: A Framework for Future Research," in L.L. Cummings and B.M. Staw (eds.), *Research in Organizational Behavior* (Greenwich, CT: JAI Press, 1985), pp. 367–408; J.M. Beyer and H.M. Trice, "A Field Study of the Use and Perceived Effects of Discipline in Controlling Work Performance," *Academy of Management Journal* 27 (1984): 743–764; P.M. Podsakoff, "Determinants of a Supervisor's Use of Rewards and Punishments: A Literature Review and Suggestions for Further Research," *Organizational Behavior and Human Performance* 29 (1982): 58–83; and B.S. Klaas and H.N. Wheeler, "Managerial Decision Making about Employee Discipline: A Policy-Capturing approach," *Personnel Psychology* 43 (1990): 117–134.

95. For two very comprehensive but readable chapters on this subject, see B.M. Staw, "Motivation in Organizations: Toward Synthesis and Redirection," pp. 55–95, and P.S. Goodman, "Social Comparison Processes in Organizations," pp. 97–132, in B.M. Staw and G.R. Salancik, eds., *New Directions in Organizational Behavior* (Chicago: St. Clair, 1977).

96. L. Festinger, "A Theory of Social Comparison Process," *Human Relations* 7 (1954) 117–140. See also A. Nauta and K. Sanders, "Causes and Consequences of Perceived Goal Differences between Departments within Manufacturing Operations," *Journal of Occupational and Organizational Psychology* 74, no. 3 (2001): 321–342.

97. See J.S. Adams, "Inequity in Social Exchange," in L. Berkowitz, ed., *Advances in Experimental Social Psychology*, vol. 2 (New York: Academic Press, 1965), pp. 267–299. For illustrative research supporting equity theory, see J.S. Adams and W.E. Rosenbaum, "The Relationship of Worker Productivity to Cognitive Dissonance about Wage Inequities," *Journal of Applied Psychology* 55, no. 1 (1971): 161–164; and S.C. Carr, D. McLoughlin, M. Hodgson, and M. MacLachlan, "Effects of Unreasonable Pay Discrepancies for Under- and Overpayment on Double Demotivation," *Genetic, Social, and General Psychological Monographs* 122 (1996): 474–494. For research that argues against equity theory, see E.R. Valenzi and I.R. Andrews, "Effect of Hourly Overpay and Underpay Inequity When Tested with a New Induction Procedure," *Journal of Applied Psychology* 55, no. 1 (1971): 22–27; and R.T. Mowday, "Equity Theory Predictions of Behavior in Organizations," in R.M. Steers and L.W. Porter, eds., *Motivation and Work Behavior* (New York: McGraw-Hill, 1991), pp. 111–131.

98. R.C. Huseman, J.D. Hatfield, and E.W. Miles, "A New Perspective on Equity Theory: The Equity Sensitivity Construct," *Academy of Management Review* 12, no. 2 (1987): 222–234; W.C. King and E.W. Miles, "The Measurement of Equity Sensitivity," "*Journal of Occupational and Organizational Psychology* 67 (1994): 133–142; and L.Y. Fok, S.J. Hartman, M.F. Villere, and R.C. Freibert, "A Study of the Impact of Cross-Cultural Differences on Perceptions of Equity and Organizational Citizenship Behavior," *International Journal of Management* 13 (1996): 3–14.

99. See J. Greenberg, "Looking Fair vs. Being Fair: Managing Impressions of Organizational Justice," in B.M. Staw and L.L. Cummings, eds., *Research in Organizational Behavior*, vol. 12 (Greenwich, CT: JAI Press, 1990), pp. 111–157; C. Lee, "Prosocial Organizational Behaviors: The Roles of Workplace Justice, Achievement Striving, and Pay Satisfaction," *Journal of Business and Psychology* 10 (1995): 197–206; and R.S. Glass and W.A. Wood, "Situational Determinants of

Software Piracy: An Equity Theory Perspective," *Journal of Business Ethics* 15 (1996): 1189–1198.

100. See P.S. Goodman and A. Friedman, "An Examination of Adam's Theory of Inequity," *Administrative Science Quarterly* 16 (1971): 271–288; and J. Greenberg, "A Taxonomy of Organizational Justice Theories," *Academy of Management Review* 12, no. 1 (1987): 9–22.

101. The discussion of social learning theory draws heavily from R. Kreitner and F. Luthans, "A Social Learning Approach to Behavioral Management: Radical Behaviorists 'Mellowing Out,'" *Organizational Dynamics* 13, no. 2 (1984): 47–65. See also W.H. Bommer, E.W. Miles and S.L. Grover, "Does One Good Turn Deserve Another? Coworker Influences on Employee Citizenship," *Journal of Organizational Behavior* 24, no. 2 (2003): 181–196.

102. See A. Bandura, *Social Learning Theory* (Englewood Cliffs, NJ: Prentice Hall, 1977).

103. B.M. Staw, *Intrinsic and Extrinsic Motivation* (Morristown, NJ: Silver Burdett, 1976); E.L. Deci, *Intrinsic Motivation* (New York: Plenum, 1975); and R. Benabou and J. Tiole, "Intrinsic and Extrinsic Motivation," *Review of Economic Studies* 70, no. 244 (2003): 489–520.

104. See, for example, J.E. Mathieu and D.M. Zajac, "A Review and Meta-Analysis of the Antecedents, Correlates, and Consequences of Organizational Commitment," *Psychological Bulletin* 108, no. 2 (1990): 171–194; and W.R. Boxx, R.Y. Odom, and M.G. Dunn, "Organizational Values and Value Congruency and Their Impact on Satisfaction, Commitment, and Cohesion: An Empirical Examination within the Public Sector," *Public Personnel Management* 20, no. 1 (1991): 195–205.

105. See, for example, P.C. Jordan, "Effects of an Extrinsic Reward on Intrinsic Motivation," *Academy of Management Journal* 29, no. 2 (1986): 405–412; B.M. Staw, "The Attitudinal and Behavior Consequences of Changing a Major Organizational Reward," *Journal of Personality and Social Psychology* (June 1974): 743–751; K.B. Boone and L.L. Cummings, "Cognitive Evaluation Theory: An Experimental Test of Processes and Outcomes," *Organizational Behavior and Human Performance* 20 (1981): 289–310; E.L. Deci, R. Koestner, and R.M. Ryan, "A Meta-Analytic Review of Experiments Examining the Effects of Extrinsic Rewards on Intrinsic Motivation," *Psychological Bulletin* 125, no. 6 (1999): 627–668; and G.B. Moneta and C.M.Y. Siu, "Trait Intrinsic and Extrinsic Motivations, Academic Performance and Creativity in Hong Kong College Students," *Journal of College Student Development* 43, no. 5 (2002): 664–683.

106. J.S. Phillips and R.G. Lord, "Determinants of Intrinsic Motivation: Locus of Control and Competence Information as Components of Deci's Cognitive Evaluation Theory," *Journal of Applied Psychology* (April 1980): 211–218; Boone and Cummings, op. cit.; M.R. Lepper, J.M. Henderlong, and I. Gingras, "Understanding the Effects of Extrinsic Rewards on Intrinsic Motivation—Uses and Abuses of Meta-Analysis: Comment on Deci, Koestner, and Ryan (1999)," *Psychological Bulletin* 125, no. 6 (1999): 669–676.

107. J.E. Hamerstone, "How to Make Gainsharing Pay Off," *Training and Development Journal* 41, no. 4 (April 1987): 80–81; V. Kafka, "A New Look at Motivation—For Productivity Improvement," *Supervisory Management* 31, no. 4 (1986): 19–24; B. Geber, "Saturn's Grand Experiment," *Training* 29, no. 6 (1992): 27–35; and M. Osterloh, J. Frost and B.S. Frey, "The Dynamics of Motivation in New Organizational Forms," *International Journal of the Economics of Business* 9, no. 1 (2002): 61–78.

108. The following discussion of gainsharing and the Scanlon Plan is drawn from C.S. Miller and M.H. Schuster, "Gainsharing Plans: A Comparative Analysis," *Organizational Dynamics* 16 (Summer 1987): 44–67; M.H. Schuster, "Gainsharing: Doing it Right the First Time," *Sloan Management Review* (Winter 1987): 17–25; and T.M. Welbourne and L.R. Mejia, "Gainsharing: A Critical Review and a Future Research Agenda," *Journal of Management* 21, no. 3 (1995): 559–609.

109. F. Lesieur, ed., *The Scanlon Plan: A Frontier in Labor-Management Cooperation* (Cambridge: MIT Press, 1958); J.W. Driscoll, "Working Creatively with a Union: Lessons from the Scanlon Plan," *Organizational*

Dynamics (Summer 1979): 61–80; and J. Kenneth White, "The Scanlon Plan: Causes and Correlates of Success," *Academy of Management Journal* 22, no. 2 (1979): 292–312.

110. See L. Hatcher and T.L. Ross, "From Individual Incentives to an Organization-Wide Gainsharing Plan: Effects on Teamwork and Product Quality," *Journal of Organizational Behavior* 12 (1991): 169–183; C.R. Gowen and S.A. Jennings, "The Effects of Changes in Participation and Group Size on Gainsharing Success: A Case Study," *Journal of Organizational Behavior Management* 11 (1991): 147–169; H.C. Handlin, "The Company Built upon the Golden Rule: Lincoln Electric," *Journal of Organizational Behavior Management* 12 (1992): 151–163; T.M. Welbourne, D.B. Balkin, and L.R. Gomez-Mejia, "Gainsharing and Mutual Monitoring: A Combined Agency-Organizational Justice Interpretation," *Academy of Management Journal* 38, no. 3 (1995): 881–899; and J.B. Arthur and L. Airman-Smith, "Gainsharing and Organizational Learning: An Analysis of Employee Suggestions over Time," *Academy of Management Journal* 44, no. 4 (2001): 737–754.

111. E.H. Schein, *Organizational Psychology*, 2nd ed. (Englewood Cliffs, NJ: Prentice Hall, 1980), pp. 44, 98–100.

112. K. Thomas, "Managing the Psychological Contract," Intercollegiate Case Clearing House, Harvard Business School, Case No. 9-474-159, 1974; Schein, *Organizational Psychology*, see Chapters 3 and 5.

113. A. Etzioni, *A Comparative Analysis of Complex Organizations* (Glencoe, IL: Free Press, 1961).

114. See N. Nicholson and G. Johns, "The Absence Culture and the Psychological Contract—Who's in Control of Absence?" *Academy of Management Review* 10, no. 3 (1985): 397–407; S.E. Markham and G.H. McKee, "Group Absence Behavior and Standards: A Multilevel Analysis," *Academy of Management Journal* 38, no. 4 (1995): 1174–1190; and W.H. Turnley, M.C. Bolino, S.W. Lester and J.M. Bloodgood, "The Impact of Psychological Contract Fulfillment and the Performance of In-Role and Organizational Citizenship Behaviors," *Journal of Management* 29, no. 2 (2003): 187–206.

115. T.E. Becker, "Foci and Bases of Commitment: Are They Distinctions Worth Making?" *Academy of Management Journal* 35, no. 1 (1992): 232–244.

116. See T.W. Lee, S.A. Ashford, J.P. Walsh, and R.T. Mowday, "Commitment Propensity, Organizational Commitment, and Voluntary Turnover: A Longitudinal Study of Organizational Entry Processes," *Journal of Management* 18, no. 1 (1992): 15–32; and L. Larwood, T.A. Wright, S. Desrochers, and V. Dahir, "Extending Latent Role and Psychological Contract Theories to Predict Intent to Turnover and Politics in Business Organizations," *Group & Organization Management* 23, no. 2 (1998): 100–123.

117. D.E. Guest and N. Conway, "Communicating the Psychological Contract: An Employer Perspective," *Human Resource Management Journal* 22, no. 2 (2002): 22–39.

118. K. Thomas, "Managing the Psychological Contract"; and B. Schneider, S.K. Gunnarson, and K. Niles-Jolly, "Creating the Climate and Culture of Success," *Organizational Dynamics* 23, no. 1 (1994): 17–29.

119. See M. Cooper, B.S. Morgan, P.M. Foley, and L.B. Kaplan, "Changing Employee Values: Deepening Discontent?" *Harvard Business Review* 57, no. 1 (1979): 117–125; D. Yankelovich, *New Rules: Searching for Self-Fulfillment in a World Turned Upside Down* (New York: Random House, 1981); T.F. O'Boyle, "Loyalty Ebbs at Many Companies as Employees Grow Disillusioned," *The Wall Street Journal*, July 11, 1985, p. 27; and J. Byrne, "In Search for the Young and Gifted: Why Talent Counts," *Business Week*, October 4, 1999, pp. 108–116.

120. E.W. Morrison and S.L. Robinson, "When Employees Feel Betrayed: A Model of How Psychological Contract Violation Develops," *Academy of Management Review* 22, no. 1 (1997): 226–256.

121. See K.P. DeMeuse and W.W. Tornow, "The Tie That Binds—Has Become Very, Very Frayed" *Human Resource Planning* 13, no. 3 (1990): 203–213; A.F. Buono, "Moral Corporate Cultures in a Down-Sized, Restructured World," in W.M. Hoffman and R.E. Frederick, eds., *Business Ethics*, 3rd ed. (New York: McGraw-Hill, 1995), pp. 226–233; "It's Your

Choice," *Fast Company* (January/February 2000): 200–210; and S.W. Lester, J.R. Kickul, T.J. Bergmann, and K.P. DeMeuse, "The Effects of Organizational Resizing on the Nature of the Psychological Contract and Employee Perceptions of Contract Fulfillment," in K.P. DeMeuse and M.L. Marks (Eds.), *Resizing the Organization: Managing Layoffs, Divestitures, and Closings—Maximizing Gain while Minimizing Pain* (San Francisco: Jossey-Bass, 2003), pp. 78–107.

122. This discussion is based on M.G. Evans, "Organizational Behavior: The Central Role of Motivation," *Journal of Management* 12, no. 2 (1986): 203–222; and F.J. Landy and W.S. Becker, "Motivation Theory Reconsidered," in L.L. Cummings and B.M. Staw, eds., *Research in Organizational Behavior*, vol. 9 (Greenwich, CT: JAI Press, 1987), pp. 1–38.

123. See D.L. Cherrington, H.J. Reitz, and W.E. Scott, Jr., "Effects of Reward and Contingent Reinforcement on Satisfaction and Task Performance," *Journal of Applied Psychology* 55 (1971): 531–536; and J.E. Hunter and F.L. Schmidt, "Quantifying the Effects of Psychological Interventions on Employee Job Performance and Work-Force Productivity," *American Psychologist* 38 (1983): 479–486.

124. Adapted from Mitchell, "Matching Motivational Strategies with Organizational Contexts," pp. 121–125. See also K. Hultman, "Motivational System Mapping," *Organization Development Journal* 20, no. 4 (2002): 39–50.

CHAPTER FOUR

Communication

One of the fundamental processes that is the basis for virtually all activity in organizations is communication. In one sense, communication is the process through which we conduct our lives. As soon as two individuals come together there is a need for communication between them—some way to facilitate an understanding of what each person wants and needs from the other and their situation. The importance of communication in the business world is reflected by studies that show managers spend well over 75 percent of their time communicating.[1] Even though advanced information technologies may be changing the way we communicate with our co-workers, customers, and other key stakeholders—especially our increased reliance on cellular communication and e-mail—we still spend most of the business day communicating with others. As our ability to manage information and knowledge becomes increasingly important, an understanding of how we communicate *explicit* knowledge (e.g., hard data, codified procedures, universal principles) and *tacit* knowledge (e.g., personal knowledge embedded in individual experience), and how we can improve that process have become increasingly important as well.

THE COMMUNICATION PROCESS

Communication is often defined as the exchange of information between a sender and a receiver, and the inference (perception) of meaning between the individuals involved. All models of human communication reflect this basic definition, and include an information source, a message, a receiver, and an interpretation of the message.[2] The message itself may be transmitted either through *symbols*, such as words, writing, and drawings, or the exchange of *behavior*, such as gestures, eye contact, and body language.[3] In many instances, communication efforts are both symbolic and behavioral exchanges. The key is to understand the meaning of these symbols and behaviors.

This view of communication suggests that there is a distinction between the *transmission* of information and *understanding* the meaning of that information.[4] Transmission issues initially focused on the technical problem of transmitting a signal from one point to another in spite of various interferences that could affect the signal.[5] Communication was thus seen as a largely mechanistic process concerned with getting a message to a particular destination with a minimum of distortion and error. Although

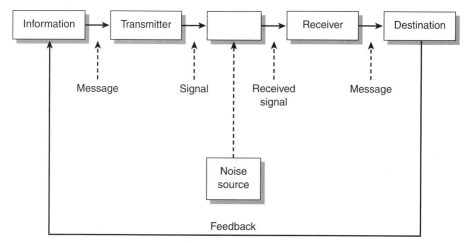

Figure 4-1 The Shannon-Weaver Communication Model

Source: Adapted from C.F. Shannon and W. Weaver, *The Mathematical Theory of Communication* (Urbana: University of Illinois Press, 1949), pp. 5 and 98.

this is a vastly oversimplified view of information theory, the key for our purposes is that in this context *communication accuracy* refers to the extent to which the basic signal transmitted by the sender is received in undistorted form by the receiver. This process is reflected in the classic Shannon-Weaver model illustrated in Figure 4-1.

Although information theory has played a vital role in solving many of the technical problems of signal transmission through noisy channels, it cannot be applied literally to human communication.[6] As suggested by Figure 4-1, an encoding process occurs— information is written down, spoken, on typed into an e-mail or text/SMS message— between the information source and the transmitter. Similarly, at the other end, the receiver *decodes* (interprets) the message and puts it into action. The signal is affected by the amount of noise—static or error—in the system. Thus, the communication is not complete until the receiver has interpreted the message; if the noise is too great (i.e., the signal-to-noise ratio is too low), the message either fails to get to its destination or it is garbled.

Communication accuracy refers to the extent to which the receiver interprets (perceives) the signal in a way that is consistent with the sender's intention. As noted in the discussion of personality in Chapter 2, each individual has his or her own unique perception, such that no two people have the exact same perception of a given issue, situation, event, and so forth. This reality can make accurate communication a challenging task. Especially in a culturally diverse workplace, it is important to realize that different people often hold different meanings for things and events. As a result, communication messages are not always perceived as they were intended.[7] Thus, in contrast to information theory, behavioral models focus on the meanings of communication and the way in which those meanings are interpreted. In this sense, communication is more complicated than simply receiving a message in an undistorted form; merely receiving a message does not ensure that the receiver will interpret it correctly (i.e., in the way the message was intended).

Because meanings grow out of social interaction, the meaning underlying a message is influenced by both the *information itself* and the *context* of the message. Thus, to understand the process of communication, six basic factors must be considered.[8]

1. Who is communicating to whom in terms of the *roles* these people play (e.g., management and labor, supervisor and subordinate, professor and student)

2. The *language* or symbol(s) used to communicate and their ability to convey information and be understood by both parties

3. The communication *channel* or medium used and how information from different channels is attended to (e.g., written versus oral communication)

4. The *content* of the communication (e.g., good news or bad news, relevant or irrelevant information, familiar or unfamiliar)

5. The *personal characteristics* of the sender (e.g., appearance, personality) and the *interpersonal relations* between the sender and receiver (e.g., trust; influence)

6. The *context* in which the communication is taking place, such as organizational structure (e.g., within or between departments or levels), physical space (e.g., distance between sender and receiver), and social surroundings (e.g., in whose office; dress codes)

INTERPERSONAL COMMUNICATION

Communication is essentially an interactive, person-to-person process. It is a dynamic transactional process in which individuals *construct meaning* and *develop expectations* about their experiences, what is occurring, and the world around them, and then share these meanings and expectations with one another through the *exchange of symbols*.[9] These symbols can be verbal or nonverbal and are influenced by intended and unintended factors (such as our emotions and sentiments).

There are five basic functions of interpersonal communication:[10]

1. *Control:* Clarifying duties, setting standards, and establishing authority and responsibility

2. *Informational:* Providing the basis for making decisions and carrying out orders and instructions

3. *Motivational:* Influencing others and eliciting cooperation and commitment to various goals and objectives

4. *Emotional:* Expressing feelings and emotions

5. *Developmental:* Sharing and learning that can provide a basis for revising beliefs, attitudes and behaviors

Thus, interpersonal communication has a number of different purposes and information is often exchanged for a variety of reasons, not all of which are focused on a specific task.

Communication Modes

During the course of a normal workday, the typical manager spends an extraordinary amount of time meeting, talking, corresponding via e-mail, and interacting with others. Yet, despite the importance of these activities, we have a tendency to take communication for granted. Even with familiar modes of communication, such as having a conversation or sending an e-mail, we tend to assume that our message has the same meaning to other people—an assumption that is often wrong. The communication process is made even more complicated when we realize that people communicate through a number of different modes or channels: verbal, nonverbal, symbolic, and electronic. In fact, much of what an individual is "saying" is communicated through body language, tone, images, and setting as well as through verbal expression.[11]

Verbal Communication

Verbal communication is the most familiar and most frequently used mode of communication. *Verbal-oral* refers to such communication activities as giving instructions to a co-worker, interviewing a job candidate, and negotiating with a supplier. *Verbal-written* communication refers to letters, memos, and written reports, procedures, and regulations.[12] Given recent advances in how we use information technology, *verbal-electronic* communication, which includes e-mail, instant messaging (IM), and text/SMS messaging, has quickly become a dominant factor in our lives. Yet, even with what we assume to be a relatively straightforward channel of communication, words can mean quite different things to different people.

Jargon   In many jobs, occupations, and organizations, we develop a specialized language that often facilitates communication between insiders but largely excludes others from understanding.[13] Consider the following conversation between the authors:

> *Jim:* What is your teaching schedule this semester?
> *Tony:* I have a section of BF503 and …
> *Jim:* 503?
> *Tony:* Your version of 702.
> *Jim:* Okay.
> *Tony:* and …

In this case, BF503 and 702 refer to the graduate-level OB courses at our respective institutions. The underlying assumption is that others will know what the jargon (the numerical designation) means. In most instances, however, outsiders and new organizational members find the use of such jargon confusing and even intimidating.

Meaning   Even if jargon is not used, linguists have shown that "common" words are interpreted quite differently by individuals because meaning exists in people's minds and not in the words themselves. Moreover, an analysis of *The Oxford Dictionary* indicates that each of the 500 most commonly used words in the English language has an average of twenty-eight different meanings.[14] Thus, we cannot necessarily assume that what we say will be received and interpreted exactly as we mean it.

Research suggests that the meaning organizational members give to organizational issues is particularly important because this meaning drives their cognition and behavior. For example, when individuals perceive an issue as an opportunity they become more actively engaged—in terms of both their attitudes and actions—with that issue. Conversely, when issues are perceived as threats, individuals minimize the energy they expend toward the issue and seek to avoid related involvement.[15] This dynamic is significant in that the majority of organizational issues are ambiguous—in other words, they do not have a fixed meaning or valence as good/bad or positive/negative. Thus managers who are able to frame organizational issues as opportunities rather than threats—and shape the ways in which they are viewed by organizational members— increase the probability of enhanced performance.

There is also a danger in interpreting business talk at face value. Career counselors, for example, have pointed out the problems recent graduates often face when things their managers say are taken literally. As an example, an executive recruiter often interprets the statement "We're a very creative department" to mean that the pay is low and promotions are scarce, but employees can wear whatever they want to work.[16]

Finally, it is also important to pay attention to the underlying meanings of language and custom that can inadvertently reinforce homogeneity and the status quo. For instance, since words such as "minority" reflect current power and status dynamics, it is recommended that they be replaced by more appropriate and inclusive language such as "African American" or "Asian American."[17]

Questions   Questions often contain assumptions that not only frame a problem in a certain way but also tend to force its resolution to conform to those underlying assumptions. For example, during a meeting in which a division vice president was attempting to develop a team management style for his top group of managers, one of the managers asked, "Who is driving the bus?"—implying that no one was. The assumption was that one person should be doing the "driving" (i.e., managing) and that the team approach would not work.[18] Thus, in many instances questions are really statements and are not as simple or as straightforward as they seem.

Symbolic Communication

Individuals surround themselves with various symbols that can communicate a lot of information to other people.[19] The places we live, clothes we wear, and cars we drive all portray certain things about us to other people. Similarly, the type of decorations a person has in an office, and the way in which chairs are arranged and physical space is used can communicate a great deal about a manager. For instance, most individuals set up their offices to encourage certain types of interaction; some managers will arrange chairs in close proximity to each other, while other managers will place chairs for visitors in front of their desk. The former suggests a desire to interact on a more egalitarian basis, while the latter portrays a situation in which the person wants it to be clear "who is the boss."

The use of place can also be an important symbol. When a manager and subordinate meet, for instance, whose office should they use? Since *place* has symbolic meaning, it is recommended that the type of meeting should influence where it is held. For example, for adversarial discussions, to emphasize hierarchy and authority, or give directions, managers should hold the meeting in their offices; to reach out to subordinates or to have conversations more on the other's terms, the manager should go to the subordinate's work area.

Since symbols communicate different things to different people, however, there are dangers in generalizing about or stereotyping people according to their symbols. In many instances, words and symbols do not match, leading to mixed messages. It is important to remember that human communication involves a complex interaction between the intended message and spontaneous, symbolic cues that can confuse rather than enhance understanding.[20] The most effective form of communication is when symbols match words and behaviors. Thus, the key for managers is to examine the symbols they are "communicating" since they may or may not be reflecting what is intended.

Nonverbal Communication

Nonverbal communication, which refers to the transmission of messages by some medium other than speech or writing, is one of the most interesting facets of communication.[21] In one sense, sign language is a form of nonverbal communication; however, nonverbal communication goes far beyond sign language and encompasses such things as the way we use our body, gestures, facial expressions, and voice to convey certain messages. Nonverbal communication occurs every day in a business environment, but it frequently goes unnoticed. Unfortunately, while nonverbal messages can be quite important, they are ambiguous and subtle. Thus, individuals often misinterpret or deny them. Yet, because these nonverbal cues are often unintended, they may provide us with insight into the true meaning of the sender's message, especially in sensitive situations. Thus, as a manager, it is important to be alert to the spatial, visual, and vocal cues involved in the communication process.

Spatial Cues   The distances people choose to sit or stand from each other can communicate quite a bit about their relationship.[22] Each of us occupies something that is referred to as our "personal space," which expands and contracts according to different situations. We tend to be uncomfortable, for instance, when someone we do not know very well comes too close to us (intimate space) or if someone we like and know very well distances himself or herself from us (public distance).

While our sense of "natural" distance is deeply ingrained in us by our culture, it tends to vary based on such factors as the gender of those involved (we tend to stand closer to members of the opposite sex), the topic or subject matter (closer during pleasant conversations), setting for the interaction (closer in informal situations), the attitudinal and emotional orientation of the people (closer in liking or friendship situations), and the personality characteristics of those involved (closer when people have a high self-concept and high affiliative needs).

Body Language   One way in which people communicate their feelings is through visual cues and body motions:[23] (1) how people carry their body; (2) how the body is postured; (3) how much and where people touch each other; (4) the extent to which people maintain eye contact; and (5) gestures. For instance, we often interpret folded arms as a sign of closed-mindedness, while open arms are a sign of openness. Individuals who feel relaxed in a conversation often have a casual, asymmetrical placement of arms and legs and/or sit in a reclined, nonerect position. There are dangers, however, in an overly simplistic interpretation of such body movements. No gesture has a single, unvarying meaning; proper interpretation depends on cultural norms, personal style, and physical setting.[24] Thus, even though an understanding of body language can be quite helpful in understanding the true meaning of a particular message (especially when there is a contradiction between what an individual says verbally and how he or she acts physically), one should be cautious in overinterpreting the meaning of body language.

Paralinguistics Paralinguistics focus on features of communication that accompany—and at times even substitute for—the spoken word, including the tone of voice, sarcasm, pacing, and other extralinguistic aspects of speech.[25] How something is said, the way in which silence is used, the use of "filled pauses" (such as "uhhh" to fill spaces between thoughts, which indicates to the receiver that you are still in the process of completing a reply), and the pitch and quality of voice have a range of meanings that they send to others. However, since we often focus on what is said rather than *how* it is said, we can miss this valuable source of information in face-to-face meetings.

Electronic Communication

An increasing amount of business-oriented communication is being done electronically as the Internet and company intranets have reinvented the basics of business life.[26] Advanced information technologies allow computer users to send and receive huge amounts of data—text, graphics, video images—through the Internet, within corporate intranets (i.e., users are all on the network of one organization and that network is closed to the public through "firewalls"), and increasingly through company-to-company extranets (e.g., links between an organization and its core suppliers). Computer-mediated communication, ranging from electronic mail (e-mail) and instant messaging, listservs, and electronic bulletin boards, to net phones, voice-mail, and desktop videoconferencing, are reshaping the way we communicate and interact with others.

E-mail and Instant Messaging   Unlike other forms of written communication, e-mail and instant messaging have a level of interactivity that combines the convenience and permanence of the written word with the immediacy and volatility of speech. In fact, research suggests that people treat e-mail as if it were an electronic telephone call, reacting immediately and often writing without thinking about organization, grammar, punctuation, and, most important, about the ramifications of their words.[27] Yet, because it embodies the casual nature and spontaneity of a telephone call but lacks the vocal inflections, gestures, and shared environment of oral communication, e-mail has a tendency to generate misunderstanding and overreactions (referred to in cybertalk as "flaming"). People are also quicker to respond in the "heat of the moment" with e-mail compared with other forms of communication. Once the "send" button is pressed, however, a message cannot be retrieved and it is often difficult to "explain" the message through further conversation and interaction. An underlying problem is that e-mail's ubiquitous connectivity has created a business culture that literally demands instant response and feedback—which readily adds to the challenge of juggling responsibilities and adhering to office protocol.

E-mail also differs from traditional means of business communication in its tendency to be an equalizer, in essence prompting the reader to focus on ideas rather than the personality or presence of the sender. Moreover, research has indicated that people who are hesitant to raise their ideas in a traditional meeting format or face to face with colleagues are more comfortable expressing their thoughts and opinions via e-mail.[28]

To a large extent, e-mail also makes it possible for organizational members to directly and immediately contact highly placed people within an organization, including a company's CEO. Within this context, recent research even suggests that e-mail actually contributes to a higher quality of exchange between subordinates and their supervisors.[29] People are encouraged to use this capability judiciously, however, carefully considering both the potential benefit and consequences of sending e-mail to these individuals, especially if it could be construed as going over someone's head or breaking accepted rules of etiquette.[30]

The growth of *instant messaging* (IM) as a key communication tool is even more phenomenal. Originally thought of as little more than a toy for teenagers, IM is becoming increasingly popular in the business world. Current estimates suggest that roughly one-half of all U.S. and Canadian firms use some form of instant messaging in their business. Mobile operators are currently launching services that enable customers to exchange instant messages across networks. There are already about 40 operators in more than 55 countries, representing over one billion customers, participating in such efforts to integrate and expand IM/text messaging capabilities.[31] Like e-mail, however, IM can create a number of organizational problems, from the technical aspects of threats to network security to the same types of misunderstandings and related difficulties associated with e-mail. Given the real instantaneous feedback and interaction that occur with IM, however, research suggests that it approaches the type of casual conversations that occur among organizational members. Chance encounters can just as easily occur online as they can in corporate hallways.[32] As a result of the ensuing conversations, employees report feeling closer and more connected with their colleagues, approaching the same type of feeling they get from casual, face-to-face contact.

Emoticons   As suggested earlier, e-mail tends to arouse emotions and generate misunderstandings more often than other communication media. One way to deal with this issue is to try to convey the type of information that is imparted in face-to-face communication through the use of *emoticons*.[33] An emoticon is a playful combination of punctuation marks that, when viewed sideways, resemble facial expressions. Four of the most common emoticons are illustrated here: a smile (meant to convey pleasure about what was written), a wink (to convey joking), a frown (meant to convey displeasure), and amazement (intended to suggest wonder and awe at what the person, group, or organization has accomplished). E-mail service providers such as Yahoo, Hotmail, and Microsoft Outlook have responded to the popularity of emoticons by including a menu of icons and symbols for users to choose from.

Smile	**Wink**	**Frown**	**Amazement**
:-)	;-)	:-(	:-o

Barriers to Effective Communication

The goal of effective communication is understanding. However, considering the complex ways in which we use verbal, symbolic, electronic and nonverbal means to send messages, such understanding is not always achieved. Even in relatively simple, face-to-face interactions, for example, while one person is talking, the other individual is often thinking about a response rather than really listening to what the person is saying. Thus, due to a failure to listen and a lack of attention to all facets of the message, the individuals involved are not truly communicating *with* one another but rather are talking *to* each other.

It is virtually impossible for people to attend to all the communications that bombard them. However, our tendency to (1) take communication for granted and (2) evaluate before understanding are significant reasons why communication efforts sometimes fail.[34] Thus, there are a number of physical, interpersonal, and intrapersonal barriers to effective communication.

Information Overload

Overload refers to a situation where we have more information than we can possibly sort out and use.[35] When an overload situation exists, we select information, delegate others to attend to the information, put off information until the overload situation is over, forget information, or even avoid it altogether. While some of these tactics are quite helpful (e.g., delegating), others (such as putting things off) reduce our capacity for action. Due to the proliferation of electronic communication—especially the volume of e-mail received in a typical day—organizational members can easily feel overwhelmed by the deluge of information they receive.[36] The increasing availability of information and the ability to process great volumes of information electronically can place serious demands on an organization's often relatively limited human resources and capacity to process and utilize such a wealth of information. Anecdotes abound of managers demanding productivity and market data with such frequency and depth that it is virtually impossible to internalize the information in a timely fashion—and, as a result, falling well short of truly informing their decision making.

Kind of Information

Information that fits our self-concept (see Chapter 3) tends to be received and accepted much more readily than data that contradict what we already "know."[37] In many instances, we deny information that conflicts with our beliefs and values, or "hear" the message in a way that is congruent with those beliefs and values (selective perception). Especially when information is sensitive, the processes of selective attention and retention frame our communication efforts.

Source of Information

Since some people are seen as more credible than others, we have a tendency to believe what those individuals tell us and discount information received from others.[38] Such credibility is influenced by the degree of trust, status, and influence of the sender and receiver. Since trust is a strong determinant of openness and accuracy, we tend to believe those individuals we trust. Similarly, we have a tendency to place more faith in what upper-status individuals tell us compared with messages we receive from those in lower-status positions. Stereotypes also influence our perception of an individual's credibility (e.g., used-car salespeople, politicians).

Imputing One's Own Knowledge to Others

To communicate effectively with other people, it is important to have a reasonably accurate sense of what they know and do not know about the subject that is pertinent to the communication.[39] Although this may appear to be a reasonably straightforward proposition, assuming that others have knowledge they do not have can readily result in miscommunication and even embarrassment. A speaker who overestimates what his or her audience knows, for example, may quickly wind up talking over their heads and losing their interest. The underlying dilemma is that underestimating the knowledge someone has, even in the interest of clarity, can be perceived as talking down to them. As such, it is important to be able to accurately infer the content of another person's thoughts and feelings, an ability referred to as *emphatic accuracy*.[40] It is, thus, useful to reflect more fully on our own knowledge base, how long we have had that knowledge and how it was developed, and to be sensitive to any nonverbal signals and cues emitted by the listener.

Physical Location and Distractions

The physical location and proximity between the sender and receiver also influence communication effectiveness.[41] Research, for example, suggests that the probability of two people communicating with each other decreases by the square of the distance between them. From an organizational perspective, this implies that how central or peripheral an individual is to others influences that person's communication ability and effectiveness. Other physical barriers such as corners, indirect paths, and stairs can also hinder communication. Although this may seem obvious, the distance between and location of different individuals and groups (departments, units, etc.) in organizations can readily create communication problems and difficulties.

A number of common distractions can reduce communication effectiveness as well. Interruptions such as telephone calls, drop-in visitors, requests from co-workers, and time constraints are all examples of everyday events that hinder communication efforts. In most instances, proper attention and planning can minimize this type of disruption; however, due to the hectic nature of the manager's job, these "simple" barriers can be significant.

Defensiveness

One of the core causes of many communication failures is for one or more of the participants to become defensive.[42] Individuals who feel that they are being threatened or are under attack tend to react in ways that reduce the probability of mutual understanding. When communication appears evaluative or judgmental, for example, instead of attempting to discuss and understand the message, the individuals involved usually act defensively to protect their self-concept by attacking the other person, resorting to sarcasm and ridicule, questioning the motives and competence of the other person, or by attempting to avoid the situation altogether. While such defensive strategies may protect the individual's self-concept, they also encourage a ritualistic approach to communication and discourage spontaneous interaction.[43] Thus, the probability of

TABLE 4-1 Defensive and Supportive Communication Styles

Defensive Style	Supportive Style	Commentary
Evaluation	Description	Evaluative or judgmental remarks tend to put people on the defensive.
Control	Problem orientation	If a communicator appears to try to control the recipients, the recipients are put on the defensive.
Strategy	Spontaneity	If the communicator appears to be trying to trap the recipient, or lead the recipient into a conclusion that might be unwarranted, the recipient will be put on the defensive.
Neutrality	Empathy	A communicator who appears to be cold and distant evokes more defensiveness than one who is warm and friendly.
Superiority	Equality	A communicator who seems to be haughty and above it all evokes defensiveness.
Certainty	Provisionalism	A communicator who "knows it all" without any shadow of a doubt creates defensiveness.

Source: Adapted from Jack Gibb, "Defensive Communication," *Journal of Communication,* vol. 3, Summer 1961, pp. 141–148.

effective communication is greatly reduced. Table 4-1 compares communication styles that are likely to either precipitate or reduce defensive responses.

Gender Differences and Styles

Women and men tend to use oral communication differently and, as a result, gender dynamics can contribute to communication difficulties between them. For men, for example, conversations in the workplace typically evolve around status issues, whereas women tend to focus more fully on creating connections.[44] These different orientations can create problems as workplace conversations take on very different meanings. For the most part, males tend to use conversation to preserve their independence and maintain their status in a hierarchical social order. Women use conversation to seek and give confirmation and support, in essence negotiating closeness with others.

Improving Interpersonal Communication

Despite the myriad barriers to interpersonal communication, there are a number of ways in which these difficulties can be minimized. Indeed, the extent to which any individual's communication efforts are effective is influenced by two basic skills: (1) *sending skills*—the ability to make yourself understood by others (e.g., use of language and other important communication symbols); and (2) *listening skills*—the ability to understand others (e.g., having empathy, focusing on what the individual is saying, reading body language and nonverbal cues).[45]

Sending Skills

A key to effective communication is to avoid the various types of communication gaps outlined earlier. This can be partly accomplished by: (1) using *appropriate* and direct language (avoiding the use of jargon and complex terms when simpler words will do); (2) providing as clear and *complete* information as possible; (3) attempting to avoid *physical interference* (e.g., the types of common office disruptions noted earlier) and *psychological interference* (e.g., preoccupation with other things, daydreaming); (4) using *multiple channels* to stimulate a number of the receiver's senses (sound, sight, etc.); and (5) using *interactive* (feedback-based) communication whenever possible.[46]

Active Listening

We often think of listening as a passive activity, where we simply sit back and receive information. Listening, however, is a multidimensional process that involves *sensing* (the physical receipt of the message), *processing* (as we assign meaning to the message), and *responding* to the sender to clarify what we have heard.[47] As the preceding discussion has pointed out, due to the probability that some distortion will occur, effective communication requires an active, two-way exchange of information. Compared with *marginal listening*, where the recipient is distracted (e.g., thinking about other things, thinking about what he or she is going to say next), the key to active or effective listening is the *willingness* and *ability* to listen to the entire message (verbal, symbolic, nonverbal) and respond appropriately to the content and intent (feelings, emotions) of the message. At times, however, people engage in *defensive or evaluative listening*, where they assume that a message is an attack on them and interpret what they "hear" in that context.[48] This tendency causes the listener to have only a superficial interpretation of what the other person is saying. Thus, as a manager it is important to create situations that help people to state what they really mean without putting them on the defensive. Only by accepting the legitimacy of another person's feelings and attempting to understand a message in the context of those feelings can individuals begin to enhance the accuracy of their communication.

Empathy Active listening requires sensitivity to the people we are trying to communicate with—their attitudes, emotions, and feelings. Empathy essentially means putting yourself in the other person's position or situation in an effort to understand that individual.[49] Although this may appear to be straightforward, it is often difficult to do because our society generally teaches people (especially males) to hide their emotions.

While empathy is often described as a trait (i.e., some people are more empathetic than others), it is also a *process* that entails empathetic resonation (sensing), received empathy (processing), and expressed empathy (responding).[50] One of the ways of enhancing this process is to understand how others see us. This can be accomplished by encouraging others to give us direct and meaningful feedback about our communication and behavior. Although risky, progressive self-disclosure and the encouragement of a dialogue with others can begin to develop an atmosphere of trust and confidence where such open communication can occur.

Reflecting Another way to apply active listening is to restate the message you have received. By reflecting on both the content and the emotion or feeling behind the content, and then restating the message in your own words, the individual with whom you are communicating is provided with an opportunity to respond with further information. When using the reflection process, however, it is important to avoid the various defensive styles outlined in Table 4-1. The key is to mirror what has been said *without* passing judgment, to test your understanding of the message.

Feedback

Since effective communication is a two-way process of exchange, the use of feedback is another way to reduce communication gaps and distortions. Basically, feedback is the process of telling another individual how you feel about something he or she said or did.[51] A problem in organizations, however, is that communication is often one-way—top-down, from managers to subordinates without any reflection or feedback.

The key is to give feedback in such a way that it is accepted and used constructively by the receiver. This is especially difficult when the feedback involves criticism of a person's work or activities. Unfortunately, what is often intended as a constructive feedback session turns into a futile confrontation, leading to defensiveness, mutual gripes, and negative feelings with no solution to the problem or the concerns that initiated the feedback effort in the first place. Although providing effective feedback is truly an art that must be developed over time, there are some basic guidelines that can make such sessions more productive and problem-oriented.[52]

- Examine your own motives to ensure that your intention is to help rather than show your perceptiveness or superiority.
- Especially in negative feedback situations, get to the point; beginning a discussion with peripheral issues and small talk usually creates anxieties rather than reduces them.
- Consider the receiver's readiness to hear the feedback.
- Describe the situation as clearly and specifically as possible; avoid evaluative openings since they prejudge the receiver's point of view and pave the way for confrontation.
- Avoid overloading the receiver with too much information and criticism; focus on what is most important and changeable.
- Agree on the source of the problem and its solution; otherwise there is little likelihood that the issue will be resolved.
- Be prepared to receive feedback yourself, since your behavior may be contributing to the receiver's behavior.
- Use active listening techniques and observe the behavior of the other person during the feedback session, which may either confirm or disconfirm the feedback. In closing, reflect upon and summarize the session to ensure that both you and the receiver are leaving the meeting with the same understanding of what was decided.

Interactional and Informational Justice

Recent organizational research has found that perceptions of justice exert significant influence on a variety of employee attitudes and behaviors and on organizational outcomes. Thus, certain aspects of justice may be particularly important with regard to communication processes. *Informational justice* focuses on the explanations provided to people that convey information about why certain procedures were used or why outcomes were distributed in a certain way.[53] Informational justice is a component of *interactional justice*, which refers to the quality of treatment received during the enactment or implementation of organizational procedures. Interactional justice represents the adequacy with which procedures are communicated or explained, which is distinct from the interpersonal component of decision makers' behavior in communicating decisions.[54] Such structural aspects of procedures are evaluated based on the extent to which decision-making authorities are perceived as truthful, exhibit proper behavior in the communication of decisions, and justify or explain the rationale for decisions.[55] Research further suggests that not only is the provision of an explanation or justification for decisions important to perceptions of fair treatment in organizations, but that explanations that are characterized as reasonable, timely, and specific also influence fairness perceptions.[56]

ORGANIZATIONAL COMMUNICATION

As was pointed out earlier in this chapter, communication is one of the fundamental processes of management. From a managerial perspective, communication can be analyzed in terms of three broad functions: (1) *production and regulation* (communication focused on getting the work done and meeting organizational output objectives such as quality control); (2) *innovation* (messages about new ideas and changing procedures that help the firm adapt and respond to its environment); and (3) *socialization and maintenance* (communication focused on the means of getting the work done rather than on the work itself, and on the personal involvement, interpersonal relationships, and motivation of individuals in the firm).[57] Each of these functions is important for an effectively and efficiently managed organization.

While the basic communication process and interpersonal communication modes, barriers, and skills obviously influence this form of communication, the key to organizational communication focuses on the arrangement and structure of *how* information is channeled to the specific individuals and groups who need it for task, problem-solving, control, or decision-making purposes. In fact, the way a group or organization is structured ultimately determines the ease with which members can communicate with one another. The different forms of organizational structure, and their strengths and weaknesses, will be discussed in Chapter 9. The main purpose of the present discussion is to examine the process and dynamics of knowledge management, and the formal and informal communication networks and roles that influence communication within organizations.

Knowledge Management

Knowledge management refers to the ways in which organizations process, capture, share, and use information. In contrast to simply managing the flow of information, the basic goal of knowledge management is to leverage and disseminate resources that already exist in an organization so that its members will be able to seek out, utilize and enhance their activities and processes. As briefly discussed in Chapter 2, one of the challenges underlying this dynamic focuses on managing the knowledge creation process itself—understanding what it is and how to create, transfer, and use it more effectively.[58] The knowledge management process typically involves:[59]

- *Explicit knowledge,* capturing, storing, retrieving, and distributing tangible knowledge assets (e.g., copyrights, patents, licenses)
- *Tacit knowledge,* gathering, organizing, and disseminating intangible knowledge (e.g., professional know-how, individual insight and intuition, and experience)
- Creation of an *interactive learning environment,* where organizational members are encouraged to readily transfer and share what they know, internalize it, and apply it to create new knowledge

Knowledge can thus be thought of as information *combined with* experience, context, interpretation, and reflection.[60]

While *explicit knowledge* is easily expressed in words and numbers and easily communicated (e.g., hard data, codified procedures, scientific formulae), *tacit knowledge* is much more difficult to formalize, communicate, and share with others. Yet, it is estimated that roughly 90 percent of the knowledge in any organization is tacit in nature, in essence contained in the heads (minds) of its people.[61] Such tacit knowledge involves the expertise people have developed over time as well as the assumptions, beliefs, perceptions, and intuitions that are so ingrained they are typically taken for granted.[62]

Knowledge versus Knowing

As summarized in Table 4-2, there are a number of issues and challenges surrounding what might be thought of as the transition between first- and second-generation knowledge management (KM). A first-generation perspective, which was the underpinning of most early KM initiatives, is the *knowledge as possession* view.[63] This perspective

TABLE 4-2 First- and Second-Generation Knowledge Management Perspectives and Challenges

First-Generation Knowledge Management (KM)	Second-Generation Knowledge Management (KM)
Knowledge as possession (Knowledge as a thing)	Knowing-in-action (Knowledge as a socially embedded phenomenon)
KM as largely a technical issue:	KM as a sociocultural, political, and technical issue:
• Complex management information systems	• Complex human systems
• Data repositories—databases and documents	• Communities of practice and knowledge zones
• Support structures largely mechanistic	• Support structures largely organic
Desire for knowledge sharing as key driver	Need for boundary spanners and cultural "mapmakers" to encourage and guide knowledge sharing

Source: Adapted from A. F. Buono and F. Poulfelt (Eds.), *Challenges and Issues in Knowledge Management.* Greenwich, CT: Information Age Publishing, 2005, p. xi. Used with permission.

assumes that knowledge is something that people possess, an entity that can be made explicit, captured, and transferred from one person or group to another. Because tacit knowledge is highly personalized (e.g., intuitions, hunches), however, the organizational challenge is to sufficiently "capture" it so that it will be available to others. As John Doyle, the former head of Hewlett-Packard Labs, reflected, "If HP only knew what HP knows."[64] The underlying assumption is that if an organization can capture the insights and experiences of key organizational members, it can enhance knowledge sharing across a wide range of individuals and groups and improve its performance. As a result of this view, organizations have increasingly adopted a series of knowledge management initiatives. The most common of these efforts attempt to capture explicit and tacit knowledge in a repository using information and computer technology: creating a company intranet, implementing data warehousing, adopting decision-support tools, and developing groupware capability.[65]

While information technology (IT) plays a major role in facilitating the knowledge creation process by making the systemic storage and dissemination of information a feasible and efficient proposition, an organization's knowledge base cannot be effectively managed through technology alone. As many companies that invested heavily in IT-based KM systems have found, they had an insufficient understanding of their internal abilities and the necessary requirements to administer and support these systems. In fact, studies suggest that organizations frequently overestimate the abilities, availabilities, and commitment of their internal staff to effectively implement and support KM initiatives,[66] and practice suggests that knowledge is often context bound. Thus, while the processes underlying knowledge transfer can be facilitated by computer-mediated communication,[67] success depends much more fully on the human element. A growing number of organizations are relying more on an exchange of stories and symbols, often embedded in the history of the organization and its members, to express the inexpressible and to disseminate and share those insights through boundary spanners, cultural guides, and "mapmakers."[68]

These latter efforts reflect a different view of knowledge and the knowledge-sharing process, viewing knowledge as socially constructed and embedded in organizational processes, which makes it difficult for individuals to fully know, understand and transfer tacit knowledge from one context to another. Thus, an alternative to the knowledge as possession view is that knowledge is not so much possessed as *embedded in practice* and as such is *inherently social*. True *knowing*, therefore, has to be generated within its own context.

Those who adopt the view that knowledge is embedded in practice argue that direct tacit knowledge transfer, as suggested in the best practice literature, is not possible because knowledge is inherently sticky and always socially constructed.[69] Within this context, the focus moves from supplying knowledge to creating and maintaining the conditions required for the production of knowing. In an effort to create understanding, people bring prior knowledge and context to the information. Given the differences in contexts across individuals, however, alternative interpretations or understandings are inevitable, even when people are presented with the same explicit knowledge.

While IT is thus clearly an enabler of knowledge management, the underlying keys are more cultural and behavioral, such as the levels of management openness and trust that exist in an organization and the extent to which *communities of practice* within an organization actually encourage knowledge sharing.[70] In fact, according to recent studies of knowledge management practices, the main obstacles and difficulties involve getting people to use and share their knowledge—including knowing what to capture, making it accessible and usable, finding the right people to manage the process, and measuring results.[71]

Knowledge Sharing versus Knowledge Hoarding

Since knowledge is often viewed as a scarce resource, people may be tempted to hoard their knowledge base, especially if they feel insecure in the organization. In fact, one view is that companies and their members are *inherently hostile* to knowledge sharing.[72] From such mildly hostile attitudes as a reluctance to spend time on knowledge sharing to far stronger orientations (e.g., attempts to survive power games, fear of hosting "knowledge parasites," trying to maintain the status quo in the face of change), organizations need to actively intervene to encourage and support knowledge sharing. Unfortunately, in all too many organizations mistakes are taboo and top-down hierarchies are all too ready to impose blame. A fundamental need, therefore, is to develop a culture that values people and fosters knowledge sharing, encouraging, supporting, and rewarding organizational members to continuously share what they know (see Chapter 10).

Given the changing nature of work and the workplace, the focus on knowledge management will continue to be an increasingly important aspect of organizational life. We have already moved away from an emphasis on the logistics of storing and sharing information and the creation of knowledge itself to the unexplored potential of the human imagination. As part of this transformation, we are entering an abstract realm of understanding that can only be guided by a sense of purpose, values, and spirit.[73] Although this change, for many, may be a difficult one, it is important to remember that as knowledge-based work increases, the only sustainable competitive advantage that organizations have is their intellectual capital, the commitment and competence of their members.[74] While data (information) allow organizational members to make informed decisions about the past, knowledge enables them to make decisions about the present. The ultimate goal, however, is the creation and sharing of *wisdom,* in essence the ability to make decisions about the future.[75]

Communication Networks

Actual communication patterns in organizations are more complex and subtle than those represented in organizational charts. Yet, despite the advances created by information technology, formal organizational structures continue to shape and constrain communication patterns.[76] Common characteristics of many bureaucratic organizations (e.g., standardization of job functions, distinct hierarchical arrangements between workers), for example, readily influence communication activities, such as the way in which reports are handled and submitted, which formal channels are relied on for reporting, and the type of information that flows through these channels. More flexible matrix and network forms of organization, in contrast, similarly determine the use of other types of information flow and communication efforts. Yet, in each of these organizational forms, informal communication networks also influence the flow of information and communication patterns. Thus, to fully understand how information is channeled in organizations and how it actually flows across organizational units, it is necessary to examine both formal communication networks and the more informal ways in which communication occurs in organizations through rumors and the "grapevine."

Formal Communications Networks

Although there are a number of different ways in which communication can be structured in organizations, research has indicated five common formal communication networks or patterns (i.e., who can talk to whom in a group or organization).[77] These patterns, which are illustrated in Figure 4-2, include the circle, all-channel, wheel, chain, and "Y" networks. The studies on which these findings were initially based typically involved small groups in laboratory settings. Thus, the conclusions are constrained by the artificial setting of the laboratory and limited to relatively small groups. Nevertheless, the consistent findings that communication networks affect task-related outcomes, such as problem solving and role satisfaction, suggest important implications for managers. Moreover, as recent work indicates, these communication patterns can either facilitate or hinder the full and effective use of an organization's information resources.[78]

One way to conceptualize these different communication patterns is to place them along a continuum based on the extent of direct communication between the members of the network. For example, in the *wheel*, while the central member can communicate with everyone in the network, the other members can only communicate with that central person. Thus, it is a highly centralized network. This pattern is quite efficient for relatively simple tasks, but satisfaction of the "outer" members tends to be low. In contrast, the *circle* and the *all-channel* patterns allow more interaction between the members. As a result, satisfaction tends to be higher but communication is usually more

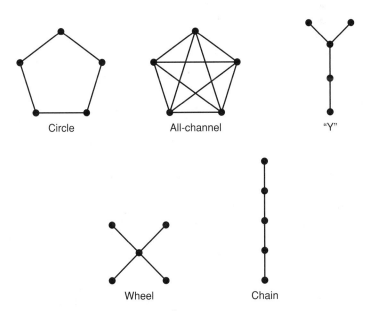

Figure 4-2   Basic Communication Networks

time consuming. Since complex tasks require a greater variety of resources, however, these decentralized networks tend to be more accurate than the centralized networks. Most knowledge management initiatives, supported by intranet-based IT systems, are based on such interactive, decentralized networks. The *chain* and "Y" patterns reflect the more traditional forms of hierarchical relationships between managers and their subordinates. Based on the criterion of centralization, the wheel, "Y," and chain are the most centralized, while the circle and the all-channel are the least centralized.

Despite the difficulties raised by the nature of the research underlying these networks (e.g., small groups, laboratory setting), some generalizations can be made. For simple tasks, highly centralized networks appear to be most effective in terms of problem solving, speed, and accuracy. For complex problems, the decentralized patterns are more accurate. Regardless of the nature of the task, however, member satisfaction appears to be higher in the decentralized networks. Decentralized networks also seem to be more adaptable and responsive to organizational changes, since the patterns are structured so people are more involved and feedback is more direct and immediate.

Current research on communication flows in organizations suggests that such generalizations are warranted.[79] The "up and down," hierarchical flow of information inherent in sequential communication patterns—the chain, the "Y", and, to a lesser extent, the wheel—for example, can readily hinder organizational innovation, knowledge creation, and change. The sequential transfer of information places excessive emphasis on a linear progression of scientific discovery. This can result in suboptimal resource allocations, slow and costly new product and process introductions, a failure to tap the creative potential of a wider range of employees, and individual interpretations that can obscure the importance of vital information. As will be discussed more fully in Chapter 9, the complexity of the knowledge creation process is rendering the highly centralized nature of such sequential communication patterns obsolete.[80] More concurrent communication arrangements—the circle and all-channel, especially when they are supported by advanced information technologies—in contrast, encourage information sharing that is more simultaneous and spontaneous, contribute to greater openness and more interactive learning across organizational members, and enhance both intra- and intergroup interactions.[81] Thus, formal communication patterns can influence the ways in which information is shared in organizations, with ramifications for the speed and accuracy of organizational problem solving, creativity and innovation, and the morale and satisfaction of organizational members.

Informal Communication Networks

The information and communication needs of organizational members are not usually fulfilled by the formal network to which they belong. Especially when information from management is not forthcoming, organizational members will tend to invent it or build "creatively" from the minimal information that is available. As a result, informal or unofficial communication patterns emerge around existing patterns of social interaction and social relationships to satisfy these needs. In virtually all organizations, rumors about what is happening or going to happen, what the "real" reasons behind certain decisions are, and other unofficial bits of information flourish in the organization's grapevine.[82] E-mail systems and the ease of communicating with large numbers of co-workers and colleagues via a keystroke have further facilitated such informal networks. As a result, *social network analysis* has emerged as a strategy for investigating social structures and the interactions between organizational or community members.[83]

Organizational and social-psychological research has found that individuals tend to develop informal communication networks with people who are similar.[84] This similarity can be based on demographic factors such as gender, ethnicity or age, and/or attitudes and interests such as politics, hobbies, and educational and professional background. As will be discussed in the following chapters, the natural formation of informal communication networks along and across demographic or other bases within organizations can have important repercussions for employee and organizational effectiveness.

The *grapevine*, which refers to the informal communication network in an organization, is the primary way in which both rumors and factual information are transmitted to individuals. In many instances, organizational members know what decisions are going to be made, who will be hired or transferred, and so forth, *before* this information is formally announced. Daily gossip and work-related conversations that occur through friendship cliques and casual associations are the most commonly used forms of the grapevine. However, as electronic communication becomes increasingly pervasive in organizations, literally permeating every aspect of how we communicate with others, grapevines are also becoming increasingly electronic in nature, especially with instant messaging systems. Depending on the size of the organization, there can be hundreds of such grapevines.

Although it is impossible to predict the speed, accuracy, direction, or final content of a message carried through the grapevine, studies have indicated that approximately 75 percent of all information received through the grapevine is accurate.[85] When such information is not factual, however, the errors tend to be dramatic and organizational members remember them quite well. Thus, the grapevine can be both functional and dysfunctional for the organization. Since these informal communication patterns cannot be eliminated, the implication for managers is to understand the grapevines that exist in their organizations, and why rumors emerge and flow through them.

Rumors, which are messages based on speculation, imagination, or certain wishes, often have a factual dimension even though they are usually constructed through limited or distorted information. As rumors flow through an organization, however, they are often perceived as quite real and "true" by organizational members. Such rumors usually emerge as a reaction to situations where there is ambiguity and anxiety about something that is important to the people involved.[86] If accurate information is not provided about these situations, rumors are created to "answer" the unanswered questions. In many instances, these rumors can have such a disrupting influence on work and work processes that organizations have to formally issue memos and statements that attempt to counteract any inaccuracies, even forcing organizations to act before they are ready.[87]

As part of the process of managing the anticipatory grapevine, it is important for managers to identify the different types of rumor as well as their content.[88] *Fantasy rumors* reflect unfulfilled or desired wishes, *bogies* are rumors that express fear and anxiety, and *aggressive rumors* are malicious stories intended to harm. While bogies and fantasy rumors can be handled through well-informed, straightforward communication, aggressive rumors require swift, truthful, and direct statements, even if the realities of the situation are negative. Since rumors and the grapevine are part of an organization's communication network, the keys are for managers to try to avoid secrecy, minimize the ambiguity and resultant anxieties that lead to rumors, anticipate that rumors will emerge (especially in change situations) and be ready to deal with them, and use the grapevine to pass factual information, even if incomplete, to organizational members.

Organizational Symbols and Rituals

Some of the most meaningful communications in organizational life occur on an implicit level. These forms of communication include rituals, customs, ceremonies, stories, metaphors, folklore, heroes, logos, and other symbolic modes of expression.[89] It is important for managers to understand how the symbolic and expressive aspects of their actions, decisions, or policies send messages to organizational members about the values and orientations of the firm. Since organizational stories and symbols create compelling images of the firm, they can readily reinforce or undermine direct, explicit communications (e.g., announcements, memos, policies) to organizational members.

If properly handled, stories and symbols can positively influence the way people view their organizations.[90] At the same time, just because widely known symbols, stories, or actions reflect important commitments and beliefs of managers and employees, it does not necessarily mean that they will help the company cause.[91] Indeed, in many instances, "negative" stories about organizational life teach employees what to be cautious about or how to "beat the system."

Organizational symbols and rituals can be especially important during and after large-scale change efforts. Through a series of mutually reinforcing processes—such as stories that reinforce a particular management philosophy, or ceremonies that signify passage from one state to another—organizational members can be indoctrinated to understand and to accept an organizational change.[92] For example, the types of social interactions required to create and establish new identities and orientations are reflected in the concept of *rites of creation*.[93] These relatively elaborate, dramatic, and planned sets of activities combine various forms of symbols and expressions in an effort to establish new patterns of attitudes and behavior and embed them in existing organizational interactions and arrangements. Other examples include: *rites of renewal,* such as organization development activities (see Chapter 11) that reassure employees that something is being done about their problems; *rites of integration,* such as office parties that permit venting of emotions while reaffirming the rightness of organizational practices; and *rites of enhancement,* such as organizational seminars and meetings that spread good news about the firm, provide public recognition of valued members, and emphasize the social value of different roles and positions.

In-House Publications

Company newsletters or publications, often referred to as *house organs*, are effective communication tools that are useful in establishing relationships between the organization and its members.[94] In essence, a house organ is a mix of persuasive messages (stories) that conveys the idea that the organization's interests are similar to those of its members. While such communications have traditionally been in printed, newsletter form, they are increasingly integrated into organizational Web sites and intranets. Effective publications emphasize the accomplishments of organizational members at all levels, espouse company values, reflect concern for individual employees, and create an image of the organization as a good place to work.[95] The underlying message is that the organization values the contributions of its members and cares about their well-being. Such themes tend to enhance the image of the organization in the eyes of its members, furthering a sense of membership and belonging to the organization.

Company newsletters can also be very useful during an organizational change as a way of ensuring that information about the change is adequately disseminated and questions about it are answered. Many organizations, for example, have redesigned or even created house organs around a change. During the merger between Delta and Western airlines, for example, Delta's newsletter, *Update,* was renamed *The Best Get Better* just two weeks after the announcement of the merger. Regular features focused on the company's plans for the merger as well as comments about the combination by both Delta and Western officials.[96] By including brief open-ended questions that could be answered anonymously (e.g., "What is your biggest concern about the merger?" and "What should management pay careful attention to during the merger?"), companies can get a general sense of employee reactions. Questions and concerns raised by the responses are often discussed in later editions.

Communication Roles

Closely related to communication networks in organizations is the concept of a *communication role,* the communication function a person serves within the network.[97] From an organizational perspective, these roles play a significant part in how information flows through an organization. From the perspective of organizational members, research indicates that highly central positions in organizational communication structures are associated with increased communication activities, power, and organizational satisfaction, while peripheral positions are related to decreased participation and lower organizational-related attitudes and behaviors. One of the key implications of these findings is that the assigned role and position, rather than any intrinsic traits of the individuals, appear to be the main determinants of these outcomes. Moreover, despite the importance of these roles, assignment of individuals is often done without explicit design. Thus, managers should pay close attention to these functions and the individuals who fill them.

There are four key communication roles: gatekeepers, liaisons, opinion leaders, and participants/isolates.

Gatekeepers

The *gatekeeper role* refers to individuals who must pass information to others or who control the flow of information as part of their job.[98] Although this is a very important position from a communication perspective, relatively lower-status employees often serve as gatekeepers (such as secretaries or administrative assistants, who often decide which issues and sources of information are brought to the attention of their managers). In many instances, a specific gatekeeping function may be an assigned activity undertaken at the specific direction of a manager. Since information overload is a problem all managers have to deal with, higher-level managers must rely on the accuracy and judgment of these assigned gatekeepers. In other instances, however, an individual can act as an informal gatekeeper (such as an overly protective administrative assistant withholding information from the manager). Thus, it is important to examine organizational communication networks to assess who is acting as formal and informal gatekeepers for different kinds of information. As a way of facilitating such assessment, there are software tools that map communication networks in organizations, pinpointing formal and informal gatekeepers and "hubs" (people at the center of important cultural communication networks).

Ideally, there appear to be three key capabilities possessed by individuals who operate as formal gatekeepers: (1) the ability to keep up with the manager's changing information needs; (2) the ability to sense when information is wanted and when it is not; and (3) the ability to evaluate the quality of information. Being human, however, gatekeepers are often prone to systematic biases that can distort the flow of information directed to particular positions. Thus, these individuals can exert significant influence over upper-level managers and executives and the information that is passed along to them. To ensure the accuracy and flow of information on a timely basis and to reduce the dependency on individual gatekeepers, therefore, organizations often rely on overlapping and, at times, redundant gatekeeper roles and information systems. While this view of gatekeepers largely reflects an internal organizational perspective, individuals who monitor the external environment of the firm also serve a critical gatekeeper function for their organization, that of *boundary spanner,* or link with outside groups or events.

Liaisons

Similar to the gatekeepers are the *liaisons* or individuals who serve as links between groups within the organization. While such roles imply a gatekeeping function, it is the primary responsibility of these positions to coordinate the activities of different groups. The OB literature refers to these roles by a variety of terms such as *linking pins, innovators,* and *integrators.*[99]

Liaisons are often formally assigned to ensure efficient communication, as when contact between three or more departments within an organization is desirable. In other instances, liaisons can informally emerge to serve as a link between different groups. This dynamic is one of the ways in which grapevines emerge between departments, units, or even divisions of a firm. Similar to gatekeepers, liaisons should ideally have certain qualities, such as the ability to convey information without distortion, the competence to know when to serve as a liaison and how to convey information without creating conflict, and the capability to maintain contact with numerous segments of the organization.

Opinion Leaders

Within any organization, some individuals have more influence than others regardless of their formal authority. These individuals are referred to as *opinion leaders* because they are often able to informally influence other organizational members. These individuals may be proactive (they provide their opinion without being asked) or reactive (they wait until they are asked) in their actions. *Pulse takers* are those individuals who regularly keep in touch with a broad cross-section of individuals and subcultures throughout the organization (see Chapter 10).[100] While such well-connected individuals were once dismissed as company "gossips," we now realize the influence they exert in "spreading the word" and shaping opinions. Regardless of their preferred style, these individuals exert a powerful influence on organizational decision making.

Although opinion leaders can be found throughout an organization, they are usually influential only in a relatively narrow sphere. Nevertheless, such individuals can shape the alternatives that a department or unit considers in its decision making and how those alternatives will be assessed. Since this is an informal role in organizations, it is important for managers to identify opinion leaders on different issues. In many instances, these are the individuals who begin and maintain rumors in the organization's grapevine. Thus, if managers know who these individuals are, they can provide those people with positive (or negative) information concerning a particular issue, depending on the opinion the manager wants communicated to others. This can be important because information coming directly from the manager may actually have less impact than the same information coming from the opinion leader. There are dangers, however, of a self-fulfilling prophecy in creating an "opinion leader." Thus, managers must carefully evaluate who the opinion leaders really are in various situations, and use discretion in terms of when to use this role as part of their communication efforts.

Participants/Isolates

The frequency with which different positions interact with others in an organization provides a good indication of the extent to which individuals take part in communication activities. *Isolates* are those individuals who have few or no contacts with other organizational members, even through the grapevine and other informal networks. *Participants*, in contrast, are those people who have active contact with others in their organization. Participants may fulfill gatekeeper, liaison, or opinion leader roles, or may simply be part of the communication network.

Although causal inferences are difficult to draw from the existing research, it appears that active participation in organizational communication efforts has positive benefits for both the people involved and the firm. While isolation is often typical of certain types of jobs (such as night shifts, telecommuters), it may also be a sign of disaffection and alienation. Thus, despite some of the causal questions that remain (e.g., "Is it the isolation that causes the dissatisfaction *or* the dissatisfaction that causes the isolation?"), research indicates that both organizations and their members will benefit if interaction and communication between individuals and between different groups and departments are encouraged and reinforced.[101]

Media Richness and Communication Effectiveness

The media richness model focuses on ways to reduce uncertainty and ambiguity in an effort to improve organizational communication efforts.[102] Different modes of communication can be arrayed along a "richness" continuum based on their relative capacity to resolve ambiguity. Media richness is determined by (1) the speed of feedback involved, (2) the variety of communication channels utilized, (3) the personal content of the source, and (4) the richness of language used.[103] As would be expected, face-to-face interaction is the richest communication medium with the greatest ability to resolve ambiguous situations, followed by the telephone, e-mail, and written documents.

This framework also proposes that media choice carries symbolic meaning that can transcend the explicit message. Written messages, for example, symbolize formality while face-to-face communication has much more informal overtones. In many instances, the influence of such symbolic meanings can interfere with decisions to use "richer" media to resolve ambiguity and clarify the task or situation. For instance, a need to convey formality may transcend the need to use a richer form of communication, which would lead to the use of a memo rather than person-to-person contact. As studies have indicated, effective managers tend to be more "media sensitive" than low-performing managers in terms of their ability to match appropriate media richness with the ambiguity involved in the communication.[104]

Application of this model suggests that managers should use "rich" modes of communication (e.g., person-to-person meetings) for nonroutine tasks, difficult communications, implementing organizational strategy, and, in general, making their presence felt in an organization. Rich media may be especially important when multiple independent parties have to carry out complex activities in an integrated fashion (e.g., partnerships and alliances, integrated business processes). Leaner media, such as memos, should be used for routine, simple communications. For critical tasks or issues, however, it is recommended that managers use multiple media to ensure that their message is correctly heard.[105]

Media Features Theory

As an offshoot of media richness theory, media features theory posits that the choice of communication channels should also be influenced by (1) the *functionality* (i.e., the way the channel supports accomplishment of the work task) and (2) the *usability* (i.e., the extent to which the channel allows a message to be transferred in a clear and readable format) of the selected communication channel.[106] For example, when the task involves the use of numerical data (e.g., sales targets, machine efficiency, share prices, depreciation rates), written forms of communication—including e-mail—are preferable to reduce the potential for misunderstanding. Moreover, there is often a need to repeat numerical information during a telephone or face-to-face conversation for clarification or to reduce ambiguity, which lowers the efficiency of that approach. Thus, some form of written communication and documentation is preferable when communicating numerical and financial information to increase accuracy.

Media Richness and Computer-Mediated Communication

Overall, research support for the relationship between media richness and communication effectiveness is stronger with respect to traditional forms of communication than it is with computer-mediated techniques such as e-mail and instant messaging. A growing number of studies, for instance, found that even though e-mail ranks comparably low in terms of its relative richness, it is frequently used for tasks that have a high socioemotional content.[107] Moreover, research on virtual teams (see Chapter 6) suggests that complex tasks can be successfully accomplished through carefully guided e-mail conferencing and exchanges.[108]

Another feature of e-mail, which is often overlooked in communication assessments, is the potential for managers to use this channel to create an audit trail.[109] Especially in the current climate of concern about corporate governance, it is often desirable to have evidence of information that has been transmitted and received. Thus, the functionality of e-mail can be extended beyond its ease of use to include tracking a wide range of activities and processes.

As computer-mediated communication continues to develop, it is increasingly approximating face-to-face conditions (e.g., use of emoticons, including a picture of the sender with electronic messages) and, when supported by broader social supports, enhances knowledge-sharing and problem-solving activities.[110] In fact, studies have found that managers prefer e-mail to telephone conversations to exchange all types of management information.[111] Thus, it appears that communication via e-mail, the Internet, and company intranets contains a higher degree of media richness than initially thought.

Social Influence Model of Technology Use

Individuals, groups, and organizations vary widely with respect to their acceptance and use of new communication technologies. As a way of understanding the impact of these new communication media, the *social influence model of technology use* suggests that (1) perceptions of electronic media differ across individuals in systematic ways, and (2) these differences are an important part of media choice.[112] This model advances the premise that views about different communication media are socially constructed; that is, they are influenced by broader social factors such as remarks by co-workers, vicarious learning experiences, and facilitating conditions and organizational norms for how different media should be evaluated and used. Thus, employee perceptions about the acceptance and use of electronic communication technologies are directly linked to social and cultural processes in their organization.

Since work groups are an important source of social support and interaction, there are likely to be similar patterns of media use *within* groups and different patterns of use *across* groups. Due to the influence of these social pressures and expectations, the actual selection of a particular communication device may not be entirely rational—that is, group pressures may influence the selection of a certain form of communication even though it may not be the most appropriate method for the task.

Managerial Implications

Although computer-based technologies such as e-mail, voice mail, teleconferencing, instant messaging, and company intranets have become increasingly popular, making some organizational tasks easier to accomplish, numerous concerns have been raised about their limitations. First, an overreliance on electronic communication technologies restricts the use of social cues that can contribute to a fuller understanding of the subtleties that permeate a particular issue or situation.[113] Recent research, however, suggests that some social cues, such as status differences, are still present in computer-mediated communication.[114] Thus, as we continue to become acclimated to these technologies, people may be able to still "read" many of the nuances inherent in the communication process. Second, research indicates that while groups that collaborate through computer-based technology perform equally well compared with groups using multiple communication media, groups that are limited to computer-based technologies report lower levels of satisfaction with their efforts.[115] Since satisfaction with communication relationships is suggested to enhance the individual's sense of membership in his or her organization,[116] this could contribute to a reduced commitment to the organization and its tasks. Finally, given the lingering apprehension that some organizational members still have about using new communication technologies, an important issue for many firms is not simply which activities new media are used for but whether and how the new media are actually used. Numerous examples continue to exist where organizations have adopted and implemented forms of electronic communication that are not utilized by their intended users nor used in their intended ways.

As the use of these new technologies continues to proliferate, it is important for managers to carefully consider the intent, impact, and context of their communication efforts.[117] First, it is important to consider the receiver(s) of the message, since some people are more attentive to face-to-face communication while others work better with ideas put in writing. Second, group and organizational norms often dictate the types of things that should be formalized and written down and those tasks that should be dealt with verbally. Third, when using new communication technologies, it is important to remember that the ways in which individuals perceive and use those systems are not simply a function of the technology itself but also how it is viewed by their co-workers and other organizational members. Thus, providing informal help sessions, using opinion leaders to support the new system, and encouraging peer training can readily improve the initial acceptance and ultimate effectiveness of the new system. Finally, it is important to recognize that a number of other factors such as organizational policies (e.g., budget constraints), individual working styles and preferences, and managerial pressures and time constraints influence media selection and the overall effectiveness of the communication process.

ENVISIONING AND COMMUNICATING ORGANIZATIONAL CHANGE

Organizational communication can be a powerful tool in shaping images of organizational change and the mindsets that accompany the change process. By envisioning the change—that is, by articulating, as clearly, concisely, and as vividly as possible, the desired future state of the organization—managers create a sense of direction and a guiding philosophy for the organization. Such visions provide direction, express organizational culture, and contribute to organizational performance by aligning opinion leaders and energizing organizational members to accomplish a common purpose. In a sense, it is a statement of an organizational dream—an attempt to stretch the imagination and to motivate people to rethink organizational possibilities. Ideally, the vision for an organization helps generate a desire for change by making a potential future more attractive than the realities of the present.[118]

Such visions, however, are meaningless without a well-thought-out plan for communicating that vision to organizational members. At the president or CEO level, the focus should be on articulating the *vision* itself, the statement of where the organization is headed. At the managerial level, in contrast, communication efforts should translate and communicate that vision through *mission statements* (the role of specific business units) and *operating principles* (guiding philosophy).[119] One of the challenges in creating and communicating an organizational vision is to avoid "concept clutter," where too many priorities and ideas are established. The preferred outcome is a clear, precise statement of what the organization is trying to accomplish.[120]

Initial communication is most effectively accomplished through the use of multiple media—giving speeches that present the vision, distributing printed copies of the vision, incorporating it on the company's Web site and intranet, holding meetings to talk about the vision, and discussing it at training events or seminars (with an emphasis on two-way communication).[121] As part of this process, it is important to encourage organizational members to express any negative thoughts or feelings about the vision. It is risky for managers to get overly excited and energized by their vision to the point where they overlook the reactions and fears of others. People often have questions and concerns about the true meaning of the values expressed by a vision (e.g., "What will employee 'involvement' really mean in practice?"), the answers to which will ultimately shape their perception and acceptance. It is important for managers to be sensitive to these issues because breakdowns in communication often result from faulty assumptions. By testing these perceptions and feelings through active listening, miscommunication and misunderstanding can be minimized.

After initial communication and discussion, a related issue concerns how to build a critical mass to promote what the organization is attempting to accomplish, especially in terms of disseminating evidence of the change and building a network to foster the change. Recommended strategies include newsletters and house organs dedicated to stories of the vision in action, organizational stories about people accomplishing specific aspects of the vision, ongoing meetings of those who are working toward the vision, and rituals and celebrations that commemorate successes related to the vision. In large, multisite organizations, these efforts can be further reinforced and supported through the application of communication technology, from company intranets to videoconferences with champions of the vision.

ETHICS IN ORGANIZATIONAL COMMUNICATION

Although it is generally accepted that people should be honest and forthright in their communications with others, in all too many instances, organizations and their managers purposefully issue false, misleading, or strategically ambiguous statements to gain an advantage in a business situation. It has even been suggested that individuals who intend to be winners in the "business game" should have the attitude of a poker player (i.e., a game where "cunning deception and concealment of one's strength and intention" are viewed as strengths) in their discussions and negotiations with everyone from employees and customers to government officials.[122] Unfortunately, as reflected by the rise and fall of companies like the Enron corporation, such behaviors can contribute to a culture of misinformation and deception.[123]

The importance of truthfulness in communications is underscored by the reality that once trust and confidence are undermined they are exceedingly difficult to restore. Indeed, as research has underscored, once credibility is undermined, employees and key stakeholders stop listening to the information coming to them, don't believe what they hear when they do listen, and create their own rumors, stories, and worst-case scenarios.[124] Thus an essential aspect of effective communication involves developing and maintaining a high level of trust among organizational members and other key stakeholders. People tend to more openly express their thoughts, feelings, opinions, information, and ideas when they trust the individuals, groups, and organizations with whom they are working. At the same time, they also tend to be more open to the thoughts, feelings, opinions, information, and ideas expressed by those whom they trust.

Research has indicated that trust is based on a number of components, most of which (integrity, consistency, loyalty, and openness) are essentially moral values.[125]

1. **Integrity:** A reputation for honesty and truthfulness
2. **Competence:** The technical knowledge and interpersonal skill needed to perform the job
3. **Consistency:** Reliability, predictability, and good judgment in handling situations
4. **Loyalty:** Benevolence, or the willingness to protect, support, and encourage others
5. **Openness:** The willingness to share ideas and information freely with others

Thus, from an ethical vantage point, managers should: (1) be sincere; (2) not deliberately alter the truth or knowingly expose an audience to falsehoods, especially those that can cause harm; (3) present the truth as they understand it; (4) increase the listener's level of expertise by providing all necessary information; (5) convey messages that are free from mental and physical coercion, both in terms of their intent and the way in which they are communicated; and (6) give full credit to the source of ideas or information.[126] At the same time, listeners have an obligation to provide a fair hearing of the message and to attempt to minimize any bias in assessing the message. By engaging in such trustworthy actions, managers can readily enhance the overall effectiveness of the communication process.

CONCLUSION

To be an effective communicator, it is important to be sensitive to how the communication process operates, the different ways in which we send messages to others, the various barriers that can distort and disrupt communication efforts, and the organizational networks and roles that further influence this process. Effective communication that helps to build trust and credibility in organizations involves a two-way exchange, and is relevant to employee needs, understandable, believable, useful, timely, and "mature" (i.e., it does not "talk down" to employees).[127] Focusing on the structure, process, and outcomes of communication efforts helps to develop a fuller understanding of this fundamental aspect of organizational life.

NOTES

1. H. Mintzberg, *The Nature of Managerial Work* (Englewood Cliffs, NJ: Prentice Hall, 1980); and A. Deutschman, "The CEO's Secret of Managing Time," *Fortune*, June 1, 1992, p. 135.

2. See, for example, C.A. O'Reilly and L.R. Pondy, "Organizational Communication," in S. Kerr, ed., *Organizational Behavior* (Columbus: Grid Publishing, 1979), pp. 121–122;

and M.T. Myers and G.E. Myers, *Managing by Communication: An Organizational Approach* (New York: McGraw-Hill, 1982), Chapter 3.

3. F. Luthans, *Organizational Behavior* (New York: McGraw-Hill, 1981), pp. 347–348; see also J.W. Gibson and R.M. Hodgetts, *Organizational Communication*, 2nd ed. (New York: HarperCollins, 1991).

4. O'Reilly and Pondy, op. cit., p. 121.

5. N. Wiener, *Cybernetics of Control and Communication in the Animal and the Machine* (New York: Wiley, 1948).

6. Myers and Myers, op. cit., pp. 64–65.

7. For a good example, see J.F. Kikoski, "Effective Communication in the Performance Appraisal Interview: Face-to-Face Communication for Public Managers in the Culturally Diverse Workplace," *Public Personnel Management* 27, no. 4 (1998): 491–513.

8. O'Reilly and Pondy, op. cit., pp. 137–144.

9. Myers and Myers, op. cit., pp. 7–8.

10. See W.G. Scott and T.R. Mitchell, *Organizational Theory: A Structural and Behavioral Analysis* (Homewood, IL: Irwin, 1976), pp. 192–203; T.E. Zorn, Jr. and S.E. Ruccio, "The Use of Communication to Motivate College Sales Teams," *Journal of Business Communication* 35, no. 4 (1998): 468–499; and T.J. Carter, "The Importance of Talk to Midcareer Women's Development: A Collaborative Inquiry," *Journal of Business Communication* 39, no. 1 (2002): 55–91.

11. M.B. McCaskey, "The Hidden Messages Managers Send," *Harvard Business Review* 57, no. 6 (1979): 135–148.

12. Myers and Myers, op. cit., p. 10.

13. H. Orlans, "Jargon," *Change* 35, no. 4 (2003): 7; and R. Goldsborough, "Learning the Lingo of the New Electronic Age," *Black Issues in Higher Education* 20, no. 9 (2003): 39.

14. See S.I. Hayakawa, *Language in Thought and Action* (New York: Harcourt, 1949); and J.J. Gumperz and D. Hymes, eds., *Directions in Sociolinguistics* (New York: Holt, Rinehart & Winston, 1972).

15. J. Dutton, "The Making of Organizational Opportunities; Interpretive Pathway to Organizational Change," *Research in Organizational Behavior* 15 (1990): 195–226.

16. M. Bralove, "Taking the Boss at His Word May Turn Out to Be a Big Mistake at a Lot of Companies," *Wall Street Journal*, June 4, 1982, p. 29.

17. M. Loden and R.H. Loeser, "Working Diversity: Managing the Differences," *The Bureaucrat: The Journal for Public Managers* (Spring 1991): 25.

18. McCaskey, op. cit., pp. 136–137.

19. This section is drawn from H. Bracey, A. Sanford, and J.C. Quick, *Effective Management: An Experience-Based Approach* (Plano, TX: Business Publications, 1981), pp. 47–48; McCaskey, op. cit., pp. 138–144; and E. Duncker, "Symbolic Communication in Multidisciplinary Cooperations," *Science, Technology and Human Values* 26, no. 3 (2001): 349–386.

20. See R. Buck and C.A. VanLear, "Verbal and Non-Verbal Communication: Distinguishing Symbolic, Spontaneous and Pseudo-Spontaneous Non-Verbal Behavior," *Journal of Communication* 52, no. 3 (2002): 522–541.

21. F. Davis, *Inside Intuition: What We Know about Nonverbal Communication* (New York: McGraw-Hill, 1973); M.L. Kapp and J.A. Hall, *Nonverbal Communication in Human Interaction*, 3rd ed. (Fort Worth, TX: Holt, Rinehart & Winston, 1992); and J.A. Russell, J. Bachorowski, and J. Ferndnez-Dols, "Facial and Vocal Expressions of Emotions," *Annual Review of Psychology* 54 (2003): 329–350.

22. See R.L. Weaver, *Understanding Interpersonal Communication*, 4th ed. (Glenview, IL: Scott, Foresman, 1987), pp. 176–179.

23. See J. Fast, *Body Language* (Philadelphia: Lippincott, 1970); G. Nierenberg and H. Calero, *How to Read a Person Like a Book* (New York: Pocket Books, 1973); P. Bull, *Body Movement and Interpersonal Communication* (New York: Wiley, 1983).

24. D.W. Hendon, "How to Negotiate with Thai Executives," *Asia Pacific Journal of Marketing and Logistics* 13, no. 3 (2001): 41–62.

25. McCaskey, op. cit.; see also S. Mealing, "Value-Added Text: Where Graphic Design Meets Paralinguistics," *Visible Language* 37, no. 1 (2003): 43–58.

26. See K. Mieszkowski, "It's a Web, Web, Web, Web World," *Fast Company* (January/February 2000): 290–303; and R. Furchgott, "Web to Go—Sort of," *Business Week*, (February 14, 2000), pp. 144–145.

27. This section draws from M.M. Extejt, "Teaching Students to Correspond Effectively Electronically," *Business Communication Quarterly* 61, no. 2 (1998): 57–67; and C. Golden, "E-Mail: Our Love-Hate Relationship," *EDUCAUSE* 38, no. 3 (2003): 68–72.

28. See, for example, L. Ku, "Social and Nonsocial Uses of Electronic Messaging Systems in Organizations," *Journal of Business Communication* 33, no. 3 (1996): 297–325.

29. A.H. Huang, "E-Mail Communication and Supervisor-Subordinate Exchange Quality: An Empirical Study," *Human Systems Management* 21, no. 3 (2002): 193–204.

30. See V.I. Polley, "A Model Electronic Communications Policy for the Workplace," *Practical Lawyer* 44, no. 7 (1998): 25–46.

31. N. Schwartz, "Instant Messaging Goes Corporate," *Information Management Journal* 37, no. 4 (2003): 8–10; and GSM Association, "Operators Exchange Instant Messages across Networks," www.gsmworld.com/news/press_2007/press07_16.shtml, accessed March 10, 2007.

32. See C.L. Pascal, "Enabling Change Interactions through Instant Messaging," *IEEE Transactions on Professional Communication* 46, no. 2 (2003): 138–141.

33. See Extejt, "Teaching Students to Correspond Effectively Electronically"; and K. Carter, "Tell Me How You Feel: Quasi-Nonverbal Cues in Computer-Mediated Communication," *et Cetera* 60, no. 1 (2003): 29–39.

34. Bracey et al., op. cit., pp. 46–49; and J. McCambridge, "12 Angry Men: A Study in Dialogue," *Journal of Management Education* 27, no. 3 (2003): 384–401.

35. G. Miller, "The Magical Number 7, Plus or Minus Two: Some Limits on Our Capacity for Processing Information," *Psychological Review* 63, no. 1 (1956): 81–97.

36. See D.E. Vinton, "A New Look at Time, Speed, and the Manager," *Academy of Management Executive* 6, no. 4 (1992): 7–16; E.J. Hunt, "Communicating in the Information Age," *Canadian Business Review* 23, no. 2 (1996): 23–28; and D.D. Dawley and W.P. Anthony, "User Perceptions of E-Mail at Work," *Journal of Business and Technical Communication* 17, no. 2 (2003): 170–200.

37. See Weaver, op. cit., pp. 256–257; and E.F. Huse and J.L. Bowditch, *Behavior in Organizations: A Systems Approach to Managing* (Reading, MA: Addison-Wesley, 1977), p. 134.

38. H. Burke and T. Weir, "Helper Perceptions of Effective, Ineffective, and Non-helpers" (paper presented at 35th Annual Meeting of the Academy of Management, New Orleans, August 1975); and O'Reilly and Pondy, op. cit., pp. 140–142.

39. This section is drawn from R.S. Nickerson, "How We Know—and Sometimes Misjudge—What Others Know: Imputing One's Own Knowledge to Others." *Psychological Bulletin* 125, no. 6 (1999): 737–759.

40. See W. Ickes, ed., *Emphatic Accuracy* (New York: Guilford Press, 1997).

41. J. Allen, "Communication Networks in R&D Laboratories," *R&D Management* 1, no. 1 (1970): 14–21.

42. See C. Argyris, "Teaching Smart People How to Learn," *Harvard Business Review* 69 no. 3 (1991): 5–15. Se also J.R. Gibb, "Defensive Communication," *Journal of Communication* 11, no. 3 (1961): 141–148; C.R. Rogers and F.J. Roethlisberger, "Barriers and Gateways to Communications," *Harvard Business Review* 30, no. 4 (1952): 46–52; and J. Schimel, J. Arndt, T. Pyszczynski, and J. Greenberg, "Being Accepted for Who We Are: Evidence That Social Validation of the Intrinsic Self Reduces General Defensiveness," *Journal of Personality and Social Psychology* 80, no. 1 (2001): 35–54.

43. Myers and Myers, op. cit., pp. 164–166; W. Bennis, *Interpersonal Dynamics: Essays and Readings in Human Interaction* (Homewood, IL: Dorsey Press, 1969), pp. 211–212.

44. See D. Tannen, *Talking 9 to 5* (New York: William Morrow, 1995).

45. See R.L. Katz, "Skills of an Effective Administrator," *Harvard Business Review* 33, no. 5 (1974): p. 91; and Bracey et al., op. cit., p. 46.

46. Costley and Todd, op. cit., pp. 144–155; and P. Maguire and C. Pitceathly, "Key Communication Skills and How to Acquire Them," *British Medical Journal* 325, no. 7366 (2002): 697–700.

47. L.B. Comer and T. Drollinger, "Active Empathic Listening and Selling Success: A Conceptual Framework," *Journal of Personal Selling & Sales Management* 19, no. 1 (1999): 15–29.

48. C. Rogers and R.E. Farson, "Active Listening," in A.R. Cohen, S.L. Fink, H. Gadon, and R.D. Willits, *Effective Behavior in*

Organizations (Homewood, IL: Irwin, 1976): and T.F. Mader and D.C. Mader, *Understanding One Another: Communicating Interpersonally* (Dubuque, IA: Wm. C. Brown, 1990), pp. 282–288.

49. Myers and Myers, op. cit., pp. 168–171; C. Rogers, "Communication: Its Blocking and Facilitating," *Northwestern University Information* 20 (1952): 9–15; and K.B. Clark, "Empathy: A Neglected Topic in Psychological Research," *American Psychologist* 35, no. 2 (1980): 187–190.

50. See Comer and Drollinger, "Active Emphatic Listening."

51. J. Anderson, "Giving and Receiving Feedback," in P.R. Lawrence, L.B. Barnes, and J.W. Lorsch, *Organizational Behavior and Administration*, 3rd ed. (Homewood, IL: Irwin, 1976), pp. 103–111; H.J. Leavitt and R.H. Mueller, "Some Effects of Feedback on Communication," *Human Relations* 4 (1951): 401–410; and D.N. Den Hartog and R.M. Verburg, "Service Excellence from the Employees' Perspective: The Role of First Line Supervisors," *Managing Service Quality* 12, no. 3 (2002): 159–164.

52. Adapted from Anderson, op. cit., p. 109; J.S. Morris, "How to Make Criticism Sessions Productive," *Wall Street Journal*, October 12, 1981, p. 26; and Cohen et al., op. cit., p. 230.

53. J. Greenberg, "Organizational Justice: Yesterday, Today and Tomorrow," *Journal of Management* 16 (1990): 399–432.

54. J. Greenberg, "Justice and Organizational Citizenship: A Commentary on the State of the Science," *Employee Responsibilities and Rights Journal* 4 (1993): 249–256.

55. R.J. Bies and J.S. Moag, "Interactional Justice: Communication Criteria for Fairness," in B. Sheppard (ed.), *Research on Negotiation in Organizations* (Greenwich, CT: JAI Press, 1986), pp. 43–55.

56. See Bies and Moag, "Interactional Justice"; D.L. Shapiro, E.H. Buttner, and B. Barry, "Explanations: What Factors Enhance Their Perceived Adequacy?" *Organizational Behavior and Human Decision Processes* 58 (1994): 346–368; and Q.M. Roberson and M.M. Stewart, "Understanding the Motivational Effects of Procedural and Informational

Justice in Feedback Processes," *British Journal of Psychology* 97 (2006): 281–298.

57. Myers and Myers, op. cit., pp. 16–18.

58. See, for example, I. Nonaka and H. Takeuchi, *The Knowledge-Creating Company: How Japanese Companies Create the Dynamics of Innovation* (New York: Oxford University Press, 1995); and W. Halal, ed., *The Infinite Resource: Creating and Leading the Knowledge Enterprise* (San Francisco: Jossey-Bass, 1998).

59. L. Wah, "Knowledge Management: Behind the Buzz," *Management Review* (April 1999): 16–19, 24–26.

60. T.H. Davenport, D.W. DeLong, and M.C. Beers, "Successful Knowledge Management Projects," *Sloan Management Review* 39, no. 2 (1998): 43–57.

61. L. Wah, "Making Knowledge Stick," *Management Review* (May 1999): 24–29.

62. For a good illustration of how tacit knowledge is embedded in organizational culture, see E. Schein, *The Corporate Culture Survival Guide* (San Francisco: Jossey-Bass, 1999), Chapter 2.

63. This section draws heavily from S. Newell, "The Fallacy of the Simplistic Notions of the Transfer of 'Best Practice,'" in A.F. Buono and F. Poulfelt (eds.), *Challenges and Issues in Knowledge Management* (Greenwich, CT: Information Age Publishing, 2005), pp. 69–106. See also M.W. McElroy, "Integrating Complexity Theory, Knowledge Management and Organizational Learning," *Journal of Knowledge Management* 4, no. 3 (2000): 195–210.

64. Reported in T.H. Davenport and L. Prusak, *What's the Big Idea? Creating and Capitalizing on the Best Management Thinking* (Boston: Harvard Business School Press, 2003), p. 189.

65. See R. Ruggles, "The State of the Notion: Knowledge Management in Practice," *California Management Review* 40, no. 3 (1998): 80–89; M. Alvai and D.E. Leidner, "Knowledge Management and Knowledge Management Systems: Conceptual Foundations and Research Issues," *MIS Quarterly* 25, no. 1 (2001): 107–136; and Davenport, DeLong and Beers, "Successful Knowledge Management," p. 45.

66. C. Davis, "A Roadmap for Long-Term Knowledge Management Success," *AIIM E-Doc*, 18, no. 1 (2004) 36–38.

67. S.W. Sussman and W.S. Siegal, "Informational Influence in Organizations: An Integrated Approach to Knowledge Adoption," *Information Systems Research* 14 no. 1 (2003): 47–66.

68. See Nonaka and Takeuchi, *Knowledge-Creating Company*, pp. 11–13; and E. Ransdell, "The NIKE Story: Just Tell It!" *Fast Company* (January–February 2000): 44–46.

69. See G. Szulanski, "Exploring Internal Stickiness: Impediments to the Transfer of Best Practice within the Firm," *Strategic Management Journal* 17, (Winter 1996): 27–44; S.Z. Shariq, "How Does Knowledge Transform as It Is Transferred? Speculations on the Possibility of a Cognitive Theory of Knowledgescapes," *Journal of Knowledge Management* 3, no. 4 (1999): 243–251; and Newell, "The Fallacy of Simplistic Notions of the Transfer of 'Best Practice.'"

70. See J.O. Iverson and R.D. McPhee, "Knowledge Management in Communities of Practice," *Management Communication Quarterly* 16, no. 2 (2002): 259–267.

71. See "MR Research: Survey on Knowledge Management," *Management Review* (April 1999): 20–23.

72. K. Husted and S. Michailova, "Diagnosing and Fighting Knowledge-Sharing Hostility," *Organizational Dynamics* 31, no. 1 (2002): 60–73.

73. Wah, "Making Knowledge Stick," p. 28; and Halal, *The Infinite Resource*.

74. D. Ulrich, "Intellectual Capital × Competence = Commitment," *Sloan Management Review* 39, no. 2 (1998): 15–26.

75. See Wah, "Making Knowledge Stick," p. 29.

76. See O'Reilly and Pondy, p. 130; J.B. Bush, Jr. and A.L. Frohman, "Communication in a 'Network' Organization," *Organizational Dynamics* 20, no. 2 (1991): 23–36; and P. Sevcik, "Flow-Oriented Management—The Next Level of Management," *Business Communication Quarterly* 33, no. 5 (2003): 8–9.

77. O'Reilly and Pondy, op. cit., pp. 130–132; B.E. Collins and B.H. Raven, "Group Structure: Attraction, Coalitions, Communication, and Power," in G. Lindzey and E. Aronson, eds., *Handbook of Social Psychology*, vol. 4 (Reading, MA: Addison-Wesley, 1969), pp. 137–155; M.E. Shaw, "Communication Networks," in L. Berkowitz, ed., *Advances in Experimental Social Psychology* (New York: Academic Press, 1964), pp. 111–147; and J. Allen, op. cit.

78. Bush and Frohman, op. cit., pp. 23–28.

79. See ibid; R. Nelson, "The Strength of Strong Ties: Social Networks and Intergroup Conflict in Organizations," *Academy of Management Journal* 32, no. 3 (1989): 377–401; and T.J. Allen and O. Hauptman, "The Substitution of Communication Technologies for Organizational Structure in Research and Development," in J. Fulk and C. Steinfeld, eds., *Organizations and Communication Technology* (Newbury Park, CA: Sage, 1990), pp. 275–294. See also P.S. Adler, "Building Better Bureaucracies," *Academy of Management Executive* 13, no. 4 (1999): 36–47, especially his discussion of the features of enabling bureaucracies.

80. See Nonaka and Takeuchi, *The Knowledge-Creating Company*; and Halal, *The Infinite Resource*.

81. C.L. Michaels, "Circle Communication: An Old Form of Communication Useful for 21st Century Leadership," *Nursing Administration Quarterly* 26, no. 5 (2002): 1–10.

82. K. Davis, "Management Communication and the Grapevine," *Harvard Business Review* 31, no. 5 (1953): 43–49; and H. Brimm and A. Murdock, "Delivering the Message in Challenging Times: The Relative Effectiveness of Different Forms of Communicating Change to a Dispersed and Part-Time Workforce," *Total Quality Management* 9, nos. 2–3 (1998): 167–182.

83. See E. Otte and R. Rousseau, "Social Network Analysis: A Powerful Strategy, Also for the Information Sciences," *Journal of Information Science* 28, no. 6 (2002): 441–454.

84. See L.K. Larkey, "Toward a Theory of Communicative Interactions in Culturally Diverse Workgroups," *Academy of Management Review* 21 (1996): 463–491; and S.B. Bacharach, P.A. Bamberger, and D. Vashdi, "Diversity and Homophily at Work: Supportive Relations among White and

African-American Peers," *Academy of Management Journal* 48 (2005): 619–644.

85. E. Walton, "How Efficient Is the Grapevine?" *Personnel* (March–April 1961): p. 48; and R. Rowan, "Where Did That Rumor Come From?" *Fortune*, August 13, 1979, p. 134. See also R. Cross, N. Nohria, and A. Parker, "Six Myths about Informal Networks—and How to Overcome Them," *Sloan Management Review* 43, no. 3 (2002): 67–76.

86. See R.L. Rosnow and G.A. Fine, *Rumor and Gossip: The Social Psychology of Hearsay* (New York: Elsevier, 1976).

87. See S.H. Applebaum, R. Lopes, L. Audet, and A. Steel, "Communication during Downsizing of a Telecommunications Company," *Corporate Communications* 8, no. 2 (2003): 73–96.

88. See L.A. Isabella, "Managing the Challenges of Trigger Events: The Mindsets Governing Adaptation to Change," in T.D. Jick, *Managing Change: Cases and Concepts* (Homewood, IL: Irwin, 1993), pp. 24–25.

89. See L.R. Pondy, P.J. Frost, G. Morgan, and T.C. Dandridge, eds., *Organizational Symbolism* (Greenwich, CT: JAI Press, 1983).

90. See J.M. Beyer and H.M. Trice, "How an Organization's Rites Reveal Its Culture," *Organizational Dynamics* 15, no. 4 (1987): p. 6; P.C. Nystrom and W.H. Starbuck, "Managing Beliefs in Organizations," *Journal of Applied Behavioral Science* 20, no. 3 (1984): 227–287; and B.E. Ashforth, "Climate Formation: Issues and Extensions," *Academy of Management Review* 10, no. 4 (1985): 837–847.

91. A.L. Wilkins, "The Creation of Company Cultures: The Role of Stories and Human Resource Systems," *Human Resource Management* 23, no. 1 (1984): 41–60.

92. T.E. Deal and A.A. Kennedy, *Corporate Cultures: The Rites and Rituals of Corporate Life* (Reading, MA: Addison-Wesley, 1982); T.J. Peters, "Symbols, Patterns, and Settings: An Optimistic Case for Getting Things Done," *Organizational Dynamics* 7, no. 2 (1978): 3–23; and T.E. Deal and A.A. Kennedy, *The New Corporate Cultures: Revitalizing the Workplace after Downsizing, Mergers, and Restructuring* (Reading, MA: Persus Books, 1999).

93. Beyer and Trice, op. cit., pp. 5–24.

94. See G. Cheney, "The Rhetoric of Identification and the Study of Organizational Communication," *Quarterly Journal of Speech* 69 (1983): 143–158; and J.M. Putti, S. Aryee, and J. Phua, "Communication Relationship Satisfaction and Organizational Commitment," *Group & Organization Studies* 15, no. 1 (1990): 44–52.

95. R. Eisenberger, R. Huntington, S. Hutchinson, and D. Sowa, "Perceived Organizational Support," *Journal of Applied Psychology* 71 (1986): 500–507.

96. See R.M. Kanter, C. Ingols, and P. Myers, "The Delta–Western Merger: The Best Get Better," *Management Review* (September 1987): 24–26.

97. The section on communication roles is based on O'Reilly and Pondy, op. cit., pp. 132–134; T.V. Bonoma and G. Zaltman, *Psychology for Management* (Boston: Kent Publishing, 1981), pp. 263–270; and L.P. Morton, "Gatekeepers as Target Publics," *Public Relations Quarterly* 40, no. 2 (1995): 21–24.

98. See G.T. Lau, M.A. Razzaque, and A. Ong, "Gatekeeping in Purchasing: An Empirical Investigation," *Journal of Business and Industrial Marketing* 18, no. 1 (2003): 82–103; and Deal and Kennedy, *The New Corporate Cultures*, pp. 218–219.

99. See R. Likert, *The Human Organization* (New York: McGraw-Hill, 1967); E.G. Rogers and F. Schoemaker, *Communication of Innovations* (New York: Free Press, 1971); and P.R. Lawrence and J.W. Lorsch, *Organization and Environment: Managing Differentiation and Integration* (Homewood, IL: Irwin, 1969). For a current example of how liaisons function, see R. Weiss, "Don't Forget about the Office Staff," *Marketing Health Services* 23, no. 2 (2003): 10–11.

100. See Deal and Kennedy, *The New Corporate Cultures*, p. 218.

101. See, for example, J. Pfeffer and J.F. Veiga, "Putting People First for Organizational Success," *Academy of Management Executive* 13, no. 2 (1999): 37–48.

102. This discussion is based on J. Fulk and B. Boyd, "Emerging Theories of Communication in Organizations," *Journal of Management* 17, no. 2 (1991): 409–411; and S.S. Kahai and R.B. Cooper, "Exploring the Core Concepts of

Media Richness Theory: The Impact of Cue Multiplicity and Feedback Immediacy on Decision Quality," *Journal of Management Information Systems* 20, no. 1 (2003): 263–300.

103. See R.L. Daft and R.H. Lengel, "Information Richness: A New Approach to Managerial Behavior and Organizational Design," in L.L. Cummings and B.M. Staw, eds., *Research in Organizational Behavior*, vol. 6 (Greenwich, CT: JAI Press, 1984), pp. 191–233; and R.L. Daft and R.H. Lengel, "Organizational Information Requirements, Media Richness and Structural Design," *Management Science* 32 (1986): 554–571.

104. R.L. Daft, R.H. Lengel, and L.K. Trevino, "Message Equivocality, Media Selection, and Manager Performance: Implications for Information Systems," *MIS Quarterly* 11 (1987): 355–366.

105. R.H. Lengel and R.L. Daft, "The Selection of Communication Media as an Executive Skill," *Academy of Management Executive* 2 (1988): 225–232.

106. S.K. Vickery, C. Droge, T.P. Stank, T.J. Goldsby, and R.E. Markland, "The Performance Implications of Media Richness in a Business-to-Business Service Environment: Direct versus Indirect Effects," *Management Science* 50, no. 8 (2004): 1106–1119.

107. See Fulk and Boyd, op. cit., p. 411; and C. W. Steinfeld, "Computer-Mediated Communication in an Organizational Setting: Explaining Task-Related and Socio-Emotional Uses," in M. McLaughlin, ed., *Communication Yearbook*, vol. 9 (Newbury Park, CA: Sage, 1986), pp. 777–804.

108. See G. Rasters, G. Vissers, and B. Dankbaar, "An Inside Look: Rich Communication Through Lean Media in a Virtual Research Team," *Small Group Research* 3, no. 6 (2002): 718–755.

109. This section is drawn from S. Salamon and T.A. Joiner, "Toward an Understanding of Communication Channel Preferences for the Receipt of Management Information," *Journal of the American Academy of Business* 7, no. 2 (2005): 56–62.

110. See S.P. Weisband, S.K. Schneider, and T. Connolly, "Computer-Mediated Communication and Social Information: Status Salience and Status Differences," *Academy of Manage-* *ment Journal* 38, no. 4 (1995): 1124–1151; M. Morris and C. Ogan, "The Internet as Mass Medium," *Journal of Communication* 46, no. 1 (1996): 39–49; and N. Kock and R. Davison, "Can Lean Media Support Knowledge Sharing: Investigating a Hidden Advantage of Process Improvement," *IEEE Transactions on Engineering Management* 50, no. 2 (2003): 151–163.

111. M.L. Markus, "Electronic Mail as the Medium of Managerial Choice," *Organization Science* 5, no. 4 (1994): 502–527.

112. This discussion is drawn from Fulk and Boyd, op. cit., pp. 411–412; J. Fulk, J.A. Schmitz, and C.W. Steinfeld, "A Social Influence Model of Technology Use," in J. Fulk and C.W. Steinfeld, eds., *Organizational and Communication Technology* (Newbury Park, CA: Sage, 1990); and J.L. Yu, C. Liu and J.E. Yao, "Technology Acceptance Model for Wireless Internet," *Internet Research* 13, no. 3 (2003): 206–222.

113. See, for example, R. Watson, G. DeSanctis, and M.S. Poole, "Using a GDSS to Facilitate Group Consensus: Some Intended and Unintended Consequences," *MIS Quarterly* 12 (1988): 463–478; and G. Kelly and R.P. Bostrom, "A Facilitator's General Model for Managing Socioemotional Issues in Group Support Systems Meeting Environments," *Journal of Management Information Systems* 14, no. 3 (1998): 23–44.

114. C. Saunders, D. Robey, and K. Vaverek, "The Persistence of Status Differentials in Computer Conferencing," *Human Communication Research* 20 (1994): 443–472; and R. Spears and M. Lea, "Panacea or Panoptica? The Hidden Power in Computer-Mediated Communication," *Communication Research* 21 (1994): 427–459.

115. R.C. King, "The Effects of Communication Technology on Group Collaboration," in J.L. Wall and L.R. Jauch, eds., *Academy of Management Best Paper Proceedings 1991* (Academy of Management, 1991), pp. 246–250; and B.A. Jain and D.N. Ross, "Assessing the Impact of Integrated Group Support Systems on the Performance of Teams," *American Business Review* 16, no. 1 (1998): 105–111.

116. Putti, Aryee, and Phua, op. cit., pp. 44–52.

117. This discussion is based on Fulk and Boyd, op. cit., p. 415; J. Webster and L.K. Trevino, "Rational and Social Theories as Complementary Explanations of Communication Media Choices: Two Policy-Capturing Studies," *Academy of Management Journal* 38, no. 6 (1995): 1544–1572; D. Taylor, "Not Much Traffic on Your Intranet? Try These Strategies," *InfoWorld* 18, no. 26 (1997): 82; and F. Deroian, "Formation of Social Networks and Diffusion of Innovations," *Research Policy* 31, no. 5 (2002): 835–851.

118. W.P. Belgrad, K.K. Fisher, and S.R. Rayner, "Vision, Opportunity, and Tenacity: Three Informal Processes That Influence Formal Transformation," in R.H. Kilmann, T.J. Covin, and Associates, *Corporate Transformation* (San Francisco: Jossey-Bass, 1988), p. 135; G.E. Ledford, Jr., J.R. Wendenhof, and J.T. Strahley, "Realizing a Corporate Philosophy," *Organizational Dynamics* 23, no. 3 (1995): 5–19; and L. Larwood, C.M. Falbe, M.P. Kriger, and P. Miesing, "Structure and Meaning of Organizational Vision," *Academy of Management Journal* 38, no. 3 (1995): 740–769.

119. M.L. Marks, *Charging Back up the Hill: Workplace Recovery after Mergers, Acquisitions, and Downsizings* (San Francisco: Jossey-Bass, 2003), pp. 202–209.

120. See D. Ulrich, "Strategic and Human Resource Planning: Linking Customers and Employees," *Human Resource Planning* 15, no. 2 (1992): 57–58; and B. Nanus, *The Vision Retreat: A Facilitator's Guide* (San Francisco: Jossey-Bass, 1995).

121. This discussion is drawn from D. Richards and S. Engle, "After the Vision: Suggestions to Corporate Visionaries and Vision Champions," in T.D. Jick, *Managing Change: Cases and Concepts* (New York: McGraw-Hill, 1993), pp. 86–89.

122. See, for example, A. Carr, "Is Business Bluffing Ethical?" *Harvard Business Review* 46, no. 1 (1968): 45, 144. See also J. Paul and C.A. Stribak, "The Ethics of Strategic Ambiguity," *Journal of Business Communication* 34, no. 2 (1997): 149–160.

123. J.A. Cohan, " 'I Didn't Know' and 'I was Only Doing My Job': Has Corporate Governance Careened out of Control? A Case Study of Enron's Information Myopia," *Journal of Business Ethics* 40, no. 3 (2002): 275–299.

124. E.F. Harshman and C.L. Harshman, "Communicating with Employees: Building on an Ethical Foundation," *Journal of Business Ethics* 19 (1999): 3–19.

125. J.K. Butler and R.S. Cantrell, "A Behavioral Decision Theory Approach to Modeling Dyadic Trust in Superiors and Subordinates," *Psychological Reports* 55 (1984): 19–28; and L.T. Hosmer, "Trust: The Connecting Link between Organizational Theory and Philosophical Ethics," *Academy of Management Review* 20, no. 2 (1995): 379–403.

126. This discussion is drawn from R.M. Berko, A.D. Wolvin, and R. Curtis, *This Business of Communicating* (Dubuque, IA: Wm. C. Brown, 1990), p. 189; and R.A. Nelson, "Ethics and Social Issues in Business: An Updated Communication Perspective," *Competitiveness Review* 12, no. 1 (2003): 66–74.

127. Harshman and Harshman, "Communicating with Employees," pp. 16–17.

Group Dynamics

*E*ver since the Hawthorne Studies and the Human Relations movement, researchers have increasingly focused their attention on the structure, dynamics, and impact of group behavior. This growing body of research has indicated the numerous ways in which groups can positively and negatively affect member satisfaction and performance, productivity, product and service quality, and a range of other organizational goals and outcomes. Indeed, the overall success of a complex organization is significantly influenced by the performance of a number of interacting groups throughout the firm's hierarchy.

Despite the centrality of groups in our lives and their importance and inevitability in organizations, we often take them for granted. We rarely take the time or effort to observe what is going on in a group, why different members behave in certain ways, why some groups appear more effective than others, how one group may affect another, and so forth. In order to have a fuller understanding of organizational behavior (OB), however, it is critical to develop an awareness of and ability to analyze the influence of groups on their individual members, interpersonal relations, and organizational activities. It is also important for managers to have insight into the problems as well as the potentialities associated with using and working with groups.[1]

As a foundation for such an understanding, this chapter will focus on *intragroup* processes and dynamics. The discussion focuses on different types of groups, basic group attributes, the stages and behaviors often found in group development, and the ways in which we can observe and improve group process and interaction. Chapter 6 takes an applied look at a variety of work-related teams, including problem-solving teams, cross-functional teams, self-managed teams, learning teams, and virtual teams, and examines the interaction between different groups and teams in an organization.

TYPES OF GROUPS

Although there are probably as many definitions of groups as there are OB researchers, they appear to have certain common characteristics. Some of the research examining organizational group phenomena distinguishes between dyads (social units consisting of two people) and groups (social units comprised of more than two people); however, for our purposes, a *group* consists of (1) *two or more people* who are

(2) *psychologically aware of each other* and who (3) *interact* to fulfill a (4) *common goal.* Thus, a group is more than a simple collection of people; these four basic conditions must be fulfilled. The goals of a group may be either task oriented (as in a work group) or socially oriented (as in friendships and clubs). Thus, a collection of people on an airplane would not really be considered a group, whereas individuals who are part of a charter flight would be considered a group because they fulfill the preceding conditions.

There are five basic distinctions that are made in the literature about groups: (1) primary and secondary; (2) formal and informal; (3) heterogeneous and homogeneous; (4) interacting and nominal; and (5) temporary and permanent. Although other classifications of groups are sometimes used (e.g., task versus social or friendship groups), such categorizations are based on these distinctions.

Primary and Secondary Groups

Sociologists make a distinction between groups in terms of the types of relationships that exist between members.[2] *Primary groups* are predominantly oriented toward close, interpersonal relationships, whereas *secondary groups* are more task or goal oriented. The family and small face-to-face friendship groups are examples of primary groups. Work groups and public interest groups, which are more impersonal and task oriented, are examples of secondary groups. It is possible, of course, for primary groups to emerge out of secondary groups, as when close friendships develop at work. When analyzing groups within organizations, the focus should be on both secondary groups and primary groups.

Formal and Informal Groups

Not all the groups that exist within organizations are formally sanctioned by management and the organization itself.[3] *Formal groups* are those that have established task-oriented goals and are explicitly formed as part of the organization—such as work groups, departments, and project teams. *Informal groups,* by contrast, are those that emerge over time through the interaction of organizational members. Although such groups do not have any formally assigned or stated goals, they do have implied or implicit goals, which are frequently recreational and interpersonal in nature. A rough distinction between these types of groups is that formal groups are represented on an organization chart, while informal (self-enacted) groups are not.[4] In relation to the previous discussion, formal groups are secondary in nature, while informal groups are usually considered primary groups.

Organizational members can be part of a number of formal and informal groups at the same time. An organization's marketing department, for example, is a formal group with specific goals and requirements. If individuals within that department get together on a regular basis for other, socially oriented reasons, however, that particular group is considered informal. Informal groups frequently cut across formal group lines as well. Both formal and informal groups have goals, interactions, and interpersonal awareness. Moreover, both types of groups may be functional (contribute to) or dysfunctional (a hindrance) for organizational goal accomplishment. An informal group, for example, can set standards (high or low) that govern the amount of work its members will accomplish, despite formal policies and standards set by management. The discussion of the Hawthorne Studies in Chapter 1 provides a good example of the influence of such informal groups in the workplace.

Heterogeneous and Homogeneous Groups

Another way of viewing groups is based on their degree of similarity (homogeneity) or dissimilarity (heterogeneity).[5] If one considers all possible dimensions, of course, virtually all groups are heterogeneous. However, we usually consider the heterogeneity or homogeneity of a group with regard to a specific set of dimensions, viewpoints, or characteristics. A *homogeneous group* is a group whose members have key aspects in common, in terms of either personal (e.g., attitudes, values, goals) or sociodemographic (e.g., education, age, gender, race) characteristics. *Heterogeneous groups* are those that differ along significant dimensions.

The key to heterogeneity and homogeneity in a group depends on the relative importance of the dimension in question. For example, while sociodemographic characteristics might make a group appear to be heterogeneous, the group might be quite homogeneous with respect to a given set of issues around which they share common values or goals, as in the environmental protection movement. Moreover, research has indicated that individuals with homogeneous attitudes and values tend to interact more with each other and are more likely to form informal group attachments.[6]

It is important to emphasize that much of our knowledge about how group composition influences group dynamics and performance is based on research with culturally homogeneous samples.[7] As our labor force becomes increasingly diverse and business activities take place in a global environment, however, the idea of heterogeneous groups takes on new and broader meanings.[8] Yet, while groups composed of individuals with diverse cultural backgrounds may be becoming more commonplace, the research on the long-term performance of such groups has yielded conflicting results. Some studies have shown that culturally diverse groups tend to experience initial performance difficulties due to interpersonal stresses and self-oriented behaviors. Over time, however, these issues are often resolved, resulting in enhanced performance.[9] Other studies yield the opposite results. Culturally diverse groups perform better in the beginning due to a greater willingness to focus on team-oriented behaviors (such as relationship building and information sharing) at the expense of self-oriented behaviors. Over time, however, culturally diverse teams can experience a reversal, as individual members shift their attention back to self rather than to team.[10] A managerial challenge, therefore, is to further our understanding of such differences, to achieve a balance between team- and self-oriented behaviors, and to develop our ability to integrate the divergent perspectives associated with sociodemographic and cultural heterogeneity.

Interacting and Nominal Groups

Interacting groups are those in which the participants are *directly* and *actively* involved in an exchange with each other. *Nominal groups,* by contrast, are those in which members interact through *controlled* and relatively *indirect* interactions with each other, either through a structured group meeting, a third party, or computer-mediated environments. Although interacting groups are obviously more common than nominal groups, the latter serve as an alternative to direct (interacting) group decision making and, with the proliferation of electronic communication technologies, are becoming increasingly commonplace.[11]

There are two basic variations in the use of noninteracting groups in decision making: the nominal group technique and the Delphi technique.[12] In the *nominal group technique* (NGT), members meet formally but discussion or interpersonal communication between members is restricted. This is done to minimize the influence of personal and interpersonal factors on the types of ideas and arguments a person might form. Thus, prior to any discussion or collaboration, members first record their ideas and comments and then openly share them *before* any discussion or evaluation takes place. The *Delphi technique* is a variant of the nominal group technique in that it does not require its members to be physically present; as such, it is often used for decision making among individuals and groups who are geographically scattered. In this approach, a particular problem is identified and group members are requested to provide potential solutions or analyses. This process is done anonymously and independently. The information is then compiled at a central location, transcribed, and fed back to the individual members. After reviewing the results, members are again asked for their analyses or solutions. This process usually goes through a number of iterations (cycles) before it is stopped. The main advantages of this approach are that it controls for the effect of individual and interpersonal influences on the decision-making process, and reduces the costs and problems associated with bringing a broad range of knowledgeable people together. The process, however, is time consuming, and it may not develop the richness of ideas that comes from discussion and debate in direct group interaction or even the more limited interaction provided by the nominal group technique. Moreover, due to the lack of actual interaction between group members, there is typically a low level of satisfaction within Delphi groups.[13]

Electronic Brainstorming and Decision Making

Advanced communication technologies, often referred to as *groupware*, have contributed to the use of nominal groups in organizations through the development of group decision–support systems (GDSS).[14] These systems—ranging from Lotus Notes to electronic mail–based voting tools, activity modelers, and topic commentators—facilitate group information needs in complex, unstructured, and dynamic environments. In essence, these systems help group members to develop and coordinate ideas by categorizing, re-sorting, and annotating items for further analysis. As an idea is submitted to a computer-mediated (virtual) group, for example, it appears in a window on a computer screen next to the window of ideas raised by the other participants. Group members can glance at and respond to the contributions of the others at any time, without necessarily interrupting their own train of thought. This process is suggested to be effective because there is less *production blocking* (e.g., when listening to a group member talk you have less time to come up with original ideas of your own). Moreover, computer-mediated environments typically overcome the inhibition often associated with face-to-face meetings, enabling people to express their thoughts without direct criticism or retribution.[15]

A related advantage of this type of information sharing and decision making is that exchanges are asynchronous (i.e., there is no pressure for an immediate response), allowing more time for reflection.[16] Instead of quick responses, which are often influenced by immediate pressures and demands, there is greater potential that the slower and often more creative process in which thoughts literally "nag away" in the back of one's mind can lead to new connections and innovative solutions. At the same time, however, such asynchronicity may not always be helpful, especially when messages and ideas build up over time and those involved feel pressured to focus on more immediate and pressing matters. Thus, it is important to emphasize that such support systems are not panaceas: Most of these systems are still relatively unsophisticated; they require extensive training to capture their full potential; existing systems offer very different combinations of features that complicate implementation; and different groupware tools appear to contribute to different aspects of the decision-making process (e.g., brainstorming and idea creation versus decision quality).

Permanent and Temporary Groups

The final distinction between types of groups refers to the expected duration of their existence. A *temporary group* is one that is formed with a specific problem or task in mind, and the expectation that once that task is completed the group will disband. *Permanent groups* are those that are expected to continue through different tasks or issues. Traditionally, organizations used permanent groups to fulfill the company's goals and objectives. Thus, we have specific departments, work units, and offices that focus on a particular function or set of functions (e.g., accounting department, research and development department, human resources department). In some instances, however, a particular group may not have the expertise or resources to address a specific task or problem. In these situations, temporary task groups are formed, drawing on others who belong to other groups within the organization or persons outside the organization, such as consultants. These groups are sometimes referred to as task forces or cross-functional groups since their membership cuts across group, departmental, or functional lines (as in bringing together people from research and development, production, and sales to deal with problems related to a new product).

Temporary task groups involve an unusual mix of autonomy and dependence.[17] They are typically free, within fairly broad limits, to proceed with their task as the group decides. Since their work is done at the request of some other individual (or group), however, they are dependent on that client's directions and preferences. Such groups are typically given a deadline for accomplishing their task(s), and as problems are resolved the groups disband and the members return to their original groups. As business organizations increasingly utilize contingent (part-time) workers and consultants assigned to specific projects as a way to augment their full-time labor force, the management of such temporary groups will continue to grow in importance.

BASIC ATTRIBUTES OF GROUPS

A number of factors influence and constrain the behavior of individual group members as well as the overall effectiveness of the group itself. This section focuses on some of the ways in which an individual's and group's status and role can affect respective behaviors, and the ways in which norms, cohesiveness, and other tendencies such as groupthink and choice-shift (risky-shift) phenomena influence group effectiveness.

Individual and Group Status

Status refers to the level or position of a person in a group, or a group in an organization. We often talk about individuals and groups as having either high or low status in an organization. In this respect, status can come from either a formal position or individual qualities. It reflects how the individual or group is perceived by others in the organization, usually in terms of relative influence and prestige. Since most groups are made up of members of unequal status (and organizations are made up of groups of unequal status), the notion of status involves a social comparison.[18]

In most group and organizational situations, we expect *status congruence*, that is, a person's job title defines his or her status within a group. A manager, for example, would be expected to have more status than an assistant manager. Similarly, within hospitals, attending physicians have more status than medical interns. In some instances, however, the attributes or qualities of individuals will overshadow their formal position within an organization, and they may actually exert more influence than someone above them in the organization's hierarchy. In others, situational factors can enhance a particular person's status. Since higher-status people tend to find it difficult to take orders from lower-status people, such *status-incongruent* situations can lead to conflict and anxiety in the workplace. This is one of the reasons, for example, why nurses have traditionally been reluctant to give suggestions to a doctor, even though they may have spent more time with a particular patient. The relative status of different groups, however, can change over time and modify such potential incongruence. Nursing, for instance, has gone through a significant evolution as nurses are asserting more autonomy in hospitals, conducting more nursing research, and advancing their academic training at both the master's and doctoral levels. As such, there is less of a status difference between doctors and nurses in hospitals today.

Electronic Communication and Status Equalization

An interesting phenomenon associated with group interaction via computer-mediated communication is *status equalization*, the tendency for one's ideas to carry more weight than one's socioeconomic position.[19] Since status cues are much more difficult to read in electronic messages, especially those posted on the Internet, there is a tendency for perceptions about status to converge. Since you cannot easily determine an individual's status in an online conversation, the tendency is to think of that person as having a status similar to your own, especially if you find the expressed ideas appealing. In these instances, status is linked much more fully to one's opinions and expertise than ascribed or acquired characteristics.

Roles

The concept of a *role* refers to the various behaviors people expect from a person or a group in a particular position.[20] These behavioral expectations are influenced by the place of a role in the organization's hierarchy, the activities associated with the role, and its social interaction patterns, which determine the range of behaviors that are perceived as acceptable. As an example, think about your expectations about how professors and students, or managers and their subordinates, "should" behave. When people in these roles engage in behaviors that go beyond these expectations, we feel that they are not acting "properly." The power of roles on our behaviors and attitudes is reflected by research indicating that when people's roles change their attitudes tend to change as well, and revert to their initial state when roles are changed back to their original position.

Role Conflict, Ambiguity, and Overload

It would be relatively easy to fulfill role expectations if we had only one role in life. Each of us, however, plays several roles that elicit certain expectations that often contradict one another. The result of these divergent role expectations is referred to as *role conflict*. We may know what is expected of us in a particular position, but due to different sets of expectations about other roles we occupy, compliance can be difficult.

In other situations, we may receive unclear or ambiguous signals about what is expected of us in a particular role. In these instances, we may experience some confusion or *role ambiguity* since we are not fully clear about how we should behave or what we should do. Role ambiguity can be especially problematic during large-scale organizational change, such as merging with or acquiring another company, as people are often confused about how they should carry out their responsibilities. Finally, organizational members can also experience *role overload*, when they lack the resources needed to fulfill commitments, obligations, and/or other job requirements. Role conflict, ambiguity, and overload are associated with lower levels of job satisfaction and performance, increased experiences of stress and burnout, decreased commitment toward the group and organization, and, in general, an increased propensity to withdraw from the situation (e.g., tardiness, absenteeism, quitting).[21]

Recent research has focused on how managers deal with such role-related difficulties.[22] Managers tend to either alter their own behaviors so that they are more consistent with expectations, attempt to change the expectations that others have of them, or try to explain the reason for their actions to relevant stakeholders. While such strategies are helpful to reduce the stresses and tensions associated with role conflict, ambiguity, and even overload, at times individuals simply attempt to avoid dealing with the situation (e.g., hoping the problem will go away, avoiding key people, changing jobs). Unfortunately, this latter tactic typically only postpones problems and is related to negative stakeholder perceptions and evaluations.

Social Identity Theory

Research indicates that group membership clearly affects members' sense of who they are—how they see themselves, how they feel about themselves, and how they act in the group.[23] Within this context, recent work in the area of *social identity theory* suggests that people become what salient others expect them to be.[24] Since group membership tends to lower self-awareness while heightening group-awareness, the roles that we play within different groups, especially those that are important to us, readily influence and shape our attitudes and behaviors. This dynamic is sufficiently powerful that it is argued that social groups cannot be conceptualized as the sum of the individual properties of their members. Instead, there is a blurring of the psychological separation between the individual (personal self) and the group (the collective self). Groups thus involve a combination of partially individual and partially structured characteristics of the group members.[25]

This notion of group identification also applies to organizational group membership(s). Workgroup identification is an individual's perception of oneness with the workgroup, and the tendency to internalize the group's successes and failures.[26] Research on workgroup dynamics has established that individuals who are more highly identified with their workgroup are more committed to the group, are more likely to take the workgroup's perspective and act in its interest, and exhibit more favorable attitudes and behaviors toward other workgroup members. They are also less likely to engage in social loafing and other dysfunctional behaviors than those who are less identified with the group.[27] Thus, the establishment of positive and salient workgroup identification among group members holds the potential of yielding positive results for organizational groups.

Norms

Norms are the common standards or ideas that guide member behavior in established groups.[28] Although in some instances norms may be formalized and written (e.g., codes of conduct), for the most part they are *unwritten rules* concerning those behaviors that are appropriate and acceptable to other group members. Norms are often more implicit than explicit in nature; that is, it is often assumed that group members understand what is expected of them. In such situations, the only way a norm may be observable is when a member inadvertently breaks it and experiences the negative reactions of other group members. It was once a group norm, for example, for men working in certain companies to wear ties, white shirts and conservatively tailored business suits. Any man who wore a colored shirt without a tie was regarded as a group *deviant*—that is, someone who goes against a norm of the group—and was pressured to conform to the group's standard. If the deviation is significant enough, the group can ostracize the member and essentially make that person a group *isolate*.

Not all norms carry the same weight. *Pivotal norms* are those that are considered to be particularly important to the group or organization. They are central to the workings and interactions of group members. *Peripheral norms,* by contrast, are those that are not as important to group members. While the distinction between pivotal and peripheral norms does vary from group to group, pivotal norms are frequently those that focus on task-related behaviors (such as being a "rate-buster" or a "slacker") or socially related behaviors that are central to the functioning of the group. Deviation from peripheral norms is not sanctioned as severely as deviation from those norms that the group feels are pivotal in nature. Such sanctions can range from ridicule and sarcasm to ostracism and physical abuse. The key to joining a new group is to understand the norms of the group and their implications for your own behaviors. Since most norms are implicitly understood, however, they must be inferred from observation of the behavior of other members.

Conformity

Research on the impact of social or group influence on individual attitudes and behaviors has found that the desire to be accepted by the group can make individuals susceptible to conformity effects. In essence, individuals can experience strong pressure to change their attitudes and behaviors to conform to the group's norm(s) or operative standard(s). Seminal research conducted by Asch placed individuals in groups that participated in several sets of matching activities.[29] During the early activities, all of the participants gave the correct response. However, during the third matching exercise, the first participant—a confederate (i.e., someone covertly working with the researcher)—provided an obviously incorrect response, which was followed by a number of other confederates (depending on the strength of the manipulation), until it was time for the unsuspecting subject to provide his or her response. Even though the subject could clearly see that the responses of her or his teammates were incorrect, subjects conformed and provided the obviously incorrect response 35 percent of the time. These results, and those of considerable additional research,[30] suggest that there are compelling group normative pressures that encourage us toward conformity.

Member Status and Conformity to Group Norms

Although conformity to norms, especially pivotal norms, is expected among group members, conformity tends to be greater when people perceive they have a relatively low status in the group or if they feel that they are not fully accepted by the other members. Higher-status members acquire the right to dissent through their position in the group. The effect among low-status members can be different. There is evidence that low-status individuals can be less committed to the group and its goals, and thus be more likely to eschew conformity to the group's norms. Thus, though for different reasons, low-status members may deviate from group norms just as high-status members do. However, lower-status members can perceive the need to earn the "right" to occasional nonconformity. These latter individuals can also feel the need to prove themselves worthy of membership.[31]

The pressures that lower-status individuals feel, however, can lead to expedient conformity rather than private acceptance of a norm.[32] *Expedient conformity* is when a group member expresses attitudes and engages in behaviors that are acceptable to the group while holding private beliefs that are at odds with the group. In essence, the conformist desires to avoid sanctions for noncompliance or achieve reward or recognition for following or appearing to identify with the group's position. This type of conformity, however, usually holds only when the individual is under scrutiny. *Private acceptance,* in contrast, is when an individual's public *and* private attitudes and beliefs are compatible with the group's norms. In this instance, external surveillance is unnecessary since the individual identifies with the group, internalizing group values and norms.

Cohesiveness

Cohesiveness refers to the degree to which group members are attracted to one another and the resulting desire to remain in the group.[33] A *cohesive group* is one whose members reflect feelings of closeness that are manifested in similar views, attitudes, liking, performance, and behavior. Cohesive groups tend to have stronger norms and harsher ways of dealing with group deviants than those groups that are less cohesive. Since cohesiveness does vary considerably from group to group, it is important to understand some of the factors that can exert an influence on a group's cohesiveness:

- The degree to which members *agree* on the goals and purpose of the group (agreement leads to cohesiveness; disagreement decreases cohesiveness).

- When group members *interact frequently* with one another, but not past the point of "diminishing returns" when groups can become stale (e.g., when groups have too many meetings).

- The extent of *mutual attraction* between group members (attraction leads to increased cohesiveness).

- When there is *intergroup conflict* that pulls members together and encourages cooperation; such conflict, however, can become too powerful, leading to *intragroup* competition that reduces cohesiveness.

- The degree of *success* a group has in meeting its goals and objectives; successful performance tends to increase cohesiveness, while poor performance often leads to scapegoating, projecting the blame onto others, and so on, which reduces cooperation and cohesiveness.

- *Perceived fairness* in terms of how group members are treated, both by members of the group and the larger organization of which the group is a part.

The cohesiveness of a group is a powerful determinant of the intensity of the group's performance. However, not all cohesive groups necessarily focus on organizational objectives. Work-group cohesion that emerges from the attractiveness of a group's goals or objectives can enhance job satisfaction and group and organizational productivity.[34] In contrast, cohesiveness that emerges from the personal attractiveness or friendliness of group members may lead to social behaviors and interactions that focus on maintaining group membership rather than accomplishing task objectives. Since social cohesion is suggested to be a continually changeable state,[35] group members may direct more of their energies toward sustaining those relationships that are important to them.

Group Cohesiveness in Cyberspace

Some observers have questioned whether groups can truly become cohesive in a computer-mediated environment.[36] Given the lack of social cues and the transitory nature of most online interactions, critics contended that it is unlikely for genuine and satisfying group relationships to develop. Membership in most of the thousands of online mailing lists, chat rooms, discussion forums, and electronic newsgroups that exist today tends to be temporary, with many of these "e-groups" drawing only occasional curious visitors.

Despite the ephemeral and largely fragile nature of these electronic forums, there is growing evidence to suggest that a strong sense of cohesiveness can develop in these online groups. What is less clear, however, is why this sense of closeness emerges in some of these groups and not others. People who participate in such electronic exchanges report that the ability to *gather information* was the most satisfying and useful aspect of such groups. Many of these individuals, however, also mentioned a "sense of community" and the ability to share "personal experiences."[37] Thus, some people do report developing deep commitments to their online group mates, although others continue to report ambivalent feelings and even a lingering sense of strangeness about the experience.[38]

It appears that just as real-life groups vary a great deal, the same is true of virtual groups. Virtual groups can range from people who have never met but are drawn together by common interests to people assigned specific tasks by their employers, working with others whom they may not have any real expectation of ever meeting in real life. As we will explore in more detail in Chapter 6, over time as people continue to work with others on virtual teams they report feelings of belonging and closeness similar to those reported in interacting teams.

Group (Organizational) Commitment

Commitment reflects the relative strength of an individual group member's feelings of identification with and attachment to a group's goals or tasks.[39] Commitment is based on the degree of (1) belief or acceptance of group goals, (2) willingness to exert significant effort on the part of the group, and (3) desire to remain a group member.[40]

While the idea of group or organizational commitment is linked with such variables as job satisfaction and likelihood of turnover,[41] research suggests a difference between affective commitment and continuance commitment.[42] Group members with a strong *affective commitment* maintain their membership because they *want* to (e.g., high levels of group or organizational comfort, job challenge), while those individuals with *continuance commitment* remain because they *need* to (e.g., concerns about potential loss of pension benefits, lack of other alternatives). Research suggests that the consequences of these different types of commitment are quite different. Studies, for example, have found that while affective commitment is positively related to supervisor ratings of job performance and a willingness to engage in organizational citizenship behaviors, continuance commitment is negatively related to these outcomes.[43] Considering the level of organizational downsizing, retrenchment, and restructuring that characterizes corporate America and the resultant feelings of fear and cynicism in the workforce, this distinction raises important concerns about the actual level of commitment that individuals may have to their work group and organization. This perspective also helps to explain the significant rise in "free agent" behaviors. Similar to the movement of professional athletes from team to team, a growing number of business professionals are moving from job to job and organization to organization, placing much greater emphasis on satisfying their own needs and career development, often at the expense of their employer organizations.

Groupthink

While cohesiveness is usually viewed as a positive force in groups and organizations, it can lead to a pattern of behaviors referred to as *groupthink*, a dynamic that diminishes the decision-making capability of the group.[44] As groups become increasingly cohesive, they can develop a "clubby" atmosphere characterized by feelings of superiority, exclusiveness, and invulnerability. Groups with high status and/or very powerful leaders can also be more vulnerable to groupthink. High-status leaders bring prestige to groups, which can increase desire to maintain affiliation with these groups. This often occurs in homogeneous groups that begin to systematically shut out divergent opinions. Thus, any new information brought to the attention of group members may be viewed as inappropriate, irrelevant, or even threatening, and thus subsequently ignored. The resulting unwillingness to examine divergent views and alternatives leads to a type of self-censorship, as group members tend not to be open to new ideas.

As an example of the power of groupthink, early research by Irving Janis suggested that the reason the United States so badly miscalculated Cuban military strength during the 1960s Bay of Pigs invasion was that President Kennedy and his closest advisers (willingly or unwillingly) did not tolerate any dissent about the situation. The result was that available intelligence information was discounted and the advisory group made incorrect assumptions about Cuban resistance, leading to a disastrous military intervention. Unfortunately, the same dynamic appears to have contributed to two recent NASA disasters involving the 1986 *Challenger* and 2003 *Columbia* space shuttles. In the 1986 catastrophe, Morton Thiokol engineers initially discussed but then suppressed information about the effect of low temperatures on the reliability of the shuttle's O-rings. Even though the *Challenger* space shuttle sat on the launch pad for hours at subfreezing temperatures, it was ultimately launched, despite concerns that the O-rings would not seal at those temperatures. This critical piece of information was discounted in the launch decision, however, and twenty-two seconds after takeoff the shuttle exploded, killing all seven astronauts on board.[45] Roughly seventeen years later, Boeing engineers at NASA appeared to fall into the same trap as they decided early on that falling foam would not endanger the *Columbia* shuttle, while it was ultimately concluded that the foam led to the craft's breakup during reentry.[46]

Janis's work helps us to understand how such faulty decisions are made. First, there is an *illusion of invulnerability* that leads to overoptimism and encourages high risk taking by group members. There are collective efforts at rationalization of the group's decisions so other members are "warned" not to question these decisions, and pressure is exerted on members who disagree. An *illusion of morality* (i.e., a feeling that the group has the highest goals in mind and should, therefore, not be criticized) emerges as further justification of the group's actions. Finally, self-censorship emerges as there is a shared *illusion of unanimity* concerning the judgments and opinions of the majority of group members and self-appointed "mind guards" emerge to protect the group from divergent information that might disrupt the group's "shared complacency about the effectiveness and morality" of the decision.

Subsequent research on the groupthink phenomenon has raised questions about its potential impact in the workplace.[47] Efforts to induce the groupthink phenomenon in laboratory studies, for example, have been generally unsuccessful, which has raised questions about the extent to which the concept is a typical group occurrence. There is, however, a strong basis on which to criticize these studies, since the threat of groupthink appears to be greatest in long-term, highly cohesive groups that (1) expect compliance with group decisions and (2) have been isolated by external pressures and stresses. As studies have found, in long-term work groups levels of consensus were positively related to the psychological well-being of group members, while identical analyses performed with "pseudogroups" (i.e., temporary, experimental groups) found that consensus and psychological well-being were not related. Recent studies have also found that there is a distinction between socially oriented and task-oriented cohesion in groups. Groups whose cohesiveness is based primarily on socioemotional factors tend to be more susceptible to groupthink than groups that are more task-focused.[48]

An important implication that emerges from Janis's work is that while cohesiveness can be a positive force in groups, overly cohesive groups can become less effective because of demands for loyalty and conformity to group norms. Managers should, therefore, be aware of the symptoms of groupthink. By encouraging group members to express doubts or criticisms of decisions, assigning a rotating role of "devil's advocate" to question solutions, showing that you are willing to accept criticism, periodically bringing in qualified outsiders to meet with the group, and alerting group members to the dangers of groupthink, the constraining aspect of group cohesiveness can be reduced.

Choice-Shift (Risky-Shift) Phenomenon

Another tendency in group decision making is when discussion intensifies and "pushes" the individual leanings of group members toward an extreme position. It was initially thought that groups would take a more daring or riskier position with respect to a particular issue than any one of its members would as individuals, hence the term *risky shift*.[49] In effect, group members might be thought of as hiding behind the anonymity of the group. Subsequent studies, however, have found that group discussion tends to reinforce prevailing attitudes within the group, and is influenced by the propensity of group members to either take or avoid risk. Thus, initially conservative attitudes tend to produce even more conservative opinions, while initially favorable attitudes toward risk taking tend to produce a willingness to assume even riskier positions.[50] This research suggests that cultural and situational factors may produce a conservative shift in group decisions. The majority of studies in this area, however, indicate a shift toward greater risk taking.[51]

The risky-shift phenomenon might be thought of as a special case of groupthink.[52] Since the decisions of a group reflect norms that have developed over time, these decision-oriented norms may tend toward the assumption of more aggressive and riskier alternatives than members would reach as individuals. Although there is no consensus on why such a shift occurs, a number of plausible explanations exist. As optimistic information is shared, individuals are more willing to take risks since they perceive themselves to be more informed. Similarly, group norms might encourage such aggressive behaviors, and the responsibility for potential loss is spread out over a number of people. It seems that group members are more willing to take extreme positions when others will "share the blame" if something goes wrong. As people increasingly communicate via information technology, it has also been suggested that there is a loss of the moderate voice in computer-mediated exchanges. Research has also shown, for example, that compared to face-to-face groups, computer-mediated groups took more time to reach consensus, used more uninhibited language (e.g., swearing, name calling, trading insults), and made larger decision shifts from their initial individual positions.[53]

Finally, it has also been suggested that the group context facilitates the use of critical defense mechanisms (e.g., denial, projection, rationalization, suppression) by individual members, increasing the amount of risk that members are willing to take or avoid.[54] This propensity can be especially problematic when combined with organizational tendencies that place: (1) an excessive faith in established systems and organizational policies and protocols (e.g., strict conformity to established procedures; obedience to the chain of command); (2) a narrow emphasis on one's job; (3) short-range preoccupation and myopic self-interest (e.g., overemphasis on short-term goals; obsession with meeting immediate goals); and (4) suppression or distortion of bad news.[55]

While no one is immune to the myriad structural, cultural and political forces that exist in organizations, ultimately it is important for managers to realize that groups often make decisions that contain a greater element of extremism compared to decisions made by an individual. It is thus critical to ensure an open decision-making environment, attempting to capture as much information as possible, encouraging and rewarding questions and dissent, and ensuring that those delivering bad news do not get "shot."

Social Loafing

Social loafing refers to the reduced efforts of individual group members when they perform as part of a group.[56] The tendency toward diminished performance in groups appears to be a universal phenomenon. It has been observed in a variety of groups working on an array of different tasks, among both males and females, across people of all ages, and in many different cultures. Recent research, however, does suggest that males tend to engage in social loafing more than women.[57] It is important to note that reluctance to participate due to shyness or discomfort is not considered social loafing. The concept refers to the inclination to "goof off" in a group, and loafers withhold their effort due to such factors as low motivation, disinterest, or group apathy.[58]

Recent research has focused on the conditions under which social loafing will and will not occur.[59] The phenomenon appears to center on the extent to which *individual member performance* can be identified. In instances where some form of evaluation of such achievement was used—whether self-evaluation or more objective assessment by others—social loafing was minimized. *Group size* is another important factor—individual effort decreases with increased size. This dynamic may occur because individuals are less noticeable in larger groups than they are in smaller ones. As work groups get larger, however, research indicates that members are more likely to be dissatisfied and feel that their contributions are dispensable, and group leaders focus more on task rather than maintenance needs. *Perception of loafing* by other group members also tends to increase the likelihood of one's own loafing. Finally, loafing is related to the *nature of the task* involved—social loafing declines as group members are involved in important, motivating task assignments.

Cross-cultural research has also found variance in the occurrence of social loafing as a function of cultural value orientations such as individualism and collectivism.[60] For example, research with U.S. and Chinese managerial trainees showed that social loafing was observed among those holding individualistic beliefs (U.S. managers), but not among those with collectivistic beliefs (Chinese managers). Results of this study suggest that social loafing may be a predominantly Western phenomenon, but at the very least it is associated with the extent to which individuals are concerned with maximizing personal return (in which case social loafing is a logical decision and practice) or are more concerned with benefiting the group or collective.

From a managerial perspective, the social loafing phenomenon raises a number of implications for the increased use of work teams as part of a strategy to improve product and service quality, productivity, and employee morale. Although *moral suasion* (i.e., calling for cooperative behavior based on moral values) and *supportive structures* (e.g., cooperative group goals, interdependent division of labor, equal distribution of reward) are important, cooperation and effort in a group also emerge from self-interest.[61] Thus, it is important to ensure that group members understand the importance of their assignment as well as to have mechanisms for both *group* and *individual accountability* in order to encourage active participation and discourage loafing.

GROUP PROCESS AND DEVELOPMENT

In an attempt to examine how groups operate, it is important to differentiate between the *content* of group activity and the *process* the group undertakes to fulfill its goals and objectives. A focus on a group's tasks, the topic of decision making, or the specific issues a group is working on are examples of the content of group activity. By contrast, a focus on *how* a group undertakes its tasks, the dynamics of how decisions are made, or the ways in which a group decides what issues it will deal with reflect concerns about group process. Thus, the emphasis is not on what the group is doing, but rather on *how* the group is doing it.

Group Development

Groups go through a number of developmental phases over time. Since groups are dynamic entities, they can be thought of as being in a continual state of activity and change. When a group is initially formed, the dynamics and processes underlying the interaction between its members are quite different from the patterns that would be expected after the group has been in existence for a longer period of time. Groups cannot be expected to be fully effective immediately, as it takes time and the management of the group development process to enhance the interactions between their members.

An extensive review of the literature on group development points to a series of stages that groups and their members go through: forming, storming, norming, performing, and reforming or adjourning[62] (see Figure 5-1). In general, research further suggests that groups that have been functioning for longer periods of time tend to function at the higher levels of group development.[63]

Figure 5-1   Group Development Stages and Member Socialization

Source: Adapted from G.L. Stewart, C.C. Manz, and H.P. Sims, *Team Work and Group Dynamics* (New York: John Wiley & Sons, 1999), p. 90.

Forming

People join groups for a number of reasons, including attraction to a group's goals, activities, or members; as a way of establishing meaning and identity in their lives; as a way of fulfilling unrelated needs (e.g., résumé enhancement); or simply being assigned to a particular group. At the outset, or the *forming* stage, group members find out what they will be doing, the kind of leadership and behaviors that are acceptable, and the range of interpersonal and task relationships that are possible. This phase of group development is typically marked by courtesy, confusion, caution, and commonality. The motivation for joining a group, however, exerts a strong influence on a member's productivity and the subsequent cohesiveness of the group. For example, if a person joins a group because he or she is attracted to its goals, cohesiveness and productivity are likely to be higher than if that individual joined to satisfy other needs that fall outside of the group.

Storming

The *storming* stage, or what might be described as the "shakedown" period, is where individual styles come into conflict. People begin resisting the influence of the group, and there tends to be conflict over competing approaches to reaching the group's goals. This phase is characterized by tension, criticism, and confrontation between members. While intense, long-lasting confrontation can be dysfunctional for groups, in general, tension and conflict are positive forces. A lack of stress or contention, for example, can result in lethargy, haphazard attention to the group's task, and social loafing.

As part of this process, a distinction should be made between primary and secondary social tension.[64] *Primary tension,* which overlaps the forming and storming periods, refers to the normal anxiety and uneasiness that people experience when first joining a group. Social inhibitions often make people hesitant in their interactions with others, and we tend to be very careful to avoid controversy. *Secondary tension* reflects the stresses and strains that emerge when group members grapple with defining their roles and status, making decisions about how a task should be accomplished, and coping with different opinions and attitudes.

Norming

During the *norming* stage, resistance is overcome as the group establishes its rules and standards, develops intragroup cohesiveness, and delineates task standards and expectations. This phase is marked by cooperation, collaboration, cohesion, and commitment. On one level, the norming process begins almost immediately when a group is formed as members try to determine which behaviors are acceptable. As recent research suggests, however, group norms typically evolve from a fairly general to a more explicit, operationalized state that begins to guide group interactions and performance.[65]

There are three primary sources of norms in groups. The most prevalent source of norms is the group itself. While some norms are explicitly negotiated, most norms emerge implicitly through trial-and-error interaction between group members as different behaviors are tested (storming). Second, norms can be influenced by other groups or organizations outside the group in question (e.g., charters and chapter by-laws of national or state organizations, professional codes of conduct, industry benchmarking). Finally, norms can emerge from the influence of a single member, as when an individual inspires a group to adopt higher (or lower) standards of behavior or performance.

Performing

When groups are at the *performing* stage, the group is ready to focus its attention on accomplishing its tasks. Issues concerning interpersonal relations, member status, and division of task assignments are settled, and the primary energies of the group are oriented toward working on the task. Typical characteristics of this phase include challenge, creativity, group consciousness, and consideration among members.

Reforming or Adjourning

Over time, stable work groups often develop entrenched work habits that make it difficult for them to respond to changes in their environment.[66] At this point, the group is literally at a crossroad. Group members must either reassess their mission, roles, and processes or prepare for the dissolution of the group. While such reassessment can revitalize and refocus a group on its tasks, leading to renewed vigor and higher-level performance, it can also create internal dissent as some members cling to an outmoded vision of the group. When this happens, performance suffers, the group slips back into the storming phase and, unless ultimately resolved, the group can burst from internal tensions, "die" a protracted death, or simply disband as its members focus their energies elsewhere.

 While some groups are disbanded due to poor performance, even successful groups can be terminated, as when a task force achieves its objectives or a department is closed due to a merger or acquisition. The final *adjourning* stage is marked by compromise, communication, consensus, and closure. Especially important during this phase is the use of parting rituals and metaphors that allow members to express their feelings and perceptions and share emotional support while attempting to understand their group experience.[67]

Punctuated Equilibrium Model

Although initial conceptualization of these phases suggested that they occur in se-quence, subsequent work indicates that groups do not necessarily travel directly from forming to storming to norming, and so forth.[68] Although groups do undergo different stages where people initially join as a group (forming), experience tension and conflict among members (storming), develop standards and rules that govern behavior (norm-ing), and focus on goal achievement (performing), groups often cycle back and forth between these phases. Groups have been found to go through more of an iterative process, alternating between periods of inertia and revolution, being influenced by their members' perceptions of time, deadlines, and their socioemotional ties to the group (see Figure 5-2).

 In some instances, groups may appear to be "frozen" at one of these stages, due to the emergence of new problems or the influx of new members. And some groups may go through these phases more quickly than others. The key for managers is to realize that groups go through such developmental processes and to be aware that different issues will be of concern to members during these different stages. Since progress through these phases is not inevitable, managers should pay close attention to the concerns of group members to facilitate the development of the group from

Figure 5-2 Punctuated Equilibrium Model of Group Development

the forming through the performing phases. As discussed later in this chapter, one of the ways this can be accomplished is through team-building activities.

Group and Organizational Socialization

The process of group development discussed earlier reflects the different stages that groups go through when they are initially formed. Membership in most groups, however, is not stagnant. If there is a sufficient turnover of members, the group will usually repeat the forming, storming, norming, and performing process. Yet, even relatively stable, "performing" groups have to deal with the entry of new members and the need to orient them into the ways of the group. This process is referred to as *organizational socialization,* a process of adaptation during which entrants learn the values, norms, expectations, and established procedures for assuming a particular role and for becoming an accepted member of the group or organization.[69] As such, there are two basic purposes underlying this process. From the perspective of new members, it reduces role ambiguity and increases feelings of security since group expectations are clarified. From the perspective of the group or organization, the socialization process creates more behavioral uniformity among its members, thereby developing a basis for understanding and collaboration and reducing the potential for conflict.

On a general level, organizational socialization is characterized by a three-stage process: anticipatory socialization, organizational or group encounter, and the acquisition of group norms and values. *Anticipatory socialization* can be thought of as a preliminary or preparatory stage during which time a person should be provided with a realistic view of organizational goals and expectations, what the person's duties and responsibilities will be, and necessary task-related skills and abilities. During this phase, entrants can then (at least initially) assess the extent of fit between their own values and needs and those of the organization.

The second phase of socialization occurs when the newcomer actually joins the group or organization. This *encounter* stage (forming) is a type of initiation period during which the individual is confronted with the need to balance a number of personal and work-related demands that may conflict with one another. *Simultaneously,* the newcomer is learning new tasks, clarifying role expectations, and becoming acquainted with peers. As part of this "initiation," individuals must learn the relative importance of and appropriate time allocations for their assigned tasks. This is when expectations about what membership or the job would be like are tested with the realities of the situation. If the expectations formed during the preparatory phase were accurate, actual encounter serves to reaffirm these initial perceptions. In many instances, however, what people expect from a group or organization does not fit what they actually find. This can readily lead to the type of "storming" activity discussed earlier.

During the encounter phase, individuals attempt to work out the various problems that may have emerged through group membership. Organizational socialization, however, is not complete until newcomers are able to balance conflicting role demands, achieve sufficient mastery over their tasks, and make appropriate *adjustments to group norms and values.* If this is successfully accomplished, the new member feels accepted by the group as a valued and trusted member, and perceives a sense of security in membership. Successful socialization has also been shown to have a positive influence on the individual's productivity and commitment to the group or organization.

Organizational socialization programs can be formal or informal, focused on particular individuals or groups of individuals, and accomplished within shorter or longer periods of time. The important point is that newcomers to a group are provided with the opportunity to learn what the group or organization expects of them, their roles and role assignments, and the implications of the group's norms and values.

Socialization and Realistic Job Previews

Realistic job previews are based on the premise that accurate and realistic communications about job duties and responsibilities are an important component of socializing newcomers to an organization.[70] People entering into an organization need to know what to expect on their jobs so they can prepare themselves to cope effectively with work-related pressures and demands. Moreover, by receiving an accurate appraisal of what their jobs will be like, employees are less likely to be disappointed when unrealistic expectations go unfulfilled. While some research has suggested that realistic job previews do not always reduce turnover and increase satisfaction,[71] most of the empirical evidence is promising. In general, people who are provided with factual depictions of what their jobs will be like tend to be more satisfied and committed to their firms, with less stress and likelihood of turnover, than employees who do not receive such information.[72]

Newcomer Strategies

Regardless of the emphasis that organizations place on realistic job previews and the socialization process, there are a number of specific strategies that new group members can use to enhance their probability of acceptance.[73] First, newcomers should undertake a thorough reconnaissance of the group. Newcomers should utilize all available sources of information about the group in order to have a reasonably accurate appraisal of the group. An initial examination of the potential fit between personal and organizational goals and values is important here.[74] Second, it is useful to act out the newcomer role, seeking the advice of long-time members and initially avoiding disagreements or conflicts with them. While this sort of subservient role should be viewed as a temporary one, it is important to gain acceptance by the group prior to directly confronting others or pushing for change. Third, seeking out influential group members, often referred to as mentors, can assist one's entry into and learning about the group or organization. Finally, it is useful to collaborate with other newcomers as a source of emotional support, encouragement, and information.

Socialization and Group Mentoring

As the preceding discussion suggests, there is a link between newcomer socialization and mentoring. As studies have shown, newcomers often seek out established members to act as role models or organizational sponsors, in essence to act as mentors who can facilitate their acceptance and development in an organization.[75] Multiple newcomers can also form a peer group and collaborate with each other to facilitate their socialization into the larger organization. Yet, while mentoring has typically been viewed as an interpersonal phenomenon (between the mentor and the individual he or she is mentoring), it appears that there are group processes going on as well. *Group mentoring*—the group influence that emerges from its norms and roles—provides a greater sense of psychosocial support for newcomers, facilitates their inclusion and sense of belonging, enhances professionalism, allows greater networking, and provides more role models.

Organizational socialization can thus be thought of as an important part of a group or organization's efforts to establish order and consistency. The overall impact that such processes have on different individuals, however, can be quite diverse.[76] As recent research suggests, identical socialization processes can affect different people in disparate ways, and are often moderated by prior work experiences, the age of the individuals, and the extent to which entrants are introverted or extraverted (e.g., willingness to seek out information on their own). At the same time, as noted earlier, newcomers are becoming more proactive agents in their own socialization, placing greater emphasis on information seeking, self-managing their own behavior, networking, and negotiating their roles.[77] Nevertheless, it is becoming increasingly clear that since socialization is a continuous process, it involves ongoing subtle changes and adjustments over time rather than abrupt transformations.[78]

Observation of Group Process

In order to survive over time, groups must fulfill two basic sets of activities: (1) groups must be productive in terms of accomplishing their goals and objectives; and (2) groups must meet the personal welfare and emotional needs of their members.[79] *Task functions* are those actions and behaviors that are related to productivity and are concerned with accomplishing the group's tasks. This reflects the rational, work-oriented aspect of group activity. *Maintenance functions* are those actions and behaviors that attend to the social and emotional needs of group members. Since different individuals will have varying needs for belonging, control, and intimacy among other aspects of group interaction, these functions reflect the nonrational, emotional aspect of group activity. The emphasis is to establish and maintain cooperative interpersonal relationships, cohesiveness, and a favorable orientation to the group.

Both sets of activities are important for the long-term effectiveness of a group. In some instances, however, groups may neglect or sacrifice the social and emotional needs of their members for the sake of task accomplishment. When this occurs, individuals may reorient their efforts toward *self-centered* actions (such as repeatedly raising objections to block the group's progress, attacking the competence of other members, attempting to dominate the group, etc.) to fulfill their personal needs. These behaviors tend to be harmful to group cohesiveness and task accomplishment. Thus, while an overemphasis on task functions may increase a group's short-term performance, a continued focus on task needs alone can undermine the long-term effectiveness of the group. This can also lead to unsuccessful attempts at socializing new members and the "freezing" of a group at one of the early stages of development.

As *participant-observers,* group members can facilitate the successful development of the groups to which they belong. The participant-observer is an individual who is a regular member of a group and actively engages in its activities. At the same time, however, the individual is also observing, evaluating, influencing, and adapting to the group's processes and procedures. Thus, by understanding the importance of both task and maintenance activities in a group and by being aware of the types of behaviors and actions that fulfill these different needs, group members can act as participant-observers and contribute to their group's performance and stability.

Sociograms

A sociogram is a way to measure patterns of interaction, influence, and activity within a group.[80] This approach is based on group members' perceptions of each other in terms of liking, influence, productivity, and so forth. The method involves both *asking* group members whom they prefer to work with, whom they like and dislike, and so forth, and *observing* the actual interaction patterns during group activity. Based on these data, attractiveness and interaction patterns can be represented in schematic form.

Figure 5-3 illustrates a simple sociogram. The diagram shows which members are preferred by others, who talks to whom, how often members participate, subgroup formation, domination by particular members, and other patterns of group interaction. Each time a person interacts with another member in the group, an arrow is drawn that connects those individuals. The head of the arrow indicates the direction of the remarks or preference. Subsequent remarks focused toward the same person are indicated by short cross marks on the base of the arrow. If an individual directs a comment to the group as a whole, the arrow is drawn toward the center of the group.

Sociograms provide a way to identify attractions, preferences, and interactions among group members. They can also be used as a measure of the cohesiveness of the group by examining the number of people attracted to each other in a group divided by the number of possible "attractions." The greater the fraction, the more cohesive the group.[81] It is more important to note, however, that such preferences and interaction patterns can change, especially as groups evolve over time. Thus, observations at one stage of a group's development might not reflect the preferences and interactions of members at a later stage of the group's existence.

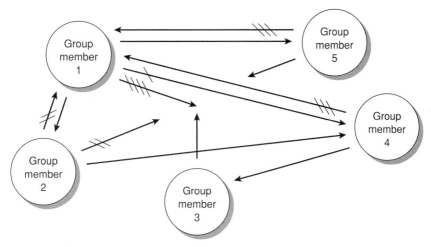

Figure 5-3 Illustration of a Sociogram

Interaction Process Analysis

Another approach to classifying behaviors of members during group activity is *interaction process analysis.*[82] This method involves observing the interactions that take place between group members and classifying them into task-oriented and maintenance-oriented roles, and the extent to which the behavior supports or detracts from group performance. Group behavior, for example, can be classified along such dimensions as asking for or giving suggestions, opinions, or information (task) and being friendly or unfriendly (maintenance). This information can be very useful in aligning roles in groups as well as helping members better understand the dynamics that are occurring in their groups.

A simplified version of the interaction process analysis scheme provides observers with an easy, straightforward model that has been found to be quite adequate for understanding group behavior and interaction.[83] Rather than focusing on particular behaviors or roles, this approach examines basic patterns and attributes of the group process. Each observation area is translated into a set of questions that serves as a guide for observation and analysis:

- *Participation:* Who does and does not participate? What is the nature of the participation? How does the group deal with members who do not participate?
- *Influence:* Who is influential? Is there competition for influence?
- *Decision Making:* How are decisions made? How are members' opinions solicited? Do majority opinions overwhelm minority positions?
- *Task Functions:* Does someone summarize proceedings? Does someone suggest or ask for ways to proceed? Does someone keep the group focused on the task?
- *Maintenance Functions:* Who is helpful to others? How are ideas and opinions accepted or rejected?

- *Feelings:* What kinds of nonverbal cues reflect the feelings of group members? Are negative feelings expressed or blocked?

- *Norms:* Do members avoid confrontation? Do members fall into "groupthink" patterns? Are members overly polite to each other?

Although this list is not exhaustive, it does provide the beginning observer with an idea of the type of interactions and attributes that can be observed in groups.

Managerial Application: Process Consultation and Team Building

While these different approaches can provide managers with an indication of the level of satisfaction, cohesiveness, and effectiveness of a group, the key to improving group performance is to feed back this information to the group in such a way that group members can use the data. Keeping in mind that such feedback may result in defensive behaviors by group members, it is useful to reflect on the discussion in Chapter 4 on defensive communication and the guidelines for effective feedback.

Process consultation is a set of activities designed to facilitate a group's ability to perceive, understand, and act on its processes. The aim is to help managers understand how group and organizational processes operate so that they can solve problems and improve those processes.[84] Four basic approaches are typically used in process consultation:

1. *Agenda-setting interventions* that direct attention to interpersonal issues, test group procedures, and analyze process. This is usually accomplished through low-key, question-and-answer sessions through which process consultants attempt to heighten group members' sensitivity to their own internal processes.

2. *Data feedback* of observations and/or other sources of information to members during meetings or to individuals after meetings.

3. *Counseling or coaching* of group members that sometimes follows data feedback sessions. An underlying key is the *receptiveness* of the group or individual to such coaching.

4. *Structural interventions* are sometimes required that pertain to group membership or interaction patterns. Although this approach is often seen as inconsistent with the "self-awareness" and "self-change" philosophy of process consultation, such direct intervention is sometimes necessary to deal with the problems involved.

A growing number of process consultants emphasize that the first two approaches—agenda-setting interventions and data feedback—are no longer sufficient in today's business environment. Owing to the rapid and at times volatile changes taking place in the business world, organizations and their management want, and need, further interpretation of the data's meaning. While managers will have their own ideas and interpretations, they are expecting more from process consultants than simply feedback and facilitation. Thus, coaching and related structural interventions that emerge from data gathering and feedback discussions are becoming increasingly important dimensions of process consultation.[85] When employed in such areas as organizational strategy, for example, process consultation skills must be buttressed by business and strategic knowledge and expertise (content skills) that can provide the organization and its management with appropriate direction and insight. While there should still be a sufficient Socratic process involved that the managers perceive ownership of the strategic challenge and prescription, the key is to achieve a blend of process and content foci.[86]

Process consultation is often used as part of *team building*, a process in which a group analyzes and evaluates its interactions with the intent of improving the process through which its members work together.[87] There are four major *goal categories* of team-building activities:[88]

1. *Goals:* To set various goals and/or priorities for the group
2. *Roles:* To analyze and/or allocate the way in which work is performed
3. *Processes:* To examine the way a group is working (its norms, decision making, and communication patterns)
4. *Interpersonal Relations:* To examine and enhance the relationships among the people actually doing the work

Although all of these purposes normally occur in a team-building effort, it is important to identify the one that is the primary purpose of the intervention. Unless this is accomplished, there will tend to be a considerable diffusion of the group's energy.

A number of conditions can serve as a guideline for effective team building.[89] First, the primary goal or outcome of the team-building session must be explicit and well articulated to group members. Second, the group's leader must perceive *ownership* of the primary goal and it must be fully *understood* and agreed to by group members. Finally, if change agents and consultants are utilized to work with a team, they should assist the leader in defining and sharing the primary purpose of the intervention as explicitly as possible.

In summary, team building is a process through which group members (1) develop a fuller understanding of the nature of group dynamics and effective teamwork, with particular emphasis on the interrelationship of process and content, and (2) learn to apply various group process principles and skills toward enhancing group effectiveness.

CONCLUSION

The importance and implications of groups for managers and their organizations are clear. As we will explore in the next chapter, one of the most significant illustrations of the importance of understanding group and intergroup dynamics in the workplace is the movement toward cross-functional, learning, self-managed and virtual work teams. An increasing number of corporations are assigning groups of workers day-to-day responsibility for managing themselves and their work. Many of these companies, however, are still in the process of learning how to effectively use these work teams and what must be done to ensure their success. In today's complex organizations, a successful firm requires the effective and efficient interaction of a number of different groups throughout its hierarchy. Considering that virtually all of our activities take place in a group context, a broad understanding of groups and their dynamics is an essential part of management education.

NOTES

1. K.L. Baettenhausen, "Five Years of Groups Research: What Have We Learned and What Needs to Be Addressed," *Journal of Management* 17, no. 2 (1991): 346; and A.P. Hare, "Roles, Relationships and Groups in Organizations: Some Conclusions and Recommendations," *Small Group Research* 34, no. 2 (2003): 123–155.

2. R.E. Park and E.W. Burgess, *Introduction to the Science of Sociology* (Chicago: University of Chicago Press, 1970), pp. 47–51. First published in 1921, this book contains a good overview of the foundations of sociology and the implications for individuals, groups, and society.

3. See M. Knowles and H. Knowles, *Introduction to Group Dynamics*, rev. ed. (New York: Association Press, 1972) for a basic treatment of group dynamics; see also S.L. Tubbs, *A Systems Approach to Small Group Interaction*, 3rd ed. (New York: Random House, 1988).

4. The distinction between work teams and self-enacted groups is drawn from R.E. Walton and J.R. Hackman, "Groups Under Contrasting Management Strategies," in P.S. Goodman, ed., *Designing Effective Work Groups* (San Francisco: Jossey-Bass, 1990), pp. 168–201. See also L. Argote and J.E. McGrath, "Group Process in Organizations: Continuity and Change," in C. Cooper and I.T. Robertson, eds., *International Review of Industrial and Organizational Psychology,* vol. 8 (New York: Wiley, 1993), pp. 333–389.

5. See Park and Burgess, op. cit., pp. 30–33.

6. G. Homans, *Social Behavior: Its Elementary Forms* (New York: Harcourt, Brace & World, 1961).

7. See Bettenhausen, op. cit., pp. 371–372.

8. L.L. Martin, F.J. Milliken, B.M. Wisenfeld, and S.R. Salgado, "Racioethnic Diversity and Group Members' Experiences: The Role of the Racioethnic Diversity of the Organizational Context," *Group & Organization Management* 28, no. 1 (2003): 75–107.

9. See, for example, W.E. Watson, K. Kumar, and M.K. Michaelsen, "Cultural Diversity's Impact on Interaction Process and Performance: Comparing Homogeneous and Diverse Task Groups," *Academy of Management Journal* 38, no. 2 (1993): 590–602; D.R. Ilgen, J.A. LePine, and J.R. Hollenbeck, "Effective Decision Making in Multinational Teams," in P.C. Earley and M. Erez, eds., *New Perspective on Industrial/Organizational Psychology* (San Francisco: New Lexington Press, 1997), pp. 377–409; and R.J. Volkeman and R.H. Gorman, "The Influence of Cognitive-Based Group Composition on Decision-Making Process and Outcomes," *Journal of Management Studies* 35, no. 1 (1998): 105–122.

10. W.E. Watson, L. Johnson, and D. Merritt, "Team Orientation, Self Orientation, and Diversity in Task Groups: Their Connection to Team Performance Over Time," *Group & Organization Management* 23, no. 2 (1998): 161–188.

11. See J. Fulk and B. Boyd, "Emerging Theories of Communication in Organizations," *Journal of Management* 17, no. 2 (1991): 415–423.

12. A. Van de Ven and A. Delbecq, "The Effectiveness of Delphi and Interacting Group Decision Making Process," *Academy of Management Journal* 17, no. 4 (1974): 605–621; A.R. Dennis and J.S. Valacich, "Group, Sub-Group and Nominal Group Idea Generation: New Rules for a New Media?" *Journal of Management* 20, no. 4 (1994): 723–735; B.L. Neiger, M.D. Barnes, R. Thackeray, and N. Lindman, "Use of the Delphi Method and Nominal Group Technique in Front-End Market Segmentation," *American Journal of Health Studies* 17, no. 3 (2001): 111–119; and C. Zopounidis and M. Doumpos, "Multicriteria Classification and Sorting Methods: A Literature Review," *European Journal of Operations Research* 138, no. 2 (2002): 229–246.

13. For good examples of the Delphi technique in action, see D. Hamilton and S. Breslawski, "Knowledge Acquisition for Multiple Site, Related Domain Expert Systems: Delphi Process and Applications," *Expert Systems with Applications* 11, no. 3 (1996): 377–389; M.M. Greenstein and D. Hamilton, "Critical Factors to Consider in the Development of an Audit Client Engagement Decision Expert Support System: A Delphi Study of Big Six Practicing Auditors," *Intelligent Systems in Accounting, Finance, and Management* 6 (1997): 215–234; and D. Hamilton, D. McFarland, and D. Mirchandani, "A Decision Model for Integration Across the Business Curriculum in the twenty-first Century," *Journal of Management Education* 24, no. 1 (2000): 102–126.

14. This discussion is based on Fulk and Boyd, op. cit., pp. 422–423; G.K. Easton, J.F. George, J.F. Nunamaker, and D.R. Vogel, "Using Two Different Electronic Meeting System Tools for the Same Task: An Experimental Comparison," *Journal of Management Information Systems* 7 (1990): 85–100; R.S. Hiltz and B. Wilman, "Asynchronous Learning Networks: As a Virtual Classroom," *Communications of the ACM* 40, no. 9 (1997): 44–49; and B.A. Jain and D.N. Ross, "Assessing the Impact of Integrated Group Support Systems on the Performance of Teams," *American Business Review* 16, no. 1 (1998): 105–111.

15. See T. Connolly, "Electronic Brainstorming: Science Meets Technology in the Group Meeting Room," in S. Kiesler, ed., *Culture of the Internet* (Hillsdale, NJ: Lawrence Erlbaum Associates, 1997), pp. 263–276; and W.L. Tullar, P.R. Kaiser, and P.A. Balthazard, "Group Work and Electronic Meeting Systems: From Boardroom to Classroom," *Business Communication Quarterly* 61, no. 4 (1998): 53–68.

16. R. Wegerif, "The Social Dimension of Asynchronous Learning Networks," *Journal*

of Asynchronous Learning Networks 2, no. 1 (1998): 34–49; and N.W. Coppola, S.R. Hiltz, and N.G. Rotter, "Becoming a Virtual Professor: Pedagogical Roles and Asynchronous Learning Networks," *Journal of Management Information Systems* 18, no. 4 (2002): 169–190.

17. G.D. Coleman and E.M. Van Aken, "Applying Small-Group Behavior Dynamics to Improve Action-Team Performance," *Employee Relations Today* (Autumn 1991): 343–353.

18. See M. Smith, *Persuasion and Human Interaction: A Review and Critique of Social Influence Theories* (Belmont, CA: Wadsworth, 1982).

19. P. Wallace, *Psychology of the Internet,* pp. 99–102.

20. See R.L. Kahn, E.M. Wolfe, R.P. Quinn, J.D. Snoek, and R.A. Rosenthal, *Organizational Stress Studies in Role Conflict and Ambiguity* (New York: Wiley, 1964); and S. Lieberman, "The Effects of Changes in Roles on the Attitudes of Role Incumbents," *Human Relations* 9 (1956): 385–402.

21. C. Fisher and R. Gitelson, "A Meta-Analysis of the Correlates of Role Conflict and Ambiguity," *Journal of Applied Psychology* 68 (1983): 320–333; M.F. Peterson, P.B. Smith, A. Akande, S. Ayestaran, S. Bochner, V. Callan, N.G. Cho, et al., "Role Conflict, Ambiguity, and Overload: A 21-Nation Study," *Academy of Management Journal* 38, no. 2 (1995): 429–452; and R. Caldwell, "The Changing Roles of Personnel Managers: Old Ambiguities, New Uncertainties," *Journal of Management Studies* 40, no. 4 (2003): 983–1005.

22. A.S. Tsui, S.J. Ashford, L. St. Clair, and K.R. Xin, "Dealing with Discrepant Expectations: Response Strategies and Managerial Effectiveness," *Academy of Management Journal* 38, no. 6 (1995): 1515–1543; and P.M. Valcour, "Managerial Behavior in a Multiplex Role System," *Human Relations* 55, no. 10 (2002): 1163–1188.

23. H. Arrow and J.E. McGrath, "Membership Dynamics in Groups at Work: A Theoretical Framework," in L.L. Cummings and B.M. Staw, eds., *Research in Organizational Behavior,* vol. 17 (Greenwich, CT: JAI Press, 1995), pp. 373–411.

24. See Bettenhausen, op. cit., pp. 347–348; J.C. Turner and P.J. Oakes, "The Significance of the Social Identity Concept for Social Psychology with Reference to Individualism, Interactionism and Social Influence," *British Journal of Social Psychology* 25 (1986): 237–252; and P.C.L. Heaven, "Group Identities and Human Values," *Journal of Social Psychology* 139, no. 5 (1999): 540–545.

25. M. Bornewasser and J. Bober, "Individual, Social Group and Intergroup Behavior: Some Conceptual Remarks on the Social Identity Theory," *European Journal of Social Psychology* 17 (1987): 267–276; M. Yuki, "Intergroup Comparisons versus Intragroup Relationships," *Social Psychology Quarterly* 66, no. 2 (2003): 166–183; and M.A. Hogg, "Social Identity Theory," in M.R. Leary and J.P. Tangney, eds., *Handbook of Self and Identity* (N.Y.: Guilford Press, 2003), pp. 462–479.

26. See C.M. Riordan and W.E. Weatherly, "Defining and Measuring Employees' Identification with Their Work Groups," *Educational and Psychological Measurement* 59 (1999): 310–324.

27. C.M. Riordan, "Relational Demography within Groups: Past Developments, Contradictions, and New Directions," *Research in Personnel and Human Resources Management* 19 (2000): 131–173; and P. Chattopadhyay, M. Tluchowska, and E. George, "Identifying the Ingroup: A Closer Look at the Influence of Demographic Dissimilarity on Employee Social Identity," *Academy of Management Review* 29 (2004): 180–202.

28. For a classic illustration of the effect of group norms on member performance see F.J. Roethlisberger and W.J. Dickson, *Management and the Worker* (Cambridge, MA: Harvard University Press, 1939), p. 387 ff; this section is also drawn from E. Schein, "Organizational Socialization and the Profession of Management," in D.A. Kolb, I.M. Rubin, and J. McIntyre, eds., *Organizational Psychology: A Book of Readings* (Englewood Cliffs, NJ: Prentice Hall, 1971).

29. See E. Asch, "Effects of Group Pressure upon the Modification and Distortion of Judgments," in H. Guetzkow (ed.), *Groups, Leadership and Men* (Pittsburgh, PA: Carnegie Press, 1951), pp. 177–190; and S.E. Asch, "Studies of Independence and Conformity: I. A Minority of One against a Unanimous Majority, *Psychological Monographs* 70 (Whole No. 416) (1956).

30. See, for example, L. Ross, G. Bierbrauer, and S. Hoffman, "The Role of Attribution Processes in Conformity and Dissent: Revisiting the Asch Situation," *American Psychologist* 31, no. 2 (1976): 148–157; and E. Lee and C. Nass, "Experimental Tests of Normative Group Influence and Representation Effects in Computer-Mediated Communication: When Interacting via Computers Differs from Interacting with Computers," *Human Communication Research* 28, no. 3 (2002): 349–381.

31. J.D. Rothwell, *In Mixed Company: Small Group Communication* (Fort Worth, TX: Harcourt Brace Jovanovich, 1992), pp. 66–67.

32. Smith, op. cit.

33. See C.R. Shepard, *Small Groups* (San Francisco: Chandler, 1954); L. Festinger, S. Schacter, and K. Baek, *Social Pressure in Informal Groups* (New York: Harper & Row, 1959). This section was also drawn from D.A. Cartwright, "The Nature of Group Cohesiveness," in D.A. Cartwright and A. Zander, eds., *Group Dynamics* (New York: Harper & Row, 1968); and P.A. Chansler, P.M. Swamidass, and C. Cammann, "Self-Managing Work Teams: An Empirical Study of Group Cohesiveness in 'Natural Work Groups' at a Harley-Davidson Motor Company Plant," *Small Group Research* 34, no. 1 (2003): 101–120.

34. See I. Summers, T. Coffelt, and R.E. Horton, "Work Group Cohesion," *Psychological Reports* 63 (1988): 627–636.

35. H.J. Grubb, "Social Cohesion as Determined by the Levels and Types of Involvement," *Social Behavior and Personality* 15 (1987): 87–89.

36. This section is based on P. Wallace, *The Psychology of the Internet* (New York: Cambridge University Press, 1999), pp. 55–59.

37. See S.C. Herring, ed., *Computer-Mediated Communication: Linguistic, Social and Cross-Cultural Perspectives* (Amsterdam: John Benjamins, 1998).

38. See M.R. Parks and K. Floyd, "Making Friends in Cyberspace," *Journal of Communication* 46, no. 1 (1996): 80–97.

39. Bettenhausen, op. cit., pp. 364–365.

40. See R.T. Mowday, L.W. Porter and R.M. Steers, *Employee-Organization Linkages: The Psychology of Commitment, Absenteeism, and Turnover* (San Diego: Academic Press, 1982); S.I. Tannenbaum, J.E. Mathieu, E. Salas, and J.A. Cannon-Bowers, "Meeting Trainees' Expectations: The Influence of Training Fulfillment on the Development of Commitment, Self-Efficacy, and Motivation," *Journal of Applied Psychology* 76, no. 6 (1991): 759–760; and D.G. Allen, L.M. Shore and R.W. Griffeth, "The Role of Perceived Organizational Support and Supportive Human Resource Practices in the Turnover Process," *Journal of Management* 29, no. 1 (2003): 99–118.

41. See, for example, R.J. Vandenberg and C. E. Lance, "Examining the Causal Order of Job Satisfaction and Organizational Commitment," *Journal of Management* 18, no. 1 (1992): 153–167.

42. J.P. Meyer, N.J. Allen, and I.R. Gellatly, "Affective and Continuance Commitment to the Organization: Evaluation of Measures and Analysis of Concurrent and Time-Lagged Relations," *Journal of Applied Psychology* 75, no. 6 (1990): 710–720; and L. Rhoades, R. Eisenberger, and S. Armeli, "Affective Commitment to the Organization: The Contribution of Perceived Organizational Support," *Journal of Applied Psychology* 86, no. 5 (2001): 825–837.

43. See, for example, J.P. Meyer, S.V. Paunonen, I.R. Gellatly, R.D. Goffin, and D.N. Jackson, "Organizational Commitment and Job Performance: It's the Nature of the Commitment That Counts," *Journal of Applied Psychology* 74 (1989): 152–156; and P.G. Irving and D.F. Coleman, "The Moderating Effect of Different Forms of Commitment on Role Ambiguity–Job Tension Relations," *Canadian Journal of Administrative Sciences* 20, no. 2 (2003): 97–120.

44. See I. Janis, *Victims of Groupthink* (Boston: Houghton Mifflin, 1972); and P.A. Kowert, *Groupthink or Deadlock: When Do Leaders Learn from Their Advisors?* (Albany, NY: State University of New York Press, 2002).

45. G. Moorhead, R. Ference and C.P. Neck, "Group Decision Fiascoes Continue: Space Shuttle Challenger and a Revised Groupthink Framework," *Human Relations* 44 (1991): 539–550; and D. Vaughan, *The Challenger Launch Decision: Risky Technology, Culture and Deviance at NASA* (Chicago: University of Chicago Press, 1996).

46. J. Schwartz and M.L. Wald, "'Groupthink' Is 30 Years Old, and Still Going Strong," *New York Times*, March 9, 2003, pp. 4–5.

47. See, for example, C.R. Leana, "A Partial Test of Janis' Groupthink Model: Effects of Group Cohesiveness and Leader Behavior on Defective Decision Making," *Journal of Management* 11 (1985): 5–7; and J. Eaton, "Management Communication: The Threat of Groupthink," *Corporate Communications* 6, no. 4 (2001): 183–192.

48. See, for example, P.D. Bliese and R.R. Halverson, "Group Consensus and Psychological Well-Being: A Large Field Study," *Journal of Applied Social Psychology* 28, no. 7 (1998): 563–581; C. MacCauley, "The Nature of Social Influence in Groupthink: Compliance and Internalization," *Journal of Personality and Social Psychology* 57 (1989): 250–260; P.R. Bernthal and C.A. Insko, "Cohesiveness Without Groupthink: The Interactive Effects of Social and Task Cohesion," *Group & Organization Management* 18, no. 1 (1993): 66–87; and Y. Kim, "A Comparative Study of the 'Abilene Paradox' and 'Groupthink'," *Public Administrative Quarterly* 25, no. 2 (2001): 168–190.

49. This section is based on N. Kogan and M.A. Willach, "Risk Taking as a Function of the Situation, the Person, and the Group," in *New Directions in Psychology III* (New York: Holt, Rinehart & Winston, 1967); A. Vinokur, "Distribution of Initial Risk Levels and Group Decision Involving Risk," *Journal of Personality and Social Psychology* 13 (1969): 207–214; and R.D. Clark III and E.P. Willems, "Where Is the Risky Shift? Dependence on Instructions," *Journal of Personality and Social Psychology* 13 (1969): 215–221.

50. R.F. Bordley, "A Bayesian Model of Group Polarization," *Organizational Behavior and Human Performance* 32 (1983):

262–274; A. Vinokur and E. Burnstein, "Effects of Partially Shared Persuasive Arguments on Group Induced Shifts," *Journal of Personality and Social Psychology* 29 (1974): 305–315; S.B. Sitkin and L.R. Weingart, "Determinants of Risky Decision-Making Behavior: A Test of the Mediating Role of Risk Perceptions and Propensity," *Academy of Management Journal* 38, no. 6 (1995): 1573–1592; and N.E. Friedkin, "Choice Shift and Group Polarization," *American Sociological Review* 64, no. 6 (1999): 856–875.

51. See Tubbs, op. cit., pp. 338–339; J.E. McGrath and D.A. Kravitz, "Group Research," *Annual Review of Psychology* 33 (1982): 195–230.

52. See S. Robbins, *Organizational Behavior: Concepts, Controversies, and Applications* (Englewood Cliffs, NJ: Prentice Hall, 1983), p. 246.

53. Wallace, *Psychology of the Internet*, pp. 73–78.

54. O. Dahlback, "A Conflict Theory of Group Risk Taking," *Small Group Research* 34, no. 3 (2003): 251–289.

55. See M. Maier, "Ten Years After a Major Malfunction . . .: Reflecting on 'The Challenger Syndrome'," *Journal of Management Inquiry* 11, no. 3 (2002): 282–293.

56. B. Latane, K. Williams, and S. Harkins, "Many Hands Make Light Work: The Causes and Consequences of Social Loafing," *Journal of Personality and Social Psychology* 37 (1979): 822–832; and D.R. Comer. "A Model of Social Loafing in Real Work Groups," *Human Relations* 48, no. 6 (1995): 647–667.

57. See N. Kugihara, "Gender and Social Loafing in Japan," *Journal of Social Psychology* 139, no. 4 (1999): 516–526.

58. D. Forsyth, *Group Dynamics* (Pacific Grove, CA: Brooks/Cole, 1990); and Rothwell, op. cit., pp. 75–76.

59. This discussion was drawn from Bettenhausen, op. cit., pp. 360–361; S.G. Harkins and K. Szymanski, "Social Loafing and Group Evaluation," *Journal of Personality and Social Psychology* 56 (1989): 934–941; B. Mullen, C. Symons, L. Hu, and E. Salas, "Group Size, Leadership Behavior, and Subordinate Satisfaction," *Journal of General Psychology* 116 (1989): 155–170; K.H. Price, "Working Hard to Get People to Loaf." *Basic and Applied Social Psychology* 14, no. 3 (1993): 329–344; B. Guerin, "Social Behaviors as Determined by Different Arrangements of Social Consequence: Diffusion of Responsibility Effects with Competition," *Journal of Social Psychology* 143, no. 3 (2003): 313–330; and S.M. Murphy, S.J. Wayne, R.C. Liden, and B. Erdogan, "Understanding Social Loafing: The Role of Justice Perceptions and Exchange Relationships," *Human Relations* 56, no. 1 (2003): 61–84.

60. P.C. Earley, "Social Loafing and Collectivism: A Comparison of the United States and the People's Republic of China," *Administrative Science Quarterly* 34 (1989): 565–581; and P.C. Earley, "East Meets West Meets Mideast: Further Explorations of Collectivistic and Individualistic Work Groups," *Academy of Management Journal* 36 (1993): 319–348.

61. See Rothwell, op. cit., pp. 98–101.

62. The discussion of stages in group development is based on B. Tuckman, "Developmental Sequence in Small Groups," *Psychological Bulletin* 63, no. 6 (1965): 384–399; M.F. Maples, "Group Development: Extending Tuckman's Theory," *Journal for Specialists in Group Work* 13 (1988): 17–23; and Rothwell, op. cit., pp. 55–80. It remains the basis for recent work on teams and team development; see, for example, G.L. Stewart, C.C. Manz, and H.P. Sims, *Team Work and Group Dynamics* (New York: Wiley, 1999), pp. 82–88.

63. S.A. Wheelan, B. Davidson, and F. Tilin, "Group Development Across Time: Reality or Illusion?" *Small Group Research* 34, no. 2 (2003): 223–246.

64. E. Bormann, *Small Group Communication: Theory and Practice* (New York: Harper & Row, 1990).

65. See C.R. Graham, "A Model of Norm Development for Computer-Mediated Teamwork," *Small Group Research* 34, no. 3 (2003): 322–342.

66. The discussion of the reforming stage is drawn from J.G. Clawson, *Level Three Leadership* (Upper Saddle River, NJ: Prentice Hall, 2003), pp. 193–194.

67. See, for example, S.G. Harris and R.I. Sutton, "Functions of Parting Ceremonies in Dying Organizations," *Academy of Management Journal* 29 (1986): 5–30; P.M. Ginter, W.J. Duncan, and L.E. Swayne, "When Merger Means Death: Organizational Euthanasia and Strategic Choice," *Organizational Dynamics* 20, no. 3 (1992): 21–33; and V. LaFarge and A.J. Nurick, "Mourning Becomes Elective: Teaching About and Managing Termination in the Classroom," *Journal of Management Education* 17, no. 1 (1993): 27–38.

68. See C.J. Gersick, "Time and Transition in Work Teams: Toward a New Model of Group Development," *Academy of Management Journal* 31, no. 1 (1988): 9–41; C.J. Gersick, "Marking Time: Predictable Transitions in Group Tasks," *Academy of Management Journal* 32, no. 2 (1989): 274–309; and A. Chang, P. Bordia, and J. Duck, "Punctuated Equilibrium and Linear Progression: Toward a New Understanding of Group Development," *Academy of Management Journal* 46, no. 1 (2003): 106–125.

69. This section is based on Schein, op. cit.; and D.C. Feldman, "The Multiple Socialization of Organizational Members," *Academy of Management Review* 6 (1981): 309–318. See also R.T. Pascale, "The Paradox of 'Corporate Culture': Reconciling Ourselves to Socialization," *California Management Review* 27, no. 2 (1985): 26–41.

70. See J.P. Wanous, *Organizational Entry,* 2nd ed. (Reading, MA: Addison-Wesley, 1992).

71. See R.M. Guion and W.M. Gibson, "Personnel Selection and Placement," *Annual Review of Psychology* 36 (1985): 573–611.

72. S.L. Premack and J.P. Wanous, "A Meta-Analysis of Realistic Job Preview Experiments," *Journal of Applied Psychology* 70 (1985): 706–719; J.A. Breaugh, "Realistic Job Previews: A Critical Appraisal and Future Research Directions," *Academy of Management Review* 8, no. 4 (1983): 612–619; and B.R. Kupperschmidt, "Unlicensed Assistive Personnel Retention and Realistic Job Previews," *Nursing Economics* 20, no. 6 (2002): 279–283.

73. R. Moreland and J. Levine, "Group Dynamics Over Time: Development and Socialization in Small Groups," in J. McGrath, ed., *The Social Psychology of Time* (Beverly Hills: Sage, 1989).

74. J.B. Vancouver and N.W. Schmitt, "An Exploratory Examination of Person-Organization Fit: Organizational Goal Congruence," *Personnel Psychology* 44, no. 2 (1991): 333–352; and T.N. Bauer and S.G. Green, "The Effect of Newcomer Involvement in Work-Related Activities: A Longitudinal Study of Socialization," *Journal of Applied Psychology* 79 (1994): 211–223.

75. See K.H. Dansky, "The Effect of Group Mentoring on Career Outcomes," *Group & Organization Management* 21, no. 1 (1996): 5–22; and A. Ritchie and P. Genoni, "Group Mentoring and Professionalism: A Programme Evaluation," *Library Management* 23, nos. 1/2 (2002): 68–78.

76. See G.R. Jones, "Psychological Orientation and the Process of Organizational Socialization: An Interactionist Perspective," *Academy of Management Review* 8, no. 3 (1993): 464–474; M.R. Louis, B.Z. Posner, and G.N. Powell, "The Availability and Helpfulness of Socialization Practices," Personnel Psychology 36 (1983): 857–881; D.C. Feldman and J.M. Brett, "Coping with New Jobs: A Comparative Study of New Hires and Job Changers," *Academy of Management Journal* 26 (1983): 258–272; and L.M. Finklestein, T.D. Allen, and L.A. Rhoton, "An Examination of the Role of Age in Mentoring Relationships," *Group & Organization Management* 28, no. 2 (2003): 249–280.

77. See, for example, B.A. Ashford, A.M. Saks, and R.T. Lee, "Socialization and Newcomer Adjustment: The Role of Organizational Context," *Human Relations* 51, no. 7 (1998): 897–926.

78. E.W. Morrison, "Longitudinal Study of the Effects of Information Seeking on Newcomer Socialization," *Journal of Applied Psychology* 73 (1993): 173–183.

79. K.D. Benne and P. Sheats, "Functional Roles of Group Members," *Journal of Social Issues* 4 (1948): 41–49; I.D. Steiner, *Group Process and Productivity* (New York: Academic Press, 1972), pp. 7–9; and "Group Dynamics: Who's Who in Groups," *International Journal of Bank Marketing* 9, no. 6 (1991): 21–24.

80. J.L. Moreno, "Contributions of Sociometry to Research Methodology in Sociology," *Sociological Review* 12 (1947): 287–292; and J. Goczol and C. Scoubeau, "Corporate Communication and Strategy in the Field of Projects," *Corporate Communications* 8, no. 1 (2003) 60–67.

81. See J.L. Moreno, *Who Shall Survive?* (Beacon, NY: Beacon House, 1953); and C.C. Foster, "A Study of a Large Sociogram 111: Reciprocal Choice Probabilities as a Measure of Social Distance," *Behavioral Science* 16, no. 5 (1971): 429–435.

82. R.F. Bales, *Interaction Process Analysis* (Reading, MA: Addison-Wesley, 1950); and R.F. Bales, S.P. Cohen, and S.A. Williamson, *SYMLOG: A System for the Multiple Level Observation of Groups* (New York: Free Press, 1980).

83. For the complete discussion of these observation categories, see P.G. Hanson, "What to Look for in Groups," in L.P. Bradford, *Making Meetings Work* (La Jolla, CA: University Associates, 1976), pp. 104–107; and J.W. Pfeiffer and J.E. Jones, eds., *The 1972 Annual Handbook for Group Facilitators* (San Diego, CA: Pfeiffer, 1972).

84. The following discussion is drawn from E.H. Schein, *Process Consultation* (Reading, MA: Addison-Wesley, 1969).

85. See E.H. Schein, "A General Philosophy of Helping: Process Consultation," *Sloan Management Review* 31, no. 3 (1990): 57–64; E.A. Fagenson and W.W. Burke, "The Activities of Organization Development Practitioners at the Turn of the Decade of the 1990s," *Group & Organization Studies* 15, no. 4 (1990): 376–377; and D.T. Hall, K.L. Otazo, and G.P. Hollenbeck, "Behind Closed Doors: What Really Happens in Executive Coaching," *Organizational Dynamics* (Winter 1999): 39–53.

86. J.J. O'Connell, "Process Consulting in a Content Field: Socrates in Strategy," *Consultation* 9, no. 3 (1990): 199–208; and R. Bouwen, "Developing Relational Practices for Knowledge Intensive Organizational Contexts," *Career Development International* 6, no. 7 (2001): 361–369.

87. Much of the following discussion is drawn from W. Dyer, *Team Building: Issues and Alternatives* (Reading, MA: Addison-Wesley, 1971); and M.S. Plovnick, R.E. Fry, and W.W. Burke, *Organization Development: Exercises, Cases and Readings* (Boston: Little, Brown, 1982), Chapter 13. See also J. Bradley, B.J. White, and B.E. Mennecke, "Teams and Tasks: A Temporal Framework for the Effects of Interpersonal Interventions on Team Performance," *Small Group Research* 34, no. 3 (2003): 353–374.

88. R. Beckhard, "Optimizing Team-Building Efforts," *Journal of Contemporary Business* 1, no. 3 (1971): 23–32. See also, S. Lembke and M.G. Wilson, "Putting the 'Team' into Teamwork: Alternative Theoretical Contributions for Contemporary Management Practice," *Human Relations* 51, no. 7 (1998): 927–944; and J. Gordon, "A Perspective on Team Building," *Journal of American Assembly of Business* 2, no. 1 (2002): 184–188.

89. Beckhard, "Optimizing Team-Building Efforts," pp. 23–24; and P. Whitehead, "Team-Building and Culture Change: Well-Trained and Committed Teams Can Successfully Roll Out Culture Change," *Journal of Change Management* 2, no. 2 (2001): 184–192.

Work Teams and Intergroup Relations: Managing Collaboration and Conflict

As the twenty-first century continues to unfold, it is becoming increasingly clear that business organizations will have to continue to become more customer and stakeholder focused, using employee talent to create, share, and utilize information as part of a broad-based competitive strategy. As we will explore in Chapter 9, as part of this transition organizations are undergoing significant structural change, developing horizontal networks of task-focused teams leading to "delayered," flatter organizational structures.[1] The resultant twenty-first-century organization will be increasingly dependent on team performance, organized around processes rather than tasks, and driven by customer needs and inputs.[2]

WORK TEAMS

Although there are still many jobs in firms today that can be handled more effectively and efficiently by one person, a basic aspect of modern organizational life is that fewer work assignments are fully performed by one individual alone. Indeed, teams are increasingly being employed in literally every type of organization in every industry, from restaurants and traditional assembly-line manufacturing environments to service-oriented and high-technology companies.[3]

Just as there are differences between amalgamations of individuals and groups, there is significant variability in the ways workgroups and teams are structured, with important implications for team functioning. In an ideal sense, work teams should be structured to (1) maximize member and team proficiency and success in task-related assignments and (2) coordinate and integrate each member's efforts with those of the other team members.[4] In practice, however, teams run the gamut from arrangements where members are assigned to a team, yet are still largely accountable for individual contributions and report to a manager, to teams in which members are mutually empowered and accountable for group outcomes. There are also a variety of ways work teams are structured, ranging from teams that have distinct formal hierarchies, to truly self-managed nonhierarchical teams, to virtual teams.

179

TABLE 6-1 **Work Groups and Teams: Similarities and Differences**

	Workgroups	**Teams**
Accountability	Individual accountability	Individual and team accountability
	Accountable to a manager	Members are mutually accountable to each other
Orientation	Fulfill narrowly defined duties	Focus on broader, external needs (e.g., serving customers)
	Group members as individuals	Cognitive and emotional investment of members where they identify themselves as a team
Leadership	Assigned to single person	Shared leadership
Work Assignments	Individually based	Collective work products
	goals and objectives assigned	Team understands organizational strategy and creates goals and objectives within that context
	Organization controlled	Team controlled
Meetings	Focused on efficiency	Focused on open-ended discussion and problem-solving
	Discuss, decide, and delegate	Discuss, decide, and engage in collaborative, real-time work
Decision Making	Social pressures impede divergent thinking	Divergent thinking is encouraged
	Group members screen/filter outside information	Information from outside the team is sought

Source: Adapted from R. Katzenbach and D.K. Smith, *The Wisdom of Teams: Creating the High Performance Organization* (New York: Harper Business, 1993); S. Lembke and M.G. Wilson, "Putting the 'Team' into Teamwork: Alternative Theoretical Contributions for Contemporary Management Practice," *Human Relations*, vol. 51, no. 7 (1998), 927–944; and G.L. Stewart, C.C. Manz, and H.P. Sims, *Team Work and Group Dynamics* (New York: John Wiley & Sons, 1999).

Table 6-1 captures some of the key distinctions in the literature between workgroups and true teams. Although teams share some of the characteristics of workgroups, ideal teams are nonhierarchical entities designed to provide a supportive, egalitarian environment that encourages and facilitates sharing information and ideas among members. While workgroups typically have a strong, clearly focused leader, teams often have shared leadership responsibilities among their members. Similarly, in workgroups individual accomplishments are typically recognized and rewarded, while teams emphasize team-related accomplishments and individual efforts that contribute to the team's success.[5]

Managing Teams

As discussed in Chapter 5, Richard Beckhard's seminal work on team building[6] has influenced researchers and practitioners to focus on the importance of providing teams with a clear sense of (1) their goals and objectives, (2) the roles expected of individual members, (3) the procedures and processes through which team members interact with one another, and (4) the interpersonal relationships and potential conflicts that develop among team members. As we will explore, in addition to these intragroup development processes, research indicates that team effectiveness (in terms of performance and viability) is also influenced and shaped by team-related boundaries and boundary-spanning roles (e.g., work team differentiation, external integration) and the broader organizational context (e.g., culture, structure, operating systems, reward systems) in which the team operates.[7]

Although it is important to fulfill these various needs and requirements, business organizations and their managers often make a number of common errors when attempting to use teams.[8] Many managers, for example, refer to a group of organizational members as a team, but manage them as individuals. In such situations, "team" performance is typically limited to the sum of individual outputs rather than the collaborative combination of member knowledge, skills, and abilities. Similarly, those responsible for overseeing teams often focus either on providing too much direction rather than ensuring team-based authority or tearing down existing structure(s) without creating or providing enabling team supports and/or resources. Related difficulties focus on encouraging participation in a decision that has already been made, assuming that people are eager to work in teams, and that individuals have the requisite skills to be effective team members. Such shortsighted decisions and assumptions constrain the willingness and ability of team members to fully interact and collaborate with each other, readily limiting team effectiveness.

Teams and Social Identity Theory

The effectiveness of any organizational team is, to a large extent, influenced by the extent to which these basic requirements are fulfilled. It is important to remember, however, that introducing teamwork and team-based activities into an organization is a complex process involving a number of interacting dynamics that are typically difficult to control. As such, some observers suggest that these realities make it difficult to directly apply the traditional group dynamics model—forming, storming, norming, and performing (see Chapter 5)—to team development.[9]

As suggested by Table 6-1, for teams to be truly effective their members must have sufficient emotional attachment to the team that it creates a sense of dedication and commitment to team activities. This dedication and commitment, in turn, facilitates the development of enhanced cognitive capabilities as members effectively pool their knowledge and strive to achieve superior performance. *Social identity theory* suggests that this cognitive change and emotional investment, in contrast to membership and interaction per se, are the critical parts of the unification process that discourage members from thinking of themselves as individuals pursuing their own personal motives and agendas.[10] Team formation is, thus, increasingly described as an adaptive psychological process, captured by the transition from feeling and thinking as individuals (personal identity), to feeling and thinking as representatives of the team (social identity). *Personal identity* refers to an individual's concern about personal benefits, while *social identity* is defined in terms of concern about the benefits of the larger social unit.[11] Once a team identity is adopted, the team rather than the individual members becomes the unit of analysis.

This perspective on team development raises a number of implications for managers and their organizations.[12] While member familiarization (e.g., forming, norming) may gradually improve performance, team identification—in essence one's self-categorization as a team member—is the key to enhanced innovation and productivity. Thus, it is important that managers ensure that team members are fully aware of the interdependence of their roles and responsibilities. Team activities should also be presented in ways that (1) are attractive to team members (enhancing the emotional component of *wanting* to be part of the team) and (2) increase member expectations that the team will achieve valued outcomes (e.g., the team will be provided with the resources it needs to succeed; team output is expected to receive appropriate recognition by the organization). Team members thus require a high level of conceptual information to gain a fuller understanding and appreciation of their contribution to the team, what the team is trying to achieve, and its relationship to the broader organizational context (e.g., other organizational teams, organizational strategy). Social identity theory provides us with insights into the cognitive and emotional elements involved in teamwork, emphasizing the need for managers to change the ways in which they interact with and provide information to team members.

Trust Building and Teamwork

Mutual trust among team members has been established as an important aspect of effective work teams. Trust facilitates individual behaviors that help establish norms that are important for creating value from teams, such as openness and cognitive conflict. Trust also allows team members to raise and discuss divergent ideas, which is important for creativity and innovation.[13] Moreover, trust is positively associated with extra-role behavior in work teams, which further contributes to favorable team performance.[14]

When people are first placed on a team, they may not simply assume that their teammates are trustworthy.[14] Instead some people initially suspend the belief that the others share common values and are trustworthy. Whereas stereotyping or perceptions of value incongruence can readily lead to distrust (see Chapter 2), most people start their membership on a team with tentative or conditional trust. *Conditional trust* is a willingness to interact with others as long as each behaves appropriately, uses a similar interpretive scheme to define the situation, and can take the role (empathy) of the other. This level of trust is usually sufficient to facilitate a wide range of social and economic exchanges, and appears to be the most common form of trust that exists in organizations today. *Unconditional trust*, in contrast, reflects a much higher level of trust where shared values not only structure the social situation but become the primary mechanism through which team members experience trust. Rather than simply suspending belief, one's teammates' trustworthiness is assumed, based on confidence in the others' values and repeated behavioral interactions, further contributing to a sense of mutual identification.

Team member demographic diversity has been found to be closely associated with the development of trust and mutually beneficial efforts among team members. A long line of research on the similarity-attraction paradigm has established that similarity with regard to salient or contextually relevant social group memberships tends to foster assumptions of competence and shared values and goals among individuals.[16] These shared beliefs lead more easily to positive expectations of each other and of the group experience, and thus to mutual trust and positive group norms and performance.[17]

Indeed, research has found homogeneous groups to develop functional performance norms more quickly than diverse groups, often outperforming diverse groups, especially in the short run.[18]

As the business world places greater emphasis on the need for collaboration and teamwork, the role of trust, especially at the team level, becomes an increasingly important factor in performance and effectiveness. Part of the challenge for managers is to create a setting in which appropriate levels of trust are nurtured over time.[19] To what extent does the work environment and broader organizational context promote positive attitudes, moods, and emotions? Does the organization's culture encourage an expression of the values underlying trust? Are organizational members provided with the opportunity to explore shared values? Is information widely shared with organizational members? Does the reward system support and encourage sharing and collaboration? To what extent does the organizations' structure provide appropriate task and reporting relationships that facilitate the development of favorable attitudes? As we will explore in subsequent chapters, it takes considerable time, effort, and resources to satisfactorily respond to these questions. As organizations choose to undertake a team-based approach to their work activities, however, these efforts are necessary to develop the level of collaboration and teamwork that creates high levels of performance and competitive advantage.

Teams in Action

As illustrated in Table 6-2, work teams range from task forces and project teams that have a relatively narrow and temporary focus, to problem-solving teams such as quality circles that focus on a broader set of goals, problems, and solutions, to self-managed teams that fully control their work processes and procedures. As an illustration of the subtleties and complexities associated with these different types of teams, this section briefly looks at the key aspects of each of these teams.

TABLE 6-2 Types of Teams

Team Type	Focus	Degree of Autonomy
Project Teams	Emphasis is placed on solving a particular problem or finishing an assigned project	Low–Moderate
Problem-Solving Teams	Emphasis is placed on solving problems in the work area and/or improving work processes	Moderate
Self-Managed Teams	Emphasis is placed on managing the overall internal work processes of the team, oriented toward increased productivity, innovation, and meeting the needs of key stakeholders (owners, customers, other employees, and teams)	High

Source: Adapted from T.P. Moses and A.J. Stahelski, "A Productivity Evaluation of Teamwork at an Aluminum Manufacturing Plant," *Group & Organization Management,* vol. 24, no. 3 (1999), p. 393.

Project Teams

Project teams are typically made up of individuals from different departments or work units. While such teams can be permanent fixtures in an organization, project teams are typically temporary and focused on a particular problem or project. Once the problem is resolved or the project is completed, the team disbands and its members return to their original work unit.

A specific type of project-oriented team is the *cross-functional team.* Multidisciplinary cross-functional teams share many of the characteristics of conventional teams, but they differ in important ways.[20] First, they are typically composed of individuals who are members of another subunit of the organization. Such teams promise improved integration across the diverse skills and expertise that exist in research and development, production, marketing, and other key functional groups. The driving force underlying the use of these teams is the belief that when representatives from all relevant areas of expertise are brought together, team decisions and actions will be more likely to address the full range of perspectives and vantage points necessary for the success of a collective venture.[21] However, even though team members may identify with the particular cross-functional team they are assigned to, they have another, potentially competing social identity with another organizational unit. Thus, it is important that a cross-functional team work on creating strong interpersonal ties among its members. Care must be taken, however, that such social cohesion is not overemphasized as it can undermine the team's focus on its relevant tasks.

Second, because they are often temporary and highly task-focused, these teams are faced with significant pressure to perform. Since there can be initial conflict across the different perspectives and orientations of team members, the early development of effective group processes is critical. Thus, it is important that these teams quickly receive the requisite training, coaching, and organizational support that will facilitate collaboration. Finally, performance expectations tend to be highly focused as these teams are often called upon to reduce cycle time, create knowledge, develop new products, and disseminate organizational learning. Thus, it is important for team leaders to actively monitor team projects and progress, encourage risk taking by team members, and ensure input from customers and other key stakeholders.

Problem-Solving Teams: Quality Circles

Problem-solving teams consist of organizational members who volunteer to examine problems affecting their work. Perhaps the most well-known problem-solving team is the *quality circle,* a team that is specifically aimed at improving the quality of production or service through highly committed and involved organizational members. A quality circle (QC) is a group of approximately ten relatively autonomous workers who volunteer to meet regularly to assess ways to improve the quality of products (or service), the production process in their part of the organization, and their working environment. The long-term objectives of QCs are: (1) to create a sense of responsibility for improving product and service quality; (2) to generate concern over productivity and production costs; (3) to enhance the motivation of employees; and (4) to develop supervisory and managerial talent. A more immediate goal is simply to foster an exchange of ideas and enhance knowledge sharing that is uninhibited by such barriers as company rank or age.[22]

The concept underlying QCs is that, provided with the proper training, organizational members can discover and correct previous quality problems. Thus, instead of leaving quality control to the province of quality control engineers, this concern is made the responsibility of *all* employees. However, while the concept itself is disarmingly simple, its effective application is not. Unfortunately, this apparent simplicity has led to an overselling of the technique as a panacea for worker-related and quality problems.[23]

Most successful problem-solving teams share a number of key elements:[24]

1. *Employee-development oriented:* Since a key purpose of these teams is to foster employee growth and development, management should not "use" these teams to further their own pet ideas or projects. Team members should identify, select, and solve problems from their areas of expertise and focus on projects related to their actual job responsibilities.

2. *Upper-level management support:* Top management must be willing to support, encourage, and listen to team recommendations. Recognition must also be granted for ideas emerging from team discussions and analyses. One of the quickest ways for the necessary trust underlying a problem-solving team to be undermined is if a manager attempts to manipulate team members or tries to take credit for improvements made by the team.

3. *Voluntary membership:* Members who are forced to join the team are rarely active participants. The team itself should deal with issues around membership and member effectiveness—the energy and enthusiasm of team members are crucial for the ultimate success of the team.

4. *Information sharing:* Members must have access to critical information (such as warranty, production, and scrap data in a manufacturing environment, or customer satisfaction surveys in a service environment) if they are to actually solve organizational problems. Very often such information is not made available in a timely fashion or in a form usable by team members.

5. *Evaluation:* Finally, problem-solving teams should be evaluated as a way of improving their effectiveness. Such evaluations should be as comprehensive as possible, focusing on input, process, and output variables and providing direct feedback to the team. Information used should include both self-reported data from team members and objective measures of the team's performance.

Self-Managed Work Teams

Self-managed work teams are groups of employees who are given substantial responsibility for the planning, organizing, scheduling, and production of work processes and outcomes.[25] As we will explore in the next chapter, the idea of empowered, self-managed work teams emphasizes a move away from leader dominance and expert problem solving to a system where organizational members, as the new experts, are continuously involved in organizational decision processes. While traditional models of power and authority were based on position and status, self-managed teams emphasize the involvement of all organizational members in efforts to continuously improve work systems and outcomes. As illustrated in Figure 6-1, team leadership roles can

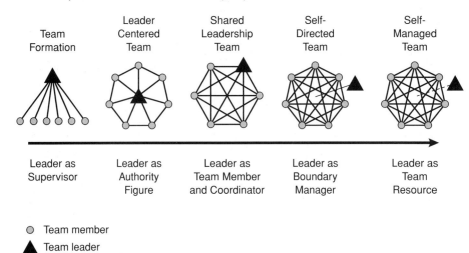

Figure 6-1 Evolution of Leadership in Collocated Teams

Source: Adapted from C.C. Manz and J.W. Newstrom (1992). "Self-Managing Teams in a Paper Mill: Success Factors, Problems, and Lessons Learned," in R. Glazer (ed.), *Classic Readings in Self-Managing Teamwork.* King of Prussia, PA: Organization Design and Development, 1992, pp. 443–462.

range from early stage leader-centered teams to teams that are more self-directed and self-managed. This team evolution reflects very different roles for team leaders, from an initial "leader as supervisor" orientation to "leader as team resource" where they provide support for team efforts as necessary. The implication is that as the team "matures" it requires less directive leadership.[26] Emphasis is placed on team building and development, and over time, team leaders increasingly share power with the team and its members as a way to enhance team performance.

Members of self-managed teams typically do not have a direct supervisor and often make many of the management decisions previously made by first-line supervisors. Team members set goals, solve problems, resolve conflicts, assess performance, initiate change, and communicate upward in the organization. It is the responsibility of managers to provide accurate information to the teams, creating a culture that supports open communication and knowledge creation.[27]

There are a number of keys to supporting and empowering such self-managed work teams.[28] First, it is important for employees to have accurate and timely information on organizational performance and outcomes (e.g., firm operating results, competitor performance). Second, team members must be provided with the knowledge and skills that will enable them to understand and contribute to organizational performance. Third, these individuals must be rewarded for their contributions to organizational performance (e.g., stock ownership, gainsharing). Fourth, team members must also be given the power to make decisions that influence work procedures and organizational direction. Finally, a high level of trust building must take place between the organization, its management, and its members. The organization must make a firm commitment to its workforce, eliciting and responding to worker input and concerns, as it creates a base for resolving inevitable conflicts and promoting risk taking among the teams.

Learning Teams

As part of the rapid, often tumultuous, change that is taking place in our global business world, organizations are being pressured to speed up their learning processes, learning how to adapt faster and faster to the world that surrounds them.[29] Teams, as well as teams of teams, need to learn how to develop such knowledge bases, in essence learning how to learn together, effectively sharing information and building on each other's knowledge to create generative (double-loop) rather than simply adaptive (single-loop) learning patterns.[30] *Single-loop learning* is a routine process of using past experience to accomplish current objectives, without any significant analysis of that experience or change in its underlying assumptions. *Double-loop learning*, in contrast, uses past experience not only to reevaluate current objectives and ways to accomplish those objectives, but to question the underlying values and culture as well. Double-loop learning not only asks questions about objective facts but also explores the reasons and motives underlying those facts.[31]

In order to accomplish such double-loop learning, *learning teams* should: (1) have an environment in which individual members are encouraged to experiment, learn from each other, and develop their full potential; (2) extend this learning to include key stakeholders such as customers and suppliers as well as other organizational teams; (3) have a significant human resource development component; and (4) continually undergo a process of development and transformation.[32] As reflected in Figure 6-2, true team learning is the ability of members to share and build on their individual knowledge such that their collective knowledge enables them to continually improve team and organizational performance as well as to discover, develop, and implement

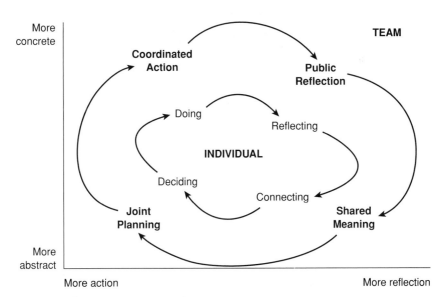

Figure 6-2   The Team Learning Cycle

Source: From *The Fifth Discipline Fieldbook,* by Peter Senge, Charlotte Roberts, et al., copyright © 1994 by Peter M. Senge, Art Kleiner, Charlotte Roberts, Richard B. Ross, and Bryan J. Smith. Used by permission of Doubleday, a division of Random House, Inc.

new ways of doing business. It builds on the learning cycles of individual team members (reflecting, connecting, deciding, doing), incorporating public reflection, developing shared meanings across team members, joint planning, and coordinating the actions and efforts of team members.[33] In addition to such *within-team* learning, effective teams also draw on *cross-team* learning (where the experience gained by one team is transplanted to another) and *market* learning (drawing on the knowledge gained from such external stakeholders as customers, suppliers, and competitors).[34] Finally, true learning teams also have the capability to revitalize themselves on an ongoing basis. Within this context, "unlearning" (i.e., discarding obsolete and misleading knowledge) can be just as important a process as developing and learning new knowledge.[35]

Successful learning teams require the mastery of a range of skills—self-knowledge, interpersonal, teamwork, problem solving, negotiating, and political—that demand significant exposure and practice.[36] Accordingly, for the level of sharing and knowledge building that is required in learning teams to occur, there are four critical success factors that facilitate and prepare team members to develop and bring these skills to their teams: (1) building a culture that supports learning; (2) building teams whose outcomes require innovation or paradigm shifts; (3) building teams that know, value, and use their individual and collective strengths; and (4) building teams whose members possess sufficient self-knowledge and self-mastery that they are able to develop extraordinary communication and process skills.[37]

It is important to underscore that the processes through which teams create new knowledge and understandings are nonlinear and highly interactive in nature. As we will explore in the next chapter, the creation and development of self-managed and learning teams requires managers to rethink their role, achieving a balance between being the "expert" and a coach-facilitator. In all too many instances, managers and first-level supervisors may find team-based management threatening, being more concerned with their own new roles and career paths than they are with the success of the team.[38] True peer learning, however, requires voluntary communication links within and across teams (which should be openly encouraged), open and honest communication (which should be modeled by the manager), and the belief that team members can learn from each other—that the knowledge and background of their colleagues can add value to the learning process. The way in which managers treat mistakes— as opportunities for development and insight rather than something to be avoided or punished—also shapes and influences the openness that team members have to learning and sharing. An underlying dilemma, especially in a downturn environment, is that as teams become leaner and have fewer resources at their disposal, they have less opportunity to learn.[39] Thus, for this approach to work, managers must foster, encourage, and continually reinforce such learning and interaction, creating a shared context in which individual members can interact with and learn from each other.

Virtual Teams

Our global business environment and the time pressures associated with completing projects and getting new products to worldwide markets are prompting organizations to tap the best people for those projects, regardless of where they are located. This development has given rise to a rapid increase in distributed workgroups, or virtual teams as they are more commonly known.[40] Like any team, a *virtual team* is a group of people who work on interdependent tasks guided by a common purpose. But unlike traditional, collocated teams, a virtual team works across space, time, and organizational boundaries that often extend across nations on a global basis. Facilitated by advanced information and communication technologies and groupware (project-management software that electronically links team members), virtual teams are developing the ability to "work together apart," completing assigned tasks while rarely, if ever, meeting face to face.[41] They are connected by e-mail, desktop video-conferencing, company intranets, and collaborative software/group support systems (such as Lotus Notes). Depending on the task involved, the duration of virtual teams can range from one to two weeks to several years. While many companies might still prefer to develop new products by pulling people together in a cross-functional team at one location for the duration of the project, this traditional strategy is becoming increasingly impractical—especially if a new product or process has to be simultaneously recast for markets around the world.

There are five primary reasons why companies are turning to virtual teams:[42]

1. The increasing prevalence of flat or horizontal organizational structures
2. Environmental pressures that require interorganizational cooperation (see Chapter 8)
3. The ongoing shift from production to service/knowledge work environments
4. The transnationalization of trade and business activity
5. Heightened worker expectations about participation and involvement

A basic managerial challenge is to get team members to work together—compatibly and productively—as a team even though face-to-face contact is limited and communication is largely confined to advanced technological devices. Such teams, however, can have different degrees of "virtualness," depending on: (1) the proportion of time that team members actually spend working virtually compared with face-to-face; (2) the proportion of team members at any one location; (3) the proportion of time that team members devote to the virtual team compared with time spent on other assignments; and (4) the extent to which there are existing relationships among team members. In reality, many teams are only moderately, rather than completely, virtual, interspersing traditional person-to-person interaction with technology-based communication to initiate and complete their tasks.[43]

Global Virtual Teams

As illustrated in Figure 6-3, there are several powerful centrifugal forces that act to pull apart global virtual teams, permanent challenges that do not fade over time: (1) pressures due to the immediacy of local versus corporate needs and pressures; (2) time-related problems as a result of different time zones; (3) cultural differences across different societies; and (4) a general sense of detachment from the team due to the lack of casual, face-to-face contact.[44] Pressure to pursue local priorities, for example, is perhaps the most powerful force encouraging team members to subordinate corporate objectives to the more immediate needs of colleagues in the same business unit and physical location. Casual, face-to-face contact occurs with local colleagues rather than with team members, undoubtedly encouraging the pursuit of local priorities rather

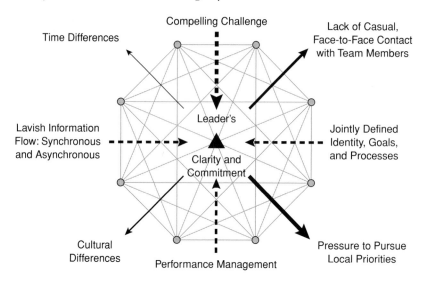

Figure 6-3   Dynamics in a Global Virtual Team

Source: K.W. Kerber and A.F. Buono, "Leadership Challenges in Global Virtual Teams: Lessons from the Field," *Sam Advanced Management Journal* 69, no. 4 (2004), p. 8. Used by permission of the authors.

than team objectives. This focus on meeting local needs is further reinforced by cultural differences that justify attention to local priorities and by time differences that reduce the opportunities for the team leader and team members to discuss team goals. In a virtual environment, these centrifugal forces tend not to diminish over the life of the team. They remain permanent forces pulling the team apart and must be counteracted on an ongoing basis.

While advanced information and communication technologies are crucial to overcoming these *centrifugal forces,* such technology is largely a pathway or enabler that allows the leader and the team to create counteracting forces that bring the team together. Creation of highly focused *centripetal forces* (see Figure 6-3) is critical to the ultimate success of these teams.

In order to build a high-performing global virtual team, members must first be faced with a *compelling business challenge* that is personally relevant and energizes them to overcome the difficulties associated with spatial distance, technological mediation, and a lack of direct interpersonal interaction. Second, a compelling challenge becomes that much more energizing when each team member is charged with determining how to achieve it, as team members *jointly define* the team's identity, goals, and processes. Third, *performance management* systems that define a clear context and set of expectations, rather than seeking tight management control, provide team members with the flexibility to consider (and balance) both corporate and local business unit needs. Fourth, the complex and challenging tasks faced by a virtual team require critical attention to team communication. While a lack of clarity around goals, tasks, and procedures can hinder any team, such ambiguity is heightened in global virtual teams. Finally, the effort needed by a team leader to build and maintain cohesiveness and trust in a virtual team may be greater than that required for collocated teams. This reality may place an additional burden on the virtual team leader's *commitment to* and *accountability for* the team and its outcomes. Demonstrating high levels of personal commitment, which may be among the most challenging and most highly leveraged methods for achieving virtual collaboration, sends a clear message to team members about the trustworthiness and sincerity of the team leader.

Facilitating Virtual Team Interaction

As with any team, early team-building interventions (clarifying goals, roles, processes, and relationships) are important. This process can help the team establish its mission and agree to a list of norms (e.g., how to share project information, how to deal with disagreements) that will guide its operation—especially during the formation of the team, when possible personal contact and socializing between team members are important contributing factors to the team's success. Paradoxically, the more virtual an organization is in practice, the more its people need to meet in person, creating a sufficient level of trust to facilitate subsequent virtual interactions.[45] Similar to the dynamics underlying learning teams, virtual team members must also have a good understanding of the knowledge, skills, and abilities of their teammates. Along these lines, it is important for team leaders to monitor the way in which the team works and ensure that information is passed along. It is also important to ensure that all important communications are kept in the team's shared database so that it can serve as a historical document of the team's work as well as a source to help socialize and inculcate new members. In fact, a good sign that a virtual team is not working well together is when the team database does not hold all the latest information. As companies that use virtual teams are quickly discovering, tending to the human factors underlying the arrangement greatly facilitates the success of the teams' projects.

Preparing virtual team leaders and members for their roles on a virtual team, helping them to develop the skills necessary to launch and sustain the team is a critical component of team success. Yet, research has suggested that the majority of organizations that utilize virtual teams do not provide any training for either leaders or team members.[46] Moreover, very few of the organizational training programs that do provide instruction on and preparation for virtual teams are rated as "very" or "extremely effective" by their members. Based on an extensive assessment of current and future training needs and practices, a prototype training program for virtual teams should include training modules for team leaders and members focused on:
Virtual Team Leaders:

- Selecting technology appropriate to the task
- Setting expectations, measuring and rewarding team contributions
- Coaching and mentoring virtual team members
- Modeling desired virtual team behaviors (e.g., responsiveness, using groupware to share information)

- Managing external team relations (e.g., with on-site managers, sponsors)

Virtual Team Leaders and Members:

- Face-to-face team-building sessions prior to launch that establish team identity, create a mission statement, establish team norms, and help to build trust
- Mastering virtual team technology (e.g., groupware, teleconference and videoconference protocols)
- Communication skills (e.g., electronic etiquette, cultural awareness, electronic brainstorming, decision making)
- Team management (e.g., virtual meeting logistics, clarifying roles and expectations, resolving conflict, setting and meeting milestones, evaluating team process and progress)

As reflected in Figure 6-4, differences in the time and location associated with various forms of information exchange possibilities among team members raise very different sets of communication issues and challenges. While facilitators are typically highly skilled in dealing with same time/same place (Quadrant I) types of interactions, they have far less experience, and are often less effective, in dealing with interactions in the other three quadrants. Most facilitation dealing with Quadrant I situations is what might be termed "active facilitation." In these situations, the facilitator applies process-oriented techniques (see Chapter 5) to guide team processes and interactions (e.g., initially leading the discussion, identifying key issues to be addressed, providing guidance on how the team might proceed), modifying the agenda, and/or raising questions or issues as deemed necessary. Far too many facilitation efforts in Quadrant IV, in contrast, tend to be "fixed-scripted" approaches, where the facilitator provides technical assistance, arranges the agenda and might even assist during initial process facilitation. Unlike "active facilitation" processes, however, the facilitator does not respond directly to evolving team needs, especially since most of the planning and

	Same Place	**Different Place**
Same Time	*Co-Located/Synchronous* • Face-to-face meetings and casual conversations • Technography • Decision-support rooms I	*Distributed/Synchronous* • Telephone conferencing • Video and Web conferencing • Distance whiteboarding • Instant messaging II
Different Time	III *Co-Located/Asynchronous* • Resource center • Team room • Operations center	IV *Distributed/Asynchronous* • Voice mail, e-mail • Computer conferencing • Groupware tools

Figure 6-4   Time and Place Dimensions of Team Information Exchange

intervention is performed prior to the actual interaction. Instead, such "fixed script facilitation" is far more prescriptive than interactive, and in some instances may even be embedded within the technology itself.[47]

As organizations increasingly turn to virtual teams, the challenge is to take what we know about Quadrant I facilitation and adapt it to the other three quadrants in Figure 6-4, especially in distributed/asynchronous interaction (Quadrant IV). Building on the basic strengths of good facilitation—observing behaviors, attending to both overt and symbolic content of team member behavior, and monitoring the emotions and feelings of team members—it is important to translate these skills into the asynchronous world of information technology systems. Some companies, for example, are experimenting with "hybrid meetings," where part of the meeting is physical and part virtual, with some team members physically present at the meeting and others "attending" from their offices via desktop videoconferencing and instant messaging technologies.[48] Especially as companies attempt to move beyond using such virtual teams as information sharing mechanisms (often referred to as *communities of practice*) to have them directly focused on completing organizational tasks and resolving project-related issues, facilitating teams that are geographically "distributed" raises unique challenges.

Team Conflict

Team conflict is generally defined as team members' awareness of discrepancies, incompatible wishes, or desires that are perceived to be irreconcilable.[49] Research on conflict within teams has established that not only is conflict an essential group process with regard to team effectiveness, but that conflict is multidimensional, including task (or cognitive) and affective (or emotional) dimensions.[50] *Task or cognitive conflict* emerges as a function of expressed differences in perspective related to a team's task. Some research suggests that this form of conflict is essentially unavoidable in teams, but that task conflict is functional and generally focused on judgmental differences about how best to achieve common goals and objectives. *Affective conflict* involves disagreements that are interpreted as, or become, personalized. Though this form of conflict is generally dysfunctional for work teams, affective conflict can emerge from individuals' misinterpretation of cognitive conflict, or a failure to recognize the difference between task-related (cognitive) and emotional (affective) conflicts.

As with trust among team members discussed above, demographic differences among members can lead to perceived and real differences in interpretations of the task and relational processes that occur in workgroups, resulting in conflict between team members. In-group members may hold negative expectations and stereotypes of out-group members, making them more likely to interpret out-group members' perspectives as diverging from their own, giving rise to intrateam affective conflict.[51]

INTERGROUP RELATIONS

As the preceding discussion suggests, work team performance is highly dependent on the extent to which team members (1) are willing to change, (2) are capable of communicating in an open and honest manner, (3) perceive themselves to be part of the team, (4) are willing to take initiative on behalf of the team, and (5) perceive that they have a future together.[52] Work teams, however, do not exist in a vacuum and it is necessary to examine the larger organizational context within which they operate. In fact, one way to think about an organization is to conceptualize it as a series of interrelated groups operating at various levels in a hierarchy. To this end, some researchers suggest that the study of all interpersonal interactions, from individual-level relations to macro-level organizational analysis, must be done with an understanding of the larger membership that these entities hold.[53] For instance, to fully understand the behavior and performance of a marketing department in a particular organization, we need to go beyond the interaction of its members per se and examine the department's interactions with other departments in the same organization as well as the interactions between the organization and its external stakeholders. Whenever there is an interaction between two groups or teams, an interface is formed that creates a new context within which the groups and teams must be understood.

Group Interdependence

An important determinant of organizational goal accomplishment is the extent to which both formal and informal groups view their goals as being congruent with those of the organization. Such perceived goal congruence is one of the underlying bases for cooperation and collaboration. Obviously, the greater the number of these different groups in a particular organization, the more difficult it can be to develop a sense of shared goals. This problem does vary, however, depending on the pattern of *interdependence* between the groups (i.e., the extent to which an action or change in one group affects another group).

As illustrated in Figure 6-5, there are four basic types of such interdependence: pooled, serial or sequential, reciprocal, and team.[54] *Pooled interdependence* describes a situation where two or more groups operate on parallel lines, sharing a common or

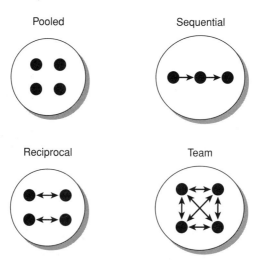

Figure 6-5   Types of Intergroup Interdependence

pooled resource, and doing the same set of tasks that is coordinated by a superordinate group. An example is a bank with a home office and a number of branches. Such pooled interdependence has little likelihood of conflict because the geographical areas served by the branches are different and intergroup interaction is largely through the total organization. In this instance, the interdependence is based on *results:* for the organization to be successful, individual units have to work well, but they do not have to work together.[55]

Sequential interdependence refers to a situation where one group must complete a task before another group can begin its task. A subassembly, such as an engine, must be completed before a car or a truck can be built. The engine manufacturing group has to finish its job before the assembly group can undertake its tasks. Since greater coordination and planning are required, there is an increased probability for conflict to develop.

Reciprocal interdependence refers to a situation where work done by one group is necessary to keep another group's work continuing, and this process has a feedback effect on the work of the former group. This can be thought of in terms of mutual interdependence among the two groups involved. In the IT world, for example, sales and technical support typically have reciprocal interdependence: Software sales relies on the technical support staff to resolve user-related problems, while technical support relies on software sales to identify application-related difficulties experienced by their customers.

Finally, *team interdependence* refers to those situations where multiple groups interact with each other. In essence, reciprocal interdependencies multiply as each group influences and is influenced by the other groups. An example is the product innovation process where research and development, production, purchasing, and marketing are involved in product changes. Given the high level of interaction, mutual support, and collaboration necessary, this type of interdependence has the greatest probability of conflict since coordination can be difficult. Thus, conflict between groups can emerge if these interdependencies are not effectively managed.

A related way of thinking about interdependence and intergroup interaction differentiates task and outcome interdependence.[56] *Task interdependence* refers to the interconnections between tasks such that the performance of one dimension of work depends on the completion of other work activities. Within this context, *initiated* task interdependence reflects the work flowing from one group to another (sequential interdependence), while *received* task interdependence refers to the extent to which an individual group is affected by the work flow from one or more other work activities. *Outcome interdependence* is the extent to which group members believe that their personal benefits and costs depend on successful goal attainment by other groups. *Positive* outcome interdependence occurs when a group believes that it will benefit from the success of other organizational groups. *Negative* outcome interdependence, in contrast, occurs when a group feels that the success of other organizational groups will make it less likely that it will achieve its goal (e.g., competition over scarce resources, dual proposals for a single client). As illustrated by a rich body of research, groups working under conditions of positive, rather than negative, outcome interdependence are much more open-minded regarding input and ideas from other groups, more concerned about each others' outcomes, and more inclined to collaborate and search for solutions or compromises.

A group's task (complexity, interdependence, predictability, and standardization) and technology (long-linked, mediating, and intensive) are also suggested to be keys to understanding the interaction between groups.[57] Since different types of work situations have different sets of technology dimensions, the way in which a particular group will function can vary considerably. For example, *intensive technologies,* such as a hospital that provides a variety of services to a client, are characterized by continuous interaction and mutual adjustment between group members and with members of different groups (reciprocal and team interdependence). A *mediating technology,* in contrast, provides products or services that link clients from the external environment. As a result, each group tends to work independently from the other, as in the case of real estate offices that mediate between buyers and sellers, independent of other offices within the larger company (pooled interdependence). Finally, *long-linked technology,* which combines successive stages of production, leads to structured interactions between groups since the output of one group becomes the input of another (sequential interdependence).

Intergroup Conflict

Intergroup conflict refers to the disagreement or differences between the members or representatives of two or more groups over authority, goals, territory, resources, or values.[58] Conflict between groups can occur for a variety of reasons: disputes over roles, scarcity of resources, misunderstandings, differentiation of tasks, and differences in orientations to time, structure, and interpersonal relations. Increased globalization and workforce diversity further contribute to conflict as they spawn differing goals, perceptions, values, commitments, and demands on resources.[59]

As reflected in Figure 6-6, conflict between groups is not necessarily dysfunctional or "bad." In fact, a lack of any conflict can reflect the systematic exclusion of certain information or "groupthink." As research indicates, pressures for early consensus during group decision processes often lead to poor choices.[60] Conflict can also lead to new ideas about novel approaches to organizational processes, the surfacing of

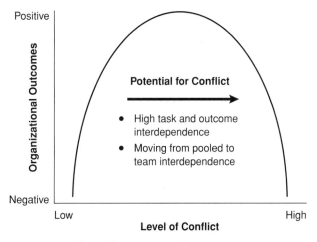

Figure 6-6 Intergroup Conflict and Organizational Outcomes

longstanding problems that can be resolved, the opportunity for people to test their capabilities, and heightened interest and creativity in dealing with organizational problems. Such conflict becomes "negative" when it escalates to the point where people begin to feel defeated, a climate of distrust and suspicion develops, resistance rather than cooperation becomes the norm, and people begin to react defensively.

One view of intergroup conflict sees it as inevitable due to the innate differences in perceptions and goals across individuals and groups.[61] Instead of viewing organizations as cooperative systems that occasionally experience discord, organizations are pictured as a means for internalizing conflicts, containing them within specific boundaries so that they can be controlled and dealt with. While organizational harmony and collaboration do occur, the parties that typically call for such accord, the "in-group" or organizational "establishment," also set the terms for the cooperation. Within this conflict-laden view of organizations, such calls for harmony are viewed as managerial tactics for dealing with ongoing conflicts with lower-level organizational members. Managers are seen as "orchestrators of conflict," in terms of being both "fight promoters" who oversee bouts and "referees" who regulate them.

Rather than representing a "breakdown" in the system, this perspective suggests that intergroup conflict is part of the inherent nature of organizational life. Organizations are conceptualized as systems that consist of myriad pairs of opposing tendencies—for example, risk-taking versus risk-avoiding and creativity versus efficiency. Without dynamic conflict within these paired tendencies, one of the dimensions would eventually become dominant in each case. As a result, the range of organizational skills and responses would become restricted, the organization would lose its ability to adapt to a changing environment, and it would run the risk of eventual failure. Conflict is thus not only a functional part of organizations—it is a critical determinant of their existence.

Managing Intergroup Conflict

As the preceding discussion indicates, conflict between groups and teams in organizations is not only inevitable, but it can also be beneficial. Given the differentiation that exists in today's complex organizations and the challenges that confront them, the integration and coordination of different groups within an organization can be a difficult process. Thus, rather than thinking in terms of totally resolving or eliminating such conflict, we can examine a number of different ways in which groups deal with conflict.

As indicated in Figure 6-7 there are two main dimensions underlying the intentions of the groups involved in a conflict situation: (1) *cooperativeness* (willingness to satisfy the other group's concerns), and (2) *assertiveness* (attempts to satisfy the group's own concerns).[62] These two dimensions are reflected in five conflict-handling modes:

1. **Avoiding** is an unassertive, uncooperative approach in which both groups neglect the concerns involved by sidestepping the issue or postponing the conflict by choosing not to deal with it.

2. **Competing** is an assertive, uncooperative mode in which each group attempts to achieve its own goals at the expense of the other through argument, authority, or threat (*forcing*).

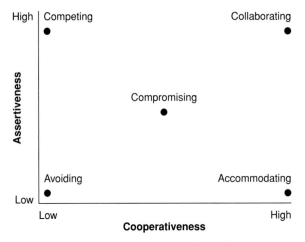

Figure 6-7   Two-Dimensional Model of Ways to Handle Conflict

Source: Adapted from T. Ruble and K. Thomas, "Support for a Two-Dimensional Model of Conflict Behavior," *Organizational Behavior and Human Performance,* vol. 16, 1976, p. 145.

3. **Accommodating** is an unassertive, cooperative position where one group attempts to satisfy the concerns of the other by neglecting its own concerns or goals.

4. **Compromising** is an intermediate approach in which partial satisfaction is sought for both through a "middle-ground" position that reflects mutual sacrifice. This stance is thus intermediate between assertiveness and cooperativeness because each group makes some concessions but also receives some concessions from the other.

5. **Collaborating** is an assertive, cooperative mode that attempts to satisfy the concerns of both groups (*problem solving*). Such mutual satisfaction involves an agreement to confront the conflict, identification of the concerns of the different groups, and problem solving to find alternatives that would satisfy both groups.

Each of these modes is used at one time or another, and the appropriateness of the style depends on the nature of the situation. If the conflict is relatively minor, for example, avoiding it altogether or accommodating the concerns of the other group may be in the best interests of the different parties. In other situations where quick, decisive action is vital and when you know your group is "right," competing appears to be more appropriate. For more significant situations, where the concerns of the groups involved are too important to be compromised, collaboration may be the ideal. This can lead to greater learning, commitment, and insight into the different perspectives.[63] Thus, while a problem-solving orientation is often viewed as the best way to proceed, the relative effectiveness of these approaches is largely determined by the context and nature of the conflict. Moreover, research indicates that reaction to conflict typically consists of multiple behavioral responses rather than a single or pure mode of behavior (e.g., competing *and* collaborating, forcing *and* problem solving).[64]

While a sizable literature has emerged from this framework, the five conflict-handling modes have been interpreted in a number of different ways, including being viewed as orientations, behaviors, and strategies. Recent work even suggests that a preference for a particular style or subset of styles is a reflection of one's personality (see Chapter 2)—for example, conscientiousness appears to be related to a preference for collaboration and compromise, while extroversion is related to a tendency toward confrontation and competing.[65] Other refinements of this model propose that these modes actually represent the *strategic intention* of the parties involved in terms of what they are *attempting* to accomplish in satisfying their own and others' goals.[66] While this is a subtle distinction, it raises some important implications for the ways in which we think about conflict management.

Focusing on intentions places more emphasis on the underlying interests of the parties involved rather than their organizational positions. Intentions are shaped by two basic forms of reasoning: rational/instrumental reasoning and normative reasoning. *Rational/instrumental* reasoning contends that individuals opt for those behaviors that they perceive will lead to a desired outcome (see, for example, the discussion of expectancy theory in Chapter 3). *Normative reasoning*, in contrast, reflects what people think is the "proper" (i.e., ethical, fair) thing to do. This form of reasoning emphasizes the intrinsic goodness of the act itself rather than its consequences. Thus, instead of viewing conflict management solely as a rational process, this perspective integrates emotion into the conflict process. Our emotions can affect both our rational/instrumental and normative reasoning and can influence us to deal with conflict in different ways. The goals of conflict management and, as a consequence, the usefulness of a particular conflict-handling mode, are also dependent on the choice of *beneficiary* (e.g., enhance the position of one of the parties, both of the parties, or the larger system of which both parties are a part). For example, a consultant who is advising a client on a dispute will have a different set of conflict management goals than someone who is attempting to mediate the situation.

Consequences of Intergroup Conflict and Competition

The American business culture has traditionally viewed conflict as being dysfunctional (or harmful) and harmony between different groups as functional (or beneficial). As we mentioned earlier, however, there are dysfunctional consequences of never having conflict or suppressing conflict, just as there are dysfunctional consequences of having too much conflict. Sometimes there can be functional and dysfunctional consequences of conflict occurring at the same time. An example of simultaneous functional and dysfunctional conflict can be seen in the ongoing debate between the automobile industry and the federal government over pollution and safety standards and regulation. Some of the benefits (functional aspects) of this conflict are safer cars and newer, more efficient engines. One of the costs (systemic dysfunctions) has been increasingly expensive automobiles due, in part, to the enforced research and development into safety and pollution control. Thus, the outcome or consequence of this conflict process has both benefits and costs for the groups involved, which can be shared by the groups through compromise or reduced through collaboration (e.g., joint exploration of innovative safety and pollution devices).

Although a large body of research suggests that collaboration can lead to better conflict resolution outcomes for individuals (e.g., improved self-esteem, satisfaction), interpersonal relations (e.g., respect, trust, affection), and groups and organizations (e.g., integrative decisions, open exchanges of information), there are instances where collaborative endeavors are naive and impractical.[67] A key factor between the normative preference for collaboration and contingency theories concerns the *time frame* involved—whether resolution of the conflict involves short- or long-term goals. Contingency theories of conflict management attempt to give us insight into the short-term problems associated with dealing with conflict. Since these perspectives are based on the realities of the situation as they presently exist, they have a decidedly pragmatic orientation. Within this context, collaboration does not make sense if competitive incentives are part of the situation, the parties involved have poor problem-solving skills, time and deadlines are too constrained, and/or neither one trusts the other. In these instances, compromise or competition may be more effective ways to deal with the conflict. Over the longer term, however, efforts to enhance the situation and improve the conditions we are operating under require interventions that move away from competition to more collaborative forms of conflict resolution.

When conflict is dealt with mainly through competition, the outcomes for the groups involved may not only reduce the potential for future cooperation and collaboration, but could alter the dynamics and interactions of both intra- and intergroup behaviors as well. In fact, a number of observable phenomena occur within and between competing groups, and within winning and losing groups. Table 6-3 summarizes the various things that happen to groups in competition. If a group perceives itself to be losing, it can begin to take on the characteristics of losing groups. This tendency, however, depends more on a group's self-perception of how it is doing than on the actual fact of winning or losing.

CONCLUSION: IMPLICATIONS FOR MANAGERS

It is clear that organizations are becoming increasingly dependent on team performance and the successful interaction of different groups and teams. However, as organizational processes are becoming more interdependent, external forces are also constraining the resources available to many firms (e.g., transnational competition, e-commerce). This mix of heightened interdependence and constrained resources is likely to precipitate a growing number of intergroup and interteam conflicts.[68]

As Table 6-3 suggests, the long-term consequences of continued competition and conflict between groups in an organization are more harmful than beneficial. Thus, managers are cautioned not to promote conflict under the assumption that a little "healthy competition" is beneficial. Although it may appear to be desirable to have groups compete against one another (e.g., sales contests between different departments), the resulting tensions, perceptual distortions, and negative stereotyping can create a host of organizational problems. Indeed, as noted earlier, a reality of organizational life today is that increased interdependencies and reduced resources will create conflict on their own—conflict that will be increasingly difficult for organizational members to self-manage. While employees may have been willing to avoid, tolerate, suppress, or self-manage conflict in the past, much of this willingness has been tested by organizational downsizing and retrenchment. As downsizing turns into resizing and what appears to be a permanent change in the nature and size of our organizations and institutions,[69] growing numbers of employees feel insecure in their

TABLE 6-3 Observable Consequences of Intergroup Competition

Within Competing Groups	Between Competing Groups
1. Groups become more cohesive.	1. Each group perceives other groups as the enemy, not as a neutral group.
2. Group norms demand more loyalty from members; deviance is not tolerated.	2. Each group perceives the best in itself and the worst in other groups—"groupthink" and negative stereotypes occur.
3. Group climate becomes very businesslike—task needs increase and social needs are left unattended.	3. Hostility increases while communication decreases.
4. Group members tolerate more task-oriented, autocratic leadership as opposed to democratic leadership.	4. When competing groups are forced into interaction, group members listen to their own spokespersons and arguments, and not those of the competing group.
5. Group structure becomes apparent; roles are more formalized.	

Within Winning Groups	Within Losing Groups
1. Groups remain cohesive and become more tightly knit.	1. Groups find ways to attribute loss to others, the situation, the judges, and so forth.
2. Social needs are addressed at this point; members become more playful and more relaxed.	2. Tend to splinter; unresolved personal conflict surfaces about strategy, what led to the loss, and so forth.
3. High intragroup cooperation, low task interest.	3. If the group is not completely demoralized, it tends to work harder, to learn the rules, to become political.
4. Group members think that their stereotypes about themselves and others have been confirmed—they are "good" and others are "bad."	4. Group members tend initially toward low intragroup cooperation and concern for member needs, and more concern for working harder.
	5. Group members learn about themselves from having their self-image disconfirmed by the loss; loser is likely to regroup and be more effective if the loss is realistically accepted.

Source: Adapted from Edgar Schein, *Organizational Psychology.* Englewood Cliffs, NJ: Prentice Hall, 1980, pp. 172–176.

jobs and less trustful of their managers and organizations. As a result, they are less likely to collaborate with other groups and manage resultant conflicts for the sake of the larger organization.

It is, therefore, important for managers to be aware of the ways in which dysfunctional intergroup conflict can be minimized: the use of *liaisons* or linking pins to coordinate the activities of the groups; *overlapping group memberships* that can develop in each group an appreciation of the concerns of the other group; *joint meetings* or task forces that can provide a common frame of reference; locating a *common enemy* external to the organization that can shift the foci of intergroup competition from inside the firm to outside competitors; and the development of *superordinate goals* that require a collaborative effort and reflect mutually rewarding outcomes. Managers can also operate as *mediators* to help resolve organizational conflicts by focusing on their underlying causes.[70] Such mediation has been found to decrease conflict and enhance the interaction between the parties by improving communication, reducing stress, and introducing problem-solving skills into the situation. Finally, it is important to realize that the quality of interpersonal relationships that exist among members of different work units is an important factor in perceptions of intergroup conflict. Negative relationships within a group appear to "spill over" and are associated with high levels of perceived conflict across groups.[71] Given the realities inherent in today's workplace, managers must be prepared to deal with the resulting strains and pressures that will inevitably emerge from intergroup conflict and to create conditions (through organizational leadership, structure, and culture) that will contribute to greater cross–work unit collaboration and cooperation.

NOTES

1. See J. Lipnack and J. Stamps, *The Teamnet Factor: Bringing the Power of Boundary Crossing into the Heart of Your Business* (Essex Junction, VT: Oliver Wright Publications, 1993); and R. Benson-Armer and T. Hsieh, "Teamwork across Time and Space," *The McKinsey Quarterly, 4* (1997): 18–27.

2. "The Horizontal Organization," *Business Week*, December 20, 1993; W.E. Halal, "From Hierarchy to Enterprise: Internal Markets Are the New Foundation of Management," *Academy of Management Executive* 8, no. 4 (1994): 69–83; and R. Jacob, "The Struggle to Create an Organization for the 21st Century," *Fortune*, April 3, 1995, pp. 90–92, 94, 96, 98–99.

3. See, for example, G. Imperato, "Their Specialty? Teamwork," *Fast Company* (January/February 2000): 54–56; C. Sittenfeld, "Powered by the People," *Fast Company* (July/August 1999): 178–189; and J. Byrne, "The Search for the Young and Gifted," *Business Week*, October 4, 1999, pp. 108–116.

4. D.W. Johnson and F.P. Johnson, *Joining Together: Group Theory and Group Skills* (Boston: Allyn & Bacon, 1994), p. 505.

5. See, for example, E. Hopkins, "Effective Teams: Camels of a Different Color," *Training & Development* 48, no. 12 (1994): 35–37; and J. Katzenbach and D. Smith, *The Wisdom of Teams: Creating the High Performing Organization* (Cambridge, MA: Harvard Business School Press, 1993).

6. R. Beckhard, *Organization Development: Strategies and Models* (Reading, MA: Addison-Wesley, 1960); and "Optimizing Team Building Efforts," *Journal of Contemporary Business* 1, no. 3 (1971): 23–32.

7. See E. Sundstrom, K.P. De Meuse, and S.J. Liebowitz, "Work Teams: Applications and Effectiveness," *American Psychologist* 45, no. 2 (1990): 120–133; S.I. Tannenbaum, R.L. Beard, and E. Salas, "Team Building and Its Influence on Team Effectiveness: Conceptual and Empirical Developments," in K. Kelley, ed., *Issues, Theory, and Research in Industrial/Organizational Psychology* (Amsterdam: North-Holland, 1992), pp. 117–153; M. Pagell and J.A. LePine, "Multiple Case Studies of Team Effectiveness in Manufacturing Operations," *Journal of Operations Management* 20, no. 5 (2002): 619–640; and J.N. Choi, "External Activities and Team Effectiveness: Review and Theoretical Developments," *Small Group Research* 33, no. 2 (2002): 181–208.

8. See R. Hackman, *Groups That Work (and Those That Don't)* (San Francisco: Jossey-Bass, 1986); R.M. Kanter, "Dilemmas of Managing Participation," *Organizational Dynamics* 11, no. 1 (1982): 5–27; and S.M. Herman, *A Force of Ones: Reclaiming Individual Power* *in a Time of Teams, Work Groups and Other Crowds* (San Francisco: Jossey-Bass, 1994).

9. See S. Lembke and M.G. Wilson, "Putting the 'Team' Into Teamwork: Alternative Theoretical Contributions for Contemporary Management Practice," *Human Relations* 51, no. 7 (1998): 927–944; and D.L. Miller, "The Stages of Group Development: A Retrospective Study of Dynamic Team Processes," *Canadian Journal of Administrative Science* 20, no. 2 (2003): 121–149.

10. H. Tajfel, "Social Identity and Intergroup Behavior," *Social Science Information*, 13 (1974): 65–93; and M.A. Hogg and D.J. Terry, "Social Identity and Self-Categorization Processes in Organizational Contexts," *Academy of Management Review* 25, no. 1 (2000): 121–140.

11. See H. Tajfel and J.C. Turner, "The Social Identity Theory of Intergroup Behavior," in S. Worchel and W.G. Austin, eds., *The Psychology of Intergroup Relations* (Chicago: Nelson-Hall, 1986), pp. 7–24; and Lembke and Wilson, "Putting the 'Team' into Teamwork."

12. The remainder of this section is drawn from Lembke and Wilson, "Putting the 'Team' into Teamwork"; and Hogg and Terry, "Social Identity and Self-Categorization Processes in Organizational Contexts." See also J.E. Salk and O. Shenkar, "Social Identities in an International Joint Venture: An Exploratory Case Study," *Organization Science* 12, no. 2 (2001): 161–178.

13. A.C. Amason, "Distinguishing the Effects of Functional and Dysfunctional Conflict on Strategic Decision Making: Resolving a Paradox for Top Management Teams," *Academy of Management Journal* 39 (1996): 123–148; A.C. Amason and H.J. Sapienza, "The Effects of Top Management Team Size and Interaction Norms on Cognitive and Affective Conflict," *Journal of Management* 2 (1997): 495–516; and R.J. Ely and D.A. Thomas, "Cultural Diversity at Work: The Effects of Diversity Perspectives on Work Group Processes and Outcomes," *Administrative Science Quarterly* 46 (2001): 229–273.

14. See D.J. Koys, "The Effects of Employee Satisfaction, Organizational Citizenship Behavior, and Turnover on Organizational Effectiveness: A Unit-Level, Longitudinal Study," *Personnel Psychology* 54 (2001): 101–114; and H. Wang, K.S. Law, R.D. Hackett, D. Wang, and Z.X. Chen, "Leader-Member Exchange as a Mediator of the Relationship between Transformational Leadership and Followers' Performance and Organizational Citizenship Behavior," *Academy of Management Journal* 48 (2005): 420–432.

15. This section draws heavily from G.R. Jones and J.M. George, "The Experience and Evolution of Trust: Implications for Cooperation and Teamwork," *Academy of Management Review* 23, no. 3 (1998): 531–546.

16. See D.E. Byrne, *The Attraction Paradigm* (New York: Academic Press, 1971); and C.M. Riordan, "Relational Demography within Groups: Past Developments, Contradictions, and New Directions," *Research in Personnel and Human Resources Management* 19 (2000): 131–173.

17. K.Y. Williams and C.A. O'Reilly, "Demography and Diversity in Organizations: A Review of 40 Years of Research," *Research in Organizational Behavior* 20 (1998): 77–140.

18. E.E. Watson, K. Kumar, and L.K. Michaelson, "Cultural Diversity's Impact on Interaction Processes and Performance: Comparing Homogeneous and Diverse Task Groups," *Academy of Management Journal* 36 (1993): 590–602; and D.A. Harrison, K.H. Price, J.H. Gavin, and A.T. Florey, "Time, Teams and Task Performance: Changing Effects of Surface- and Deep-Level Diversity on Group Functioning," *Academy of Management Journal* 45 (2002): 1029–1045.

19. See, for example, S. Vangen and C. Husham, "Nurturing Collaborative Relations: Building Trust in Interorganizational Collaboration," *Journal of Applied Behavioral Science* 39, no. 1 (2003): 5–31.

20. This section is based on D.R. Dension, S.L. Hart and J.A. Kahn, "From Chimneys to Cross-Functional Teams: Developing and Validating a Diagnostic Model," *Academy of Management Journal* 39, no. 4 (1996): 1005–1023; A.R. Jassawalla and H.C. Sashittal, "Building Collaborative Cross-Functional New Product Teams," *Academy of Management Executive* 13, no. 3 (1999): 50–63; R. Sethi, D.C. Smith, and C.W. Park,

"Cross-Functional Product Development Teams, Creativity and the Innovativeness of New Consumer Products," *Journal of Marketing Research* 38, no. 1 (2001): 73–85; and R. Sethi, D.C. Smith, and C.W. Park, "How to Kill a Team's Creativity," *Harvard Business Review* 80, no. 4 (2002): 16–18.

21. G.S. van der Vegt and J.S. Bunderson, "Learning and Performance in Multidisciplinary Teams: The Importance of Collective Team Identification," *Academy of Management Journal* 48, no. 3 (2005): 532–547.

22. E.G. Yager, "The Quality Control Circle Explosion," *Training & Development Journal* (April 1981): 98–105; K. Ohmae, "Quality Control Circles: They Work and Don't Work," *Wall Street Journal*, March 29, 1982, p. 18; G. Munchus III, "Employer-Employee Based Quality Circles in Japan: Human Resource Policy Implications for American Firms," *Academy of Management Review* 8, no. 2 (1983): 255–261; and S. Zetie, "The Quality Circle Approach to Knowledge Management," *Managerial Auditing Journal* 17, no. 6 (2002): 317–328.

23. D. Hutchins, "Quality Circles: The Missing Link," *Leadership and Organization Development Journal* 1, no. 4 (1980): v–viii; M.L. Marks, P.H. Mirvis, E.J. Hackett, and J.F. Grady, "Employee Participation in a Quality Circle Program: Impact on Quality of Work Life, Productivity, and Absenteeism," *Journal of Applied Psychology* 71, no. 1 (1986): 61–69; E.E. Lawler III and S.A. Mohrman, "Quality Circles: After the Honeymoon," *Organizational Dynamics* 15, no. 4 (1987): 42–55; and B.G. Dale, M.B.F. Elkjaer, A. van de Wiele, and A.R.T. Williams, "Fad, Fashion and Fit: An Examination of Quality Circles, Business Process Re-Engineering and Statistical Process," *International Journal of Production Economics* 73, no. 2 (2001): 137–152.

24. This discussion is based on H.H. Greenbaum, I.T. Kaplan, and W. Metlay, "Evaluation of Problem-Solving Groups: The Case of Quality Circle Programs," *Group and Organization Studies* 13 (1988): 113–147; J.W. Fairfield-Sonn, "Influence of Context on Process Improvement Teams: Leadership from a Distance," *Journal of Business and Economic Studies* 5, no. 2 (1999): 47–66; E.E. Lawler III, S.A. Mohrman, and G.E. Ledford, Jr., *Employee Involvement and Total Quality Management* (San Francisco: Jossey-Bass, 1992); and J.C. Williams, "Energy and Expertise: Keys to Avoiding Project Management Pitfalls," *Information Strategy* 20, no. 1 (2003): 15–25.

25. See F. Shipper and C.C. Manz, "Employee Self-Management without Formally Designated Teams: An Alternative Road to Empowerment," *Organizational Dynamics* 21 (Winter 1992): 48–61; D.E. Yeats, M. Hipskind, and D. Barnes, "Lessons Learned from Self-Managed Work Teams," *Business Horizons* 37, no. 4 (1994): 11–18; G.M. Spreitzer, S.G. Cohen, and G.E. Ledford, Jr., "Developing Effective Self-Managing Work Teams in Service Organizations," *Group & Organization Management* 24, no. 3 (1999): 340–366; and W.A. Randolph and M. Sashkin, "Can Organizational Empowerment Work in Multinational Settings?" *Academy of Management Executive* 16, no. 1 (2002): 102–115.

26. C.C. Manz and J.W. Newstrom, "Self-Managing Teams in a Paper Mill: Success Factors, Problems, and Lessons Learned," in R. Glazer (ed.), *Classic Readings in Self-Managing Teamwork* (King of Prussia, PA: Organization Design and Development, 1992), pp. 443–462.

27. C.E. Nicholls, H.W. Lane, and M.B. Brechu, "Taking Self-Managed Teams to Mexico," *Academy of Management Executive* 13, no. 3 (1999): 15–25.

28. See D.E. Bowen and E.E. Lawler III, "The Empowerment of Service Workers: What, Why, How, and When," *Sloan Management Review* 33, no. 3 (1992): 35–36; M.A. Verespej, "No Empowerment without Education," *Industry Week*, April 1, 1991, pp. 28–29; and P.A. Chansler, P.M. Swamidass, and C. Cammann, "Self-Managing Work Teams: An Empirical Study of Group Cohesiveness in 'Natural Work Groups' at Harley-Davidson Motor Company Plant," *Small Group Research* 34, no. 1 (2003): 101–121.

29. E.H. Schein, "How Can Organizations Learn Faster? The Challenge of Entering the Green Room," *Sloan Management Review* (Winter 1993): 85–92; and R. Teare and D.F. Pantin, "Cascading Organizational Learning,"

International Journal of Contemporary Hospitality Management 14, no. 7 (2002): 349–353.

30. See C. Argyris, *Overcoming Organizational Defenses: Facilitating Organizational Learning* (Needham Heights, MA: Simon & Schuster, 1990); and P. Senge, *The Fifth Discipline: The Art & Practice of the Learning Organization* (New York: Doubleday/Currency, 1990).

31. See C. Argyris, "Good Communication That Blocks Learning," *Harvard Business Review* 72, no. 4 (1994): 77–85.

32. M. Dodgson, "Organizational Learning: A Review of Some Literatures," *Organization Studies* 14, no. 3 (1993): 375–394; and C.L. Wang and P.K. Ahmed, "Organisational Learning: A Critical Review," *The Learning Organization* 10, no. 1 (2003): 8–17.

33. See P.M. Senge, C. Roberts, R.B. Ross, B.J. Smith, and A. Kleiner, *The Fifth Discipline Fieldbook: Strategies and Tools for Building a Learning Organization* (New York Currency/Doubleday, 1994), pp. 59–64.

34. G.S. Lynn, "New Product Team Learning: Developing and Profiting from Your Knowledge Capital," *California Management Review* 40, no. 4 (1998): 74–93. See also A. Jashapara, "Cognition, Culture and Competition: An Empirical Test of the Learning Organization," *The Learning Organization* 10, no. 1 (2003): 31–50.

35. R.A. Zawacki and C.A. Norman, "Successful Self-Directed Teams and Planned Change: A Lot in Common," in W.L. French, C.H. Bell, Jr., and R.A. Zawacki, eds., *Organization Development and Transformation: Managing Effective Change* (Burr Ridge, IL: Irwin, 1994), pp. 309–316; and Dodgson, op. cit.

36. C.D. O'Brien and A.F. Buono, "Creating a Networked, Learning Organization in the Classroom," *Journal of Management Education* 20, no. 3 (1996): 369–381.

37. C.D. O'Brien and A.F. Buono, "Building Effective Learning Teams: Lessons from the Field," *Sam Advanced Management Journal* 61, no. 3 (1996): 4–9.

38. See, for example, J.T. Buck, "The Rocky Road to Team-Based Management," *Training & Development Journal* 49, no. 4 (1995): 35–38.

39. See D. Clutterbuck, "How Teams Learn," *T&D* 56, no. 3 (2003): 67–69.

40. See B. Geber, "Virtual Teams," *Training* 32, no. 4 (1995): 36–40; A.M. Townsend, S.M. DeMarie and A.R. Hendrickson, "Are You Ready for Virtual Teams?" *HR Magazine* 41, no. 9 (1996): 122–123; and B.S. Bell and S.W.J. Kozlowski, "A Typology of Virtual Teams," *Group & Organization Management* 27, no. 1 (2002): 14–49.

41. R. Greiner and G. Meters, *Enterprise Networking: Working Together Apart* (Bedford, MA: Digital Press, 1992).

42. A.M. Townsend, S.M. DeMarie, and A.R. Hendrickson, "Virtual Teams: Technology and the Workplace of the Future," *Academy of Management Executive* 12, no. 3 (1998): pp. 18–20.

43. See M.L. Maznevski and K.M. Chudoba, "Bridging Space over Time: Global Virtual-Team Dynamics and Effectiveness," *Organization Science* 11, no. 5 (2000): 473–492; and B.L. Kirkman, B. Rosen, C.B. Gibson, P.E. Tesluk, and S.O. McPherson, "Five Challenges to Virtual Team Success: Lessons from Sabre, Inc.," *Academy of Management Executive*, 16, no. 3 (2002): 67–79.

44. The following discussion draws heavily from K.W. Kerber and A.F. Buono, "Leadership Challenges in Global Virtual Teams: Lessons from the Field," *Sam Advanced Management Journal* 69, no. 4 (2004): 4–10.

45. See C. Handy, "Trust and the Virtual Organization," *Harvard Business Review* 73, no. 3 (1995): 40–49; and J.L. Creighton and J.W.R. Adams, "The Cybermeeting's About to Begin," *Management Review* 87, no. 1 (1998): 29–31.

46. This section draws from B. Rosen, S. Furst, and R. Blackburn, "Training for Virtual Teams: An Investigation of Current Practices and Future Needs," *Human Resource Management* 45, no. 2 (2006): 229–247.

47. B.A. Jain and D.N. Ross, "Assessing the Impact of Integrated Group Support Systems on the Performance of Teams," *American Business Review* 16, no. 1 (1998): 105–111.

48. C. Olofson, "So Many Meetings, So Little Time," *Fast Company* (January/February 2000): 48.

49. K.A. Jehn and E.A. Mannix, "The Dynamic Nature of Conflict: A Longitudinal

Study of Intragroup Conflict and Group Performance," *Academy of Management Journal* 44 (2001): 238–253.

50. A.C. Amason, "Distinguishing the Effects of Functional and Dysfunctional Conflict on Strategic Decision Making: Resolving a Paradox for Top Management Teams," *Academy of Management Journal* 39 (1996): 123–148; A.C. Amason and H.J. Sapienza, "The Effects of Top Management Team Size and Interaction Norms on Cognitive and Affective Conflict," *Journal of Management* 2 (1997): 495–516; and K.A. Jehn, G.B. Northcraft, and M.A. Neale, "Why Differences Make a Difference: A Field Study of Diversity, Conflict, and Performance in Workgroups," *Administrative Science Quarterly* 44 (1999): 741–763.

51. See T. Cox, Jr., *Cultural Diversity in Organizations: Theory, Research & Practice* (San Francisco: Berrett-Koehler Publishers, 1993); L.H. Pelled, "Relational Demography and Perceptions of Group Conflict and Performance: A Field Investigation," *The International Journal of Conflict Management* 7 (1996): 230–246; L.H. Pelled, K.R. Xin, and A.M. Weiss, "No Es Como Mi: Relational Demography and Conflict in a Mexican Production Facility," *Journal of Occupational & Organizational Psycchology* 74 (2001): 63–84; and P. Garcia-Prieto, E. Bellard, and S.C. Schneider, "Experiencing Diversity, Conflict, and Emotions in Teams," *Applied Psychology: An International Review* 52 (2003): 413–440.

52. See M. Bassin, "From Teams to Partnerships," *HR Magazine* 41, no. 1 (1996): 84–86; and B.J. Alge, C. Weithoff and H.J. Klein, "When Does the Medium Matter? Knowledge-Building Experiences and Opportunities in Decision-Making Teams," *Organizational Behavior and Human Decision Processes* 91, no. 1 (2003): 26–37.

53. C.P. Alderfer, "An Intergroup Perspective on Group Dynamics," in J. Lorsch, ed., *Handbook of Organizational Behavior* (Englewood Cliffs, NJ: Prentice-Hall, 1983), pp. 190–222; see also L.D. Brown, *Managing Conflict at Organizational Interfaces* (Reading, MA: Addison-Wesley, 1983).

54. J. Thompson, *Organizations in Action* (New York: McGraw-Hill, 1967); and A.H. Van de Ven, A.L. Delbecq, and R. Koenig, Jr., "Determinants of Coordination Modes within Organizations," *American Sociological Review* 41 (1976): 322–338.

55. A.B. Drexler and R. Forrester, "Interdependence: The Crux of Teamwork," *HR Magazine* 43, no. 10 (1998): 52–62.

56. G.S. van der Vegt, B. Emans, and E. van de Vliert, "Motivating Effects of Task and Outcome Interdependence in Work Teams," *Group & Organization Management* 23, no. 2 (1998): 124–143. See also C.W. Langfred, "Work-Group Design and Autonomy: A Field Study of the Interaction between Task Interdependence and Group Autonomy," *Small Group Research* 31, no. 1 (2000): 54–70.

57. P.S. Goodman, E. Ravlin, and M. Schminke, "Understanding Groups in Organizations," in L.L. Cummings and B.M. Staw, eds., *Research in Organizational Behavior*, vol. 9 (Greenwich, CT: JAI Press, 1987), pp. 121–173; and R. Wageman, "Interdependence and Group Effectiveness," *Administrative Science Quarterly* 40, no. 1 (1995): 145–180.

58. See A. Rahim and T.V. Bonoma, "Managing Organizational Conflict: A Model for Diagnosis and Intervention," *Psychological Reports* 44 (1979): 1323–1344.

59. See A. Donnellon and D.M. Kolb, "Constructive for Whom? The Fate of Diversity Disputes in Organizations," *Journal of Social Issues* 50 (1994): 139–155; and J.A. Wall, Jr. and R.R. Callister, "Conflict and Its Management," *Journal of Management* 21, no. 3 (1995): 515–558.

60. See R.L. Priem, D.A. Harrison, and N.K. Muir, "Structured Conflict and Consensus Outcomes in Group Decision Making," *Journal of Management* 21, no. 4 (1995): 691–710.

61. This section is adapted from L.R. Pondy, "Reflections on Organizational Conflict," *Journal of Organizational Behavior* 12 (1992): 257–261.

62. See K. Thomas, "Conflict and Conflict Management," in M.D. Dunnette, ed., *Handbook of Industrial and Organizational Psychology* (Chicago: Rand McNally, 1976);

and T. Ruble and K.W. Thomas, "Support for a Two-Dimensional Model of Conflict Behavior," *Organizational Behavior and Human Performance* 16 (1976): 143–155.

63. See K.W. Thomas, "Toward Multi-Dimensional Values in Teaching: The Example of Conflict Behaviors," *Academy of Management Review* 2 (1977): 484–490.

64. E. van de Vliert, A. Nauta, E. Giebels, and O. Janssen, "Constructive Conflict at Work," *Journal of Organizational Behavior* 20 (1999): 475–491.

65. P.J. Moberg, "Linking Conflict Strategy to the Five-Factor Model: Theoretical and Empirical Foundations," *International Journal of Conflict Management* 12, no. 1 (2001): 47–68.

66. This discussion is drawn from K.W. Thomas, "Conflict and Conflict Management: Reflections and Update," *Journal of Organizational Behavior* 13 (1992): 265–274.

67. The following discussion of time frame and conflict management is based on Thomas, "Conflict and Conflict Management," pp. 271–272.

68. This discussion is adapted from Wall and Callister, op. cit., pp. 548–550.

69. For an excellent overview of the myriad issues surrounding organizational resizing, see K.P. DeMeuse and M.L. Marks, eds., *Resizing the Organization: Managing Layoffs, Divestitures, and Closings—Maximizing Gain While Minimizing Pain* (San Francisco: Jossey-Bass, 2003).

70. See J.A. Wall and A. Lynn, "Mediation: A Current Review," *Journal of Conflict Resolution* 37 (1993): 160–194.

71. See G. Labianca, D.J. Brass, and B. Gray, "Social Networks and Perceptions of Intergroup Conflict: The Role of Negative Relationships and Third Parties," *Academy of Management Journal* 41, no. 1 (1998), 55–67.

Leadership, Power, and the Manager

*L*eadership has been a major topic for research in organizational behavior and its related fields (e.g., psychology, sociology) since the 1930s, and continues to be a prominent focus of research. In 2001, the *Harvard Business Review* dedicated its first special issue to "breakthrough leadership," which has been followed by two additional issues dedicated to leadership.[1] Research and writing on organizational leadership has progressed from theories that depict the personal characteristics or traits of effective leaders through the basic functions that delineate what effective leaders *should* do, to a situational or contingency approach that suggests more of a flexible, adaptive style for effective leadership. Research in the field gradually returned to personal traits and the idea of the heroic or "magic" leader, only to see the business world become disenchanted with "celebrity" chief executive officers (CEOs). Much of the work on leadership has been criticized as being too narrow in focus, concerned more with explaining leader behaviors vis-à-vis subordinates rather than examining leaders in the larger context of their organizations and large-scale organizational and environmental change.

Leadership as traditionally defined was seen as only a small part of the manager's role and that leadership was depicted as being very different from management. This traditional demarcation—casting management as an administrative function and leadership as a strategic function—has become increasingly blurred. Part of this blurring is due to the increasingly widespread use of team-based processes in organizations, requiring managers to coordinate and motivate entire teams in addition to individuals. The trend to leading teams has been sufficiently pervasive that some observers have asserted that the "pendulum has swung," such that the prevailing paradigm has shifted from individual to team leadership.[2] In addition, though the idea of leadership teams has been known throughout recorded history, recent attention has turned to leadership teams as potentially effective means of dealing with the rapid pace of change and the presumption of uncertainty and change as the status quo.[3]

Since much of the current work on leadership is an attempt to make leadership more useful to practitioners and to provide prescriptive advice to future managers, the chapter integrates theories about what managers as leaders *should do* and research on what managers *actually do* in their organizations. The chapter begins with a definition of leadership and an examination of the concept of power as both an independent and dependent variable. A historical overview of the various approaches to the study of leadership is then presented, and the chapter concludes with an examination of leadership in the context of transforming organizations and the other roles fulfilled by managers.

LEADERSHIP AND POWER

Although the terms *leader* and *leadership* are frequently used in the OB literature, there is often a great deal of misunderstanding about what is actually meant by these concepts. Although there are numerous definitions of the term, leadership can be thought of as a *process of influence,* usually by one person, whereby another individual or group is oriented toward setting and achieving certain goals. There are, of course, a number of ways in which this influence can be accomplished, just as there are different types of leadership, several of which can operate at the same time. Similarly, groups and organizations often have multiple objectives that may be addressed by different leaders. The key, however, is the three underlying themes in all definitions of leadership. First, leadership is a *relationship* between people (leaders and followers) in which influence and power are unevenly distributed on a legitimate basis (contractual or consensual). Second, leadership does not occur in isolation; there is a *context* surrounding this relationship (e.g., formal versus informal, social versus task). Third, the leader–follower relationship creates a variety of *outcomes* (e.g., respect, animosity, goal attainment, customer satisfaction). Thus, understanding leadership and the leadership process is based on an understanding of the relationship between a leader and his or her followers, the context of their interaction, and its resulting by-products.[4]

Power and Authority

As suggested earlier, power and authority are closely related to the concept of leadership. *Power* is the ability to influence various outcomes. If this is formally sanctioned by an organization (contractual) or informally supported by individuals or groups (consensual), it is described as *legitimate power.* *Authority* refers to situations in which a person (or group) has been formally granted a leadership position. Within this context, *executive* or managerial power is often distinguished from "raw" power by its unique focus. It refers to power directed toward creating and sustaining an active organization, with the ideal of transforming the organization to its fullest potential. Thus, executive power consists of understanding what the organization is, envisioning what it can or should become, and initiating those processes that close the gap between organizational ideals and actual practice.[5]

Although an individual may be granted a formal leadership position, this does not mean that the person will necessarily be effective in "leading" others or exerting influence on them.[6] This distinction is often referred to in terms of the difference between appointed leaders and emergent leaders. *Appointed leaders* refers to those individuals who occupy a particular organizational role, such as executive, manager, or supervisor. The job description of this role gives the individual the authority to carry out certain organizational tasks. In many instances, however, other individuals are defined as leaders by organizational members. These *emergent leaders* may not have the formal role or positional authority of the appointed leader, but they are accorded power by other organizational members due to their ability either to get the task accomplished or to maintain the social network of the group.[7]

Types of Power

While appointed and emergent leadership in a particular group or organization may reside in the same individual, they are often fulfilled by different people with different sources of power at their disposal.[8] As suggested earlier, the most common form of power for appointed leaders is *position* power or formal authority. This form of power is impersonal and not based on the individual's personal characteristics. Appointed leaders can also utilize formal organizational reward systems (e.g., promotions, merit raises) or sanctions (e.g., threat of dismissal) that can influence individuals to do certain things. These power bases are respectively referred to as *reward* and *coercive* power. While emergent leaders may also have some control over certain rewards (e.g., respect and esteem) and sanctions (e.g., social censure), their power is based more fully on personal rather than organizational characteristics.

Expert power is based on an individual's knowledge about relevant issues, which is perceived to be a valuable resource. Since such expertise may reside in lower-status individuals, their informal influence can create the type of status-incongruent situations discussed in Chapter 5. *Referent* power is based on personal magnetism or charisma. In many instances, people identify with a particular individual because of certain personality traits or personal characteristics. Such charisma can be quite potent in influencing people even though they may not be under direct or formal control of that individual. Emergent leaders often have a combination of referent and expert power, which can create a strong and forceful basis for exerting influence on others.

Each of these five definitions treats power as an *independent variable*, that is, power as the ability to make things happen and to get things accomplished. Power, however, has also been viewed as a *dependent* or *situational* variable (in terms of the nature of a particular setting within an organization that provides a group or individual with power). In this context, individuals or groups within an organization are presumed to have power based on such factors as:[9]

- **Ability to cope with uncertainty.** If a forecasting unit of a sales organization can accurately predict the demand cycle for a particular product, the capability to "control" the uncertainty gives this unit power.

- **Substitutability.** The greater the extent to which someone else in the organization can substitute for a particular individual or group, the lesser the power (the lower the substitutability, the greater the power).

- **Organizational centrality.** The more central a person or group is to the tasks or processes of an organization, the greater the power (see, for example, the discussion of organizational communication and gatekeepers in Chapter 4).

- **Role and task interdependence.** If the activities of a person or group depend on the activities of another person or group, the latter is presumed to have greater control over relevant contingencies, which is another dimension of power.

Power can thus be conceptualized as being the *cause* of certain behaviors or as a *result* of certain situational factors. It is probably most accurate to think of power as both an independent and a dependent variable. In a real sense, the study of power is part of a means-end process of interpretation and evaluation.

The Need for Power in Managerial Performance

Effective leaders tend to have a high motivation for power. As research indicates, they also often have a relatively low need for affiliation coupled with high activity inhibition. In other words, a person likely to be a leader desires power, does not have very strong social needs, and should be able to operate independently. At the same time, leaders must be able to comfortably constrain their use of power so that they are not perceived as being impulsive, coercive, or manipulative. This overall pattern is referred to as the *leadership motive syndrome.*[10] The ideal is a person who uses power carefully, viewing power as the ability to accomplish things for others or for a cause, instead of for personal gain or dominance. At the same time, this syndrome suggests that the need for power must be higher than the need for affiliation, as leaders should remain somewhat socially distant from others. As research suggests, leaders who fit this leadership motive profile tend to be more satisfied and more effective than those who do not.[11]

Current trends and pressures facing managers underscore the relevance of Chester Barnard's classic assessment of managers—managers are essentially powerless until their followers grant them the authority to lead.[12] This creates a paradox for managers in that power is effectively exercised in an organization only when those who are the target of the power give their consent to its use.[13] The reality of complex organizations is that the formal authority vested in a particular position rarely provides an individual with enough power to get things done. Because of two basic organizational "facts of life"—the division of labor and limited resources—managers, to varying degrees, are dependent on their superiors, subordinates, peers in other parts of the organization, the subordinates of those peers, and a host of external stakeholders (e.g., suppliers, customers, regulatory agencies) to accomplish their tasks. In fact, one of the realities of the increasing diversity of values and goals among employees and the increasing interdependence of their tasks is that the effectiveness of formal authority in organizations is diminishing. The resulting "power gap"—that is, the difference between the power granted through position and the power required to accomplish organizational goals—dictates that managers must be able to acquire and maintain sufficient power so the inevitable conflicts that will emerge across such diverse, interdependent groups can be managed in positive ways.

The additional bases of power necessary to fulfill organizational goals effectively, however, are not freely given to managers. The reality is that they must be gradually accumulated by a wide array of actions and skills such as: (1) acquiring and sharing information and knowledge; (2) assessing who really has power that is relevant to particular issues; (3) creating good working relationships across stakeholders; (4) envisioning and creating valued agendas for action; (5) honing diagnostic and interpersonal skills; (6) building cooperative and supportive networks; (7) maintaining a good image and track record by using these influence tactics with sensitivity, flexibility, and high levels of communication; (8) developing a reputation as a knowledgeable, trustworthy person; and (9) being able to submerge one's ego and get along with others.[14] The use of power in this context is far removed from the idea of lonely individuals with flashes of brilliance; instead power is part of a systematic, behavioral process that is innately intertwined with leadership.[15]

THEORIES OF LEADERSHIP

Much of the research on leadership can be grouped into three categories: the trait approach, the behavioral or functional perspective, and the situational or contingency view. Although some of these theories are currently more popular than others, none of these orientations by itself seems to fully explain all of the dynamics underlying leadership. Moreover, even the theories that have been criticized as being too narrowly focused or inconsistent across different situations (such as the trait approach) seem to describe certain types of leadership. Thus, our purpose is to examine these different perspectives and to focus on their critical aspects for an understanding of leadership theory.

Trait Theory

The early approaches to leadership focused on those personal characteristics and attributes—physical, mental, and cultural—that seemed to differentiate between leaders and followers. This research is often termed the "Great Person" theory of leadership, since it was assumed that leaders were quite different from average people in terms of a number of personality and physical characteristics. Based on comprehensive reviews of the leadership research, for example, five personal characteristics seemed to be related to effective leadership: intelligence, dominance, self-confidence, high levels of energy and activity, and task-relevant knowledge.[16] Certain sociodemographic characteristics (e.g., education, social class) have also been suggested to be related to leadership. The relationship between these characteristics and evidence of effective leadership, however, is not particularly strong. In fact, in the case of each characteristic, there have been significant studies that have either *not* shown any relationship with effective leadership or found a negative relationship. Thus, while some common attributes have been suggested, much of the research in this area is contradictory and it provides an incomplete picture of leadership.

Trait Theory, Emotional Intelligence, and the "Magic" Leader

Although trait theories were held in disrepute for a number of years, they have reemerged as a promising research area, especially in terms of examining the specific traits related to effectiveness and success in different types of organizational settings. Many of the popular studies of management in the 1980s and 1990s, for example, pointed to the importance of strong corporate leaders and their ability to develop a shared sense of values and mission as a significant part of an organization's search for excellence.[17]

Recent research suggests that there are, in fact, a number of traits that do contribute to effective leadership:

- *Drive*, reflection of a high effort level (achievement orientation, ambition, energy, tenacity, initiative)

- *Leadership motivation,* a strong desire to lead
- *Honesty and integrity,* being truthful and following through on verbal commitments
- *Self-confidence,* including emotional stability and the ability to arouse confidence in followers
- *Resonance,* the ability to drive emotions positively, creating and spreading enthusiasm throughout the organization
- *Cognitive ability and knowledge of the business,* especially in terms of strong analytic skills, good judgment, and the capacity to think strategically and multidimensionally

It seems that although these traits—which bear a relationship to many of the traditional characteristics noted earlier—alone do not guarantee leadership success, they help leaders acquire and develop the requisite skills and abilities necessary for success.[18]

In an increasing number of instances, successful large-scale organizational change appears to be guided by individual leaders who embody these traits, authentic leaders with high levels of emotional intelligence (see Chapter 2) who are able to serve as a focal point for the change, and whose presence, actions, and touch have a special feel or "magic" to them.[19] Within this context, *magic* does not refer to mystical or illusory powers, but rather to those special qualities and traits that enable an individual to mobilize and sustain organizational effort over time. Three key dimensions of leader behavior—envisioning, energizing, and enabling—appear to characterize these individuals. *Envisioning* involves the creation and communication of a strategic image of the future that people can understand, accept, and get excited about. *Energizing* refers to the ability of leaders to motivate and inspire others through their own personal excitement, energy, and self-confidence, personal contact with organizational members, and use of organizational successes to celebrate progress toward the vision. Finally, *enabling* reflects the ability to empower others, helping them to perform on their own in the face of challenging goals through empathy, support, and expressions of confidence. These individuals often take on legendary status, "expanding the envelope" by testing themselves and their organizations, creating a "bigger than life" stature in the process.[20] The idea of magic or heroic leaders—their strengths as well as their limitations—will be explored more fully in the section on transformational leadership.

Attributes and Results

One of the limitations of looking solely at leadership traits or attributes is that it emphasizes an inwardly focused, partial view of leadership.[21] As a recent perspective suggests, it is not enough to simply master the attributes of leadership—effective leaders must also *connect* attributes to desired results and outcomes. In essence, *effective leadership = attributes × results.* Based on this formulation, the two variables in the equation multiply each other; they are not cumulative. Thus, a low score on one dimension considerably lessens a leader's effectiveness. A sole focus on leadership development through attributes falls short of paying sufficient attention to results. Organizations that pressure their leaders to do whatever it takes to meet short-term objectives, in contrast, rarely attain sustainable results over time. The basic thrust of this perspective is that leadership competencies and organizational capabilities must lead to, and be directly connected with, desired results over the long term.

Similar to the dimensions of "magic" or resonant leaders, the key attributes associated with effective leadership in this formulation fall into four areas: (1) *setting direction* (e.g., creating a vision, customer orientation, future orientation); (2) *demonstrating personal character* (e.g., integrity, trust); (3) *mobilizing individual commitment* (e.g., engaging and energizing others, sharing power); and (4) *engendering organizational capabilities* (e.g., building teams, valuing diversity, managing change). To be truly effective, however, these attributes must contribute to *desired* results, which are based on four key criteria. First, results should be *balanced* across key stakeholders (see Chapter 8): customers, investors, employees, and the organization itself (e.g., learning, speed, boundary spanning, accountability). Long-term prosperity is rarely gained by achieving success with one of these stakeholders while ignoring the others. Second, results should be *strategic,* ultimately contributing to organizational distinctiveness and competitive advantage. Third, results should be *lasting,* not sacrificing long-term success for short-term gains. Finally, results should be *selfless,* focused on the benefit of the larger whole rather than a single individual, area, or department. This link between attributes and results (organizational outcomes) enriches our understanding of the relationship between leader traits and leadership effectiveness.

Behavioral and Functional Theories

Another major thrust in leadership research has focused on the various behavioral patterns or styles used by different leaders and the functions fulfilled by these individuals. Early research on small groups, for example, attempted to assess the effect of three different leadership styles on member performance and satisfaction: *autocratic* (leading by command), *democratic* (leading through group input and decision making), and *laissez-faire* (leading through minimal participation by the leader and allowance of total group freedom) leadership. In one set of studies of boys' clubs, adult leaders of different groups used these styles to focus on the completion of a particular set of tasks.[22] One leader told the boys exactly what to do (*autocratic*), another engaged in a participative approach encouraging the boys to make suggestions about how to do the task (*democratic*), while a third leader let the boys do exactly what they wanted (*laissez-faire*). The study found that the autocratic group produced the most by a small amount, but the democratic group produced higher-quality goods and had higher levels of member satisfaction. The laissez-faire group fared the least well of the three groups in terms of task quantity, quality, and member satisfaction. Although there have been a number of criticisms of these studies (e.g., with adult advisers working with young boys during the 1930s and 1940s, what you actually have are three variations of authoritarian leadership), the results were generalized to industrial settings and spawned a host of related empirical investigations.

Researchers at Ohio State University and the University of Michigan continued this research into the behavioral aspects of leadership. The Michigan studies were concerned with two different leader orientations: one toward *employees* and the other toward *production.*[23] The results of this research suggested that a strong orientation to production resembled the autocratic leadership style, while a strong employee orientation was indicative of the democratic leadership style. In a similar way, the Ohio State studies developed two dimensions of leadership based on questionnaires given to supervisors and their subordinates that focused on how the leaders perceived their own styles and how the styles were perceived by the people they were supervising. Two basic factors were derived: *initiating structure* and *consideration* for others.[24] Leaders high on initiating structure tended to tell their subordinates what to do and how to do it. Leaders high on consideration focused on their subordinates' satisfaction, interpersonal needs, and general comfort. Thus, leaders high on initiating structure and low on consideration were viewed as authoritarian, while leaders who were high on consideration and low on initiating structure were perceived as democratic—although these relationships are not perfect fits. It is also possible for a leader to be high or low on *both* these dimensions at the same time.

The initial outcome of these studies suggested that consideration for others was more effective than initiating structure, especially in terms of maintaining member satisfaction and performance, and reducing absenteeism and turnover. Subsequently, it was argued that effective leadership and management were characterized by being high on both dimensions.[25] However, the "high-high" style did *not* lead to high member performance and satisfaction in all situations; research found inconclusive and at times contradictory findings. It appeared that the style that was high on both initiating structure and consideration was generally the most favorable, but there were enough exceptions to suggest that other situational factors needed to be considered. Recent meta-analysis, including 130 studies up to 2001, indicated that both consideration and initiating structure were significantly related to leadership outcomes. The results suggest that consideration is more closely related to employee satisfaction, motivation, and leader effectiveness, while initiating structure is more closely related to leader job performance and group and organization performance.[26]

Managerial Grid®

During the 1960s, Robert Blake and Jane Mouton developed two attitudinal dimensions: a *concern for people* and a *concern for production*.[27] These two dimensions were combined to form the Managerial Grid. This theory initially argued that the 9,9 approach—a high concern for both people and production—is the most effective leadership style. This "team" orientation was viewed as superior to those leadership orientations that are controlling and solely task-oriented (9,1), highly accommodating and "country clubbish" (1,9), impoverished (1,1), or "middle of the road"/status quo (5,5), because effective leadership involves both working with people and accomplishing various tasks.

As seen in Figure 7-1, this theory is now referred to as the Leadership Grid. In addition to the concern-for-people and concern-for-production dimensions, the theory also includes the issue of motivation ("Why do I do what I do?"). The new framework provides a basis for exploring and understanding personal motivations and allows for two additional leadership styles. These latter styles are combinations of the five orientations noted earlier. Paternalistic (or Maternalistic) management (9,9) links the production orientation (9) of the Authority-Compliance style (9,1) with the people orientation (9) of the Country Club style (1,9). The motivation underlying the Paternalistic style is domination, mastery, and control exercised in a manner that is intended to gain admiration. Opportunism incorporates several or all of the other Grid styles, including paternalism, in an effort to gain maximum advantage in a given situation. Given the "what's in it for me" orientation of this style, however, this orientation can lead to unethical behavior, especially when two opportunists interact with one another.

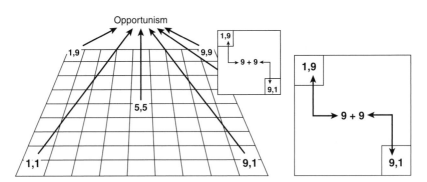

In Opportunistic Management, people adapt and shift to any Grid style needed to gain the maximum advantage. Performance occurs according to a system of selfish gain. Effort is given only for an advantage for personal gain.

9 + 9: Paternalism/Maternalism Reward and approval are bestowed to people in return for loyalty and obedience; failure to comply leads to punishment.

Figure 7-1   The Leadership Grid

Source: The Leadership Grid figure, Paternalism figure, and Opportunism figure from *Leadership Dilemmas—Grid Solutions*, by Robert H. Blake and Anne Adams McCanse (formerly the Managerial Paternalism figure, p. 30; Opportunism figure, p. 31). Copyright © 1991 by Scientific Methods, Inc. Reproduced by permission of the owners.

One of the unique aspects of this particular approach is the assumption that each Grid style represents a pattern of thinking about or analyzing a situation. Since these orientations are not personality characteristics or fixed traits, they can be affected by training. People, therefore, can be trained to become 9,9 leaders and an elaborate framework, referred to as *Grid Organization Development,* has been developed for such training. While this model has influenced our thinking about leadership for over forty years, an underlying difficulty is that research findings have been inconclusive, it has a Western/North American orientation, and there is still a lack of substantive evidence that the 9,9 approach is actually the most effective form of leadership in all situations.[28]

Nevertheless, Blake and Mouton's breakthrough approach integrated an empirical theory of behavior with a learning methodology that brought about significant change in how we thought about and approached leadership. Their framework promoted excellence through leadership and how leaders might enhance the effectiveness of those around them.[29]

Immaturity-Maturity Theory

A different way to examine leader behavior is to look at the effects of leadership on subordinate behavior. One perspective is Chris Argyris's developmental psychological approach, which analyzes behavioral differences from childhood to adulthood.[30] Argyris argued that seven basic personality changes must occur if people are to develop into mature individuals. These changes, which are summarized on the immaturity-maturity continuum in Figure 7-2, represent general tendencies among people. In some instances, however, the norms of a particular culture may inhibit the development of an individual's "maturity," even though this process continues with chronological aging.

The implications of this theory are reflected in the ways in which we have structured organizations. Since many organizational settings continue to operate under bureaucratic (or hierarchical) value systems (based on Theory X assumptions), employees are often treated as immature children. As a consequence, many problems

Argyris assumes that the developmental continuum from childhood to adulthood has the following characteristics:

Immature, Childlike Behavior	Mature, Adult Behavior
1. Passivity	Activity, increasing self initiation
2. Few ways of behaving	Many ways of behaving
3. Dependency on others	Relative independency, but acknowledging healthy dependencies
4. Erratic, shallow, quickly dropped interests	Deeper, more challenging interests
5. Short time focus, mainly on the present	Extended time focus, on past, present, and future
6. Subordinate in relevant hierarchies (family, society)	Equal or superordinate in relevant hierarchies
7. Lack of self-awareness	Aware of self, has self worth, own decisions determine outcome of effort

Figure 7-2 Argyris's Immaturity-Maturity Continuum

Source: Adapted from Chris Argyris, *Personality and Organization* (New York: Harper Brothers, 1957), pp. 50–53.

that appear to be related to worker apathy or even laziness are actually caused by managerial practices that constrain people from "maturing." Thus, leadership behaviors that attempt to increase organizational effectiveness by creating relatively simplistic jobs and straightforward requirements actually restrict the creativity and initiative of their subordinates. Argyris subsequently challenged many of these managerial practices and called for organizational leaders to establish those conditions that favored participation and employee involvement, such as more democratic and participative leadership styles based on Theory Y assumptions.

Linking Pin Theory

Another approach to examining the behaviors and functions of managers is through Rensis Likert's concept of a *linking pin*.[31] In his examination of organizations, Likert found that the traditional view of management (close supervision, high structure) only partly explained the roles fulfilled by managers. He argued that managers are actually members of two different workgroups—one group that the person is responsible *for* (traditional view of supervision) and another that the person is responsible *to* (see Figure 7-3). Thus, managers can be thought of as *leaders* of one group and *subordinates* of another. Effective leadership, therefore, is characterized by the ability to exert influence *upward* and *lateral* (peer managers) as well as "leading" those below. Since this linking pin role is an important aspect of management, by creating conditions that will encourage the development of maturity among subordinates, managers will

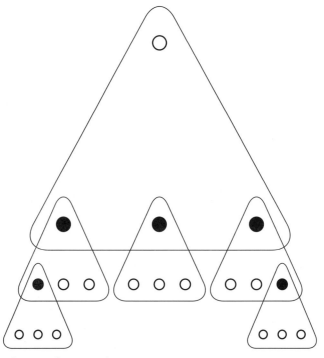

Figure 7-3   Likert's Linking Pin Theory

Source: Rensis Likert, *New Patterns of Management*, 1961 (New York: McGraw-Hill), p. 105. Reprinted with permission.

be able to develop their own leadership abilities in terms of longer-range planning and interdepartmental coordination.

Due to the traditional top-down orientation in organizations, the idea of exerting influence upward—in essence managing your boss—is often viewed somewhat skeptically, something that people would typically do for political or personal reasons.[32] Within the context of the linking pin theory, however, this idea refers to the process of consciously working with those above you in the organizational hierarchy to achieve the best possible results for yourself, your boss, and your company. The key is to (1) develop a good understanding of your boss and yourself, especially in terms of strengths, weaknesses, needs, and personal working styles; and (2) then use this information to develop and manage a compatible, healthy, and mutually supportive working relationship. It is important to underscore the significance of this aspect of leadership. The ability to represent a group upward in an organization and to establish and effectively manage organizational relationships with others—including one's boss—is a vital dimension of management.[33]

System 4

Subsequent work by Likert focused on various patterns of leadership behaviors, structures, and controls, and their effect on employee attitudes, motivation, and perceptions. Based on a series of questions that graphically illustrated organizations in terms of these different patterns, Likert identified four profiles of organizational characteristics: *System 1* (Exploitative-Authoritative); *System 2* (Benevolent-Authoritative); *System 3* (Consultative); and *System 4* (Participative).[34] While System 1 and System 4 have respective parallels to McGregor's Theory X and Theory Y, Likert stressed the environment in which the manager works, the organization, and the group in addition to the manager's assumptions about the workers.

In System 1, supervisors do not trust their subordinates, and the chain of command from the top down is used to convey organizational goals and decisions. From the perspective of employees, this system leads to suspicion, strong covert resistance to organizational goals, and the emergence of an informal system that resists the formal one. In System 4, by contrast, supervisors trust their subordinates and goal setting and decision making are collaborative activities. As a result employees tend to be more receptive to communication—both downward and upward—and there is little or no resistance to organizational goals and decisions.

Likert is quite clear in his preference for the ideal pattern of organization—System 4. By ideal, Likert refers to organizational performance in terms of satisfaction, morale, and the more traditional business criteria associated with productivity and effectiveness. Using what is now referred to as a Likert-type scale ("strongly agree" to "strongly disagree"; see Appendix A) he asked people to complete a survey that compared their existing organization on a number of dimensions (ranging from leadership and motivation to goals and control) with their ideal or preferred organization. As illustrated in Figure 7-4, in most cases there was a distinct gap between the authoritative reality of organizational life and the level of consultation and participation that people desired. Accordingly he argued that a change in leader behavior is one of the important determinants that can influence a shift to System 4 patterns. His view is increasingly being reflected in recent discussions of efforts to empower organizational members and reenergize mature organizations in both the private and public sectors.[35]

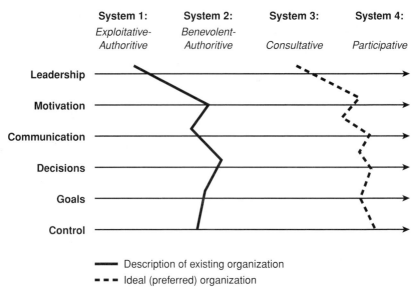

Figure 7-4 Typical Patterns in Organizational Profile Ratings

Managerial Application: Leadership Styles

A recent application of the work on leader behavior links the various styles leaders employ with their emotional intelligence (see Chapter 2).[36] Daniel Goleman and his associates suggest that there are six distinct leadership styles that exert a significant, direct, and unique impact on the work atmosphere in an organization:

1. The **visionary style** focuses on moving people toward shared dreams and mobilizing organizational members toward the vision. This style is most effective when an organizational change requiring a new vision or clear direction is needed, and it emphasizes self-confidence, empathy, and being a change catalyst.

2. **Coaching** connects what people want with the organization's goals and develops their potential. Emphasis is placed on helping organizational members improve their performance by building long-term capabilities, and it draws on the leader's empathy, self-awareness, and willingness to help others.

3. An **affiliative style** attempts to create harmony by connecting people to each other and creating strong emotional bonds and attachments. Focus is placed on healing rifts within a team or helping people cope with stressful situations. This style draws on the leader's empathy and relationship-building and communication skills.

4. A **democratic style** values people's input and gaining commitment and consensus through participation. This set of behaviors is very useful to create buy-in and build consensus, generating input from valued employees, and it draws on the leader's collaborative and communication skills.

5. **Pacesetting** lays out challenges and exciting goals, setting high performance standards and demanding excellence from organizational members in the process. While this approach can get quick results from highly motivated and competent teams and individuals, it can induce stress in the organization. This style reflects the leader's conscientiousness, achievement drive, and initiative.

6. **Commanding** ensures clear direction and demands immediate compliance with objectives. This style is most effective in a crisis situation or dealing with problem employees, and it draws on the leader's drive to achieve, initiative, and self-control.

Effective leaders should be able to draw on a number of these styles, depending on the circumstances around them. As Goleman and his colleagues suggest, four of these styles—visionary, coaching, affiliative, and democratic—create the type of atmosphere and resonance that engages people and boosts performance. The pacesetting and commanding styles, in contrast, while powerful in moving an organization forward, can have a negative impact on organizational climate and lead to dissonance among organizational members and should, therefore, be used with caution. To be effective, however, leaders should be able to draw on the emotional intelligence abilities that drive these different styles, switching their style—including pacesetting and commanding—in response to the cues and challenges around them.

Summary

Although there are obvious differences between these behavioral approaches to leadership, a number of common themes can be drawn. First, all of these theories are based on the belief that *leader style* is a key determinant of the leadership process. Second, an underlying assumption is that there are two primary functions of leadership: (1) an orientation to task structure, direction, and production; and (2) an orientation to people, and support for their needs and the maintenance needs of groups. Finally, these different perspectives strongly suggest that there is "one best way" to approach leadership over the long term: an orientation to teamwork, participation, and a concern for democratic processes in decision making, or a high concern for *both* people and production processes.

These theories have been criticized, however, for failing to capture the true complexity of the leadership process.[37] Although the behavior approach seems to go beyond the trait theory of leadership, what these theories actually do is provide a list of styles or behaviors instead of a list of traits. Moreover, since empirical investigation has led to inconsistent findings, it appears that we must continue to systematically explore the influence of individual differences and situational constraints on the leadership process.

Contingency Theories

As reflected in Goleman's work noted earlier, as researchers continued to explore leadership in different organizational settings it appeared that in some circumstances an authoritative production-oriented style was quite effective. In other circumstances, however, it appeared that an affiliative people-oriented style was more effective. Yet, although these observations began to suggest that managers needed to be flexible in their approach to leadership, an initial concern was raised that people in leadership positions might not able to change their styles very easily. In fact, it was suggested that it was more effective to design a specific leadership situation to fit the style of a particular leader or even to change leaders when a style change seemed to be needed than to attempt to change an individual's leadership style.

This perspective suggests that there is *no* "one best way" to lead in all situations; rather, the most effective style of leadership is *contingent* or dependent on the situation. In effect, contingency theories combine the trait approach and the behavioral/functional theories to suggest that the most effective leaders are those individuals who can *adapt* their styles to the demands of a particular situation, group, and their own personal values.[38] While researchers have questioned the extent to which situational factors actually serve as moderators of a leader's effectiveness, these variables do exert an influence on job- and organization-related attitudes (e.g., job involvement, intrinsic satisfaction) and behaviors (e.g., group effectiveness, product quality, organizational change).[39]

Fiedler's Contingency Theory

One of the classic contingency theories, based on the work of Fred Fiedler, proposes that effective leadership is based on the degree of fit between a leader's style and the extent to which a particular situation enables that person to exert influence over the group (*favorableness of a situation*).[40] According to Fiedler's model, there are three basic situational variables that influence the favorableness of a situation for a leader:

1. Leader-member relations, the personal relationships leaders have with members of their group in terms of trust, confidence, and respect

2. Task structure, how well the task of the group is defined (e.g., structured or unstructured; clear or ambiguous)

3. Position power of the leader, the degree of power and influence a leader has over subordinates

Based on extensive research, Fiedler and his associates found that when the overall situation was either very favorable (good leader-member relations, structured task, strong position power) or very unfavorable (poor leader-member relations, unstructured task, weak position power), the most effective leadership style was authoritarian in nature (*task oriented*). However, when the situation was intermediately favorable, such as when leader-member relations were good, but the task was unstructured and the leader had weak position power, the most effective style was more democratic in nature (*relationship oriented*). Subsequent studies have suggested that other salient factors should be considered, such as the interaction between the personal compatibility among leaders and followers and their ability to collaborate on the work task.[41]

An underlying problem with Fiedler's theory is that the situational (favorability) variables are often difficult to assess (such as how good relations are between leader and subordinates, or how structured or unstructured a particular task is). Second, Fiedler constructed a least-preferred co-worker (LPC) scale (a relatively simple questionnaire that asks leaders to describe the person they work least well with in terms of sixteen extremes such as helpful-frustrating, efficient-inefficient) that purports to measure the extent to which a person is task- or relationship-oriented. Although Fiedler used the LPC to classify leadership styles, the rationale underlying the LPC and the instrument itself has been questioned, and research has found that a particular leader's LPC scores can vary. Finally, despite the more recent development (e.g., leader-follower compatibility; task collaboration), this model has been criticized as being overly simplistic in its analysis of the situational complexities of leadership. Nevertheless, Fiedler's approach significantly influenced our thinking about leadership and prompted further research into the contingencies of the leadership process.

Cognitive Resource Utilization

Although research has suggested that leader success was generally related to a leader's intelligence, technical competence, and job-relevant knowledge, a number of studies found that these factors did not necessarily predict leader success. Based on an extension of the least preferred co-worker (LPC) research, Fiedler explored these concerns and found that leaders effectively used such cognitive resources only when they (1) were directive (authoritative), (2) were not under stress, (3) had good relationships with their subordinates, and (4) possessed relevant task knowledge.[42] When leaders are under stress (e.g., due to poor relationships with their subordinates), they will tend to rely more on past experiences rather than attempting to diagnose and understand their present situation. In these cases, Fiedler found that intelligence was actually *inversely* related to leadership effectiveness.

The dynamic underlying such reliance on prior experiences is similar to what happens when a person attempts to defend a position that is no longer tenable and must rely on more primitive, less well-developed defenses in order to maintain that position. While both practices are typically unsuccessful, a significant feature of this research emphasizes the role of stress and the importance of stress management in leadership. Moreover, by beginning to combine situational variables with personality characteristics and the concept of emotional intelligence (see Chapter 2), this line of research provides us with more insight into leadership dynamics.[43]

Path-Goal Theory

Another contingency theory that was developed through empirical research is the path-goal model.[44] This approach emerged from an attempt to clarify the discrepancies in the earlier Ohio State studies, which found that although effective leaders tended to be high on both the initiating structure and consideration dimensions of leadership, there were a number of exceptions. Thus, the research focused on the circumstances under which the "high-high" approach or a greater focus either on initiating structure or consideration would be most effective.

Path-goal theory, which as discussed in Chapter 3 is also used as a motivation model, is based on expectancy theory. The concept is derived from a leader's ability to clarify a subordinate's path to a desired goal or outcome. In other words, a leader could attempt to create a clear path to a particular objective as a way of increasing motivation toward reaching an important (valent) and attainable goal. If, however, the route to the goal is already clear, any additional clarifying information could be regarded by subordinates as redundant, and satisfaction with the leader will diminish. Thus, high consideration appears to be important (i.e., leads to greater satisfaction) when individuals are working on routine or structured tasks, while initiating structure is more effective in ambiguous task situations.

While path-goal theory has effectively predicted the outcomes of a number of task structures, there have also been inconsistent research results. Further investigation is continuing to add to our understanding of underlying dynamics and interactions, for example, the influence of subordinates' locus of control, the level and determinants of goal commitments, and the complexities of the tasks involved. It also appears that this theory is more effective in describing leader-subordinate behaviors than leader-peer relations.[45]

Life-Cycle Theory of Leadership

One of the more recent contingency theories is an attempt to integrate the different perspectives discussed thus far into a comprehensive model. This situational approach, which is referred to as the *Life-Cycle Theory of Leadership,* is focused on three basic factors: (1) the amount of task-oriented behavior (guidance and direction) a leader gives; (2) the amount of relationship-oriented behavior (socioemotional support) a leader provides; and (3) the readiness level that organizational members exhibit in performing a specific task, function, or objective.[46] Thus, similar to the earlier Ohio State studies, Paul Hersey and Ken Blanchard delineate two dimensions of leader behavior: task (initiating structure) and relationship (consideration) activities. As indicated in Figure 7-5, these two dimensions form four possible leadership styles. While this basic view of leadership patterns is similar to Blake and Mouton's managerial (leadership) grid, this approach suggests that the most appropriate (effective) style of leadership depends on the relative task readiness of the leader's subordinates.

Within this context, readiness is defined in terms of subordinates':

- Level of achievement motivation
- Willingness and ability to assume responsibility
- Task-relevant education and experience

These basic readiness variables are combined with the leader's assessment of the past and present performance of the group, and how well group members interact with one another (e.g., handling conflict, decision making) to determine the appropriate leadership style. As indicated in Figure 7-5, the style that is preferable for relatively "immature" subordinates (in terms of the three readiness dimensions) is different from the style preferred with more "mature" group members.

One of the interesting features about this model is that a leadership pattern can emerge (or be developed over time) where there is a sufficient level of trust that delegation of authority and responsibility (for highly mature members) reflects a higher developmental stage than one with high concern for tasks and people ("high-high"). The ultimate point is that the organization and its managers can be so confident in the subordinates and *vice versa* that less time is required for task or relationship considerations.

While this model has impressive scope, it is a *post hoc* model, which limits its ability as a predictive framework. Although many studies have supported this approach, there have also been criticisms of the methodology of these studies as well as of the model

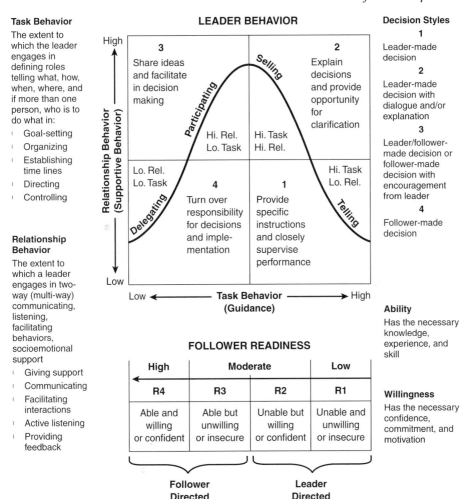

Figure 7-5 Situational Leadership Model

Source: Paul Hersey and Kenneth H. Blanchard, *Management of Organizational Behavior: Utilizing Human Resources,* 5th edition, Englewood Cliffs, NJ: Prentice Hall, 1988, p. 182. Copyrighted materials from Leadership Studies, Inc. All rights reserved. Used by permission.

itself (e.g., the "high-high" approach in this model does not reflect the true sentiment of the "team" orientation of the managerial grid).[47]

Leader-Participation Style Model

Another contingency approach to leadership focuses on an examination of leader behavior and group participation in making decisions.[48] This model, which is based on the work of Vroom and Yetton, attempts to delineate a "rational way" of deciding on the form and amount of participation in decision making that *should* be used in different situations.

Based on this approach, there are five basic leadership decision styles, which range from highly autocratic (A), through consultative (C), to group-oriented (G). These five styles are summarized as follows:[49]

AI: You solve the problem or make the decision yourself, using information available to you at that time.

AII: You obtain the necessary information from your subordinates, then decide on the solution to the problem yourself. You may or may not tell your subordinates what the problem is in getting the information from them. The role played by your subordinates in making the decision is clearly one of providing the necessary information to you, rather than generating or evaluating alternative solutions.

CI: You share the problem with relevant subordinates individually, getting their ideas and suggestions without bringing them together as a group. Then you make the decision, which may or may not reflect your subordinates' influence.

CII: You share the problem with your subordinates as a group, collectively obtaining their ideas and suggestions. Then you make the decision, which may or may not reflect your subordinates' influence.

GII: You share a problem with your subordinates as a group. Together you generate and evaluate alternatives and attempt to reach agreement (consensus) on a solution. Your role is much like that of chairperson. You do not try to influence the group to adopt your solution and you are willing to accept and implement any solution that has the support of the entire group.

The model assumes that any one of these styles *may* be appropriate in a given situation. However, since this can vary from situation to situation, it is necessary to have a framework to guide the choice of an appropriate style. The model is thus extended to include a series of situational variables in decision-tree or flowchart form (see Figure 7-6). By responding to the series of questions raised in this framework, a leader goes through the decision-making tree until an end point is reached, suggesting an appropriate decision style for that particular situation. Thus, depending on the presence (or absence) of various contingencies, one particular decision style is argued to be more appropriate for solving problems than another.

Conceptually, there are three dimensions underlying this approach: (1) the quality or rationality of the decision; (2) the acceptance or commitment on the part of subordinates necessary for effective implementation; and (3) time constraints. The questions that are illustrated in Figure 7-6 serve to protect the quality and acceptance

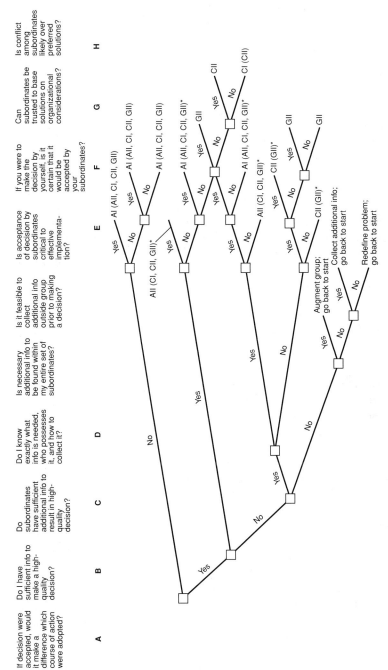

Figure 7-6 Stakeholder Map of Major Oil Company in the Present Environment

Note: The primary decision style is for the short-term model. Appropriate decision styles for the long-term model are indicated in the parentheses following the primary styles. Long-term decision styles marked by asterisks are appropriate only when the answer to question G is positive.

Source: Adapted from *Leadership and Decision Making* by Victor Vroom and Philip Yetton by permission of the University of Pittsburgh Press. Copyright © 1973 by University of Pittsburgh Press.

of the decision by eliminating particular decision styles that might risk one of these outcomes. There is a difference, however, in what is termed the short-term versus long-term implications of this approach. The decision tree seeks to protect the quality of a decision (if relevant) and to create the necessary acceptance of the decision by subordinates. Yet, the particular decision approach that may be effective in the short-term may not be that effective over a longer time frame (as when a highly autocratic manager needs subordinates to make a decision on their own, yet they might not have developed the expertise). Thus, *when appropriate* and *when time permits,* the long-term model suggests moving toward a developmental, participative orientation to decision making (e.g., using CII when AI is acceptable).

Most of the research on this model has focused on its development rather than on testing it in actual managerial situations.[50] One of the main findings, however, is that the model recommends that managers should change their decision styles more than most managers do and that a lack of information sharing and consensus building can result in serious disadvantages. Thus, some of Fiedler's early arguments that it may be easier to alter a situation to fit a particular leader, rather than the reverse, appear to have some validity. Moreover, it has been argued that the series of decision rules, even in decision tree format, makes it unlikely that managers will be able to use such an approach in practice. Nevertheless, the model provides an interesting view of participation in decision making and a basis to evaluate when a particular style of leadership may be appropriate.

Attribution Theory

Another way of viewing the dynamics of the leadership process is through attribution theory.[51] Although this perspective is more speculative than the preceding contingency models, it is similar to the discussion of attribution theory in the chapters on motivation and perception. If a subordinate (or an observer) has an implicit idea of what constitutes "good" (or "poor") leadership and its behavioral effects, then leadership characteristics may be attributed to a person who is related to the situation in question. In other words, if a certain leadership act initially causes a behavioral result, then every time an observer sees that result, the observer will attribute leadership to a person close to the outcome of the behavior.

As an example, imagine a production group that currently produces high-quality goods. As observers, we may have noticed that in the past one of the primary factors that led to this high-quality output was participative leadership and its effect on group cohesiveness. Due to selective perception and our view that participative leadership was important (in the earlier period), we may attribute participative qualities to the present leader because the outcome is unchanged from earlier production quality. However, this may *not* be the case. While the leader *may* (or *may not*) be participative, the fact that we attribute a certain type of leadership to this person determines how we react to that individual. Thus, the perception and attribution of leadership qualities and style are just as important from the perspective of others in the organization (perceivers) as they are from the perspective of the leader.

The effects of leadership attributions on member evaluations of organizational performance have been found to be quite profound. As research suggests, we have a sufficiently romanticized conception of leadership that we often attribute more influence to leadership than may be warranted.[52] While nonleadership factors—such as environmental forces, other characteristics of the firm, or even chance—may have been influential determinants of a particular outcome, especially under ambiguous conditions, people have a bias toward viewing leadership as a likely causal force when trying to explain organizational performance. This type of halo effect tends to be greatest when a firm's performance is at the extremes (either positive or negative), with leadership credited for very good performance and blamed for very poor performance. Thus much of what is referred to as leadership is perceptual in nature, in the "eye of the beholder."

Leader-Member Relations

A final way of looking at leadership is to examine the nature of the relationships that a leader has with his or her subordinates. There has been an increased emphasis on the relational aspects of leadership and associated outcomes, producing a flurry of studies utilizing leader-member exchange theory. *Leader-member exchange* (LMX) theory posits that differential social exchange relationships exist between leaders and their subordinates, and that the quality of those relationships influences subordinate outcomes. High levels of leader support and guidance exhibited toward a follower characterize high-quality or favorable LMX, which exerts a positive influence on subordinate outcomes; low levels of leader support and guidance indicate low-quality LMX, with a concomitant negative influence on subordinate experiences.

The underlying mechanism incorporated by LMX from vertical dyad linkage (VDL) and social exchange theories is the *norm of reciprocity*:[53] According to this norm, individuals treated favorably by others experience a sense of obligation to respond in kind.[54] Research has supported this dynamic in leader-member relationships, as LMX has been positively associated with subordinate job satisfaction, commitment, empowerment, extra-role behaviors, and performance.[55]

By definition, LMX research has focused on dyadic leader-member relationships (e.g., supervisor-subordinate) and the impact of these relationships on individual outcomes. However, recent research has begun to consider the influence of LMX at the group level. This research has considered the implications of two aspects of LMX: LMX *quality* (i.e., the quality of the LMX relationships established between a leader and his or her workgroup members, averaged across workgroup members); and LMX *differentiation* (i.e., the extent to which the quality of LMX relationships varies within a group). In general, the research suggests that higher aggregated LMX (or more high-quality relationships developed between a leader and group members) should be associated with performance advantages in workgroups. This prediction is based on the premise that LMX creates feelings of obligation among subordinates to reciprocate leader treatment in ways that benefit the leader. Thus, to the extent that group members are aware that contributions to workgroup success are desired by or valuable to the leader, group members should engage in behavior that contributes to group effectiveness:[56] Considerable support for this idea can be gleaned from the preponderance of studies that have found a positive relationship between dyadic LMX quality and subordinate extra-role behavior such as organizational citizenship behavior (OCB)—those efforts that go beyond formal contractual obligations and benefit the collective.[57] In teams with high aggregated LMX, the relationships between members and the leader are characterized by trust and respect, thus group members may feel more empowered and able to perform effectively.[58]

A key premise underlying LMX, however, is the notion that due to resource constraints, leaders tend to establish high-quality exchange relationships only with a select group of trusted subordinates. Due to time limitations and related pressures, they tend to have lower quality, transaction-based relationships with the majority of organizational members.[59] As a result, it is suggested that members of workgroups (1) need to work collaboratively or "act by consensus" in order to be effective, and (2) their ability to act by consensus is determined by the extent to which they share norms and perceptions of climate.[60] Research has found that dispersion within a group (across, for example, demographic variables, skills, perceptions) is negatively related to social integration, which can impair the speed of decision making and implementation.[61]

LMX differentiation also has the potential to affect interaction processes via the formation of in- and out-groups *within* a workgroup. Research has found that employees who share similar perceptions with regard to the quality of their LMX relationships (e.g., of similarly high or low quality) report higher quality relationships with each other. Conversely, employees engaged in very different LMX relationships (e.g., an employee in a high-quality LMX relationship and an employee in a low-quality LMX relationship) report lower quality relationships with one another.[62] Thus, LMX differentiation may affect the development of within-group agreement with regard to expectations and group climate.

Other LMX research has drawn on role theory (see Chapter 5) to understand LMX differentiation effects. It is argued that group performance should be enhanced by LMX differentiation because it helps to establish and clarify subordinate roles. Workgroup tasks generally run the gamut from routine activities to those requiring greater skills. Leaders rely on low-status members (those in low-quality LMX relationships) to perform mundane work, and high-status members (those in high-quality LMX relationships) to perform more important tasks. Thus, role differentiation and clarity among workgroup members has the potential to yield optimal group performance.[63]

The basic idea of an in-group and an out-group reflects a type of social distance—in this instance, a continuum of supervisor-subordinate relations—that provide us with a fuller sense of the effect of leadership in different situations. An implication of this type of analysis is that managers should attempt to balance the time spent in each of their critical organizational relationships according to the needs of the work rather than on the basis of habit or social preference.

LEADERSHIP AND MANAGEMENT

Thus far, the discussion in this chapter has implied that people in leadership positions are virtually unconstrained in their choice of behaviors. Indeed, the contingency theorists argue that effectiveness is ultimately determined by the extent to which leaders can adapt their behaviors to fit the demands of a given situation. Some theorists even suggest that a willingness to adapt and change is a core value of principled, diplomatic leadership.[64] Research on what managers actually do, however, suggests that leaders operate in a social context that must be maintained and negotiated with other groups. In fact, given many of the conflicting expectations and prescriptions concerning what managers *should do* in different circumstances, the resulting high levels of role conflict that may be experienced by people in these leadership roles lead to questions concerning the relationship between leadership and management.[65]

A manager is usually thought of as an organizational member with legitimate power (authority) to direct the work-related activities of at least one subordinate. In this context, a manager is viewed as a leader. There is more to management and leadership, however, than this type of direct supervision—initiating structure and consideration for others. Even the traditional view of management suggests that managers plan, organize, staff, direct, control, and coordinate.

Empirical research on what upper-level managers *actually do* in their organizations captures the complex realities of organizational life. Thus, in order to place the concept of leadership in its broader managerial context, we will examine two views of top managerial behavior. In contrast to the traditional view of management, leader behavior typically involves fragmented activities, long hours, and a preference for live action and oral communication with organization members.

Mintzberg's Managerial Role Set

In an effort to describe what CEOs actually do in their jobs, Henry Mintzberg undertook a series of intensive structured observations of the daily activities of such top-level managers.[66] Rather than finding that these individuals engaged in behaviors that could be characterized as planning, controlling, staffing, and so forth, Mintzberg found that their actions were much more concerned with relationships (*interpersonal roles*), the transfer of information (*information roles*), and decision making (*decision roles*) that emerged from their formal status and authority in the organization. He argued that these different roles formed a *gestalt*. In practice, the roles constitute an integrated whole—based on a manager's formal status and authority, certain interpersonal relationships emerge that lead to various informational inputs that, in turn, lead to informational and decisional outputs.

The first set of roles, interpersonal in nature, describes the manager's relationships with others in the organization and its environment. Most basic of all managerial roles is that of *figurehead*, the symbolic and ceremonial aspects of management ("ribbon cutting," going to formal dinners). Because organizations look to their formal head for guidance and motivation, another interpersonal role is that of *leader*, which defines manager-subordinate relationships. Finally, there is the *liaison* role, which encompasses the interpersonal network of dealings with peers and external stakeholders. Even though these three activities are different, each one links directly to the manager's formal status and authority, and each involves the development of interpersonal relationships.

The next set of roles relates to receiving and transmitting information. The three informational roles characterize the manager as a nerve center of the organization. As a *monitor*, a manager continually seeks, and is bombarded with, information concerning what is taking place in the organization (internal operations) and its environment (market changes, political interactions, technological developments, etc.). The second informational role is that of *disseminator*, which involves the dispersal of information to subordinates. This information can be both factual and value-oriented (e.g., what "ought" to be). Finally, while the disseminator role focuses on transmitting information downward in organizations, the *spokesperson* role concerns sharing information with the groups in the organization's environment. This outside communication is largely focused on two types of groups—key influencers (e.g., board of directors in terms of the chief executive, upper-level executives in terms of a middle manager) and relevant external stakeholders (e.g., customers, suppliers, governmental agencies).

The final set of roles encompasses the decision-making aspects of managerial work. Such decisions can be arranged along a continuum from those that are purely voluntary and innovative (e.g., introduction of a new product) to those that are involuntary and reactive (e.g., responding to a crisis). In the *entrepreneur* role, the manager takes responsibility for organizational change, acting as initiator and designer of specific changes, such as exploiting new market opportunities. This type of decision is closely related to the monitoring information role. In contrast to the proactive nature of the entrepreneurial role, a manager also operates as a *disturbance handler,* a person who must deal with involuntary situations and changes that are often beyond the manager's control. Such reactive situations may involve conflicts between subordinates, competitive problems between organizations, or resource losses or threats. There are two additional decisional roles that can be placed between the extremes of entrepreneur and disturbance handler. The manager also operates as a *resource handler* deciding "who gets what" in the organization in terms of money, time, materials, equipment, personnel, reputation, and so forth. Finally, in the role of *negotiator,* the manager is responsible for representing the organization at routine and major negotiations (e.g., negotiating an acquisition, consulting contract, or labor agreement).

Although Mintzberg argues that the amount of activity in any one of these roles varies depending on the particular type of job an individual manager may fulfill, this overview of managerial work presents quite a different picture of management compared with traditional definitions. It also suggests that leadership involves a much broader set of activities than a focus solely on task and maintenance considerations.

The Role of the General Manager

In another attempt to understand what general managers actually do in their jobs, John Kotter undertook an extensive investigation with a number of general managers from a broad range of different industries. Similar to Mintzberg, he found that it was hard to fit the behaviors of these individuals into the traditional categories of planning, organizing, controlling, and so forth. Overall, he found that there were two basic challenges and dilemmas in managerial work: (1) figuring out what to do in spite of uncertainty, ambiguity, and information overload; and (2) accomplishing things through a large and diverse group of people despite having little direct control over most of them. Kotter analyzed effective responses to these challenges in terms of agenda setting, network building, and agenda implementation.[67]

Based on his research, Kotter argues that effective managers initially engage in *agenda setting.* Such agendas are made up of loosely connected goals and plans that address long-term as well as short-term responsibilities across a broad range of financial, market, and organizational issues. Unlike the formal planning process, which is a functional area in many large organizations, managerial agendas often contain lists of goals or plans that are not as explicitly connected as the formal planning process would suggest. Managers rely more heavily on discussions with others than on reports, books, and other informational sources in formulating these plans. Moreover, much of the information used in agenda setting is applied in both conscious (analytical) and unconscious (intuitive) ways.

In addition to setting their agendas, effective managers spend considerable time and effort in developing networks of cooperative relationships with others they feel are necessary to fulfill their agendas. This type of *network building* activity is focused on a much larger group than the person's direct subordinates. Kotter found that effective managers develop cooperative relationships with such varied groups as peers, organizational outsiders, their bosses' boss, their subordinates' subordinates, and so forth. Moreover, managers also attempt to shape these networks by creating different types of relationships among people in different parts of the network. In other words, managers attempt to create an appropriate atmosphere (in terms of norms and values) that will encourage people to implement their agendas.

Once a manager's agenda and network have been established, the next set of behaviors is focused on using the network to implement the agenda. Such implementation is based on the manager's interpersonal skills, budgetary resources, information base, and ability to use symbolic communications to influence people and events in both direct and indirect ways. In most instances, *agenda implementation* will involve virtually the entire network of relationships that has been developed over time. Kotter also found that general managers who relied on a broader range of influence techniques (motivation skills, use of different types of power, communication skills, etc) were more effective than those who relied more heavily on traditional sources of influence (e.g., use of formal status and authority).

Implications for Management and Leadership

One of the main themes that emerges from these research studies is that there is considerable difference between what traditional theories of management suggest managers should do compared with the actual behaviors of successful managers. Although there are differences in the way in which these behaviors are categorized, relationships can be drawn between agenda setting and informational roles, network building and interpersonal roles, and agenda implementation and decisional roles. Both studies characterize management as being very demanding, fast paced, and less systematic and more informational than implied by basic textbook interpretations. Finally, these findings suggest that management is more of an art than a science, although the formal skills, functions, and quantitative techniques developed to train managers are important tools of managerial work.

If this research is an indication of managerial behavior, much of the leadership research that has been discussed in this chapter can be more properly classified as supervision rather than management or leadership. This difference appears to be the case, especially since the individuals whom Mintzberg and Kotter focused on in their research were upper-level executives and general managers with responsibilities across organizational functions.

Organizational Application: Executive Coaching

When viewing management and leadership in terms of your own career growth and development, it is important to keep in mind many of the broader issues and concerns that are involved in today's complex organizations. As a way of facilitating this process, a growing number of organizations are providing a "coach" to meet privately with leaders to discuss and work on their personal learning and development issues.[68] Areas covered by executive coaching programs range from relatively easy issues such as validating strengths, setting priorities, and assessing staff needs, to increasingly difficult problems such as improving a relationship with a boss, improving interpersonal skills, or how to facilitate a merger or implement a layoff. The major categories involved in such coaching concern feedback coaching, in-depth development coaching, and content coaching.

Feedback coaching, which typically involves ten to twenty hours spread out over a one- to six-month period, entails giving feedback to a person in a leadership position and assisting that individual in developing an action plan to address the needs or problems that are observed. This approach usually includes a 360-degree assessment instrument with which the coach helps the leader to identify strengths and areas needing development. *In-depth development coaching,* which can last from six months to a year, involves a closer, more intimate relationship between the leader and coach. Multiple assessments, observations, and face-to-face discussions are extensively used to develop the leader's interpersonal skills, including such objectives as improving his or her relationships with others, enhancing team-building skills, and developing personal style and behavior. At times, the coach will "shadow" the leader, observing the individual in meetings, in discussions with others, making presentations, and so forth. This information (observations) is then shared and discussed with the executive. Finally, *content coaching* involves providing leaders with knowledge and skills in specific areas. The amount of time involved varies considerably and is based on the complexity of the issue and background of the leader (e.g., global marketing strategies, advanced information technologies for supply chain management). The coaching process often combines these categories. A leader going through a merger for the first time, for instance, might draw on the experience and insights of a coach who has studied the dynamics associated with the merger and acquisition process (content coaching) as well as that individual's views on how he or she is dealing with her subordinates, peers, and boss (development coaching).[69] As the demands placed on organizational leaders become increasingly complex, it appears that this type of support will continue to grow in importance. In fact, one of the reasons why executive coaching has recently increased in popularity is that the process allows leaders to focus on and address the kinds of issues that often go unattended in the rush of day-to-day business life.

Substitutes for Leadership as Supervision

As this chapter underscores, leadership research has proliferated with many competing models that attempt to explain leader behaviors and outcomes. Unfortunately, attempts to create comprehensive, generalizable models of leadership have not been very successful in actually predicting subordinate behaviors, productivity, and related outcomes. In fact, as suggested earlier, (1) there has been a paucity of attention to *results,* and (2) many of the *perceptions* about leader effectiveness can be explained more effectively by the types of things we attribute to our leaders than by their actual behavior or attitudes.[70]

These concerns have led researchers to examine the types of factors that can augment or compensate for a lack of effective leadership at the supervisory level.

These "substitutes" for leadership encompass three basic sets of characteristics of the subordinate, the task, and the organization.[71] Particular *subordinate characteristics* that can modify the type of leadership or managerial control required for effective performance include a subordinate's (1) ability (the greater the level of ability, the lower the need for direct leadership); (2) experience (in general, the greater the experience, the less oversight required); (3) training and knowledge (less supervision is associated with higher levels of training and knowledge); (4) professional orientation (the more professionally oriented a person is, the less need for direct leadership); (5) need for autonomy (the greater the need for independence, the less direct supervision needed); and (6) orientation to organizational rewards (the greater the indifference, the greater the need for closer supervision and control).

Task characteristics that may substitute for leadership as supervision include high levels of (1) task repetitiveness and clarity; (2) intrinsic satisfaction; and (3) built-in feedback as part of the work process. The greater the degree these factors are in existence, the less need for direct oversight and control. Finally, *organizational characteristics* that may modify the types of leadership required in different work settings encompass (1) formalization (the greater the bureaucratic nature of an organization, the less discretion held by individual workers); (2) cohesive workgroups where norms significantly influence member behaviors; (3) organizational reward systems (the lower the degree of control over organizational rewards, the less influential a particular leader will tend to be); and (4) the actual distance between leaders and their subordinates (the greater the distance, the more difficult it is to exert influence).

As this discussion suggests, research on substitutes for leadership focuses on *whether* subordinates are being provided sufficient task guidance and incentives for performance instead of assuming that the formal leader must be the primary source of such direction. Emphasis is being placed on closely knit teams of highly trained individuals, intrinsically satisfying work that is self-motivating, computer-integrated manufacturing and networked computer systems that take over many of the supervisor's leadership functions, and the influence of higher levels of professional education among organizational members (e.g., sufficient formal education to complete work tasks without technical guidance from a supervisor).[72]

Leadership, Empowerment, and Self-Directed Work Teams

One way to conceptualize the idea of team-centered as opposed to leader-centered decision making and work direction is Tannenbaum and Schmidt's classic continuum of leader behavior.[73] As illustrated in Figure 7-7, work-related decisions can range from those in which the manager has complete control to those in which the decision-making process is centralized in the group. Consistent with these analyses, scholars continue to emphasize the importance of workgroup structure with regard to leader approach and effectiveness. Specifically, internal leaders of hierarchically structured groups can likely lead via individualized leadership of employees and the coordination of individuals' efforts. In this context, the supervisory leader is the conduit for coordinating employee effort. In contrast, nonhierarchical self-managing work teams require a different leadership approach and alternative means of coordinating effort. In this context, leaders are external to the group and are called on to facilitate team functioning via empowered organizational members.[74]

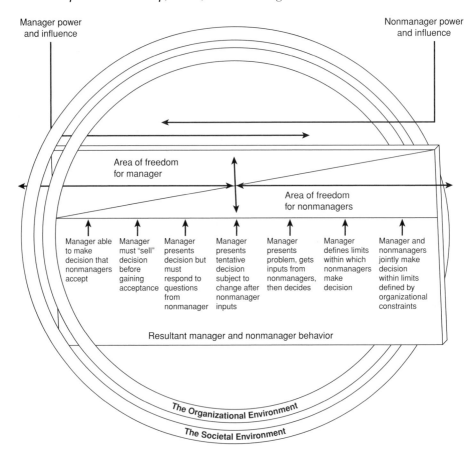

Figure 7-7   Continuum of Manager-Nonmanager Behavior

Source: Reprinted by permission of the *Harvard Business Review*. An exhibit from "How to Choose a Leadership Pattern: Retrospective Commentary," by Robert Tannenbaum and Warren H. Schmidt (May/June 1973). Copyright © 1973 by the President and Fellows of Harvard College; all rights reserved.

The idea of worker and team *empowerment* emphasizes a move away from leader dominance and expert problem solving to a system where organizational members, as the new experts, are continuously involved in organizational decision processes. While traditional models of power and authority were based on position and status, empowerment and self-directed teams emphasize the involvement of all organizational members in efforts to continuously improve work systems and outcomes. As a growing body of research indicates, especially for complex unprogrammed tasks, directive leadership is relatively ineffective when compared with the efficacy of work experience and training of members of close-knit, self-directed teams.[75]

Empowerment, in essence, reflects increased task motivation resulting from an individual's positive orientation to his or her work role.[76] There are four keys to effective empowerment strategies.[77] First, it is important for employees to have information on organizational performance and outcomes (e.g., firm operating results, competitor performance). Second, these individuals must be rewarded for their contributions to organizational performance (e.g., stock ownership, gainsharing). Third, team members must be provided with the knowledge and skills that will enable them to understand and contribute to organizational performance. Finally, these individuals must be given the power to make decisions that influence work procedures and organizational direction.

By developing alternative sources of task guidance and incentive systems to guide performance and empower employees, substitutes for leadership (as supervision) can increase the satisfaction, motivation, and accomplishments of organizational members. These same actions, however, may also have a negative effect on the morale among those leaders who perceive a loss of power. Although strong, self-confident leaders understand and are comfortable with the idea of empowering others, weak, "power-hungry" leaders typically view such substitutes as personally frustrating and organizationally dysfunctional.[78] These latter individuals mistakenly believe that the more power is granted to their subordinates, the less they will have for themselves. Power and influence, however, are not part of a zero-sum game where one party gains only at the expense of another. Moreover, if organizational members perceive their leader as being threatened by such change or using it as a temporary balm to soothe low morale and maximize productivity in the short term, they will readily withhold their commitment.[79]

A question that emerges from the use of work teams and the type of empowerment strategies and leadership substitutes discussed earlier focuses on the nature of leadership in what are essentially leaderless groups. Although the supervisory aspects of leadership literally disappear, the need for enlightened leadership—broadening and elevating the interests and skills of organizational members, generating awareness and acceptance of the organization's purpose and mission, creating and maintaining an environment of trust, and inspiring employees to look beyond their own self-interest— becomes increasingly important for these groups.[80]

Transformational Leadership and Organizational Change

As the previous discussion indicates, there is a much broader set of functions associated with being a leader than directly overseeing the activities and behaviors of subordinates. This distinction has led to assessments of transformational and transactional leadership.[81] A *transactional leader* (manager) views the leader-follower relationship as a process of exchange—work for specified rewards, a favor for a favor, and so forth. Transactional leadership reflects the relatively narrow view of management and leader as supervisor and is increasingly being replaced by the substitutes for leadership discussed earlier. *Transformational leaders*, in contrast, are more visionary, inspirational figures who are consumed with specific ideals and goals and able to engender intense emotions in their followers. Such individuals have both the ability to articulate and communicate a vision that identifies superordinate goals for an organization, and the charisma to energize and motivate people to accomplish these broader goals. Transformational leaders also appear to have sufficiently strong empathy and self-awareness skills (emotional intelligence) that they tend to be quite accurate in their perceptions of others—they often know what their subordinates' needs are, even when the followers themselves may not be fully aware of these needs.[82]

Recent research on this broader aspect of leadership has identified a number of characteristics that differentiate these individuals from transactional leaders.[83]

1. **Identification as a change agent.** Their personal and professional image is to make a difference, to create an organization that is adaptive, entrepreneurial, innovative, and successful.

2. **Courage and outspokenness.** These individuals are able to take risks and stand against the status quo in an organization. Intellectually, they are able to confront reality even if it is painful. Emotionally, they are able to reveal the truth to others who may not want to hear it.

3. **Belief in people.** Although powerful, these individuals are sensitive to the needs of others, seeking to empower others instead of acting in a dictatorial role.

4. **Value-driven.** These individuals typically articulate a set of core values and exhibit behaviors that are quite congruent with those value positions.

5. **Lifelong learning.** Transformational leaders tend to view failures as learning experiences, with a strong desire for continuous self-learning and development. They are capable of being self-reflective, with the ability to make rather dramatic shifts in their styles and approaches to management when necessary.

6. **Ability to deal with complexity, ambiguity, and uncertainty.** Such individuals are able to cope with and frame problems in a complex, changing world. They are able to deal with the sociocultural and political aspects of organizations as well as their technical dimensions.

7. **Visionary.** Finally, these individuals are visionaries in the sense that they are not only capable of creating a dream, but they can translate that dream and image so that others can share them.

Transactional leaders may have been quite sufficient for an era of continually expanding markets and nonexistent competition from abroad. Given the often painful realities of our present business environment, in contrast, the brand of leadership necessary for success in a more turbulent, often chaotic world, is quite different. Within this context, strong leaders create effective internal change processes that enable their organizations to cope with external change by:[84] (1) creating a sense of urgency by identifying and discussing crises, potential crises, or major opportunities; (2) building a guiding coalition of organizational members with sufficient power to lead the change; (3) developing a vision to direct the change effort and strategies to achieve the vision; (4) communicating and modeling the vision; (5) empowering others and encouraging risk-taking; (6) creating short-term wins (e.g., visible performance improvements) and recognizing and rewarding people who make those accomplishments; (7) consolidating gains and reinvigorating the process, in essence producing more change; and (8) anchoring new approaches in the organization's culture.

The Dark Side of Transformational Leadership

As the preceding discussion strongly suggests, transformational leaders are often characterized as organizational heroes, "magic" leaders who can orchestrate turn-arounds, launch new enterprises, inspire organizational renewal, and obtain extraordinary performance from organizational members.[85] Through their personal charisma, these individuals inspire trust, faith, and belief in themselves, their vision, and their actions. Yet, while the virtues of these charismatic leaders are frequently praised in the popular management press, there can be a "dark side" to such forms of leadership.

Despite good intentions, "magic" leaders may become sufficiently captivated by their vision of what is best for the organization that they unintentionally overlook internal and external signals that their vision might not be appropriate. In many instances, these individuals seek out the information they want to hear, do not learn easily from those around them, and focus relentlessly on tasks and goals—at times to the point where they actually damage organizational performance.[86] Numerous cautionary tales exist of leaders who got so carried away with their personal vision that they literally destroyed their companies in the process.

Narcissism and Ethics in Leadership

A far more insidious issue concerns narcissistic tendencies and unethical leader behavior.[87] Instead of attempting to align their visions with the long-term interests of the organization and follower aspirations, these individuals censure critical or opposing views, often with brutal force and demands that their decisions be accepted and implemented without question. Such narcissistic leaders pursue their own selfish agendas with such pathological egoism and disregard for those around them, that they literally suck the life out of the companies they purportedly serve.[88] Unfortunately, these individuals often use the ambiguities associated with organizational change to further their personal interests.

While most of us have probably worked for a bad boss, research points to six basic characteristics of truly narcissistic leaders: (1) reliance on manipulation and exploitation (e.g., lying, domination ploys, bullying, scapegoating); (2) impulsive and unconventional behavior (e.g., temper tantrums, fierce and sadistic attacks on subordinates); (3) excessive impression management (e.g., exaggerating accomplishments, credit-stealing); (4) poor administrative practices (e.g., vacillation between loose delegation and micromanagement); (5) inability to recognize a flawed vision (e.g., personal agendas versus true visions, illusion of invulnerability); and (6) failure to plan for succession. Taken together, these six characteristics reveal a pathological level of narcissism that can prove extremely destructive for organizations and their members.

The ultimate power of these individuals is reflected in the limited ways in which subordinates can respond to the pressure they create. While avoidance is a viable short-term coping strategy, it can easily become self-defeating over the longer term, precipitating increased stress, cynicism, and bitterness. Another prescription is to keep a well-documented "paper trail," taking care to protect your information (and yourself) from the possibility of being seized (and misused) by the narcissist. Being more proactive, other advice includes building a coalition of supporters, end runs to higher ups and formal complaints. These latter recommendations are risky and should be thought of as last-resort options, especially since narcissistic leaders often have good political and, when they choose, interpersonal skills, and are capable of manipulating organizations and those around them to further their own agendas and personal goals.

Thus ethical leadership, which entails an emphasis on creating the most good and least harm for a broad range of stakeholders, must be considered a crucial component of the leadership process.[89] It is important to remember that charisma can be charged with explosive, unpredictable potential that is often beyond our control. Executives and managers need to be aware of its dangers as well as its enlightening potential.

A final concern is that the magic or heroic leader, no matter how well intentioned, might not be the most effective form of leadership in today's complex organizations.[90] In a growing number of instances, recent research suggests that the most appropriate leader is the individual who can *lead others to lead themselves.* Instead of an organizational hero, this view conceptualizes the leader as a "hero-maker," someone truly capable of empowering individuals, teams, and organizations. This perspective underscores a new way of thinking about a leader's strength. Instead of focusing on the leader's ability to influence the will of others, emphasis is placed on the leader's ability to maximize the contributions of others through the recognition of their right to guide their own destiny. The resulting sense of "self-leadership" in organizational members encourages innovation and creativity as well as enabling work teams to perform at their greatest potential.

Gender, Power, and Leadership

One of the questions that often emerges around issues of power and leadership concerns potential differences between men and women in the workplace. Despite the fact that women are playing an increasingly prominent role in the executive suite, the basic stereotypes continue to persist—reinforced by study after study on gender roles and managerial characteristics—as we tend to identify "masculine" (i.e., aggressive) characteristics as managerial and "feminine" (i.e., cooperative and communicative) characteristics as nonmanagerial in nature.[91] Traditionally, the underlying belief was that because business organizations reflect our society's definition of maleness (e.g., competitiveness, team spirit, sharing risks), women were not as capable as men of being effective leaders because little in their upbringing prepares them for this role.[92] Even attempts to refute such gender-based stereotypes have encountered rather strong evidence that men and women may indeed differ in personality characteristics which could, in fact, affect leadership style.[93] Ironically, an interesting twist to the argument that men and women differ with respect to the qualities that they bring to organizations is that given the changing demands being placed on organizations today, women may actually be better-suited for managerial and leadership roles due to such "female qualities" as intuitive and empathetic skills, affiliation, attachment, cooperativeness, and nurturance.[94]

Research, however, suggests that men and women with high needs for power tend to have similar characteristics—they hold more offices and prestigious positions, and pursue occupations that allow them greater influence over others—compared with people with lower power needs.[95] While male leaders tend to receive higher effectiveness ratings than women, this is only true in laboratory settings. In actual organizational settings, women and men in similar positions receive similar ratings.[96] The main reason that more women have not been represented in organizational positions of power and leadership has been suggested to be due to a type of institutional sexism that has kept them on the periphery of the executive suite and prevented them from moving up the organizational hierarchy.[97] As recent research has underscored, while CEOs typically point to a lack of experience as the main reason more women are not found among the highest ranking executives, the women themselves argue that organizational culture factors (e.g., male stereotyping, exclusion from formal and informal networks) are the real reasons.[98]

One difference that has been found, however, is that women—even those with high needs for power—tend to be less assertive, less competitive and less comfortable in hierarchical arrangements compared with their male counterparts. Although gender role expectations are suggested as the underlying reason—society has traditionally expected women to be less aggressive and more caring than men—gender roles are changing and women, especially those who take their cues from themselves instead of the outside world, are increasingly exhibiting work patterns and profiles similar to those of their male counterparts.[99] Yet, as noted earlier, as our business system becomes much more global and international in nature, it seems that many of the orientations our society has traditionally characterized as "feminine" are becoming increasingly important components of organizational success. The types of abilities necessary for success in a global marketplace—for example, relationship building, communication, and social sensitivity across cultural differences—are skills in which women have been traditionally strong. In fact, even in countries we routinely think of as being "sexist," expatriate women managers appear to be succeeding *because* they are women, not in spite of their gender.[100]

LEADERSHIP: A SYNTHESIS

As this chapter has demonstrated, leadership research has proliferated over the past several decades with numerous competing theories and models that attempt to explain leader behaviors and outcomes. We have gone from denouncing early trait theories of leadership in favor of attitude- and behavior-related theories, moving on to contingency and situational frameworks, only to return to personal characteristics and "special qualities" in our emerging fascination with "magic" and "heroic" leaders. Along the way, researchers have attempted to differentiate executive power from other forms of organizational influence and control, contrast transformational leadership with transactional management, and emphasize the need for empowering others, in essence creating self-directed leaders throughout the organization. Today, prominent leadership scholars assert that the number one question facing leadership scholars is not whether, but the conditions under which, leadership matters. This inquiry begs the age-old question of leader behavior versus situational explanations for organizational, group, and individual outcomes. The key is to distinguish—both conceptually and empirically—those circumstances that facilitate leader influence and those that render leadership essentially moot.[101]

As this chapter has indicated, while we have numerous middle-range theories and models of leader attitudes and behavior, the field has been less successful in creating a comprehensive, generalizable model of leadership. We can, however, develop an integrative framework that encompasses these different perspectives, differentiating leadership at the *systems* (ten- to twenty-year and beyond time frame), *organizational* (two- to ten-year time frame), and *direct production* (under two-year time span) levels.[102] The model suggests that at upper-organizational levels, leadership is more strategic in nature, focused on broader responsibilities for an organization and its future. This view of leadership reflects the activities of the CEOs and general managers researched by Mintzberg and Kotter, and the concept of the transformational leaders. At the other end of the spectrum, direct production leadership, with its emphasis on lower-level, face-to-face interaction, captures the essence of leader as supervisor. Organizational leadership, which falls between these two extremes, stresses the concerns and activities of middle-level managers with an emphasis on strategic business units within larger corporate bodies, and developing product lines, operating procedures, and product/service strategies. As this framework suggests, there is a relatively orderly progression of complexity—marked by increasing cognitive demands and time spans for decisions—as leadership moves from supervision (direct production) to middle-management (organizational) to top-management (systems) levels.

This view of leadership also underscores the influence of both internal (individual capabilities and skills) and external (environment, organizational culture, and climate) factors on leadership performance. Along these lines, examination of leadership research over the past three decades reveals four enduring themes associated with derailed executive careers and leadership-related failure:[103] (1) problems with interpersonal relationships (e.g., insensitivity to others, isolation, being overly ambitious, betrayal of trust); (2) failure to meet business objectives (e.g., performance problems, lack of follow-through); (3) inability to build and lead a team; and (4) inability to personally develop or adapt as one's responsibilities move from direct production to organizational to systems-level demands. Similarly, based on interviews with more than 40,000 leaders over a thirty-year period, a related perspective provided by the Gallup Organization emphasizes twenty key leadership talents or "themes" that are grouped into four main categories:[104]

1. **Direction:** A leader's ability to provide direction to his or her subordinates and organization. This dimension is composed of *vision* (the ability to create and project beneficial images), *concept* (ability to provide the best explanation of key events), and *focus* (the capacity to focus on important goals).

2. **Drive to execute:** The leader's ability to motivate others. This category includes *ego drive* (self-definition of oneself as significant), *competition* (the desire to win), *achiever* (energy), *courage* (relishes challenge), and being an *activator* (proactive).

3. **Relationships:** The capacity to develop positive relationships with others. Specific roles include *relater* (can build trust and be caring), *developer* (desire to help people grow), *multirelater* (has a wide circle of relationships), *individualized perception* (recognizes peoples' individuality), *stimulator* (can create good feelings in others), and being *team-oriented* (ability to get people to help each other).

4. **Management systems:** Relates to general management abilities. Specific themes involve *performance orientation* (results oriented), *discipline* (capable of structuring time and the work environment); *responsibility and ethics* (able to take psychological ownership of own behavior), *arranger* (coordinate people and their activities), *operational* (can administer systems that help people be more effective), and *strategic thinking* (able to engage in "what if?" thinking, creating "paths" to future goals).

As this chapter has indicated, it is increasingly apparent that there is *no* one style of leadership that is the most effective in all situations. While we have begun to understand more about the complexities of leadership, we still need to learn much more about the various constraints placed on people in leadership roles, the type of behaviors that are more effective in different positions and situations, and the real consequences of effective (competent) and ineffective (incompetent) leadership in team and organizational performance. As we continue to gain further insight into the actual behaviors, activities, and outcomes of people in managerial positions, the concept of leadership in contemporary organizations will continue to develop, especially in terms of cultivating more productive and effective teams and organizations. As you develop your own leadership style, the best advice is to read, reflect, observe, and adapt these different perspectives to fit your particular situation and context.

NOTES

1. See *Harvard Business Review* issues on "Breakthrough Leadership," vol. 7, no. 1 (2001), "Inside the Mind of the Leader," vol. 82, no. 1 (2004), and, most recently, "The Tests of a Leader," vol. 85, no. 1 (2007). In addition, the American Psychological Association has also carried the leadership torch with a special issue on leadership in *American Psychologist*, vol. 62, no. 1 (2007).

2. J.R. Hackman, *Leading Teams: Setting the Stage for Great Performance* (Boston: Harvard Business School Press, 2002); and G. Chen, B.L. Kirkman, R. Kanfer, D. Allen, and B. Rosen, "A Multilevel Study of Leadership, Empowerment, and Performance in Teams," *Journal of Applied Psychology* 92 (2007): 331–346.

3. See, for example, S.A. Miles and M.D. Watkins, "The Leadership Team: Complementary Strengths or Conflicting Agendas?" *Harvard Business Review* 85 (2007): 90–98.

4. See F.E. Fiedler and M.M. Chemers, *Leadership and Effective Management* (Glenview, IL: Scott, Foresman, 1974), pp. 3–5; and J.L. Pierce and J.W. Newstrom, *Leaders and the Leadership Process* (New York: McGraw-Hill, 2000), pp. 4–5.

5. See S. Srivastva and D.L. Cooperrider, "Ways of Understanding Executive Power," in S. Srivastva and Associates, *Executive Power: How Executives Influence People and Organizations* (San Francisco: Jossey-Bass, 1986), pp. 2–3.

6. J.R.P. French and B. Raven, "The Bases of Social Power," in D. Cartwright, ed., *Studies in Social Power* (Ann Arbor: Institute for Social Research, University of Michigan, 1959).

7. See R.F. Bales and P.E. Slater, "Role Differentiation in Small Decision-Making Groups," in T. Parsons and R.F. Bales, eds., *Family, Socialization and the Interaction Process* (New York: Free Press, 1955); and R.M. Stogdill, *Handbook of Leadership* (Glencoe, IL: Free Press, 1975).

8. French and Raven, op. cit.

9. See, for example, D.J. Hickson, C.R. Hinings, C.A. Lee, R.E. Schneck, and J.M. Pennings, "A Strategic Contingencies Theory of Intraorganizational Power," *Administrative Science Quarterly* 16 (1971): 216–227. See also S.M. Goltz and A. Hietapelto, "Using the Operant and Strategic Contingencies Models of Power to Understand Resistance to Change," *Journal of Organizational Behavior Management* 22, no. 3 (2002): 3–22.

10. D.C. McClelland, *Human Motivation* (Glenview, IL: Scott, Foresman, 1985).

11. See D.C. McClelland and D.H. Burnham, "Power Is the Great Motivator," *Harvard Business Review* 54, no. 2 (1976): 100–110, 159–166; D.C. McClelland and R.E. Boyatzis, "Leadership Motive Pattern and Long-Term Success in Management," *Journal of Applied Psychology* 67 (1982): 737–743; and W.D. Spangler and R.J. House, "Presidential Effectiveness and the Leadership Motive

Profile," *Journal of Personality and Social Psychology* 60, no. 3 (1991): 439–455.

12. C. Barnard, *The Functions of the Executive* (Cambridge, MA: Harvard University Press, 1938).

13. The following discussion is drawn from J. Kotter, "Why Power and Influence Issues Are at the Very Core of Executive Work," in Srivastva and Associates, op. cit., pp. 20–32; and J. Kotter, "Power, Dependence, and Effective Management," *Harvard Business Review* 55, no. 3 (1977): 125–136. See also D.N. Sull, "Managing by Commitments," *Harvard Business Review* 81, no. 6 (2003): 82–94.

14. This discussion is drawn from B. Keys and T. Case, "How to Become an Influential Manager," *Academy of Management Executive* 4, no. 4 (1990): 38–51; J. Pfeffer, *Managing with Power: Politics and Influence in Organizations* (Cambridge, MA: Harvard University Press, 1992); and S. Srivastva and F. Barrett, "Functions of Executive Power: Exploring New Approaches," in Srivastva and Associates, *Executive Power*, p. 313.

15. See N.M. Tichy and M.A. Devanna, "The Transformational Leader," *Training and Development Journal* 40 (July 1986), p. 27.

16. The following discussion is drawn from R.M. Stogdill, *Handbook of Leadership* (New York: Free Press, 1974); and R.J. House and M.L. Baetz, "Leadership: Some Empirical Generalizations and New Research Directions," in B.M. Staw, ed., *Research in Organizational Behavior*, vol. 1 (Greenwich, CT: JAI Press, 1979).

17. See T. Peters and R.H. Waterman, *In Search of Excellence* (New York: Random House, 1982); M. Maidique, "The New Management Thinkers," *California Management Review* (Fall 1983); and D.E. Berlew, "Managing Human Energy: Pushing Versus Pulling," in Srivastva and Associates, op. cit., pp. 33–50.

18. S.A. Kirkpatrick and E.A. Locke, "Leadership: Do Traits Matter?" *Academy of Management Executive* 5, no. 2 (1991): 48–60.

19. See D.A. Nadler, "Organizational Frame Bending: Types of Change in the Complex Organization," in R.H. Kilmann, T.J. Covin, and Associates, *Corporate Transformation: Revitalizing Organizations for a Competitive World* (San Francisco: Jossey-Bass, 1988),

pp. 77–79; D.A. Nadler and M.L. Tushman, "Leadership for Organizational Change," in A.M. Mohrman, Jr., S.A. Mohrman, G.E. Ledford, Jr., T.G. Cummings, E.E. Lawler III, and Associates, *Large-Scale Organizational Change* (San Francisco: Jossey-Bass, 1989), pp. 104–108; and D. Goleman, R. Boyatzis, and A. McKee, *Primal Leadership: Realizing the Power of Emotional Intelligence* (Boston: Harvard Business School Press, 2002). See also B. George and P. Sims, *True North: Discover Your Authentic Leadership* (San Francisco: Jossey-Bass, 2007).

20. See H. Rubin, "Living Dangerously," *Fast Company* (January–February 2000): 248–252.

21. The discussion in this section is drawn from D. Ulrich, J. Zenger, and N. Smallwood, *Results-Based Leadership: How Leaders Build the Business and Improve the Bottom Line* (Boston: Harvard Business School Press, 1999).

22. R. Lippitt and R.K. White, "An Experimental Study of Leadership and Group Life," in T.M. Newcomb and E.L. Hartley, eds., *Readings in Social Psychology* (New York: Holt, Rinehart & Winston, 1947).

23. See R. Kahn and D. Katz, "Leadership Practices in Relation to Productivity and Morale," in D. Cartwright and A. Zander, eds., *Group Dynamics Research and Theory*, 2nd ed. (Elmsford, NY: Row, Peterson, 1960).

24. E.A. Fleishman, E.F. Harris, and R.D. Burtt, *Leadership and Supervision in Industry* (Columbus: Ohio State University Press, 1955).

25. E.A. Fleishman and E.F. Harris, "Patterns of Leadership Behavior Related to Employee Grievances and Turnover," *Personnel Psychology* 15 (1962): 45–53.

26. T.A. Judge, R.F. Piccolo, and R. Ilies, "The Forgotten Ones? The Validity of Consideration and Initiating Structure in Leadership Research," *Journal of Applied Psychology* 89 (2004): 36–51.

27. R. Blake and J. Mouton, *The Managerial Grid* (Houston: Gulf, 1964); see also R. Blake and J. Mouton, "The Managerial Grid III," *Personnel Psychology* 39 (Spring 1986): 238–240; and R. Blake, B. Carlson, R. McKee, P. Sorensen, and T.F. Yaeger, "Contemporary

Issues of Grid International: Sustaining and Extending the Core Values of OD," *Organization Development Journal* 18, no. 2 (2000): 54–61.

28. See W. Bennis and B. Nanus, *Leaders: The Strategies for Taking Charge* (New York: Harper & Row, 1986); G. Yukl, *Leadership in Organizations* (Englewood Cliffs, NJ: Prentice Hall, 1981); J. Owens, "A Reappraisal of Leadership Theory and Training," *Personnel Administrator* 26 (November 1981): 78–82; L.S. Pheng and B.S.K. Lee, "'Managerial Grid' and Zhuge Liung's 'Art of Management': Integration for Effective Project Management," *Management Decision* 35, no. 5 (1997): 382–391; and D. Coghlan and R.K. McKee, "Aligning Grid Organization Development and Interlevel Dynamics for Systemic Change," *Organization Development Journal* 18, no. 3 (2000): 37–48.

29. "In Memoriam: Robert Blake 1918–2004," *T+D* 58, no. 10 (2004): 9.

30. See C. Argyris, *Personality and Organization* (New York: Harper & Row, 1957); C. Argyris, *Interpersonal Competence and Organizational Effectiveness* (Homewood, IL: Irwin, 1962); and C. Argyris, *Integrating the Individual and the Organization* (New York: Wiley, 1964).

31. See R. Likert, *New Patterns of Management* (New York: McGraw-Hill, 1961).

32. J. Kotter, "Managing Your Boss," *Harvard Business Review* 58, no. 1 (1980): 92–100.

33. See L. Johnson and A.L. Frohman, "Identifying and Closing the Gap in the Middle of Organizations," *Academy of Management Executive* 3, no. 2 (1989): 107–114; D.M. Malone, "The Integration of Internal Operating Systems: An Application of Systems Leadership," in R.L. Phillips and J.G. Hunt, eds., *Strategic Leadership: A Multiorganizational-Level Perspective* (Westport, CT: Quorum Books, 1992), pp. 219–236; and J. Laabs, "Managing-Up Secrets: I Did It the Boss's Way," *Workforce* 79, no. 8 (2000): 22.

34. R. Likert, *The Human Organization* (New York: McGraw-Hill, 1967).

35. See D. Harry, "Managing the Bossless Team: Lessons in Distributed Leadership," *Organizational Dynamics* 20, no. 1 (1991): 31–47; R.W. Beatty and D.O.

Ulrich, "Re-Energizing the Mature Organization," *Organizational Dynamics* 20, no. 1 (1991): 16–30; and S. Kim, "Participative Management and Job Satisfaction: Lessons for Management Leadership," *Public Administration Review* 62, no. 2 (2002): 231–241.

36. See D. Goleman, "Leadership That Gets Results," *Harvard Business Review,* 78, no. 2 (2000): 78–90; and D. Goleman, R. Boyatzis, and A. McKee, *Primal Leadership: Realizing the Power of Emotional Intelligence* (Boston: Harvard Business School Press, 2002).

37. See, for example, Fiedler and Chemers, op. cit., Chapter 3; Stodgill, op. cit.

38. See T.V. Bonoma and D. Slevin, *Executive Survival Manual* (Boston: CBI Publishing, 1978).

39. P.M. Podsakoff, S.B. MacKenzie, M. Ahearne, and W.H. Bonner, "Searching for a Needle in a Haystack: Trying to Identify the Illusive Moderators of Leadership Behaviors," *Journal of Management* 21, no. 3 (1995): 422–470; and L.L. Paglis and S.G. Green, "Leadership Self-Efficacy and Managers' Motivation for Leading Change," *Journal of Organizational Behavior* 23, no. 2 (2002): 215–235.

40. F.E. Fiedler, *A Theory of Leadership Effectiveness* (New York: McGraw-Hill, 1967).

41. F.E. Fiedler, M.M. Chemers, and L. Maher, *Improving Leadership Effectiveness: The Leader Match Concept* (New York: Wiley, 1976). See also S. Shiflett, "Is There a Problem with the LPC Score in Leader Match?" *Personnel Psychology* 34, no. 4 (1981): 765–769; and A.P. Hare, S.E. Hare, and H.H. Blumberg, "Wishful Thinking: Who Has the Least Preferred Co-worker?" *Small Group Research* 29, no. 4 (1998): 419–435.

42. F.E. Fiedler and J.E. Garcia, *New Approaches to Leadership: Cognitive Resources and Organizational Performance* (New York: Wiley, 1987).

43. See R.J. House and J.V. Singh, "Organizational Behavior: Some New Directions for IO Psychology," *Annual Review of Psychology* (1987): 669–718; M.F.R. Kets de Vries, *Life and Death in the Executive Fast Lane: Essays on Irrational Organizations and Their Leaders* (San Francisco: Jossey-Bass, 1995); and D. Goleman, *Working with Emotional Intelligence* (New York: Bantam Books, 1998).

44. R.J. House and T.R. Mitchell, "Path-Goal Theory of Leadership," *Journal of Contemporary Business* 3 (1974): 31–99.

45. See, for example E.A. Locke, G.P. Latham, and M. Erez, "The Determinants of Goal Commitment," *Academy of Management Review* 13, no. 1 (1988): 23–39; D.J. Campbell, "Task Complexity: A Review and Analysis," *Academy of Management Review* 13, no. 1 (1988): 40–52; A. Sagie and M. Koslowsky, "Organizational Attitudes and Behaviors as a Function of Participation in Strategic and Tactical Change Decisions: An Application of Path-Goal Theory," *Journal of Organizational Behavior* 15, no. 1 (1994): 37–47; and C. Silverman, "A Test of the Path-Goal Theory in Taiwan," *Leadership and Organization Development Journal* 22, no. 4 (2001): 151–168.

46. P. Hersey and K. Blanchard, *Management of Organizational Behavior: Utilizing Human Resources*, 5th ed. (Englewood Cliffs, NJ: Prentice Hall, 1988).

47. See P. Hersey, A.L. Angelini, and S. Carakushansky, "The Impact of Situational Leadership and Classroom Structure on Learning Effectiveness," *Group & Organization Studies* 7, no. 2 (1982): 216–224; and R.K. Hambleton and R. Gumpert, "The Validity of Hersey and Blanchard's Theory of Leader Effectiveness," *Group & Organization Studies* 7, no. 2 (1982): 225–242. For a good overview of the debate between Hersey and Blanchard, and Blake and Mouton (Managerial Grid), see the two articles comparing "Grid Principles and Situationalism" in *Group & Organization Studies* 7, no. 2 (1982): 207–215. Recent assessments include T.D. Cairns, J. Hollenback, R.C. Preziosi, and W.A. Snow, "Technical Note: A Study of Hersey and Blanchard's Situational Leadership Theory," *Leadership and Organization Development Journal* 19, no. 2 (1998): 113–118; and G.C. Avery and J. Ryan, "Applying Situational Leadership in Australia," *Journal of Management Development* 21, no. 3/4 (2002): 242–262

48. V.H. Vroom and P.W. Yetton, *Leadership and Decision Making* (Pittsburgh: University of Pittsburgh Press, 1973).

49. V.H. Vroom, "A New Look at Managerial Decision Making," *Organizational Dynamics* (Spring 1973).

50. V.H. Vroom and A.G. Jago, "On the Validity of the Vroom-Yetton Model," *Journal of Applied Psychology* 63 (1978): 151–162; R.H. Field and R.J. House, "A Test of the Vroom-Yetton Model Using Manager and Subordinate Reports," *Journal of Applied Psychology* 751, no. 3 (1990): 362–366; and W.J. Duncan, K.G. LaFrance, and P.M. Ginter, "Leadership, and Decision Making: A Retrospective Application and Assessment," *Journal of Leadership and Organizational Studies* 9, no. 4 (2003): 1–20.

51. B.J. Calder, "An Attribution Theory of Leadership," in B.M. Staw and G.R. Salancik, eds., *New Directions in Organizational Behavior* (Chicago: St. Clair, 1977), Chapter 5, pp. 179–204.

52. J.R. Meindl and S.B. Erlich, "The Romance of Leadership and the Evaluation of Organizational Performance," *Academy of Management Journal* 30, no. 1 (1987): 91–109; J.R. Meindl, S.B. Erlich, and J.M. Dukerich, "The Romance of Leadership," *Administrative Science Quarterly* 30 (1985): 78–102; and R. Weber, C. Camerer, Y. Rottensteich and M. Knez, "The Illusion of Leadership: Misattribution of Cause in Coordinated Games," *Organization Science* 12, no. 5 (2001): 582–598.

53. G.B. Graen and M. Uhl-Bien, "Development of Leader-Member Exchange (LMX) Theory of Leadership over 25 Years: Applying a Multi-Level Multi-Domain Perspective," *Leadership Quarterly* 6 (1995): 219–247.

54. See S.J. Wayne, L.M. Shore, W.H. Bommer, and L.E. Tetrick, "The Role of Fair Treatment and Rewards in Perceptions of Organizational Support and Leader-Member Exchange," *Journal of Applied Psychology* 87 (2002): 590–598; and M. Uhl-Bien and J.M. Maslyn, "Reciprocity in Manager-Subordinate Relationships: Components, Configurations, and Outcomes," *Journal of Management* 29 (2003): 511–532.

55. Graen and Uhl-Bien, "Development of Leader-Member Exchange Theory"; C.R. Gerstner and D.V. Day, "Meta-Analytic Review of Leader-Member Exchange Theory: Correlates and Construct Issues," *Journal of Applied Psychology* 82 (1997): 827–844; G. Chen, B.L. Kirkman, R. Kanfer, D. Allen, and

B. Rosen, "A Multilevel Study of Leadership, Empowerment, and Performance in Teams," *Journal of Applied Psychology* 92 (2007): 331–346; and B. Erdogan and J. Enders, "Support from the Top: Supervisors' Perceived Organizational Support as a Moderator of Leader-Member Exchange to Satisfaction and Performance Relationships," *Journal of Applied Psychology* 92 (2007): 321–330.

56. D.A. Hofmann, F.P. Morgeson, and S.J. Gerras, "Climate as a Moderator of the Relationship between Leader-Member Exchange and Content-Specific Citizenship: Safety Climate as an Exemplar," *Journal of Applied Psychology* 88 (2003): 170–178; and L. Bossidy, "What Your Leader Expects from You," *Harvard Business Review* 85 (2007): 58–65.

57. R.C. Liden and G. Graen, "Generalizability of the Vertical Dyad Linkage Model of Leadership," *Academy of Management Journal* 23 (1980): 451–465; and H. Wang, K.S. Law, R.D. Hackett, D. Wang, and Z.X. Chen, "Leader-Member Exchange as a Mediator of the Relationship between Transformational Leadership and Followers' Performance and Organizational Citizenship Behavior," *Academy of Management Journal* 48 (2005): 420–432.

58. See, for example, K. Boies and J.M. Howell, "Leader-Member Exchange in Teams: An Examination of the Interaction between Relationship Differentiation and Mean LMX in Explaining Team-Level Outcomes," *Leadership Quarterly* 17 (2006): 246–257.

59. S.G. Green, S.E. Anderson, and S.L. Shivers, "Demographic and Organizational Influences on Leader-Member Exchange and Related Work Attitudes," *Organizational Behavior and Human Decision Processes* 66 (1996): 203–214; and R.C. Liden, B. Erdogan, S.J. Wayne, and R.T. Sparrowe, "Leader-Member Exchange, Differentiation, and Task Interdependence: Implications for Individual and Group Performance," *Journal of Organizational Behavior* 27 (2006): 723–746.

60. L.R. Ford and A. Seers, "Relational Leadership and Team Climates: Pitting Differentiation versus Agreement," *The Leadership Quarterly* 17 (2006): 258–270.

61. K.J. Klein, A.B. Conn, D.B. Smith, and J.S. Sorra, "Is Everyone in Agreement? An Exploration of Within-Group Agreement in Employee Perceptions of the Work Environment," *Journal of Applied Psychology* 86 (2001): 3–16.

62. K.M. Sherony and S.G. Green, "Coworker Exchange: Relationships between Co-workers, Leader-Member Exchange, and Work Attitudes," *Journal of Applied Psychology* 87 (2002): 542–548; and B. Schyns, "Are Group Consensus in LMX and Shared Work Values Related to Organizational Outcomes?" *Small Group Research* 37 (2006): 20–35.

63. See Liden, Erdogan, Wayne, and Sparrowe, "Leader-Member Exchange, Differentiation, and Task Interdependence."

64. See M. London, *Principled Leadership and Business Diplomacy: Values-Based Strategies for Management Development* (Westport, CT: Quorum Books, 1999).

65. See Evans, op. cit., pp. 236–237; J. Seltzer and B.M. Bass, "Transformational Leadership: Beyond Initiation and Consideration," *Journal of Management* 16, no. 4 (1990): 693–703; J.A. Champy, "The New Work of Managers," *Directors & Boards* 19, no. 1 (1994): 37–38; and J.P. Doh, "Can Leadership Be Taught? Perspectives from Management Educators," *Academy of Management Learning & Education* 2, no. 1 (2003): 54–67.

66. H. Mintzberg, *The Nature of Managerial Work* (Englewood Cliffs, NJ: Prentice Hall, 1973).

67. J. Kotter, *The General Managers* (New York: Free Press, 1982). See also J. Kotter, "What Leaders Really Do," *Harvard Business Review*, 79, no. 11 (2001): 85–96.

68. This section is based on L. Thach and T. Heinselman, "Executive Coaching Defined," *Training & Development* (March 1999): 35–39; and D.T. Hall, K.L. Otazo, and G.P. Hollenbeck, "Behind Closed Doors: What Really Happens in Executive Coaching," *Organizational Dynamics* (Winter 1999): 39–53. See also J.M. Hunt and J.R. Weintraub, *The Coaching Manager: Developing Top Talent in Business* (Thousand Oaks, CA: Sage, 2002).

69. For an example of executive coaching, see A.F. Buono, "When the Client Dies: Reflecting on the Personal and Professional

Ramifications of a Sudden Tragedy," in R.T. Golembiewski & G. Varney, eds., *Cases in Organization Development: Four Perspectives on Value-Guided Consultation* (Itasca, IL: F.E. Peacock, 2000), pp. 145–155.

70.   See Calder, op. cit., pp. 179–204; and Ulrich et al., *Results-Based Leadership*.

71.   S. Kerr and J.M. Jermier, "Substitutes for Leadership: Their Meaning and Measurement," *Organizational Behavior and Human Performance* 22 (1978): 375–403.

72.   J.P. Howell, D.E. Bowen, P.W. Dorfman, S. Kerr, and P.M. Podsakoff, "Substitutes for Leadership: Effective Alternatives to Ineffective Leadership," *Organizational Dynamics* 19, no. 1 (1990): 21–38; and E. Cohen and N. Tichy, "Operation Leadership," *Fast Company* (September 1999): 278–288. For methodological concerns about the focus of this research focus see S.D. Dionne, F.J. Yammarino, L.E. Atwater, and L.R. James, "Neutralizing Substitutes for Leadership Theory: Leadership Effects and Common-Source Bias," *Journal of Applied Psychology* 87, no. 3 (2002): 454–464.

73.   R. Tannenbaum and W.H. Schmidt, "How to Choose a Leadership Pattern: Retrospective Commentary," *Harvard Business Review* 51, no. 3 (1973): 162–175, 178–180.

74.   See, for example, Chen, Kirkman, Kanfer, Allen, and Rosen, "Multilevel Study of Leadership, Empowerment, and Performance in Teams."

75.   See, for example, B. Dumaine, "Who Needs a Boss?" *Fortune* (May 7, 1990), pp. 52–60; Barry, op. cit., pp. 31–47; E.E. Lawler III, "The New Plant Approach: A Second Generation Approach," *Organizational Dynamics* 20, no. 1 (1991): 5–14; and M. Maccoby, "Creating an Empowered Organization," *Research-Technology Management* 35, no. 3 (1992): 50–51.

76.   G.M. Spreitzer, S.C. De Janasz, and R.E. Quinn, "Empowered to Lead: The Role of Psychological Empowerment in Leadership," *Journal of Organizational Behavior* 20 (1999): 51–526.

77.   See D.E. Bowen and E.E. Lawler III, "The Empowerment of Service Workers: What, Why, How, and When," *Sloan Management Review* 33, no. 3 (1992): 35–36;

W.A. Randolph, "Navigating the Journey to Empowerment," *Organizational Dynamics* 23, no. 4 (1995): 19–32; and M. Pardo del Val and B. Lloyd, "Measuring Empowerment," *Leadership and Organization Development Journal* 24, no. 1/2 (2003): 102–109.

78.   Howell, Bowen, Dorfman, Kerr, and Podsakoff, op. cit., p. 24.

79.   See P.E. Brauchle and D.W. Wright, "Fourteen Team Building Tips," *Training & Development* (January 1992): 32–36; and K. Mattes, "Empowerment: Fact or Fiction," *HR Focus* (March 1992): 1, 6.

80.   See C. Manz and H. Sims, "Leading Workers to Lead Themselves: The External Leadership of Self-Managing Work Teams," *Administrative Science Quarterly* 32, no. 1 (1987): 106–128; B.M. Bass, "From Transactional to Transformational Leadership: Learning to Share the Vision," *Organizational Dynamics* 18, no. 3 (1990): 19–31; C. Carr, "Managing Self-Managed Workers," *Training & Development* 45, no, 9 (1991): 36–42; and L. Holdsworth and S. Cartwright, "Empowerment, Stress and Satisfaction: An Exploratory Study of a Call Centre," *Leadership and Organization Development Journal* 24, no. 3 (2003): 131–152.

81.   See J.M. Burns, *Leadership* (New York: Harper & Row, 1978); and W.W. Burke, "Leadership as Empowering Others," in Srivastva and Associates, *Executive Power*, pp. 63–75.

82.   See J.J. Sosik and L.E. Megerian, "Understanding Leader Emotional Intelligence and Performance: The Role of Self-Other Agreement on Transformational Leadership Perceptions," *Group & Organization Management* 24, no. 3 (1999): 367–390.

83.   N.M. Tichy and M.A. Devanna, *The Transformational Leader* (New York: Wiley, 1986); J.M. Howell and C.A. Higgins, "Champions of Change: Identifying, Understanding, and Supporting Champions of Technological Innovation," *Organizational Dynamics* 19, no. 1 (1990): 40–57; and K. Boehnke, N. Bontis, J.J. DiStefano, and A.C. DiStefano, "Transformational Leadership: An Examination of Cross-National Differences and Similarities," *Leadership and Organization Development Journal* 24, no. 1/2 (2003): 5–15.

84. See J. Kotter, *Leading Change* (Boston: Harvard Business School Press, 1996); J. Kotter, "Change Leadership," *Executive Excellence* 16, no. 4 (1999): 16–17; and R. Gill, "Change Management—or Change Leadership?" *Journal of Change Management* 3, no. 4 (2003): 307–318.

85. This discussion is adapted from J.M. Howell and B.J. Avolio, "The Ethics of Charismatic Leadership: Submission or Liberation" *Academy of Management Executive* 6, no. 2 (1992): 43–54.

86. See J.A. Conger, "The Dark Side of Leadership," *Organizational Dynamics* 19, no. 2 (1990): 44–55; M. Maccoby, "Narcissistic Leaders: Their Incredible Pros, the Inevitable Cons," *Harvard Business Review* 78, no. 1 (2000): 68–77; T.L. Price, "The Ethics of Authentic Transformational Leadership," *Leadership Quarterly* 14, no. 1 (2003): 67–82; and S.W. Spreier, M.H. Fontaine, and R.L. Malloy, "Leadership Run Amok: The Destructive Potential of Overachievers," *Harvard Business Review* 84, no. 3 (2006): 72–82.

87. Howell and Avolio, op. cit. See also, H.B. Jones, Jr., "The Ethical Leader: An Ascetic Construct," *Journal of Business Ethics* 14, no. 10 (1995): 607–632.

88. The discussion of narcissistic leaders is drawn from D.B. Farlin and P.D. Sweeney, *House of Mirrors: The Untold Truth About Narcissistic Leaders and How to Survive Them* (London: Kogan Page, 2000).

89. See, for example, A.L. Minkes, M.W. Small, and S.R. Chatterjee, "Leadership and Business Ethics: Does It Matter? Implications for Management," *Journal of Business Ethics* 20 (1999): 327–335; and London, *Principled Leadership and Business Diplomacy*.

90. This discussion is drawn from C.C. Manz and H.P. Sims, Jr., "Super-Leadership: Beyond the Myth of Heroic Leadership," *Organizational Dynamics* 19, no. 4 (1991): 18–35; P. Tierney, S.M. Farmer, and G.B. Graen, "An Examination of Leadership and Employee Creativity: The Relevance of Traits and Relationships," *Personnel Psychology* 52, no. 3 (1999): 591–620; and W. H. Weiss, "Leadership," *Supervision* 60, no. 1 (1999): 6–9. For an assessment of the ideal of shared leadership see, J.A. Raelin, *Creating Leaderful Organiza-*tions: How to Bring Out Leadership in Everyone (San Francisco: Berrett-Koehler, 2003).

91. G.N. Powell and D.A. Butterfield, "The 'Good Manager': Masculine or Androgynous?" *Academy of Management Journal* 22, no. 2 (1979): 395–403; and S.H. Appelbaum, L. Audet, and J.L. Miller, "Gender and Leadership? Leadership and Gender? A Journey Through the Landscape of Theories," *Leadership & Organization Development* 24, no. 1/2 (2003): 43–51.

92. See M.D. Fottler and T. Bain, "Sex Differences in Occupational Aspirations," *Academy of Management Journal* 23, no. 1 (1980): 144–149; and L.R. Gallese, "Women and the Race Up the Corporate Ladder," *The Wall Street Journal*, November 3, 1980, p. 30.

93. For a good summary of this literature, see G.H. Dobbins and S.J. Platz, "Sex Differences in Leadership: How Real Are They?" *Academy of Management Review* 11, no. 1 (1986): 118–127; A.H. Eagly, S.J. Karau, J.B. Miner, and B.T. Johnson, "Gender and Motivation to Manage in Hierarchic Organizations: A Meta-Analysis," *Leadership Quarterly* 5 (1994): 135–159; and N.Z. Stelter, "Gender Differences in Leadership: Current Social Issues and Future Organizational Implications," *Journal of Leadership & Organizational Studies* 8, no. 4 (2002): 88–99.

94. See J. Grant, "Women as Managers: What They Can Offer to Organizations," *Organizational Dynamics* 16, no. 3 (1988): 56–63; M. van der Boon, "Women in International Management: An International Perspective on Women's Ways of Leadership," *Women in Management Review* 18, no. 3/4 (2003): 132–146; and L. Grisoni and M. Beeby, "Leadership, Gender and Sense-Making," *Gender, Work & Organization* 14, no. 3 (2007): 191–209.

95. See D.G. Winter, *The Power Motive* (New York: Free Press, 1975); S. Wilsnack, "The Effects of Social Drinking on Women's Fantasy," *Journal of Personality* 42 (1974): 43–61; and R.P. Vecchio, "Leadership and Gender Advantage," *Leadership Quarterly* 13, no. 6 (2002): 643–670.

96. See L. McFarland Shore and G.C. Thornton, "Effects of Gender on Self- and Supervisory Ratings," *Academy of Management*

Journal 29, no. 1 (1986): 115–129; K. Bartol, "The Sex Structuring of Organizations: A Search for Possible Causes," *Academy of Management Review* 3 (1978): 805–815; and A.H. Eagly, S.J. Karau, and M.G. Makhijani, "Gender and the Effectiveness of Leaders: A Meta-Analysis," *Psychological Bulletin* 117, no. 1 (1995): 125–145.

97. A.F. Buono and J.B. Kamm, "Marginality and the Organizational Socialization of Female Managers," *Human Relations* 36, no. 12 (1983): 1125–1140; R.M. Kanter, *Men and Women of the Corporation* (New York: Basic Books, 1977); N.C. Zane, "The Glass Ceiling in the Floor My Boss Walks On," *Journal of Applied Behavioral Science* 38, no. 3 (2002): 334–354; and M.K. Ryan and S.A. Haslam, "The Glass Cliff: Exploring the Dynamics Surrounding the Appointment of Women to Precarious Leadership Positions," *Academy of Management Review* 32, no. 2 (2007): 549–572.

98. B.R. Raggins, B. Townsend, and M. Mattis, "Gender Gap in the Executive Suite: CEOs and Female Executives Report on Breaking the Glass Ceiling," *Academy of Management Executive* 12, no. 1 (1998): 28–42; and G. Morse, "The Emancipated Organization," *Harvard Business Review* 80, no. 9 (2002): 20–22.

99. T.D. Jick and L.M. Mitz, "Sex Differences in Work Stress," *Academy of Management Review* 10, no. 3 (1985): 408–420; D.D. Bowen and R.D. Hisrich, "The Female Entrepreneur: A Career Development Perspective," *Academy of Management Review* 11, no. 2 (1986): 393–407; D.G. Winter and A.J. Stewart, "Power Motivation," in H. London and J. Exner, eds., *Dimensions of Personality* (New York: Wiley, 1982); G.N. Powell, "One More Time: Do Female and Male Managers Differ?" *Academy of Management Executive* 4, no. 3 (1990): 68–75; R.L. Kent and S.E. Moss, "Effects of Sex and Gender Role on Leader Emergence," *Academy of Management Journal* 37, no. 5 (1994): 1335–1346; and E.E. Duehr and J.E. Bono, "Men, Women and Managers: Are Stereotypes Finally Changing?" *Personnel Psychology* 59, no. 4 (2006): 815–846.

100. M. Jelinek and N.J. Alder, "Women: World-Class Managers for Global Competition," *Academy of Management Executive* 2, no. 1 (1988): 11–19.

101. J.R. Hackman and R. Wageman, "Asking the Right Questions about Leadership: Discussion and Conclusions," *American Psychologist* 62 (2007): 43–47.

102. The following discussion is based on J.G. Hunt, *Leadership: A New Synthesis* (Newbury Park, CA: Sage, 1991); and R.L. Phillips and J.G. Hunt, *Strategic Leadership: A Multiorganizational-Level Perspective* (Westport, CT: Quorum, 1992).

103. E. Van Velsor and J.B. Leslie, "Why Executives Derail: Perspectives Across Time and Cultures," *Academy of Management Executive* 9, no. 4 (1995): 62–72; and J. Harrison, "How to ... Prevent Executive Derailment," *People Management* 12, no. 19 (2006): 50–51.

104. R.M. Fulmer and S. Wagner, "Leadership: Lessons from the Best," *Training & Development* (March 1999): 29–32.

Macro-Organizational Behavior: The Organization's Environment

$\mathbf{A}$ s the contents of this book thus far suggest, a main focus of organizational behavior (OB) has been on individuals, small groups, and their leaders. This traditional or micro-OB perspective was significantly influenced by two factors: the founders of the field who largely came from psychology and social psychology; and, as discussed in Chapter 1, the social context that shaped the Classical and Neoclassical traditions. As OB continued to evolve, the work of other social scientists, most notably sociologists and political scientists, was gradually incorporated. This focus began to raise questions concerning patterns of behavior at the organizational level, focusing on organizations as entities interacting with other organizations and their larger environments. The result has been a broader conceptualization of the field and the development of models for understanding, designing, and managing these macro-level behaviors.

The importance of such macro-behavior is reflected in our recent emphasis on adapting the structure of organizations to meet various environmental constraints and pressures, managing linkages across organizations, creating organizational cultures that reflect the overall mission and goals of the organization, and managing the growing influence of external factors on organizational decision making, effectiveness, and micro-level behaviors in general. Within this context, this chapter will explore the changing nature of the environment, organization-environment relations, and the international environment.

ORGANIZATIONAL ENVIRONMENT

In classical management thought, organizations were viewed as relatively closed systems. Since effectiveness and success were argued to be dependent on the efficiency of internal operations, organizational policies were designed to fulfill a stable set of tasks and goals. Relatively little attention was focused on organizational adaptation to changes in the external environment.

As discussed in Chapter 1, however, contemporary organizational theory takes a much broader perspective of organizations and their management. Organizations are viewed as open systems, ones that have to adapt to changing external conditions. Studies of companies over the long term, for example, indicate that successful firms are able to maintain a workable equilibrium for several years or even decades, but as their environments shift these companies are also capable of initiating and carrying out widespread change and realignment.[1] While some of these environmental shifts may still be relatively simple and predictable, others tend to be much more complex and dynamic in nature.

Since organizations are conceptualized as being part of a larger universe or environment, it can be argued that anything that happens in that larger environment can affect the organization (and vice versa) in at least a subtle way. Indeed, especially at the large corporation level, there is scarcely any trend—social, economic, political, technological, or international—that does not, to some degree, affect internal operations.[2] Although specific environmental occurrences, of course, may have little direct effect on any one particular organization, significant environmental events can affect organizations far more profoundly than internal policies and improvements. The economic deregulation of the banking, telecommunication, and airline industries, for example, has drasticall changed the ways in which companies in those industries operate.

Defining Organizational Environment

Environment, like many areas in OB, is not a firmly defined topic.[3] Theorists disagree as to what actually constitutes an organization's environment and the types of issues that should be included in an assessment of organizational environments. Yet, while there are numerous definitions of the concept of environment, the underlying theme is a focus on those factors external to the organization. One definition, for example, describes organizational environment as "all elements existing outside the boundary of the organization that have the potential to affect all or parts of the organization."[4] Another even broader view is that environment is "anything not part of the organization itself."[5] Other definitions are more focused and look at the specific institutions or forces that affect organizational performance, but over which organizations have little or no direct control.[6]

As a way of defining organizational environment more precisely, we will draw on three analytic distinctions made by many organizational theorists: (1) how a firm's boundary is determined, (2) the general versus specific environment, and (3) the actual versus perceived environment.

Organizational Boundary

Senior-level managers can exert a great deal of influence in determining the boundary of their organization, in essence the distinction between where the organization ends and the external environment begins. An organization creates its own domain by deciding what products or services it is going to produce, which customers it is going to focus on, and how it is going to manage relationships and transactions across the value chain in its industry (i.e., the complete range of activities from the creation and securing of raw materials through production and distribution to the end user).[7] Basic strategic questions—such as "Which business activities should be brought inside the firm?" and "Which activities should be outsourced?"—are also instrumental in setting an organization's boundary.[8] As we will see later in this chapter, the decision to outsource a particular function or activity is often made to achieve greater flexibility and agility in a rapidly changing environment. Companies that fail to maintain the "right" business activities within their boundaries, however, also risk losing their competitive advantage.

General and Specific Environment

The *general organizational environment* refers to the broad factors, trends, and conditions that concern all organizations.[9] It includes such forces as technological development and change, social and cultural factors, political interactions, economic conditions, demographic factors, the legal structure, the ecological system, and market factors (see Figure 8-1). The general environment focuses on those conditions that may *potentially* affect organizations. In many instances, however, the relevance of these factors for a particular organization may not be exactly clear. Yet, because such changes can have far-reaching effects on an organization (e.g., the shift from an economically regulated to a deregulated environment, as witnessed in the telecommunications industry), it is important for organizations to monitor general societal trends and changes.

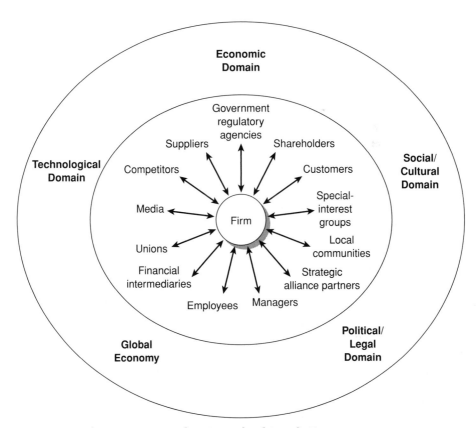

Figure 8-1 The Organization and Its General and Specific Environment

In contrast to the relative ambiguity and uncertainty concerning the effect of the general environment on a particular organization, the *specific (or task) environment* focuses on those external factors, groups, and organizations that have immediate relevance for an organization. Such a specific environment usually includes an organization's customers, suppliers, unions, government regulatory agencies, public interest groups, trade associations, and other relevant publics or critical constituencies (see Figure 8-1). While the general environment is similar for all organizations, the specific environment will vary depending on the specific domain (i.e., range of products or services offered, markets served) an organization has chosen. Thus, the distinction between the general and specific environment is dependent or contingent upon the core tasks of a particular organization.

Organizational Stakeholders The concept of a specific organizational environment points to the need to understand the relationship between organizations and the different social groups that are affected by their operation: shareholders, employees, unions, customers, suppliers, local communities, government agencies, and so forth. The exact nature of the bond between corporations and these groups, as one would expect, is quite variable in terms of its intensity, duration, and significance.[10]

Throughout most of our history, the *shareholder model* has been our basic business gospel—a corporation is essentially viewed as a piece of private property owned by those who hold its stock. These owners elect a board of directors, whose responsibility is to serve the best interests of the owners. This model assumes that the interactions between business organizations and the different groups affected by their operations (employees, consumers, and suppliers) are most effectively structured as marketplace transactions. The forces of supply and demand—the pressures of a competitive market—will ensure the best use of business and its economic resources. In essence, the board of directors and its appointed managers are fiduciary *agents* or trustees for the owners. They fulfill their basic obligations when they operate in the best financial interests of the stockholders, in other words, when they act to maximize profits. The other groups in a firm's environment are relegated to secondary consideration.

In contrast to the shareholder view, the *stakeholder model* recognizes that expanding demands are being placed on business organizations that include a wider variety of groups not traditionally defined as part of the corporation's immediate self-interest. These groups are referred to as stakeholders. In a narrow sense, stakeholders are those identifiable groups or individuals on which an organization is dependent for its survival—internal stakeholders such as shareholders and employees, and external stakeholders such as customers, suppliers, and key government agencies. On a broader level, however, a stakeholder is any identifiable group or individual who can affect or is affected by organizational performance in terms of its products, policies, and work processes. In this sense, public interest groups, protest groups, local communities, trade associations, competitors, unions, and the media are also organizational stakeholders. Shareholders continue to occupy a place of prominence, but their specific interests are placed within the broader context of stakeholder needs and pressures.

A recent conceptualization of the influence of stakeholders suggests that the capacity of a business to generate sustainable wealth, in essence long-term value, is determined by its relationships with critical stakeholders.[11] Managers, therefore, need to improve their skills and abilities to work with key stakeholders across all the dimensions of their strategic environment, from *resource-based stakeholders* (investors/owners, employees, customers), to *industry structure stakeholders* (supply chain associates, joint venture and strategic alliance partners, unions, competitors, regulatory authorities), to broader *sociopolitical stakeholders* (local communities, special interest groups, the media).

Stakeholders and Managerial Decision Making　As will be explored later in this chapter, business organizations are currently experiencing a high degree of environmental turbulence. Indeed, over the past two decades, business organizations and their management have faced many new demands from a host of stakeholders that are based on changing societal expectations about the appropriate role of the corporation in the larger society. As a result, the ability to effectively manage potentially competing interests across a variety of stakeholder groups has become a critical part of management. As research has indicated, the ability to address stakeholder concerns and to foster positive connections with key stakeholders can enhance a firm's reputation and financial performance.[12] Thus, these pressures and concerns, far from being temporary events that merely happen and then go away, require corresponding shifts in the minds and orientations of managers.[13]

The stakeholder framework provides managers with a way of thinking about business's environment, especially in terms of the specific individuals, groups, and organizations in that environment, how they "see" the organization (image), and how the resulting interaction can shape how organizational insiders view their own firm (identity).[14] The underlying key is to be able to understand the ways in which different stakeholders are or might be affected by organizational policies and practices, how they are likely to respond, and what your own options are in dealing with these varied stakeholder groups.

Actual and Perceived Environment

Another important analytic distinction is the difference between the actual (objective) environment and the one that managers perceive (subjective).[15] The *actual environment* consists of those entities, objects, or conditions that exist outside the firm. By focusing on the general and specific environments of a particular organization, individuals can go "outside" the organization and through the use of objective indicators (e.g., specific number of task components, rate of change, technological and market volatility) develop a useful description of this environment. Every organization has an objective environment that is real, measurable, and external to the firm. This reality places certain constraints on the way in which the organization operates (e.g., any industry group has definite technical characteristics that it must attend to, regulations define acceptable business practices). The *perceived environment,* in contrast, reflects the subjective interpretation of that environment. Although these perceptions are also "real" events in their consequences, they take place *within* an organization.

Although we might assume that there is close correspondence between these two dimensions, empirical research has indicated that the correlation between measures of a firm's actual environment and measures of the perceived characteristics of that environment by the firm's managers is not very high. In fact, managers often have a badly distorted picture of their business and environment.[16] This gap is significant since people react according to their perceptions rather than what is actually "out there." The influence of perceived environment is further reflected in the concept of the *enacted environment*. An organization "creates" the environment to which it adapts by selectively choosing those stakeholders and aspects of the environment it will deal with and those stakeholders and concerns that it will, at least temporarily, ignore. Since it is basically through managerial perceptions that the environment is "known" to an organization, many theorists argue that the perceived environment is more important than the actual environment. However, as knowledge from both industry economics and marketing theory readily indicates, when decisions are made on inaccurate perceptions of the actual environment the results can be severe.

Despite the importance of both the objective and perceived environment, most studies have emphasized only one perspective. Research focusing on objective environments as determinants of organizational responses, for example, has tended to disregard the potential influence of managers' perceptions of that environment. Similarly, studies looking at the role of perception have tended to ignore the influences of objective environments. Theoretical work in this area, however, has emphasized the importance of the interaction between objective environmental attributes and managers' perceptions, as well as other moderating variables such as individual characteristics and values, organizational slack, and degree of managerial discretion as distinct components of organizational responses.[17] Thus, both the actual and perceived environments of organizations are important aspects of environmental analysis that should be explicitly recognized in decision-making processes.

Environmental Change and Uncertainty

As the distinction between the general and specific environment implies, not all organizational environments are the same. Such environments vary from the nearly static (e.g., no new competitors or technological breakthroughs; little social or political pressure) to the very dynamic (e.g., rapid, often unpredictable change as experienced in the shakeout in the world of e-commerce). In some instances, however, the transition from a relatively static to a rapidly changing environment can be quite sudden, as evidenced by recent events in the publishing industry. While the major chains have dominated the industry in the recent past, the growth of Amazon.com, the online presence of a host of other book companies, and the introduction of online publishing and e-books have altered competitive practices, strategy considerations, and external opportunities and constraints.

Stability, Complexity, and Resource Availability

One way of assessing the potential effect of environmental change on an organization is based on three dimensions: degree of stability, complexity, and resource availability.[18] The *stability* dimension refers to the extent to which elements in the environment are dynamic. An environment is considered stable if it remains relatively the same over a given period of time (e.g., such as with a public utility). Unstable environments, by contrast, are those that experience abrupt changes that are rapid and often unexpected.

The *complexity* dimension refers to the number and similarity of external elements and different stakeholders in an organization's environment. A complex environment consists of a large number of diverse elements that exert a significant influence on the organization, while a simple environment is characterized by only a few important external factors. A local convenience store, for example, has a relatively simple environment (suppliers, customers, and local competitors are the main influential external elements); large corporations, by contrast, have much more complex environments that are characterized by such multiple stakeholders as governmental regulatory agencies and legislators, unions and employee groups, public interest groups, and local community groups as well as stockholders, suppliers, creditors, and vendors.

Resource availability refers to the level of resources available to firms in the environment. An important aspect of *munificence* (i.e., the extent to which an environment can provide sufficient resources for the firms in that environment) is competition for those resources. A market with little growth may still be munificent if it contains few competitors for those resources, while a rapidly growing market might pose problems for individual firms if it contains many competitors.

Uncertainty

The stability, complexity, and resource availability dimensions outlined above are significant for organizations in that they determine the amount of *uncertainty* an organization must confront in its environment. Environmental uncertainty essentially refers to the lack of information that organizational decision makers have about trends and changes in environmental conditions.[19] Thus, the decision-making process—from a consideration of alternative decisions to an assessment of their potential outcomes—becomes increasingly unpredictable with greater environmental uncertainty, which also creates more risk for organizations. In general, unstable and complex environments present more uncertainty than stable and simple ones. As the discussion of behavioral decision theory (Chapter 2) suggests, considering our cognitive limitations and their influence on our perceptual processes, such uncertainty significantly influences the way in which managers attempt to make their decisions.

A Typology of the Environment

One of the landmark contributions that reflects much of our thinking about organizational environment is Emery and Trist's four-environment model of uncertainty.[20] This classic typology depicts rates of environmental change ranging from relatively stable environments to those that are constantly changing. The model is based on the assumption that as environments develop, their parts become increasingly interdependent, which creates greater complexity. Consider, for example, our fuel needs prior to the Industrial Revolution. During our agrarian era, coal and wood (our primary fuels) were used mainly for heating purposes. When individuals required wood, they simply chopped it themselves or went to someone who had a woodlot. There was little need for any systematic forest management or reseeding plans. After industrialization, however, our fuel needs changed significantly as coal, wood, and eventually oil were used not only for home heating but for industry energy requirements as well. As multiple sectors in society became increasingly dependent on the same energy source, the resulting network of interdependencies that emerged created many potential difficulties, often in unanticipated ways, to the point where any change in supply can be highly disruptive. Today, as global warming and climate change are capturing increased attention, energy planning and sustainable business practices have become critical components of corporate strategy.

Based on this perspective, four types of increasingly complex environments are identified: (1) placid, randomized; (2) placid, clustered; (3) disturbed, reactive; and (4) turbulent field. The *placid, randomized* environment is relatively unchanging and there is no significant interdependence among its parts. Thus, this type of environment poses little threat to organizations. Change takes place slowly over time (high environmental stability) and it is predictable (low complexity). The next stage is the *placid, clustered* environment. This environment also changes slowly (stability), but there is increased interdependence (growing complexity) of parts of the environment into different clusters (e.g., coalitions of suppliers or distributors). Events in the firm's environment are no longer fully random as they are in the first type of environment. Thus, the placid, clustered environment begins to present a threat (uncertainty as to the clustered relationships) for organizations.

The *disturbed, reactive* environment is much more complex than the two previous ones. The main aspect of this environment is the emergence of a number of similar organizations (competitors) that are sufficiently large to exert control over their own and *other* organizations' environments. This dynamic creates a situation in which an organization tries to influence, as well as react to, its environment. Disturbed, reactive environments are characteristic of oligopolies (industries dominated by three or four companies). In the automotive industry, for example, the "horsepower race" of the 1950s, the "guarantee race" of the 1960s (where a relatively small automobile company introduced a very comprehensive guarantee, only to have the others follow suit), the "efficiency race" of the late 1970s, and the "quality race" of the 1980s and 1990s reflect how companies create part of the industry environment, forcing others to react in a similar way.

In the final type of environment, the *turbulent field*, conditions are so complex that it is difficult to understand the combination of forces that create constant change. This environment is the most dynamic and it has the highest degree of uncertainty. It is difficult to provide an adequate illustration of a turbulent field since theoretically the environment does not "sit still" long enough for examination. However, the rapid growth of the Internet and the turbulent rise and fall (and subsequent reemergence) of e-business is a good example of the types of change that can quickly occur. As a growing number of corporate giants quickly discovered, a slow response to such disruptive technologies[21] can result in significant losses and shifts in power.

Environmental Turbulence

A number of theorists have observed that organizations are being confronted with increasingly *turbulent fields,* characterized by high levels of instability and complexity. Faced with making decisions in Internet time, coping with destructive technologies that are revamping entire industries, and responding to rapidly changing stakeholder demands, among a host of other volatile changes, managers are increasingly being encouraged to embrace the inevitability of instability, learning to succeed at the "edge of chaos."[22] Such forces and relentless pressures have created a situation where a realization of and an emphasis on the environment is an increasingly important aspect of managing organizations and the behaviors that occur within them.

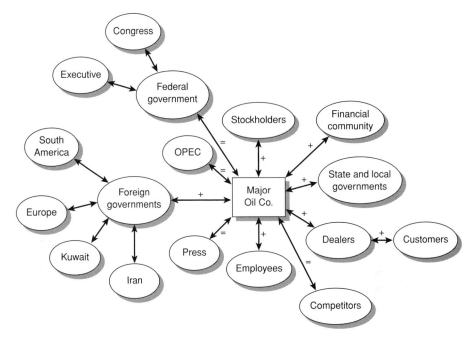

Strategic Issues:
- New sources of production
- Diversification "downstream"
- U.S. government policy

Notes:
"+" means "generally positive relationship"
"–" means "generally negative relationship"
"=" means "generally neutral relationship"

Figure 8-2 Stakeholder Map of Major Oil Company in the Past (1950s—Early 1960s)

Source: Reprinted from R. Edward Freeman, *Strategic Management: A Stakeholder Approach.* Harper & Row Publishers, 1984. Reprinted by permission of the author.

An example of increasing environmental turbulence is provided by an internal assessment by a major oil company.[23] As a way of helping its managers better understand the firm's environment and its implications for the organization, "Major Oil" undertook a comparative study of changes in the company's environment over several decades. Based on this analysis, the corporation created a *stakeholder map* for each period. As illustrated in Figure 8-2, in the past (1950s–early 1960s) the firm enjoyed neutral to favorable relationships with a relatively small number of generally supportive stakeholders. Due to the myriad changes that took place over the next few decades, however, this relatively stable picture evolved into a much more turbulent one. As Figure 8-3 indicates, not only did many of the positive and neutral relationships between the firm and key stakeholder groups deteriorate to neutral and negative ones, but the sheer number and types of groups and constituencies drastically increased as well. A comparison between these two "worlds" readily portrays the levels of instability and complexity faced by managers today compared with those of previous generations.[24] A basic characteristic of the twenty-first century is that such turbulence and the intensifying dynamics between companies and their stakeholders make the need to understand and cope with uncertainty that much more important.

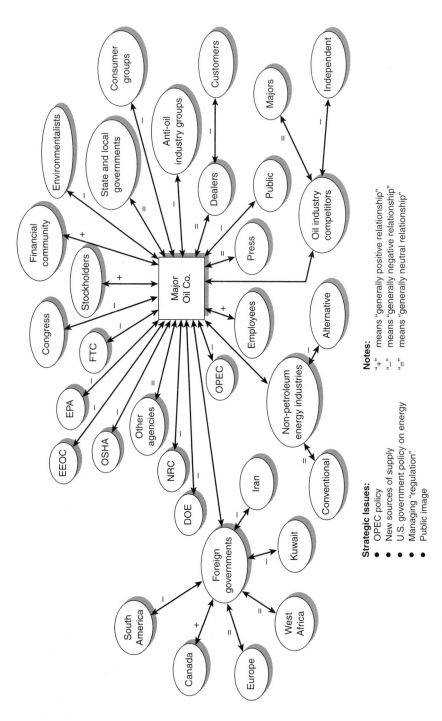

Figure 8-3 Stakeholder Map of Major Oil Company in the Present Environment

Notes:

"+" means "generally positive relationship"
"−" means "generally negative relationship"
"=" means "generally neutral relationship"

Strategic Issues:

• OPEC policy
• New sources of supply
• U.S. government policy on energy
• Managing "regulation"
• Public image

Source: Reprinted from R. Edward Freeman, *Strategic Management: A Stakeholder Approach.* Harper & Row Publishers, 1984. Reprinted by permission of the author.

ORGANIZATION-ENVIRONMENT RELATIONS

Managers and organizations attempt to deal with their environments in a number of different ways. This section examines managerial efforts to reduce uncertainty by: (1) controlling the environment, (2) managing the organization's boundary, (3) creating interorganizational linkages or alliances, and (4) responding to environmental decline. Chapter 9 extends this discussion and examines attempts to structure organizations so they "fit" environmental pressures and demands.

Controlling the Environment

Since environmental uncertainty poses a threat to an organization's effectiveness, managers often attempt to minimize this phenomenon by attempting to influence—or create—their environment. Companies like Amazon.com and Barnes & Noble, for example, have a significant impact on the publishing industry in both their respective countries and in world markets. What is less well known is the extent to which such organizations are also capable of influencing other aspects of their environment, such as controlling suppliers or attempting to introduce new product trends (e.g., the failed attempt at e-books).[25]

There are five basic ways in which organizations attempt to exert control over their environment to reduce the level of uncertainty in their planning.[26] First, under "norms of rationality," organizations try to *buffer* or isolate their core technologies (internal operations) from external influences. Through both input (e.g., stockpiling of inventories) and output (e.g., marketing campaigns) mechanisms, managers attempt to ensure that the core task of the organization is not directly affected by external conditions such as scarcity of materials (input) or changes in consumer preferences (output).

If buffering strategies fail to reduce uncertainty, organizations may attempt to control environmental fluctuations by *smoothing* or leveling their input and output transactions. Scheduling nonemergency operations in hospitals or offering reduced airline fares during the "off-season" are examples of ways in which organizations try to keep their internal operations going at an even, predictable rate.

If buffering and smoothing are not sufficient, managers may turn to a third, more proactive strategy—*forecasting*, an attempt to better anticipate and adapt to environmental changes. In the automotive industry, for example, sales tend to increase following the introduction of a new model, usually during the fall season; sales then tend to decline until early spring. If an automobile company can adjust its production to forecasted periods of high and low demand, it will not have huge inventories of unsold cars or demands for cars that are not built. Obviously, close congruence between the actual and perceived environment is especially important for effective forecasting.

Even prediction and anticipation, however, do not always work. When all else fails, organizations may resort to *rationing*, the allocation of products or services based on a priority system. Consumers often see this as "one item per buyer." Stores that place sales limits on popular toys around the holiday season are a good example of this kind of tactic.

Managers can also engage in a series of *interorganizational coping strategies* to allow for organizational adjustment in times of severe environmental change. This can be accomplished through coalition formation (e.g., inter-firm joint ventures), cooptation (e.g., mergers and acquisitions), competition (e.g., major sales and rebates), or bargaining (e.g., contracting certain services or functions to another organization). The main consideration is that organizational autonomy and discretion over goal setting are reduced according to the degree of involvement with other organizations.

Managing Organizational Boundaries

As suggested earlier, senior-level managers can exert significant influence over the determination of the boundary of their organizations.[27] A well-developed approach for making such decisions is based on *transaction cost economics.* The three main dimensions of this perspective are: *governance* (the process through which a firm manages an economic exchange), *opportunism* (when a party in an exchange attempts to take unfair advantage of the other parties involved), and *transaction-specific investment* (an investment that is significantly more valuable in one particular exchange than another).

Firms rely on *market governance* when they use market-determined prices to manage specific exchanges. Oil refineries, for example, rely on market-determined prices when they purchase crude oil on the spot market; electronics firms use market governance to obtain standardized electrical components from component distributors. The boundary between the organization in question and the other firms it is doing business with is clearly delineated. Companies use *intermediate governance* when they rely on interorganizational arrangements (such as long-term supply contracts or strategic alliances) to manage an exchange. In these instances, complex agreements and contracts replace the more independent, arm's-length market relationship, and the boundary between firms is often blurred. Finally, organizations use *hierarchical governance* to bring an exchange within their own boundary. By acquiring another firm, for example, a company gains greater control over that particular area, as when a manufacturer purchases one of its suppliers or distributors. Firms also exert hierarchical governance through internal growth, as when a retail firm owns, develops, and operates its own stores.

Transaction cost economics suggests that the most effective way to manage a firm's boundary is determined by two factors: the cost of a particular governance mechanism and the threat of opportunism in an exchange. In general, the more complex the form of governance (going from market to intermediate to hierarchical), the more costly it will be. Thus, from a cost perspective, nonhierarchical forms of governance are preferable. However, if there is a *threat of opportunism* (when the other party might try to develop an unfair advantage), the tendency is to try to bring the activity in question within the boundary of the firm. Threats of opportunism are greater when *only one* of the parties has made a *transaction-specific investment* in the exchange. For example, if an oil pipeline company builds a pipeline from an oil field to an oil refinery owned by a second firm, the pipeline only creates value when it is pumping crude oil. Because the refinery has not made a similar investment, it can try to take advantage of the other company, for instance, by demanding that the pipeline company reduce the price of its crude oil, increase its quality, or share in the expense of upgrading facilities in the refinery. Since the pipeline company made a transaction-specific investment and the refinery did not, the oil refinery is in a position to behave opportunistically. By weighing these factors, firms can choose a more complex form of governance to mitigate the threat of opportunism as needed. Especially in rapidly evolving, high-technology industries, however, firms are increasingly attempting to gain access to capabilities through nonhierarchical forms of governance (especially partnerships and alliances), despite the threat of opportunism that may exist due to the significant costs involved (e.g., acquiring another firm, the cost of internal development, time delays).[28]

Boundary-Spanning Roles

The basic purpose of boundary-spanning roles is to connect and position the firm with key elements in its external environment—by channeling information back and forth—so that organizational plans and actions can be more effectively coordinated and uncertainty reduced.[29] The underlying premise is that as a result of such interaction, the organization will be in a better position to adapt to its environment, and that some environmental components and stakeholders might be influenced to adapt to the needs of the organization.

Boundary-spanning roles serve two fundamental purposes.[30] First, they attempt to detect and process information about changes in the environment, and relate that information to the organization. Many corporations, for example, have *issues management* roles and *community relations* functions that seek to identify emerging trends, concerns, or issues that are likely to affect the organization over the next few years, and to develop appropriate organizational responses toward that future.[31] Second, boundary-spanning roles represent the organization to its environment by sending out information and attempting to influence that environment. For example, many firms and industries employ lobbyists to promote and further their interests in public policy decisions. The *public affairs* departments of large organizations often attempt to fulfill both purposes, detecting and processing information and disseminating information in an effort to influence the environment.[32] This function reflects an evolution of the traditional public relations area, with greater emphases on information gathering, environmental analysis, interactions with key stakeholder groups, and appropriate modifications to company policies and strategies. By attempting to influence other people's perceptions of the organization, they seek to manage the way in which key stakeholders will interact with the organization.

Interorganizational Alliances

Interorganizational alliances are organizational arrangements that employ resources from two or more organizations. Sometimes referred to as "hybrid" organizations, these inter-firm linkages range from formalized relationships between organizations (e.g., outsourcing, licensing agreements), to partnerships, to the actual creation of formal joint ventures.[33] Since such alliances are simultaneously uniting organizations and products of single organizations, they create a unique set of advantages and disadvantages. Because "hybrids" (*intermediate governance*) draw on the capabilities of multiple, independent organizations, they offer a wide range of solutions to deal with such problems as operational inefficiency, resource scarcity, and lack of facilities to take advantage of economies of scale. At the same time, there is an inherent fragility in such inter-firm arrangements, which makes them quite complex to manage.[34] The potential clash of organizational cultures, "we-they" conflicts between members of the different firms, different management styles and expectations, unrealistic projections or expectations about the alliance, low levels of employee involvement and coalition building, ineffectual leadership, and related concerns can easily undermine the most "ideal" alliance. In fact, studies have pointed to the relatively low level of success in partnerships and joint ventures, where only one out of three such combinations proves to be successful over the long term.[35] Yet, despite these difficulties, the growing pressures on firms for greater efficiency and flexibility are increasingly influencing firms to experiment with such hybrid, interorganizational arrangements.

The ambiguities and uncertainties created by a rapidly changing environment are influential in interorganizational alliance decisions. A vertical integration partnership (e.g., an agreement between a manufacturer and a supplier, or between a product design company and a contract manufacturer), for example, is associated with attempts to absorb industry interdependencies and reduce value chain–related uncertainties. In general, the larger the degree of uncertainty, the greater the tendency to pursue such inter-firm arrangements.[36] Underlying keys to making these ventures work focus on understanding creation (strategic), maintenance (relationship building), and performance (outcome) related issues, achieving sufficient confidence in the partner's cooperation that the firms are able to develop a balance between trust and control.[37]

Organizational Responses to Environmental Decline

For the past two decades, the potential for organizational decline, which is generally defined as a deterioration in the organization's ability to adapt to its environment, has been a stark reality for many firms.[38] It is important to distinguish between downsizing and organizational decline. Downsizing is an intentional, proactive management strategy to respond to current market conditions, while decline is an involuntary environmental phenomenon that leads to the erosion of an organization's resource base. Organizational decline results when a firm is faced with reduced influence and control over environmental resources (e.g., loss of market share due to increased international competition), the environment itself has changed (e.g., changing demographics and consumer preferences leading to a shrinking market for blue jeans), or a company has become inefficient due to reliance on past successes (organizational atrophy)[39]—as exemplified by the deep recession in our traditional, "smokestack" industries (e.g., steel, automobiles) from the late 1970s to mid-1980s, the consolidation of the personal computer industry in the 1990s, and the technology slide during the early 2000s. Managers need to understand the reasons underlying organizational decline, develop strategies to attempt to avoid decline, and be knowledgeable about how to manage requisite retrenchment if it does occur. Unfortunately, research has indicated that most managers—including top management teams—are ill prepared to deal with such decline.[40]

Population Ecology Theory   One approach to understanding the emergence or decline of populations of organizations is referred to as *population ecology*. Sometimes referred to as a "natural selection" theory, this perspective argues that the environment "chooses" certain types of organizations to survive and others to perish based on the degree of fit between the firms' structural characteristics and the characteristics of their environment.[41]

Organizations competing in an open environment are viewed as having a particular niche—a place or position in the marketplace.[42] This niche may be either large or small, and it is determined by such variables as technology, concentration, and resource availability that give the niche a certain "shape" (characteristics). Organizations must fit their particular niche or they will fail. For example, although numerous factors contributed to the situation in the automobile industry in the late 1970s and early 1980s, three variables played key roles: the oil crisis, changing technology, and international competition. The oil crises of 1972 and 1979 changed the focus of the industry from larger cars to smaller, more fuel-efficient ones. Technological changes—for instance, front-wheel drive and fuel injection as opposed to rear-wheel drive and carburetion—as well as the ability of Japanese and German manufacturers to quickly adapt to take advantage of these needs and preferences, further influenced the size and shape of the niche. Over a relatively short period of time, the large-car niche shrank and the small-car niche grew. However, it was not only the size of the niche that changed, but its shape as well—it was not a small-car, rear-wheel drive niche, but rather a small-car, front-wheel drive niche with considerable technological sophistication. Due to these changes, automobile makers had to quickly adapt or face decline. Continued adaptation is necessary, however. The niche can move in very different directions, as witnessed by the juxtaposition of the popularity of trucks and sport utility vehicles (SUVs) and the emergence of fuel-efficient hybrid cars.

According to this perspective, there are four types of niche declines based on the continuity of the change and the impact on niche size and shape. *Erosion* is where niche size gradually shrinks over time (continuous change). In this situation, organizations often take an offensive strategy, attempting to redistribute or fine-tune their efforts, resizing (shrinking) the organization to meet the new realities of the marketplace. *Contraction*, in contrast, is where niche size shrinks suddenly and organizations are placed in a defensive position, typically characterized by substantial cutbacks either in selected areas or throughout the entire organization. *Dissolution* is where the shape of the niche changes over time. In this situation, firms attempt to initially protect what they currently have and gradually undertake a diversification strategy. This pattern is characteristic of the cigarette industry as our society's growing awareness of and concern with smoking-related health problems have prompted many firms to seek out new products (e.g., recent experiments with smokeless cigarettes) and investment opportunities in other industries. Finally, *collapse* is where a particular niche suddenly disintegrates, as happened when the market for mainframe computers gave way to the personal computer revolution.

A basic finding of many studies in this area is that the failure to effectively adapt to changes in the environment can be understood by examining certain characteristics of each firm's managers, structure, culture, strategy, and environment.[43] For example, once highly innovative Digital Equipment Corporation (DEC), which was second only to IBM as a computer manufacturer, faltered when its engineering-driven culture and orientation failed to respond to the emerging reality of the commoditization of personal computers. Despite the fact that the firm was responsible for the invention of speech recognition technology, the minicomputer, and local area networking, DEC ultimately failed as a business and was acquired by Compaq Corporation.[44]

While population ecology theory provides us with insights into industry dynamics, it has been criticized for its extreme environmental determinism.[45] The theory posits that an industry's life cycle, much like human growth and development, shapes later growth and adaptive capabilities. Essentially, this approach also suggests that luck, chance, and randomness play an important role in the success of a firm—if a company proposes a new product or service and the environment supports it, it will be successful; if not, it will fail. Thus, an idea that worked extremely well in the 1990s might fail miserably in the 2000s. Based on this theory, therefore, critics contend that organizational success or failure is determined more by characteristics of the environment and the particular niche than by management skills and organizational strategies.

Managing Decline   There are two basic approaches to dealing with the effects of organizational decline: recentralization and reallocation.[46] Since decline-related decisions need to be made at the top of an organization, upper-level executives usually reclaim authority to make related decisions (*recentralization*). Employees often have to be laid off, departments eliminated, pay and benefits cut, and so forth. The remaining resources in the firm must then be *reallocated* for maximum effect. If the firm has a particular niche, resources are often channeled to take advantage of that area. Yet, while such reallocation may mean strengthening a specific component of the company, it also means further weakening or drawing from another area or department. As a result, decline-related decisions typically lead to a host of organizational problems and tensions: increases in conflict, secrecy, scapegoating, withdrawal, rigidity, and turnover; decreases in morale, participation, innovativeness and creativity, and long-term planning.[47] Successful turnaround strategies, however, are well documented,[48] and strategies for managing the impact of organizational decline are presented in Chapter 11.

Managing Growth   While population ecology theory suggests that organizations are constrained in their ability to adapt, a competing perspective emphasizes a much more adaptive process of strategic change. The strategic adaptation view focuses on the role that managers can play in monitoring environmental changes and modifying organizational strategy to better match environmental contingencies, leading to organizational change and growth.[49] As will be explored in the following chapters, senior-level managers can exert significant influence on overcoming organizational inertia and internal resistance to change, setting the stage for an assessment of the organization's capabilities and weaknesses, and, in turn, strategic adaptation, renewal, and/or redirection of the organization.

THE INTERNATIONAL ENVIRONMENT

A quick look at the past few decades reveals that the business world is no longer confined by national boundaries. Globalization—noted as creating a "borderless" and "flat" world—is suggested to be "leveling the playing field," leading to significantly lessened barriers to competition for countries, companies, and even individual entrepreneurs.[50] Increased emphasis is also being placed on new markets with billions of people—the "aspiring poor"—in developing nations who are entering the market economy for the first time. These "bottom of the pyramid" strategies are influencing companies to rethink traditional price-performance relationships for products and services, potentially creating the foundation for highly distributed small-scale operations across the world.[51]

Prior to the early to mid-1970s, the United States was clearly the dominant industrial power in the world. Toward the end of the 1970s, however, the U.S. position of industrial dominance in the world began to wane. During the 1980s, industrialized countries such as Japan and West Germany achieved impressive successes in capturing increasing shares of many markets. A number of newly industrializing countries (NICs)—such as South Korea, Taiwan, China, Brazil, Argentina, and India—also emerged as a powerful economic force in world trade. During the 1990s, regional trade blocs—for example, the European Community (EC) and the North American Free Trade Association (NAFTA)—began to exert significant influence on business competition. Today, information technology is continuing to transform the business world to the point where virtually all but the smallest organizations operate across national boundaries. China and India—often referred to as "Chindia"—have become true economic powers, as their companies and markets attract increased attention across the world.

Historically, trade between nations was largely *complementary* (e.g., England sold wool to Portugal while Portugal sold wine to England, neither of which the other could produce) and *competitive* (e.g., the United States and Germany bought and sold chemicals and electrical machinery from each other) in nature. During the 1980s and 1990s, however, trade took on an increasingly *adversarial* character as exemplified by U.S.-Japan tensions.[52] While complementary trade seeks to establish partnerships (courtship) and competitive trade attempts to create a customer (winning battles), adversarial trade aims at industry domination (destruction of the other's industry). The shifts from complementary exchange to competitive trade to adversarial trade have challenged our conventional assumptions about trade, raised questions about the need for new laws and authority structures (e.g., market reciprocity as opposed to free markets or protectionism), and influenced the economic block formation noted above. The heightened globalization in the twenty-first century has further created the need for greater *diplomacy* in international trade, the capability to build bridges between a firm's core businesses, other companies in that niche and related niches, and the complex political environments within which the global company conducts its business.[53] These changes are continuing to challenge many of the assumptions underlying our traditional notions of management and organization, and competition and collaboration.

Due to the early dominance of the United States in world trade, most of our understanding of management and organization came from the American experience.[54] The underlying assumption was that the work-related attitudes and behaviors of U.S. workers were similar to those in other countries. This rather simplistic "assumption of universality" has been tested by the new realities of the business world. For instance, while different economic systems and management practices may be partly accountable for some of the changes in worldwide business behaviors and successes, research suggests that Japan and other Asian countries may have an advantage over the United States and Europe due to the Eastern emphasis on belonging and the art of synthesis that is embedded in their culture.[55] At the very least, such analyses point to the need to become more aware of cross-cultural differences and the implications they hold for managerial and organizational practices.

Globalization and Organizational Behavior

When we think about international business, most of us tend to think in terms of *multinational corporations* (MNCs). An MNC is typically defined as a company headquartered in one country but which engages in foreign production and related activities through affiliates located in other countries.[56] Most firms examining the feasibility of establishing operations in another country tend to focus on the economic conditions and market analyses of the country under consideration: the availability, adequacy, and current utilization of a nation's resources (land, labor, and capital); the potential to create new markets for goods and services; income distribution and patterns of personal consumption; labor costs; and political risk and government attitudes toward private investment. Many firms, however, still overlook or underestimate the sociocultural and political-legal factors involved in the success of such ventures.

A growing reality of today's global environment is the *transnational enterprise* (TNE), a firm that attempts to achieve the local responsiveness of an MNC while capturing the scale and efficiencies of a global corporation.[57] In a TNE, distinctions between the parent organization and its affiliates are blurred. Instead of centralizing key activities and resources in the parent company or decentralizing them so that each local subsidiary can fully carry out its own tasks, specialized resources and activities are dispersed across national boundaries as necessary to simultaneously achieve maximum efficiency and flexibility. One of the ramifications is the need for intensive organization-wide coordination and shared decision making.

There are some important organizational characteristics that differentiate TNEs from MNCs.[58] First, TNEs are characterized by concerted efforts to build on and legitimize the diverse perspectives held by worldwide organizational members. *National subsidiary managers* are relied on to sense and represent the changing needs of local populations and influences from host governments. *Global business managers* track the strategies of global competitors, providing the necessary coordination for response. Finally, *functional managers* focus on organizational information and expertise, facilitating the dissemination of this knowledge across appropriate organizational units. The guiding objective is to build a multidimensional organization that develops and balances the influence of each of these different management groups.

Second, instead of viewing national units as a pipeline for company products or implementers of centrally defined strategies, the TNE regards each of its worldwide units as a source of ideas, skills, capabilities, and knowledge that can serve the total organization. In this sense, the TNE can be conceptualized as an integrated network of globally distributed and interdependent resources and capabilities. Within this context, traditional functional organizational structures (see Chapter 9) have become increasingly obsolete, and TNEs are characterized by a flat organizational structure embedded with transnational teams and boundaryless information networks.[59]

Finally, transnational management must have the ability to differentiate its operating relationships and alter its decision-making roles across functions, businesses, and geographic units. Within this context, it is top management's role to create an organizational culture that is supportive of diversity and delegated decision making and has the ability to adapt across different countries. Although the idea of TNEs is typically linked with corporate giants, as will be explored in Chapter 9, even small and middle-sized firms are increasingly operating without regard for national boundaries through network structures and partnership arrangements.

The emergence of MNCs and TNEs raises a number of questions concerning the idea of cross-cultural management:[60] (1) Do organizational behaviors vary across cultures? (2) How much of any observed difference can be attributed to cultural determinants? (3) Is the variance in organizational behaviors worldwide increasing, decreasing, or remaining the same? (4) How can managers best operate when working in different cultures? (5) How can managers best handle cultural diversity, including using that diversity as an organizational resource?

If companies are to maintain their positions as successful world competitors, it is crucial that we develop managers and business professionals who not only understand the dynamics associated with a global economy, but who can act accordingly. There is a critical need for managers who are mobile and adaptable, who can effectively deal with highly heterogeneous groups and individuals, and who feel at ease and knowledgeable in different cultures.[61] The importance of training and development in this area is underscored by studies that indicate that close to one-third of placement decisions in U.S. MNCs are deemed mistakes, largely because of the employees' failure to adjust to the new culture. As a result, companies are undertaking intercultural training efforts that include such dimensions as (1) area studies, or documentary programs, that expose employees to a new culture through written materials on the country's history, geography, economics, and cultural institutions; (2) cultural assimilation efforts—programmed instruction that exposes people to specific incidents that are important for successful interaction in different countries; (3) language preparation; (4) sensitivity training, in which employees' self-awareness is increased; and (5) field experiences, in which people are exposed to "mini-cultures" within their own country.[62] What remains unclear, however, is whether typical predeparture training initiatives (where individuals tend to be less involved and committed to the training) are more effective than postarrival training (in essence, on-site exposure where people are more emotionally invested in the training).[63]

Transferability of Management Practices

The globalization of business has led to numerous analyses of different management models and business systems from around the world. Questions about cultural differences across societies raise concerns about the transferability of management practices from one country to another. Due to the processes underlying industrialization and postindustrialization (see Chapter 1), some researchers argue that work-related values and goals are becoming increasingly similar across societies, implying *convergence*.[64] For instance, while long-term, closely linked relationships between companies and their suppliers are still more common in Japan than in the United States, research indicates that the basic nature of supplier relations in the two countries is converging.[65] Similarly, the phenomenal success of Japanese manufacturing practices influenced many U.S. firms to transplant and adapt these practices to their own operations.[66] Other studies, however, point to persistent *divergence*, underscoring that cultural differences across societies persist even after controlling for industrial organizational differences.[67] This view suggests the need for more indigenous management theories (i.e., the creation of management theory and practice embedded in local conditions and sociocultural factors).[68] Thus, the debate over convergence and divergence continues, as comparative analyses across different countries continues to contribute to the development of international management thought.

Business Practice and National Culture

Sociologists and anthropologists talk in terms of national character, the "relatively enduring personality characteristics, cultural attributes or institutional structures sufficiently distinctive in their incidence or distribution to distinguish one society from another."[69] While national character is not unimodal (i.e., every person in a particular country does not necessarily have all the characteristics associated with that culture) and the characteristics in question may not be unique to a particular society, the interdependence between personality, culture, and social system has gained increased acceptance.

Based on an extensive study of IBM employees in forty different countries, for example, Hofstede found significant differences across the national characters (or cultures) of the countries he studied.[70] On the basis of his analysis, he found four basic dimensions that could be used to describe and differentiate the national cultures of these countries: (1) *power distance,* the degree to which hierarchical power places people at a psychological distance from each other; (2) *uncertainty avoidance,* the degree to which ambiguity is perceived to be threatening or anxiety arousing; (3) *individualism-collectivism,* the extent to which individuals or groups are regarded as primary resources for work and problem solving; and (4) *masculinity,* the extent to which those values and behaviors that are stereotypical masculine traits (e.g., independence and achievement) are valued in contrast to more stereotypically feminine values and behaviors (e.g., nurturance and sympathy). His subsequent work added a fifth dimension, initially referred to as "Confucian dynamism," which reflects a *long-term* versus *short-term orientation* (e.g., propensity toward thrift and saving versus immediate consumption).[71]

NAFTA provides a good context to explore the implications of Hofstede's findings. Although the trade agreement has sparked a significant increase in business activity between the United States, Canada and Mexico, the ability to manage cross-cultural differences is more critical than ever.[72] Compared with Mexico, for example, the United States was found to be low to average on power distance (e.g., rank has only a few privileges), quite low on uncertainty avoidance (risk is generally encouraged and conflict is viewed as having potentially constructive outcomes), very high on individualism (people are expected to take care of themselves and autonomy is cherished), and above average on masculinity (e.g., people should be driven by ambition, achievement should be rewarded). Mexican society, in contrast, was found to be high on power distance (e.g., those in power should look and act powerful), high on uncertainty avoidance (e.g., a tendency to avoid bad news, or make unrealistic promises to avoid conflict and/or disappointing one's business partner), low on individualism (organizational goals are more important than individual goals, personal networks play an important role in business success), and, similar to the United States, high on masculinity.

Especially in U.S.-Mexican joint ventures, these differences can readily impact business practices and relationships. A recent study of such partnerships found that Mexican workers and managers, as a group, were more likely to emphasize form over substance compared with their U.S. counterparts. This tendency often produces such counterproductive behaviors as reluctance to admit to failure or error and aversion to inform the joint-venture partner of bad news. While U.S. managers often suffer from the same problem, it is significantly more pronounced in Mexico than in the United States. At the same time, perceived arrogance on the part of U.S. organizations and their management exacerbates face-saving behaviors on the part of Mexican joint-venture partners. U.S. managers have experienced similar types of differences and related problems in their dealings with European managers and joint ventures with Chinese companies.[73] It is clear that U.S. managers must continue to become more culturally aware and knowledgeable about different societies.

Societal Culture and Management

To fully appreciate the dynamics associated with the globalization of business, it is important to understand the role of culture, since a society's culture reveals the values, attitudes, and behaviors of its members. Anthropologists and sociologists have long recognized the significance of culture as a major determinant of a population's beliefs, attitudes, and behaviors. Indeed, most definitions of culture used today are modifications of E.B. Tylor's definition of the concept in 1871: "That complex whole which includes knowledge, belief, art, morals, law, custom, and any other capabilities and habits acquired by (people) as members of a society."[74] In its broadest sense, culture can be thought of as that part of the entire repertoire of human action and its products that is socially, as opposed to genetically, transmitted.

Two central themes emerge from analyses of culture.[75] First is the integrative concept of custom—that is, traditional and regular ways of doing things. Culture can be thought of as being *learned* rather than genetic or biological in nature. It is *shared* by people as members of social groups rather than being idiosyncratic in nature. Culture is also *transgenerational* and *cumulative* in that it is passed from one generation to the next. Finally, it is *symbolic* in nature and *patterned* (i.e., organized and integrated) in our lives. Second, there is a distinction between material or objective culture and ideational or subjective culture. *Objective culture* refers to the artifacts and material products of a society. *Subjective culture* refers to a society's characteristic way of perceiving its environment, its rules, and its norms, roles, and values.

As illustrated in Figure 8-4, individuals express culture and its normative qualities through the values that they hold about life and the social world around them. These values, in turn, affect attitudes and what are viewed as appropriate behaviors in a given situation. As the discussion of Theory X and Theory Y in Chapter 3 emphasized, the types of beliefs that people hold about the nature of human behavior greatly influence the way in which they approach management and organization. This relationship also holds for the way in which management and organizations are viewed in different societies.

The extent to which management practices are truly transferable across societies thus remains an intriguing question. In countries where members of MNCs and TNEs are accustomed to working with nationals in their home country environment, foreign companies are more likely to include locals in management decisions and use the same type of management approaches that they practice at home. At the same time, anyone who has lived in a different culture can appreciate the myriad differences involved. Comparative studies of top-level managers from the U.S. and the Pacific Rim, for example, have pointed to different styles of strategic decision making and different patterns of time usage.[76] Senior-level American managers were found to spend almost one-half of their time on activities in fragmented, short periods of fewer than nine minutes, and only 10 percent of their time on issues that lasted more than one hour.

Figure 8-4 Culture's Influence on Behavior

Source: Adapted from Nancy J. Adler, *International Dimensions of Organizational Behavior* (Boston: Kent, 1986), p. 9; © by Wadsworth Inc.; and Boris W. Becker and Patrick E. Connor, "A Course on Human Values for the Management Curriculum," *Exchange: The Organization Behavior Teaching Journal* 8, no. 1 (1983), 10–16.

Japanese and Korean senior managers, by contrast, had virtually opposite time profiles. U.S., Japanese, and Chinese managers were also found to have different ways of analyzing and conceptualizing strategic decisions. Although these style differences may be appropriate for each particular culture, such differences can be particularly acute in international dealings and negotiations. In such situations, it is critical that members of a negotiating team study the other team's culture to gain a better understanding and appreciation of the perspectives from which they are negotiating.[77]

Along similar lines, culture exerts an influence on how leadership itself is conceptualized. In Western culture, for example, much of the early writings focused on those qualities necessary to become a "great" leader (see Chapter 7). In Islamic culture, in contrast, the emphasis was placed more on the relationship between leaders and their followers, the duties of the leader, and the demand for integrity and trustworthiness in leaders.[78] Within this context, the ideal leader was seen as being both humble and exalted, capable of vision while dedicated to the needs of the people. Of course, as events of the past several decades have indicated, there can be a gap between this leadership ideal and its reality. Nevertheless, the notions of servant leadership and followership, which the Islamic tradition has long emphasized, have entered the Western assessment of leadership, pointing to the ways in which management concepts benefit from ideas from different cultures.

Cultural differences also continue to shape a number of generalities about management and management practices—for instance, "The French hate management by objectives," "Family is vital to Norwegians," "Success in Asia means family first," "Organizational loyalty in Japan is the key to its success," and "The British are highly individualistic with a low commitment to their firms."[79] While present data suggest that many of these stereotypes are generally supportable, it is also clear that much more research and insight are needed into cross-cultural differences and preferences in management and organization, especially as TNEs continue to expand their influence. As studies have shown, such stereotypes, which are constructed as a result of direct interaction with other managers *and* as a product of exposure to indirect information sources, do have an impact on how business is carried out.[80]

Culture, Context, and Information Technology

Although advanced information technologies have made communication across national borders easier, they have not necessarily made such communication more effective. Indeed, while many Western companies are investing significant resources in information technology to make their global communication efforts more efficient, such tools are often underutilized, misunderstood, and even counterproductive in cross-cultural business exchanges.[81]

The United States, Canada, and northern European nations are defined as *low-context* cultures, that is, the actual content of the message is more important than the medium itself (the setting in which the message is communicated).[82] Thus, video-conferencing or e-mail is usually accepted as an efficient substitute for face-to-face meetings. In *high-context cultures,* such as in Asia and the Middle East, in contrast, the context (setting) itself, with its myriad nonverbal cues and personal touches, often conveys more meaning than the literal words of the message itself. In these countries, business transactions are often ritualized, and the style in which these interactions are carried out is significant. A high value is placed on personal interaction, and after-hours socializing with key stakeholders is almost a daily experience. Thus companies that rely on low-context communication technologies to replace more context-rich forms of human interaction may unwittingly place themselves and their colleagues at a disadvantage. While high-context forms of communication are not necessarily the better choice (see the discussion of media richness in Chapter 4), it is important to place the use of advanced information technologies in their larger culture context.

When using information technology for cross-cultural communication, it is important to find ways to create greater context to enhance participation and understanding. Prior to a videoconference, for example, managers can circulate an agenda, written background information, a seating chart, and biographical information about the participants. During the videoconference itself, a facilitator could be used to introduce people and act as a gatekeeper to draw everyone into the discussion, define unfamiliar terms and concepts, work toward greater understanding across the different parties, and so forth. The key is to adapt the technology to fit people's preferences, work habits, and emotional reactions to different communication media by understanding how these variables vary across cultures. This area is where our deepening experience with diversity-related human resource practices can help to avoid cross-cultural misunderstandings by sensitizing organizational members to these differences.[83]

Management Practices and Dual-National Hybrid Cultures

Given the growth of MNCs and TNEs, it is clear that we are facing a truly global business world. While the actual cross-cultural transfer of management practices and organizational systems from one society to another will never be an easy process, it can be done. Cross-cultural differences do not necessarily mean that it is impossible to harmonize different managerial and organizational systems, but they do point to the need to "bridge" these differences. For example, rather than attempt to directly transfer standard Western management practices to local offices in different countries, successful global managers appear to use local cultural understandings as a starting point for interpreting and operationalizing those practices. In essence, by creating a hybrid organizational orientation—through communication, the promotion of mutual recognition and respect, and an appreciation of local customers—managers can achieve a harmonization of diverse cultural elements, creating, in effect, a hybridization of management values and practices.[84]

It appears that the successful transfer of management and organization orientations and techniques is based on this type of dual-nation, hybrid approach. In fact, recent research points to the long-term success of creating hybrid team cultures within transnational work teams as a way of facilitating group interaction.[85] There is a clear need to understand the cultural orientations and dynamics of each society and to adapt different practices as appropriate. Indeed, as Hofstede has argued, a "disregard of other cultures is a luxury only the strong can afford . . . as far as management theories go, cultural relativism is an idea whose time has come."[86]

CONCLUSION

A central theme in this chapter focuses on the significant effect that the external environment can have on management practices and organizational functioning. As discussed in Chapter 1, organizations are *open systems* that are influenced by a multitude of environmental forces and changes. As this chapter has illustrated, a number of environmental factors influence management philosophy and practice, and ultimately managerial and organizational effectiveness. As we will explore in the next chapter, these pressures and forces have significantly influenced the ways in which we think about appropriate forms of organization. An increased emphasis on social and political changes in addition to traditional considerations of economic and technological change, a growing awareness of organizational stakeholders and related tensions, and the growing pressures from hyper-competition in a truly global marketplace reflect some of the main external factors that have influenced the ways in which managers attempt to deal with and respond to the environment.

It is important to realize that while organizations can learn and adapt to their environment, they also, to varying degrees, attempt to change and control their environment. While these latter strategies are particularly true for large corporations, the rapid diffusion of information technology has enabled much smaller organizations to exert a significant influence on their environments as well. As the discussion on managing the environment emphasizes, it is important for organizations to change and adapt when necessary, but it is just as important for them to be able to manage their boundaries, neutralizing or altering problematic aspects of their environment when necessary.

NOTES

1. See M.L. Tushman, W.H. Newman, and E. Romanelli, "Convergence and Upheaval: Managing the Unsteady Pace of Organizational Evolution," *California Management Review* 29, no. 1 (1986): p. 29.

2. For a good overview of these concerns see D.P. Baron, "Integrated Strategy: Market and Nonmarket Components," *California Management Review* 37, no. 2 (1995): 47–65; and D.L. Walker, "Forces That Will Shape America's Future: Themes from GAO's Strategic Plan, 2007–2012," *GAO Reports*, April 2, 2007, pp. 1–38.

3. J. Frishammar, "Organizational Environment Revisited," *International Studies of Management & Organization* 36, no. 3 (2006): 22–49.

4. R.L. Daft, *Organization Theory and Design* (St. Paul, MN: West, 2001), p. 130.

5. R. Miles, *Macro Organizational Behavior* (Santa Monica, CA: Goodyear, 1980), p. 195.

6. See, for example, C.W. Churchman, *The Systems Approach* (New York: Dell, 1968).

7. H. Aldrich, *Organizations and Environments* (Englewood Cliffs, NJ: Prentice Hall, 1979); and M. Porter, *Competitive Advantage: Creating and Sustaining Superior Performance* (New York: Free Press, 1985).

8. See J. Barney, "How a Firm's Capabilities Affect Boundary Decisions," *Sloan Management Review* (Spring 1999): 137–145; and R.L. Cross, A. Yan, and M.R. Louis, "Boundary Activities in 'Boundaryless' Organizations: A Case Study of a Transformation to a Team-Based Structure," *Human Relations* 53, no. 6 (2000): 841–868.

9. This section is based on Miles, op. cit., pp. 195–198.

10. This section is based on A.F. Buono and L.T. Nichols, *Corporate Policy, Values and Social Responsibility* (New York: Praeger, 1985); R.E. Freeman, *Strategic Management: A Stakeholder Approach* (Boston: Pitman, 1984); and T.M. Jones, "Instrumental Stakeholder Theory: A Synthesis of Ethics and Economics," *Academy of Management Review* 20, no. 2 (1995): 404–437.

11. See J.E. Post, L.E. Preston and S. Sachs, *Redefining the Corporation: Stakeholder Management and Organizational Wealth* (Stanford, CA: Stanford University Press, 2002).

12. S.L. Berman, A.C. Wicks, S. Kotha, and T.M. Jones, "Does Stakeholder Orientation Matter? The Relationship Between Stakeholder Management Modes and Firm Financial Performance," *Academy of Management Journal* 42, no. 5 (1999): 488–506; and B.A. Neville, S.J. Bell, and B. Mengüc, "Corporate Reputation, Stakeholders and the Social Performance–Financial Performance Relationship," *European Journal of Marketing* 39 no. 9/10 (2005): 1184–1198.

13. See Freeman, op. cit., pp. 22–24, G.T. Savage, T.W. Cox, C.J. Whitehead, and J.D. Blair, "Strategies for Assessing and Managing Organizational Stakeholders," *Academy of Management Executive* 5, no. 2 (1991): 61–75; and S.A. Waddock and M.E. Boyle, "The Dynamics of Change in Corporate Community Relations," *California Management Review* 37, no. 4 (1995): 125–140.

14. See B.R. Agle, R.K. Mitchell, and J.A. Sonnenfeld, "Who Matters to CEOs? An Investigation of Stakeholder Attributes and Salience, Corporate Performance, and CEO Values," *Academy of Management Journal* 42, no. 5 (1999): 507–525; and S.G. Scott and V.R. Lane, "A Stakeholder Approach to Organizational Identity," *Academy of Management Review* 25, no. 1 (2000): 43–62. For an insightful discussion of concerns about stakeholder management, see R.A. Wolfe and D.S. Putler, "How Tight Are the Ties That Bind Stakeholder Groups?" *Organization Science* 13, no. 1 (2002): 64–82.

15. L.J. Bourgeois III, "Strategy and Environment: A Conceptual Integration," *Academy of Management Review* 5, no. 1 (1980): 23–39; K. Weick, "Enactment Processes in Organizations," in B.M. Staw and G.R. Salancik, *New Directions in Organizational Behavior* (Chicago: St. Clair, 1977), pp. 277–300; and K.M. Sutcliffe, "What Executives Notice: Accurate Perceptions in Top

Management Teams," *Academy of Management Journal* 37, no. 5 (1994): 1360–1378.

16. J.M. Mezias and W.H. Starbuck, "What Do Managers Know, Anyway?" *Harvard Business Review* 81, no. 5 (2003): 16–17.

17. See M. Yasai-Ardekani, "Structural Adaptations to Environments," *Academy of Management Review* 11, no. 1 (1986): 9–21; K.M. Sutcliffe, "What Executives Notice: Accurate Perceptions in Top Management Teams," *Academy of Management Journal* 37, no. 5 (1994): 1360–1378; P.R. Duimering and F. Safayeni, "The Role of Language and Formal Structure in the Construction and Maintenance of Organizational Images," *International Studies of Management & Organization* 28, no. 2 (1998): 57–77.

18. R.B. Duncan, "Characteristics of Organizational Environment and Perceived Environmental Uncertainty," *Administrative Science Quarterly* 17 (1972): 313–327; R. Jurkovich, "A Core Typology of Organizational Environments," *Administrative Science Quarterly* 19 (1974): 380–394; and M.P. Sharfman and J.W. Dean, Jr., "Conceptualizing and Measuring the Organizational Environment: A Multidimensional Approach," *Journal of Management* 17, no. 4 (1991): 681–700.

19. See J.F. March and H.A. Simon, *Organizations* (New York: Wiley, 1958), pp. 136–142.

20. F.E. Emery and E.L. Trist, "The Causal Texture of Organizational Environments," *Human Relations* 18 (1965): 21–32.

21. G. Broekstra, "A Synergetics Approach to Disruptive Innovation," *Kybernetes* 31, no. 9/10 (2002): 1249–1259.

22. See R.T. Pascale, "Surfing on the Edge of Chaos," *Sloan Management Review* (Spring 1999): 83–94; M. Santos, "Inevitably Chaos," *CMA Management* 78, no. 9 (2005): 37–39; and R.B. Mason, "Coping with Complexity and Turbulence: An Entrepreneurial Solution," *Journal of Enterprising Culture* 14, no. 4 (2006): 241–266.

23. See Freeman, op. cit., pp. 119–122.

24. See T. Modis, *Conquering Uncertainty: Understanding Corporate Cycles and Positioning Your Company to Survive the Changing Environment* (New York: McGraw-Hill, 1998); and R.M. Grant, "Strategic Planning in a Turbulent Environment: Evidence from the

Oil Majors," *Strategic Management Journal*, 24, no. 6 (2003): 491–517.

25. For a conceptual analysis of this phenomenon, see C.B. Perrow, *Organizational Analysis: A Sociological View* (Monterey, CA: Wadsworth/Brooks-Cole, 1970).

26. J.D. Thompson, *Organizations in Action* (New York: McGraw-Hill, 1967); and J.D. Thompson and W.J. McEven, "Organizational Goals and Environment: Goal-Setting as an Interaction Process," *American Sociological Review* 23 (1958): 23–31.

27. This section draws heavily from Barney, "How a Firm's Capabilities Affect Boundary Decisions."

28. See, for example, M.D. Whinston, "On the Transaction Cost Determinants of Vertical Integration," *Journal of Law Economics and Organization* 19, no. 1 (2003): 1–23; and H.C. Dekker, "Value Chain Analysis in Inter-Firm Relations: A Field Study," *Management Accounting Research* 14, no. 1 (2003): 1–24.

29. See Daft, *Organization Theory and Design*, p. 141.

30. D.B. Jemison, "The Importance of Boundary Spanning Roles in Strategic Decision-Making," *Journal of Management Studies* 21 (1984): 131–152; and A.M. Walsh, "Managing Environmental Uncertainty: An Analysis of Executive Behavior in the Health and Social Service Sector," *Journal of Healthcare Management* 44, no. 1 (1999): 47–55.

31. For a good discussion of the role of responsibilities of the issues management function see J.F. Coates, V.T. Coates, J. Jarratt, and L. Heinz, *Issues Management: How You Can Plan, Organize, and Manage for the Future* (Mt. Airy, MD: Lomond Publications, 1986); and M. Palese and T.Y. Crane, "Building an Integrated Issue Management Process as a Source of Sustained Competitive Advantage," *Journal of Public Affairs* 2, no. 4 (2002): 284–292.

32. L.E. Preston, *Social Issues and Public Policy in Business and Management* (College Park, MD: Center for Business and Public Policy, University of Maryland, 1986), pp. 8–9; and O. Ihlen, "Rhetoric and Resources: Notes for a New Approach to Public Relations and Issues Management," *Journal of Public Affairs* 2, no. 4 (2002): 259–269.

33. B. Borys and D.B. Jemison, "Hybrid Arrangements as Strategic Alliances: Theoretical Issues in Organizational Combinations," *Academy of Management Review* 14, no. 2 (1989): 234–249; and A.F. Buono, "Managing Strategic Alliances: Organizational and Human Resource Considerations," *Business in the Contemporary World* 3, no. 4 (1991): 92–101.

34. See S. Waddock, "Building Successful Social Partnerships," *Sloan Management Review* 29, no. 3 (1988): 17–23; and A.F. Buono, ed., *Enhancing Inter-Firm Strategies and Interorganizational Networks* (Greenwich, CT: Information Age Publishing, 2003).

35. See A.F. Buono, "Managing Joint Ventures: Inter-Firm Tensions and Pitfalls," *SAM Advanced Management Journal* 55, no. 2 (1990): 28–32; N. Alster, "Dealbusters: Why Partnerships Fail," *Electronic Business* 12 (April 1986): 70–75; and W. Bergquist, J. Betwee, and D. Meuel, *Building Strategic Relationships* (San Francisco: Jossey-Bass, 1995).

36. M. Brenner and Z. Shapira, "Environmental Uncertainty as Determining Merger Activity," in W.H. Goldberg, ed., *Mergers: Motives, Modes, and Methods* (Aldershot, England: Gower), 1983, pp. 51–65; J. Pfeffer, "Merger as a Response to Organizational Interdependence," *Administrative Science Quarterly* 17 (1972): 382–394; and M.S. Kraatz, "Learning by Association: Interorganizational Networks and Adaptation to Environmental Change," *Academy of Management Journal* 41, no. 6 (1998): 621–641.

37. See A.F. Buono, "Enhancing Strategic Partnerships: Intervening in Network Organizations," *Journal of Organizational Change Management* 10, no. 2 (1997): 251–266; and T.K. Das and B. Teng, "Between Trust and Control: Developing Confidence in Partner Cooperation in Alliances," *Academy of Management Review* 23, no. 3 (1998): 491–512.

38. See, for example, J.P. Sheppard, "Strategy and Bankruptcy: An Exploration into Organizational Death," *Journal of Management* 20, no. 4 (1994): 795–833; and Y. Neumann and E. Finaly-Neuman, "Management Strategy, The CEO's Cognitive Style and Organizational Growth/Decline: A Framework for Understanding Enrollment Change in Private Colleges," *Journal of Educational Administration* 32, no. 4 (1994): 66–76.

39. See D.A. Whetten, "Sources, Responses, and Effects of Organizational Decline," in J.R. Kimberly and R.H. Miles, eds., *The Organizational Life Cycle* (San Francisco: Jossey-Bass, 1980), pp. 342–374; S.J. Freeman and K.S. Cameron, "Organizational Downsizing: A Convergence and Reorientation Framework," *Organization Science* 4 (1993): 10–29; and W. McKinley, J. Zahao, and K.G. Rust, "A Sociocognitive Interpretation of Organizational Downsizing," *Academy of Management Review* 25, no. 1 (2000): 227–243.

40. D. Whetten, "Organizational Decline: A Neglected Topic in Organizational Behavior," *Academy of Management Review* 5, no. 4 (1980): 577–588; R.I. Sutton, K.M. Eisenhardt, and J.V. Jucker, "Managing Organizational Decline: Lessons from Atari," *Organizational Dynamics* 14, no. 4 (1988): 17–29; M.A. Mone, W. McKinley, and V.L. Barker III, "Organizational Decline and Innovation: A Contingency Framework," *Academy of Management Review* 23, no. 1 (1998): 15–33; J.C. Edwards, W. McKinley, and G. Moon, "The Enactment of Organizational Decline: The Self-Fulfilling Prophecy," *International Journal of Organizational Analysis* 10, no. 1 (2002): 55–75; and A. Carmeli and J. Schaubroeck, "Top Management Team Behavioral Integration, Decision Quality, and Organizational Decline," *Leadership Quarterly* 17, no. 5 (2006): 441–453.

41. Aldrich, *Organizations and Environment.*

42. This discussion is based on R.F. Zammuto and K.S. Cameron, "Environmental Decline and Organizational Response," in L.L. Cummings and B.M. Staw, eds., *Research in Organizational Behavior* (Greenwich, CT: JAI Press, 1985), pp. 223–262. See also S.D. Dobrev, T. Kim, and G.R. Carroll, "The Evolution of Organizational Niches: U.S. Automobile Manufacturers, 1885–1981," *Administrative Science Quarterly* 47, no. 2 (2002): 233–263.

43. See J. Hage, "Responding to Technological and Competitive Change: Organizational and Industry Factors," in D.D. Davis, ed., *Managing Technological Innovation*

(San Francisco: Jossey-Bass, 1986), pp. 44–71; and D.D. Davis, "Technological Innovation and Organizational Change," in D.D. Davis, ed., *Managing Technological Innovation*, pp. 8–9.

44. See E. Schein, P.J. Kampas, P.S. Delisi, and M.M. Sonduck, *DEC Is Dead, Long Live DEC: The Lasting Legacy of Digital Equipment Corporation* (San Francisco: Berrett-Koehler, 2004).

45. See M. Hannan and G. Carroll, *Dynamics of Organizational Populations: Density, Legitimation, and Competition* (New York: Oxford University Press, 1992); and A. Lomi, "The Population Ecology of Organizational Founding: Location Dependence and Unobserved Heterogeneity," *Administrative Science Quarterly* 40, no. 1 (1995): 111–144.

46. C.H. Levine, I.S. Rubin, and G.G. Wolohojian, "Managing Organizational Retrenchment," *Administration & Society* 14 (1982): 101–136; and B. Baack and J.B. Cullen, "Decentralization in Growth and Decline: A Catastrophe Theory Approach," *Behavioral Science* 39 (1994): 213–228.

47. K.S. Cameron, D.A. Whetten, and M.U. Kim, "Organizational Dysfunctions of Decline," *Academy of Management Journal* 30, no. 1 (1987): 126–138; A.F. Buono, "Moral Corporate Cultures in a Downsized, Restructured World," in W.M. Hoffman and R.E. Frederick, eds., *Business Ethics* (New York: McGraw-Hill, 1995), pp. 226–233; T.M. Amabile and R. Conti, "Changes in the Work Environment for Creativity During Downsizing," *Academy of Management Journal* 42, no. 6 (1999): 630–640; and Z. Rosenblatt and Z. Sheaffer, "Brain Drain in Declining Organizations: Toward a Research Agenda," *Journal of Organizational Behavior* 22, no. 4 (2001): 409–424.

48. See, for example, V.L. Barker and I.M. Duhaime, "Strategic Change in the Turnaround Process: Theory and Empirical Evidence," *Strategic Management Journal* 18 (1998): 13–38; and R.M. Kanter, "Leadership and the Psychology of Turnaround," *Harvard Business Review* 81, no. 6 (2003): 74–81.

49. W. Boeker, "Strategic Change: The Influence of Managerial Characteristics and Organizational Growth," *Academy of Management Journal* 40, no. 1 (1997): 152–170; and T. Levitt, "Creativity Is Not Enough," *Harvard Business Review* 80, no. 8 (2002): 137–151.

50. See K. Ohmae, *The Borderless World: Power and Strategy in the Interlinked Economy* (New York: HarperInformation, 1990); and T.L. Friedman, *The World Is Flat: A Brief History of the Twenty-First Century* (New York: Farrar, Straus and Giroux, 2005).

51. C.K. Prahalad and S.L. Hart, "The Fortune at the Bottom of the Pyramid," *Strategy + Business*, no. 26 (2002): 1–14; and J. Brugmann and C.K. Prahalad, "Cocreating Business's New Social Compact," *Harvard Business Review* 85, no. 1 (2007): 80–90.

52. See P.F. Drucker, *The New Realities* (New York: Harper & Row, 1989), pp. 129–132.

53. R. Saner, L. Yiu, and M. Sondergaard, "Business Diplomacy Management: A Core Competency for Global Companies," *Academy of Management Executive* 14, no. 1 (2000): 80–92.

54. See N.J. Adler, *International Dimensions of Organizational Behavior* (Boston: Kent, 1986).

55. See, for example, G. Hofstede and M.H. Bond, "The Confucius Connection: From Cultural Roots to Economic Growth," *Organizational Dynamics* 14, no. 4 (1988): 4–21; M. Kotabe, "Efficiency vs. Effectiveness Orientation of Global Sourcing Strategy: A Comparison of U.S. and Japanese Multinational Companies," *Academy of Management Executive* 12, no. 4 (1998): 107–119; and H. Shibata, "Productivity and Skill at a Japanese Transplant and Its Parent Company," *Work and Occupations* 28, no. 2 (2001): 234–260.

56. J.J. Miller and J.A. Kilpatrick, *Issues for Managers: An International Perspective* (Homewood, IL: Irwin, 1987), p. 1.

57. See Drucker, op. cit., Chapter 9; D. Gold and K.P. Sauvant, "The Future Role of Transnational Corporations in the World Economy," *Business in the Contemporary World* 2, no. 3 (1990): 55–62; and D.A. Rondinelli, "Transnational Corporations: International Citizens or New Sovereigns?" *Business and Society Review* 107, no. 4 (2002): 391–413. See also R. Pinheiro-Alves, "Transnational Corporations and

International Production: Concepts, Theories and Effects," *Economic Issues* 11, no. (2006): 85–86; and M.R. Haas, "Acquiring and Applying Knowledge in Transnational Teams: The Roles of Cosmopolitans and Locals," *Organization Science* 17, no. 3 (2006): 367–384.

58. This discussion is drawn from C.A. Bartlett and S. Ghoshal, *Transnational Management* (Homewood, IL: Irwin, 1992), pp. 522–525.

59. See C.C. Snow, S.A. Snell, S.C. Davison, and D.C. Hambrick, "Using Transnational Teams to Globalize Your Company," *Organizational Dynamics* 24, no. 4 (1996): 50–67; M.F.R. Kets de Vries with E. Florent-Treacy, "*The New Global Leaders* (San Francisco: Jossey-Bass, 1999); and B. Hunter, "What Does It Mean to Be Globally Competent?" *Journal of Studies in International Education* 10, no. 3 (2006): 267–285.

60. See N.J. Adler, R. Doktor, and S.G. Redding, "From the Atlantic to the Pacific Century: Cross-Cultural Management Revisited," *Journal of Management* 12, no. 2 (1986): 297; and P.C. Earley and H. Singh, "International and Intercultural Management Research: What's Next?" *Academy of Management Journal* 38, no. 2 (1995): 327–340.

61. R.M. Steers and E.L. Miller, "Management in the 1990s: The International Challenge," *Academy of Management Executive* 2, no. 1 (1988): 21–22; I. Torbiorn, "Operative and Strategic Use of Expatriates in New Organizations and Market Structures," *International Studies of Management & Organization* 24, no. 3 (1994): 5–17; and C.A. Bartlett and S. Ghosal, "What Is a Global Manager?" *Harvard Business Review* 81, no. 4 (2003): 101–108.

62. See P.C. Earley, "Intercultural Training for Managers: A Comparison of Documentary and Interpersonal Methods," *Academy of Management Journal* 30, no. 4 (1987): 685–698; R.L. Tung, "Selection and Training of Personnel for Overseas Assignments," *Columbia Journal of World Business* 16 (1981): 68–78; and J.C. Baker, "Foreign Language and Predeparture Training in U.S. Multinational Firms," *Personnel Administrator* 29 (1984): 68–72.

63. J. Selemer, "The Preference for Predeparture or Postarrival Cross-Cultural Training: An Exploratory Approach," *Journal of Man-*

agerial Psychology 16, no. 1 (2001): 50–58. See also G.M. Hernández, "Cultural Training: Crucial to Relocation," *Caribbean Business* 35, no. 3 (2007): S2; and V. Peltokorpi, "Intercultural Communication Patterns and Tactics: Nordic Expatriates in Japan," *International Business Review* 16, no. 1 (2007): 68–82.

64. M.E. Arias and M.F. Guillen, "The Transfer of Organizational Management Techniques Across Borders," in J.L. Avarez, ed., *The Diffusion and Consumption of Business Knowledge* (London: Macmillan, 1998), pp. 110–137; and M.C. Galand, "The Transferability Question: Comparing HRM Practices in the Philippines with the US and Canada," *International Journal of Human Resource Management* 15, no. 7 (2004): 1207–1233.

65. See S.R. Helper and M. Sako, "Supplier Relations in Japan and the United States: Are They Converging?" *Sloan Management Review* 36, no. 3 (1995): 77–84.

66. See J.K. Liker, W.M. Fruin, and P.S. Adler, eds., *Remade in America: Transplanting and Transforming Japanese Manufacturing Systems* (New York: Oxford University Press, 1999).

67. See D.A. Ricks, B. Toyne, and Z. Martinez, "Recent Developments in International Management Research," *Journal of Management* 16, no. 2 (1990): 223–226; I. Vewrtinsky, D.K. Tse, D.A. Wehrung, and K. Lee, "Organizational Design and Management Norms: A Comparative Study of Managers' Perceptions in the People's Republic of China, Hong Kong, and Canada," *Journal of Management* 16, no. 4 (1990): 853–867; O. Shenkar and M.A. von Glinow, "Paradoxes of Organizational Theory and Research: Using the Case of China to Illustrate National Contingency," *Management Science* 40, no. 1 (1994): 56–71; J. Rafferty, "The Synthesis of Economic Organisation and the Management of Change: Intercultural Transferability and the Japanese Paradigm," *Management Decision* 39, no. 5/6 (2001): 415–420; and L.C. Thang, C. Rowley, T. Quang, and M. Warner, "To What Extent Can Management Practices Be Transferred between Countries? The Case of Human Resource Management in Vietnam," *Journal of World Business* 42, no. 1 (2007): 113–127.

68. See C. Gopinath, "Alternative Approaches to Indigenous Management in India," *Management International Review* 35, no. 3 (1998): 257–276; M.F. Guillen, "International Management and the Circulation of Ideas," in C.L. Cooper and D.M. Rousseau, eds., *Trends in Organizational Behavior*, vol. 5 (New York: Wiley, 1998), pp. 47–63; V. Miroshnik, "Culture and International Management: A Review," *Journal of Management Development* 21, no. 7/8 (2002): 521–543; and M. Vaadi and M. Suuroja, "Training Retail Sales Personnel in Transition Economies: Applying a Model of Customer-Oriented Communication," *Journal of Retailing and Consumer Services* 13, no. 5 (2006): 339–349.

69. G.D. Mitchell, *A Dictionary of Sociology* (London: Routledge & Kegan Paul, 1973), p. 123.

70. G. Hofstede, *Culture's Consequences: International Differences in Work-Related Values* (Beverly Hills, CA: Sage, 1980). See also G. Hofstede and J. Soeters, "Consensus Societies within Their Own Character: National Cultures in Japan and the Netherlands," *Comparative Sociology* 1, no. 1 (2002): 1–16; and L. Kolman, N.G. Noorderhaven, G. Hofstede, and E. Dienes, "Cross-Cultural Differences in Central Europe," *Journal of Managerial Psychology* 18, no. 1/2 (2003): 76–93.

71. G. Hofstede, *Cultures and Organizations: Software of the Mind* (New York: McGraw-Hill, 1991); and R. Hodgetts, "A Conversation with Geert Hofstede," *Organizational Dynamics* 21, no. 4 (1993): 53–61. For an interesting application of this framework, see L. Lu, G.M. Rose, and J.G. Blodgett, "The Effects of Cultural Dimensions on Ethical Decision Making in Marketing: An Exploratory Study," *Journal of Business Ethics* 18 (1999): 91–105; and A.M. Soares, M. Farhangmehr, and A. Shoham, "Hofstede's Dimensions of Culture in International Marketing Studies," *Journal of Business Research* 60, no. 3 (2007): 277–284.

72. This discussion draws heavily on G.K. Stephens and C.R. Greer, "Doing Business in Mexico: Understanding Cultural Differences," *Organizational Dynamics* 24, no. 1 (1995): 39–55. See also I. Berdrow, "Complex Learning Partnerships: Creating the Connections in International Alliances," in A.F. Buono, ed., *Enhancing Inter-Firm Networks and Interorganizational Strategies* (Greenwich, CT: Information Age Publishing, 2003), pp. 117–136.

73. See R. Calori and B. Dufour, "Management European Style," *Academy of Management Executive* 9, no. 3 (1995): 61–71; and I. Bjorkman and Y. Lu, "The Management of Human Resources in Chinese-Western Joint Ventures," *Journal of World Business* 34, no. 3 (1999): 306–320.

74. E.B. Tylor, *Primitive Culture: Researches into the Development of Mythology, Philosophy, Religion, Language, Art and Custom*, vol. 1 (New York: Holt, 1871), p. 1.

75. See A.F. Buono, J.L. Bowditch, and J.W. Lewis, "When Cultures Collide: The Anatomy of a Merger," *Human Relations* 38, no. 5 (1985): 477–500; H.D. Triandis, V. Vassilou, G. Vassilou, Y. Tanka, and A.V. Shanmugan, *The Analysis of Subjective Culture* (New York: Wiley-Interscience, 1972); and N.C. Morey and F. Luthans, "Refining the Displacement of Culture and the Use of Scenes and Themes in Organizational Studies," see Adler, op. cit., Chapter 1.

76. R.H. Doktor, "Asian and American CEOs: A Comparative Study," *Organizational Dynamics* 18, no. 3 (1990): 46–56; and M.G. Martinsons and R.M. Davidson, "Strategic Decision Making and Support Systems: Comparing American, Japanese and Chinese Management," *Decision Support System* 43, no. (2007): 284–300.

77. See J.M. Brett and T. Okumura, "Inter- and Intracultural Negotiations: U.S. and Japanese Negotiations," *Academy of Management Journal* 41, no. 2 (1998): 495–510; and D. Martin, P. Herbig, C. Howard, and P. Borstaff, "At the Table: Observations on Japanese Negotiation Style," *American Business Review* 17, no. 1 (1999): 65–71.

78. This discussion is drawn from M. Witzel, "Islamic Leadership: Extolling Humility, Justice and Community," *European Business Forum* no. 28 (Spring 2007): 50–51.

79. J.W. Hunt, "Commentary: Do American Theories Apply Abroad?" *Organizational Dynamics* 10, no. 1 (1981): 62.

80. N. Zaidman, "Stereotypes of International Managers: Content and Impact on Business Interactions," *Group & Organization Management* 25, no. 1 (2000): 45–66.

81. See M. Boudreau, K.D. Loch, D. Robey, and D. Straud, "Going Global: Using Information Technology to Advance the Competitiveness of the Virtual Transnational Organization," *Academy of Management Executive* 12, no. 4 (1998): 120–128; and J.Y. Weissinger and E.M. Trauth, "Situating Culture in the Global Information Sector," *Information Technology & People* 15, no. 4 (2002): 306–320.

82. The following discussion is based on E. Gundling, "How to Communicate Globally," *Training & Development* (June 1999): 28–31.

83. Y. Fujimoto, N. Bhafen, J. Fermelis, and C.E.J. Härtel "The Global Village; Online Cross-Cultural Communication and HRM,"

Cross Cultural Management 14, no. 1 (2007): 7–22.

84. B. Shimoni and H. Bergmann, "Managing in a Changing World: From Multiculturalism to Hybridization—The Production of Hybrid Management Cultures in Israel, Thailand, and Mexico," *Academy of Management Perspectives*, 20, no. 3 (2006): 76–89.

85. See P.C. Earley and H. Mosakowski, "Creating Hybrid Team Cultures: An Empirical Test of Transnational Team Functioning," *Academy of Management Journal* 43, no. 1 (2000): 26–49.

86. G. Hofstede, "Do American Theories Apply Abroad?: A Reply to Goodstein and Hunt," *Organizational Dynamics* 10, no. 1 (1981): 68. See also, R. Hodgetts, "A Conversation with Geert Hofstede," *Organizational Dynamics* 21, no. 1 (1993): 53–61.

Organization Structure and Design

It is increasingly being recognized that we are in the midst of a significant organizational revolution. The hypercompetitive, technology-based global business environment that encompasses today's organizations has prompted a growing number of firms and their management to move away from centrally coordinated, multileveled hierarchies toward a variety of organizational forms that bear a greater resemblance to intricate, diamond-like structures and rotating spheres than traditional pyramids. Business organizations, which in the not too distant past were defined almost exclusively by internal functions and boundaries, now focus on a range of external stakeholders including vendors and suppliers, the ultimate consumer, their surrounding communities, and government regulatory agencies. Some theorists even argue that this historic transition away from inwardly focused, mechanistic bureaucracies toward flatter, more organic structures that focus on markets rather than hierarchy represents one of the most striking changes in management thought.[1]

As changes in the broader environment begin to accumulate, existing organizational forms become less and less capable of meeting the demands placed on them. When this occurs, new organizational types begin to emerge in an attempt to meet these environmental opportunities and constraints.[2] Over the past two decades, a number of new organizational forms have emerged, including the "horizontal" organization, the "infinitely flat" organization, the "cluster organization," the "spider web," "inverted pyramid," "starburst," "hypertext organization," "virtual corporation" and the modular organizational form.[3] Yet, despite the variety of organizational configurations that exist today, the basic theory underlying organizational structure is a relatively simple one—an organization's structure should divide its tasks and then coordinate them, in essence balancing job-related specialization with group-, intergroup-, and organization-based integration as necessary.[4] The ways in which such specialization (differentiation, decentralization) and coordination (integration, centralization) can be most effectively achieved, however, have changed and evolved over time.

As discussed in Chapter 1, historically there was a distinct demarcation between what happened *inside* an organization and *outside* its boundaries.[5] Organizations were viewed as *closed systems*, which meant that they were managed as self-contained entities (i.e., what took place outside the organization was perceived to have little effect on what transpired on the inside). The dominant mechanism for controlling organizations, therefore, was the *hierarchy*, which focused largely on organizing people in their roles as employees as the primary means of maintaining order, harmony, and stability. The dominant mechanism for controlling activities outside organizations and between organizations and their stakeholders, in contrast, is the *market*. Markets essentially regulate business relationships, typically disrupting harmony and stability, stimulating the rise of self-interest, and threatening to cause discontinuities within the organization and between an organization and its stakeholders. Within this context, organizations are viewed as *open systems* (i.e., they are influenced by a wide variety of environmental forces). In fact, as we have witnessed during the past two decades, what occurs outside and inside organizations is increasingly converging. Volatile, literally seismic changes in the external environment are forcing managers and their organizations to move away from an emphasis on controlling, organizing, and closely supervising people to one based on process, flexibility, and collaboration. In essence, today's rapidly changing business environment has created the need for organizations to continuously transform themselves in order to maintain and reinforce their ability to compete successfully.

ORGANIZATIONAL STRUCTURE

Organizational structure can be broadly defined as the sum total of the ways in which an organization divides its tasks and then coordinates them. In essence, organizational structure defines the firm's decision-making authority and serves as the connecting fiber between the company's strategy and the actions and behaviors of its members. An organization's structure:[6]

1. Designates formal reporting relationships, encompassing the number of levels in the hierarchy and the span of control held by managers and supervisors

2. Identifies groupings of individuals into specific positions, work units, teams, departments, divisions and so forth, as well as the grouping of these subunits into the total organization

3. Comprises the design of systems in an attempt to ensure effective communication, coordination, and integration of effort across these subunits

In order to fully appreciate the design-related decisions facing an organization's management, three key dimensions of organizational structure—complexity, formalization, and centralization—should be examined.[7] These variables not only differentiate organizations, but they can also be used to examine differences between main units within a particular organization. In reality, of course, organizations are not complex or simple, formal or informal, or centralized or decentralized. Each of these core dimensions should be conceptualized as a continuum and, as will be explored throughout the chapter, organizational structures can be analyzed in terms of their *degree* of complexity, formalization, and centralization.

Complexity

Complexity refers to the different number of components or extent of *differentiation* that exists in a particular organization. More complex organizational structures have a greater degree of differentiation compared with organizations having less complex structures. The more complex a particular organizational structure, the greater the need for both direct and indirect control (integrative) mechanisms. In highly complex organizational structures, therefore, managers are required to spend more significant amounts of time and attention in dealing with communication, coordination, and control needs.

Differentiation

One of the key concepts underlying the complexity of an organizational structure is *division of labor,* the ways in which tasks are divided across organizational members.[8] In a large automobile service station, for instance, one might see general mechanics, service attendants, front-end mechanics, engine mechanics, and transmission specialists. In a smaller service station, one mechanic may do multiple tasks, making this individual's work less differentiated than in the larger service station. *Differentiation* is thus concerned with the amount of work segmentation of an organizational system into component parts. Organizations may be differentiated in a number of ways (see Figure 9-1):[9]

1. *Horizontal differentiation,* where work is divided on a particular level of an organizational hierarchy.

2. *Vertical differentiation,* where work is divided by levels of the organizational hierarchy; the distinction between a tall and flat organization refers to whether it has many or few levels of hierarchy.

3. *Personal differentiation,* where work is divided according to the personal specialty (e.g., a law firm may have trial lawyers, probate lawyers, patent lawyers, corporate lawyers).

4. *Spatial differentiation,* where work is divided according to geographical location (such as one company's automobile assembly plants scattered throughout the country).

Integration

Given the specialization and segmentation of organizational activities brought about by such differentiation, organizational structure must also allow for the coordination or integration of these activities. *Integration* is defined as "the quality of the state of collaboration that exists among departments that are required to achieve unity of effort by the demands of the environment."[10] Organizations differ in the ways that they coordinate or integrate such specialization through the use of various types of *integrative mechanisms.*

Integrative mechanisms may be roughly categorized into two types based on the extent of face-to-face interaction: indirect and direct mechanisms. *Indirect* integrative mechanisms (no face-to-face interaction between participants) are appropriate for organizations in stable environments that are not highly differentiated. Because there is a high degree of similarity across work assignments (low differentiation), relatively

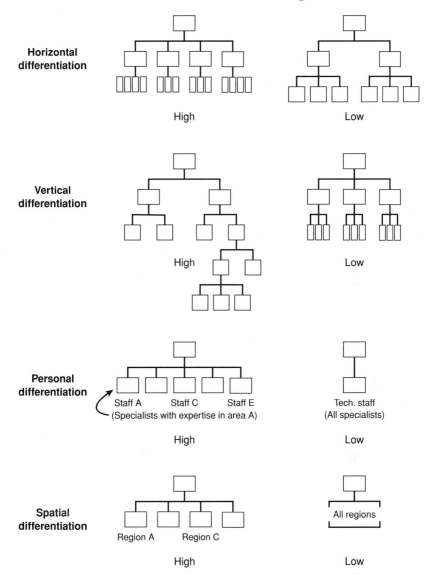

Figure 9-1 Types and Degrees of Differentiation

Source: A Diagnostic Approach to Organizational Behavior, 5/e by Judith Gordon © 1996, p. 9.
Reprinted by permission of Prentice Hall, Inc., Upper Saddle River, New Jersey.

indirect ways of coordination are sufficient: organizational policies and rules, goals, standard operating procedures, hierarchical referral, and so forth. For organizations with highly differentiated structures in a changing environment, however, such indirect mechanisms are not sufficient. In these situations, conventional means of coordination must be supplemented with more *direct* forms of integration, such as the creation of integrator or liaison roles, cross-functional teams, and inter-work unit memberships.[11] As we will see later in this chapter, in rapidly changing, dynamic environments (especially where technology and information needs are changing), effective organizations appear to simultaneously have high differentiation *and* high direct integration.

Formalization

Formalization refers to the extent to which an organization relies on rules and standardized procedures to direct the behavior of its members. The clearer and more detailed these specifications are for a particular role or task, the greater the degree of formalization. This dimension of organizational structure, thus, reflects the amount of discretion that is built into particular roles and positions. Professional positions, for example, tend to have a greater amount of freedom of activity than less skilled, more routine work (e.g., assembly-line jobs that require relatively simple and repetitive behavior).

Formalization can also vary depending on organizational function. As suggested earlier, some positions have much more standardization in their activities (standard procedures and methods of work accomplishment) than others. Accounting and finance and operations (e.g., manufacturing) units, for example, follow more standard operating procedures than members of marketing, human resources, or research and development departments (which typically face less stable and less repetitive activities).

Centralization

Centralization focuses on the locus of decision-making authority within the organization—the level at which decisions are made and the extent of involvement of organizational members in the decision-making process. A *centralized* organization is one in which decisions are concentrated at one or a few points, typically at the top of the organizational hierarchy; a *decentralized* structure disperses authority (low concentration) for making decisions throughout a number of positions in the organization.

Authority for making decisions can be centralized or decentralized, and the *chain of command* delineates the path of decentralization (extent of participation and input from lower-level individuals or units). Within this context, a distinction can be made between horizontal and vertical decentralization.[12] *Vertical decentralization* refers to the distribution of formal decision-making power down the hierarchy or chain of command. Although such power is still vested at a higher organizational level, the individual involved may choose to disperse—or *delegate*—the authority to make certain decisions to others at lower organizational levels. *Horizontal decentralization,* in contrast, focuses on the extent to which people in nonmanagerial positions—analysts, support specialists, technicians—control decision processes. The continued growth and utilization of information technology are readily exerting influence on enterprisewide standards and practices that facilitate both vertical and horizontal decentralization.[13]

Key Organization Structure Challenges

These basic structural dimensions give rise to three fundamental questions concerning the most appropriate ways to organize people and tasks:[14]

1. What is the appropriate way to divide and coordinate work and work-related processes throughout the organization (**differentiation and integration**)?

2. Where will these decisions be made in the organization (**centralization versus decentralization**)?

3. How will the organization attempt to control (formalize) the actions and activities of its members (**standardization versus mutual adjustment**)?

Differentiation and Integration

A basic rule of organizational theory is that as organizations differentiate (either horizontally, vertically, personally, or spatially) a key management task is to ensure an appropriate level of coordination (integration) across the various operations. While successful companies differentiate themselves into suborganizations, ensuring that expertise accumulates around core organizational processes, these firms also adopt appropriate integrating mechanisms to coordinate work across these different subunits. Depending on the level and nature of differentiation that exists in an organization, such integration can range from (1) relatively indirect mechanisms such as the exchange of information through memos and standard operating procedures, or (2) a reliance on the chain of command and formal hierarchy, to (3) more direct forms such as specific integrative roles (individuals or departments) whose primary activity is to coordinate the efforts across different departments, or even (4) temporary or permanent cross-functional teams.

Especially in highly differentiated operations, managing integration through interpersonal-intensive mechanisms—direct contact, liaison roles, task forces, cross-functional teams—has become increasingly important.[15] In fact, designing integrative mechanisms that actually coordinate and integrate rather than merely control is, perhaps, one of the greatest challenges in today's organizations. Given the rapidity of change precipitated in large part by advanced information technologies, successful integrative mechanisms must be able to: (1) collect and disseminate information in "real time"; (2) understand the language and perspectives of the individuals or work units that are being integrated, with the ability to balance diverse points of view; and (3) influence the actions taken by organizational members.[16] As we will explore later in this chapter, in rapidly changing, dynamic environments, effective organizations appear to simultaneously have high differentiation *and* high direct integration.

Centralization versus Decentralization

There are advantages and disadvantages associated with either centralizing or decentralizing organizational decision-making processes. As indicated earlier, centralization allows top management to coordinate organizational activities and to ensure that the organization stays focused on its goals and objectives. Yet, while classical theorists, such as Frederick Taylor and his system of scientific management (Chapter 1), strongly favored centralized operations, with planning and decision making occurring at the top of organizations, there are four primary disadvantages associated with highly centralized organizations:[17]

1. The decision-making capacity of top management is limited and is consequently subject to overload.

2. Top management frequently lacks specific knowledge about conditions at the subunit level.

3. Moving information up and down the hierarchy is time consuming and can delay decision making.

4. Centralization can have a negative effect on the motivation of subunit managers.

Although it may seem paradoxical, despite the common stereotype of bureaucracies as highly centralized, monolithic organizations, delegation of authority (decentralization) is a prerequisite for efficient bureaucratic operations.[18] A general principle in centralizing or decentralizing decision making is that the person or unit with most relevant information should make the decision. A primary advantage of decentralization is that it promotes flexibility and responsiveness by allowing unit-level managers to use local knowledge to make "on-the-spot" decisions.[19] This capability not only speeds up the decision process, but providing unit-level managers with the power and authority to make decisions is also a strong motivational factor. The main drawback associated with decentralization is when so much authority is delegated throughout the organization that managers at all levels are able to make their own decisions, making system-level planning and coordination difficult at best. In this instance, organizations can begin to lose control over their decision-making processes.

One of the realities of today's rapidly changing business environment is that most organizations are neither fully centralized nor fully decentralized. Even in highly centralized organizations, most routine decisions are still decentralized to lower-level staff. In fact, one of the characteristics of highly bureaucratized organizations is the ability of clerks, supervisors, and employees to handle the day-to-day tasks of the organization without involving their managers. Such delegation allows the organization to reap the benefits from differentiation and formalization because it minimizes communication costs and demands on scarce managerial time.[20] In largely decentralized operations, in contrast, it is often appropriate to centralize certain value-adding activities (e.g., procurement, sales) that cut across a range of work units. The success of such *partial centralization* is based on management's ability to create a systemwide awareness of the value of the interrelationship, as well as the creation of a mix of indirect and direct integrative mechanisms between the centralized activities and the business units involved.[21]

Simultaneous Loose-Tight Properties

One way to attempt to balance the competing needs of centralization and decentralization is through the use of simultaneous loose-tight properties.[22] A *loose coupling* of organizational elements refers to the absence of tight and rigid connections (low centralization) among organizational components and the assumption that organizational subunits are capable of autonomous action (decentralization).[23] By decentralizing decision making in this fashion, allowing the structures of the subunits to vary independently, each unit has the capability to be more sensitive to changes in its immediate environment. At the same time, however, *tight coupling*—often achieved through the imposition of hierarchy—creates a set of rules that guide the delegated decision process. In essence, central direction at the organizational level coexists with autonomy at the individual level.[24] As part of the transformation of the 3M corporation, for example, the company formulated a set of broad, general guidelines (central direction)—creating patentable products that were new to the world, would lead to specified gross margins, and have a significant impact on sales within five years—and then allowed managers to make operational decisions (individual autonomy) in conjunction with their technical staffs.[25] As we will explore in Chapter 10, one of the ways in which organizations attempt to exert control over the decision-making process while allowing organizational members autonomy in making those decisions is through the organization's culture, the systemwide dissemination and internalization of core beliefs and values. Creating shared beliefs and values among managers and employees makes it more likely that, even in the absence of formal oversight by company officials, employees will use their specific local knowledge and resources to pursue the interests of the organization as a whole rather than just their own partisan interests.

Standardization versus Mutual Adjustment

Organizational control is also achieved through various mechanisms that organizations use to coordinate their work, ranging from the standardization of work processes, work outputs, and/or worker skills and knowledge, to direct supervision, to the mutual adjustment between organizational members.[26] *Work processes* can be *standardized* when the actual work itself is specified or programmed. Standardized work processes range from the assembly instructions provided with many children's toys to coordination of work on an assembly line. *Work outputs* are standardized when the results or outcomes of the work are specified. Many services, for example, can be delivered in different ways but the end result is expected to be the same. The final way to standardize work focuses on the individuals doing the tasks rather than the way in which they are done or the outcomes that are expected. *Worker skills and knowledge* are standardized when specific training and education are necessary to perform the work. *Direct supervision* coordinates work through hierarchical referral, having one individual assume responsibility for the work of others, giving them directions and monitoring their efforts.

Mutual adjustment secures the coordination of work through relatively simple processes of informal communication and interaction. Mutual adjustment can be used to coordinate work in the simplest (e.g., the interaction of two people in a pottery studio) to the most complicated (e.g., scientists on a research team) organizations. In fact, as work and work processes become increasingly elaborate and unprogrammed, the ability of specialists to adapt to one another in ambiguous situations is a critical component of work unit and organizational success.

The main design challenge confronting managers is to find a way to use norms, guidelines, and rules to standardize behavior (formalization) while simultaneously providing their employees with the opportunity and encouragement to experiment, innovate, and discover new and better ways to achieve organizational goals. As indicated earlier, standardization provides organizations with control over specified organizational activities, while mutual adjustment allows organization members to participate in decisions that are related to their jobs and to act spontaneously when confronting organizational problems.[27] In general, as organizations and their tasks become increasingly complicated, coordination tends to shift from mutual adjustment to direct supervision to standardization, reverting back to mutual adjustment for the most complex tasks. A basic tenet is that people who fulfill roles at higher organizational levels and in functions that perform complex, uncertain tasks rely more on mutual adjustment than standardization to coordinate their activities. In today's rapidly changing environment, however, companies are increasingly designing their structures to facilitate mutual adjustment and minimize the limiting effects of standardization at all organizational levels.

Concept Application: Mechanistic and Organic Organizational Forms

Many discussions of organization structure refer to organizations as either rigid (mechanistic) or flexible (organic) in nature.[28] As illustrated in Figure 9-2, mechanistic organizations are highly structured entities, with centralized decision making and largely vertical information flows. Organic structures, in contrast, are more loosely structured, with more decentralized decision making and lateral information flows. In general, mechanistic organizations tend to be effective under relatively stable environmental conditions (low complexity), while organizations with organic structures tend to fare better in rapidly changing, more unpredictable environments.

A *mechanistic* organizational structure reflects the traditional description of a bureaucracy (Chapter 1), where (1) there is a clear definition of jobs (high formalization); (2) senior administrators have more knowledge of problems facing an organization than those at lower levels (a condition conducive to centralization); (3) standardized policies and procedures govern organizational decision making (indirect integrative mechanisms, standardized work processes); and (4) rewards are determined by adherence to instructions from (direct) supervisors.

Organic organizational structures, sometimes referred to as adhocracies, are designed to be flexible and to cope with rapidly changing environments.[29] Adhocracies are characterized by: (1) decreased emphasis on formal job descriptions and specialization (low formalization); (2) there is *no* assumption that people in higher

MECHANISTIC ORGANIZATIONS	**ORGANIC ORGANIZATIONS**

Characteristics

- Tall structure, many levels of management
- Information flows up and down the hierarchy
- Decision making centralized at upper levels
- Emphasis on standardized policies and procedures and indirect integration

Characteristics

- Flat structure, few levels of management
- Information flows horizontally across departments
- Decision making decentralized to point where work is done
- Emphasis on mutual adjustment and direct integration

Figure 9-2   Characteristics of Mechanistic and Organic Organizations positions are necessarily better informed than those lower in the organization (decentralization); (3) horizontal relationships (across departments) are equal or more important than vertical, chain of command, relationships (direct integrative mechanisms, mutual adjustment); (4) organizational atmosphere is more collegial (mutual adjustment, trust-based relationships); and (5) the formal structure of the organization is fluid and changeable.

Consider the difference between management in a textile mill (likely to be mechanistic) and management in a computer network company (likely to be organic). In the textile mill, plant managers are likely to be near the top of a tall organization where much is written down (standardized work processes) and formalized (direct supervision). Experience in the field provides managers with their expertise (centralization). Managers in a computer network company, in contrast, are likely to operate in a flat organization where the technology is changing rapidly and relatively little is written down. Because these managers are less likely to know as much about state-of-the-art network developments as their newest engineers, they typically provide general guidelines while relying on those engineers to solve problems (simultaneous loose-tight properties), even if a particular engineer is not in the "right" department (direct integrative mechanisms, mutual adjustment).

Determinants of Structure

As illustrated by Figure 9-3, there are four main factors that influence decisions about organizational structure: the environment, the size of the organization, its dominant technology, and the organization's strategy. Chapter 8 focused on the environment, and as was emphasized, the more complex the environment the greater the need for differentiation. Accordingly, this section turns to issues surrounding organization size, technology, and strategy.

Organization Size

Organization size is typically defined in terms of the total number of members.[30] This definition follows from the assumption that organizations are social entities; since it is people and their interactions that are patterned, their number should be more closely related to the way in which the organization is structured than other size measures.

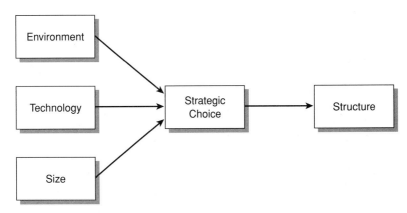

Figure 9-3   Determinants of Organizational Structure

While other measures, such as total assets, sales, or capacity (e.g., number of hospital beds),[31] also reflect magnitude, critics argue that they do not truly indicate the size of the human dimension of the system.

Although the total number of employees is a good indicator of the size of an organization, this measure still has limitations. For instance, some companies use a relatively small number of full-time employees, but rely quite heavily on part-time and contingent workers. Similarly, the total number of employees in a seasonal business can vary quite extensively depending on the time of year. Questions linger as to how such part-time and seasonal workers should be counted. Finally, accurate assessments about the relative size of a firm—whether it is large, medium, or small—require a sense of industry norms. A garage with only two mechanics, for example, would be quite small compared to one with 25 employees; however, while a manufacturing plant with 250 employees may initially appear large, if other plants in the same industry typically employ thousands of people it would actually be relatively small.

While size in and of itself does not necessarily lead to a particular type of structure, it is an important predictor of some of its key dimensions. For instance, size typically generates differentiation in organizations: There is a strong relationship between size and vertical differentiation, and a moderate relationship between size and horizontal differentiation. Although the association between size and spatial differentiation has also been found to be quite strong (the larger the firm, the more its operations tend to be geographically dispersed), this relationship seems to be explained more fully by the kind of organization involved rather than size per se. Larger organizations also tend to have more formalized authority structures than smaller ones. Moreover, size tends to lead to decentralization. In small organizations, management can usually maintain control by centralizing the decision-making process. As organizations become increasingly large, however, managers find that they can no longer physically maintain control in this manner. While the resultant problems often lead to increased decentralization, this decision is typically accompanied by increased formalization as part of the control process. Organizational size has also been found to be related to innovation adoption, especially the use and dissemination of IT systems.

Size, Subunit Size, and Productivity Although size is an important determinant of an organization's structure, the relationship between organizational size and productivity is less clear.[32] While it is generally expected that larger organizations should produce more units or generate greater dollar returns in *absolute* terms than smaller ones, studies examining *relative* performance (i.e., units produced per organizational member) reflect inconsistent results. Moreover, anecdotal accounts and case studies reported in the popular management literature are increasingly taking the position that "small is better." Given these findings, it is important to differentiate between total organizational size and *subunit size*. Within the pharmaceutical industry, for example, a growing number of companies are rethinking their traditional integrated research and development (R&D) structures, moving toward smaller, more flexible R&D teams and units.[33]

A growing number of our large corporations are creating structures that encompass relatively small work units—sometimes referred to as "skunkworks"—that facilitate the mutual adjustment of organizational members. Especially in an era of hypercompetition, these smaller work units are being lauded because their members (1) have greater psychological ownership of and commitment to their tasks; (2)

are more accountable for their performance; (3) are more creative and resourceful, especially in the context of lower organizational slack; (4) have greater information since information sharing is easier; and (5) are more motivated and fast-acting.[34]

Organizational Technology

Organizational technology is based on the nature of the task in the production or service subsystem, and encompasses the actions, knowledge, and techniques used to transform various inputs into outputs.[35] Although we tend to think of technology in terms of "high-tech"—computer networks, fiber optics, robotization—technology covers a vast array of activities that organizations employ to produce their products or services. In this sense, technology can range from microcomputers, to hand-processing different forms, to the pedagogical technologies (lecture, case method, experiential exercises) chosen by your instructor. Moreover, in large, complex organizations, different functional areas often rely on different technologies, with varying degrees of complexity, as they undertake their activities.

Once we move beyond this general sense of technology, a number of conceptual and definitional problems begin to emerge as researchers have used quite different technology classifications. This section briefly summarizes some of the main paradigms in the technology-structure arena: technical complexity, knowledge-based technology, technological uncertainty, and the organizational context of technological innovation.

Technical Complexity   Technical complexity refers to the extent of mechanization and predictability of a manufacturing process: High technical complexity means that most of the work is performed by machines and is quite predictable; low technical complexity means that employees play a more significant role in the production process. Based on Joan Woodward's classic study of management and technology, there are three basic technology categories.[36]

1. **Small-batch and unit production.** Job-shop operations that manufacture and assemble small orders that meet specific customer specifications. Since custom work is the norm, organizational members fulfill a central role—the process is not highly mechanized, and the predictability of outcomes is relatively low (e.g., made-to-order manufacturing products).

2. **Large-batch and mass production.** Companies that engage in long production runs of standardized parts as found in most assembly lines. Since customers do not have special needs, output usually goes into inventory from which orders are filled.

3. **Continuous-process production.** The most complex technological group in which the entire process is mechanized. Essentially, there is no starting or stopping the process, which is based on a level of mechanization and standardization that goes beyond an assembly line (e.g., oil refineries, chemical plants); accordingly, organizations have a high level of control over the process and the outcomes are highly predictable.

Woodward found that there was a distinct relationship between these technological categories and the resultant structure of the firm. For instance, mass-production (large batch) technology companies tended to be highly differentiated with extensive formalization and little delegation of authority. The small-batch and continuous-process firms, in contrast, were structured more loosely. Since high formalization and centralization did not appear to be feasible due to the custom-made, nonroutine technology found in the small-batch companies, flexibility was achieved through less differentiation, less division of labor, more group activities, more widely defined role responsibilities, and decentralized decision making. Similarly, due to the heavily automated, continuous-process technology (which creates tight control) in other firms, extensive formalization and centralization were not necessary. Advanced manufacturing and information technologies, however, are changing these dynamics, especially as cellular manufacturing techniques provide organizations with the ability to capture the efficiencies of large-batch mass production with the flexibility and customization associated with small-batch production.[37]

Knowledge-Based Technology   In contrast to Woodward's focus on production technology, sociologist Charles Perrow examined the knowledge base of the technology on two dimensions: task variability and problem analyzability.[38] *Task variability* refers to the number of exceptions in a person's work. Jobs that are highly routine tend to have few exceptions (e.g., working on an assembly line), while jobs that involve a high degree of variety (many unexpected situations, frequent problems) tend to have a large number of exceptions (e.g., managerial work). *Problem analyzability* focuses on how decisions about the work are made. At one extreme, jobs and work processes are well defined, the work itself can be reduced to mechanical steps, and job incumbents can follow objective, specified procedures in their work (e.g., standard operating procedures, instruction manuals). In contrast to such highly analyzable technologies, other jobs involve problems and activities that are difficult to analyze and find the "correct" solution. In these work efforts, individual judgment, expertise, and experience are more valuable in solving problems than step-by-step, predetermined procedures.

Based on these two dimensions, Perrow formed four types of technology: routine, engineering, craft, and nonroutine. *Routine technologies* have few exceptions and easy-to-analyze problems as found in most mass-production and lower-level service (e.g., bank customer service representatives) jobs. *Engineering technologies* involve a large number of exceptions that can be resolved through established, systematic procedures and techniques (e.g., engineering, accounting). *Craft technologies* have a relatively stable set of activities, but with fairly difficult, not easily analyzed demands. The tasks thus require extensive training and experience because job incumbents must deal with job-related problems on the basis of their background and expertise (e.g., glassmaking, furniture restoring). Finally, *nonroutine technologies* are characterized by many exceptions with difficult-to-analyze problems (e.g., research, strategic planning).

Perrow argued that organizational control and coordination efforts should be based on the degree of routineness involved in the technology. Since there is a strong correlation between task variability and problem analyzability (i.e., it is unusual to find situations where tasks have few exceptions and problems are clearly unanalyzable, or tasks have a high number of exceptions with well-defined and clearly analyzable problems), the four technologies could be combined into a single routine–nonroutine continuum. In order to most effectively accomplish their tasks, therefore, organizations with highly routine technologies should be highly structured. Nonroutine technologies, in contrast, dictate greater structural flexibility in terms of: (1) the degree of discretion given to employees in completing tasks; (2) the degree of power given to groups and departments to control their goals and strategies; (3) the level of interdependence between these groups; and (4) the degree to which intergroup coordination is accomplished through feedback and sharing of planning and strategy efforts.

Technological Uncertainty   While the work of both Woodward and Perrow suggests that technology should determine the appropriate organizational structure, Thompson's research on technological uncertainty argues that technology determines strategic choice. The selected strategy, which is designed to reduce this uncertainty, then leads to decisions about appropriate structural arrangements.[39] As part of his work, Thompson developed a typology based on the type of tasks performed by an organization: mediating, long-linked, and intensive technologies.

Mediating technology provides products or services that act as an exchange function, which links clients that are otherwise independent (e.g., banks, brokerage firms, real estate offices). As part of the work process, each unit works independently of the other (e.g., while different real estate offices within the same company mediate between buyers and sellers, they work independently within the organization). *Long-linked technology* is characterized by a fixed sequence of repetitive steps in which one work unit must complete its activities and pass them along to the next unit before it can begin its efforts, and so forth, as found in an assembly line. Finally, *intensive technology* involves activities where the outcome of one unit becomes the input of another and vice versa. Since intensive technologies provide a diverse set of products or services (e.g., hospitals, research laboratories, universities), the exact nature of response from the different units depends on the nature of the problem and the degree of mutual adjustment between the units. As illustrated in Table 9-1, each technology creates a type of interdependence (see Chapter 6), which, in turn, requires a certain kind of coordination and has different structural considerations.

Historically, organizations were largely characterized by pooled and sequential interdependencies, where time frames were slower and coordination was hierarchically structured. Today, however, we are increasingly witnessing reciprocal and team

TABLE 9-1   Technology, Interdependence, and Structural Considerations

Type of Technology	Level of Interdependence	Appropriate Integrative Mechanism	Complexity	Formalization
Mediating	Pooled	Rules; standard operating procedures	Low	High
Long-linked	Sequential	Meetings; planning; scheduling	Moderate	Moderate
Intensive	Reciprocal	Mutual adjustment between two units	High	Low
	Team	Mutual adjustment between more than two units	High	Low

Source: Adapted from J.D. Thompson, *Organizations in Action* (New York: McGraw-Hill, 1967); and Stephen P. Robbins, *Organization Theory: Structure, Design, and Applications*, 2nd edition, © 1987, pp. 136–137. Reprinted by permission of Prentice Hall, Inc., Englewood Cliffs, N.J.

interdependence in much tighter time frames, with interunit boundaries that change as task demands change.[40] Advanced manufacturing technologies (AMT), such as computer-integrated manufacturing (CIM), flexible manufacturing systems (FMS), and computer-aided design and computer-aided manufacturing (CAD/CAM), and advanced information technologies (such as company intranets) are heightening the complexity and level of interdependence that exist in organizations.[41] Although AMT significantly reduces the amount of physical work necessary for managing and operating production processes, the knowledge, skills, and abilities required for effective implementation have become much more sophisticated and success is increasingly contingent on more organic organizational structures and a high degree of cross-functional integration. Such changes require organizations to balance simultaneous demands and pressures for centralized control (e.g., focused development of design and technology enhancements, continuous improvement efforts), decentralized decision making (e.g., fast response, ability to exploit emerging but unanticipated opportunities), and coordinating value-adding activities (e.g., relationships with suppliers, distributors and customers).[42]

Organizational Context of Technological Innovation   While advanced manufacturing and information technologies hold significant promise for enhanced organizational performance, they have become so complex that they often stretch the ability of managerial and organizational systems to absorb them.[43] In fact, a basic problem is that while such technologies are becoming increasingly commonplace, many firms have been slow to fully adopt them and those that have often view them as little more than turnkey systems requiring almost no modification of present organizational structures and practices. Organizations, however, are far more likely to effectively use such advanced technologies when appropriate modifications are made in strategies that stress technological progress and structures that facilitate their introduction, acceptance, and diffusion. In fact, research suggests that competitive advantage is likely to result only when managers understand the need to redesign their organizational processes and structures to exploit the full benefits of technological innovation efforts.[44]

Strategy

Historically, strategy has been defined as the "determination of the basic long-term goals and objectives of an enterprise, and the adoption of courses of action and the allocation of resources necessary for carrying out those goals."[45] As this definition implies, strategy requires sound diagnostic skills and astute judgment. Based on an analysis of the external environment and organizational resources, managers identify organizational goals and objectives and then generate systematic plans and structures to accomplish those goals and objectives.[46] As illustrated in Figure 9-3, this view, which is influenced by the early work of Alfred Chandler, suggests that strategy determines structure.

In his research, Chandler found that companies usually begin operations with a single product or service (concentration strategy). Since the goals and objectives of the firm, and in turn its strategy, are thus relatively narrow, the organization's structure is typically high on centralization and low on complexity and formalization. As firms grow and develop, however, such simple structures become increasingly ineffective and inefficient. Chandler found that highly centralized structures became increasingly impractical for dealing with the added complexity in the firm, and that new organizational structures were needed. Thus, as the firms in his study grew and diversified, he found that they also adapted their structures accordingly, becoming more decentralized with greater complexity and formalization. While recent research has found that the strategy-structure interaction is more complex than commonly supposed in multiproduct firms (influenced, for example, by different control arrangements, different levels of decentralization, organizational span of control, and environmental uncertainty), strategy was still found to be an influential factor in determining structure.[47]

The need for new organizational strategies and structures is reflected by the shifting consumer demands and hypercompetitive pressures characteristic of today's technology-driven, global marketplace. There have been dramatic changes in the types of product demands being placed on business organizations—from shorter product life cycles and increased demands for product choice and customization, to growing pressures for technological innovation—that are challenging existing notions of strategy and structure. Managers are being called upon to meet what have been typically thought of as contradictory requirements, for instance, quickly delivering customized, high-quality goods (and services) while holding down costs. As a result, some organizational theorists suggest that our business firms should be conceptualized as being *dynamically stable*—that is, being able to respond to these changes and challenges with stable and long-term, yet flexible and responsive strategies, structures, and processes.[48] Firms should be strategically designed to serve a broad range of customers and changing product demands (dynamic) while building on existing organizational capabilities, experience, and knowledge (stability).

Although most theorists agree with the proposition that strategy should drive structure, actual implementation of this principle is often complicated by the different levels of strategy that exist in organizations. Firms tend to have a series of strategies, both documented (formal) and undocumented (informal), that shape their business. As a result, such multiple-strategic concerns and their implications often create a number of ambiguities for organizational members. Moreover, recent research has also begun to question the idea that strategy is necessarily as systematic, carefully planned, and well thought out as suggested earlier.[49] A *behavioral view of strategy* suggests that it actually evolves over time as part of a pattern of important incremental decisions. In fact, some critics suggest that given the turbulence that exists in today's business environment, top executives should spend less time attempting to create the ideal strategy and focus more of their energies on developing the knowledge, skills, and abilities of their managers, encouraging them to develop new competencies and insights as necessary.[50] As an organization's strategy changes over time, however, regardless of whether the changes are part of a systematically derived plan or something that has implicitly evolved, structural changes typically follow.

ORGANIZATION DESIGN

The basic idea of organization design focuses on the management side of organization theory—constructing and changing an organization's structure to achieve its goals. As the earlier discussion of mechanistic and organic forms of organization, and the concepts of differentiation and integration pointed out, there is *no* one ideal way to structure an organization. In fact, most organization theorists today argue for a *contingency theory* of organization design; that is, the way in which an organization should be designed depends on its environment, especially its market and technology dimensions. The most effective structure is one that adjusts to these environmental requirements—a mechanistic form of organization in stable, certain environments, and an organic design in more unpredictable, turbulent fields.[51] Similarly, in more complex and turbulent environments, more internal differentiation is needed among the organization's subsystems. This high degree of differentiation in turn creates greater demands for integration, which cannot be sufficiently achieved by indirect, conventional mechanisms.[52] Thus, one type of structure is appropriate when the environment is stable and simple, while another type appears to be more appropriate when the environment is rapidly changing and complex (see Table 9-2).

This section examines the five basic organizational forms: (1) the simple (or agency) model, (2) the functional organization, (3) the divisional firm, (4) the adhocracy, and (5) market-based, network organizations. While there are variations on these forms, such modifications are essentially *organizational hybrids,* that is, a mix or blending of two or more of these basic types. Some theorists even argue that the matrix form is essentially a mixed or hybrid structure since it simultaneously utilizes functional departments and "divisionalized" project or product teams.

Simple Structure

In the simple structure (agency) form, which is characteristic of new, entrepreneurial companies, the organization is composed of a top manager (owner) and a relatively small number of organizational members (technical workers, support personnel).[53] The main coordinating mechanism is direct supervision. The simple structure is low in complexity, has little formalization, and its authority is typically centralized in one individual. As illustrated in Figure 9-4, it is often depicted as a flat organization with virtually all members reporting to the top manager. While this form of organization is most often found in a firm's early stage of development, it becomes increasingly ineffective as the organization grows.

This form is well suited for a relatively simple, though dynamic environment. Since organizational members usually have little discretion and input in decision making, the environment must be sufficiently simple to be comprehended by the top manager (who makes the decisions). Some simple structures, however, utilize delegation and decentralized decision making. Research has shown that the tendency for small business owners to centralize or decentralize power and decision making is related to such

Figure 9-4 Simple Organization Form

personality and psychological factors as an internal or external locus of control (see Chapter 2) and the extent to which they feel secure in their close personal relationships (e.g., with spouse, with parents).[54] Such firms, however, are still highly dependent on the top individual.

The Functional Organization

Functional structures group organizational members based on the focus of their work activity (see Figure 9-5). A manufacturing firm, for example, would typically group workers into a number of different departments, including research and

TABLE 9-2 A Conceptualization of Environmental Uncertainty and Appropriate Organizational Structure

		Low Uncertainty Environment	Low–Moderate Uncertainty Environment
Environmental Change	**Stable**	Small number of external elements	Large number of external elements
		Elements remain the same or change slowly	Elements remain the same or change slowly
		Organization Structure	Organization Structure
		Mechanistic (formal, centralization)	Mechanistic (formal, some decentralization)
		Few departments	Many departments
		Indirect integrative mechanisms	Mostly indirect with some direct integrative mechanisms
		Moderate–High Uncertainty Environment	**High Uncertainty Environment**
	Unstable	Small number of external elements	Large number of external elements
		Elements are continuously changing	Elements are continuously changing
		Organization Structure	Organization Structure
		Organic (informal, mostly decentralization)	Organic (informal, decentralization)
		Few departments with boundary spanning roles	Many departments, high boundary spanning roles (high differentiation)
		Mostly indirect with some direct integrative mechanisms	Mostly direct integrative mechanisms
		Simple	**Complex**

Environmental Complexity

Source: Adapted by permission of the publisher, "What Is the Right Organization Structure? Decision Tree Analysis Provides the Answer," by Robert Duncan, *Organizational Dynamics,* Winter 1979, p. 63 © 1979 by AMACOM, a division of American Management Association, New York. All rights reserved. P.R. Lawrence and J.W. Lorsch, *Organization and Environment: Managing Differentiation and Integration.* Boston: Division of Research, Harvard Business School, 1967; and Henry Mintzberg, *The Structuring of Organizations: A Synthesis of the Research,* © 1979, pp. 286, 446–447. Adapted by permission of Prentice Hall, Inc., Englewood Cliffs, N.J.

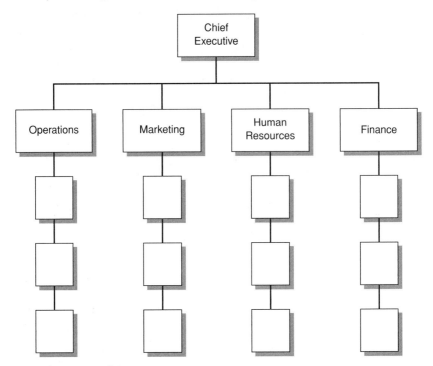

Figure 9-5 Functional Organization

development, operations, purchasing, marketing, finance, human resources, and so forth. In each of these departments, further grouping by specialization also typically occurs. For example, a large human resources (HR) department would have separate individuals/groups for compensation and benefits, training and development, employee relations, HR information systems, diversity/affirmative action, and so forth.

There are two basic types of functional organizations: the machine bureaucracy and professional bureaucracy.[55] The *machine bureaucracy* is characteristic of Weber's bureaucratic organization (see Chapter 1). This form is appropriate for large organizations that utilize routine technology in simple and stable environments. Extensive specialization and formalization are present: highly routine operating tasks, highly formalized rules and regulations, centralized authority, and a sharp demarcation between line and staff activities. Coordination (integration), which is mainly achieved through the standardization of work processes, is accomplished through policy manuals, explicit job descriptions, and task specialization by functional area. The machine bureaucracy is a mechanistic organization and is often found in the textiles, automobile and steel industries, large retail organizations, and large service organizations with repetitive activities (e.g., insurance and telephone companies, post office).

Although there are a number of criticisms of the machine bureaucracy—a lack of control by lower-level employees, low level of interdepartmental communication, lack of innovation, employee alienation—this structure does seem to be well suited for large organizations in stable environments. Because most of the contingencies have previously occurred, they are predictable and can be effectively dealt with by formalized procedures.

The *professional bureaucracy* shares many of the features of the machine bureaucracy, especially formalization and standardization. However, instead of standardization of work processes (machine), this form utilizes standardization of skills for coordination (i.e., complex work done by individuals with highly developed knowledge and skills). Since organizational members are highly trained specialists doing complex tasks and their work cannot be easily regulated, the professional bureaucracy is characterized by decentralized decision making and less formalization than the machine bureaucracy.

This structural form appears to be most appropriate for organizations that provide knowledge-related services rather than tangible products. The environment is likely to be complex but relatively stable and predictable. It is characteristic of groups of lawyers, physicians, architects with different specialties, and universities. The professional bureaucracy is relatively flat (low vertical differentiation), with some horizontal and a high degree of personal differentiation.

The Divisionalized Form

Divisionalized organizations tend to be extremely large firms that are subdivided into market or product groups (see Figure 9-6).[56] Thus, instead of grouping employees based on functional expertise, this market-oriented structure groups them according to the specific market they serve (e.g., product; geographical area). Coordination is based on standardization of outputs based on these product or market lines. Overall, the divisionalized form is mechanistic in nature, but it may have some relatively organic components (e.g., research and development units). There is some horizontal and vertical differentiation, and there is a high degree of formalization within divisions because the technologies are often routine. Centralization exists largely within the divisions rather than at corporate headquarters, although a corporate staff may retain some functions (such as strategic planning).

The divisionalized structure seems to be most appropriate for organizations with relatively simple and stable markets, although the overall firm may serve diverse markets. Many large organizations such as General Motors, Ford, Procter & Gamble, and Disney have divisionalized structures.

Adhocracy

Adhocracies are designed to be flexible and to be able to adapt to complex, rapidly changing environments.[57] This is an organic form of organization and coordination is largely achieved through mutual adjustment. The adhocracy is characterized by cross-functional grouping, liaisons, and other direct integrative roles and structures. In general, it has low-to-moderate complexity, low formalization, and highly decentralized decision making. Because this organizational form attempts to provide flexibility it tends to be flat, since many levels of administration would restrict its ability to adapt.

Matrix Organizations

The most well-known form of adhocracy is the matrix (see Figure 9-7). Although the concept of a matrix organization has eluded a precise definition, it generally refers to those organizational forms that (1) have a mix or overlay of traditionally separated functional authority and lateral (project, product, or business-based) authority and (2) operate on a relatively permanent basis.[58] Internally, the matrix has two loci of control.

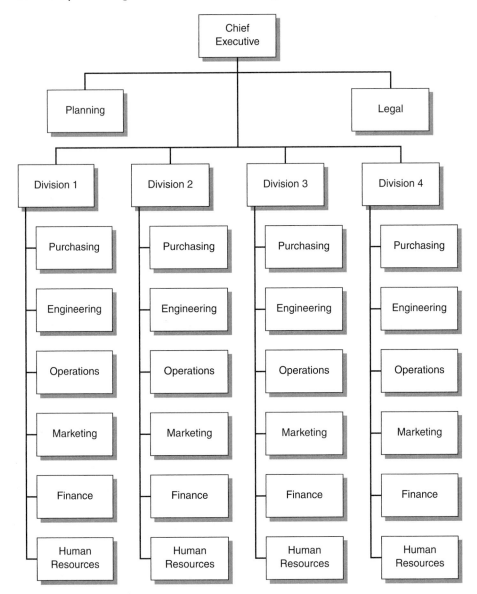

Figure 9-6   Divisional Organization

Since the parts of the organization are fully differentiated on both a functional and project or product basis, they require direct forms of integration to function effectively. Organizational members often have two bosses, their appropriate functional manager (e.g., production, sales, research and development) and their product or project manager (e.g., the product managers of different types of personal computers). The relative permanence of these arrangements also differentiates matrix organizations from cross-functional structures that develop such overlays through temporary teams or assignments.

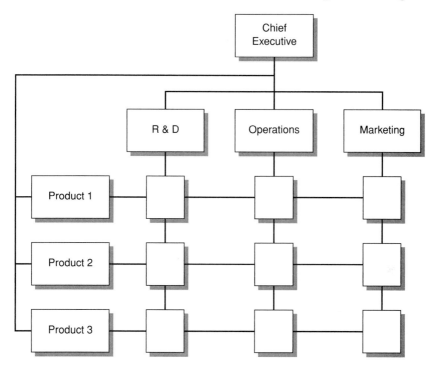

Figure 9-7   Matrix Organization

Each project group has members from the different functional areas, but the main focus is their particular project line. As an example, a personal computer group would have members from sales, research and development, operations and other appropriate functions. Unlike the situation of the machine bureaucracy (where experience gained from producing a product leads to greater expertise because things change slowly), in turbulent environments experience is often of less help with new and changing technologies. In fact, people with the most recent high-technology training are often more knowledgeable about the technical aspects of new projects. Therefore, people with specific knowledge of particular functions are brought together in a product group. Even though the participants in the group may be at different hierarchical levels, the group is formed around the people with the most expertise on a given subject and not necessarily the most experience overall.

Most of the advantages associated with matrix organizations emerge from the cross-functional (horizontal) communication linkages and interactions that are virtually nonexistent in the classic bureaucratic form. In essence, the matrix forces managers to maintain close contact with other organizational groups whose support is necessary for successful task accomplishment. By grouping people with different areas of expertise, matrix organizations can also facilitate innovative solutions to complex problems, discourage departmental parochialism, and build flexibility into the organization's response to a changing environment.

Research on matrix organizations, however, indicates that in many instances dual reporting leads to conflict and confusion and increased stress, the expansion of communication channels and committee assignments overloads and bogs down organizational members, and overlapping responsibilities generate turf battles and a general loss of accountability. Accordingly, operating in a matrix form places a much greater emphasis on developing interpersonal and communication skills and competencies as an important part of the mutual adjustment process, and a greater orientation toward transformational leadership as opposed to transactional management (see Chapter 7). It has become increasingly clear that implementing a matrix organization is a complex process that goes well beyond structural change per se, involving concomitant changes in organizational strategies, processes and training programs, as well as attitudes, behaviors, and culture.[59]

The Horizontal Organization

A growing number of organizations are undergoing significant structural change, developing horizontal networks of task-focused teams leading to "delayered," flat organizational structures.[60] The resultant "horizontal organization" is (1) organized around processes rather than tasks, (2) driven by customer needs and inputs, (3) heavily dependent on team performance, and (4) characterized by significant human resource development efforts (e.g., training; information sharing) (see Figure 9-8). In its pure form, this adhocracy consists of two core groups: (1) senior management responsible for strategic decisions and policies, and (2) groups of empowered employees working together in different process teams (e.g., product development, quality assurance, customer service). The main objective is to reorient the focus of organizational members from coordinating and reporting to (1) the flow and nature of work, and (2) those activities that add value for customers.[61] Teams literally take over basic management functions and maximize contact with key stakeholders, especially customers and suppliers.

GE, which has referred to itself as a "boundaryless organization," provides a good example of the horizontal organization. The corporation has essentially replaced its hierarchy with more than 100 processes and programs, breaking down traditional barriers between departments and seeking to create an intricate network where people seek out "better and newer and bigger idea(s)" literally every time they meet

Figure 9-8 Horizontal Organization

someone. The emphasis on horizontal processes and interactions supports the company's tradition—"imagination at work"—encouraging organizational members to interact and share ideas with minimal bureaucracy.[62]

To ensure that different functions operate seamlessly across groups of employees, firms must also emphasize concomitant changes in the organization's reward systems, performance appraisal processes, and training programs to reflect teamwork, customer satisfaction, and information sharing. As these horizontal networks of organizational units and people replace traditional hierarchies of authority, knowledge becomes the main organizational resource.[63] Thus to be successful, these horizontal teams must have (1) shared goals; (2) shared expertise; (3) shared work across groups not normally part of the local structure; (4) shared decision making through enhanced access to critical information across the firm; (5) shared timing and issue prioritization; (6) shared responsibility, accountability, and trust; and, finally (7) shared recognition and reward for collaborative efforts.[64]

Parallel Organization Structures

Even though many management theorists predicted the demise of traditional bureaucratic organizations due to their inability to adapt to rapidly changing internal and external environments, this traditional organizational form has exhibited a high level of resistance to change. Attention has thus turned to interventions that can assist organizations in dealing with such change while accommodating traditional bureaucratic structures. One approach is the creation of a form of adhocracy within the traditional structure, referred to as a parallel organization.

In essence, a *parallel organization structure* creates a series of rotating teams directed by a steering committee to the conventional organization.[65] The main objective is to fill in the gaps created by traditional bureaucratic structures by focusing on such issues as employee concerns, data gathering, diagnosis and problem solving, organizational interventions, and strategy planning and implementation. Similar to a matrix organization, these structures undercut traditional authority relations since those involved hold dual positions and roles. Unlike matrix organizations, however, parallel structures are not anchored in products or projects per se as much as they are in the ongoing reexamination and reevaluation of organizational routines, exploring new options and developing new techniques, tools, and approaches for dealing with changing organizational conditions. A key component of the success of this form is that organizational members need to know that new ideas, which may challenge existing sets of policies and procedures, will not be stifled or suppressed.[66]

There are five key elements of parallel organizational structures.[67] First, their essential purpose is to improve existing or introduce new organizational practices that affect more than one or two functional units. These concerns can range from strategic decision making to operational issues in daily work life. Second, the operating norms and procedures within the parallel structure tend to be different from those in the formal organization, explicitly promoting collaboration, effective nonhierarchical relations, and group problem solving. Third, members of parallel organizations are also members of the formal organization, though within their roles in the parallel structure they operate outside the formal chain of command.

CONSORTIUM

Figure 9-9 Technology Transfer Structure

Source: Reprinted from Anthony F. Buono, "Managing Strategic Alliances: Organizational and Human Resource Considerations," *Business in the Contemporary World,* vol. 3, no. 4 (1991), p. 94. Reprinted with permission.

Fourth, a senior-level steering committee is used to control and legitimize the activities of the parallel structure. Finally, specific mechanisms are devised (e.g., use of facilitators and liaisons) to ensure that the parallel structure is linked to the formal organization.

An example of how such parallel organization structures operate is provided by high-technology firms that are involved in industry-based research consortia. As a way of facilitating communication flow and information dissemination to appropriate organizational members, the type of technology transfer structure illustrated in Figure 9-9 is utilized.[68] First, a program office is established that serves as a liaison between the consortium and the individual member firm. Second, a series of project development groups are formed as a way of readying the company to make the most efficient use of the basic research emerging from the consortium. The program office is responsible for initially assessing the technological developments, research insights, and breakthroughs produced through the consortium, and channeling that information to appropriate project development groups throughout the organization. Any training or other support necessary for the full utilization of this new knowledge or experimentation is also set up and coordinated by this office. The project development groups, in turn, are responsible for generating potential product offerings and prototypes, which are shared, as appropriate, with the consortium through the program office. This type of structure reduces the probability that pertinent information will be lost between the consortium and its individual members, and provides a mechanism to enable subsequent requirements for new product advances to be funneled back to the consortium in a timely manner.

Although such parallel structures appear to hold promise as facilitators during periods of large-scale organizational change and transformation (e.g., a merger transition team), there is a danger in making such committees top heavy. If such steering committees are to be successful, there has to be an explicit emphasis on data gathering, problem finding, and problem solving. Moreover, it is important that the task force's members are both laterally (different functions and departments at the same level) and vertically (different levels) integrated. While it is critical to have the support and guidance of top management, by restricting the membership of such structures to those at the top echelons much of the potential and effectiveness of these groups will be minimized. Moreover, the change that the parallel organizational structure is supporting should also be aligned—both strategically and operationally—with appropriate management development initiatives.[69]

Market-Based, Network Organizational Forms

During the early part of the twenty-first century, technology-based global competition has created myriad pressures on corporations to reduce costs while increasing innovation and quality, precipitating the downsizing and delayering of organizational structures. At the same time, advanced information technologies have literally shattered the traditional organizational boundaries created by time, territory, and technology. Whether people work during the same shift, in the same building, or even in the same country has become far less important to such boundaries than the actual interdependencies and linkages that exist between these individuals and their organizational roles. Indeed, recent developments in information and communication technology have led to the development of organizational forms that are characterized by cooperative networks along the entire industry value chain (e.g., encompassing the different stages from raw materials through delivery to the end customer, delivering public services).[70] In essence, these new forms are characterized by (1) an emphasis on bottom-up entrepreneurship and (2) a reliance on cooperative networks that allow these entrepreneurial units to share their competencies with one another.[71] Thus, the need to effectively coordinate the activities of discrete organizational subunits is becoming significantly greater in the mid-2000s than it was even in the late-1990s. Such demands are prompting managers to create horizontal arrangements that facilitate cooperation and information sharing both within and across organizations.

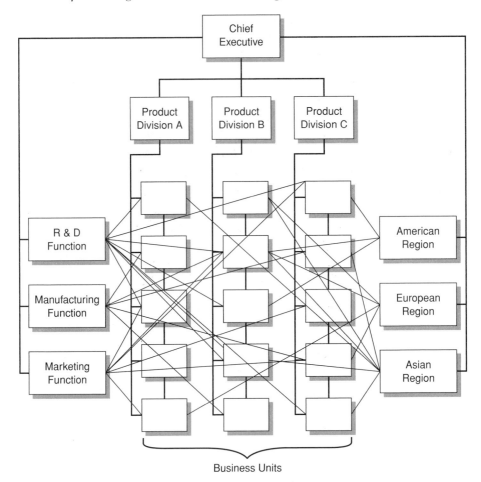

Figure 9-10 Internal Market Organization

Source: W.E. Halal, "From Hierarchy to Enterprise: Internal Markets Are the New Foundation of Management," *Academy of Management Executive,* 1994, vol. 8, no. 4, p. 70.

Internal Market Organizations

Going beyond the market orientation of the divisional form and the dual focus (function, project) of the matrix, this organizational form is composed of a series of "internal enterprises" or markets.[72] The internal market form, which is illustrated in Figure 9-10, is based on three principles:

1. The hierarchy is transformed into *internal enterprise units,* the entrepreneurial equivalents of departments and divisions. Each unit, which is treated as a small, separate company, services both internal and external customers with tight controls on performance (e.g., customer satisfaction, product quality, sales) in exchange for autonomy of operations.

2. An *economic infrastructure* guides decisions. Since operating decisions are delegated to internal enterprise units, executives focus on creating an

infrastructure of performance measures, financial incentives, communication systems, an entrepreneurial-oriented culture, and related organizationwide systems that guide decisions by market forces rather than administrative authority. The resulting organizational architecture is closely monitored for weaknesses and market failures, and adapted as necessary to improve performance.

3. Leadership focuses on developing *collaborative synergy.* Although upper-level managers give up a good deal of their formal authority in such internal market systems, they must still lead by ensuring accountability, resolving conflict, encouraging cooperation, forming alliances, and providing inspiration and other general forms of strategic guidance that shape the system into a productive community.

Johnson & Johnson (J&J) is a good example of an internal network organization. J&J has approximately 190 separate companies that are fiercely autonomous, yet are coordinated through a series of "customer support centers" that operate as internal distributorships to coordinate sales, logistics, and service for each of J&J's major retailers (e.g., one support center for Wal-Mart, another for Kmart). Success is heavily dependent on the extent to which organizational leadership is able to foster high levels of cooperation across individual units. In essence, the organization is transformed from a hierarchy of decision makers to a "confederation of intrapreneurs" capable of both innovating on their own and learning from the innovations of other organizational members. As part of this dynamic, it is important to ensure that the psychological contract (see Chapter 3) that binds the organization, its subunits, and their members reinforces appropriate understandings of and commitments to such high levels of collaboration and cooperation.[73]

Dynamic Network Organizations

Network organizations are central core firms that utilize other companies to perform basic business functions and collaborate in the innovation process.[74] Traditionally, large corporations vertically integrated multiple stages of an industry chain—from raw materials to final product delivery—leading to increased direct control over operations but also creating unwieldy conglomerate structures in the process. Today, in contrast, a growing number of firms have reversed this process, entering into a series of alliances with other organizations as part of their strategy to lower overhead costs, obtain new technologies, increase responsiveness to customers, enter new markets, and, in general, enhance their flexibility. Many of these companies are continuing to downsize to their core competencies, delayering management hierarchies, and strategically outsourcing a wide range of activities.

In their ideal-type form, network organizations are integrating entities that rely on other companies to perform basic design, supply, manufacturing, marketing, and distribution functions on a contractual and relationship basis. As illustrated in Figure 9-11, one company in the network might research and design a product, while another would engineer and manufacture it, another firm would oversee distribution, and so forth. The construction industry has relied on such interorganizational relationships for years, with a central contractor performing the broker role, integrating

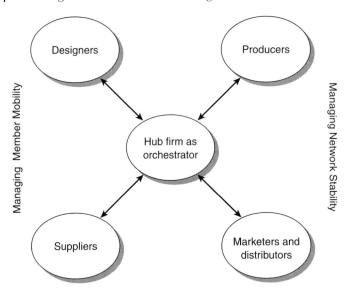

Figure 9-11   Network Organizational Structure

Source: Adapted from *Organizational Dynamics,* C.C. Snow, R.E. Miles, and H.J. Coleman, Jr., "Managing 21st Century Network Organizations," Winter/1992; and C. Dhanaraj and A. Parkhe, "Orchestrating Innovation Networks," *Academy of Management Review,* vol. 31, no. 3 (2006), p. 661.

masonry, construction, plumbing, electrical and related services as needed for a project.

Designed to be flexible and adaptable to rapidly changing environments, network organizations have a number of advantages over traditional, more bureaucratic and hierarchical forms of organization. In addition to being more agile and fast moving, network firms require less capital to operate, carry lower overhead expenses, are able to tap outside technology with relative ease, and, in general, are relatively entrepreneurial in character. As a result, an increasing number of organizations are becoming, in effect, multiorganizational in nature, comprising a nexus of relationships (e.g., joint ventures, value-added partnerships, subcontracting, licensing activities) with both domestic and foreign firms.

Although these inter-firm arrangements offer companies the opportunity to expand their strategic options beyond existing capabilities and/or current product-market domains, they also create a number of organizational and managerial challenges. As experience with such organizational forms has shown, network firms tend to be vulnerable to competition from suppliers, have less control over the production process, can lose design and manufacturing expertise, have less security of supply, and have volatile earnings since they often ride waves of fashion or technology. Thus, while network organizational forms provide a useful way for organizations to cope with rapidly changing environments, such change demands the development of new perspectives and understanding of management.[75] These interorganizational forms call for a complex set of management skills and abilities, including building relationships, negotiating mutually rewarding deals, finding the "right" partners with compatible goals and values, and providing the partnered organizations with the appropriate balance of freedom and control. Managers will have to be more prepared to (1) act as orchestrators and brokers, securing and negotiating relationships with other firms; (2) recognize their interdependence and be willing to share information and cooperate with their partners; (3) customize their product or service on a continual basis to maintain their position within the network; and (4) invest in the development of inter-firm capabilities, human resource skills and competencies, relationship building, and trust at the individual, team, firm, and network levels; as well as (5) successfully compete against other network organizations.

These mechanisms and systems go well beyond the type of conventional, arm's-length relationships usually associated with interactions between independently owned firms. Instead, the network must be structured so that the member firms recognize their interdependence and are willing to cooperate with other member firms, sharing information and customizing their products or services as needed. If interorganizational networks are to survive over time, the interaction between their members must be characterized by trustworthy transactions and a sense of mutual reciprocity. Successful network firms typically describe the relationship between the companies in collegial rather than business terms, while negative relationships between key players is suggested to be detrimental to the network, especially over the long term, since they undermine cooperative tendencies and behaviors.[76] Such partnering ventures depend on inter-firm expectations that are based on mutual commitment to mutual benefit. Coercion (e.g., "You must do it this way to work with us") or tactical submission (e.g., "In the spirit of cooperation, we'll go along with you this time") undermine the development of long-term mutual effectiveness.[77] Most contemporary network organizations expect a highly proactive role among the participants, with an emphasis on knowledge sharing, innovation, inter-firm trust, and voluntary behavior focused on improving the final product or service rather than simply fulfilling a contractual obligation.

Cellular Organizations

In a number of emerging settings—particularly in the professional services arena—minimalist organizations are being formed that essentially facilitate the interaction and activities of a network of entrepreneurial professionals.[78] As illustrated in Figure 9-12, while each "cell" is capable of acting alone, by acting in concert with other cells the outcome is a far more potent and competent organization. Each individual member brings specialized skills and capabilities to the larger organization, providing the overall entity with the knowledge, skills and abilities (KSAs) that go well beyond the KSA set of any individual member. As members of the network, they also have an entrepreneurial responsibility to their peers and the system as a whole.

In the cellular form, the organization functions more as a facilitating mechanism than an employer. Emphasis is placed on promoting, enhancing, and applying the knowledge and capabilities of its members. This form shares many of the key properties of professional associations, where people are drawn together to share information and take personal responsibility for member competency and performance. Within the cellular form, people take charge of their own careers, benefiting from the learning opportunities and development opportunities provided by their interaction with fellow

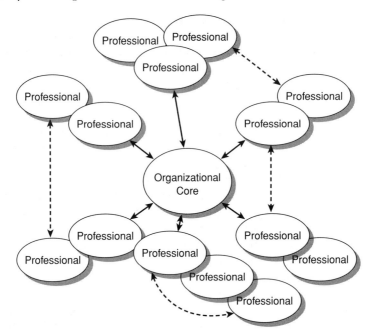

Figure 9-12   The Cellular Organization

members. An emergent and agreed upon set of norms promotes and reinforces self-governance as well as personal and professional allegiance to the larger system.

An illustration of the cellular form is Gennova Group, a collaborative community of management and business consultants. The Gennova Group is envisioned as a seamless alliance of trusting, purposeful and mutually beneficial relationships between members (referred to as trading partners) and their clients.[79] The network consists of (1) a broad array of professionals who act as business partners, (2) a choreographer, as the organizational core, who builds and ties the community together, and (3) knowledgeable and powerful customers. Described as the "professional community of the future," the network strives to meet the needs of both clients (companies that have become disenchanted with traditional professional services firms) and its members (professional service providers who work on their own but desire the resources and fellowship offered by a large firm). The underlying challenge of this type of organization is to sufficiently understand the end customer's needs and to translate that insight into trusting and profitable "win-win" relationships for all parties.

CONCLUSION

As this chapter has shown, there are several ways of structuring and designing organizations. It is important to remember that each form has its own advantages and disadvantages. The key is to ensure that the structure is appropriate for the type of environment and organization in question. As changes in the broader environment—technological, economic, sociocultural, political, and international—begin to accumulate, however, existing organizational forms become less and less capable of meeting the demands placed on them. When this occurs, new organizational types be-gin to emerge in an attempt to meet these environmental opportunities and constraints. Thus, over time new forms begin to take shape as organizational leaders attempt to correct the principal deficiencies of the form currently in use.[80] However, while many people seem to have a bias for newer organizational forms, it is just as inappropriate to create a matrix or network type of organization for a stable environment as it is to create a tall, functional structure for a highly turbulent one.

Each of the organizational forms discussed in this chapter emerged during a particular time period, is based on a specific production and market strategy, and is supported by a particular approach to management. It is important to reemphasize that although these forms will continue to evolve and change, all of these organizational paradigms are still in existence today. While an increasing number of our business organizations may be moving toward the right-hand side of Figure 9-13, simple and functional organizations are still amply represented in the business world. By adapting and focusing their strategies, organizations are often able to *enact* an environment

Figure 9-13 Evolution of Organizational Forms

that is supportive of their existing form. A highly specialized, simple structure (e.g., an owner-managed convenience store) or functionally structured organization (e.g., a department store), for example, may continue to focus on a narrow market niche and remain successful, even in an increasingly turbulent environment.[81] Thus, organizations operating in relatively simple and stable environments, where there is little uncertainty in decision making, can be more mechanistic and less differentiated in nature.

Organizations operating in diverse and dynamic environments, in contrast, can be expected to be more effective if they have flexible (organic), highly differentiated, *and* highly integrated structures. It should be noted, however, that structural differentiation can also occur *within* organizations and departments. Different parts of an organization may be confronted with subenvironments that create unique problems vis-à-vis the ones faced by other departments. Thus, it is quite possible to find an organization with a hybrid structure, having some departments with mechanistic and routinized structures (e.g., finance, production), while others tend to be more organic and nonroutinized (e.g., research and development, long-range planning). The important consideration is that the way in which an organization or department is structured should fit the particular demands, constraints, and uncertainties posed by its environment.

NOTES

1. See R.E. Miles and C.C. Snow, "Internal Markets and Network Organizations," in W.E. Halal, A. Geranmayeh, and J. Pourdehnad, eds., *Internal Markets: Bringing the Power of Free Enterprise Inside Your Organization* (New York: Wiley, 1993), pp. 68–69; R.E. Miles and C.C. Snow, *Fit, Failure & The Hall of Fame: How Companies Succeed or Fail* (New York: Free Press, 1994), Chapter 8; W.E. Hall, "The Transition from Hierarchy to ... What?" in W.E. Halal, A. Geranmayeh and J. Pourdehnad, eds., *Internal Markets*, p. 40.
2. See Miles and Snow, "Internal Markets and Network Organizations," pp. 68–69; and B. Chakravarthy and M. Gargiulo, "Maintaining Leadership Legitimacy in the Transition to New Organizational Forms," *Journal of Management Studies* 35, no. 4 (1998): 437–457.
3. See H. Mintzberg, *Mintzberg on Management: Inside Our Strange World of Organizations* (New York: Free Press, 1989); J.A. Byrne, "The Horizontal Corporation," *Business Week* (December 20, 1993), pp. 76–81; G. Stalk, Jr. and J.E. Black, "The Myth of the Horizontal Organization," *Canadian Business*

Review 21, no. 1 (1994): 26–31; J.B. Quinn, *Intelligent Enterprise: A Knowledge and Service Based Paradigm for Industry* (New York: Free Press, 1992); D.Q. Mills, *Rebirth of the Corporation* (New York: Wiley, 1991); I. Nonaka and H. Takeuchi, *The Knowledge-Creating Company: How Japanese Companies Create the Dynamics of Innovation* (New York: Oxford University Press, 1995); W.H. Davidow and M.S. Malone, *The Virtual Corporation: Lessons from the World's Most Advanced Companies* (New York: HarperCollins, 1992); M.A. Schilling and H.K. Steensma, "The Use of Modular Organizational Forms: An Industry-Level Analysis," *Academy of Management Journal* 44, no. 6 (2001): 1149–1168; and C. Paradeise, "French Sociology of Work: From Shop Floors to Labor Markets to Networked Careers," *Organization Studies* 24, no. 4 (2003): 633–654.
4. See R.H. Waterman, Jr., T.J. Peters, and J.R. Phillips, "Structure Is Not Organization," *Business Horizons* 23, no. 3 (1980): p. 19. See also M. Harris and A. Raviv, "Organization Design," *Management Science* 48, no. 7 (2002): 852–865.

5. The following discussion is adapted from J. Swieringa and A. Wierdsma, *Becoming a Learning Organization: Beyond the Learning Curve* (Reading, MA: Addison-Wesley, 1992), pp. 145–146. For a detailed examination of the interaction between organizational hierarchies and markets, see O.E. Williamson, *Markets and Hierarchies* (New York: Free Press, 1971).

6. See J. Child, *Organization* (New York: Harper & Row, 1984); and J. Pfeffer, "Organization Theory and Structural Perspectives on Management," *Journal of Management* 17, no. 4 (1991): 789–803.

7. This section draws from S. Robbins, *Organization Theory: Structure, Design, and Applications*, 2nd ed. (Englewood Cliffs, NJ: Prentice Hall, 1987), Chapters 3–5; and R. Miles, *Macro Organizational Behavior* (Santa Monica, CA: Goodyear, 1980), pp. 23–25.

8. D.S. Pugh, D.J. Hickson, C.R. Hinings, V.M. MacDonald, C. Turner, and T. Lupton, "A Conceptual Scheme for Organizational Analysis," *Administrative Science Quarterly* 8 (1963): 189–315.

9. P.R. Lawrence and J.W. Lorsch, "Differentiation and Integration in Complex Organizations," *Administrative Science Quarterly* 12 (1967): 1–47.

10. P.R. Lawrence and J.W. Lorsch, *Organization and Environment* (Cambridge, MA: Harvard University Press, 1967), p. 11.

11. See Lawrence and Lorsch, *Organizations and Environments*; Miles, op. cit., pp. 21–22; J. Galbraith, *Designing Complex Organizations* (Reading, MA: Addison-Wesley, 1973); and D. Dougherty, "Reimagining the Differentiation and Integration of Work for Sustained Product Innovation," *Organization Science* 12, no. 5 (2001): 612–631.

12. This discussion is adapted from H. Mintzberg, *Structure in Fives: Designing Effective Organizations* (Englewood Cliffs, NJ: Prentice Hall, 1993), pp. 99–100.

13. See P.S. Kahai, H.H. Carr, and C.A Snyder, "Technology and the Decentralization of Information Systems," *Information Systems Management* 20, no. 3 (2003): 51–60.

14. See G.G. Dess, A.M.A. Rasheed, K.J. McLaughlin, and R.L. Priem, "The New Corporate Architecture," *Academy of Management Executive* 9, no. 3 (1995): 7–18; G. Jones, *Organization Theory* (Reading, MA: Addison-Wesley, 1995), see Chapter 2.

15. See J.L. Galbraith, *Organizational Design* (Reading, MA: Addison-Wesley, 1977); and I. Lu and T. Chang, "A Contingency Model for Studying R&D-Marketing Integration in NPD Context," *International Journal of Technology Management* 24, no. 2/3 (2002): 143–164.

16. W.A. Pasmore, *Creating Strategic Change: Designing the Flexible, High-Performing Organization* (New York: Wiley, 1994), see pp. 257–258.

17. See Mintzberg, *Structure in Fives*, pp. 95–97; and R.J. Hershock, "Cross-Functional Teams: The Driving Force to Change," in H.B. Thorelli, ed., *Advances in Strategic Management* (Greenwich, CT: JAI Press, 1995), pp. 206–207.

18. See H.E. Aldrich, *Organizations and Environments* (Englewood Cliffs, NJ: Prentice Hall, 1979), p. 11.

19. Mintzberg, *Structure in Fives*, pp. 96–97; Jones, *Organization Theory*, pp. 65–66; and N. Nohria and S. Ghoshal, "Differentiated Fit and Shared Values: Alternatives for Managing Headquarters-Subsidiary Relations," *Strategic Management Journal* 15, no. 6 (1994): 491–502.

20. Aldrich, *Organizations and Environments*, p. 11.

21. M. Porter, *Competitive Advantage: Creating and Sustaining Superior Performance* (New York: Free Press, 1985), pp. 398–399. See also Z. Lin and C. Hui, "Should Lean Replace Mass Organization Systems? A Comparative Examination from a Management Coordination Perspective," *Journal of International Business Studies* 30, no. 1 (1999): 45–64.

22. T.J. Peters and R.H. Waterman, Jr., *In Search of Excellence: Lessons from America's Best-Run Companies* (New York: Warner Books, 1982), see Chapter 12; and L.G. Bolman and T. Deal, *Reframing Organizations: Artistry, Choice and Leadership* (San Francisco: Jossey-Bass, 2003), pp. 71–72.

23. See K. Weick, "Educational Organizations as Loosely Coupled Systems,"

Administrative Science Quarterly 21, no. 1 (1976): 1–19.

24. Aldrich, *Organizations and Environments*, pp. 80–86; and Peters and Waterman, *In Search of Excellence*, pp. 318–319.

25. See R.J. Hershock, "Cross-Functional Teams: The Driving Force to Change," in H.B. Thorelli, ed., *Advances in Strategic Management* (Greenwich, CT: JAI Press, 1995), p. 208.

26. Mintzberg, *Structure in Fives*, pp. 4–7.

27. See Jones, *Organizational Theory*, pp. 71–72.

28. See T. Burns and G.M. Stalker, *The Management of Innovation* (London: Tavistock, 1966); C.R. Gullet, "Mechanistic vs. Organic Organizations: What Does the Future Hold?" *Personnel Administrator* 20 (1975): 17; and C. Wang and P.K. Ahmed, "Structure and Structural Dimensions for Knowledge-Based Organizations," *Measuring Business Excellence* 7, no. 1 (2003): 51–62.

29. H. Mintzberg, *The Structuring of Organizations* (Englewood Cliffs, NJ: Prentice Hall, 1979), pp. 431–467; and Gullet, op. cit., p. 17.

30. This discussion is based on S. Robbins, *Organization Theory* (Englewood Cliffs, NJ: Prentice Hall, 1987) Chapter 5; and R.L. Daft, *Organization Theory and Design* (St. Paul, MN: West, 1986), Chapter 5.

31. See R.Z. Gooding and J.A. Wagner III, "A Meta-Analytic Review of the Relationship between Size and Performance: The Productivity and Efficiency of Organizations and Their Subunits," *Administrative Science Quarterly* 30 (1985): 462–481; and J.E. Yao, X. Xu, C. Liu, and J. Lu, "Organization Size: A Significant Predictor of IT Innovation Adoption," *Journal of Computer Information Systems* 43, no. 2 (2002/2003): 76–82.

32. This discussion is based on P.M. Carillo and R.E. Kopelman, "Organization Structure and Productivity: Effects of Subunit Size, Vertical Complexity, and Administrative Intensity on Operating Efficiency," *Group & Organization Studies* 16, no. 1 (1991): 44–59.

33. See O. Gassmann and G. Reepmeyer, "Organizing Pharmaceutical Innovation: From Science-Based Knowledge Creators to Drug-Oriented Knowledge Brokers," *Creativity and Innovation Management* 14, no. 3 (2005): 233–245.

34. Carillo and Kopelman, op. cit., pp. 55–57; and R.N. Yeaple, "Why Are Small R&D Organizations More Productive?" *IEEE Transactions on Engineering Management* 39, no. 4 (1992): 332–346; M. Bommer, R. DeLaPorte, and J. Higgins, "Skunkworks Approach to Project Management," *Journal of Management in Engineering* 18, no. 8 (2002): 21–28; and H.K. Ping, "Skunkworks May Be Way Ahead to Create Fresh Programming," *Media Asia*, February 11, 2005, p. 12.

35. The following discussion is adapted from Robbins, op. cit., Chapter 6; and Daft, op. cit., Chapter 4.

36. J. Woodward, *Industrial Organizations: Theory and Practice* (London: Oxford University Press, 1965); and *Management and Technology* (London: Her Majesty's Stationery Office, 1958).

37. See C. Evans, G.O. Hammersley, and M. Robertson, "The HRM Consequences of Cellular Manufacturing at Dowell Remcraft," *Human Resource Management International Digest* 10, no. 2 (2002): 17–20; and F. Al-Mubarak, B.M. Khumawala, and C. Canel, "Focused Cell Manufacturing: An Alternative to Cellular Manufacturing," *International Journal of Operations and Production Management* 23, no. 3/4 (2003): 277–299.

38. C. Perrow, "A Framework for the Comparative Analysis of Organizations," *American Sociological Review* 32 (April 1967): 194–208; *Organizational Analysis: A Sociological Approach* (Belmont, CA: Wadsworth, 1970).

39. J.D. Thompson, *Organizations in Action* (New York: McGraw-Hill, 1967).

40. See R. House, D.M. Rousseau, and M. Thomas-Hunt, "The Meso Paradigm: A Framework for the Integration of Micro and Macro Organizational Behavior," in L.L. Cummings and B.M. Staw, eds., *Research in Organizational Behavior*, vol. 17 (Greenwich, CT: JAI Press, 1995), p. 108; and C.W. Langfred, "Autonomy and Performance in Teams: The Multilevel Moderating Effect of Task Interdependence," *Journal of Management* 31, no. 4 (2005): 513–529.

41. See M. Ebers and M. Lieb, "Computer Integrated Manufacturing as a Two-Edged

Sword," *International Journal of Operations and Production Management* 9 (1989): 69–92; D. Lei, M.A. Hitt, and J.D. Goldhar, "Advanced Manufacturing Technology: Organizational Design and Strategic Flexibility," *Organization Studies* 17, no. 3 (1996): 501–523; and K. Ghani, V. Jayabalan, and M. Suguman, "Impact of Advanced Manufacturing Technology on Organizational Structure," *Journal of High Technology Management Research* 13, no. 2 (2002): 157–176.

42. M.A. Hitt, R.E. Hoskisson, and R.D. Nixon, "A Mid-Range Theory of Interfunctional Integration, Its Antecedents and Outcomes," *Journal of Engineering and Technology Management* 10 (1993): 161–185; Lei, et al., "Advanced Manufacturing Technology," pp. 509–510; and K.J. Klein, A.B. Conn, and J.S. Sorra, "Implementing Computerized Technology: An Organizational Analysis," *Journal of Applied Psychology* 86, no. 5 (2001): 811–824.

43. See D.D. Davis, "Technological Innovation and Organizational Change," in D.D. Davis and Associates, *Managing Technological Innovation* (San Francisco: Jossey-Bass, 1986), pp. 1–22; and Y.C. Gagnon and J. Dragon, "The Impact of Technology on Organizational Performance," *Optimum* 28, no. 1 (1998): 19–33.

44. See T.H. Davenport, "On Tomorrow's Organizations: Moving Forward, or a Step Backwards?" *Academy of Management Executive* 8, no. 3 (1994): 93–95; J.D. Goldhar and D. Lei, "Variety Is Free: Manufacturing in the Twenty-First Century," *Academy of Management Executive* 9, no. 4 (1995): 73–86; M. Boudreau, K.D. Loch, D. Robey, and D. Straud, "Going Global: Using Information Technology to Advance the Competitiveness of the Virtual Transnational Organization," *Academy of Management Executive* 12, no. 3 (1998): 120–128; and S.L. MacDougall and R.H. Pike, "Consider Your Options: Changes to Strategic Value During Implementation of Advanced Manufacturing Technology," *Omega* 31, no. 1 (2003): 1–16.

45. A.D. Chandler, *Strategy and Structure: Chapters in the History of the Industrial Enterprise* (Cambridge, MA: MIT Press, 1962), p. 13.

46. The following discussion is adapted from Robbins, op. cit., Chapter 4.

47. C.W. Bill and R.E. Hoskisson, "Strategy and Structure in the Multiproduct Firm," *Academy of Management Review* 12, no. 2 (1987): 331–341; and G. Hult, M. Tomas, S. Cavusgil, S. Tamer, T. Kiyak, S. Deligonul, and K. Lagerström, "What Drives Performance in Globally Focused Marketing Organizations? A Three-Country Study," *Journal of International Marketing* 15, no. 2 (2007): 58–85.

48. This discussion is based on A.C. Boynton and B. Victor, "Beyond Flexibility: Building and Managing the Dynamically Stable Organization," *California Management Review* 34, no. 1 (1991): 53–66. For a further development of the concept of dynamic stability, see E. Abrahamson, "Change Without Pain," *Harvard Business Review* 78, no. 4 (2000): 75–80.

49. See for example, G.G. Dess and N.K. Origer, "Environment, Structure, and Consensus: A Conceptual Integration," *Academy of Management Review* 12, no. 2 (1987): 313–330; H. Mintzberg, *The Rise and Fall of Strategic Planning* (New York: Free Press, 1994); and D. Lozeau, A. Langley, and J. Denis, "The Corruption of Managerial Techniques by Organizations," *Human Relations* 55, no. 5 (2002): 537–564.

50. See C.A. Bartlett and S. Ghoshal, "Matrix Management: Not a Structure, a Frame of Mind," *Harvard Business Review* 68, no. 4 (1990): 138–145; M.S. Van Clieaf, "Strategy and Structure Follow People: Improving Organizational Performance through Effective Executive Search," *Human Resource Planning* 15, no. 1 (1992): 33–46; S.W. Floyd and P.J. Lane, "Strategizing Throughout the Organization: Managing Role Conflict through Strategic Renewal," *Academy of Management Review* 25, no. 1 (2000): 154–178; and A. Styhre, "How Process Philosophy Can Contribute to Strategic Management," *Systems Research and Behavioral Science* 19, no. 6 (2002): 577–588.

51. See Burns and Stalker, op. cit. See also W.R. Scott, "Reflections of a Half-Century of Organizational Sociology," *Annual Review of Sociology* 30 (2004): 1–21.

52. Lawrence and Lorsch, op. cit.

53. Mintzberg, *Structure in Fives*, see Chapter 8.

54. See M.A. Johnson, "Delegation and Organizational Structure in Small Businesses: Influences of a Manager's Attachment Patterns," *Group & Organization Management* 25, no. 1 (2000): 4–21.

55. Mintzberg, *Structure in Fives*, see Chapters 9 and 10.

56. Mintzberg, *Structure in Fives*, see Chapter 11.

57. Mintzberg, *Structure in Fives*, see Chapter 12.

58. This discussion is based on Bartlett and Ghoshal, op. cit; R.C. Ford and W.A. Randolph, "Cross-Functional Structures: A Review and Integration of Matrix Organization and Project Management," *Journal of Management* 18, no. 2 (1992): 267–294; R.E. Numerof and M.N. Abrahams, "Matrix Management: Recipe for Chaos?" *Directors and Boards* 26, no. 4 (2002): 42–43.

59. See W.D. Rees and C. Porter, "Matrix Structures and the Training Implications," *Industrial & Commercial Training* 36, no. 5 (2004): 189–193.

60. J.A. Byrne, "The Horizontal Corporation," *Business Week* (December 20, 1993), pp. 76–81; G. Stalk, Jr. and J.E. Black "The Myth of the Horizontal Organization," *Canadian Business Review* 21, no. 1 (1994): 26–31; and F. Ostroff, *The Horizontal Organization: What the Organization of the Future Actually Looks Like and How It Delivers Value to Customers* (N.Y.: Oxford University Press, 1999).

61. See R.K. Chung, "The Horizontal Organization: Breaking Down Functional Silos," *Business Credit* 96, no. 5 (1994): 21–24.

62. See Byrne, ibid; N.M. Tichy and S. Sherman, *Control Your Destiny or Someone Else Will* (New York: Free Press, 1994); For an update on GE's system see "Imagination at Work," accessed May 10, 2007: http://www.ge.com/en/company/companyinfo/at_a_glance/operating_system.htm.

63. C.M. Savage, *The Fifth Generation Management: Integrating Enterprises Through Human Networking* (Maynard, MA: Digital Press, 1990).

64. J.F. Rockart and J.W. Short, "The Networked Organization and the Management of Interdependence," in M.S. Morton, ed., *The Corporation of the 1990s: Information Technology and Organizational Transformation* (New York: Oxford University Press, 1991), p. 196; and W. Brockbank and D. Ulrich, "The Work of HR Part Two: The Flow of Information and Work," *Strategic HR Review* 4, no. 6 (2005): 20–23. See also X.A. Koufteros, A.Y. Nahm, T.C. Edwin Cheng, and K. Lai, "An Empirical Assessment of a Nomological Network of Organizational Design Constructs: From Culture to Structure to Pull Production to Performance," *International Journal of Production Economics* 106, no. 2 (2007): 468–492.

65. See M.L. Moore, "Designing Parallel Organizations to Support Organizational Productivity Programs," in J.J. Famularo, ed., *Handbook of Human Resources Administration* (New York: McGraw-Hill, 1986), pp. 4-1–4-18. See also G.A. Moore, "Darwin and the Demon: Innovating within Established Enterprises," *Harvard Business Review* 82, no. 7/8 (2004): 86–92.

66. See D. Lei and J.W. Slocum, "Organization Designs to Renew Competitive Advantage," *Organizational Dynamics* 31, no. 1 (2002): 1–18.

67. G.R. Bushe and A.B. Shani, "A Review of the Literature on the Use of Parallel Learning Structure Interventions in Bureaucratic Organizations," in F. Hoy, ed., *Best Papers Proceedings 1988: Forty-Eighth Annual Meeting of the Academy of Management*, pp. 258–262.

68. A.F. Buono, "Managing Strategic Alliances: Organizational and Human Resource Considerations," *Business in the Contemporary World* 3, no. 4 (1991): 92–101.

69. See A.F. Buono and J.L. Bowditch, *The Human Side of Mergers and Acquisitions* (San Francisco: Jossey-Bass, 1989), pp. 218–220. See also B. Burnes, "Managing Change and Changing Managers from ABC to XYZ," *Journal of Management Development* 22, no. 7 (2003): 627–642.

70. See R. House, D.M. Rousseau, and M. Thomas-Hunt, "The Meso Paradigm: A Framework for the Integration of Micro and Macro Organizational Behavior," in

L.L. Cummings and B.M. Staw, eds., *Research in Organizational Behavior*, vol. 17 (Greenwich, CT: JAI Press, 1995), p. 108; A. Picot, "Management in Networked Environments: New Challenges," *Management International Review* (October 1999): 19–23; and P.M. Jackson and C. Stainsby, "Sector Networked Organizations," *Public Money & Management* 20, no. 1 (2000): 11–16.

71. Chakravarthy and Gargiulo, "Maintaining Leadership Legitimacy in the Transition to New Organizational Forms," pp. 437–457.

72. The discussion of internal network organizations is adapted from W.E. Halal, "The Transition from Hierarchy to . . . . What?" in W.E. Halal, A. Geranmayeh, and J. Pourdehnad, eds., *Internal Markets: Bringing the Power of Free Enterprise inside Your Organization* (New York: Wiley, 1993); and W.E. Halal, "From Hierarchy to Enterprise: Internal Markets Are the New Foundation of Management," *Academy of Management Executive* 8, no. 4 (1994): 69–83.

73. See N. Llewellyn, "The Role of Psychological Contracts within Internal Service Networks," *Services Industries Journal* 21, no. 1 (2001): 211–226.

74. This section is adapted from H. Thorelli, "Networks: Between Markets and Hierarchies," *Strategic Management Journal* 7 (1986): 37–51; C.C. Snow, R.E. Miles, and H.J. Coleman, Jr., "Managing 21st Century Network Organizations," *Organizational Dynamics* 20, no. 3 (1992): 5–20; and R.E. Miles and C.C. Snow, "The New Network Firm: A Spherical Structure Built on a Human Investment Philosophy," *Organizational Dynamics* 23, no. 4 (1995): 5–17. See also C. Dhanaraj and A. Parkhe, "Orchestrating Innovation Networks," *Academy of Management Review* 31, no. 3 (2006): 659–669.

75. R.E. Miles and C.C. Snow, "Causes of Failure in Network Organizations," *California Management Review* 34 (1992): 53–72; J. Sydow, "On the Management of Strategic Networks," in H. Ernste and V. Meier, eds., *Regional Development and Contemporary Industry Response* (London: Belhaven Press, 1992), pp. 114–129; Miles and Snow,

"The New Network Firm"; and M.D. Hutt, E.R. Stafford, B.A. Walker, and P.H. Reingen, "Defining the Social Network of a Strategic Alliance," *Sloan Management Review* 41, no. 2 (2000): 51–63.

76. See R. Gulati and D. Kletter, "Shrinking Core, Expanding Periphery: The Relational Architecture of High-Performing Organizations," *California Management Review* 47, no. 3 (2005): 77–104; and G. Labianca and D.J. Brass, "Exploring the Social Ledger: Negative Relationships and Negative Asymmetry in Social Networks in Organizations," *Academy of Management Review* 31, no. 3 (2006): 596–614.

77. See F. Hull and E. Slowinski, "Partnering with Technology Entrepreneurs," *Research-Technology Management* (November–December 1990): 16–20; and J.D. Lewis, *Partnerships for Profit: Structuring and Managing Strategic Alliances* (New York: Free Press, 1990). See also S.A. Carlsson, "Knowledge Management and Knowledge Management Systems in Inter-Organizational Networks," *Knowledge and Process Management* 10, no. 3 (2003): 194–206.

78. The discussion of the cellular form is drawn from B.B. Allred, C.C. Snow and R.E. Miles, "Characteristics of Managerial Careers in the 21st Century," *Academy of Management Executive*, 1996, 10 (4): 17–27. See also J. Nebus, "Building Collegial Information Networks: A Theory of Advice Network Generation," *Academy of Management Review* 31, no. 3 (2006): 615–637.

79. See J. Twombly and J.C. Shuman, "Creating a Collaborative Community of Management Consultants," in A.F. Buono (Ed.), *Enhancing Inter-Firm Networks and Interorganizational Strategies* (Greenwich, CT: Information Age Publishing, 2003), pp. 223–237.

80. See Miles and Snow, "Internal Markets and Network Organizations," pp. 68–69.

81. See R.E. Miles and W.E.D. Creed, "Organizational Forms and Managerial Philosophies: A Descriptive and Analytic Review," in L.L. Cummings and B.M. Staw, eds., *Research in Organizational Behavior*, vol. 17 (Greenwich, CT: JAI Press, 1995), p. 349.

Organizational Culture and Effectiveness

$\mathbf{A}$s suggested by the discussion of organizational structure and design, different combinations of structural dimensions exert a significant influence on the attitudes, behaviors, and interactions of organizational members. These structural factors alone, however, do not explain all of the variation in such attitudes and behaviors. Indeed, there are a number of macro-level dynamics and phenomena that also shape and influence the attitudes and behaviors of organizational members.

These internal dynamics will be explored in the context of organizational culture. As part of this discussion, this section will also explore the related topics of organizational climate and identity. These concepts characterize the atmosphere and attributes that are unique to a particular organization in terms of how it deals with its members, its goals and objectives, its stakeholders, and its environment. The chapter concludes with an assessment of organizational effectiveness.

ORGANIZATIONAL CULTURE

Organizational culture refers to the *shared pattern* of beliefs, assumptions, and expectations held by organizational members, and their characteristic way of perceiving the organization's artifacts and environment, and its norms, roles, and values as they exist outside the individual.[1] In a way, organizational culture is a reflection of an organization's "personality," and, similar to an individual's personality, provides us with insights into attitudes and behaviors. In fact, ongoing research has underscored the potency of organizational culture, suggesting that strategy formulation, preferred leadership style, and accepted ways of accomplishing tasks, among other central facets of organizational life, are reflections of an organization's culture. As reflected in Enron's rapid decline and financial implosion, values and attitudes that support corporate smoke and mirrors, a penchant for keeping debt off the balance sheet, arm's-length partnerships, and conflicts of interest set the stage for a spiraling self-reinforcing decline.[2]

Just as culture is a central factor that influences the ways in which people act and interact in a given society, indigenous cultures evolve over time in organizations that affect individual and group behavior in predictable though subtle ways. Similar to societal culture, organizational culture is also implicitly diffused, and it is a pervasive and

TABLE 10-1 Characteristics and Consequences of Organizational Culture

Dominant Characteristics	Illustrative Consequences
Collective	Creation of organizational order and continuity
Emotionally charged	Creation of collective identity and commitment
Historically based	Creation of shared expectations
Inherently symbolic	Ethnocentrism
Inherently fuzzy	Dominant culture and subcultures
Dynamic	Dual tensions:
	Manifest and latent
	Functional and dysfunctional

Source: Adapted from Harrison M. Trice and Janice M. Beyer, *The Cultures of Work Organizations*, © 1993, pp. 5, 8. Reprinted by permission of Prentice Hall, Englewood Cliffs, New Jersey.

powerful force in shaping behavior. Moreover, although there are multiple definitions and uses of the concept at the organizational level, an underlying, integrative theme is *custom*. This "normative glue" holds an organization together through traditional ways of carrying out organizational responsibilities, unique patterns of beliefs and expectations that emerge over time, and the resulting shared understandings of reality at given points in time.

As summarized in Table 10-1, organizational culture has several dominant characteristics and consequences.[3] Culture is collective in nature in that it evolves over time as people interact with each other. Through these interactions they develop and share common beliefs, values, and uncertainties, and ways of coping with them. In essence, an organization's culture is the repository of what its members agree about. Because organizational cultures help their members manage anxieties, their substance and form are steeped with emotion, meaning, and symbolism. In contrast to organizational structure, culture reflects the expressive, rather than the mechanistic and pragmatic, dimension of organizational life.

Given the emotive and symbolic nature of organizational culture, it is also inherently fuzzy in that it is not a monolithic, unitary set of ideas. As will be discussed later in this section, while researchers differentiate between "thick" and "thin" cultures, all organizational cultures involve contradictions, ambiguities, and paradoxes.[4] At the same time, however, cultures can create social order from the potential chaos that permeates the open-ended nature of human behavior and interaction. Custom and continuity begin to emerge over time as organizational members construct and internalize "proper" attitudes and behaviors, and socialize new entrants. The resulting sense of unified ideas enhances members' feelings of belonging and commitment. As reviewed in Chapter 6, empirical research has found evidence that within-group agreement with regard to team and organization climate is positively associated with performance outcomes[5] (e.g., Ford & Seers, 2001), suggesting the importance of climate perceptions among organization members.

There is, however, a "dark side" to this type of identification in that people often distrust, fear, and/or dislike those with "other" ideas or ways of doing things. In fact, in some instances an organization's culture can discourage change by forcing organizational members to work within the same set of beliefs.[6] A strong (thick) culture may promote change, but only within its own, carefully defined boundaries. As numerous organizations have found, the cultural ideology that enables it to be successful at one point in time can also make it difficult to adapt and move into a different niche as their industry changes. As the story of Digital Equipment Corporation underscores, the very culture that makes an organization a great company can quickly become dysfunctional in the rapidly changing world of information technology.[7] As the dual nature of (and tension in) this discussion suggests, the outcomes or consequences of organizational culture are not always "positive," manifest, or functional.

For a fuller understanding of the subtleties of culture, three conceptual issues need to be briefly examined: (1) the uniqueness of organizational cultures, (2) the differences between objective and subjective organizational culture, and (3) organizational subcultures.

Uniqueness of Organizational Cultures

Although popular use of the concept of culture suggests that differences between organizational cultures exist primarily across industries rather than between organizations in the same industry, this focus is too restrictive. Early work in this area focused on creating types of corporate cultures, typically drawing on certain industry-specific characteristics such as degree of risk and speed of feedback involved in corporate decision making. For example, industries in which typical decisions involve major stakes and fast results (e.g., as found in advertising, entertainment, construction) were characterized as having "tough guy/macho" cultures in which the ability to take risks and succeed were highly prized. In contrast, industries that are characterized by low risks and long-term feedback (e.g., insurance, utilities) tend to have "process" cultures in which the ability to manage details is the key to success.[8] Although it was recognized that intra-firm differences might exist based on functional area differences (e.g., cultural differences across sales, research and development, finance) and location (e.g., regional operations, international offices), it was suggested that general cultural patterns evolved to meet the specific demands of the workplace.[9]

As discussed in Chapter 8, the general environmental forces in a particular industry do exert a significant influence on the development of an organization's culture. Research has suggested that basic cultural commonalities can be found across different industries.[10] However, while such general differences do exist and are useful for initial framing of different companies, cultural differences between firms in the same industry can be just as great as cultural differences across industries.[11] Today, it is generally recognized that successful companies continue to adapt to changes in their environment, honing and blending different aspects of their culture, in essence creating unique cultural configurations.[12]

Cultural differences between organizations in the same industry are readily apparent when one company attempts to acquire, merge with, or even partner with another firm. The merger between automobile giants Daimler-Benz and Chrysler, for example, was initially touted as a paradigm-breaking move forward in the cost-efficient manufacture and development of cars and trucks. The combination was cast as a perfect way of capturing significant synergies through the combination of Mercedes-Benz's highly engineered luxury cars with Chrysler's mass-market vehicles. The merger, however, was later described as more of a takeover, laden with fears, anxieties, clashes, and frustrations as the two companies operated with widely different styles, cultural orientations, and strategies.[13] Similar dynamics have been observed in the mega-mergers between Exxon and Mobil, and AOL and Time Warner.

Objective and Subjective Organizational Culture

Culture exists on a number of levels and organizations have both subjective and objective cultures (see Figure 10-1). *Subjective organizational culture* refers to the shared patterns of beliefs, assumptions, and expectations held by organizational members, and the group's characteristic way of perceiving the organization's environment, artifacts and its values, norms, and roles as they exist outside the individual.[14] This includes such things as organizational heroes (i.e., those people who personify the culture's values and provide tangible role models for others); myths and stories about the organization and its leadership; organizational taboos, rites, and rituals; and perceptions of "Mecca" (i.e., important symbolic locations and prideful extensions of the organization).

Subjective organizational culture also encompasses what may be termed a *managerial culture*—the leadership styles and orientations, mental frameworks, and ways of behaving and solving problems that are influenced by the values supported by the organization.[15] Although some aspects of the managerial culture may be shared across organizations, crucial though subtle facets tend to be indigenous to particular organizations. Thus, while two organizations may assert that "quality customer service" is the key to their success, managerially there may be significant differences in terms of what "quality" actually means in practice or how to best achieve that end.

Objective organizational culture refers to the artifacts created by an organization. For instance, 3Com Corporation's modular, open-office configuration, and the chassis assembly team bays complete with sauna, coffee room, and entrance at Volvo's Kalmar

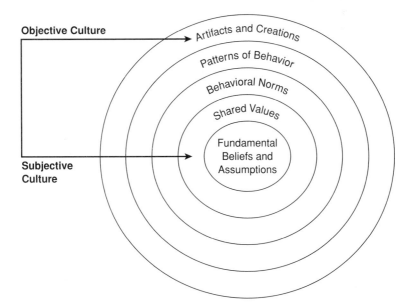

Figure 10-1 Levels of Organizational Culture

plant are objective (material) reflections of each organization's culture. Such physical settings, office locations and decor, and even the fleet of cars an organization leases for its executives can reflect the values of the organization.

Although both aspects of culture are important for a full understanding of a particular organization, what we have termed subjective organizational culture provides a more distinctive basis for characterizing and interpreting similarities and differences among and between people and organizations. While objective culture may contain similarities across organizations, subjective organizational culture is unique to a particular enterprise. At times, however, something that is part of the objective culture of an organization can begin to take on a life of its own. When this occurs, there is a distorted magnification of the importance of the artifact that then becomes part of the subjective culture of the organization. This is one of the ways in which myths concerning organizational life are created.

Organizational Subcultures

The discussion thus far has treated organizational culture as if it were a monolithic phenomenon, that is, one culture to a setting. It is important to realize, however, that multiple cultures often exist in organizations. While organizations typically have a dominant culture (i.e., the core values and norms that are shared by the majority of organizational members), corporations, divisions, plants, and departments may have cultures that are distinct from the larger group.[16] In fact, as recent research suggests, these subcultures appear to exert a more powerful influence than the larger organizational culture on employee behavior.[17] When examining an organization from a cultural perspective, therefore, it is important to distinguish the organization's dominant culture and the various *subcultures* that coexist with it.

While organizations will typically have one or more subcultures, they are usually *enhancing* (an enclave where adherence to the core values of the dominant culture is more fervent than in the rest of the organization) or *orthogonal* (members simultaneously accept the core values of the dominant culture and a separate, nonconflicting set of values particular to themselves) in nature.[18] This configuration is often found in functionally structured organizations where different functional cultures coexist within the dominant organizational culture.[19] Members of research and development departments, for example, often hold very different beliefs and expectations about organizational life compared with those members in accounting and finance departments. Although these different groups might still share many of the overall cultural values of the organization (e.g., "Employees are our most important asset"), they can also be expected to differ along certain lines (e.g., "We don't follow any routines in *this* department"). An important implication that stems from such subcultural variation is that corporatewide integrative solutions, especially those that depend on advanced information technologies, may prove to be more difficult to implement than initially envisioned.[20] Managers must recognize these subcultural differences, and facilitate sharing and discussion to enhance understanding across the different groups. Emphasis should be placed on how these differences might limit the acceptance and effectiveness of technology implementation as a way of building a stronger foundation to maximize the long-term benefits of these systems.

Organizational Countercultures

As indicated earlier, organizational subcultures are typically enhancing or orthogonal in nature. However, just as societies may have groups whose norms, values, and behaviors sharply contradict dominant societal norms, values, and behaviors,[21] organizations may also have subgroups that strongly reject what the organization stands for and/or what it is attempting to accomplish. Referred to as organizational countercultures, these groups usually engage in three forms of dissent:[22] (1) direct opposition to the firm's dominant values; (2) opposition to the dominant culture's power structure; and (3) opposition to the patterned exchanges and interactions that are intertwined with the values of the dominant culture. Since countercultural values and behaviors are inconsistent with what the dominant culture is attempting to accomplish, they can influence people to either consciously or subconsciously work against the success of the organization.

Organizational countercultures tend to emerge when individuals or groups are living under sets of conditions that they strongly feel cannot provide them with their accustomed or hoped-for satisfactions. In one sense, organizational countercultures can be thought of as calls for help in stressful times, when existing cultural support systems have broken down and people are attempting to regain some sense of control in their lives. Such countercultural groups can be especially prevalent during large-scale organizational transformations—such as in mergers and acquisitions—that involve significant changes in the nature, shape, or character of the organization.

Summary

Organizational culture tends to be unique to a particular organization, composed of an objective and subjective dimension, and concerned with custom, tradition, and shared beliefs about organizational life. It is a powerful determinant of individual and group behavior. Organizational culture affects virtually all aspects of organizational life from the ways in which people interact with each other, perform their work, and dress, to the types of decisions made in a firm, its organizational policies and procedures, and strategy considerations.

Diagnosing Organizational Culture

Not all organizational cultures are equally strong. There are, in fact, three basic factors that make a significant difference in how influential a culture will be in shaping the attitudes and behaviors of its members.[23] First, cultural strength is based on the *extent* of shared beliefs and values that exist in an organization. The greater the degree of shared beliefs and values, the stronger the culture's influence since there are more basic assumptions that guide behavior. IBM, Procter & Gamble, and Morgan Guaranty, for example, are described as having "thick" cultures due to a high level of shared beliefs and values that organizational members are socialized to accept as their own. "Thin" or "pseudocultures," in contrast, have few shared assumptions and, as a result, have much less influence on organizational life.[24]

Second, organizational cultures whose beliefs and values are *more widely shared* across organizational members tend to have a more powerful effect because more people are guided by them. Finally, in cultures where beliefs and values are *clearly ordered* (i.e., where the relative significance of different assumptions is widely known), the effect on member behavior will be more pervasive since there is less ambiguity about which beliefs and values should prevail in conflict situations. For instance, in "thick" cultures the distinction between central and pivotal values is clear and people respond accordingly, while in "thin" cultures there tends to be greater disagreement and ambiguity.

The ability to diagnose an organization's culture is important since it is difficult on the surface to predict whether a company will have a strong or weak culture. As a general rule, smaller organizations that operate on a localized basis tend to have strong cultures because it is easier for beliefs and values to become more widely shared between members. However, significantly larger organizations with worldwide operations, such as IBM, GE, and Johnson & Johnson, can have very strong cultures. Especially if there has been a continuity of strong leadership, an ongoing emphasis of the same values and beliefs through socialization practices, and a relatively stable workforce, a consistent set of beliefs and values can take hold and become widely known and shared.

Deciphering an organization's culture is a highly interpretive, subjective process that requires insights into historical as well as current activities. One cannot simply rely on what people verbally report about their culture. While such self-reports are important, the ways in which people act and interact with each other, how top management deals with various situations, how people actually spend their time, what the company says about itself in annual reports, house organs, and other documents, and the organization's physical setting all contribute to a fuller understanding of a particular firm's culture.

Although a number of different "interpretive frameworks" are proposed in the literature, there are several aspects of culture that ethnographic researchers typically focus on:[25]

1. **Cultural artifacts and creations (objective culture).** The material artifacts created by an organization and its physical layout often reflect its values and orientations. These can range from various icons such as luxury executive automobiles and designer furniture to images (e.g., logo, corporate dress styles) and building structure (open versus closed offices, assigned parking). Organizations try to create settings and images that make a statement about their company. Employee perceptions of "Mecca," those important symbolic locations of the organization, also signal important values and orientations. Employees are usually quite explicit about where the office power base is located, where people can establish their reputation, and so forth. Similarly, specific job assignments and locations typically signify longer-term intentions and plans to employees from advancement potential to a "dead-end" career.

2. **Organizational heroes.** Organizations tend to have role models who personify the cultural value system and define the organization's concept of success in a tangible way. Although such heroes are frequently part of upper management, they may be identified throughout the organization. The key is that these individuals represent what the company stands for and reinforce the values of the culture by underscoring that success is

attainable, acting as a role model for others, providing a symbol to the external world, setting a standard of performance, and motivating organizational members.

3. **Organizational myths and stories.** In many instances, employees do not speak directly of values, beliefs, and assumptions but instead imply them through a diverse set of concrete examples and stories. These narratives organize beliefs about the organization and its value system by acting as a "map" that facilitates a person's understanding of how things are done.[26] Such stories and myths are often filtered through a "cultural network" that continues to reinforce and remind people of "why we do things that way." Organizational storytellers spread the corporate folklore and dramatize the exploits of the firm's heroes and heroines. It is important to note that widely known stories do not necessarily support organizational needs. "Negative stories" can teach people what aspects or individuals of an organization to be wary of or how to "beat the system." Myths and stories, therefore, can be either functional or dysfunctional for the organization. The key is that they provide a strong indicator of how employees view the company, its culture, and its management.

4. **Behavioral norms and expectations: rituals, rites and organizational taboos.** Organizations also have norms (see Chapter 5) that shape expectations about appropriate behaviors, which are social manifestations of the dominant beliefs and values of the culture. Thus, it is useful to observe *behavioral regularities* that characterize the way in which organizational members interact with each other, including the common language that they use. Social rituals, sometimes referred to as the "dance of culture," define everyday interaction and reinforce the basic orientations of the organization. Special ceremonies, such as awards or honors dinners, annual parties and gatherings, and daily rites and rituals, such as departmental and committee meetings, symbolically convey the relative importance of organizational values, functions, and activities to employees. However, just as "negative stories" inform organizational members about activities or individuals to avoid, organizational taboos convey boundaries concerning acceptable behaviors and interactions. Insight into such taboos, the "rules of the game" for getting along in an organization, are often found in organizational socialization processes where newcomers are exposed to those things they are expected to learn to become accepted members.

5. **Shared values.** A firm's underlying values and beliefs are the essence of the organization's philosophy for achieving success. They reflect the basic view of "the way things should be" in a company that is shared by organizational members. A firm's philosophy provides a sense of common direction for its members and guidelines as to acceptable behaviors in their daily operations. As a reflection of the organization's values, the *managerial culture* concerns the basic concept of authority that exists in the organization in terms of dominant leadership styles and orientations, mental frameworks, and ways of behaving and solving problems that are influenced by the values supported by the organization. As part of this level of analysis, it is important to examine

the *dominant espoused values/theories* (what people say ought to be done) that exist in an organization in contrast to the *dominant values/theories-in-use* (what is actually done).

Given the interpretive, subjective nature of the process of deciphering these different dimensions, a number of guidelines are suggested.[27] First, cultural diagnosis should be an *iterative process* (observations, interviews), beginning with an initial emphasis on objective organizational culture phenomena, gradually moving toward the deeper, subjective dimensions of culture (see Figure 10-2). Second, the process should be *triangulated,* that is, checking each piece of information against other pieces of information (e.g., archival data, observations, interviews) until a pattern begins to reveal itself. Third, it is beneficial to include joint assessments between insiders and outsiders to avoid subjectivity biases and to overcome any internal visibility problems. Finally, it is important to underscore that dangers are inherent in reporting what we have observed about a particular organization's culture. Organizational members can "hear" very different things when an outsider discusses their culture. There is also a need to be wary of lecturing insiders about their own culture since it is difficult for outsiders to know where cultural sensitivities may lie.

Culture Change in Organizations

Organizational cultures do change. Because culture is an integral part of a group's learning process and experience, changes occur over time as people cope with shifts in the external environment and problems created by internal integration efforts. Since the assumptions underlying a culture do not easily change, however, it is important to note that cultural transformation is typically an incremental and evolutionary process. Efforts to create a particular type of culture must be guided by committed leaders who envision compelling missions for their organizations. These leaders must carefully cultivate and nurture these purposes, and attend to and empower the people who make them work.[28] True culture change is often a time-consuming, expensive, and emotionally draining experience. In fact, most successful culture change efforts appear to be based on incremental "redirections" and efforts to "honor" the company's past.[29]

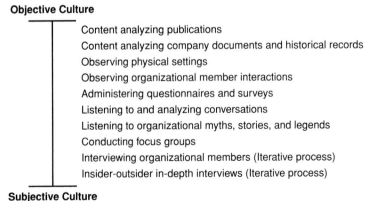

Objective Culture

Content analyzing publications
Content analyzing company documents and historical records
Observing physical settings
Observing organizational member interactions
Administering questionnaires and surveys
Listening to and analyzing conversations
Listening to organizational myths, stories, and legends
Conducting focus groups
Interviewing organizational members (Iterative process)
Insider-outsider in-depth interviews (Iterative process)

Subjective Culture

Figure 10-2 Methods for Deciphering Organizational Culture

As a context for examining how to change an organization's culture, it is useful to understand how a culture takes hold in an organization. Schein differentiates between primary embedding mechanisms and secondary reinforcement mechanisms.[30] *Primary embedding mechanisms,* the dominant forces that shape a particular organization's culture, consist of (1) those things that leaders pay systematic and consistent attention to, measure, and control; (2) leader reactions to critical incidents and organizational crises; (3) deliberate role modeling, teaching, and coaching by leaders; (4) criteria for allocating rewards and status; and (5) criteria for recruitment, selection, and promotion. *Secondary mechanisms* that reinforce the culture include (1) the way in which the organization is structured and designed, (2) organizational systems and procedures, (3) design of physical space, facades, and buildings, (4) use of stories, legends, myths, and parables about important events and people, and (5) formal statements of organizational philosophy, creeds, and charters. An underlying key is that these secondary factors must be consistent with, and a reflection of, the primary embedding mechanisms noted above.

There are two fundamental ways to effect culture change in an organization: (1) by getting organizational incumbents to "buy into" a new configuration of beliefs and values, and (2) by recruiting and socializing new people into the organization (with an emphasis on those new beliefs and values) while removing past members as necessary. As illustrated in Figure 10-3, five key intervention points and processes can be utilized to create such change: (1) changing organizational member behaviors; (2) justifying

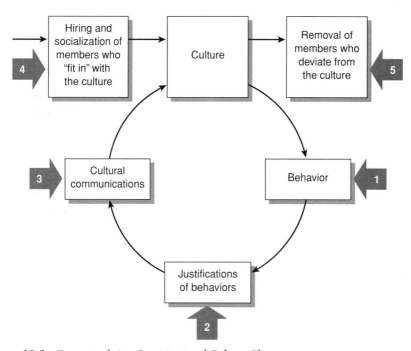

Figure 10-3 Conceptualizing Organizational Culture Change

Source: Reprinted from V. Sathe, *Culture and Related Corporate Realities.* Homewood, IL: Richard D. Irwin, 1985, p. 385. Reprinted by permission of the author.

the behavioral changes; (3) communicating cultural messages about the change; (4) hiring and socializing new members who "fit in" with the desired culture; and (5) removing those incumbents who deviate from the desired culture.[31] Managers seeking to create change in an organization's culture should intervene at these main points.

Behavior Change

Managers attempting to introduce major change in an organization often begin by assessing and then trying to change employee attitudes. This approach is consistent with the conventional wisdom that beliefs and values influence behavior. As a significant body of social science research underscores, however, one of the most effective ways of changing beliefs and values is to begin with changes in related behaviors. While attitudes do influence behavior, it is important to emphasize that behavior also influences attitudes.[32]

Individual values and attitudes, especially those that are deeply held, are notoriously difficult to change directly since people's values tend to be part of an interrelated system in which each value is tied to and reinforced by other values. Thus, managers must realize that it is virtually impossible to change a particular value in isolation from an individual's other values. By focusing on relevant behaviors and interactions, in contrast, managers can begin to shape the desired outcomes by setting explicit expectations and performance standards, rewarding appropriate behaviors and providing channels through which people can contribute to goals and objectives.[33] Changes in behaviors in and of themselves, however, do not necessarily translate into culture change. In fact, changes in culture may lag behavioral changes for a considerable period of time, or in some instances may never occur. Especially when a firm relies solely on extrinsic motivators, organizational members can easily rationalize why they "accepted" the change, leaving present cultural values and orientations intact. If organizational members can see the inherent value of the change, they are much more likely to accept and identify with what the organization is attempting to accomplish.

Justifying the Behavior Change

While behavior change is an important, initial step, for true culture change to take effect, over the longer term the beliefs, values, and attitudes held by organizational members must be consistent with and reinforce the new desired behavior (culture change). Indeed, as previously suggested, while organizational members may appear to "buy into" proposed changes through their actions, they may be simply rationalizing their behavior because "it was required to keep my job" or "that's what is rewarded." Thus, while they may behave in a certain way desired by the organization, they may still cling to the beliefs and values of their old culture. In this sense, there may be overt behavioral compliance, but there is little, if any, real acceptance of or commitment to the culture change.

If culture change is to take place, therefore, managers should make every effort to support relevant behavioral changes with intrinsic motivators. As part of this process, explanations for and justifications of the culture change must be made to organizational members. One approach is to convince organizational members to probe their present beliefs and values by showing them that their assumptions conflict with what is happening around them.[34] For culture change to take hold, however, managers must also articulate and communicate the new organizational beliefs and values and get people to adopt them.[35]

Using Cultural Communications

Cultural communications take place on both explicit and implicit levels. *Explicit cultural messages* include announcements, memos, speeches, and other direct forms of communication. While managers often rely on these overt forms of intercourse, *implicit cultural messages*—rituals, ceremonies, stories, metaphors, heroes, logos, decor, dress, and other symbolic actions—also act as significant communication devices about changes in the organization's culture. Both explicit and implicit forms of communication are important and should be used to induce people to adopt the new cultural beliefs and values. The underlying strategy should be to promote a sense of common purpose among organizational members.

A significant problem in bringing about employee acceptance of cultural communications, however, concerns the credibility of both the message and the sender. Explicit and implicit communications often conflict with each other as managers say one thing and then do the opposite. Since ongoing, consistent cultural communications are necessary for culture change to occur, it is important that promises, images, and messages are supported by deeds and actions. Consider the example of a computer company that attempted to create an awareness of and commitment to product quality as part of the firm's culture. However, while the idea of high-quality, defect-free products was verbally supported and given a great deal of ballyhoo at company meetings, departments were still shipping defective software packages. Virtually nothing was done to encourage or support employee actions in the quality-improvement area. The result was a highly cynical assessment among employees of the gap between the actual and "official" culture. As one of the company's managers argued: "We do have a zero-defect program: Don't test the product and you'll find zero defects."[36] As this brief illustration underscores, actual strategies, behaviors and practices must reflect the cultural messages if organizational members are going to buy into the change.[37]

In most instances, actions and symbols have a more potent impact on people than speeches by upper-level managers. The president and CEO of a major health care system that attempted to expand his company's focus from community health services to regional networks, for example, stresses the importance of transition rituals that allow people to express their feelings and "mourn" the change.[38] One of the values his company expressed—"people matter more than technology"—was reflected in its actions in terms of the way people were supported, trained, and encouraged during the change effort. As a way of further getting the "message" across, the firm used a "video newsletter," tapes of employees talking about their experiences and how they were innovating and changing, to relay to other employees what the organization was attempting to accomplish. Overall, the best way to ensure that cultural communications are credible and successful is to back them with consistent actions and behaviors that correspond to the espoused beliefs and values.

Hiring and Socialization

Organizational culture change is also significantly impacted by the extent to which newcomers "fit" and are socialized into the new culture. Especially if tensions exist among the present group of organizational members, it is important to ensure that there are no irreconcilable mismatches between new people being hired and the desired culture. While a "perfect" person-culture fit is highly unlikely and largely undesirable since it can contribute to a lack of critical thinking,[39] careful attention should be given to the selection and socialization process. Procter & Gamble (P&G), for example, well known for its "thick" culture, uses an exhaustive application and screening process for new hires.[40] Interviewers, who are part of a highly trained cadre, probe potential applicants and reveal the reality of working for P&G in terms of its pluses *and* minuses. In this sense, P&G facilitates an applicant's "deselection," based on the assumption that the candidate has the best understanding of whether the company meshes with his or her own beliefs, values, and objectives.

Removal of Deviants

Perhaps the most controversial aspect of culture change concerns dealing with those individuals who continually resist the change and what the organization is attempting to accomplish. While terminations are often involuntary as when a person is asked to resign or is fired outright, in major culture-change efforts some of this turnover will be voluntary, especially among those who feel particularly uncomfortable with the change. A high degree of turnover, whether voluntary or involuntary, however, can have negative repercussions. First, it is difficult to assimilate a significant number of new people in a short time period. Moreover, a large inflow of new hires can escalate internal political maneuvers as people jockey for position, especially at the managerial levels. Removal of deviants can also reduce the level of critical analysis that exists in an organization, precipitating the type of groupthink behavior discussed in Chapter 5.

Managerial Application

As the preceding discussion suggests, culture analysis can be challenging and very time consuming. As a way of accelerating the assessment and change process, Ed Schein, an expert in the field of organizational culture, has created a useful framework that is based on group discussion and analysis (see Figure 10-4).[41] This approach suggests that rather than trying to decipher and change a culture in its totality, it is more useful and pragmatic to look at the culture as it relates to a specific strategy, involving as many organizational members as needed to understand the culture and to set out a course of action to align the culture with the strategy in question. Emphasis in the assessment process should be placed on understanding the underlying cultural assumptions in terms of whether they are strengths or constraints on what the organization is attempting to accomplish.

Resistance

As a cautionary note, it is important to return to the caveat at the beginning of this section: While organizational cultures do change and evolve over time, the process of managed change can be difficult and time consuming. A high level of anxiety and uncertainty typically accompanies any substantial organizational change. While organizational members often resist any major change initiatives, cultural change is among the most difficult for human beings to accept.

Resistance to organizational culture change efforts is influenced by: (1) the magnitude of the change in the content of the culture (radical vs. incremental) and (2)

1. **Define the "Business Problem"**
   - Delineate context: create a learning organization, strategic alliance, acquisition, quality initiative

2. **Review the Concept of Culture**
   - Brief lecture and overview

3. **Culture Delineation**
   - Identify organizational artifacts
   - Identify practices and espoused values: strategies, goals, philosophies, key norms, and justifications
   - Identify underlying organizational values and assumptions

4. **Culture Analysis**
   - Comparison of values, practices, and artifacts

5. **Culture Assessment**
   - What does the culture mean in terms of the "Business Problem" defined in Step 1?

6. **Creation of Action Plan**

Repeat process with other groups as needed

Figure 10-4 A Framework for Deciphering and Changing Organizational Culture

Source: Adapted from E.H. Schein, *The Corporate Culture Survival Guide* (San Francisco: Jossey-Bass, 1999), pp. 65–68.

by the strength of the prevailing culture (thick versus thin).[42] Member resistance will be much greater in those instances where a radical change in a strong or thick culture is being attempted compared with incremental changes in relatively weak or thin cultures. It is important to underscore, however, that resistance to such change is not purely emotional and, in many instances, organizational members resist change for reasonable and predictable reasons: (1) People often perceive a loss of control (e.g., too much change is done *to* people rather than *by* them); (2) key decisions are sprung literally without warning; (3) organizational members worry about their competence and ability to be effective after the change; (4) legacies of distrust based on past resentments and broken promises can make it difficult to be positive about an impending change; (5) latent effects often disrupt unintended behaviors or plans; (6) more work and pressures are involved, requiring more energy, time, meetings, and learning; (7) the uncertainties about the future create anxiety; and (8) the change brings genuine pain or loss to the individual(s) involved.[43] As will be discussed in Chapter 11, it is necessary, therefore, for managers and executives who are thinking about cultural innovation and change to take these potential sources of resistance into account. Unless carefully envisioned and implemented, even those culture change efforts that are aimed at increased member involvement and improved competitive position in the marketplace can fail.

Culture as Sustained Competitive Advantage

Many organizations are attempting to change their cultures as part of a broader set of strategies intended to encourage innovation, incorporate advanced information technologies, enhance quality and productivity, ensure transparency and compliance with new laws and regulations, and, in general, revitalize their operations. Whether organizations can actually manage their cultures to become a sustained competitive advantage, however, is still unclear.[44] It appears that in order for a company's culture to offer competitive advantages over time, three basic conditions must be met: (1) The culture must enable the organization to undertake activities that lead to economic value, (2) it must be unique or rare relative to other competitors, and (3) it must be "imperfectly imitable" so that competing firms cannot easily change their own cultures to capture the desired characteristics. While the first two conditions reflect the pragmatic view that organizational culture can be used as a managerial tool to improve firm performance, the third point raises a cautionary note. If firms can, in fact, adopt or create a valuable and unique culture, the culture is not "imperfectly imitable"; that is, other firms could develop similar cultures. This research implies that organizations which already have a rare and valuable culture can manage to *sustain* it over time, but firms attempting to develop such cultures will be unable to actually create any sustained competitive advantage since, in principle, any of its competitors could do the same thing.

As environments change, however, organizations as open systems also need to change if they are to ensure a continued fit with their surrounding world. Before an organization can be altered—whether the focus is on structural change, cultural change, or a combination of the two—there has to be some general agreement on what the organization is about—its basic mission, goals, values, and so forth. Different views and perceptions of an organization can readily result in quite disparate goals, psychological contracts, and assumptions as to what is important. As research has indicated, if we are to manage the cognitive processes through which an organization invests its resources for competitive advantage, it is important to attend to the identities that people use to make sense of what they do in relation to the organization and its norms.[45]

Ethical Considerations and Organizational Culture

While the preceding discussion provides a framework for conceptualizing the culture change process, concerns have been raised about whether such managerial tactics are ethical. Critics, for example, view explicit attempts to manage and change an existing culture as insidious and subtle ways of manipulating organizational members and reducing their individual freedom and autonomy.[46] In fact, many of the doubts about changing employee beliefs and values are laden with connotations of "company brainwashing." Although the emphasis is placed on organization-related beliefs and values, not personal ones, the two sets are interrelated. As discussed in Chapter 2, since our beliefs and values are not randomly ordered, a change in one or more of them typically requires changes in related belief and values. Critics also contend that as our workforce becomes increasingly diverse, there is a concomitant obligation to ensure that the cultures of our organizations reflect and appreciate that diversity.[47] Recommendations include creating mechanisms that allow and build on member dissent and diversity (e.g., internal review procedures) and sensitizing managers to be aware of the ethical issues inherent in these efforts.

Despite these concerns and reservations, it is important to underscore that the nature of the manager's job is to influence organizational behavior in a responsible and professional manner.[48] As part of this process, it is necessary to conscientiously shape organizational beliefs and values as appropriate. As research has indicated, upper-level management's ability to create organizational cultures that are consistent with environmental pressures, trends, and underlying expectations has a significant influence on the firm's performance.[49] The key is to channel such culture change efforts into constructive responses to the changing environment, being aware of the ethical concerns involved.

A related issue concerns the extent to which organizational members are forced to violate their individual values by organizational cultural pressures.[50] A growing body of evidence suggests that employees are often placed in situations where unethical or even illegal actions are encouraged, either implicitly or explicitly, by their peers and supervisors. Recent scandals in a growing number of industries suggest that many organizational members can be induced either to directly engage in ethically dubious activities or to provide indirect support by "looking the other way" and failing to report obvious wrongdoings. Since individuals do not exist in a vacuum, it is important for organizations to create cultures that facilitate and support ethical behaviors—through role modeling at the top of the organization, fair treatment of employees, codes of conduct, ethics officers and committees that provide avenues to address ethical concerns, ethics workshops and training, and ethics audits.[51]

Organizational Climate

Although the terms *organizational culture* and *organizational climate* are sometimes used interchangeably, there are important differences between these concepts. *Organizational climate* is a measure of the extent to which people's expectations about what it should be like to work in an organization are being met.[52] As initially conceptualized, organizational climate referred to the psychological environments that people interacted in, and research in this area focused on the individual perceptions of this environment rather than the actual, shared experiences of organizational members.[53] In the context of the preceding discussion, organizational culture is concerned with the *nature* of beliefs and expectations about organizational life, whereas climate is an *indicator* of whether those beliefs and expectations are being fulfilled. It is a summary perception of the organization's atmosphere and environment, and has implications for organizational and job satisfaction, performance, group interaction, and withdrawal behaviors (e.g., absenteeism and turnover).

Although there has been some disagreement as to whether climate is descriptive or evaluative, it appears that it is a bit of both.[54] Many climate researchers, for example, ask people to *describe* what they see in their work environment, rather than explicitly evaluate what they see as "good" or "bad." Climate, however, is a perceptual measure. Since such perceptions can vary across organizational members and may differ from actual organizational conditions, people are really evaluating rather than describing their organizations. Moreover, the strong relationship between measures of climate and measures of job and organizational satisfaction emphasizes its evaluative nature.

There has also been a debate as to whether climate operates as an independent, intervening, or dependent variable.[55] Although some of this confusion can be clarified by differentiating climate and culture, research indicates that climate can be a *dependent variable* (reflecting the fulfillment of cultural expectations), an *independent variable* (such fulfillment leads to feelings of satisfaction in the organization and the job), or an *intervening variable,* for example, perception of a supportive climate that encourages the application of managerial training programs (independent variable) and subsequent performance and satisfaction (dependent variable).

Relationship with Organizational Culture

Climate is generally viewed as a quantifiable concept, while culture is seen as more qualitative and less tangible in nature.[56] As such, climate is frequently measured by questionnaires that are aggregated across individuals to provide a database profile of the organization on a number of different dimensions (e.g., support, warmth, peer relationships, rewards, and relationship between performance and rewards). Different organizational cultures, however, may produce similar climate profiles. Organizational members view their situation depending on their expectations, which are based on the type of psychological contract formed at entry, organizational socialization processes, and their own prior experiences and perceptions of the larger environment. For example, one organization may have a relatively autocratic managerial style and be perceived as autocratic, while another may be more democratic in nature and perceived as such. Yet, responses to the survey statement "My manager involves me in decisions that affect me whenever appropriate" can produce similar ratings in the two organizations. Even though the actual situations and cultures may be quite different, if they are congruent with the nature of employee expectations about what life in the organization *should be like,* aggregate climate profiles will be similar.

ORGANIZATIONAL EFFECTIVENESS

A significant challenge for organizational evaluation efforts is to differentiate between effective and ineffective organizations. Unfortunately, such endeavors often prove to be quite elusive in nature, and researchers often disagree about the most important criteria for making such decisions. Some theorists have even suggested that to a large extent being effective essentially means "doing the right thing as well as doing things right."[57] Thus, given the diverse interpretations of what actually constitutes an effective organization, it is important to understand the different views of organizational effectiveness.

One-Dimensional Views of Effectiveness

As illustrated in Figure 10-5, there are four main, unitary approaches to evaluating organizational effectiveness:[58] Goal accomplishment, system resource, internal processes and operations, and strategic constituencies. Each of these approaches provides some useful guidelines for systematically thinking about organizational effectiveness. None of them, however, is appropriate for all organizations in all situations.

ORGANIZATIONS AS INPUT-PROCESS-OUTPUT SYSTEMS

Input	Conversion Process	Output

System Resources (Resource-based)

Internal Process
- Excellence and competency
- Efficiency

Goal Accomplishment

Strategic Constituencies (Stakeholder Model)

Figure 10-5   Single-Dimension Approaches to Organizational Effectiveness

Goal Accomplishment

The goal accomplishment method is the most widely used approach in assessing organizational effectiveness. The focus is usually on the output of the organization—effectiveness is dictated by the extent to which the organization's output meets its specified goals (e.g., profitability, product volume and quality, market share). Since this model attempts to measure an organization's progress toward fulfilling its goals, it is a logical and intuitively appealing measure of effectiveness. It is most appropriate when organizational goals are clear, consensual, and measurable (e.g., sports teams whose goal is to win games).

Most business organizations, however, have multiple, often conflicting goals that make decisions about goal effectiveness problematic at best.[59] For instance, consider the manager who wants her firm to obtain a substantial profit, while also growing in size, ensuring future profit through product improvements and developments, avoiding financial risk, paying a considerable dividend to investors, having satisfied employees, operating in a socially responsible manner, and being respected in the surrounding community. Obviously, it would be impossible to maximize all of these goals at the same time; "trade-offs" between such goals are typically made on an ongoing basis. Similarly, the increased focused on supply chain management typically involves tensions between cost-cutting and building flexibility in the supply chain. As such conflicts suggest, there are often differences between an organization's *official goals* (i.e., its basic mission, what it should be doing) and its *operative goals* (i.e., operating practices, what the organization actually does).[60]

Another limitation of this approach concerns the nature of the goals themselves. For instance, if an organization's goals are too low, it might achieve them, but does that necessarily mean that the organization is really effective? A relative problem concerns the level of subjectivity associated with many goals, such as being a socially responsible organization, enhancing employee morale, or ensuring the continued development of the firm's managers. Finally, an organization's goals may raise legal or ethical questions that can create significant problems even though it may have accomplished those goals. Microsoft's recent antitrust case is a good example. By incorporating its Internet browser in its operating system, Microsoft set out to dominate the industry and drive Netscape out of business. As our judicial system determined, however, Microsoft acted like a monopoly and engaged in unfair competitive practices, limiting the ability of computer companies and consumers to customize their machines.

System Resource

The system resource perspective views effectiveness as the extent to which an organization is able to acquire the resources needed to accomplish its goals. The focus is thus on organizational inputs rather than outputs—effectiveness is determined by the extent to which the organization is able to obtain needed resources from its external environment. This model is most appropriate for organizations that have a clear connection between their resources and their production (e.g., the more depositors a bank can generate, the more profitable it can be). It can also be used to compare organizations that have different goals. Examples of the types of measures that are used with this method include an organization's ability to:[61] (1) acquire scarce and valued resources; (2) perceive and correctly interpret the actual environment (see Chapter 8); and (3) respond to changes in its environment.

While the system resource approach provides an alternative perspective on organizational effectiveness, an underlying problem is that it provides a limited, input-based view of organizations.[62] Studies have also raised questions as to whether the acquisition of resources per se is as important as the actual use and implementation of those resources. In many instances, the flow of resources into an organization is not necessarily related to how the resources are used or to the successful accomplishment of output goals.

Internal Processes and Operations

A third perspective on organizational effectiveness focuses on internal organizational dynamics, emphasizing organizational health (harmony, competency, excellence) and efficiency (use of resources). Specific indicators might include interdepartmental cooperation and collaboration, team spirit and morale, employee-management trust and an efficient use of time, money, and people. The greater the extent to which an organization has such characteristics, the "healthier" and more effective it is thought to be. This technique is most appropriate when these dynamics are closely related to the organization's primary task.

The internal processes approach is useful since the efficient utilization of resources and agreeable relations between organizational members are important indicators of an effective organization. Moreover, similar to the systems resource method, it can be used to compare organizations with different goals and objectives. This technique, however, also provides a limited view of organizations because it omits outputs and the relationship with the larger environment, in essence providing a "closed system" perspective. Moreover, there is a high level of subjectivity with respect to the typical indicators noted above (e.g., measuring interdepartmental collaboration). Finally, while economists typically equate internal efficiency with organizational "health" and effectiveness (i.e., the most effective organizations are those that have the smoothest internal processes and produce the least waste), over the long term apparent inefficiencies can contribute to effectiveness. Long-term adaptation and innovation, for example, are often enhanced by inter-unit conflict and organizational slack (i.e., unused resources), indicators that would suggest an ineffective organization.

Strategic Constituencies (Stakeholders)

The final single-dimension approach, sometimes referred to as the reputational model, defines effectiveness as the degree to which an organization's key stakeholders are at least minimally satisfied with the organization. Effectiveness is thus determined by the extent to which an organization is able to respond to the demands and expectations of its primary stakeholders and achieve a satisfactory balance among them. Criteria include such varied concerns as return on investment (owners), satisfaction with work and compensation (employees), satisfaction with the quality and cost of goods and services (customers), contribution to community affairs and health (local community), and compliance with laws and regulations (government officials). This approach is most appropriate in situations where an organization's stakeholders have a potent influence on the organization's operations or when an organization's primary task is to react to constituency demands (e.g., a state legislature).

This method takes a broader view of effectiveness than the preceding three in that it: (1) includes the concept of social responsibility and obligation to others and (2) recognizes that different groups and stakeholders can have varied goals. The overall utility of the strategic constituencies approach, however, is also limited in evaluating an organization's effectiveness. Although the underlying assumption is that organizations will be more effective if they can at least minimally satisfy the demands of their relevant stakeholders, organizations can still be effective even when they ignore these demands or act in opposition to them. Within this context, an underlying question concerns the relative importance of different stakeholders, a reality that may influence organizations to only pay attention to a restricted set of these groups. Organizations have a variety of constituents, including industry peers and competitors, customers, suppliers, and regulators, each of whom evaluate the organization based on activities most relevant to them.[63] Successful firms appear to recognize such stakeholder interests, focus on the most important of these stakeholder groups, and adopt practices and structures that legitimize them with those particular constituents. Moreover, the strategic constituencies view assumes that the valued goals of these different groups make sense for the organization and other stakeholders, and that they can be "balanced" in a rational and satisfactory manner.[64]

Competing Values and Organizational Effectiveness

As the previous discussion indicates, organizational effectiveness involves a number of different dimensions and considerations. No single measure or indicator can truly depict an organization's overall effectiveness. Thus, much like the contingency theories of leadership and organization design discussed earlier, there is no "one best" criterion that can be used to evaluate organizational effectiveness. An effort to empirically integrate the numerous criteria reflected in the organizational effectiveness and performance literature, however, has led to the creation of an alternative model, referred to as the *competing values approach*.[65]

The competing values method emerged from a series of studies in which organizational theorists were asked to make judgments about the similarity of different organizational performance criteria. Using multidimensional scaling techniques, three dimensions or continua emerged:

1. **Control-flexibility.** Related to organizational structure, this dimension indicates the extent to which the organization places an emphasis on control (stability, order, and predictability) or flexibility (innovation, adaptation, and change).

2. **Internal-external.** The second dimension reflects the organization's focus, ranging from an internal emphasis on coordination and organizational members to an external emphasis stressing fit with the environment and the development of the overall organization.

3. **Means-ends.** The final dimension reflects different emphases on important processes and procedures (e.g., planning, goal setting) and final outcomes (e.g., productivity, profitability).

As illustrated in Figure 10-6, based on these different dimensions four different models of organizational effectiveness emerge: (1) The *human relations model* (defined by maintenance of the social system, human commitment, and decentralization-differentiation) emphasizes the development of a highly cohesive and skilled workforce; (2) the *open-systems model* (defined by decentralization-differentiation, expansion-adaptation, and the competitive position of the overall system) stresses flexibility and the ability to acquire resources; (3) the *rational-goal model* (defined by competitive position of the overall system, maximization of output, and centralization-integration) accentuates planning, efficiency, and productivity; and (4) the *internal process model* (defined by centralization-integration, consolidation-continuity, and maintenance of the social system) highlights the dissemination of information, stability, and order. This framework essentially clarifies the values that are implicit in each view of effectiveness, and juxtaposes each perspective in relation to the others.

The four quadrants illustrated in Figure 10-6 capture the conflicts or competing values inherent in organizational life.[66] While we typically want our organizations to be adaptable and flexible, we also desire stability and control; although we want growth, resource acquisition, and support from external stakeholders, we also seek tight information management and formal communications within our organizations; we want to stress the value and importance of our human resources, but we also want to emphasize rational planning and goal setting. An underlying problem is that managers often think of these four approaches as distinctly different from each other, to the point where they may even appear to be mutually exclusive. In a given situation, however, effectiveness may demand approaches that reflect both the caring orientation of the human-relations model *and* the demanding, goal orientation of the rational-goal model, or positions that simultaneously advocate change and stability. By understanding that seemingly contrasting approaches may occur concurrently, this model can help managers "reframe" their understandings of a given situation and more fully prepare themselves to deal with the complexities of managerial and organizational life.

Since the competing values paradigm has been operationalized in a set of questionnaire measures that reflect the means-ends performance criteria in the four models,

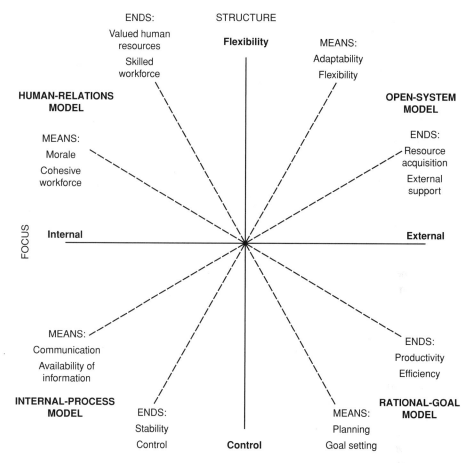

ENDS:
Valued human
resources
Skilled
workforce

STRUCTURE

Flexibility

MEANS:
Adaptability
Flexibility

**HUMAN-RELATIONS
MODEL**

**OPEN-SYSTEM
MODEL**

MEANS:
Morale
Cohesive
workforce

ENDS:
Resource
acquisition
External
support

FOCUS

Internal

External

MEANS:
Communication
Availability of
information

ENDS:
Productivity
Efficiency

**INTERNAL-PROCESS
MODEL**

ENDS:
Stability
Control

Control

MEANS:
Planning
Goal setting

**RATIONAL-GOAL
MODEL**

Figure 10-6   Competing Values Approach to Organizational Effectiveness

Source: Adapted from R.E. Quinn and J. Rohrbaugh, "A Spatial Model of Effectiveness Criteria: Toward a Competing Values Approach to Organizational Analysis," *Management Science,* Vol. 28, 1983, pp. 363–377.

it can be used as a diagnostic and intervention tool.[67] Based on these questionnaire measures, managers can assess their firm's performance, changes in that performance over time, and how different individuals and groups perceive the organization. Moreover, unlike the one-dimensional models discussed earlier, this approach does not impose a desired performance profile of the organization. Thus, it overcomes the potential deficiencies of simply using goal accomplishment, internal processes, resource attainment, or stakeholder satisfaction as a measure of the overall effectiveness of the firm.

The competing values framework is increasingly being used to understand the effectiveness of other aspects of OB, including managerial communication, leadership and managerial competency, the performance of expert teams, group decision processes, and ethical codes.[68] The dualistic nature of organizational needs is further reflected in recent work on organizational strategy and structure.[69] Organizational effectiveness is increasingly viewed in terms of the ability to successfully manage the contradictory internal forces that can literally tear organizations apart, as when initially healthy internal competition turns into dysfunctional departmental politics or pressures for efficiency begin to suppress innovation. As such, effective organizations create their own solutions to problems by understanding and working through the interaction between the multiple conflicting forces that exist in them and the different forms that they can take.

CONCLUSION

The last three chapters have taken a broad view of the main areas encompassed by macro-OB. As this discussion has indicated, the focus on these macro-dimensions of organizational life has been stimulated by ongoing changes in the larger environment and within organizations themselves. As the environment and organizations continue to evolve and change, it is clear that we do not have all the answers to the myriad questions posed by these concerns. It is also clear that the field of OB will continue to evolve and focus on defining and understanding the problems facing organizations and their management.

NOTES

1.   See A.F. Buono, J.L. Bowditch, and J.W. Lewis, "When Cultures Collide: The Anatomy of a Merger," *Human Relations* 38, no. 5 (1985): 477–500; T.E. Deal and A.A. Kennedy, *Corporate Cultures: The Rites and Rituals of Corporate Life* (Reading, MA: Addison-Wesley, 1982); A.M. Pettigrew, "On Studying Organizational Culture," *Administrative Science Quarterly* 24, no. 4 (1979): 570–581; R.S. Bhagat and S.J. McQuaid, "Role of Subjective Culture in Organizations: A Review and Directions for Future Research," *Journal of Applied Psychology* 67, no. 5 (1982): 653–685; H. Schwartz and S.M. Davis, "Matching Corporate Culture and Business Strategy," *Organizational Dynamics* (Summer 1981): 30–48; and S. Hindus, "Transparency and There Again: Lessons Learned at Digital," *Journal of Management Development* 25, no. 10 (2006): 1007–1012.

2.   See R.R. Sims and J. Brinkmann, "Enron Ethics (Or: Culture Matters More Than Codes)," *Journal of Business Ethics* 45, no. 3 (2003): 243–256.

3.   This discussion is adapted from H.M. Trice and J.M. Beyer, *The Cultures of Work*

Organizations (Englewood Cliffs, NJ: Prentice Hall, 1993), pp. 5–12.

4.   J. Martin, *Organization Culture: Mapping the Terrain* (Thousand Oaks, CA: Sage, 2002) refers to the ambiguities associated with organizational culture as the "fragmented" view of culture where there is relatively little in the way of consensus among organizational members about beliefs, values and attitudes.

5.   See L. Ford and A. Seers, "Relational Leadership and Team Climates: Pitting Differentiation versus Agreement," *The Leadership Quarterly* 17 (2006): 258–270.

6.   H. Mintzberg, "The Effective Organization: Forces and Forms," *Sloan Management Review* 32, no. 2 (1991): 64; and R. Charan, "Conquering a Culture of Indecision," *Harvard Business Reivew* 84, no. 1 (2006): 108–117.

7.   See E. Schein, *The Corporate Culture Survival Guide* (San Francisco: Jossey-Bass, 1999), p. 5; and E. Schein, P.J. Kampas, P.S. Delisi, and M.M. Sonduck, *DEC Is Dead, Long Live DEC: The Lasting Legacy of Digital Equipment Corporation* (San Francisco: Berrett-Koehler, 2004).

8. Deal and Kennedy, *Corporate Cultures*.

9. T.E. Deal and A.A. Kennedy, "Culture: A New Look through Old Lenses," *Journal of Applied Behavioral Science* 19, no. 4 (1983): 503.

10. For a concise summary of this research, see Trice and Beyer, op. cit., pp. 15–17. See also Martin, *Organization Culture* and her categorization of these different models as integration, differentiation, and fragmentation perspectives.

11. A.F. Buono and J.L. Bowditch, *The Human Side of Mergers and Acquisitions* (San Francisco: Jossey-Bass, 1989).

12. T.E. Deal and A.A. Kennedy, *The New Corporate Cultures: Revitalizing the Workplace after Downsizing, Mergers and Reengineering* (Reading, MA: Persus Books, 1999), pp. 12–16.

13. B. Vlasic and B.A. Stertz, *Taken for a Ride: How Daimler-Benz Drove Off with Chrysler* (New York: HarperCollins, 1991); and M. Landler, "Chrysler Sale Unavoidable, Zetsche Says," *New York Times*, May 15, 2007, pp. C1, C5.

14. See Buono, Bowditch, and Lewis, op. cit.; L. Smircich, "Concepts of Culture and Organizational Analysis," *Administrative Science Quarterly* 28, no. 3 (1983): 339–358; and A.L. Wilkins, "The Creation of Company Cultures: The Role of Stories and Human Resource Systems," *Human Resource Management* 23, no. 1 (1984): 41–60.

15. T.J. Peters, "Management Systems: The Language of Organizational Character and Competence," *Organizational Dynamics* (Summer 1980): 3–27.

16. J. Martin and C. Siehl, "Organizational Culture and Counterculture: An Uneasy Symbiosis," *Organizational Dynamics* 12, no. 2 (1983): 52–64; A.L. Wilkins, "The Culture Audit: A Tool for Understanding Organizations," *Organizational Dynamics* 12 (1983): 24–38; and H. Trice and D. Morand, "Cultural Diversity: Organizational Subcultures and Countercultures," in G. Miller, ed., *Studies in Organizational Sociology: Essays in Honor of Charles K. Warriner* (Greenwich, CT: JAI Press, 1991), pp. 69–105.

17. See P. Lok and J. Crawford, "Antecedents of Organizational Commitment and the Mediating Role of Job Satisfaction," *Journal of Managerial Psychology* 16, no. 7/8 (2001): 594–613; E. Ogbonna and L.C. Harris, "Organisational Culture in the Age of the Internet: An Exploratory Study," *New Technology, Work & Employment* 21, no. 2 (2006): 162–175; and T. Aherns and M. Mollona, "Organisational Control as Cultural Practice: A Shop Floor Ethnography of a Sheffield Steel Mill," *Accounting, Organizations & Society* 32, no. 4/5 (2007): 305–331.

18. Martin and Siehl, "Organizational Culture and Counterculture."

19. V.J. Sathe, *Culture and Related Corporate Realities* (Homewood, IL: Irwin, 1985).

20. See J.C. Huang, S. Newell, R.D. Galliers, and S. Pan, "Dangerous Liaisons? Component-Based Development and Organizational Subcultures," *IEEE Transactions on Engineering Management* 50, no. 1 (2003): 89–99.

21. J.M. Yinger, *Countercultures* (New York: Free Press, 1982); and P. Braunstein and M.W. Doyle, eds., *Imagine Nation: The American Counterculture of the 1960s and 1970s* (NY: Routledge, 2002).

22. Yinger, *Countercultures*, p. 25. See also P. Taylor and P. Bain, "'Subterranean Worksick Blues': Humour as Subversion in Two Call Centres," *Organization Studies* 24, no. 9 (2003): 1487–1509.

23. V.J. Sathe, "Implications of Corporate Culture: A Manager's Guide to Action," *Organizational Dynamics* 12 (Autumn 1983): 12–13.

24. R.T. Pascale, "The Paradox of 'Corporate Culture': Reconciling Ourselves to Socialization," *California Management Review* 27, no. 2 (1985): 26–41; and Sathe, *Culture and Related Corporate Realities*.

25. This discussion is synthesized from Deal and Kennedy, *Corporate Cultures*; M. Jelinek, L. Smircich, and P. Hirsch, "Introduction: A Code of Many Colors," *Administrative Science Quarterly* 28, no. 3 (1983): 331–338; Sathe, *Culture and Related Corporate Realities*; and E. Schein, *Organizational Culture and Leadership*, 2nd ed. (San Francisco: Jossey-Bass, 1992). For an illustrative application, see C. Homburg and

C. Pflesser, "A Multiple-Layer Model of Market-Oriented Organizational Culture: Measurement Issues and Performance," *Journal of Marketing Research* 37, no. 4 (2000): 449–462; and J.M. Higgins, C. McAllaster, S.C. Serto, and J.P. Gilbert, "Using Cultural Artifacts to Change and Perpetuate Strategy," *Journal of Change Management* 6, no. 4 (2006): 397–415.

26. Wilkins, op. cit.; and D.M. Bjoe, "Stories of the Storytelling Organization: A Postmodern Analysis of Disney as 'Tamara-Land,'" *Academy of Management Journal* 38, no. 4 (1995): 997–1035.

27. Schein, *Organizational Culture and Leadership*; and S. Zamanou and S.R. Glaser, "Moving Toward Participation and Involvement: Managing and Measuring Organizational Culture," *Group & Organization Management* 19, no. 4 (1994): 475–502.

28. See H. Mintzberg, "The Effective Organization," p. 64.

29. A.L. Wilkins and N.J. Bristow, "For Successful Organizational Culture, Honor Your Past," *Academy of Management Executive* 1, no. 3 (1987): 221–228; and H. Trice and J. Beyer, "The Routinization of Charisma in Two Social Movements," in B.M. Staw and L.L. Cummings, eds., *Research in Organizational Behavior*, vol. 7 (Greenwich, CT: JAI Press, 1985).

30. Schein, *Organizational Culture and Leadership*.

31. This discussion is based on Sathe, *Culture and Related Corporate Realities*, pp. 386–395.

32. See E. Aronson, *The Social Animal* (San Francisco: Freeman, 1976); D.J. Bem, *Beliefs, Attitudes, and Human Affairs* (Monterey, CA: Brooks/Cole, 1970); and P.G. Zimbardo, E.B. Ebbesen, and C. Maslach, *Influencing Attitudes and Changing Behavior*, 2nd ed. (Reading, MA: Addison-Wesley, 1977).

33. For a good illustration of how such behavior change can contribute to culture change, see R.O. Esler and D.A. Nipp, "Worker Designed Culture Change," *Nursing Economics* 19, no. 4 (2001): 161–164.

34. See E. Schein, "Personal Change Through Interpersonal Relations," in W.G. Bennis et al., eds., *Interpersonal Dynamics* (Homewood, IL: Dorsey Press, 1973).

35. For an illustration of managing with values, see S.L. Dolan and S. Garcia, "Managing by Values: Cultural Redesign for Strategic Organizational Change at the Dawn of the Twenty-First Century," *Journal of Management Development* 21, no. 2 (2002): 101–117.

36. P.C. Reynolds, "Imposing a Corporate Culture," *Psychology Today* (March 1987): 33–38.

37. R.J. Greene, "Culturally Compatible HR Strategies," *HR Magazine* 40, no. 6 (1995): 115–123.

38. M.O. Bice, "The Transformation of Lutheran Health Systems," in R.H. Kilmann, T.J. Covin, and Associates, *Corporate Transformation: Revitalizing Organizations for a Competitive World* (San Francisco: Jossey-Bass, 1988), pp. 435–450.

39. J. Falvey, "Best Corporate Culture Is a Melting Pot," *Wall Street Journal*, April 6, 1987, p. 28.

40. Pascale, "The Paradox of 'Corporate Culture.'"

41. Schein, *Corporate Culture Survival Guide*, see Chapter 4.

42. Sathe, *Culture and Related Corporate Realities*, p. 383.

43. R.M. Kanter, B.A. Stein, and T.D. Jick, *The Challenge of Organizational Change* (New York: Free Press, 1992), pp. 380–381.

44. See, for example, W. Mastenbroek, "A Dynamic Concept of Revitalization," *Organizational Dynamics* 16, no. 4 (1988): 52–61; J. Barney, "Organizational Culture: Can It Be a Source of Sustained Competitive Advantage?" *Academy of Management Review* 11, no. 3 (1986): 656–665; R. Reed and R.J. DeFillippi, "Causal Ambiguity, Barriers to Imitation, and Sustainable Competitive Advantage," *Academy of Management Review* 15, no. 1 (1991): 191–211; and L. Chan and M.A. Shaffer, "In Search of Sustained Competitive Advantage: The Impact of Organizational Culture, Competitive Strategy and Human Resource Management Practices on Firm Performance," *International Journal of Human Resource Management* 15, no. 1 (2004): 17–35.

45. C.M. Fiol, "Managing Culture as a Competitive Resource: An Identity-Based View of Sustainable Competitive Advantage," *Journal of Management* 17, no. 1 (1991): 191–211. For an interesting discussion of the critical role that human resource professionals can play in this process, see M.L. Lengnick-Hall and C.A. Lengnick-Hall, "HR's Role in Building Relationship Networks," *Academy of Management Executive* 17, no. 4 (2003): 53–63.

46. See Trice and Beyer, *The Cultures of Work Organizations*, pp. 370–372; and Sathe, *Culture and Related Corporate Realities*, pp. 380–381.

47. See B.B. Bunker, "Appreciating Diversity and Modifying Organizational Cultures: Men and Women at Work," in S. Srivastva, D.L. Cooperrider and Associates, *Appreciative Management and Leadership: The Power of Positive Thought and Action in Organizations* (San Francisco: Jossey-Bass, 1990), pp. 126–149.

48. See Trice and Beyer, *The Cultures of Work Organizations*, pp. 370–372; and Sathe, *Culture and Related Corporate Realities*, pp. 380–381.

49. See I. Goll and R.B. Sambharya, "The Effect of Organizational Culture and Leadership on Firm Performance," in P. Shrivastava and R.B. Lamb, eds., *Advances in Strategic Management*, vol. 6 (Greenwich, CT: JAI Press, 1990), pp. 183–200; J. Barney, "Looking Inside for Competitive Advantage," *Academy of Management Executive* 9, no. 4 (1995): 49–61; and R.R. Sims and J. Brinkmann, "Leaders as Moral Role Models: The Case of John Gutfreund at Salmon Brothers," *Journal of Business Ethics* 35, no. 4 (2002): 327–339.

50. See Trice and Beyer, *The Cultures of Work Organizations*, p. 372.

51. See W.M. Hoffman, "A Blueprint for Corporate Ethical Development," in E.J. Trunfio, B.C. Auday, and M.A. Reid, eds., *Developing Moral Corporate Cultures* (Wenham, MA: Gordon College Institute for Applied Ethics, 1992), pp. 37–60; A.F. Buono, "Developing Moral Corporate Cultures in a Downsized, Restructured World," in W.M. Hoffman and R.E. Frederick, eds., *Business Ethics*, 3rd ed. (New York: McGraw-Hill, 1995),

pp. 226–233; and K. Cravens, E.G. Oliver, and S. Ramamoorti, "The Reputation Index: Measuring and Managing Corporate Reputation," *European Management Journal* 21, no. 2 (2003): 200–212.

52. Schwartz and Davis, op. cit., pp. 32–34; W.F. Joyce and J.W. Slocum, Jr., "Climates in Organizations," in S. Kerr, ed., *Organizational Behavior* (Columbus: Grid Publications, 1979), pp. 317–333; B. Schneider, ed., *Organizational Climate and Culture* (San Francisco: Jossey-Bass, 1990); B. Schneider, S.K. Gunnarson, and K. Niles-Jolly, "Creating the Climate and Culture of Success," *Organizational Dynamics* 23, no. 1 (1994): 17–29; M.A. Shadur, R. Kienzle, and J.J. Rodwell, "The Relationship Between Organizational Climate and Employee Perceptions of Involvement," *Group & Organization Management* 24, no. 4 (1999): 479–503; C. Glisson and L.R. James, "The Cross-Level Effects of Culture and Climate in Human Service Teams," *Journal of Organizational Behavior* 23, no. 6 (2002): 767–783; and E. Sopow, "The Impact of Culture and Climate on Change," *Strategic HR Review* 6, no. 2 (2007): 20–23.

53. See Trice and Beyer, *The Cultures of Work Organizations*, pp. 19–20.

54. B. Schneider, "Organizational Climates: An Essay," *Personnel Psychology* 28, no. 4 (1975): 447–480; J.E. Newman, "Development of a Measure of Perceived Work Environment (PWE)," *Academy of Management Journal* 20 (1977): 520–534; M.A. Shadur, R. Kienzle, and J.J. Rodwell, "The Relationship between Organizational Climate and Employee Perceptions of Involvement," *Group & Organization Management* 24, no. 4 (1999): 479–503; and S.G. Bednar, "Elements of Satisfying Organizational Climates in Child Welfare Agencies," *Families in Society* 84, no. 1 (2003): 7–12.

55. For an overview of this debate see Joyce and Slocum, op. cit., pp. 325–331; and D. Hellriegel and J.W. Slocum, "Organizational Climate: Measures, Research, and Contingencies," *Academy of Management Journal* 17 (1974): 225–280. For an illustration of the different ways in which climate can operate as an independent or dependent variable, see R.D. Pathak, V.S. Chauhan, U. Dhar,

D.M. Pestonjee and R. Reddy, "Effect of Personal and Situational Variables on Managerial Effectiveness: An Empirical Study," *International Journal of Management* 19, no. 1 (2002): 27–37.

56. See, for example, A.J. McMurray, "The Relationship between Organizational Climate and Organizational Culture," *Journal of American Academy of Business* 3, no. 1/2 (2003): 1–8.

57. Mintzberg, "The Effective Organization," p. 54.

58. The discussion of the four organizational effectiveness models is adapted from K. Cameron, "Critical Questions in Assessing Organizational Effectiveness," in P.L. Wright and S. Robbins, eds., *Organization Theory: Readings and Cases* (Englewood Cliffs, NJ: Prentice Hall, 1987), pp. 16–31. For an application to not-for-profit organizations, see D.F. Forbes, "Measuring the Unmeasurable: Empirical Studies of Nonprofit Organizational Effectiveness from 1977 to 1997," *Nonprofit and Voluntary Sector Quarterly* 27, no. 2 (1998): 183–202.

59. See S.E. Seashore, "Criteria of Organizational Effectiveness," in L.E. Boone and D.D. Bowen, eds., *The Great Writings in Management and Organizational Behavior* (Tulsa, OK: PPC Books, 1980), pp. 432–433; W.Q. Judge, Jr., "Correlates of Organizational Effectiveness: A Multilevel Analysis of a Multidimensional Outcome," *Journal of Business Ethics* 13, no. 1 (1994): 1–10; and J. Balijko, "Agents of Change Challenged by Layoffs, Shrinking Budgets," *EBN*, January 27 (2003): 1.

60. C. Perrow, "The Analysis of Goals in Complex Organizations," *American Sociological Review* 26 (1961): 854–866. For a current application in the not-for-profit sector, see M.K. Meyers, N.M. Riccucci and I. Lurie, "Achieving Goal Congruence in Complex Organizations: The Case of Welfare Reform," *Journal of Public Administration Research and Theory* 11, no. 2 (2001): 165–201.

61. J.B. Cunningham, "A Systems-Resource Approach to Organizational Effectiveness," *Human Relations* 31 (1978): 631–656.

62. Daft, op. cit., pp. 103–104; and G.J. Castrogiovanni, "Environmental Munifi-

cence: A Theoretical Assessment," *Academy of Management Review* 16 (1991): 542–565.

63. M.C. Suchman, "Managing Legitimacy: Strategic and Institutional Approaches," *Academy of Management Review* 20 (1995): 571–610; and D.L. Deephouse, "Does Isomorphism Legitimate?" *Academy of Management Journal* 39 (1996): 1024–1039.

64. For an interesting critique of problems with such stakeholder analyses, see R.E. Freeman and D.R. Gilbert, *Corporate Strategy and the Search for Ethics* (Englewood Cliffs, NJ: Prentice Hall, 1988), Chapter 4; and J.F. Mahon and S.L. Wartick, "Dealing with Stakeholders: How Reputation, Credibility and Framing Influence the Game," *Corporate Reputation Review* 6, no. 1 (2003): 19–35.

65. The discussion and application of the Competing Values Approach is adapted from R.E. Quinn and J. Rorbaugh, "A Competing Values Approach to Organizational Effectiveness," *Public Productivity Review* 5 (1981): 122–140; R.E. Quinn and M.R. McGrath, "Moving Beyond the Single Solution Perspective: The Competing Values Approach as a Diagnostic Tool," *Journal of Applied Behavioral Science* 18 (1982): 463–472; and M.R. McGrath, "An Application of the Competing Values Approach to Organizational Analysis as a Diagnostic Tool," in J.A. Pearce and R.B. Robinson, eds., *Academy of Management Proceedings 1984*, pp. 254–257. See also K.S. Cameron and R. Quinn, *Diagnosing and Changing Organizational Culture: Based on the Competing Values Framework* (San Francisco: Jossey-Bass, 2005).

66. The following discussion is drawn from R.E. Quinn, H.W. Hildebrandt, P.S. Rogers, and M.O. Thompson, "A Competing Values Framework for Analyzing Presentational Communication in Management Contexts," *The Journal of Business Communication* 28, no. 3 (1991): 217–218.

67. See R.E. Quinn and M.R. McGrath, "Moving Beyond the Single Solution Perspective: The Competing Values Approach as a Diagnostic Tool," *Journal of Applied Behavioral Science* 18 (1982): 463–472; M.P. Thompson, M.R. McGrath, and J. Wharton, "The Competing Values Approach," *Public Productivity Review* 2 (1981): 188–200; P. Rogers and

H. Hildebrandt, "Competing Values Instruments for Analyzing Written and Spoken Management Messages," *Human Resource Management* 32, no. 1 (1993): 121–143; G.B. Jordan, L.D. Streit, and J.S. Binkley, "Assessing and Improving the Effectiveness of National Research Laboratories," *IEEE Transactions on Engineering Management* 50, no. 2 (2003): 228–235; and D. Lee and R.S. Brower, "Pushing the Envelope on Organizational Effectiveness: Combining an Old Framework and a Sharp Tool," *Public Performance & Management Review* 30, no. 2 (2006): 155–178.

68. See R.E. Quinn, Hildebrandt, Rogers, and Thompson, ibid.; R.E. Quinn, S.R. Saerman, M.P. Thompson, and M.R. McGrath, *Becoming a Master Manager: A Competency Framework*, 2nd ed. (New York: Wiley, 1996); P. Reagan and J. Rohrbaugh, "Group Decision Process Effectiveness: A Competing Values Approach," *Group & Organization Studies* 15, no. 1 (1990): 20–43; B. Stevens, "Using the Competing Values Framework to Assess Corporate Ethical Codes," *Journal of Business Communication* 33, no. 1 (1996): 71–84; A.S. Dunk and A.F. Lysons, "An Analysis of Departmental Effectiveness, Participative Budgetary Control Process and Environmental Dimensionality within the Competing Values Framework: A Public Sector Study," *Financial Accountability & Management* 13, no. 1 (1997): 1–16; R. Cacioppe, "An Integrated Model and Approach for the Design of Effective Leadership Programs," *Leadership & Organization Development Journal* 19, no. 1 (1998): 44–54; and T. Vilkinas and G. Cartan, "The Integrated Competing Values Framework: Its Spatial Configuration," *Journal of Management Development* 25, no. 6 (2006): 505–521.

69. See Mintzberg, "The Effective Organization," pp. 54–67.

Organization Development and Change

As the previous chapters have indicated, our understanding of human behavior has been greatly enhanced by the development and refinement of a number of theoretical frameworks. In addition to these conceptual models, the increasing number and sophistication of empirical research studies have further contributed to our overall knowledge of this area. As illustrated by the managerial applications interspersed throughout the book, however, the full utility of OB theory is in its actual application in organizations. Moreover, as ongoing work has underscored, our understanding of sources of sustained competitive advantage and effective strategic change is dependent on our understanding of fundamental OB concepts that underlie such phenomena as active listening, trust building, teamwork, and organizational culture.[1]

An integrative theme throughout this book is the idea of organizational competency. How can business organizations become more *effective* (e.g., improving internal processes, attaining goals, managing stakeholders) and more *efficient* (e.g., controlling the financial and psychological costs associated with these goals and processes) in rapidly changing environments? As a way of responding to this question, the concluding chapter will draw on the material covered thus far and explore the areas of organization development and organizational change, including the challenges posed by organizational consolidation and retrenchment and the continued growth of information technology in the workplace.

ORGANIZATION DEVELOPMENT

One of the main areas in which OB theory has been put into action is the field of organization development (OD), a process through which planned and systematic attention is given to developing greater organizational competence, improving organizational effectiveness, and enhancing organizational functioning in general. The foundations of OD in the United States emerged during the mid-1940s from two basic sources: (1) laboratory training and (2) survey research and feedback.[2] A central influence in both of these areas was Kurt Lewin's work in developing a field theory of social psychology and his interest in applied behavioral science. Although Lewin died before the field of OD was formally established in the mid-1950s, his legacy is intellectual (many of today's frameworks have been influenced by his work), personal (e.g., he worked with many influential social psychologists early in their careers, including Ronald Lippett and Kenneth Benne), and institutional (e.g., he was co-founder of the Research Center for Group Dynamics at MIT and the journal *Human Relations*).[3]

Laboratory Training

Laboratory training involves unstructured small-group activities in which participants learn from their own interactions and the evolving dynamics of their group in order to facilitate change—in attitudes and behavior—in "back home" situations. Lewin, who had established the Committee on Community Interrelations of the American Jewish Congress, worked closely with the Connecticut Interracial Commission, undertaking research and training for community leaders. A series of workshops were designed that brought various community leaders together to discuss their problems while researchers observed and assessed the interactions of the groups. Based on these observations, the first *T-group* was formed to feed back this information to group participants and to examine how group members reacted to data about their own behavior. As a result of this experience, the researchers drew two main conclusions about the process: (1) Feedback of information about group interaction is a rich learning experience, and (2) the process of "group building" had potential for learning that could be transferred to organizational situations.

Based on this initial experience, the Office of Naval Research and the National Education Association financed continued work in this area and the National Training Laboratories (NTL) at Bethel, Maine, was created. Although there were a number of problems and frustrations involving the transfer of skills from T-group experiences to actual organizational situations, the training of teams from the same organization is linked with today's focus on the total organization.

During the 1950s, three main trends developed: (1) the emergence of regional training laboratories, which began to conduct year-round sessions; (2) the expansion of T-group training into business and industry; and (3) the growing emphasis on intergroup as well as interpersonal relations. Subsequently, T-groups, which were often referred to as "development groups," were increasingly used in organizational training efforts. Thus, based on this intervention and many of the insights that emerged during this period, OD emerged as a new approach to organizational improvement.

Survey Research and Feedback

The second major thrust in the history of OD, which parallels the laboratory-training stem, is the use of attitude surveys and data feedback sessions. The application of survey research in organizations also evolved from the work of Kurt Lewin and the Research Center for Group Dynamics, which he founded at MIT in 1945. Following Lewin's death in 1947, his staff moved to Michigan to join with the University of Michigan's Survey Research Center to form the Institute for Social Research.

An early example of this type of research was the work of Floyd Mann at the Detroit Edison Company during the late 1940s and early 1950s.[4] Mann and his associates began a systematic feedback of data from an organizationwide management and employee attitude survey. The process that emerged, which was referred to as an "interlocking chain of conferences," involved reporting the survey's major findings to the top management group and then to other involved groups down the organization's hierarchy. The feedback sessions were conducted in task groups, with each supervisor and immediate subordinates discussing the data together. Based on this experience, it was concluded that intensive group discussions of the information generated by an employee survey could be an effective tool for introducing positive change in organizations, especially since it dealt with the system of human relations as a whole.

Managerial Application

As one of the principal methodologies in OD, survey feedback programs have gained increased prominence in contemporary business organizations. On a more general level, survey feedback has also been suggested as a way for improving overall organizational effectiveness, for forming data-based profiles of organizational climate, for enlightening management-labor relations, and for establishing a pragmatic approach to dealing with people-related problems in the workplace.[5]

Survey feedback consists of the collection of data from a specific work unit or total organization through the use of a structured questionnaire. The data generated from this questionnaire are summarized, fed back to the participants through reports and workshops, and ultimately used by different groups and managers to confront existing and potential organizational problems.[6] The initial survey feedback approach employed a standardized questionnaire for data collection.[7] Since this type of instrument is prepackaged and based on a theoretical framework, it has usually been through an extensive validity testing process. Thus, there is a high degree of confidence that the questions are generating data about the specific issues on which they are focused. Since the survey items are prepackaged, however, questions sometimes overlook issues that are important and emphasize others that may be relatively minor in nature for that particular organization. Research has indicated that although these types of "canned" instruments can be highly efficient, surveys that reflect a greater familiarity with key issues for a particular organization seem to achieve better information in terms of both its quality and quantity.[8]

One approach to survey feedback entails five interrelated stages that form the basis of a participative OD process (see Figure 11-1):[9]

1. *Entry* into the client organization: Contracting between change agents and management is accomplished (e.g., what are the goals and roles involved; what is the timetable involved; what kinds of data will be needed; who will have access to the data; how feedback will be handled), and preliminary diagnosis (e.g., interviews with managers and executives; analyses of unobtrusive organizational measures such as recent copies of the house organ and absenteeism data) is undertaken.

2. *Planning and development phase:* Meetings with key human resource and appropriate line personnel and cross-sectional small group sessions with randomly selected employees are held to identify important organizational concerns.

3. *Implementation and administration phase:* The questionnaire is pilot tested and then given to a sample of employees (in very large firms) or all organizational members (preferable).

4. *Analysis and feedback phase:* A preliminary analysis of the data is undertaken and fed back as early as possible through reports and meetings, followed by more in-depth analyses and feedback to workgroup planning committees.

5. *Program continuation and organization development:* The information generated through the survey process is used to deal with such organizational concerns as job redesign, training needs, organizational restructuring efforts, and so forth. It is suggested that the process be repeated on a two- to three-year cycle.

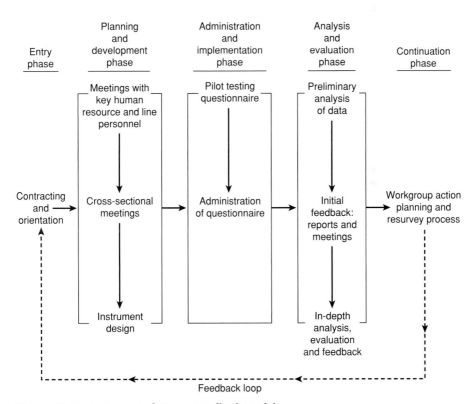

Figure 11-1 An Integrated Survey-Feedback Model

Source: Adapted from J.L. Bowditch and A.F. Buono, *Quality of Work Life Assessment: A Survey-Based Approach* (Boston: Auburn House, 1982). Copyright © J.L. Bowditch and A.F. Buono. Used by permission.

Although survey feedback is a practical OD tool that is quite useful in diagnosing existing organizational problems, identifying potential conflicts, and formulating a forum for two-way communication, employee opinion and attitude surveys are often viewed solely as an information-gathering tool for management's use. Moreover, even within this rather narrow orientation, many managers fail to utilize survey results to improve employee satisfaction and organizational performance. There is an important distinction between simply authorizing a survey and fully applying the results to organizational concerns. When employees take the time and effort to participate in a survey feedback program, expectations will rise that the information generated will be used to improve various facets of organizational life. If managers ignore survey results, employees can subsequently experience an increased sense of frustration, which can manifest itself in such dysfunctional job-related behaviors as turnover, absenteeism, job apathy, cynicism, and even sabotage, among other problems. It must be remembered that survey feedback is *not* a panacea to all organizational problems. Properly used, however, it can increase the probability of managerial and employee involvement, commitment, and effectiveness in the workplace.

Sociotechnical Systems

Although the evolution of OD in the United States was primarily influenced by the laboratory training and survey research stems discussed earlier, OD in Europe, especially in the Scandinavian countries, was influenced by the sociotechnical orientation of London's Tavistock Institute of Human Relations. Instead of viewing organizations as "closed" technical systems to which people were forced to adapt, a key Tavistock concept was the "open sociotechnical system" that focused on the interaction and interrelatedness of the human and technical dimensions of work. This research influenced the restructuring of work and redesigning of work systems on the group and organizational levels along the lines of autonomous and self-governing workgroups rather than an emphasis on management and individual development as found in the United States.

In the United States, an implicit belief in technical determinism appeared to influence early management decisions to get workers to adapt to the technology rather than the reverse. The more holistic approach taken by the Tavistock group, in contrast, evolved more easily due to the cultural acceptance in Europe of the mutual influence of both the technological and social requirements of work. In fact, the concern with the organization as a whole and the realization of the importance of the organization's environment emerged much later in the United States than in Western Europe. In the 1960s, for example, relatively few OD researchers in the United States intervened at the shop-floor level or concerned themselves with organizational structural problems. During this same period in Norway, joint concerns at both the managerial and union levels focused on working conditions and originated the concept of "industrial democracy." These Scandinavian experiments received relatively little attention in the United States at the time, and it wasn't until the late 1960s and early 1970s that the sociotechnical approach to OD began to gather momentum in the United States.[10]

During the 1980s, the sociotechnical systems approach was increasingly emphasized in the United States due to efforts to "jointly optimize" the technical and social structures of our organizations.[11] Traditional OD values that centered on the importance of people and their roles in the organization, although still quite influential, began to give way to the realization that the key to organizational improvements was to focus on both human and performance factors. In fact, an increasing number of influential OD scholars began to argue that performance issues should be the predominant focus, with a concern for people part of a long-range strategic vision for the firm but not explicitly part of the operational component of OD efforts. This focus has added increased support for the sociotechnical systems approach due to its underlying integration of task and process variables.

During the 1990s, the "whole systems" orientation of the sociotechnical systems approach began to dominate OD practice, focusing on such areas as strategic planning and forecasting, strategy implementation, organizational integration, and transformational leadership development.[12] The cornerstone of many of these interventions is still embedded in the development of interpersonal and team-oriented process skills.[13] A key difference, however, is that large group sessions, often referred to as *search conferences* and *interactive dialogue,* increasingly replaced T-groups.[14] Yet, despite this trend and the "open systems" orientation of this approach, critics contended that there had been relatively little attention placed on the outside world and its impact on the structure and functioning of organizations.[15] During the early 2000s, this focus led to the idea of "fast-cycle" OD, with a growing emphasis on rapid, whole-system interventions that were embedded in the strategic context of the organization.[16] This evolution has continued as contemporary OD increasingly focuses on its relevance to organizations and pragmatic approaches to organizational change, placing greater attention on assessing the effectiveness of these changes.[17] The underlying goal is to accelerate change-related processes, facilitating the ability of organizations to keep pace with the rapidity and complexity of today's globally integrated, technology-driven economy.

The Nature of Organization Development

The practice of OD focuses on (1) a method of inquiry (the various techniques and skills employed to facilitate change), (2) the relationship between the change agent and organizational members, and, above all, (3) humanistic values that reflect a concern for the health and well-being of the individual in a large social system.[18] Its two primary aims are directed toward improvements in organizational performance and in the overall "human condition" within organizations.[19] As depicted in Figure 11-2, OD is increasingly characterized by the integration of structure and process variables and interventions. As the field has become increasingly intertwined with organizational improvement efforts, there has also been a growing emphasis on organizational culture and culture change.

A number of characteristics differentiate OD from other types of traditional organizational change efforts:[20]

1. A dual focus on culture and process as well as the human/social and technical/structural sides of the organization

2. An emphasis on collaboration between organizational members and the change agent, enabling the client system to solve problems on its own by

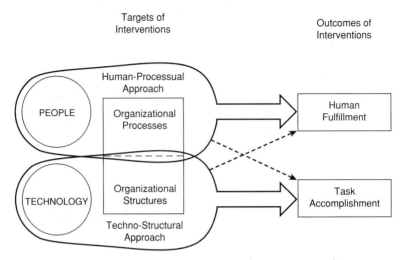

Figure 11-2 Relationship between Organization Development Approaches

Source: Reprinted with permission from M. Sashkin and W.W. Burke, "Organizational Development in the 1980s," *Journal of Management*, vol. 13, no. 2 (1987), p. 396.

teaching the skills and knowledge of continuous learning through self-analytic methods

3. Accent on participation and involvement in problem solving and decision making at all organizational levels

4. A view of OD practitioners as facilitators, collaborators, and co-learners with the client system

5. A focus on the total system, with a developmental view that seeks the mutual betterment of individuals and the organization

OD and Employee Participation

One of the central facets of OD is the idea of involving organizational members in collaborative problem solving and decision making. The rationale underlying this approach is that participation empowers organizational members, increasing (1) knowledge about organizational activities, (2) feelings of personal control and trust of management, (3) job satisfaction and organizational commitment, (4) performance, and (5) acceptance of organizational changes.[21] Recent meta-analyses, however, suggest that while participation may have a statistically significant relationship with performance and satisfaction, its actual effect in organizations is questionable.[22] An underlying problem with these studies, though, is that the actual manner and magnitude of participation are often limited. Studies of quality circles, for example, have found significant differences between active and inactive quality circles, in some instances finding that members actually spent less than 3 percent of their time on circle-related activities.[23]

Some management experts suggest participation is more effective when (1) there is a high level of interdependence between different jobs and (2) the organization's

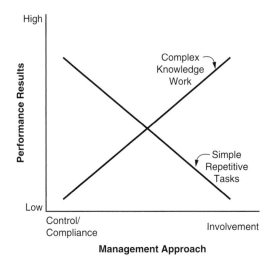

Figure 11-3 Performance Effectiveness of Management Approaches

Source: Reprinted with permission from E.E. Lawler III, "Transformation from Control to Involvement," in R.H. Kilmann, T.J. Covin, and Associates, *Corporate Transformation: Revitalizing Organizations for a Competitive World* (San Francisco: Jossey-Bass, 1988), p. 54.

environment is dynamic.[24] As illustrated in Figure 11-3, employee involvement strategies are thus most appropriate for complex knowledge work (high interdependence; dynamic environment), while more traditional management control and compliance approaches are effective with simple, repetitive tasks (low interdependence; stable environment). As indicated in the chapters on macro-OB, however, highly interdependent jobs and dynamic environments driven by rapid changes in information technology are becoming the rule rather than the exception of corporate life.

Employee participation and empowerment have been, and continue to be, central values and goals of OD.[25] However, participation in OD efforts does not necessarily mean full participation in making all organizational decisions. The focus is on involving individuals in specific interventions as appropriate, facilitating collaborative problem solving and decision making especially in those areas that affect them personally and where they have specific expertise.[26]

Quality of Work Life and OD

The term *Quality of Work Life* (QWL) was initially introduced in the late 1960s as a way of focusing on the effects of employment on worker health and general well-being, and ways to enhance the quality of a person's on-the-job experience.[27] While some theorists have suggested that QWL is little more than an elaborate definition of OD, others have argued that QWL is much broader and more diverse than OD, a way of ensuring adequate and fair compensation, safe and healthy (physical and psychological) working conditions, opportunities for personal growth and development, satisfaction of social needs at work, protection of employee rights, compatibility between work and nonwork responsibilities, and the broader social relevance of work life.[28]

There are three distinctive elements of QWL-related interventions:[29] (1) a concern about the impact of work on people as well as organizational effectiveness, (2) the idea of worker participation in organizational problem solving and decision making, and (3) the creation of reward structures in the workplace which consider innovative ways of rewarding employee input into the work process (e.g., gainsharing). As practiced during the 1980s, emphasis was increasingly placed on the relationship between QWL efforts and employee-centered productivity programs.[30] While the harsh realities of the early to mid-1990s (e.g., downsizing, corporate restructuring) raised a number of challenges to the QWL arena, it has reemerged as a critical area in the early part of the twenty-first century. Today's employees, especially in the rapidly changing world of high technology and resized organizations, are seeking out more meaning in their work and balance in their lives.[31]

Managerial Application: QWL and the Context of Work

The context or conditions under which employees fulfill their work obligations is a salient feature of the overall climate of the workplace. As our labor force becomes increasingly diverse, managers will have to deal with a greater variety of lifestyles, family structures, legal considerations and employee rights, and employment backgrounds.[32] Thus, the broader work context in which human resource–related decisions are made will continue to become increasingly important. As an illustration of these contextual issues, this section briefly looks at employee assistance programs, modified work schedules, career planning and development, managing employee stress, and facilitating employee health and "wellness."

Employee Assistance Plans   Employee Assistance Plans (EAPs) are internal organizational programs designed to help employees cope with their personal and family problems. Although most organizational members may never need such assistance, research has indicated that approximately one-fifth of our workforce does experience some kind of personal problem severe enough to precipitate job- and work-performance-related difficulties.[33] The growing use of EAPs stems from the widespread realization of the dysfunctional effects of various stressors and personal problems in the workplace such as alcohol and drug abuse, financial difficulties, marital problems, and burnout.[34] Demographic trends are also influencing organizations to expand the types of EAP offerings they provide, including more attention to both child care and elder care concerns, and seminars on home buying and retirement planning. Especially in the wake of the September 11 catastrophe and ongoing concerns about terrorism, the role of EAPs has further expanded to include crisis-related grief counseling and general assistance in helping organizational members to refocus on their work.[35]

   The underlying rationale for this type of program is that in terms of both organizational productivity and QWL it is more effective to aid employees during difficult periods rather than fire them or have them handle the problems alone. Considering the expense of hospitalization, sick and severance pay, and the managerial time spent disciplining and counseling organizational members who are beset by personal problems, EAPs ensure that employees have quick and easy access to help whenever it is needed. This does not suggest, of course, that an employee with a personal problem should never be fired. After an employer has provided a "problem employee" with a reasonable opportunity for rehabilitation, termination is a last resort. However, considering the grievance procedures often followed in unionized organizations, the lawsuits that may be filed even in nonunion organizations if the firing appears to be arbitrary, and the employee replacement and training costs involved, EAPs seem to be an effective and increasingly popular intermediate step. Moreover, since research has indicated that many personal problems experienced by employees are work induced, organizations have a responsibility to help individuals confront these difficulties.[36]

Modified Work Schedules *Flexitime* allows employees to select their hours of work within set organizational limits. The basic form incorporates "core periods," usually two to three hours in the morning and afternoon when all employees are required to be at work. Outside of these periods, flexibility is allowed (during starting, lunch, and quitting times) and employees can create their own schedules as long as they work an eight-hour day.[37]

Facilitated by increases in telecommuting, a related form of flexitime, the *compressed work week*, condenses the hours worked each week into fewer days. The most common of these programs is the 4/40 system, under which employees work four 10-hour days rather than the traditional five 8-hour days. A less common variation is the 3/36 system, in which individuals work three 12-hour days.[38] Some organizations use the compressed work week on a full-year basis, while others use it only during certain times of the year (e.g., summer hours).

Research has indicated that flexible work arrangements can (1) increase morale and job satisfaction; (2) significantly reduce tardiness; (3) reduce absenteeism and turnover (although less dramatic for the latter); (4) reduce overtime costs; (5) reduce commuting and increase personal time; (6) improve employee productivity (although most of these results are based on employee and supervisor opinion rather than hard data); and (7) improve attitudes toward modified work arrangements.[39] Disadvantages include the costs and time associated with implementing new systems, potential negative reactions among employees to the introduction of any formal timekeeping system (especially if the timekeeping system becomes a symbol of inferior status), the need to ensure adequate employee coverage (especially in service-oriented firms), and the challenge inherent in managing individuals who maintain variable hours.[40] While a growing number of organizations have experimented with modified work arrangements, the increased use of *contingent workers* (temporary or contract workers) who provide organizations with flexibility without long-term commitment from the organization reflects a very different type of modified work arrangement.

Career Planning and Development Programs Career planning and development is part of a conscious process undertaken by organizations to facilitate the work careers of their employees, by promoting a healthy adjustment to that career choice, and assisting the individual to grow and become more involved in that role.[41] The process can result in decisions to enter or leave certain occupations, accept or decline job opportunities (including promotions, transfers, or relocations), or even leave a particular company for another position or for early retirement. Traditionally, personal initiative and knowledge have influenced career planning, while education and work experience, personal contacts, and luck ("being in the right place at the right time") have generally been the keys to career progress. Today, however, while many organizations are taking greater interest in assisting employees to analyze and assess their abilities and interests and to implement their career planning activities, it is becoming increasingly clear that individuals must also assume greater responsibility for their own career development, ensuring a sufficient knowledge and experience base to remain employable.[42] In contrast to the conventional career model, where people worked steadily full-time for the same employer, the realities of the twenty-first century suggest a *protean model* of career development, where careers continue to develop throughout one's life as new skills and knowledge are continually sought in accordance with individual goals and job changes.[43]

Thus, the intent of organizational career planning practices is *not* to plan employee careers for them. Rather, the focus of these programs is to:[44]

- Help employees conduct their own career planning by raising questions and providing information on available opportunities and resources, and helping them construct narratives that capture their experiences and future hopes.
- Guide organizational members in taking advantage of systems available for career development, such as job posting, training, and education assistance programs.
- Increase employee confidence in the organization's career management, and demonstrate to outside parties that the firm is concerned with career development, particularly for women and minorities.

Although actual career planning and development practices vary widely from firm to firm, these interventions can be broadly defined as any activity or set of activities designed to enhance employee knowledge of, satisfaction with, or performance in their present (or future) positions. As our workforce continues to become more diversified, dual-career families become the norm, and flatter organizational structures and changing job requirements demand more carefully planned staffing needs, such career planning activities on both the individual and organizational levels will become increasingly important.

Managing Work-Related Stress Although there is always a certain degree of strain and tension in our daily lives, the impact and control of stress in organizational life have received increasing attention and concern. Indeed, the negative, often costly, consequences of stress in the workplace are reflected in rising numbers of work-related accidents, heightened turnover and absenteeism rates, escalating health-care costs, falling quantity and quality of production and services, and rising legal fees.[45] As a result, many organizations have begun to realize that significant savings could be achieved by decreasing the amount of stress experienced by their members. The growing focus on and use of employee assistance plans reflects some of the concern in this area.

Stress is a psychological state that develops when an individual is confronted with situations that exhaust or exceed his or her perceived internal and external resources.

Work-related stressors can occur at several organizational levels, including those (1) *intrinsic to the job* (e.g., role conflict, ambiguity, overload, insufficient control); (2) associated with *structure and control* of the organization (e.g., "red tape," rigid policies, organizational politics); (3) related to facets of the *reward and feedback system* involving concerns about equity and fairness; (4) associated with *human resource concerns* about training, development, and career advancement; and (5) connected with *leadership relations.* While extra-organizational stressors (e.g., familial relations, life-cycle changes, or economic difficulties) can also have a significant effect on the individual, whether they have an impact on the person at work depends on a number of factors, including how well the individual can cope with the stressors, various affective and cognitive attributes (e.g., need levels, locus of control, and personality type), and sociodemographic variables (e.g., age, education, and health status).

Although stress can have severe consequences for both individuals and work organizations, stress in and of itself is not necessarily harmful. Moderate levels of stress, for example, can heighten a person's interest, amount of effort expended, and ultimately performance, growth, and development. Moreover, as suggested earlier, people vary significantly in terms of their ability to handle and cope with stress.[46] Something that might be perceived as extremely stressful to one person might be viewed as irrelevant or even favorable by another. The increasing attention on work-related stressors, however, focuses on those activities, events, and conditions that produce stressful situations for most organizational members.

On an individual level, stressful situations may lead to physiological problems (e.g., coronary heart disease, hypertension, migraine headaches, insomnia), psychological difficulties (e.g., anxiety, depression, fear), and adverse behavioral reactions (e.g., drinking, drug use, increased smoking). While stress can manifest itself in many different ways, one of the more significant symptoms from an organizational perspective is employee *burnout*, deteriorating job performance, and decreasing energy levels caused by the cumulative effect of continuous daily pressures.[47]

Given these concerns, increasing management attention and intervention have focused on controlling the negative effects of stress at work. Various approaches to managing stress and burnout typically focus on attempts to (1) *change the environment* in which the stress exists (e.g., transfers from highly stressful jobs; reassignment of responsibilities); (2) *change the individual's appraisal* of the environment (e.g., suggest ways they might exert more control over the situation; counseling; stress-reduction workshops); and/or (3) *change activities or behaviors* that can modify the environment (e.g., change organizational policies; develop social-support networks). Further management policies and strategies that can reduce negative stress include: (1) increased two-way communication with employees to reduce uncertainty; (2) performance appraisal and reward systems that reduce role conflict and role ambiguity; (3) increased participation in decision making to provide employees with a sense of greater control over their work; (4) job enrichment efforts that develop a sense of meaning and significance in work assignments; and (5) improved matching of skills, personality, and work through carefully constructed career development programs and counseling.[48] Current initiatives also include helping employees increase their resilience to stress through stress management training, career development programs, and by encouraging healthier lifestyles.[49]

Corporate Fitness and Wellness Programs   Health and well-being in the workplace have become an increasingly important dimension of organizational life.[50] As part of many stress management efforts, *corporate fitness programs* focus on developing the overall health and well-being of organizational members. Although physical recreation-related efforts to improve employee loyalty, morale, and physical and mental vitality have been traced back to the late 1880s,[51] these programs rapidly expanded during the past few decades. Recent studies, for example, report that two-thirds of all companies with fifty or more employees currently run some type of campaign for improving the health of their employees—encouraging workers to assess health risks, stop smoking, control blood pressure, screen their cholesterol and modify their diets, and exercise.[52]

While questions have been raised about the overall effectiveness of these programs, a widely publicized study by the Prudential Insurance Company points to significant benefits.[53] Comparing a group of sedentary employees with a group that was actively involved in an organizationally sponsored exercise program, Prudential found that the "fit" employees averaged fewer disability and sick days each year, had higher levels of productivity, and reported more positive feelings and self-descriptions than the sedentary group. By enhancing the mental and physical health and well-being of organizational members, companies attempt to favorably influence individual-level (e.g., physical, psychological, behavioral) and organization-level (e.g., health insurance costs, productivity, absenteeism) outcomes.[54]

Most proponents argue that a balanced approach is needed, that so-called wellness and fitness efforts should supplement and not substitute for broader safety efforts. The ultimate success of these programs is determined by the extent of employee buy-in and the way in which the programs are communicated throughout the organization.[55] A growing controversy, however, is reflected by those firms that have taken a more punitive role in the wellness area, for example, by refusing to hire smokers or charging them more for health insurance.[56] Yet, while wellness programs should not be considered as a panacea for organizational and work-related ills, they represent another way in which the context of work and the workplace continues to evolve and develop.

Spirituality in the Workplace   Historically, the human spirit—with its hopes, dreams, and aspirations—has largely been excluded from the workplace. We are beginning to realize, however, that people must be able to express their values and share their hopes if they are to fully tap into their creative potential.[57] While such expression can take many different forms, the role of spirituality in the workplace has begun to take on increased prominence. According to popular business magazines, a literal spiritual revival has been sweeping across corporate America as a rapidly growing number of executives are mixing mysticism into their management endeavors.[58] From company-sponsored "vision quests" to prayer breakfasts and "passing the rock" rituals (a Native American talking circle custom when only the person holding the stone can speak), organizational members are increasingly drawing on references to "spirit" and "soul" as they reflect on work-related challenges.

Especially as information technology is prompting increased interest in systems thinking and the nonlinear nature of the Internet is pushing people to take unconventional, intuitive approaches to their work, people appear to be seeking a deeper sense of meaning and fulfillment on the job. While critics raise questions and concerns about the promotion of traditional religion in our secular institutions, present trends suggest that workplace spirituality is increasingly becoming a fundamental part of the quality of work life experienced by organizational members.

Intervention Strategies and Change

An intervention strategy is a planned effort involving a set of structured activities or techniques to bring about improvement (change) in individual, group, or organizational functioning.[59] Such intervention strategies have usually been developed along the lines of Kurt Lewin's three-step change framework: unfreezing, moving, and refreezing.[60]

Unfreezing refers to a decrease in the strength of old values, attitudes, or behaviors which results from new or different experiences or data that challenge individual perceptions of self, others, and/or events. Change agents can employ various techniques (e.g., T-group experiences, survey questionnaires) to increase such awareness and to stimulate self-questioning of present behaviors and attitudes (own versus induced change) that can lead to a greater readiness for change. Once people become dissatisfied with the status quo (unfreezing), the potential for successful change is increased. In essence, this step can be thought of as preparing people for change.

Moving (changing) takes place after people "unfreeze," when they are prepared to undertake new values, attitudes, and/or behaviors. These values, attitudes, or behaviors are usually oriented toward the values, attitudes, or behaviors of some role model, and either through identification or internalization they are accepted by the group and its members. This process often requires some facilitation (helping people to understand why a change is needed) and training (showing people how they will be affected by the change, what will be expected of them) to minimize resistance.

Finally, *refreezing* is the stabilization of the change effort. The changes are now integrated into the group or organization's normal processes and operating procedures. It is important to reinforce these changes to ensure that they become an accepted part of the organization's functioning. This does not imply, of course, that refreezing means becoming rigid in the new or changed situation; rather, structures should be developed to allow the organization to integrate and internalize the desired changes.[61]

Lewin's framework has influenced an array of subsequent phase-oriented models of the change process that reflect three major themes: (1) awakening the organization to a new reality, disengaging it from the past and recognizing that the "old way" of doing things is no longer acceptable; (2) creating and embracing a new vision of the future, and uniting behind the various steps necessary to achieve that vision; and (3) reinforcing and solidifying the changed attitudes and behaviors.[62] In essence, before any lasting organizational change can take place, it is necessary to prepare people for the change, carefully monitor its progress, and provide support and reinforcement for the new attitudes, practices, and policies that emerge.

Given the rapid and volatile nature of change in today's globally interdependent business world, however, some critics contend that Lewin's notion of unfreezing and refreezing has become obsolete.[63] Organizational systems, in effect, are changing so rapidly that "unfreezing" them is simply not as significant as it once was. Rather than

TABLE 11-1 Episodic versus Continuous Change

	Episodic Change	Continuous Change
Perspective	Change reflects an occasional divergence from equilibrium. Driven externally, change is part of a reactive adaptation to the external environment.	Change is a pattern of ongoing modifications of work processes and social practice. Driven internally, change reflects organizational instability and the need to continuously react to daily contingencies.
Intervention Approach	1. Unfreeze 2. Change/Move 3. Refreeze	1. Freeze 2. Rebalance 3. Unfreeze
Role of Change Agent	Managing Change: Create the Change	Guiding Changing: Redirect Changes

Source: Adapted from: K.W. Weick and R.E. Quinn, "Organization Development and Change," *Annual Review of Psychology,* vol. 50 (1999), p. 366.

change being an episodic, infrequent dimension of organizational life, change today is far more continuous and embedded in the day-to-day reality of the workplace. As reflected in Table 11-1, today's organizations experience a sufficient multitude of overlapping changes that the change process has become an ongoing redirection of what is already under way.[64] Instead of having a clear beginning and end point, change is cyclical. Because there is no real beginning, it is important to *"freeze"* the continuous changes, attempting to make sequences of events visible to people (i.e., a symbolic "snapshot" of the organization) and to show patterns of what is happening in the organization. Freezing, in this sense, is typically done through the creation of conceptual maps, schemas, or war stories that capture events, activities, and relationships. The next step is to *rebalance* the system, reinterpreting, relabeling, and resequencing organizational patterns to remove obstacles and barriers. In this phase, problems should be reframed as opportunities, drawing out the attractiveness of the change. Instead of simply telling people what to do (*logic of replacement*) the key is to inspire organizational members so that they are drawn to the change (*logic of attraction*). By making sense of the change dynamics already under way, organizational leaders can then *unfreeze* the system as organizational members resume improvisation and learning within the context of the clarified direction. As will be discussed later in the chapter, this perspective suggests that instead of managing change, managerial interventions should be focused on *guiding changing*, the appreciation that change is a constant reality of organizational life.[65]

Planned Change Intervention

The basic strategy for conceptualizing and planning change, which emerges from Lewin's three-step framework, has been developed and modified into a seven-step framework often referred to as planned change.[66]

   1. *Scouting:* A joint exploration of a particular organizational problem or situation by the change agent and management.

2. *Entry:* Mutual development of a contract and related expectations by the change agent and organizational members that establishes the relationship between these individuals in terms of how subsequent stages will be carried out.

3. *Diagnosis:* Identification of specific goals for improvement beginning with the client's perceived problems.

4. *Planning:* Joint development of an action plan and ways to deal with potential resistance to the planned changes.

5. *Action:* The implementation of the plan formulated in stage four.

6. *Evaluation:* Assessment of the success of the change program and a determination of the need for further actions or termination.

7. *Termination:* The end of the particular change program; the change agent either leaves the organization or moves on to a different project.

Thus, the basis of planned change is oriented toward conscious and deliberate efforts to improve a particular organizational system.

Action Research

In contrast to the process underlying planned change, another intervention strategy known as *action research* refers to a cycle of data-based problem solving that replicates the process of scientific inquiry. This approach involves a continuously unfolding interplay between diagnosis, solution, results, rediagnosis, and new solutions to organizational problems. Although there are similarities between action research and planned change models, action research places more emphasis on the diagnosis of organizational concerns and the development of specific actions to deal with those problems, while planned change (although still data based) usually emphasizes the use of preplanned techniques. The cyclical nature of the action research model is illustrated in French's framework, presented in Figure 11-4. The significant elements of an action research design are:[67]

1. Identification of a problem that individuals or groups are sufficiently concerned about that they are prepared to take some action.

2. Involvement of those concerned/affected to select the problem and formulate a prediction (hypothesis) that has a goal (outcome) and a procedure for reaching it. This goal must also be viewed in relation to the total situation.

3. Careful recording of actions taken and accumulation of evidence to determine the degree to which the goal has been achieved.

4. Analysis and inference from this evidence of generalizations regarding the relations between the actions and the desired goal.

5. Continuous retesting of these generalizations in action situations.

As these interrelated steps suggest, the goal of action research is to improve practice as well as contribute to our insights into and understanding of organizational dynamics.[68] The action research approach continues to provide the foundation for most OD approaches to studying and simultaneously changing social

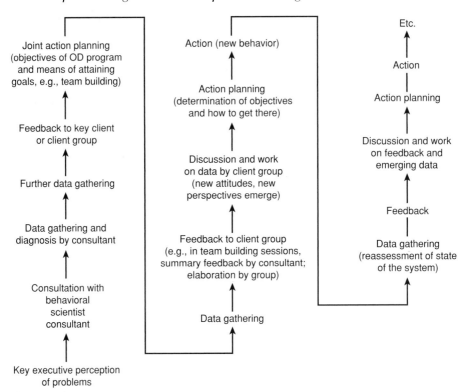

Figure 11-4 Action-Research Model for Organization Development

Source: Wendell L. French, "Organization Development: Objectives, Assumptions, and Strategies," © 1969 by the Regents of the University of California. Reprinted from *California Management Review*, vol. XII, no. 2, p. 26 by permission of the Regents.

systems. Current practice, however, goes beyond this initial conceptualization and emphasizes: (1) full client-change agent partnership, (2) collaborative learning throughout the action research process, (3) the importance of drawing on local tacit knowledge, and (4) a willingness to examine assumptions in the system.[69]

Appreciative Inquiry A continued development of the action research approach toward increasingly collaborative and inclusive intervention is *appreciative inquiry*, a process that focuses on organizational success rather than problems and failures.[70] Instead of beginning with a problem that people want to resolve, appreciative inquiry (AI) emphasizes what is "right" with an organization: what works well, *why* it works well, and how that success can be extended throughout the organization. In general, AI is an integrated, four-step process that draws on participants' emotional energy, imagination, and vision for the future:

1. A *discovery* phase that emphasizes data collection through interviews that shift the focus from what is wrong with the system to what is going well for the organization. Common themes are assessed that point to organizational strengths and "peak experiences," all stated in a positive manner.

2. Sometimes referred to as the *dream* stage, participants are then encouraged to think about what "could be," challenging them to think outside the traditional boundaries of what has been done in the past. Participants are asked to build on existing strengths, developing "provocative propositions" that draw out favorable possibilities envisioned for the organization.

3. The *design* phase builds on the possibilities created in the first two steps, moving toward implementation planning and an assessment of the resources the organization currently has and additional resources that might be needed. A significant outcome of this stage is development of an action agenda, with specified action plans and commitments.

4. The final stage is *delivery*, sometimes referred to as the "destiny" phase, where the action plan is implemented, commitments are solidified, and results are assessed.

While AI is still a relatively new approach to organizational intervention and system change, its power clearly lies in the positive energy that is unleashed when people focus on what is working well. While reports from the field suggest that it is a highly effective approach to change, its greatest challenge is moving from vision (dream and design) to implementation (delivery) and ensuring the sustained and supportive energy and commitment from those on implementation teams.[71]

OD Interventions

Although there are a number of different ways of classifying OD interventions,[72] a comprehensive review of the literature suggests that OD interventions can be grouped into four basic classifications:[73]

1. *Human process interventions* that focus on organizational members and the processes through which they accomplish organizational goals (e.g., T-groups, process consultation, team building, organization confrontation meetings, and intergroup relations).

2. *Technostructural interventions* that examine the technology (e.g., task methods) and structure (e.g., division of labor) of organizations and emphasize both productivity and human fulfillment (e.g., quality circles, cross-functional teams, work redesign).

3. *Human resource management interventions* that center on personnel practices used to integrate and socialize organizational members (e.g., career planning and development, goal setting, performance appraisal, diversity programs, employee wellness).

4. *Strategic interventions* that link internal organizational functioning to the environment and transform the organization to keep pace with changes in the larger environment (e.g., open-systems planning, culture change, integrated approaches to strategic change).

In practice, these methods are not mutually exclusive. In fact, most successful OD efforts take an eclectic approach and will typically involve a mix of these components at one point or another.[74]

Depth of Intervention

A slightly different way of thinking about OD interventions is based on the depth of individual emotional involvement in the change process.[75] Although emotional involvement may be present at any given level of intervention, the typology in Figure 11-5 is concerned with the extent to which a particular intervention is directly related to such involvement. Strategies that deal with the more external aspects of the individual and focus on the more formal and public aspects of role behavior fall toward the surface end of the depth continuum, whereas strategies that touch the deep, personal, private, and central aspects of the individual or the individual's relationships with others fall toward the deeper end of the continuum. The main advantage of this type of framework is that it provides a rational basis for the selection of an appropriate intervention strategy. In essence, two basic criteria should be used to assess the appropriate depth of intervention. One should not intervene at any level deeper than: (1) required to produce a solution to the problem(s) at hand; and (2) the client has the energy, willingness, and resources to commit to problem solving and to change. Intervention strategies that are selected should not only be appropriate for the particular problems the organization is confronting, but they must be carefully gauged

Figure 11-5 Depth of Intervention Typology

Source: Adapted from Roger Harrison, "Choosing the Depth of Organizational Intervention," *Journal of Applied Behavioral Science*, vol. 6, no. 2 (1970), pp. 181–202. Copyright © 1970. Used with permission.

in terms of the degree of emotional impact they will have on individual organizational members as well.

Transorganization Development

As suggested by the earlier discussion of interorganizational alliances and network organizations in Chapters 8 and 9, these multiorganizational forms require a level of consultation and collaboration that goes well beyond conventional patterns of management and organization. Indeed, the traditional American management and organization paradigm—based on assumed needs for hierarchical control and organizational stability—appears to be increasingly outdated for such alliances and needs to shift toward one based more on involvement and continuous change.[76] As a way of coping with these changes and emergent structures, the field of OD has begun to focus on ways to mobilize and bring order to such inter-firm alliances.

While traditional OD practices and interventions have focused on what may be referred to as "over-organized" systems, these interorganizational arrangements are more appropriately conceptualized as "under-organized" systems.[77] Inter-firm alliances are typically characterized as loosely coupled systems, with leadership and power dispersed among autonomous organizations with sporadic member commitment to inter-firm collaboration efforts. Thus, interventions designed to facilitate such linkages are guided by a transorganizational perspective, focusing on the dynamics associated with this higher systems level.[78] Compared to the typical phases of planned change—entry, diagnosis, intervention, and evaluation—transorganization development emphasizes the process of change across organizational boundaries, the need to create new systems, and the need to assimilate those involved. It incorporates traditional OD interventions in a broader three-phase process of (1) *identification* of relevant systems and appropriate representatives (e.g., stakeholder analysis, survey feedback, focus groups, active listening, and small group discussions); (2) *convention* of representatives (a form of search conference) and initiation of linkage processes (e.g., staged communication, transition teams, parallel organizational structures, intergroup mirroring, and team building); and (3) *organization* of the system to regularize behaviors (e.g., team building, strategic use of organizational symbols and rituals, management of retention and dismissal processes, joint evaluation, and integration review).[79]

A problem, however, is that we are still just beginning to fully comprehend and understand the nature and underlying dilemmas involved in such inter-firm interactions. For instance, although reactive change is largely viewed in negative terms, especially when contrasted to proactive management efforts, given the uncertain nature of these interorganizational forms significant questions linger as to whether managers can accurately predict exactly what will happen in such linkages.[80] In fact, it has been suggested that the nature of the relationship between inter-firm partners should model the change process.[81] Accordingly, it seems that being prepared to *cope* with the resultant processes and changes appears to be a more realistic posture than one of directly managing (controlling) such dynamics.

Next-Generation OD

Critics of OD are increasingly pointing to the need to develop a greater understanding of why and how organizations change and develop as they do. The field has been admonished for placing most of its emphasis on a rather narrow range of interventions and normative models at the expense of broader assessments of when such methods are actually useful and beneficial to the organization and when their costs may not warrant such an investment.[82]

Given the rapidity of change and the turbulence associated with the hyper-competitive world of globalization and information technology, the practice of OD is going through a concomitant revolution. While practitioners still rely heavily on the OD techniques discussed earlier, the field itself is reaching far beyond what might be thought of as these first- and second-generation approaches, especially in the sense that many OD applications are far more complicated and multifaceted than they have been in the past.[83] Today, OD's emphasis is increasingly placed on organizations operating on the "edge of chaos" and the need to create complex adaptive systems, especially through (1) introducing and disseminating advanced information and manufacturing technologies, (2) creating team-based, continuous learning, (3) visioning and creating future orientations, (4) valuing diversity, and, in general, (5) focusing on large-scale organizational transformation and redirection. Organization Development practices are increasingly being integrated into basic human resource management and human resource development strategies.[84] While some critics have questioned the current relevance of OD, the field's ongoing focus on change, change management, and leadership is clearly at the top of organizational and CEO agendas.[85]

MANAGING ORGANIZATIONAL CHANGE

Most discussions of organizational change, which reflect a planned change orientation, focus on top-management strategies and tactics for conceptualizing and introducing that change. Recent work, however, has raised questions about the extent to which successful large-scale change initiatives can actually be implemented through such well-laid plans or whether it emerges through a process of logical incrementalism, as strategies arise as part of an iterative process based on repeated interactions between organizations, their leaders, organizational members, and the environment. Moreover, as we study the process of such change and transformation it appears that it involves a multitude of skills and abilities. No one individual, no matter how skilled he or she may be as a leader and change agent, will necessarily have the full range of skills, contacts, and power necessary to successfully create major transformations of their organizations. While such individuals may be able to "set the wheels in motion," they must rely on a network of supporters—managers and specialists both inside and outside the company—to bring about the change.[86]

Within this context, while such large-scale change efforts might be conceptualized as carefully orchestrated, planned, systems-level change, most successful change initiatives appear to involve a series of continuous but relatively small change efforts that involve the ongoing enhancement and reconfiguration of existing processes and business models.[87] While there are times when companies require significant, all-encompassing change—what might be thought of as "creative destruction"—this type of pacesetting, revolutionary change can readily lead to resistance, burnout, chaos, and cynicism, as one set of changes seems to overlap and cascade into others.

Changemakers

When conceptualizing organizational change, three key "changemakers" should be considered: (1) *strategists* who identify the need for change, laying its foundation and creating a vision of the desired outcome; (2) *implementers* who develop specific steps, championing the day-to-day process of executing the change; and (3) *recipients*, the largest number of organizational members, who must adopt, adapt, and adjust to the change.[88] Each of these groups brings a very different role, mindset, orientation, and focus to the change process. For example, while strategists focus on the external environment and preparing the organization for change, implementers focus on internal coordination and related problems and demands (e.g., overcoming resistance, managing specific change projects) that accompany the change. Recipients, who ultimately institutionalize the change, typically focus on what they perceive to be the personal benefits *and* costs related to the change.

Approaches to Organizational Change

From a conceptual vantage point, there are three interrelated approaches to organizational change: directed change, planned change and guided changing.[89]

Directed Change

Directed change is driven from the top of the organization and relies on authority and compliance. Leaders (change strategists) create and announce the change and seek to persuade organizational members to accept it based on business necessity, logical arguments, and/or emotional appeals. Directed change reflects a quick, decisive approach to introducing change in an organization. This type of change is most appropriate in situations where both *business complexity* (e.g., number of interdependencies, size, geographical dispersion, number of products and services, array of critical stakeholders) and *sociotechnical uncertainty* (i.e., amount of information processing and decision making required for implementation, extent to which solutions are known and established) are low. If the change involves well-known and well-accepted actions that are implemented in a relatively simple, routine environment, then directed change can make the best use of limited organizational resources.

Within this context, persuasive and ethical communication is critical, ensuring both the clarity of the message and the honesty and trustworthiness of the change agent. If organizational members do not trust the change implementer and his or her message, their acceptance of the change is unlikely. Another important dimension of such communication is responding to the *"so that" question*—"We are changing *X* so that we will be able to accomplish *Y*"—making certain that organizational members fully understand the reason, rationale, and expected outcome of the change.[90] Although explaining reasons for change might seem obvious, research indicates that employees, including many managers, often have little or no objective knowledge of the intention and/or outcomes of their change efforts.[91]

This approach to change has clear limitations and, as will be explored later in the chapter, if used inappropriately or too frequently, managers and employees throughout the organization are inevitably forced to cope with resistance.

Planned Change

Planned change may arise from any level in the organization, but ultimately must be sponsored at the top. Change strategists and implementers seek involvement in and commitment to the change by making extensive use of specific actions, identified through research and experience, which mitigate the typical resistance and productivity losses associated with directed change. As discussed earlier, underlying most planned change efforts is Lewin's three-stage process of unfreezing, changing, and refreezing.[92] Rather than simply creating and announcing the change, planned change provides a project management approach to the change process. It attempts to create the conditions for people to become more involved in the change process, identifying and encouraging key stakeholders to participate in both the form and implementation of the change.

As the business complexity of the implementation process increases, a planned change approach is needed, especially when key stakeholders differ about what actions may be most effective in different parts of the organization. Effectively and appropriately engaging people in the planning process can ameliorate implementation problems and generate acceptance of the change. This effort is especially important when commitment to the decision is critical for successful implementation. Although an underlying concern might be that increasing participation simply adds more complexity to a situation that is already highly complex, the planned change approach increases the probability of buy-in and support for the change.

The planned change approach creates an important capability in today's organizations. The burden for initiating and sustaining the change, however, is still placed directly on the change strategists, from identifying the need for change and creating a vision of desired outcomes to deciding which changes are ultimately feasible.

Self-Organizing, Guided Changing

Self-organizing, guided changing is an iterative process in which organizational members assume responsibility for the change, including initial interpretation and design, implementation and improvisation, learning from the change effort, and sharing that learning system-wide, leading to ongoing reinterpretation and redesign of the change. The resulting spiral of learning, innovation, and development can contribute to both continuous improvement of existing change efforts as well as the ability to generate novel changes and solutions.

The primary driver of this approach to change is sociotechnical uncertainty. If the future state or change solution is unknown, even in what appear to be relatively simple situations, managers do not have the answers and are unable to meaningfully direct the change or carefully plan the change process. Instead, they must draw on the tacit knowledge and capabilities of organizational members. The iterative nature of such self-organizing, guided changing encourages the type of improvisation and experimentation needed to identify the most effective actions, solutions, and outcomes. While planned change has clearly provided us with implementation-related tools and participative strategies to get people involved in the change process, it does not go far enough in those situations where a solution to the change problem is unknown or unclear. The dynamics inherent in self-organizing change are crucial as organizational members create, test, experiment, and mutually adjust to each other's efforts. In effect, guided changing is an attempt to break through the constraints imposed by hierarchy and closely managed change processes, dispersing awareness much more broadly throughout the organization and ensuring that the right talent and appropriate resources are applied to continuous changing.[93] An underlying challenge, especially as excitement about change possibilities begin to emerge, is to harness the energy of organizational members around those aspects of the organization that require changing while maintaining continuity where appropriate.[94]

Although self-organizing change can have a transformational effect on organizations, it can also contribute to organizational chaos, because continuous changes and transitions confuse and frustrate rather than enlighten and support organizational members and other key stakeholders. The feeling of being in "permanent white water" and the need to constantly adapt and adjust can be a daunting experience.[95] Many people ultimately want organizational change to end, rather than experience changing as a way of doing business that will, in essence, never end.

Enabling Large-Scale Organizational Change

A critical challenge for twenty-first-century organizations and their leaders is the ongoing development of individuals, teams, and entire organizations that are capable of understanding these different approaches to change and adapting the change process to the complexity and uncertainty of the situation. From this perspective, the highest level of change capacity would be exemplified by an organization in which these different approaches to change—directed change, planned change, and self-organizing, guided changing—are implemented as appropriate in different situations with the full support and commitment of all organizational members because they understand the different approaches to change and challenges of change management.

Once a large-scale change has been envisioned, a number of related issues emerge that concern needed support for the actual implementation of the change. Six key enabling factors should be considered in formulating a context for the implementation of any significant change:[96]

1. Issues of *pace* focus on the length of time necessary to actually design and implement the change program, how quickly the change itself should unfold given relevant external pressures (e.g., customer demands, competitive pressures), how much adjustment should be allowed for trial-and-error learning, and the appropriate mix of big and small changes.

2. Questions of *scope* emerge directly from the vision of the change, and center on whether the change should "start small and grow" (e.g., through a pilot program) or be instituted organization-wide. If a pilot test is preferred, additional questions focus on where the change should be initiated, which component of the organization has the most appropriate subculture and climate for change, and how it might most effectively be diffused throughout the organization. Scope also includes the focus of the change (e.g., maximizing shareholder versus enhancing organizational capabilities versus a combination of the two).

3. *Depth* concerns the number of changes that can be successfully introduced in any given area. There is often a limit as to how much change people can absorb and handle before resistance to the change begins to emerge.

4. Questions about *publicity* focus on how the change should be announced, ranging from a quiet, understated introduction to all-out organizational hype (e.g., speeches, banners, and buttons) intended to rally organizational members around the change effort. It is important to emphasize that the key consideration here is the way in which communication is handled rather than the communication per se. Effective and open communication with organizational members about the change and its ramifications is critical in any large-scale change program.

5. Questions about appropriate *supporting structures* focus on the mechanisms that an organization currently has or needs to put into place to further the change. While decisions about appropriate supporting structures are directly related to the scope and pace of the change, decisions must be made concerning the extent to which the change can be introduced through normal management processes and what should be specifically developed (e.g., task forces; on/off-site meetings; use of consultants).

6. Finally, a decision must be made as to *who* will drive the change, whether it should be implemented in a top-down manner, emerge from middle- or lower-level ownership, or be introduced and facilitated by an external change agent (e.g., consultant). As part of this process, if consultants will be utilized, the role that the consultant plays in the change process must also be determined (e.g., analyzing and creating solutions versus supporting management in developing their own solutions versus empowering employees and supporting them with their expertise).

As these key factors imply, creating an appropriate context for the implementation of a large-scale change requires thoughtful planning, an assessment of who should be part of the change team, and how and to what extent organizational members should be involved in the process.

Interventions and Organizational Politics

The discussion of OD and change-related interventions thus far has largely focused on their sociocultural and structural-technical characteristics. In addition to the various problems and considerations concerning the technical design of an intervention and its broader cultural context, certain issues must also be addressed concerning the political dynamics that occur in organizations.[97] Since all organizations must confront the problem of allocating power and resources, they are often conceptualized as political arenas. Through ongoing processes of bargaining and coalition formation, a number of different groups vie for control of the organization's resources and the ways in which those resources will be used.[98] Within this context, change occurs as political adjustments are made—through negotiation and bargaining—by these coalitions.

In many instances, however, changes that would be beneficial from a technical and cultural perspective are often undermined because of political considerations: potential shifts in power centers and resistance due to the need for power, internal and external control issues, resistance to new organizational structures or management styles, concomitant changes in the reward structure and related opposition owing to real or imagined resource limitations, and so forth. This focus moves us away from the public, readily observable dimensions of organizational life to the "shadow organization." This darker side of organizations reflects the complex interactions in which covert political influences, power struggles and interpersonal tensions coexist with the legitimate system.[99] Thus, if interventions and change efforts are to be successful, these three dimensions—the technical, cultural, and political—must be understood and effectively integrated. Otherwise, the organization may be working at cross-purposes and, as a result, undermine its own ability to capitalize on the desired changes.

A number of steps should be followed as part of any change program that focuses on managing the political aspects of the transition:[100] (1) identify target individuals and groups whose commitment is needed; (2) define the critical mass needed to ensure effective implementation; (3) develop a plan for obtaining commitment from the critical mass; and (4) develop a monitoring system to assess progress. Based on an analysis of key influential people, it is important to determine the gap between their current attitudes toward the change and what their attitudes toward the change should be if it is to be carried out successfully. Analysis should focus on reasons for support or nonsupport of the change. Diagnostic questions might include such concerns as:[101] Who are formally and informally the influential people in the organization? What is at stake for them in the change? How can those significant people who support the change be mobilized? How can those significant people who are opposed to the change be influenced? Is resistance due to political, technical, and/or cultural factors? What means (e.g., involvement in the change, rewards, incentives, or bargaining) might be useful to influence key people?

By mobilizing and energizing a network of supporters, the probability that the intervention will be promoted and accepted in the organization will be strengthened. At the same time, however, a focus on political dynamics in and of itself will not ensure a successful change effort. For any large-scale change to be truly effective and productive, the technical, cultural, and political dimensions of that change must be identified, assessed, and integrated.

Resistance, Support, and Coping with Change

As part of the change process, it is important for organizations to understand the effect that large-scale change can have on their members (recipients) and to be prepared to deal with any resulting resistance in a constructive manner. A related problem concerns those middle-level managers (implementers) who are literally squeezed between the demands of top-management decisions and strategies they neither make nor influence, and the expectations, aspirations, and potential fears of subordinates.[102]

Although most people successfully adapt to change, the process is typically an evolutionary one, with different stages involving difficult, often conflicting, emotions and reactions. An underlying key in determining people's readiness for change is the degree of "felt security" (sometimes referred to as *psychological safety*) they have in their organization. Individuals who show an eagerness for change typically perceive a high level of security in their organizations, whereas those who experience anxiety have lower levels of security and, as a result, are less ready for change.[103] The reactions of these individuals have even been compared to bereavement processes, as organizational members move from initial discomfort with the change to eventual acceptance, going through shock, defensive retreat, acknowledgment, and adaptation.[104] In the initial shock stage, individuals are threatened by the anticipated change, at times even denying its existence. As the change becomes a reality, organizational members move to defensive retreat, expressing anger at the situation, attempting to "hold on" to the past and accustomed ways of doing things, and, in general, feeling uncomfortable and uneasy about the change. Over time, people stop denying the change and acknowledge their loss, often mourning the past and slowly developing a willingness to take risks associated with the change. Finally, the ideal situation is when organizational members adapt and change themselves; they reach a point where they are comfortable with the change and are prepared to "move on," assuming new responsibilities and challenges. As the discussion of organizational culture change in Chapter 10 underscores, however, not all people can adapt to such change and either voluntarily or involuntarily leave the organization.

It has become increasingly important to assist employees in coping with the pressures and strains typically associated with major organizational changes and transformations: (1) helping individuals to conceptualize and understand their sphere of influence; (2) facilitating their assessment of the potential opportunities that exist in ambiguous situations; and (3) gaining momentum from "small wins."[105]

Conceptualizing and Understanding One's Sphere of Influence

All too often during a large-scale organizational change, managers become preoccupied with those dimensions of organizational life that they cannot control. However, by (1) understanding the "controllables" and "uncontrollables" as they apply to a particular job and role in a changing organization, and (2) working within one's sphere of influence, middle managers can begin to combat a feeling of powerlessness through what may be referred to as *controlled empowerment*. The difficulty, of course, lies in gaining insight into what we can and, perhaps more important, cannot control in a large-scale change. Given the high levels of uncertainty and ambiguity that permeate such change, one's actual and perceived sphere of influence may be quite different. The key is to be as specific as possible with respect to (1) the exact nature of problems and concerns that are facing you, (2) what it will take to resolve the situation(s), and (3) whether you currently have or might be able to generate appropriate resources to deal with the task.[106]

Looking for Opportunities in Ambiguity

Much of the literature on ambiguity in organizations emphasizes the stress associated with dealing with uncertainty.[107] Given the high level of uncertainty that exists in large-scale organizational change, however, the ability to accept and work with ambiguity is an important component of successfully managing and coping with such change. The metaphor of "permanent white water" has been used to characterize modern organizations, a metaphor that is particularly fitting to the changes derived from a major organizational transformation.[108] As suggested in the preceding discussion of enabling structures and controlled empowerment, the key here is not to totally control or remove the anxiety, but rather to contain it through the use of change agents and other supporting structures. In fact, often the mere presence of a change agent in a large-scale change can serve as a containing device. Containing efforts, such as empathic listening and other process consulting skills, legitimize anxiety and stress, and can keep them from "spilling over" into other facets of organizational life.

Gaining Momentum from Small Wins

The massive scale on which many social problems are conceived precludes innovative action because the limits of bounded rationality are exceeded, and anxiety and arousal are raised to dysfunctionally high levels.[109] This dynamic often takes place during a large-scale organizational change. As arousal increases, selective attention to cues also increases (see Chapter 2), and the resultant editing makes dealing with difficult tasks even more problematic. Reformulation of change-related issues as "mere problems," however, allows managers to pursue a strategy of "small wins" wherein a series of concrete, complete outcomes of moderate importance can be used to set forces in motion that favor other small wins. One approach to building such support is to mount a grass-roots campaign by establishing visible and measurable links between unit or individual performance and organizational outcomes. It is important to underscore, however, that in complex organizations such small wins do not necessarily connect in neat linear or sequential form, with each step being a demonstrable movement toward some predetermined goal. Yet, when a solution is found for one problem, the next solvable problem often becomes more visible as new allies are created, bringing new solutions with them. By providing enabling structures that help middle managers to recast change-related problems into smaller, less threatening difficulties, a process can be facilitated through which organizational members can begin to identify a series of controllable opportunities of moderate size that produce visible outcomes, which can then be used to achieve the new organizational vision.

Participation-Related Dilemmas in Managing Change

Although the literature suggests that participation in organizational change efforts is one of the most effective ways to minimize resistance and enhance acceptance of the change, there is an underlying dilemma concerning employee participation in organizational large-scale change efforts.[110] While it is both possible and desirable to involve organizational members in the change process, once the change is implemented employee participation in the process necessarily ceases. Although this situation is acceptable for the present group of workers who were part of the process, new employees who come into the system are simply inheriting a system *created by others*. As a result, the latter group may not be as approving of the organizational change as the initial group.

Organizational Downsizing, Retrenchment, and Resizing

Organizational downsizing and retrenchment currently cut across the entire economic spectrum, affecting virtually every industry, region, company, and employees at all levels of skill and education. As a result of volatile and often chaotic changes in the external environment, of course, few companies have escaped some form of restructuring over the past two decades. In fact, part of the dilemma is that in an increasing number of instances, organizations have made these changes not by choice, but by necessity. The reality is that organizations and their members must change in order to compete and survive in a rapidly changing, globally competitive world. Unfortunately, there is a lingering tendency for companies to fall back on what they believe to be the most straightforward, direct, cost-controlled approach, namely, terminating employees, cutting costs, and selling off underperforming businesses. The current business environment is increasingly characterized by restructuring efforts to create "lean" organizations with "lean" management practices. True restructuring, however, involves much more than simply adding or selling a business, trimming staff, and relying on information technology, or reorganizing departmental configurations. Those restructuring efforts with the highest probability of creating long-term value also focus on realigning employee attitudes, values, and orientations.[111] Unfortunately, these less tangible dimensions of organizational life are usually the last factors to be addressed in a restructuring program because they are the most difficult for senior managers to control.

There are, of course, a number of benefits linked to successful resizing: lower overhead costs, less bureaucracy with faster decision making and smoother communications between organizational members, greater entrepreneurship, and increases in productivity. As research has indicated, however, the actual savings and benefits that result from an organizational restructuring and downsizing tend to fall far short of those that are anticipated.[112] In fact, far too many companies are ill-prepared to downsize, undertaking such cutbacks without appropriate retraining and/or redeployment policies in place and preparation to deal with the human resource problems that inevitably develop.

In contrast to traditional downsizing strategies, *resizing* is based on the ideal that organizational restructuring and the reallocation of resources have less to do with immediate market conditions than the emerging longer-term realities of business and industry trends.[113] The focus of resizing is to ensure that the firm is in a stronger position to respond to such shifts and transformations. Instead of using downsizing targets to drive the redesign of work processes and organizational structure, resizing begins with redesign efforts. When downsizing and cost-reduction drive work-related redesign, downsizing is the primary goal. When a redesign strategy and long-term performance improvement are the driving forces, in contrast, the primary goal is to change the way work is accomplished, literally redefining what work is important.[114] The underlying belief is that such continuous adaptation, rather than staggered layoffs and traditional approaches to downsizing, is the key to arresting decline. As research has suggested, in leading firms resizing means far more than simply paring down one's human resources. It requires a new, shared vision of the future of the organization—driven and supported by organizational redesign, retraining, and redeployment of organizational members—and a clearly articulated mission and strategy that are not only understood but "owned" by organizational members.[115] The challenge is to capture such advantages and benefits while minimizing the costs associated with such change.

Facilitating Workplace Recovery

In the wake of the lingering recession and jobless recovery of the mid-2000s, as the economy improved senior executives increasingly turned their attention to new business possibilities. As many of these individuals discovered, however, organizational members were often unprepared—both emotionally and cognitively—to pursue these emerging opportunities. The destabilizing events of the early 2000s—from the technology implosion and corporate scandals to widespread recession—have further fractured the fragile bond between companies and their members, a bond already weakened by the mismanagement of many past downsizing initiatives. Yet, even the best planned transitions have unintended, often dysfunctional, consequences for employees that, in turn, can create havoc at the organizational level. As such, it is critical for organizations to regain commitment and reenergize their workforce as part of their strategy for growth and renewal.

The idea of workplace recovery is intended to help organizational survivors of mergers, acquisitions, downsizings and related large-scale transitions by accelerating people's ability to let go of the past ("ending the old") and look toward the future ("accepting the new"). The underlying key is to address both the emotional realities (i.e., the situation as perceived from the employee perspective) and business imperatives (those actions that need to be fulfilled for business success to occur) associated with such change. A recent conceptualization of these challenges includes:[116]

- Showing *empathy* by letting organizational members know that leaders realize that things have been difficult and are likely to continue to be difficult during the transition. Key tasks include acknowledging the difficulties faced by the organization, offering workshops to raise awareness of the transition process, and using symbols, ceremonies and interactive forums to facilitate the "end of the old."

- *Engaging* people, helping them to develop an understanding of and support for the need to withdraw from the past and accept the new organizational order. Specific tasks include helping people get their work done, communicating and providing opportunities for involvement, and diagnosing and eliminating barriers to adaptation and performance.

- Creating *energy* among organizational members, getting them excited about the future direction of the organization and supporting them in working toward that future. Key challenges involve clarifying a new vision for the organization, creating a learning environment that encourages people to experiment with new ways of doing things, creating opportunities for short-term wins, and connecting with organizational members and providing them with psychological support during the change.

- *Enforcing* and solidifying the new mental models and orientations that fit the new direction of the organization. The main focus is on aligning systems and operating standards with the new direction, involving people in bringing that vision to life, and tracking and assessing the development of the new organizational order.

Within this context, research suggests that a number of issues should be considered and support structures developed prior to any restructuring or downsizing initiative.[117]

1. **Problem recognition and initial downsizing decisions:** Does the current situation reflect a temporary marketplace aberration or a permanent change? Should the focus be on a particular unit or organizationwide?

2. **Strategic planning:** What are the short-term (e.g., cost control) versus long-term (e.g., future market possibilities; size and nature of firm, ability to attract good employees) considerations? How will key stakeholder groups be affected?

3. **Consideration of alternatives:** Could there be potential reduction of nonpersonnel costs? Are there alternative courses of action (e.g., hiring freeze, pay/benefits freeze or cuts, voluntary retirement program attrition, job sharing, leaves of absence, redeployment)?

4. **Preparatory actions:** Does the downsizing plan conform to law and union agreements? How will the downsizing be communicated to organizational members? To external stakeholders? How will those affected be compensated? Has appropriate outplacement support been established?

5. **Development of specific action plans:** Have appropriate selection criteria been developed? How will affected employees be identified? Are mechanisms in place to allow for a modification of existing plans and the continued development of support systems?

6. **Downsizing program components:** Have specific programs, including financial assistance, job relocation assistance, and morale support, been formalized for "stayers"?

7. **Communication and implementation:** Have clear and concise announcements been formulated, focusing on the reasons for the downsizing, general terms and conditions, support programs, and so forth?

8. **Assistance to displaced personnel:** Are employee assistance programs in place for counseling, stress reduction, job search workshops, and placement services as needed?

9. **Follow-up and rebuilding:** Is the organization prepared to emphasize and support productivity enhancement and the morale of organizational survivors, and monitor (e.g., through focus groups) and evaluate downsizing-related outcomes? Emphasis must be placed on the future of the organization.

Although these considerations propose an enlightened approach to the difficult decisions inherent in the downsizing process, as noted earlier, in far too many instances such recommendations are not followed, leading to rising tensions and conflicts and stressful uncertainties for organizational members. There is usually (1) an overly narrow and restricted focus on technical concerns at the expense of broader organizational realities; (2) an emphasis on finances and tactics at the expense of production, service, innovation, and long-term strategies; (3) an emphasis on short-term shareholder value at the expense of broader stakeholder needs, and, perhaps most troublesome, (4) an emphasis on power and political machinations at the expense of the individuals who are caught up in the process.[118] It is important to underscore, however, that a myopic focus on the financial efficiencies that can be derived from a corporate consolidation or restructuring often serves only to disrupt the human fabric of the organization, a firm's true resource in a postindustrial world.

CONCLUSION

Organization development represents a systematic attempt to enhance organizational effectiveness through the use of planned diagnosis and intervention. The OD process usually includes some form of data collection and diagnosis, an action plan (change program) to deal with the problem(s) found in the diagnosis, and a follow-up effort to evaluate and maintain the change program. The main purpose is to "renew" the organization by enabling managers to apply behavioral science knowledge as they influence the transition of their organization from the present to the future.

As you approach organizational change, it is important to remember that a diagnostic approach is necessary. It is quite possible—and even probable—that a specific intervention that is effective in one organization will not work the same way in another firm. Although the tools and techniques discussed in these chapters have a proven track record, unless an organization's problems are sufficiently diagnosed and analyzed, and interventions are then fitted to meet those particular problems, frustration and disenchantment with the application of OB-related concepts and theories rather than personal satisfaction and organizational improvements are likely to occur.

NOTES

1. See J.B. Barney, "Integrating Organizational Behavior and Strategy Formulation Research: A Resource Based Analysis," *Advances in Strategic Management*, vol. 8 (Greenwich, CT: JAI Press, 1992), pp. 39–61; C.G. Worley, D.E. Hitchin, and W.L. Ross, *Integrated Strategic Change: How OD Builds Competitive Advantage* (Reading, MA: Addison-Wesley, 1996); P.T. Anderson and G. Ovaice, "Strategic Organization Development: A Seat at the Table," *Organization Development Journal* 24 no. 4 (2006): 29–37; R.K. Singh, S.K. Garg, and S.G. Deshmukh, "Strategy Development for Competitiveness: A Study on Indian Auto Components Sector," *International Journal of Productivity & Performance Management* 56 (2007): 285–304; and R. Biancino and C. Zevalkink, "Soft Skills: The New

Curriculum for Hard-Core Technical Professionals," *Techniques: Connecting Education & Careers* 82, no. 5 (2007): 20–22.
2. The discussion of the laboratory training and survey feedback stems of OD was drawn from W.L. French and C.H. Bell, "A Brief History of Organization Development," *Journal of Contemporary Business* (Summer 1972): 1–8; and E.F. Huse, *Organization Development and Change* (St. Paul, MN: West, 1980), pp. 30–33.
3. B. Cooke, "The Kurt Lewin–Goodwin Watson FBA/CIA Files: A 60th Anniversary There-and-Then of the Here-and-Now," *Human Relations* 60, no. 3 (2007): 435–462.
4. For a fuller discussion of this research see F.C. Mann, "Studying and Creating Change," in W. Bennis, K. Benne, and R. Chin, eds., *The

Planning of Change (New York: Holt, Rinehart & Winston, 1961), pp. 605–613.

5. See D. Sirota, "Why Managers Don't Use Survey Results," in S.W. Gellerman, *Behavioral Science in Management* (Baltimore: Penguin, 1974), pp. 86–98; R.B. Dunham and F.J. Smith, *Organizational Surveys: An Internal Assessment of Organizational Health* (Dallas: Scott, Foresman, 1979); T. Rickards and J. Bessant, "A Mirror for Change: Survey Feedback Experiences," *Leadership and Organization Development Journal* 1, no. 2 (1980): 10–14; N. Rosen, "Employee Attitude Surveys: What Managers Should Know," *Training & Development Journal* (November 1987): 50–52; and K. Liberman, "Survey Employees: Avoiding a Company Pitfall," *Journal of Compensation & Benefits* 21, no. 5 (2005): 18–20.

6. For a fuller discussion of the survey feedback process see D. Nadler, *Feedback and Organization Development* (Reading, MA: Addison-Wesley, 1977); and R. Golembiewski and R. Hilles, *Toward the Responsive Organization: The Theory and Practice of Survey Feedback* (Salt Lake City: Brighton, 1979).

7. For an example of the questionnaire see J. Taylor and D. Bowers, *The Survey of Organizations: A Machine Scored Standardized Questionnaire Instrument* (Ann Arbor: Institute for Social Research, 1972).

8. C.P. Alderfer and L.D. Brown, "Questionnaire Design in Organizational Research," *Journal of Applied Psychology* 56, no. 6 (1972): 456–460.

9. J.L. Bowditch and A.F. Buono, *Quality of Work Life Assessment: A Survey-Based Approach* (Boston: Auburn House, 1982).

10. C. Faucheux, G. Amado, and A. Laurent, "Organizational Development and Change," *Annual Review of Psychology* 33 (1982): 347–349.

11. M. Sashkin and W.W. Burke, "Organization Development in the 1980s," *Journal of Management* 13, no. 2 (1987): 393–418.

12. R.W. Woodman, "Organizational Change and Development: New Areas for Inquiry and Action," *Journal of Management* 15 (1989): 205–228; and R. Fry, F. Barrett, J. Seiling and D. Whitney, eds., *Appreciative Inquiry and Organizational Transformation:* *Reports from the Field* (Westport, CT: Quorum, 2002).

13. See A.M. Jaeger, "Organization Development Methods in Practice: A Five-Country Study," *Advances in International Comparative Management*, vol. 4 (Greenwich, CT: JAI Press, 1989), pp. 113–130; and E.A. Fagenson and W.W. Burke, "The Activities of Organization Development Practitioners at the Turn of the Decade of the 1990s: A Study of Their Predictions," *Group & Organization Studies* 15, no. 4 (1990): 366–380.

14. See, for example, M. Emery and R.E. Purser, *The Search Conference: A Powerful Method for Planning Organizational Change* (San Francisco: Jossey-Bass, 1996); and C.D. O'Brien and A.F. Buono, "Creating Learning Organizations: Working with Organizations to Access Their Collective Intelligence," *Organization Development Journal* 17, no. 4 (1999): 103–111.

15. N. Adler and P. Docherty, "Bringing Business into Sociotechnical Theory and Practice," *Human Relations* 51, no. 3 (1998): 319–345; and J. De Leede, J.K. Loosie and M. Verkerk, "The Mini-Company: A Specification of Sociotechnical Business Systems," *Personnel Review* 31, no. 3 (2002): 338–355.

16. See, for example, M.C. Anderson and Associates, *Fast Cycle Organization Development: A Fieldbook for Organization Transformation* (Cincinnati: South-Western, 2000).

17. C. Piotrowski and T.R. Armstrong, "The Research Literature in Organization Development: Recent Trends and Current Directions," *Organization Development Journal* 22, no. 2 (2004): 48–54.

18. M.S. Plovnick, R.E. Fry, and W.W. Burke, *Organization Development: Exercises, Cases, and Readings* (Boston: Little, Brown, 1982), pp. 5–6; and S. Cady, "Staying True to Purpose: The Key to Sustainability of Our Work in OD," *Organization Development Journal* 21, no. 2 (2003): 1–2.

19. See Sashkin and Burke, "Organization Development in the 1980s."

20. See W.L. French and C.H. Bell, Jr. "A Definition of Organization Development," in W.L. French, C.H. Bell, and R.A. Zawacki, eds., *Organization Development: Theory, Practice and Research* (Plano, TX: Business

Publications, 1983), pp. 27–30; and W.L. French and C.H. Bell, Jr., *Organization Development*, 5th ed. (Englewood Cliffs: Prentice Hall, 1995), p. 33.

21. See A.J. Nurick, "Participation in Organizational Change: A Longitudinal Field Study," *Human Relations* 35, no. 5 (1982): 413–430; A.J. Marrow, D.G. Bowers, and S.E. Seashore, *Management by Participation* (New York: Harper & Row, 1967); R.J. Magjuka, "Survey: Self-Managed Work Teams Achieve Continuous Improvement Best," *National Productivity Review* 11, no. 1 (1991/92): 51–57; E.E. Lawler III, S.A. Mohrman, and G.E. Ledford, Jr., *Employee Involvement and Total Quality Management: Practices and Results in Fortune 1000 Companies* (San Francisco: Jossey-Bass, 1992); and S. Kim, "Participative Management and Job Satisfaction: Lessons for Management Leadership," *Public Administration Review* 62, no. 2 (2002): 231–241.

22. For a good summary of recent work in this area see D.J. Glew, A.M. O'Leary-Kelly, R.W. Griffin, and D.D. Van Fleet, "Participation in Organizations: A Preview of the Issues and Proposed Framework for Future Analysis," *Journal of Management* 21, no. 3 (1995): 395–421. See also D.A. Harrison, D.A. Newman, and P.L. Roth, "How Important Are Job Attitudes? Meta-Analytic Comparisons of Integrative Behavioral Outcomes and Time Sequences," *Academy of Management Journal* 49, no. 2 (2006): 305–325.

23. F.M. Hill, "An Evaluative Study of the Attitudinal and Performance-Related Outcomes of Quality Circle Participation," *International Journal of Quality and Reliability Management* 10, no. 4 (1993): 28–47; and T.L. Tang, P.S. Tollison, and H.D. Whiteside, "The Case of Active and Inactive Quality Circles," *Journal of Social Psychology* 136, no. 1 (1996): 57–67.

24. See, for example, E. Locke, D. Schweiger, and G. Latham, "Participation in Decision Making: When Should It Be Used?" *Organizational Dynamics* 14, no. 3 (1986): 65–79; and E.E. Lawler III, "Transformation from Control to Involvement," in R.H. Kilmann, T.J. Covin, and Associates, *Corporate Transformation: Revitalizing Organizations for a Competitive World* (San Francisco: Jossey-Bass, 1988), pp. 46–65; and A. Somech, "Explicating the Complexity of Participative Management: An Investigation of Multiple Dimensions," *Education Administration Quarterly* 38, no. 3 (2002): 341–371.

25. French and Bell, *Organization Development*, pp. 94–97.

26. J.L. Cotton, D.A. Vollrath, K.L. Froggatt, M.L. Lengnick-Hall, and K.R. Jennings, "Employee Participation: Diverse Forms and Different Outcomes," *Academy of Management Review* 13, no. 1 (1988): 8–22; and J. Abel and L. Pries, "Shifting Patterns of Labor Regulation: Highly Qualified Knowledge Workers in German New Media Companies," *Critical Sociology* 33, no. 1/2 (2007): 101–125.

27. For a good overview of early QWL concerns see L.E. Davis and A.B. Cherns, eds., *The Quality of Working Life*, vols. 1 and 2 (New York: Free Press, 1975). See also D.A. Nadler and E.E. Lawler III, "Quality of Work Life: Perspectives and Directions," *Organizational Dynamics* (Winter 1983): 20–30.

28. See R.E. Walton, "Criteria for Quality of Working Life," in Davis and Cherns, ibid., pp. 93–97. See also L.E. Beaudoin and L. Edgar, "Hassles: Their Impact on Nurses' Quality of Work Life," *Nursing Economics* 21, no. 3 (2003): 106–112.

29. See E.E. Lawler III, "Strategies for Improving the Quality of Work Life," *American Psychologist* 37, no. 5 (1982): 486–493.

30. See, for example, A.J. Nurick, *Participation in Organizational Change: The TVA Experiment* (New York: Praeger, 1985); G.D. Kleim, "Employee-Centered Productivity and QWL Programs: Findings from an Area Study," *National Productivity Review* 5, no. 4 (1986): 348–362; P.F. Sorensen, Jr., T.C. Head, and D. Stotz, "Quality of Work Life and the Small Organization: A Four-Year Case Study," *Group & Organization Studies* 10, no. 3 (1985): 320–339; D.A. Ondrack and M.G. Evans, "Job Enrichment and Job Satisfaction in Quality of Working Life and Nonquality of Working Life Work Sites," *Human Relations* 39, no. 9 (1986): 871–889.

31. See R.E. Herman and J.L. Gioia, "Making Work Meaningful: Secrets of the Future-Focused Corporation," *The Futurist* (December 1998): 24–26, 35–38; and F.B. Green and E. Hatch, "Does Business Process Reengineering Diminish the Quality of Work Life?" *Social Indicators Research* 60, no. 1–3 (2003): 299–308.

32. R.R. Sims and S.J. Sims, *Changes and Challenges for the Human Resource Professional* (Westport, CT: Quorum Books, 1994).

33. See D.J. Reed, "One Approach to Employee Assistance," *Personnel Journal* 62, no. 8 (1983): 648–652; and D. Drehmer, "A Look at the Counseling Practices of a Major U.S. Corporation," *Personnel Administrator* 28, no. 6 (1983): 76–81, 143–146.

34. H. Shore, "Employee Assistance Programs—Reaping the Benefits," *Sloan Management Review* (Spring 1984): 69–73; and "Aetna to Provide Employee Assistance Services to Small Group Health Plans," *Managed Care Outlook* 20, no. 8 (2007): 11.

35. See P. Kiger, "Lessons from a Crisis: How Communication Kept a Company Together," *Workforce* 80, no. 11 (2001): 28–35.

36. H.K. Freudenberger, *Burn Out: The High Cost of High Achievement* (Garden City, NY: Anchor/Doubleday, 1980); and A.P. Brief, R.S. Schuler, and N. Van Sell, *Managing Job Stress* (Boston: Little, Brown, 1981).

37. For a more in-depth discussion of flexitime see D.J. Petersen, "Flexitime in the United States: The Lessons of Experience," *Personnel* (January–February 1980): 21–31; C.B. Bard, "Flexitime Under Scrutiny: Research on Work Adjustment and Organizational Performance," *Personnel Administrator* 25, no. 5 (1980): 69–74; and P. Dunne, "Introducing Flexitime," *Management Today* (September 1999): 96.

38. For more detail on the compressed work week see B.J. Hodge and R.D. Tellier, "Employee Reactions to the Four-Day Week," *California Management Review* (Fall 1975): 25–30; J.M. Ivancevich and H.L. Lyon, "The Shortened Work Week: A Field Experiment," *Journal of Applied Psychology* 62 (1977): 34–37; and M. Tan-Solano and B.H. Kleiner, "Effects of Telecommuting on Organisational Behaviour," *Management Research News* 24, no. 3/4 (2001): 123–126.

39. W.D. Hicks and R.J. Klimoski, "The Impact of Flexitime on Employee Attitudes," *Academy of Management Journal* 24, no. 2 (1981): 333–341; J.R. Turney and S.L. Cohen, "Alternative Work Schedules Increase Employee Satisfaction," *Personnel Journal* (March 1983): 199–207; M. Tippins and L.K. Stroh, "The 4/4 Work Schedule: Impact on Employee Productivity and Work Attitudes in a Continuous Operation Industry," *Journal of Applied Business Research* 9, no. 3 (1994): 136–145; and E. Heyn, "The Daddy Track," *Parenting* 17, no. 7 (2003): 150–152.

40. A.S. Glickman and Z.H. Brown, *Changing Schedules of Work: Patterns and Implications* (Kalamazoo, MI: W.E. Upjohn Institute, 1974), pp. 36–39; R.J. Donahue, "Flexible Time Systems: Flex Time Systems in New York," *Public Personnel Management* 4, no. 4 (1975): 214; and S.J. Havlovic, D.C. Lau and L.T. Pinfield, "Repercussions of Work Schedule Congruence Among Full-Time, Part-Time, and Contingent Nurses," *Health Care Management Review* 27, no. 4 (2002): 30–41.

41. D.T. Hall, *Careers in Organizations* (Santa Monica: Goodyear, 1976), p. 4; also see John Van Maanen and Edgar H. Schein, "Career Development," in Hackman and Suttle, op. cit., pp. 30–95.

42. P.O. Benham, Jr., "Developing Organizational Talent: The Key to Performance and Productivity," *SAM Advanced Management Journal* 58, no. 1 (1993): 34–39; S. Sherman, "A Brave New Darwinian Workplace," *Fortune*, January 25, 1993, pp. 50–56; and R. Aubrey and P.M. Cohen, *Working Wisdom: Timeless Skills and Vanguard Strategies for Learning Organizations* (San Francisco: Jossey-Bass, 1995).

43. See D.T. Hall and P.H. Mirvis, "The New Career Contract: Developing the Whole Person at Midlife and Beyond," *Journal of Vocational Behavior* 47, no. 2 (1995): 269–289; and S.M. MacDermid, M.D. Lee, M. Buck, and M.L. Williams, "Alternative Work Arrangements Among Professionals and Managers: Rethinking Career Development and Success," *Journal of Management* 20, no. 4 (2001): 305–317.

44. R.J. Mirabile, "New Directions for Career Development," *Training and Development Journal* 41, no. 12 (1987): 30–33; M.B. Arthur, "Career Development and Participation at Work: Time for Mating?" *Human Resources Management* 27, no. 2 (1988): 181–199; and T.K. Christensen and J.A. Johnson, "Incorporating the Narrative in Career Planning," *Journal of Career Development* 29, no. 3 (2003): 149–160.

45. The following discussion is drawn from M. Matteson and J.M. Ivancevich, *Controlling Work Stress: Effective Human Resource and Management Strategies* (San Francisco: Jossey-Bass, 1987). An interesting discussion of the stress that can be precipitated by such "positive" interventions as work teams and related Japanese management practices can be found in M. Parker and J. Slaughter, "Management by Stress," *Technology Review* (October 1988): 37–44. See also H. Neville, "Workplace Accidents: They Cost More Than You Might Think," *Industrial Management* 40, no. 1 (1998): 7–9; National Audit Office, "Workplace Accidents in NHS on the Rise," *Occupational Health* 55, no. 6 (2003): 5; and S. Edward, F. Coffield, R. Steer, and M. Gregson, "Endless Change in the Learning and Skills Sector: The Impact on Teaching Staff," *Journal of Vocational Education & Training* 59, no. 2 (2007): 155–173.

46. See B.S. Dohrenwend and B. Dohrenwend, eds., *Stressful Life Events: Their Nature and Effects* (New York: Wiley, 1974); A.P. Brief and J.M. Atieh, "Studying Job Stress: Are We Making Mountains out of Molehills?" in J.A. Pearce and R.B. Robinson, Jr., eds., *Academy of Management Best Paper Proceedings, 1986* (Academy of Management, 1986), pp. 170–174; and R.S. Lazarus and S. Folkman, *Stress, Appraisal, and Coping* (New York: Springer, 1985).

47. The following discussion is based on D. Etzion, "The Experience of Burnout and Work/Non-Work Success in Male and Female Engineers: A Matched-Pairs Comparison," *Human Resource Management* 27, no. 2 (1988): 163–179; and J.M. Angerer, "Job Burnout," *Journal of Employment Counseling* 40, no. 3 (2003): 98–107.

48. C. Dubnicki and L.D. Prince, "Personal Growth Training," in W.R. Tracey, ed., *Human Resources Management and Development Handbook* (New York: AMACOM, 1985), pp. 1211–1212.

49. See S. Newell, *Creating the Healthy Organization: Well-Being, Diversity & Ethics at Work* (London: Thomson Learning, 2002).

50. See K. Danna and R.W. Griffin, "Health and Well-Being in the Workplace: A Review and Synthesis of the Literature," *Journal of Management* 25, no. 3 (1999): 357–384; L. Esola, "Employers Cook Up Ways to Boost Healthy Living," *Business Insurance* 41, no. 15 (2007): 13–14; and J. Ingham and A.J. Norris, "Health and Wellness Programs Help Manage Human Capital," *Strategic HR Review* 6, no. 3 (2007): 10–11.

51. M.T. Murphy, "The History of Employee Services and Recreation," *Parks & Recreation* 19 (August 1984): 34–39.

52. Reported in S. Feinstein, "Labor Letter: Wellness Programs Are Promoted by More Firms," *Wall Street Journal*, January 17, 1989, p. 1. See also K. Pallarito, "Wellness Features Fused with Work/Life Programs." *Business Insurance* 40, no. 25 (2006): 11–20.

53. See B. Lau, "Corporate Fitness Programs," *NRECA Management Quarterly* (Spring 1985): 20–24; and C. Finney, "Corporate Benefits of Employee Recreation Programs," *Parks & Recreation* 19 (August 1984): 44–46, 71. See also J.A. Jacob, "Wellness Programs Help Companies Save on Health Costs," *American Medical News* 45, no. 1 (2002): 36–37.

54. Danna and Griffin, "Health and Well-Being in the Workplace," p. 360; P.J. Haynes and M.M. Helms, "Increasing Participation in Corporate Wellness Programs: A Segmentation Study of Employee Differences," *Services Marketing Quarterly* 23, no. 2 (2001): 49–60.

55. G. Gonzalez, "Employee Buy-In Viewed as Vital for Success of Wellness Programs," *Business Insurance* 41, no. 12 (2007): 4, 19.

56. See C.H. Deutsch, "Rewarding Employees for 'Wellness,'" *New York Times*, September 15, 1991, p. F21; A. Korney, "Balancing Work/Life No Longer Optional." *Accounting Technology* 23, no. 3 (2007): 10; and

M. Conlin, "Get Healthy—Or Else." *Business Week*, February 26, 2007, pp. 58–69.

57. See Herman and Gioia, "Making Work Meaningful," pp. 37–38; L.G. Bolman and T.E. Deal, *Leading with Soul: An Uncommon Journey of Spirit* (San Francisco: Jossey-Bass, 1995); M. Basadur, "Organization Development Interventions for Enhancing Creativity in the Workplace," *Journal of Creative Behavior* 31, no. 1 (1997): 59–72; J. Milliman, A.J. Czaplewski, and J. Ferguson, "Workplace Spirituality and Employee Work Attitudes: An Exploratory Empirical Assessment," *Journal of Organizational Change Management* 16, no. 4 (2003): 426–447; and Y.A. Nur and D.W. Organ, "Selected Organizational Outcome Correlates of Spirituality in the Workplace." *Psychological Reports* 98, no. 1 (2006): 111–120.

58. M. Conlin, "Religion in the Workplace: The Growing Presence of Spirituality in Corporate America," *Business Week*, November 1, 1999, pp. 150–158; and A.J. Vogl, "Can This Soul Be Saved?" *Across the Board* 42, no. 2 (2005): 26–30.

59. See C. Argyris, *Intervention Theory and Method* (Reading, MA: Addison-Wesley, 1970).

60. K. Lewin, *Field Theory in Social Science* (New York: Harper & Row, 1951), see especially pp. 228–229.

61. See E. Schein, "Mechanisms of Change," in Bennis, Benne, and Chin, op. cit., pp. 98–167; and Plovnick, Fry, and Burke, op. cit., pp. 12–14.

62. R.M. Kanter, B.A. Stein, and T.D. Jick, *The Challenge of Organizational Change: How Companies Experience It and Leaders Guide It* (New York: Free Press, 1992), pp. 375–376.

63. See, for example, M. Weisbord, "Toward Third-Wave Managing and Consulting," *Organizational Dynamics* (Winter 1987): 5–24.

64. This discussion is drawn from K.E. Weick and R.E. Quinn, "Organizational Change and Development," *Annual Review of Psychology* 50 (1999): 361–386. See also E. Abrahamson, "Change without Pain," *Harvard Business Review* 78, no. 4 (2000): 75–79.

65. See K. Kerber, "Change in Human Systems: From Planned Change to Guided

Changing," in A.F. Buono, ed., *Current Trends in Management Consulting* (Greenwich, CT: Information Age Publishing, 2001), pp. 145–169.

66. The discussion of planned change is adapted from R. Lippitt, J. Watson, and B. Westley, *The Dynamics of Planned Change* (New York: Harcourt, 1958); and Bowditch and Buono, *Quality of Work Life Assessment*, pp. 41–42.

67. For a more complete discussion of the action research model, see W.L. French, "Organization Development Objectives, Assumptions, and Strategies," *California Management Review* 12, no. 2 (1969): 23–34; and French and Bell, *Organization Development*, pp. 138–151.

68. See V. Woodell, "An Interview with Chris Argyris," *Organization Development Journal* 21, no. 2 (2003): 67–70.

69. H.L. Newman and S.P. Fitzgerald, "Appreciative Inquiry with an Executive Team: Moving Along the Action Research Continuum," *Organization Development Journal* 19, no. 3 (2001): 37–44.

70. This section is based on S. Srivastva and D. Cooperrider, *Appreciative Inquiry and Leadership: The Power of Positive Thought and Action in Organizations* (San Francisco: Jossey-Bass, 1990); S.A. Hammond, *The Thin Book of Appreciative Inquiry* (Plano, TX: Kodiak Consulting, 1996); G. Johnson and W. Leavitt, "Building on Success: Transforming Organizations Through Appreciate Inquiry," *Public Personnel Management* 30, no. 1 (2001): 129–136; J.M. Watkins and B.J. Mohr, *Appreciative Inquiry: Change at the Speed of Imagination* (San Francisco: Jossey-Bass, 2001); and C. Keers, "Using Appreciative Inquiry to Measure Employee Engagement," *Strategic HR Review* 6, no. 2 (2007): 10–11.

71. For a thoughtful critique of the appreciative inquiry process, see S. Grant and M. Humphries, "Critical Evaluation of Appreciative Inquiry," *Action Research* 4, no. 4 (2006): 401–418.

72. D.G. Bowers, J.L. Franklin, and P. Pecorella, "Matching Problems, Precursors, and Interventions in OD," *Journal of Applied Behavioral Science* 11 (1975): 391–410; R. Lippit and G. Lippit, "Consulting Process in Action," parts 1 and 2, *Training and Development Journal* 29 (May and June 1975): 48–54, 38–44 respectively; S. White and T. Mitchell, "Organization Development: A Review of Research Content and Research Design," *Academy of Management Review* 1, no. 1 (1976): 57–73; and R. A. Schmuck and M. B. Miles, eds., *Organization Development in Schools* (La Jolla, CA: University Associates, 1976), pp. 7–10.

73. See T.G. Cummings and C.G. Worley, *Organization Development and Change*, 5th ed. (Minneapolis: West, 1993), pp. 166–171.

74. E.F. Huse and M. Beer, "An Eclectic Approach to OD," *Harvard Business Review* 49, no. 5 (1971): 103–112; and R.E. Zackrison and A. Freedman, "Some Reasons Why Consulting Interventions Fail," *Organization Development Journal* 21, no. 1 (2003): 72–74.

75. The following discussion is based on R. Harrison, "Choosing the Depth of Organizational Intervention," *Journal of Applied Behavioral Science* 6, no. 2 (1970): 181–202.

76. See A.M. Mohrman, Jr. and E.E. Lawler III, "The Diffusion of QWL as a Paradigm Shift," in W. G. Bennis, K.D. Benne, and R. Chin, eds., *The Planning of Change*, 4th ed. (New York: Holt, Rinehart & Winston, 1985).

77. See, for example, R.E. Walton, "From Control to Commitment in the Workplace," *Harvard Business Review* 63, no. 2 (1985): 76–84; and E.E. Lawler III, *High Involvement Management* (San Francisco: Jossey-Bass, 1986).

78. L.D. Brown, "Planned Change in Underorganized Systems," in T. Cummings, ed., *Systems Theory for Organization Development* (New York: Wiley, 1980).

79. T.G. Cummings and K.K. Motamedi, "Transorganizational Development," in B. Staw, ed., *Research in Organizational Behavior*, vol. 6 (Greenwich CT; JAI Press, 1984); T.G. Cummings, "Transorganizational Development," *Academy of Management Organization Development Division Newsletter*, 1989 (Summer), 8–10; A.A. Halley, "Applications of Transorganization Development to Congressional-Executive Relations," *Public Relations Quarterly* 18, no. 2 (1994): 177–203; A.F. Buono, ed., *Enhancing Inter-firm Networks and Interorganizational Strategies* (Greenwich, CT: Information Age Publishing, 2003).

80. See A.M. Mohrman, Jr., S.A. Mohrman, G.E. Ledford, Jr., T.G. Cummings, E.E. Lawler III, and Associates, *Large-Scale Organizational Change* (San Francisco: Jossey-Bass, 1989); A.F. Buono, "Technology Transfer through Acquisition," *Management Decision* 35, no. 3 (1997): 194–204; and N. Clarke, "Transorganization Development for Network Building," *Journal of Applied Behavioral Science* 41, no. 1 (2005): 30–46.

81. Brown, "Planned Change in Underorganized Systems."

82. See, for example, M. Beer, "Towards a Redefinition of OD: A Critique of Research Focus and Method," *Academy of Management OD Newsletter* (Winter 1988): 6–7; and J. Mozenter, "Recent Research Links Macro Forces, Emerging Trends and OD's Expanding Role," *Organization Development Journal* 20, no. 2 (2002): 48–58.

83. This section is adapted from W.L. French and C.H. Bell, Jr., *Organization Development: Behavioral Science Interventions for Organizational Improvement*, 6th ed. (Upper Saddle River, NJ: Prentice Hall, 1999), pp. 46–50; and E.B. Dent, "The Complexity Science Organization Development Practitioner," *Organization Development Journal* 21, no. 2 (2003): 82–86.

84. W.E. Ruona and S.K. Gibson, "The Making of Twenty-First-Century HR: An Analysis of the Convergence of HRM, HRD, and OD," *Human Resource Management* 43, no. 1 (2004): 49–66.

85. See C.G. Worley and A.E. Feyerherm, "Reflections on the Future of Organization Development," *Journal of Applied Behavioral Science* 39, no. 1 (2003): 97–126.

86. R.E. Cole "Large-Scale Change and the Quality Revolution," in Mohrman et al., *Large-Scale Organizational Change*, pp. 229–254; and E.E. Lawler III, "Strategic Choices for Changing Organizations," in Mohrman, et al., *Large-Scale Organizational Change*, pp. 255–271.

87. E. Abrahamson, "Change Without Pain."

88. Kanter, Stein, and Jick, op. cit., pp. 376–382; see also S.W. Floyd and P.J. Lane, "Strategizing throughout the Organization: Managing Role Conflict in Strategic Renewal," *Academy of Management Review* 25, no. 1 (2000): 154–177.

89. This discussion draws heavily from K.W. Kerber and A.F. Buono, "Rethinking Organizational Change: Reframing the Challenge of Change Management," *Organization Development Journal* 23, no. 3 (2005): 23–38.

90. D. Ulrich, J. Zenger, and N. Smallwood, *Results-Based Leadership: How Leaders Build the Business and Improve the Bottom Line* (Boston: Harvard Business School Press, 1999).

91. See, for example, J.A. Olsson, J. Ovretveit, and P. Kammerlind, "Developing and Testing a Model to Predict Outcomes of Organizational Change," *Quality Management in Health Care* 12, no. 4 (2003): 240–249; and S.L. Walston and C. Chadwick, "Perceptions and Misperceptions of Major Organizational Changes in Hospitals: Do Change Efforts Fail Because of Inconsistent Organizational Perceptions of Restructuring and Reengineering?" *International Journal of Public Administration* 26, no. 14 (2003): 1581–1605.

92. K. Lewin, "Frontiers in Group Dynamics," *Human Relations* 1, no. 1 (1947): 5–47; and Lewin, *Field Theory in Social Science.*

93. See J.A. Oxman and B.D. Smith, "The Limits of Structural Change." *Sloan Management Review* 45, no. 1 (2003): 77–82.

94. J. Gosling and H. Mintzberg, "The Five Minds of a Manager," *Harvard Business Review* 81, no. 11 (2003): 54–63.

95. See P. Vaill, *Managing as a Performing Art* (San Francisco: Jossey-Bass, 1989).

96. The discussion of enabling change is adapted from T.D. Jick and M.A. Peipel, *Managing Change: Cases and Concepts,* 2nd ed. (Homewood, IL: Irwin, 2003); and M. Beer and N. Nohria, "Cracking the Code of Change," *Harvard Business Review* 78, no. 3 (2000): 141.

97. The following discussion is based on N. Tichy, *Managing Strategic Change: Technical, Political, and Cultural Dynamics* (New York: Wiley, 1983).

98. For a further assessment of the political nature of organizations see R.M. Cyert and J.G. March, *A Behavioral Theory of the Firm* (Englewood Cliffs, NJ: Prentice Hall, 1963); H. Mintzberg, *Power In and Around Organizations* (Englewood Cliffs, NJ: Prentice Hall, 1983); M. London, *Principled Leadership and Business Diplomacy* (Westport, CT: Quorum Books, 1999), Chapter 3; and J.M.L. Poon, "Situational Antecedents and Outcomes of Organizational Politics Perceptions," *Journal of Managerial Psychology* 18, no. 1/2 (2003): 138–155.

99. See R. Stacey, *Complexity and Creativity in Organizations* (San Francisco: Berrett-Koehler, 1996), pp. 234–237.

100. R. Beckhard and R.T. Harris, *Organizational Transitions: Managing Complex Change* (Reading, MA: Addison-Wesley, 1977); and Tichy, op. cit., pp. 347–352. See also M. Beer, "The Critical Path for Change: Keys to Success and Failure in Six Companies," in R.H. Kilmann, T.J. Covin, and Associates, *Corporate Transformation* (San Francisco: Jossey-Bass, 1988), pp. 17–45; and D. Butcher and M. Clarke, "Redefining Managerial Work: Smart Politics," *Management Decision* 41, no. 5/6 (2003): 477–487.

101. M.L. Tushman, W.H. Newman, and D.A. Nadler, "Executive Leadership and Organizational Evolution: Managing Incremental and Discontinuous Change," in Kilmann et al., op. cit., see pp. 120–121; and Tichy, op. cit., p. 348.

102. See R. M. Kanter, "The Reshaping of Middle Management," *Management Review* 75, no. 1 (1986): 19–20; T.R. Horton, "The Middle Manager—Caught in the Middle," *Management Review* 76, no. 1 (1987): 3; and R. DeWitt, L.K. Trevino, and K.A. Mollica, "Stuck in the Middle: A Control-Based Model of Managers' Reactions to their Subordinates' Layoffs," *Journal of Managerial Issues* 15, no. 1 (2003): 32–49.

103. H. Brimm and A. Murdock, "Delivering the Message in Challenging Times: The Relative Effectiveness of Different Forms of Communicating Change to a Dispersed and Part-Time Workforce," *Total Quality Management* 9, nos. 2–3 (1998): 167–180. See also, E. Schein, *The Corporate Culture Survival*

Guide (San Francisco: Jossey-Bass, 1999), Chapter 6; and D.J. Stanley, K.P. Meyer, and L. Topolnytsky, "Employee Cynicism and Resistance to Organizational Change," *Journal of Business & Psychology* 19, no. 4 (2005): 429–459.

104. See, for example, E. Kübler-Ross, *On Death and Dying* (New York: Macmillan, 1969); M.L. Marks and P.H. Mirvis, "Merger Syndrome: Stress and Uncertainty," *Mergers & Acquisitions* (Summer 1985): 50–55; and H. Woodward and S. Bucholz, *Aftershock* (New York: Wiley, 1987).

105. This discussion is adapted from A.F. Buono and A.J. Nurick, "Intervening in the Middle: Coping Strategies in Mergers and Acquisitions," *Human Resource Planning* 15, no. 2 (1992): 19–33.

106. E.H. Schein, "A General Philosophy of Helping: Process Consultation," *Sloan Management Review* 31, no. 3 (1990): 57–64; and M.J. Darling, "Coaching People Through Difficult Times," *HR Magazine* 39, no. 11 (1994): 70–73.

107. R. Kahn, D. Wolfe, R. Quinn, J. Snoek, and R. Rosenthal, *Organizational Stress: Studies in Role Conflict and Ambiguity* (New York: Wiley, 1964); J.R. Rizzo, R.J. House, and S.I. Lirtzman, "Role Conflict and Role Ambiguity in Complex Organizations," *Administrative Science Quarterly* 15 (1970): 150–163; and A. Styhre, A. Ingelgard, P. Beausang, M. Castenfors, K. Mulec, and J. Roth, "Emotional Management and Stress: Managing Ambiguities," *Organization Studies* 23, no. 1 (2003): 83–103.

108. P. Vaill, *Managing as a Performing Art*.

109. K.E. Weick, "Small Wins: Redefining the Scale of Social Problems," *American Psychologist* 39, no. 1 (1984): 40–49.

110. See W.F. Whyte, "Work Redesign and Cross-Cultural Lessons," in R. Schrank, ed., *Industrial Democracy at Sea: Authority and Democracy on a Norwegian Freighter* (Cambridge, MA: MIT Press, 1983), pp. 156–170.

111. See N.F. Whiteley, Jr., "Commentary: Why Restructurings Fail," *Across the Board* 28, no. 9 (1991): 13–14; H.P. Weinstein and M.S. Leibman, "Corporate Scale Down, What Comes Next," *HR Magazine* 36, no. 8 (1991):

33–37; Z. Jin and C. Hui, "Should Lean Replace Mass Organization Systems?" *Journal of International Business Studies* 30, no. 1 (1999): 45–68; and W. McKinley, J. Zhao, and K.G. Rust, "A Sociocognitive Interpretation of Organizational Downsizing," *Academy of Management Review* 25, no. 1 (2000): 227–243.

112. See, for example, D.A. Heenan, "The Downside of Downsizing," *Journal of Business Strategy* (November–December 1989): 18–23; R. Zemke, "The Ups and Downs of Downsizing," *Training* (November 1990): 27–34; W.F. Cascio, "Downsizing: What Do We Know? What Have We Learned?" *Academy of Management Executive* 7, no. 1 (1993): 95–104; J.R. Morris, W.F. Cascio, and C.E. Young, "Downsizing after All These Years: Questions and Answers about Who Did It, How Many Did It, and Who Benefited from It," *Organization Dynamics* (Winter 1999): 78–87; and M. Beylerian and H. Kleiner, "The Downsized Workplace," *Management Research News* 26, no. 2–4 (2003): 97–107.

113. A.F. Buono, "The Hidden Costs and Benefits of Organizational Resizing Activities," in K.P. DeMeuse and M.L. Marks, eds., *Resizing the Organization: Managing Layoffs, Divestitures, and Closings* (San Francisco: Jossey-Bass, 2003), pp. 306–346.

114. See S.J. Freeman, "The Gestalt of Organizational Downsizing: Downsizing Strategies as Packets of Change," *Human Relations* 52, no. 12 (1999): 1505–1541.

115. See P.H. Mirvis, "Human Resource Management: Leaders, Laggards, and Followers," *Academy of Management Executive* 11, no. 2 (1997): 43–56.

116. This section is drawn from M.L. Marks, *Charging Back up the Hill: Workplace Recovery after Mergers, Acquisitions, and Downsizings* (San Francisco: Jossey-Bass, 2003).

117. See L.T. Perry, "Least-Cost Alternatives to Layoffs in Declining Industries," *Organizational Dynamics* 14, no. 4 (1986): 48–61; S.H. Appelbaum, R. Simpson, and B.T. Shapiro, "The Tough Test of Downsizing," *Organizational Dynamics* 16, no. 2 (1988): 68–79; K.S. Cameron, "Strategies for Successful Downsizing," *Human Resource*

Management 33, no. 2 (1994): 189–211; W.E. Hopkins and S.A. Hopkins, "The Ethics of Downsizing: Perceptions of Rights and Responsibilities," *Journal of Business Ethics* 18 (1999): 145–156. See also M.A. Campion, T.V. Mumford, F.P. Morgeson, and J.D. Nahrgang, "Work Redesign: Eight Obstacles and Opportunities," *Human Resource Management* 44, no. 4 (2005): 367–390.

118. A.F. Buono, "Moral Corporate Cultures in a Down-Sized, Restructured World," in W.M. Hoffman and R.E. Frederick, *Business Ethics*, 3rd. ed. (New York: McGraw-Hill, 1995), pp. 226–233.

The Research Process in Organizational Behavior

One of the ways in which people attempt to simplify the world is to break down the complex sets of information that surround them into manageable portions. Within the field of organizational behavior (OB), this process often takes the form of propositions about human behavior and its causes.[1] Many managers, for example, would probably agree that job satisfaction causes high productivity, that lower-level employees care only about receiving monetary rewards for their work, and that a number of personality traits differentiate effective leaders from nonleaders. As discussed in Chapter 1, belief in such propositions has readily influenced our thinking about management. Yet, as recent research has indicated, serious questions remain concerning the general validity of many of these propositions and beliefs.

As members of organizations, of course, it *is* important to understand what our co-workers and colleagues *believe* to be true. However, it is also critical to know the extent to which such beliefs are supported by empirical research. In order to do this, it is necessary to have a basic knowledge of how organizational research is conducted and analyzed. In addition to helping make the field of OB clear so that students and practitioners will be able to comprehend the research being done, an understanding of the whys and hows of research and data analysis facilitates the ability to assess the validity of research claims and evaluate their soundness. It can also help develop a greater capacity for *applying* the research reported by others.[2]

Both research scholars and organizational practitioners engage in various research efforts to enhance their understanding of behavior. In most instances, however, their purposes will be different. Organizational researchers often design studies to develop a new theory or test an existing one, while the practitioner's main concern is usually to diagnose problems and to help the organization become more effective and efficient. Correspondingly, although the practitioner and the scientist might use the same data collection techniques, the ways in which they design their research efforts and analyze their data will usually differ. For example, practitioners may be satisfied to know that a change has occurred that made the organization more effective. Organizational researchers, on the other hand, will want to know as specifically as possible *why* the change was effective, what *caused* the change, or, if it is impossible to identify what caused the change, what is *related* to the change. These aims largely determine how research is constructed and carried out.

In order to understand the research process more fully, this appendix is devoted to an exploration about how people develop knowledge in OB and how data are gathered.

ORGANIZATIONAL RESEARCH METHODS AND TECHNIQUES

One of the basic considerations in evaluating the soundness of a given proposition (e.g., job satisfaction causes high productivity) is to assess the way in which "knowledge" about the proposition is initially established and subsequently tested. Within this context, there are two general approaches to increasing knowledge: deductive and inductive reasoning.

Deductive Reasoning

In *deductive reasoning*, the researcher observes general phenomena and develops specific premises about those phenomena. Based on these premises, the researcher creates a model and, through the principles of logic, reaches a conclusion about the phenomena in question. The conclusion is then compared to the initial observations to assess the degree of expected convergence (see Figure A-1). Essentially, this is a process of "putting two and two together" by combining bits of knowledge obtained on separate occasions or by drawing conclusions that follow from existing information.

Although this is a logical process through which valid conclusions can be made from observations and premises, a difficulty with deductive reasoning is that one must be sure that the premises are accurate. As an example, look at the following set of statements:

- John is a manager who is ineffective in dealing with his subordinates. (observation)
- Organizational behavior provides an understanding of manager-subordinate relations. (premise)
- Managers who are effective in dealing with their subordinates understand organizational behavior. (premise)
- John does not understand organizational behavior. (conclusion)

Figure A-1   Process of Deductive Reasoning

Source: Adapted from W. Jack Duncan, *Organizational Behavior,* 2nd ed. Copyright © 1981 by Houghton Mifflin Company. Adapted with permission.

Based on such reasoning, John's manager might suggest he take an OB course to improve his managerial skills. While this may appear to be an appropriate "solution" drawn from the conclusion, it might be faulty for a number of reasons. On the one hand, the premise itself may not be correct. Moreover, since there may be a number of other factors causing John's ineffectiveness, the conclusion is not fully supported by the present information. Thus, simply taking an OB course will not necessarily improve John's interpersonal and managerial effectiveness.

Inductive Reasoning

For most complex organizational problems, there is not a single "right" answer, and the requirements of the situation cannot be met simply by pulling together the available evidence. Something new must be added by the researchers (going from the known to the unknown) if they are to fully understand the situation. This process is referred to as *inductive reasoning*.

The inductive process is essentially the method of discovery. It moves from objects or critical incidents to the development of ideas. As indicated above, conclusions reached through deductive reasoning alone are valid only if they are derived from tenable premises. However, since assuring the accuracy of premises in the social sciences is quite difficult, researchers have sought a more thorough way of determining whether their observations are justified. This inductive process can thus be thought of as a way to *complement* deductive reasoning.[3]

Essentially, researchers identify an issue or behavior to analyze. These investigators then collect information (through surveys, interviews, field or laboratory experiments, and so on) about respondents, conditions, or behaviors of the particular group or phenomenon to be studied. These data are usually gathered from a *sample* (a finite set of persons, objects, or things selected for study) of the total population or universe of the larger group. Researchers then use these data to make certain inferences about the larger population or universe based on observations in the sample. This is done through statistical analysis and probabilities that certain phenomena that occur in the sample are representative of the larger population (see Appendix B).

This procedure, of course, relies on *generalization*. A basic assumption underlying this process is that if the research were repeated with other samples drawn at random from the sample population, the outcome or findings would be consistent. Thus, an important consideration is to ensure that the size and representation of the sample are adequate, and that the resulting explanation (theory) is not vulnerable to more plausible explanations. In order to do this, one must also attempt to incorporate as wide a variety of observations in a study as one would want to generalize about.

Theory Development

Since the processes of deductive and inductive reasoning help us understand and create order out of observations, researchers use both methods in developing theories. Basically, a theory is an ordered relationship of data-supported hypotheses. When a social scientist initiates a research effort, facts (earlier research, observations, literature review, etc.) about a particular theoretical or applied problem are noted. Based on these observations, a number of research questions are formulated (e.g., "What is the relationship between A and B?"; "Will improving job satisfaction improve productivity?"). These questions then serve as a guide to establish *hypotheses* (tentative explanations about the relationship between two or more variables) which are put to the test of empirical research. A strategy (*study design*) is then constructed that will guide data collection efforts and be used to test the hypotheses. The data are then analyzed (statistically or otherwise) to assess whether or not they support the hypotheses. Finally, conclusions (explanations, theories) are drawn that appear justified by the study's results, which then become "existing facts" for other research efforts.[4]

An example of this process can be seen in the satisfaction–performance controversy.[5] It was initially believed that job satisfaction causes good work performance. Although deductively this premise appears to make sense (hypothesis), empirical research has not fully corroborated the relationship (hypothesis testing). Research on the satisfaction–performance hypothesis has indicated that there is no simple, direct relationship between individual job satisfaction at one time and work performance at a later time. Although some OB researchers still argue that the satisfaction–performance causal relationship may exist in certain situations, an emergent hypothesis is that performance actually causes satisfaction when high performance is followed by valued rewards. Empirical tests on this hypothesis have generally indicated a stronger relationship than the one found between initial job satisfaction and later work performance. Thus, by probing existing facts, framing research questions, and then testing hypotheses drawn from these questions, theories about the causal relationship between job performance and job satisfaction have been developed and refined.

Types of Hypotheses

The basic building block in theory development is the creation of hypotheses. Hypotheses are always formulated in pairs—referred to as the working hypothesis and the null hypothesis—although in most journal articles the null hypothesis is usually assumed rather than explicitly stated (see Appendix B). Consider the following statement: "Reducing work hours from 40 to 36 hours per week will change productivity." This assertion is a *working hypothesis*. Since hypotheses must be in pairs that are exhaustive (they take account of all possibilities) and mutually exclusive (only one of which can be supported), the *null hypothesis* to this statement is "Reducing work hours from 40 to 36 hours per week will *not* change productivity." This pair of hypotheses is referred to as a *two-tailed hypothesis*. In this case, the working hypothesis does not specify that there will be an increase or decrease in productivity; rather it states that there will be a change in *either* direction. The null hypothesis, which is mutually exclusive and exhaustive, thus states that there will not be any change in productivity. In a two-tailed hypothesis, the null hypothesis is often referred to as the *hypothesis of no difference*. Since these two hypotheses cover all possible events, once sufficient data are gathered on organizational productivity after the change in working hours a statistical test—such as a *t-test* (see Appendix B)—can be used to "test" which hypothesis is supported.

Let us assume that instead of simply predicting a change in productivity, based on your own observations or previous research you believe that reducing work hours from 40 to 36 hours per week would actually increase productivity. Because there is now a prediction that the results will be in a specific direction (increased productivity), the working hypothesis creates a *one-tailed* test. The null hypothesis would thus have to be restated: "Reducing work hours from 40 to 36 hours per week will decrease productivity *or* not cause any change in productivity." In this case, the null hypothesis is not simply a hypothesis of no difference since it also takes into account the possibility of a decrease in productivity. Since one-tailed hypotheses are more powerful and more useful in theory building, two-tailed tests are typically used in exploratory research.

Hypothesis Generation

In OB, as in many of the social sciences, much more effort is typically placed on testing hypotheses than in generating them. Accordingly, one may reasonably question where hypotheses come from. The short answer is that they come from many places: observation of compelling natural occurrences, direct inference, complex conceptual analysis, reinterpretation of old research, and prior research looked at in new ways that require additional data collection.[6]

Returning to the satisfaction–performance relationship discussed earlier, for example, research in the 1950s suggested that if workers were satisfied on the job they would perform well. Later on it was realized that although this relationship did hold *in some instances*, it was more complex. Indeed, later research found that high performance, followed by appropriate reward to the high performers, was followed by high satisfaction. The managerial implications of these revised findings are enormous. In the 1950s, the emphasis was on making workers happy. Outcomes included the development of more pleasing work contexts, supervisors learning to be courteous to their subordinates, and so forth. When subsequent research indicated that the satisfaction–performance paradigm might work just the opposite from the way it was thought in the 1950s (in other words performance yields satisfaction), managers began to emphasize productivity and meaningful work rather than comfortable surroundings and pleasant supervisors. This change represented a complete reversal in thinking about how managers could influence job-related performance.

Replication and Theory Development

An important feature of theory development and building scientific knowledge is the extent to which research results are repeatable.[7] While replication of empirical findings in the natural sciences is a common practice, such replications are less common in the social sciences. Yet, in those instances where replications of the research have been undertaken, the results often conflict with, or at best partially support, the original findings. Unfortunately, management scholars often accept the findings of a single study whose validity is later called into question. Throughout the text, in our discussions of the various theories that constitute the OB field, we attempt to provide a sense of how that particular theory or perspective has held up over time.

Some observers contend that replication has not been sufficiently recognized as a valuable part of theory development. While to some extent this neglect is due to the biases of journal editors (e.g., replications lack creativity, novelty is prized more than "mere" replications), there are lingering doubts as to whether replication is truly possible in social science research. Since replication presupposes that an experiment or study is repeated under identical conditions, critics argue that it is impossible to achieve or create the identical circumstances in a social science experiment or study. If most social science conditions that are *likely to be relevant* are controlled for, however, it is suggested that replication has been performed.[8] Thus, while not necessarily possible in every situation, replication in organizational behavior research is both feasible and desirable as a critical part of theory development.

Designation of Variables

In behavioral science research, there are four classes of symbols that in some way identify groups of persons (or objects) or how they have been treated. These symbols are referred to as *variables*. *Independent variables* are those that occur at an earlier time, or in the case of experiments are manipulated to cause an effect. *Dependent variables* are those that are predicted or measured, and in experiment are caused by an independent variable. An *intervening variable* is an unobservable process or state, hypothetically deduced by examining the independent and dependent variables, which helps to clarify the relationship between the variables.

There are two subtypes of intervening variables: moderator and mediator.[9] A *moderator variable* is a qualitative (e.g., gender, level of management, socioeconomic class) or quantitative variable (e.g., level of compensation, time taken for training) that affects the direction and strength of relationship between an independent and dependent variable. For example, a person's position within an organization might moderate the effect of intentions on behavior. Even though we may intend to act in a certain way, the way we actually behave is often influenced by our role and status (see Chapter 5). A *mediator variable*, in contrast, recognizes that "an active organism intervenes between a stimulus and a response."[10] While moderator variables stipulate when certain effects will hold, mediator variables deal with how or why such effects occur. The underlying notion is that various processes internal to the organism (individual, group, organization) mediate the effects of a stimulus on that organism's behavior. For instance, in the previous illustration of the satisfaction–performance controversy, it was initially thought that job satisfaction (independent variable) caused work performance (dependent variable). In later theory development, it was hypothesized that work performance (independent variable) causes job satisfaction (dependent variable) when good performance is followed by valued rewards (moderator variable). Researchers also argued that enhanced job satisfaction for some individuals results in changes in the amount of motivation (mediator variable) they have to engage in work-related tasks, which results in better work performance. Unlike the values of independent and dependent variables, however, because the values of intervening variables cannot be observed they must be inferred. Thus, individual motivation to perform a task (unobservable) must be inferred from the amount of observable effort exerted in that task or from the self-reports of the respondents.

Outcome versus Process in Organizational Research

Most research in OB is focused on specific outcome variables—attitudes, job performance, work unit productivity, and so forth. As a result, many OB experts are becoming increasingly critical of the relative lack of attention research in the field has given to documenting organizational processes and change-related dynamics.[11] Thus, although it is likely that a focus on outcomes will continue to dominate organizational research, *process* and related *contextual* variables are emerging as a significant area of interest. Researchers, for example, are increasingly beginning to explore how people are socialized into their organizations, how an organization's culture develops over time, the stages in which managers develop their competencies, and, in general, why and how organizations change and develop greater effectiveness. Thus, it is becoming increasingly clear that longer-term, longitudinal studies and event-history assessments that explore the relationships among contextual, process, and outcome variables are important for sound theory development.[12]

Research Approaches and Designs

In the beginning of the chapter, we made a distinction between the type of research undertaken by organizational practitioners as compared to scholarly researchers. While both researchers and practitioners may use the same techniques to gather their data, since the aims of their research efforts are different, the overall approach or research design they employ will differ as well. In brief, the critical difference is the degree of scientific rigor involved in the process.

Table A-1 compares the type of research approaches employed by practitioners and organizational scientists. You will notice from the table that research can range from rigorous, scientific theory building to fairly systematic efforts, to unsystematic observations. Each approach has its benefits *and* problems. Although rigorous research is used in theory development, it is often problematic to generalize to practical situations because it is difficult to control multiple variables in actual situations. Action research may be valuable to a specific practical situation, but it is usually not generalizable and is less useful in theory building or advancement of the field. Similarly, while casual changes may be useful in a particular situation, there is no real attempt to measure their effectiveness. Rigor is also related to time: Scientific research takes a long time to plan and execute, whereas casual changes may be accomplished very quickly.

In planning empirical research, choices have to be made about research design (e.g., experimental vs. nonexperimental), the research setting (e.g., laboratory versus natural setting), and data collection (e.g., questionnaires; observation) as well as data analysis (see Appendix B).[13] Depending on the purpose of the study, different types of designs may be appropriate. In this section, four basic types of research designs (case studies, field studies, laboratory experiments, and field experiments) and an approach for accumulating knowledge across similar types of studies, referred to as *meta-analysis*, will be briefly discussed.

The Case Study

The case study method involves the in-depth examination of an individual, group, or organization by a researcher or team of researchers. The single case study is the most familiar version of this approach, although comparative case studies in which two or more groups are under study and phased research efforts in which the case approach is used as a pilot study are other variations. Although the case approach is usually employed for descriptive or exploratory research, there are attempts to use it for explanatory and predictive purposes.[14]

The main advantage of a case study is that researchers can get directly involved with the subject relatively quickly, and get a "feel" for what is going on. This advantage, however, is severely limited by the fact that it is not feasible to generalize to a population or universe from a sample of one. Case studies, on the other hand, are generalizable

TABLE A-1 Types of Research Approaches in Organizational Behavior

Dimension	Most Rigorous — Formal Behavioral Research	Action Research	Least Rigorous — Casual Change
1. Aims	To develop data-supported theories that will be widely generalized to other organizational settings.	To provide data that will ultimately support organizational changes needed to make an organization more effective.	To make limited "common sense" changes that focus on problems perceived by managers.
2. Sample	Scholarly researcher attempts to obtain a representative sample of the population or universe; this may be done by random or other kinds of sampling within established subsectors of the population.	The practitioner will use a portion of the organization or the entire organization as subjects for the research.	Managers may observe their work group to see whether changes implemented have been effective.
3. Experimental design	Prior to data collection, a research design is carefully planned, and subsequently followed. As many important variables as possible are controlled. Experimental bias is seriously watched.	General procedures are developed, but not adhered to if in the middle of the procedure there seems to be a "better way." There are no formal control or experimental groups. Although practitioners try to be dispassionate in their approach, bias cannot be ruled out.	There is a minimum of prior planning, and there is no formal design or common agreement as to what procedures should be used. Similarly, the results are not likely to be generalized.

4. Measurement	The most valid measures available are sought. Invariably there will be pilot studies preceding the main study in order to thoroughly check out the data collection instruments or approaches.	There are less rigorous checking measures; there usually will not be pilot testing before using the measure in a main study.	Usually there will be no formal data collection on the effectiveness of the intervention. Subjective opinion may be sought.
5. Analysis of data	Thorough quantitative and/or qualitative analysis is required. Statistical significance is usually emphasized.	Simple procedures are emphasized. There is more weight on practical significance than statistical significance. Subjective opinion counts heavily.	Opinions of the participants are sought. There is no attempt to be rigorous or dispassionate.
6. Application of results	Results are generalizable, but frequently the situation is so unique that it is difficult to generalize to a practical situation.	The results are applied to the immediate organizational situation, but there is no development of theory. The results cannot be generalized.	Decisions made are applied immediately, but no evidence is gathered that the change was effective. Changes such as these are frequently reversed.

Source: Adapted from *Educational Research: An Introduction,* first ed. by Walter R. Borg. Copyright © 1963 by Longman Inc. Reprinted by permission of Longman, Inc., New York; and adapted from *Training: Program Development and Evaluation* by I.L. Goldstein. Copyright © 1974 by Wadsworth Publishing Co., Inc. Reprinted by permission of Brooks/Cole Publishing Company, Monterey, California 93940.

to theoretical propositions.[15] Nonetheless, since the observer chooses what to report, and in fact may only see and hear certain things, care must be exercised to ensure that such perceptual biases (see Chapter 2) do not influence the direction of the findings and conclusions. Another drawback is that variables are not controlled, and people usually do not behave in a "normal" way when they know they are being watched. Finally, the most "interesting" features about a situation are usually reported, when in actuality, the less exciting features may be just as important.

The case study approach is usually considered to be an important input at the outset of a research project. A case study may identify facets of a situation that deserve to be examined in further detail using different methods. It is also a very popular teaching method in management courses. Yet by itself, the case study is not an adequate means to support or disconfirm a hypothesis, and is more useful for descriptive and exploratory research. Despite these limitations, competent case studies go far beyond casual observation or superficial description in that they require the same attention to detail, planning, and execution as do the other research designs. Effective case studies emphasize the need for precise detail and thoroughness in observation and data collection. Haphazard collection of data, careless recording of information, or superficial investigation can render a case study virtually worthless as a research device.[16]

The Field Study

Fieldwork, once the hallmark of anthropology and sociology, is increasingly being used in organizational studies. Field studies utilize the natural setting of the subject to be investigated. Data collection may entail the use of questionnaires, interviews, observations, or archival data such as measures of productivity. Basically, in a field study the researcher identifies issues to be explored, develops and pilot-tests the data collection instrument(s), and proceeds to collect the data. In most instances, field studies are *ex post facto* in nature; that is, the independent variables under study have already occurred and the researcher begins with the observation of the dependent variables. The independent variables are then studied in *retrospect* for their possible relations to the dependent variables.[17]

Given the retrospective nature of most field studies, no attempt is made to divide the respondents into different groups or to "control" the independent variable(s). As a result, while relationships between variables may be determined, it is difficult to establish causality. Moreover, when two or more variables combine, they can produce a reaction much greater than the addition of the effects of the variables taken separately (an *interaction effect*), which cannot be identified through field study alone. This dynamic has been part of the problem with the satisfaction–performance controversy discussed earlier.

Despite these limitations, the field study may be the only approach possible when it is not feasible to control variables. A main advantage of a field study is that because the data are collected in a natural setting, the results are transferable to other similar situations. If the researcher is interested in establishing patterns between variables (and not causal relationships), the field study may be the most appropriate research design to use. It is important to underscore, however, that in order to generalize to wider populations, the samples studied must be representative of those groups. Research has found, for example, that the organizational samples most frequently used in industrial and organizational studies are from a relatively narrowly defined group composed of predominantly male, professional, technical, and managerial employees. As will be discussed at the conclusion of this chapter, this orientation has precipitated growing criticism about inherent biases that underlie much of the research on and our thinking about management. Thus, the homogeneous nature of such typical organizational samples challenges the notion of generalizability to other, more diverse settings. Moreover, many experts argue that the ability to generalize to other populations, settings, and variables cannot be achieved in any one study, but is an empirical question that requires comparisons over different research efforts and sites.[18]

Organizational Ethnography

Organizational ethnographies are in-depth, highly detailed, longitudinal assessments of groups or organizations.[19] This type of research, which typically requires a long period of time in the field as the researcher becomes fully immersed in a particular situation, can provide numerous insights into the nuances of group and organizational life. Emphasis is placed on delineating the characteristic cultural patterns and orientations of the organization under study (Chapter 10), including such areas as the norms adopted and followed by organizational members (Chapter 5), how these individuals are socialized into the group or organization (Chapter 5), how organizational policies and procedures are developed, interpreted, and implemented, and, in general, how the organization functions on a daily basis.

While ethnographies are generally descriptive accounts, an underlying tension focuses on achieving a balance between the extremes of providing (1) a straight narrative account without theoretical consideration and (2) one that is more theoretical and generalized, but with fewer references to substantive accounts of actual behavior.[20] The most useful ethnographic accounts are those that go beyond a simple description of a particular organization and raise broader issues and theoretical insights that contribute to our understanding of organizational life. Given the problems inherent in assuring the objectivity of the observer in reconstructing events, however, it is critical that researchers consider many possible sources of evidence to support the importance of different events and to verify the connections between them.[21]

The Laboratory Experiment

The laboratory experiment is a study that is performed in a location *other* than the group's natural setting where the researcher can control (manipulate) the variables. This approach allows the researcher to focus on specific factors and screen out other, potentially distracting, variables. As an example, a researcher might undertake a laboratory experiment to assess the effectiveness of a training program. Using a basic experimental design, two groups of people, randomly selected, would be assigned to an experimental group and a control group. The experimental group would be given the training program, while the control group would *not* receive the training. Both the experimental and control groups would have "before" and "after" observations to assess task effectiveness related to the training. Schematically, the design is as follows:[22]

	Observation 1 (O_1)	Training	Observation 2 (O_2)
Experimental Group	O_1	Yes	O_2
Control Group	O_1	No	O_2

If the experimental group's performance during O_2 was significantly improved from its initial performance (O_1) and there was no significant difference in the control group's performance from O_1 to O_2, the researcher would conclude that the training program was effective—that it caused the improved performance of the experimental group. If, however, there were no significant differences, or if the performance of the control group improved as well, the study would be inconclusive as to the effectiveness of the training program, or (depending on the results) might even suggest that the training program was *not* effective.

There are two variations on this basic experimental design: the *one-shot* approach and the *before-after* study. Although these approaches are useful for action research, they are not appropriate for the development of scientific theory (see Table A-1).

One-Shot Approach   This technique does not use a control group, but simply measures the outcomes (e.g., performance) of a group after an intervention (e.g., a training program). It is illustrated as follows:

	Training	Observation
Experimental Group	Yes	O

One cannot determine from this approach whether the training or some other event produced the results found in O. If the researcher is not interested in *how* participants improved their performance, but simply that the performance is effective, the one-shot approach may be justified. One has to assume, however, that there was no prior knowledge about the subject matter covered by the training.

Before-After Approach   This method is similar to the basic experimental design, however, a control group is not used:

	Observation 1 (O_1)	Training	Observation 2 (O_2)
Experimental Group	O_1	Yes	O_2

Similar to the one-shot approach, this design is also of limited value because the researcher cannot determine what caused the effect in O_2—the training program or the initial observation. For example, if the training program provides an orientation to company rules and procedures, the initial questionnaire or interview (O_1) might have prompted questions concerning company rules that "caused" the results noticed in O_2. Thus, it could be a function of the initial observation and not the training program per se that improved knowledge about organizational rules and procedures.

The obvious advantages of laboratory experiments are that they provide adequate controls for theory building and the examination of causal relationships. Such controls, however, should be balanced against the artificial nature of the laboratory situation. When research examines the effects of variables that are manipulated in an artificial setting, concern should be raised about the effect that the setting in question has on the experimental manipulation itself and the outcome of the study.

The Field Experiment

Field experiments are research efforts conducted in natural settings in which one or more of the independent variables can be controlled by the researcher under as carefully controlled conditions as the situation permits.[23] Although laboratory experiments provide greater control during the research than field experiments, the natural setting in which the research is conducted in field experiments overcomes the artificiality of the laboratory.

The benefits of field experiments are clear. First, theory development can proceed because the researcher can control relevant variables and is, thus, in a position to establish causal relationships. Second, because the study is conducted in a natural setting, the results are generalizable to other natural settings. As pointed out earlier, such generalization is not always possible from a lab setting owing to its artificial nature. Thus, field experiments combine the advantages of field studies and laboratory experiments. It is often difficult, however, to find situations that allow for field experimentation.

Cross-Sectional versus Longitudinal Research

A key distinction concerning research designs is the difference between longitudinal and cross-sectional research. Frequently a theory that is supported by *cross-sectional research* (research done at one point in time) is not supported by *longitudinal research* (a study conducted over an extended period). Maslow's theory of motivation is a classic case in point. As discussed in Chapter 3, the theory posits that there is a hierarchical progression of motivational stages, as people go from basic, physiological needs to higher-order, psychological needs. While cross-sectional research acknowledged that these different stages do exist, longitudinal research found that people did not move up and down the hierarchy as posited; instead, they were sometimes at two stages at the same time, they skipped stages, and so forth. In this case, the cross-sectional research conducted at one point was inadequate to test the theory. Longitudinal research done over a longer period of time with a number of different data collection points was necessary to challenge the theory and led to a revised theory of motivation.[24]

Multiple Hypothesis Testing

As research becomes more complex, researchers endeavor to test many hypotheses at the same time. The challenge when undertaking such complex research is to make sure that the hypothesis supports the working and null hypotheses when appropriate. Research that allegedly supports the working hypothesis when it is false is referred to as a *Type I error;* research that allegedly supports the null hypothesis when it in fact is false is referred to as a *Type II error.* When multiple hypotheses are being tested at the same time (unless some correction procedure is introduced) there is a statistical tendency to support the working hypotheses (reject the null hypotheses) when, in fact, the working hypotheses should be rejected. Although recent research has improved the precision in applying techniques to appropriately support or reject the working hypotheses, these findings raise questions about older studies where multiple hypotheses were simultaneously tested as the working hypotheses may have been inappropriately accepted.[25]

Meta-Analysis

In most instances, research projects focus on a single site or body of data to develop or test a set of hypotheses. As a result, the findings of one study are often difficult to compare with the findings of another. While this problem exists for statistical analyses from different laboratory and field experiments, it is especially true of individual case and field studies. Since case studies often do not meet generally accepted standards of methodological rigor, the experience and learning from such research efforts are often not integrated into the mainstream of research. Thus, although a voluminous body of case and field studies and laboratory and field experiments exists within OB and related fields, this literature has not been assimilated into an empirical body of knowledge.

An increasingly popular analytic technique referred to as *meta-analysis* attempts to overcome this shortcoming.[26] In its most general form, meta-analysis can be thought of as a "study of studies." It is sometimes referred to as a quantitative literature review because it converts findings from similar studies into a unified set of variables that draws out the average statistical findings for the group of studies as well as the variance between the findings of individual studies (see Appendix B). The result is much stronger support for (or disconfirmation of) a given hypothesis than could be obtained from a single research effort. The process involves collecting studies that relate to a specific research question, systematically coding the findings, and analyzing the resultant variables through statistical procedures. In standard meta-analyzes, the unit of analysis is an experiment; in case meta-analysis, the unit of analysis is the individual case study.

Proponents argue that meta-analysis can combine borderline results from a number of different studies to reach more definite and valid conclusions. Yet, despite the attractiveness of cumulating many types of research findings and the appearance of scientific objectivity, significant concern has emerged concerning the many judgment calls that must be made and how they can readily affect outcomes.[27] For instance, judgments must be made with respect to such critical factors as: (1) defining the domain to be investigated (e.g., by independent variable; by causes and/or consequences of key variables); (2) determining the criteria to be used for the selection of studies (e.g., published versus unpublished; time period covered; operational definitions of variables); (3) searching for relevant studies (e.g., manual versus computer search); (4) selecting the final set of studies to be analyzed (e.g., individual versus group decision); (5) extracting data (e.g., using all the data reported versus a subset of the data); and (6) coding the information. Concern has also been raised about the extent to which meta-analysis is capable of determining the influence of moderator variables on study outcomes[28] and its subsequent limitations in drawing causal inferences.[29] In fact, given the level of subjectivity involved, critics contend it is not surprising that published meta-analyses on the same topic reach different conclusions.

Thus, while meta-analysis can be a powerful tool, care must be exercised in both data collection and interpretation. First, it is important to ensure that all relevant studies have been included, not simply those that are readily available. Second, while similar studies may include the same variables, researchers often emphasize different variables or outcomes. Thus, faulty conclusions may be reached about an apparent relationship between two variables that might better be explained by a particular bias or focus of the researchers. As meta-analysis becomes increasingly popular, however, many academic journals have begun to require methodological appendices which provide information that will facilitate future cross-study assessments. Finally, it is recommended that meta-analysis should be done by more than one person.[30] With at least two people making the judgment calls noted previously on an independent basis, each person will be prompted to think more carefully about the critical decisions involved and forced to examine differences of opinion as part of the research process.

As a growing number of researchers caution, such analysis is best thought of as an aid to, not substitute for, critical thought.[31]

DATA COLLECTION AND MEASUREMENT

A number of different techniques and methods are used to gather information for OB research. The four most frequently used techniques are questionnaires, interviews, direct observation, and unobtrusive measures. Since each of these techniques can obtain different types of data, the most appropriate method depends on the nature of the problem posed in the research.[32]

Questionnaires

Survey questionnaires are probably the most widely used of all data-gathering techniques. In addition to being used in OB research, questionnaires are the prime method of amassing large amounts of data on public opinions about a wide range of social and political issues. Questionnaire surveys are particularly useful for studies of the attitudes, beliefs, and values of a particular population. They can also provide useful information on changes in these variables. Another advantage of this approach is that the data lend themselves to rigorous statistical analysis, which can aid in analyzing trends in different situations.

Questionnaires often employ what is referred to as a *Likert-type scale*, in which people are asked to place themselves on a continuum—ranging from "strongly agree" to "strongly disagree"—in terms of their attitudes about a particular issue.

> *Question:* Overall, I am satisfied with my job.
> *Response Continuum:* Strongly Agree Neutral Disagree Strongly
> Agree   Disagree

Questionnaires have a number of potential weaknesses, which, if not carefully considered, can lead to results that may be only minimally useful. Care and attention must be given to the way in which specific questions or items are created.[33] For example, individual questions must be formulated with caution so that respondents are not led in their answers (i.e., asking a question that influences people to respond in a particular way). Because questionnaires are also impersonal, researchers are often confronted with the problem of nonresponse in which individuals (for explicit or implicit reasons not always fully understood) choose not to answer specific or large blocks of questions, or even the entire questionnaire. Since the questionnaire is privately self-administered, there is usually no way to probe this information more fully. Surveys also require a fairly high degree of trust on the part of the respondent (the person completing the questionnaire). If the people involved suspect that they can be identified or that the data may be used in a punitive manner, respondents will often choose to tell a researcher what they feel that person wants to hear. Consequently, actual thoughts about a particular issue remain unexpressed.

Interviewing

Personal interviews are another method of collecting information concerning how individuals feel about certain issues and problems. This approach is more direct than the use of questionnaires and can lend deeper insight into the actual meanings of subjective data. Because the face-to-face situation provides greater flexibility than the survey method, individuals can be questioned more fully about their attitudes and opinions about a particular issue, which can often clarify causal relationships.

Successful interviews, however, require skilled interviewers and relatively large amounts of time to fully probe pertinent aspects of the situation. It is not uncommon for an interview with one person to approach a full hour or more in duration. Such interviews can range from relatively open-ended types of questions (e.g., "What do you like most about your job?") to highly structured, formalized questions similar to those found in questionnaires (e.g., "How satisfied are you with your pay? Are you highly satisfied, moderately satisfied, slightly satisfied, or not satisfied at all?"). Even for the more structured questions, however, ensuring the comparability of data across individuals is often difficult, especially when a number of different interviewers are used. Thus, although the interview is highly direct and can produce in-depth information, it is a time-consuming and expensive process, which often generates data that are not valid for comparative purposes.

Similar to the use of questionnaires, a high degree of trust between the researcher and the respondent (the individual being interviewed) is important. Especially with respect to longitudinal studies, however, an underlying dilemma concerns the nature and quality of social relationships that evolve between a researcher and these individuals. It is important to establish a sufficient level of rapport and comfort with those you are interviewing, since this readily influences the accuracy and value of the information generated.[34] Within this context, some researchers point to the effectiveness of *common biographies*, where shared aspects of the interviewer's background and experience are used to put people at ease during the interview process.[35] Disclosing various things about oneself can provide an assurance of confidentiality and allay suspicion on the part of the respondent.

It is important to realize, however, that growing familiarity influences not only what individuals will tell you, but also what they expect from you in return. In this sense, rather than respondents just playing a role of key informant (e.g., "Let me tell you what really goes on around here"), interviewers can find themselves thrust into the role of "strategic informant."[36] The same tendencies that influence respondents to cue the researcher often cause them to question the researcher about what he or she is "finding out" about the organization (e.g., "I'm really curious about what is going on in the accounting department"). This dynamic raises a number of ethical concerns—for instance, the potential for betraying information given in confidence, or of inadvertently providing information gathered in a neutral context as ammunition in an internal conflict—and interviewers must be extremely careful in what they tell members of the host organization.

Storytelling

An emerging interviewing strategy, especially within the context of ethnographic research, involves *storytelling*—getting people to recount critical incidents that have occurred in their group or organization.[37] Stories are different from gossip, the organizational grapevine, and other forms of organizational communication (see Chapter 4) in that they typically involve a setting, a cast of characters, a plot that involves a crisis or critical incident, and an implicit moral message and shared meaning that reflects the organization's belief system. In this sense, stories act as a cultural code (see Chapter 10), helping organizational members to make sense of their workplace and pass on an organization's history, values, and vision.[38] As such, they can be extremely useful in developing deeper insights into organizations, allowing researchers to go beneath the public relations–type rhetoric that typically accompanies public discussion about an organization.

A specific type of storytelling involves *narratives*, an analytic technique that unifies a group of events into a single story. Especially useful for exploring and understanding organizational change, narratives take into account the temporal and historic nature of the numerous events that are part of a change sequence. Due to the interpretive nature of narratives, however, it is important that researchers use multiple techniques in putting together their story. Such techniques include auditing (where a second researcher independently reconstructs the events created by another researcher, clarifying assumptions about causal connections until agreement is reached), combining insider-outsider perspectives, drawing on multiple data sources, identifying and corroborating important events, and revisiting the data, probing initial interpretations.[39]

Direct Observation

One of the most effective ways of discovering how work is actually accomplished in a given group or organization is to watch people's behavior as they work or interact with others. Such observations can range from casual, informal perusals of the work process to highly structured ones that use a formal chart to outline specific activities and behaviors. The major strength of this approach is its flexibility and directness. Moreover, with observation the researcher is collecting information on the behavior itself and not reports of that behavior.

Since the researcher is placed in the role of the "measuring device," however, this technique is subject to a number of perceptual biases (see Chapter 3). Because what we see is influenced by our own feelings and experiences, we often distort reality to fit our preconceived notions of what that reality should be. Moreover, when people know that they are being observed they often act differently from "normal." This tendency is often referred to as the *Hawthorne effect* (see the discussion of the Hawthorne Studies in Chapter 1). Just as individuals singled out for special attention often end up performing as anticipated because of the expectancies created, people will attempt to provide observers with what they think the researchers are looking for. Thus, since our presence and behavior influence those around us, we must be aware of possible contamination of the "reality" we are observing.

Participant Observation

Sociologists argue that since we cannot escape participating, at least to some degree, in the experiences we observe, we are always more or less participant observers of the social phenomena that surround us. As such, the individual researcher is viewed as the key instrument of social investigation.[40] *Participant observation* refers to situations where researchers become, as much as possible, members of the group (or organization) they are studying, participating fully in the life of that group. In the extreme form, the researcher is an actual member of the group *not known* by group members to have any other role. While such presence obviously limits the influence of the Hawthorne effect, the only way to achieve this level of involvement is to assume the role of group or organizational spy, which raises obvious ethical concerns about dishonesty and deception. Thus, in most cases participant observation refers to situations in which researchers "live" in an organization, sharing in the day-to-day lives of organizational members even though their dual roles are recognized.[41]

Unobtrusive Measures

One of the main difficulties with the data collection methods discussed previously is that the researcher must interact with the individuals providing the information. As noted earlier, this can create the problem of *reactivity*, when the act of measuring something influences the response being measured.[42] To control for this potential bias, unobtrusive measures are often used.

Unobtrusive measures are highly *indirect* ways of collecting information about an issue in which the people involved are not aware of the data collection process. Such measures can take the form of observations in which people do not know they are being observed, and the use of archival data such as organizational absenteeism, production, and turnover rates. These data have the advantage that they are not being influenced by the research process. In many instances, however, these measures are generated for a specific purpose and are misleading if they are analyzed out of context. Thus, this information should not be taken at face value; rather, these measures must be refined and viewed in the appropriate situational context if they are to be fully useful.

Triangulation

As the discussion of different data-gathering techniques suggests, because each of these approaches has its own strengths and weaknesses, the most effective information collection process encompasses a combination of these methods. Although one of these techniques may be used more extensively than the others in a particular study, most successful OB research projects are based on information generated from a mix of complementary techniques.

This approach is referred to as *triangulation*, the use of multiple methods to offset the weaknesses of one type of data with the strength of another.[43] In many instances, what organizational members might say they would do in a certain situation (via questionnaires or interviews) might not necessarily correspond to their actual behaviors (observation). Thus, researchers should plan at the outset to complement their data-collection efforts. It is particularly important to check findings generated by one method with the data presented by another. This type of empirical triangulation—for instance, drawing upon and comparing archival information, self-reports and interviews with key informants, observations, and questionnaire data—can provide researchers with a more accurate understanding of the phenomena they are studying. Another form of triangulation, referred to as *metatriangulation*, involves the use of multiple paradigms or frameworks as a tool in theory building and development.[44] Especially in those areas marked by contradictory research findings and disagreements, this form of triangulation has the potential to help researchers to accommodate disparate insights and findings across different studies.

Measurement

Regardless of the type of data collection technique employed, an important concern in behavioral science research deals with the measurement properties of the information collected. In the physical sciences, when a chemist collects a pound of mercury and then reweighs it at a later time the mercury will still weigh a pound. With respect to data collected in the behavioral sciences, however, the measures we obtain often vary from one point to another. In aptitude testing, for instance, we expect that a person's IQ will remain constant over time. Psychologists, however, have been unable to devise an aptitude test that is not heavily influenced by external factors such as experience or achievement. This dynamic is why one's scores on the Scholastic Assessment Test (SAT) change over time. Thus, unlike the pound of mercury that is always a pound, IQ or SAT scores do not remain constant. The same is true of measures of job satisfaction, motivation, and other facets of organizational life.

Reliability and Validity of Data

Considering the problems inherent in collecting precise data in behavioral science research, there are two questions that should be raised concerning any measures used to collect such information: Are the measures reliable and are they valid? *Reliability* refers to the consistency or stability of the measurements in question. *Validity*, in contrast, refers to the extent to which the measure used actually measures what it purports to measure. For example, we might be able to consistently measure people's attitudes toward certain aspects of their jobs (reliability), but before we can infer the information provides a description of the level of job satisfaction we must ensure that the data collected do indeed reflect job satisfaction (validity). Thus, although both these dimensions are important, validity is more crucial because it tells us whether or not we are measuring the correct phenomenon.

There are two different uses of the term *validity*: One focuses on the difference between internal and external validity in research or experimental design, and the other on the difference between predictive and concurrent validity found in human resources selection.[45] The determination of cause-effect relationships, sometimes described as an issue of *internal validity*, is typically verified through an experimental group–control group research design. As suggested earlier, in a before-after study involving an experimental group, even if changes in an independent variable create a measurable difference on a dependent variable, questions would remain as to what actually caused the change. For instance, assume that a group of employees are initially tested on a particular area and then put through a training program, which resulted in improved performance on the test. It would not be clear whether the training program, the initial testing, or some combination of the two is responsible for the improved knowledge or performance. By using one or more control groups (e.g., no initial test and training; initial test and no training), however, the researcher will have a better sense of whether the training program was the causal factor. Similarly, if an organization uses an advertising campaign to stimulate the sale of its smoke detectors and there is a well-publicized fire during the ad campaign, one is not sure of the causal factor (the ad campaign or the fire) if there is an upsurge in smoke detector purchases.

External validity, by contrast, concerns the extent to which the results of a particular research project are generalizable to other situations. As mentioned earlier, the problem of reactivity can influence the behavior and responses of people when they know they are being studied. The Hawthorne research discussed in Chapter 1 is a classic example of the reactivity phenomenon. Since the people involved in the experiment reacted differently from the way they might have if they did not realize they were being observed, the conclusions of the research might very well have been different. Thus, in most instances, the results of one study should be replicated in another situation to ensure external validity.

The final distinction to be made concerning validity deals with the difference between concurrent and predictive validity. *Concurrent validity* refers to research findings that occur at the same time. *Predictive validity*, in contrast, refers to research efforts where a set of measures made at one point in time are correlated to (associated with) results in the future (e.g., a test that accurately separates potentially "good" workers from potentially "poor" ones).

Levels of Measurement

As part of the data-gathering process, different values are assigned to the various responses provided by respondents. The practice of assigning these values constitutes the process of measurement. Since these values are differentiated from one another on the basis of the ordering and distance properties inherent in measurement rules, distinguishing between levels of measurement is important. The four basic levels of measurement are: nominal, ordinal, interval, and ratio scales.[46]

Nominal-Level Data Nominal-level data constitute the lowest form of measurement. They are used to place things into basic, mutually exclusive categories where there is no single underlying continuum. For example, gender, race, and job classification are considered nominal data. Although numerical values are often assigned to these different categories, they have no quantitative properties and serve only to identify the category.

Ordinal-Level Data The next level of measurement assumes an underlying continuum. These data are rank-ordered according to a specific criterion; however, the amount of distance between the different categories involved is unknown. For example, in organizational surveys employees are often asked to rate the benefits they receive according to whether they are perceived to be "excellent," "good," "fair," or "poor." While it is possible to rank-order these perceptions in terms of relative value (e.g., higher or lower, more positive or less positive), we do not know how different a response of "good" is compared to a feeling that the benefit involved is "excellent." Moreover, we cannot safely assume that the difference between "good" and "excellent" is equal to the difference between "good" and "fair." The distances remain undefined.

Interval-Level Data Interval-level data differ from ordinal data in that the distances between items or articles on an interval scale are known. Thus, in addition to ordering values, the distances between categories are defined in fixed and equal units. The classic example of an interval-level scale is a thermometer, which records temperatures in terms of degrees; one degree implies the same amount of heat whether the temperature is at the higher or lower end of the scale. Moreover, the difference between 30 degrees Fahrenheit (F) and 15 F is the same as the difference between 60 F and 45 F.

Ratio-Level Data   The final level of measurement consists of an interval scale with an absolute zero point. Rulers and weight scales are examples of ratio-level measurements.

Most research efforts in the behavioral sciences deal primarily with nominal-, ordinal-, and, at times, interval-level data; the use of ratio-level data is highly infrequent. In fact, most behavioral science research data do not meet the rigorous standards of interval measurement.

Levels of Measurement and Statistical Analysis

At one time it was thought that different types of statistical analyses required an appropriate level of measurement. In other words, the level of measurement in a particular set of data determined which statistical techniques were relevant for analysis. Since higher-order statistical tests are based on the assumption that the data are interval in nature, the general rule of thumb was that ordinal and especially nominal data limited the types of statistical techniques that could be used (see Appendix B). A more recent position is that the distinction between *categorical* (nominal) and *continuous* (ordinal, interval, ratio) data is more germane to determining appropriate statistical technique than the different levels of measurement per se.[47] For instance, while information gathered by Likert-type scales (e.g., strongly agree, agree, neutral, disagree, strongly disagree) is at the ordinal level, since it is continuous data the information meets the assumptions of higher-order statistical techniques. Moreover, because studies have indicated that the reliability of these scales tends to be quite good, sophisticated statistical tests are often run on such data. Nominal-level data, however, are clearly categorical rather than continuous in nature. Thus, statistical techniques that would be appropriate for ordinal-level data might not be appropriate for nominal-level data. The important point to remember when selecting statistical methods is that the analysis is only as good as the quality and nature of the data you are using.

ETHICAL CONSIDERATIONS IN ORGANIZATIONAL RESEARCH AND DATA COLLECTION

A number of ethical issues are raised in OB-related studies that concern the conduct of the research process and utilization of the data generated.[48] It is generally accepted, for example, that it is unethical to involve individuals in a research project without their knowledge or consent. Similarly, ethical concerns emerge with respect to issues of coercing individuals (e.g., one's students) into being study participants, deceiving individuals as to the true nature of the research in which they are participating, subjecting individuals to physical or psychological harm during their involvement in a study, and maintaining the confidentiality of the study participants as well as the data generated by the research.

While these issues appear on the surface to be rather straightforward, a number of subtle factors are involved that readily complicate these decisions.[49] First, the very meaning of informed and voluntary consent is open to interpretation. The idea of informed consent means explaining the purpose and nature of the research to potential subjects, including warnings of possible harm. Since organizations are open systems, however, a research project can set a variety of organizational processes in motion that can take on their own dynamics, directly and indirectly affecting a host of organizational members without anyone knowing, with confidence, what the outcome will be. Second, although one should not purposefully deceive someone as to the nature of a research project, there are instances where full knowledge of the intent of the research might compromise the study's validity. As noted earlier, people will often attempt to provide observers with what they think the researchers are looking for. Third, although one should be careful to maintain the anonymity of subjects and respondents, the way in which data are reported can unknowingly compromise confidentiality agreements. Finally, as advances in information technology have made it much easier for researchers to amass huge amounts of data on individuals, their preferences and behaviors, issues of privacy, informed consent, and access to this information have become more problematic.

Given these concerns, it is important for researchers to examine a proposed study's design and procedures in the context of guidelines set forth in existing standards of research. The Academy of Management, the main professional association for college and university professors in the management area, for example, has incorporated such research guidelines as part of its code of conduct. Third-party review is another means that can be used to protect the interests of study participants. Most academic institutions, for instance, have a human subjects review committee whose members are sensitive to the ethical and legal ramifications associated with research. In those cases where it is felt that deception is necessary to ensure the study's validity, the researcher must be able to show that the people involved in the study are not likely to be emotionally upset or endure any psychological harm when the deception is revealed.

Researchers should exercise due care in removing any detrimental side effects from involvement in their studies.[50] As the Academy of Management's Code of Ethical Conduct notes, "It is the duty of Academy members to preserve and protect the privacy, dignity, well-being, and freedom of research participants."[51] It is expected that OB researchers design, implement, analyze, report, and present their findings as rigorously and objectively as possible. Especially when people are part of a study, it is important to carefully weigh the perceived gains from the project against any costs to human dignity.

THEORY BUILDING, POSTMODERNISM, AND THEORY DECONSTRUCTION

There is an emerging debate in management concerning the extent to which the theories and frameworks that dominate the field have inherent biases that limit the ways in which we think about organizations. As discussed in Chapter 1, management theories are best thought of as social products that are shaped by wider sociocultural, economic, political, and technological forces. Accordingly, events and changes in the larger society not only affect existing arrangements, but also influence our views on and thinking about management, behavior, and organization. Thus, the research questions we raise, the studies we design, and the types of data we collect are, to a large degree, determined by our experiences within these societal forces. In fact, this effect is so pervasive that regardless of any pretense that we approach problems as objective, value-free scientists, the reality is that the academic research process is significantly influenced by our personal as well as professional lives.[52]

Paralleling earlier debates about the transformation from industrial to post-industrial society, there are emerging tensions between what is referred to as modern and postmodern perspectives on management and organization. Although there is no simple description of *postmodernism*, it reflects a dissenting voice leveled against the contemporary view that science and reason can solve all our problems. As part of the controversy, critics are increasingly challenging the managerial bias inherent in traditional research by attempting to show how organizations operate as places of domination and exploitation. Questions are surfacing about underlying ideological and patriarchal (male-dominated) biases, the role of power in the workplace, and, in general, the ways in which organization theory favors those arrangements that reflect the status quo.[53] As a result of this dialectic, OB and management theory building are beginning to become increasingly sensitive to areas that have traditionally been left to the margins of interest—for instance, the experiences of different ethnic and racial groups in the workplace, the influence of culture and symbolism on organizational performance, emphases on sexuality, gender, and feminism in the workplace, and the utility of metaphors in understanding organizations.[54]

Modern organization theory is influenced by the functional orientation of organizational systems models (see Chapter 1), the view that organizations are extensions of human rationality. This perspective has readily shaped and influenced the type of research questions and designs that dominate the field. Emerging *postmodern* emphases, in contrast, reject this view and focus instead on the paradoxes and indeterminacy inherent in social life. Thus, rather than looking at organizations as expressions of planned thought and calculative action, the postmodern perspective is that organizations are, in essence, defensive reactions to the natural forces that constantly threaten the stability of organizational life.[55] As an example, modern theory depicts corporate strategy as a set of rational techniques for managing complex businesses in a changing environment. Postmodernists, in contrast, would question the extent to which strategy actually reflects rational processes, focusing on the social construction and political character of the strategy process and its inability to account for the uncertainties involved in organizational change.[56] This perspective has begun to change the types of questions and considerations that are involved in strategy research. Rather than focusing on information written down in formal reports and expressed in numbers, for example, a growing number of researchers are examining the meanings exchanged in informal conversations, interactions between organizations and their customers, suppliers, and other key stakeholders, and the internal politics associated with strategic initiatives.[57]

By questioning the underlying assumptions and presuppositions that are offered as "knowledge," the postmodern perspective attempts to "deconstruct" existing theory.[58] In other words, postmodernists argue that the "meaning" of existing concepts is not fixed but instead constructed through constantly shifting dichotomies (polar extremes). The basic purpose is to control the tendency to seek closure in our understanding about organizational phenomena and move us closer to the reality that multiple truths exist in pluralistic settings. As an example, an important concept in modern organization theory is *bounded rationality*, the premise that rational, goal-directed decisions are constrained due to the reality that we operate with incomplete information and are able to explore only a limited number of alternatives (see Chapter 2). Using this concept, management's efforts to enhance productivity and improve decision making translates into fragmenting and simplifying the types of decisions that most organizational members must make, reducing complexity to the point where lower-level workers are only delegated routine, programmed decisions. Upper-level executives, in contrast, are the ones who must deal with uncertainty and make decisions of true consequence. Critics contend that by defining rationality as "bounded," this concept implies that more holistic forms of reasoning, such as intuition and judgment, are "nonrational" and decisions based on emotions are "irrational."

By deconstructing this concept, postmodernists have emphasized the concept of *bounded emotionality*, where nurturing, caring, community, supportiveness, and interrelatedness constitute alternative modes of organization. In this sense, "bounded" refers to our ability to recognize the subjectivity of others; we are constrained, not by our ability to process information, but by our commitment and responsiveness to others. This reconstructed theory places much more emphasis on the role of inspiration, sentiment, intuition, and judgment-affective factors that have been devalued by more rationally oriented models. Within this context, individuals select organizational actions that are based more on a tolerance for ambiguity than they are on attempts to reduce ambiguity through "satisficing" (i.e., selecting the first option that meets organizational goals rather than continuing to search for the optimal alternative which is suggested by bounded rationality).

As this type of postmodern analysis suggests, many of the concepts presented in this volume should be thought of as contingent terms rather than the final vocabulary of OB.[59] As we continue to question our underlying assumptions, deconstruct existing theories, and become more aware of the multiple truths that exist in diverse populations, our understanding of the complexities of organizations and the behaviors that occur within and between them will continue to evolve.[60]

As you continue to explore the OB field, it will become increasingly evident that our knowledge is highly dependent on previously conducted research. It is thus important to have an understanding of how that research was formulated and conducted before either dismissing a theory as not being relevant for practicing managers or accepting a research report. The ability to make sound diagnoses and to selectively choose among the materials presented in this book are essential skills if you are to effectively *apply* these concepts in your work setting.

NOTES

1. The first part of this chapter was inspired by a very lucid discussion in W.J. Duncan, *Organizational Behavior* (Boston: Allyn & Bacon, 1981), pp. 48–68.

2. E.F. Stone, "Research Methods and Philosophy of Science," in S. Kerr, ed., *Organizational Behavior* (Columbus: Grid Publishing, 1979), pp. 16–19.

3. B. Turney and G. Robb, *Research in Education: An Introduction* (Hinsdale, IL: Dryden Press, 1971), pp. 4–5.

4. Stone, op. cit., pp. 24–26.

5. For a complete discussion of this controversy see C.N. Greene, "The Satisfaction–Performance Controversy," *Business Horizons* 15 (October 1972): 31–41; and D. Organ, "Reappraisal and Reinterpretation of the Satisfaction-Causes-Performance Hypothesis," *Academy of Management Review* 2, no. 1 (1977): 46–53.

6. For a complete review of ways of generating hypotheses in the social sciences, see

W.J. McGuire, "Creative Hypothesis Generating in Psychology: Some Useful Heuristics," *Annual Review of Psychology* 48 (1997): 1–30.

7. This section is based on E.W.K. Tsang and K. Kwan, "Replication and Theory Development in Organizational Science: A Critical Realist Perspective," *Academy of Management Review* 24, no. 4 (1999): 759–780.

8. Tsang and Kwan, "Replication and Theory Development," pp. 763–764.

9. This discussion draws heavily from R.M. Baron and D.A. Kenny, "The Moderator-Mediator Variable Distinction in Social Psychological Research: Conceptual, Strategic, and Statistical Considerations," *Journal of Personality and Social Psychology* 51, no. 6 (1986): 1173–1182.

10. Baron and Kenny, ibid., p. 1176.

11. See M. Beer, "Towards a Redefinition of OD: A Critique of Research Focus and Method," *Academy of Management OD Newsletter* (Winter 1988): 6–7; and B.M. Staw, "Organizational Behavior: A Review and Reformulation of the Field's Outcome Variables," *Annual Review of Psychology* 35 (1984): 627–666. With the increased use of computer-driven data analysis, these concerns have become especially important; see R.C. MacCallum and C.M. Mar, "Distinguishing Between Moderator and Quadratic Effects in Multiple Regression," *Psychological Bulletin* 118, no. 3 (1995): 405–421.

12. Specific strategies for how to conduct such process-oriented research are beyond the scope of this text. For a thoughtful discussion of how such research can be carried out, see A. Langley, "Strategies for Theorizing from Process Data," *Academy of Management Review* 24, no. 4 (1999): 691–710.

13. E.F. Stone-Romero, A.E. Weaver, and J.L. Glenar, "Trends in Research Design and Data Analytic Strategies in Organizational Research," *Journal of Management* 21, no. 1 (1995): 142–257.

14. J.E. Post and P.N. Andrews, "Case Research in Corporation and Society Studies," in L.E. Preston, ed., *Research in Corporate Social Performance Policy*, vol. 4 (Greenwich, CT: JAI Press, 1982), pp. 1–33; see also R.K. Yin, *Case Study Research: Design and Methods* (Newbury Park, CA: Sage, 1989).

15. Yin, op. cit., p. 21.

16. Turney and Robb, op. cit., pp. 63–64.

17. F.N. Kerlinger, *Foundations of Behavioral Research* (New York: Holt, Rinehart & Winston, 1965), p. 30.

18. See J. Greenberg, "The College Sophomore as Guinea Pig: Setting the Record Straight," *Academy of Management Review* 12, no. 1 (1987): 157–159; and R.L. Dipboye and M.F. Flanagan, "Research Settings in Industrial and Organizational Psychology: Are Findings in the Field More Generalizable Than in the Laboratory?" *American Psychologist* 34 (1979): 141–150.

19. Yin, op. cit., pp. 21–22.

20. See O. Parry, "Making Sense of the Research Setting and Making the Research Setting Make Sense," in R.G. Burgess, ed., *Studies in Qualitative Methodology: Learning About Field Work*, vol. 3 (Greenwich, CT: JAI Press, 1992), pp. 82–83.

21. P. Atkinson, *Understanding Ethnographic Texts* (Beverly Hills: Sage, 1992).

22. D.T. Campbell and J.C. Stanley, *Experimental and Quasi-Experimental Designs for Research* (Chicago: Rand McNally, 1963).

23. Kerlinger, op. cit., p. 382.

24. See, for example, E.E. Lawler III and J. Suttle, "A Causal Correlational Test of the Need Hierarchy Concept," *Organizational Behavior and Human Performance* 7, no. 2 (1972): 265–287; D.T. Hall and K. Nougaim, "An Examination of Maslow's Need Hierarchy in an Organizational Setting," *Organizational Behavior and Human Performance* 3, no. 1 (1968): 12–35; C.P. Alderfer, "An Empirical Test of a New Theory of Human Needs," *Organizational Behavior and Human Performance* 4, no. 2 (1969): 142–175.

25. For a thorough discussion of multiple hypothesis testing, see J.P. Shaffer, "Multiple Hypothesis Testing," *Annual Review of Psychology* 46 (1995): 561–584.

26. This section is based on R.J. Bullock, "A Meta-Analysis Method of OD Case Studies," *Group & Organization Studies* 11, nos. 1–2 (1986): 33–48; G.V. Glass, B. McGaw, and F.J. Smith, *Meta-Analysis in Social Research* (Beverly Hills, CA: 1981); R.A. Guzzo, S.E. Jackson, and R.A. Katzell, "Meta-Analysis Analysis," in L.L. Cummings and B.M. Staw, eds.,

Research in Organizational Behavior, vol. 9 (Greenwich, CT: JAI Press, 1987), pp. 407–442; and M. Hunt, *How Science Takes Stock: The Story of Meta-Analysis* (New York: Russell Sage Foundation, 1997).

27. This discussion is drawn from J.P. Wanous, S.E. Sullivan, and J. Malinak, "The Role of Judgment Calls in Meta-Analysis," *Journal of Applied Psychology* 74, no. 2 (1989): 259–264. For an insightful approach (the analysis of unpublished doctoral dissertations) to controlling the problem of well-executed studies not being published due to a lack of significant results, see E.L. Deci, R. Koestner, and R.M. Ryan, "A Meta-Analytic Review of Experiments Examining the Effects of Extrinsic Rewards on Intrinsic Motivation," *Psychological Bulletin* 125, no. 6 (1999): 649–650.

28. See E.R. Kemery, K.W. Mossholder, and W.P. Dunlap, "Meta-Analysis and Moderator Variables: A Cautionary Note on Transportability," *Journal of Applied Psychology* 74, no. 1 (1989): 168–170; and K.T. Trotman and R. Wood, "A Meta-Analysis of Studies of Internal Control Judgments," *Journal of Accounting Research* 29, no. 1 (1991): 180–192.

29. G.P. Knight, R.A. Fabes, and D.A. Higgins, "Concerns about Drawing Causal Inferences from Meta-Analyses: An Example in the Study of Gender Differences in Aggression," *Psychological Bulletin* 119, no. 3 (1996): 410–421.

30. Wanous, Sullivan, and Malinak, op. cit., pp. 263–264.

31. See G.F. Green and J.A. Hall, "Quantitative Methods of Literature Reviews," *Annual Review* of *Psychology* 35 (1984): 27–53; Kemery, Mossholder, and Dunlap, op. cit., pp. 168–170; and M.R. Lepper, J. Henderlong, and I. Gingras, "Understanding the Effects of Extrinsic Rewards on Intrinsic Motivation— Uses and Abuses of Meta-Analysis: Comment on Deci, Koestner, and Ryan (1999)," *Psychological Bulletin* 125, no. 6 (1999): 669–676.

32. This section is adapted from J.L. Bowditch and A.F. Buono, *Quality of Work Life Assessment: A Survey-Based Approach* (Boston: Auburn House, 1982), pp. 30–39.

33. See T.R. Hinkin, "A Review of Scale Development Practices in the Study of Organizations," *Journal of Management* 21, no. 5 (1995): 967–988.

34. C. Currer, "Strangers or Sisters? An Exploration of Familiarity, Strangeness, and Power in Research," in R.G. Burgess, ed., *Studies in Qualitative Methodology: Learning about Field Work*, vol. 3 (Greenwich, CT: JAI Press, 1992), pp. 16–18.

35. See J. Finch, "It's Great to Have Someone to Talk to: The Ethics and Politics of Interviewing Women," in C. Bell and H. Roberts, eds., *Social Researching* (London: Routledge & Kegan Paul, 1984), pp. 7–87; and C. Hughes, "A Stranger in the House: Researching the Step Family," in R.G. Burgess, ibid., pp. 48–50.

36. L. Schatzman and A.L. Strauss, *Field Research: Strategies for a Natural Sociology* (Englewood Cliffs, NJ: Prentice Hall, 1973), pp. 87–89.

37. This discussion is drawn from C.D. Hansen and W.M. Kahnweiler, "Storytelling: An Instrument for Understanding the Dynamics of Corporate Relationships," *Human Relations* 46, no. 12 (1993): 1391–1409; and D.M. Bjoe, "Stories of the Storytelling Organization: A Postmodern Analysis of Disney as 'Tamara-Land,'" *Academy of Management Journal* 38, no. 4 (1995): 997–1035.

38. B. Kaye and B. Jacobson, "True Tales and Tall Tales: The Power of Organizational Storytelling," *Training & Development* 53, no. 3 (1999): 44–50.

39. See W.B. Stevenson and D.N. Greenberg, "The Formal Analysis of Narratives of Organizational Change," *Journal of Management* 24, no. 6 (1998): 741–762; and B.T. Pentland, "Building Process Theory with Narrative: From Description to Explanation," *Academy of Management Review* 24, no. 4 (1999): 711–724.

40. See G. Jacobs, ed., *The Participant Observer* (New York: Braziller, 1970), pp. viii–ix; and R.G. Burgess, *In the Field: An Introduction to Field Research* (London: Unwin Hyman, 1984).

41. See G.D. Mitchell, *A Dictionary of Sociology* (London: Routledge & Kegan Paul,

1973), pp. 129–130; and Schatzman and Strauss, op. cit., pp. 61–65.

42. For a complete discussion on the matter of reactivity, see E.J. Webb, D.T. Campbell, R.D. Schwartz, and L. Sechrest, *Unobtrusive Measures: Non-Reactive Research in the Social Sciences*, 2nd ed. (Chicago: Rand McNally, 1966).

43. See Parry, op. cit., pp. 63–87.

44. See A.F. Buono and L.T. Nichols, *Corporate Policy, Values and Social Responsibility* (New York: Praeger, 1985), pp. 215–220; and M.W. Lewis and A.J. Grimes, "Metatriangulation: Building Theory from Multiple Paradigms," *Academy of Management Review* 24, no. 4 (1999): 672–690.

45. Campbell and Stanley, op. cit.

46. These levels of measurement were first identified by S.S. Stevens, "On the Theory of Scales of Measurement," *Science* 103 (1946): 667–680. A discussion of their properties and importance can be found in most statistics and methodology texts for the social sciences.

47. For a further discussion of the measurement controversy, see J. Gaito, "Measurement Scales and Statistics: Resurgence of an Old Misconception," *Psychological Bulletin* 87, no. 3 (1980): 564–567.

48. See Stone, op. cit., p. 38.

49. P.H. Mirvis and S.E. Seashore, "Being Ethical in Organizational Research," *American Psychologist* 34, no. 9 (1979): 778–779.

50. See J.A. Wagner and J.R. Hollenbeck, *Management of Organizational Behavior* (Englewood Cliffs, NJ: Prentice Hall, 1992), p. 74.

51. *Academy of Management Handbook*, 3rd ed. (Academy of Management, 1992), p. 39.

52. See, for example, A. Gouldner, *The Coming Crisis of Western Sociology* (New York: Basic Books, 1970); C.E. Arrington and J.R. Francis, "Letting the Chat out of the Bag: Deconstruction, Privilege and Accounting Research," *Accounting, Organizations and Society* 14, nos. 1–2 (1989): 1–28; and S. Cannon, "Reflections on Fieldwork in Stressful Situations," in R.G. Burgess, op. cit., pp. 147–182.

53. See D. Brown, "An Institutionalist Look at Postmodernism," *Journal of Economic Issues* 25, no. 4 (1991): 1092–1094; and D.K. Mumby and L.L. Putnam, "The Politics of Emotionality: A Feminist Reading of Bounded Rationality," *Academy of Management Review* 17, no. 3 (1992): 465–466.

54. M. Parker, "Postmodern Organizations or Postmodern Organization Theory?" *Organization Studies* 13, no. 1 (1992): 1–17.

55. See R. Cooper and G. Burrell, "Modernism, Postmodernism and Organizational Analysis: An Introduction," *Organization Studies* 9, no. 1 (1988): 91–112; and M. Zey, *Rational Choice Theory and Organizational Theory: A Critique* (Thousand Oaks, CA: Sage, 1998).

56. D. Knights and G. Morgan, "Corporate Strategy, Organizations, and Subjectivity: A Critique," *Organization Studies* 12, no. 2 (1992): 251–273.

57. See, for example, H. Mintzberg, *The Rise and Fall of Strategic Planning* (New York: Free Press, 1994); and L.G. Bolman and T.E. Deal, *Reframing Organizations: Artistry, Choice and Leadership* (San Francisco: Jossey-Bass, 1997).

58. See Arrington and Francis, op. cit., pp. 3–4; and Mumby and Putnam, op. cit., pp. 467–474. The comparative discussion of bounded rationality and bounded emotionality is drawn from the Mumby and Putnam article.

59. See Mumby and Putnam, op. cit., pp. 481–482; and Arrington and Francis, op. cit., pp. 3–4.

60. See M.B. Calas and L. Smircich, "Past Postmodernism? Reflections and Tentative Directions," *Academy of Management Review* 24, no. 4 (1999): 672–690.

APPENDIX B

Statistical Analysis

T here are a number of different statistical techniques commonly used in OB research.[1] These methods range from relatively simple marginal distributions and cross-tabulations of the data to more complex techniques such as correlations, regression, and analysis of variance. These more sophisticated analyses are desirable when researchers wish to determine (1) which variables are related to each other, (2) whether there are differences between subsamples of the population being studied that could be attributed to chance, and/or (3) whether certain variables are predictable by knowing the values of other variables.

The purpose of this appendix is to familiarize the reader with some of the more common statistical techniques employed in OB research. Our intent is *not* to fully discuss each of these techniques and their application. The reader is encouraged to consult some of the many sources on how to work with quantitative data for further information and clarification.

Because data are often gathered from a sample of the population of interest, most of the techniques discussed in this appendix are used to estimate which findings are applicable to the population as a whole.

SAMPLING

The basic purpose of sampling is to examine an entire population by studying a proportion of the larger group in such a way that the data gathered can be used to make accurate estimates about the whole population. To ensure such generalization, reliable procedures must be used to increase the probability that the sample studied is indeed representative of the total population. In such research efforts, selection bias can occur if (1) the sampling is accomplished on a nonrandom basis (i.e., the selection is either consciously or unconsciously influenced by human choice), or (2) the sampling frame that serves as the basis for selection does not adequately cover the population. Thus, *probability sampling* is the prime method that can be used to provide data from a subset of a population that accurately represents the responses that could be gathered from the entire population.[2]

Random Sampling

The most commonly used form of probability sampling is referred to as *simple random sampling*, a process in which any member of the population has an equal chance of being selected. This is accomplished by sampling *without* replacement; that is, an individual (or thing) cannot appear in the same sample more than once. To ensure randomness, individuals are chosen either on the basis of a table of random numbers (which can be found in any elementary statistics book), or by the "lottery method" (each member of the population is represented by a token, which is placed in a bin and drawn until the required sample size has been selected).

Although random sampling is often equated with "haphazard selection" and many people believe that as long as the researcher does not consciously select certain individuals randomness can be ensured, this is not necessarily the case. Individuals unconsciously tend to favor certain people or units in the population even if they think they are choosing randomly. Only by undertaking a procedure that is independent of human judgment can the sample be said to be truly random.

Stratified Sampling

An important variation on probability sampling that is often used in OB research is *stratified sampling*. This approach is used to increase the precision of a particular sample by ensuring that certain groups are sufficiently represented. This approach does not imply a departure from the principle of randomness. Rather, *prior to* selection, the population is divided into critical groups (e.g., gender, race, and job cluster); the next step is a random sample selected *within* each group. Thus, although this method can increase the probability that the sample will be representative of the larger population being studied, the choice within groups must be randomly made.

Cluster Sampling

A second variation on probability sampling, which is often used to reduce survey costs, is *cluster sampling*. Although this procedure is used less frequently than simple random sampling or stratified sampling, cluster sampling is a process of sampling complete groups or units within a given population. This is often done through a multistage process in which different groups are randomly selected and included in the sample. There are often questions, however, concerning what actually constitutes an appropriate cluster for analysis. Since this is a highly judgmental decision, the expertise of the researcher is especially important with this technique.

STATISTICAL SIGNIFICANCE

One of the tasks of OB research is to describe what has occurred in a particular group or organizational setting. This, however, is only the beginning of the task of such research efforts. The next step is to arrive at conclusions extending beyond the sample itself and to make generalizations about the larger population. In order to do this, researchers rely on *inferential statistics*, statistical techniques that permit inferences or inductions to be made about the larger population based on observations of the sample.

There are two critical questions in inferential statistics: (1) To what extent do uncontrolled variables (often referred to as "chance") influence the findings in the study; and (2) if the study were repeated, would we be able to predict with confidence that the same results would occur? The issue underlying these questions is where to "draw the line" that determines whether we make inferences about the larger population. The response to this concern reveals the basic nature of behavioral science research, that is, it is probabilistic rather than absolutistic in orientation. In other words, *probability* is used to determine whether "chance" influenced the research findings.[3]

Probability statements, which are printed in statistical form, are used to indicate whether the sample data can be used to make inferences about the larger population. In research articles or reports, the statement appears as follows:

$p < .05$
$p < .01$
$p < .001$
$p = NS$

These statements mean that there is a probability of less than 5 percent ($p < .05$), 1 percent ($p < .01$), or 1/10 of 1 percent ($p < .001$) that the results could have occurred by "chance." $p = NS$ means that the results are *not* statistically significant (that the probability of "chance" is greater than 5 percent). As may be evident from the preceding discussion, the 5 percent level ($p = .05$) is the point where behavioral scientists agree that there is a difference that would allow inferences to be made from the data. A probability larger than this (e.g., $p = .10$) while still not very large, is by convention too high for behavioral scientists to accept such generalizations.

One caveat should be mentioned about statistical significance.[4] Findings are regarded as significant if they meet the $p < .05$ standard. There are times, however, when researchers will attain statistical significance, but there will be no meaningful difference of practical importance (*substantive significance*). For example, an evaluation of the effectiveness of a training program for assembly workers might compare those who had taken a formal program with a control group that only received on-the-job training. The formal program would be the independent variable, and the data collected (the dependent variable) might be the error rate on the job. There could be a significant difference between the error rate of the experimental training program and on-the-job control—let's say 2 percent fewer errors made by those participating in the training program. However, while this may be statistically significant, a 2 percent reduction in errors might not be worth the effort and expense to develop the training program. Thus, this statistically significant difference has little *practical importance*. As such, many OB professionals are now calculating the cost/benefit ratios for training programs and other interventions in order to assess their overall utility.[5]

COMMON STATISTICAL TECHNIQUES

The discussion now turns to a brief examination of some commonly used statistical techniques and how to interpret them. The first two methods (frequency distributions and cross-tabulations) are *descriptive statistics*, and the latter (correlations, regression,

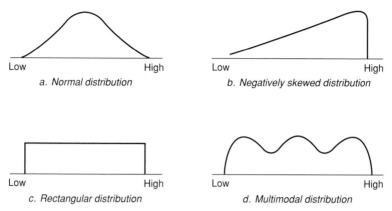

Figure B-1 Types of Frequency Distribution

t-tests, and F-tests) are *inferential statistics*. While other statistical techniques are often employed as well, a basic understanding of these methods will provide you with sufficient background to compare the results of those studies with other research efforts.

Since inferential statistics are based on certain assumptions about the data being analyzed, a few comments are in order. Inferential statistics assume that:

1. The data are interval (see Appendix A).
2. The data are normally distributed. With respect to Figure B-1, this means that the distribution of the sample forms a bell-shaped curve (a) as opposed to a skewed (b), rectangular (c), or multimodal distribution (d).
3. In addition, inferential techniques are based on *correlations* that further assume linear relationships between two variables (such as SAT scores and grade point average), and equal variance throughout the distribution of the two variables. Equal variance or dispersal throughout a distribution is referred to as *homoscedasticity*. Figure B-2 presents different distributions of hypothesized relationships between length of employment and job satisfaction: (a) illustrates a linear relationship, (b) shows a nonlinear or curvilinear relationship, (c) a nonhomoscedastic (fan-shaped) relationship, and (d) a nonhomoscedastic relationship. These types of *scatter plots* are useful to graphically display the relationship between two variables, and, more important, to indicate whether the relationship is linear or nonlinear.

Frequency Distributions

Probably the most widespread and simplest technique for describing data is the frequency distribution. Frequency distributions indicate the number and percentage of respondents, objects, or events that fall into each of the available categories. These data give a broad overview of the research data without making distinctions across different groups in the study.

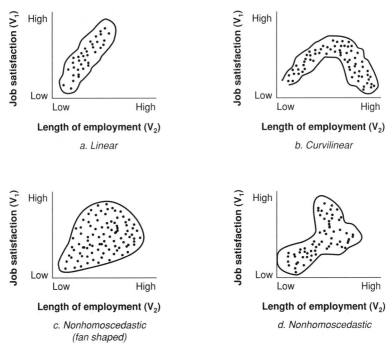

Figure B-2 Scatter Plots Showing Possible Relationships between Length of Employment and Job Satisfaction

Table B-1 presents an example of the frequency distribution of a series of job-related questions from an organizational survey we conducted. As the table indicates, this procedure readily shows the proportion of people who respond favorably or unfavorably to a particular set of questions. The distribution of response is usually indicated in percentage terms, although it can be presented in simple numbers of response as well.

Cross-Tabulations

While frequency distributions provide information that describes the overall sample or population being studied, cross-tabulation is a visual technique that enables researchers to examine relationships *between* variables. For example, in Table B-1

TABLE B-1 Frequency Distribution for Selected Survey Items

	Response (percent)				
Statement	Strongly Agree	Agree	Neutral	Disagree	Strongly Disagree
Overall, I am satisfied with my job.	15	48	19	12	6
There is sufficient challenge in my job.	20	43	17	14	6
I feel I am adequately trained for my job.	20	60	12	6	2
My daily work hours are satisfactory.	22	58	6	8	6

TABLE B-2 **Example of a Cross-Tabulation for Job Satisfaction by Job Classification**

	Statement: Overall, I am satisfied with my job				
Job Classification	**Strongly Agree**	**Agree**	**Neutral**	**Disagree**	**Strongly Disagree**
Clerical	12	42	23	15	8
Secretarial	14	46	20	10	10
Teller	13	48	16	12	11
Head Teller	8	42	38	10	2
Professional Staff	18	55	9	16	2
Assistant Managers	22	69	4	5	0
Department Heads	20	63	17	0	0

the first statement, "Overall, I am satisfied with my job," indicates that 15 percent of the group being surveyed "strongly agree" that they are satisfied with their jobs, 48 percent "agree," and so forth. Is this distribution, however, representative of all job classifications in the organization? Are long-term employees more satisfied with their jobs than those individuals who have worked for the organization for only a short period of time? Are those who report that they are *not* satisfied also the ones who feel there is insufficient challenge in their jobs?

To find out whether there are differences in job satisfaction within this particular organization, the distribution of response must be *cross-tabulated* by another variable. Through a process of "breaking down" responses by various subcategories, researchers can be more explicit in describing their findings. Table B-2, for example, takes the global question on job satisfaction discussed previously and breaks it down by job classification. As these data indicate, the level of job satisfaction is not uniform throughout the organization—the perception of job satisfaction generally increased with higher levels of organizational responsibility. Head tellers, however, were less satisfied than the employees in other job classifications. This type of analysis thus provides researchers with a clearer indication of relationships between variables. It also points to specific areas in which further analysis is needed (e.g., *why* are head tellers less satisfied?; what does the large neutral response indicate?). Beyond simple cross-tabulations, researchers will often want to do slightly more complex aggregate data analysis. One way to isolate certain groups even more precisely is to *control* certain variables. Thus, if in Table B-2 it was also desirable to assess the effect of another variable (such as gender or length of employment), one could do a "triple" cross-tabulation of these variables.

These two basic statistical techniques are used to describe the data gathered during the research. As mentioned earlier, however, this is just the beginning of the researcher's task. The next task is to explain these findings and to be able to make generalizations about the larger population. In order to accomplish this, more intricate, inferential statistics are employed.

Correlation

The first technique, which can be used either inferentially or descriptively, is referred to as *correlation*. This method describes quantitatively the association or relationship of one interval level variable with another. As an example, we can look at a hypothetical relationship between length of employment and satisfaction with pay. A correlation coefficient (r) will indicate how much correspondence there is between the two variables. The range of possible scores is between +1.00 and –1.00. Perfect correspondence would give a score of +1.00; high correspondence or correlation, a score in the range of +0.60; no correlation a score of 0.00; and high negative correlation a score in the range of –0.60.

Figure B-3 illustrates some hypothetical results of the scatter plots and related correlations between length of employment and satisfaction with pay. For each diagram, the different dots represent each respondent's length of employment with his or her pay satisfaction. Assume, for instance, that the correlation between the two variables is high. As example (a) indicates, given a particular length of employment one is then able to predict a narrow range of satisfaction with pay. In other words, in this example, workers who have been with the organization for long periods of time tend to be more satisfied with their pay than those individuals who have been with the organization for shorter periods of employment. This type of *bivariate* (two-variable) correlation analysis provides a single summary statistic describing the relationship between the variables. The *number* or *value* indicates the strength of the relationship, and the sign (1 or 2) tells whether the variables are positively or negatively related (i.e., whether both variables ascend simultaneously, or whether one ascends when the other descends).

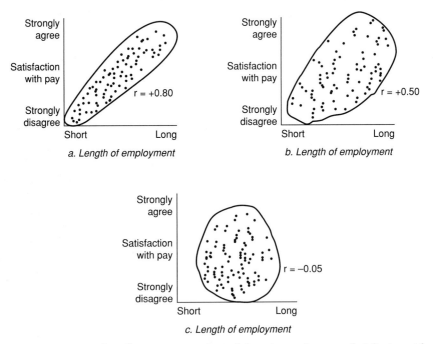

Figure B-3   Scatter Plots Illustrating Hypothetical Correlations between Satisfaction with Pay and Length of Employment

Significance of Correlations

As part of the interpretation of correlations, statistical significance should be determined. Statistical significance depends on two factors: the *strength of the relationship* (the higher the correlation, the greater the probability that it will be significant), and the *number of paired observations* that make up the correlation (the higher the number of pairs, the lower the required strength of the correlation necessary for significance). As indicated earlier, however, statistical significance should not be confused with substantive significance.

As a *rough* guide to the value of correlations, the following system has been suggested:[6]

+ or − 0.80 to 1.00 very high correlation
0.60 to 0.79 high correlation
0.40 to 0.59 moderate correlation
0.20 to 0.39 slight correlation
0.01 to 0.19 very slight correlation

Causality

One danger in using simple correlation analysis is to attribute causality to a relationship. For instance, if satisfaction with pay and length of employment were correlated at 1.70, one might be tempted to argue that the length of employment causes satisfaction with pay. Causality, however, *cannot* be determined by simple correlation. All that the preceding example indicates is that a *relationship* exists between length of employment and pay satisfaction, not that length of employment leads to pay satisfaction. While it is possible that one of these variables leads to or causes the other, it is also possible that both variables are affected by some other variable or variables (e.g., actual level of pay; adjusted occupational aspirations) and that they do not directly affect each other.*

Regression

Closely linked to the concept of correlation is regression analysis. Regression is used when researchers want to predict outcomes on certain variables by using another set of variables. In its simplest form, only two variables are involved, such as length of employment and satisfaction with the job. Simple regression would try to predict job satisfaction by length of employment on the job. Since job satisfaction is thought to be influenced by a number of other factors, however, such a two-variable equation is unlikely to produce significant findings. Rather, we would want to look at the effect of a number of different variables such as length of employment, level of job responsibility, job duties, satisfaction with pay, supervisory relationships, and so forth on job satisfaction. This process is referred to as *multiple regression*. While it is expected

---

* Tentative causality may be inferred from a more complex statistical procedure referred to as cross-lagged correlation, which requires a longitudinal or time-lagged research design. Partial correlations can also control for the influence of a third variable (or more). Since these techniques are beyond the scope of this appendix, the reader is encouraged to consult a statistics text.

that multiple regression analysis should improve the predictive ability over simple regression, caution must be exercised when adding "predictor" variables. Much like the economic concept of "diminishing returns," there is a point where adding variables to a regression analysis will not improve its predictive effectiveness.

Three basic concepts are important for an understanding of regression analysis: the regression line, intercept, and slope. The *regression line* is the hypothetical line that goes through the center of the distribution, sometimes called the "line of best fit." If one were to total all of the scores on a scatter plot in terms of how far above and below they fell from the regression line (those scores above the line having a + value and those below having a – value) the sum of these scores would equal zero (see Figure B-4). While the regression line goes through the middle of the distribution, the *intercept* (which is usually designated by the letter *a* or *c* in a regression equation) indicates the constant score required to make the mean (average) of one variable equal the mean of the other variable (e.g., length of employment and job satisfaction). The *slope* of the distribution represents the number of units of one variable needed to increase another variable by one unit. In our example, this would be the number of years of employment it takes to increase job satisfaction by one level. As indicated in Figure B-4, since the regression line is not at a 45-degree angle, the increase in length of employment by two years increases the likelihood of job satisfaction by one point. This would be calculated by multiplying the length of employment by a weight, referred to as *b* (beta), and adding the intercept constant to give the predicted level of satisfaction. Thus, in this example, the slope is the expected change in one variable for every unit of change in the other variable. In this example, if one wished to predict in reverse (i.e., predict length of employment by job satisfaction), the regression equation would be different, with a different slope and intercept.

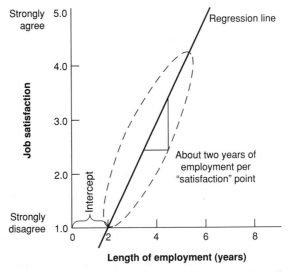

Figure B-4   A Simple Regression of Job Satisfaction with Length of Employment

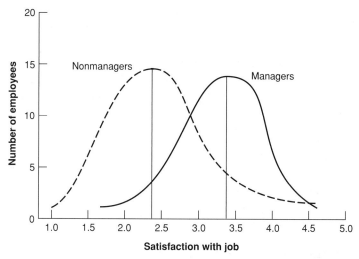

Figure B-5   Hypothetical Means and Variances of Managers and Nonmanagers on Job
Satisfaction Scores

Regression becomes an inferential statistic when a procedure referred to as *analysis of variance* is computed for the overall regression equation. The weight associated with variables in a multiple regression, *b* (beta), provides an indication of the relative importance of the variable in the predictive efficiency of the overall regression equation. In simplified manner, such as the assessment of job satisfaction between managers and nonmanagerial employees, analysis of variance allows the researcher to compute the difference around the means of these variables. In this example, the analysis provides an indication as to whether managers and nonmanagerial personnel differ significantly with respect to the expressed level of job satisfaction.

The importance of means and variance within and between distributions is reflected in Figures B-5 and B-6. Suppose we wanted to assess how managers and

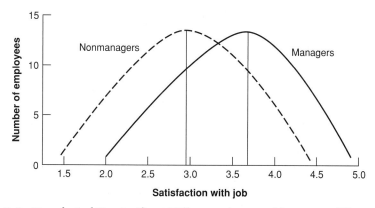

Figure B-6   Hypothetical Nonsignificant Differences between Managers and Nonmanagers

nonmanagers within a particular corporation perceived their jobs. Looking at Figure B-5, nonmanagers report a mean satisfaction level of 2.4, while managers report a mean satisfaction level of 3.4. It is also clear from the distribution, on the other hand, that there is an overlap between the two job levels. Still, if a statistical test were performed on the two groups (say, with 250 respondents in both groups), a significant difference (i.e., not due to chance) would be observed. However, consider the situation illustrated by Figure B-6, where the internal variance within the nonmanagerial sample and the managerial sample is much larger. In this instance, although the difference between the means is similar to that in Figure B-5, the large variance within each distribution causes so much overlap between the two groups that one could not say that nonmanagers are significantly lower than managers in their average scores on the job satisfaction question.

In summary, regression analysis indicates the relative importance of one or more variables in predicting a score on an outcome variable. Analysis of variance on regression indicates which of the predictor (independent) variables makes a significant contribution in forecasting a person's score on an outcome or dependent variable. When further used as an inferential statistic, analysis of variance indicates whether the variable's contribution was statistically significant or whether it could be expected to occur by chance.

t-Tests and F-Tests

A corollary to analysis of variance is the t-test. Although there is a close relationship between the two procedures, the t-test is used only for two-sample situations and does not apply to regression analysis. In some instances, researchers will want to evaluate the differences between effects, rather than the effects themselves. For example, a researcher might be interested in differences in job satisfaction for people with different levels of education. One of the most common techniques for this type of analysis is a comparison of the two groups, say those with a college education and those without, by using group means as the basis for comparison. The t-test would indicate whether the difference between the two groups is statistically significant.

In multiple regression analysis, F scores are used to indicate statistical significance. Because there are three possible F scores—one for the beta weight or slope, one for a subset of slopes, and one for the overall regression equation—the researcher must know whether one variable, a group of variables, or all of the independent variables involved make a significant contribution to the prediction of the outcome or dependent variable.

An F-test (*analysis of variance*) on the overall regression equation simply tests whether the population from which the sample is drawn is likely to have a multiple correlation (R) of zero, or whether there is a significant relationship between the predictor (independent) variables and the outcome (dependent) variables. Using the example of satisfaction with pay, job satisfaction, and length of employment, if the multiple R is significantly different from 0, there will be a significant F reported.

Using Venn diagrams, possible multiple correlations between these variables are shown in Figure B-7. The schematic inference shows that the greater the overlap

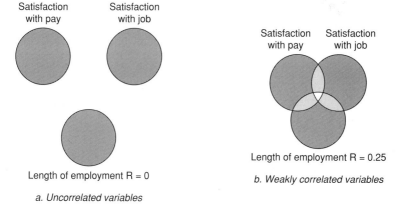

a. Uncorrelated variables

b. Weakly correlated variables

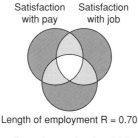

Length of employment R = 0.70

c. Strongly correlated variables

Figure B-7 Venn Diagrams Showing Relationships between Uncorrelated, Weakly Correlated, and Strongly Correlated Variables

between the variables, the higher the multiple correlation. In fact, the square of the multiple correlation (R^2) represents the amount of the variance in the dependent measure accounted for in the independent measure.

Beyond a simple test of the overall regression equation, a researcher may wish to know whether some particular regression slopes (betas) add significantly to the overall regression equation. By examining the individual betas and the F scores associated with them, it is possible to determine whether a particular variable makes a significant contribution to the overall multiple correlation.

Interactions

When conducting an analysis of variance on an experimental design testing the manipulation of two or more variables, the researcher may find that the main manipulations do not produce any effects on the outcome variable, but that the *combination* of two or more variables does produce an effect. For example, a researcher might want to study the relationship between managerial and clerical employee job satisfaction in an insurance company and the number of claim errors per week (the dependent measure). Based on attitude surveys taken for all employees, two groups among the managerial and clerical categories can be formulated—those satisfied with their jobs and those

TABLE B-3 **Mean Number of Claim Errors for Managers and Clerical Employees by Job Satisfaction (Main Effect)**

		Managers		
		Satisfied	**Unsatisfied**	**Total**
Clerical Workers	Satisfied	5	5	10
	Unsatisfied	10	10	20
	Total	15	15	30

TABLE B-4 **Mean Level of Claim Errors for Managers and Clerical Employees by Job Satisfaction (Interaction Effects)**

		Managers		
		Satisfied	**Unsatisfied**	**Total**
Clerical Workers	Satisfied	5	10	15
	Unsatisfied	10	5	15
	Total	15	15	30

who report that they are not satisfied. As indicated in Table B-3, the mean levels of errors for each group can then be compared. Based on these (hypothetical) data, the example indicates that employee job satisfaction appears to be a significant factor in the level of claim errors.

If, on the other hand, there was no difference in marginal totals but individual cells were obviously different, an interaction would be present. Consider the data in Table B-4. The marginal totals (15 each) represent equal numbers of mistakes under both levels of satisfaction for managers and clerical workers. However, when looking at the cells, clearly something is different. The data suggest that matching workers and managers with similar levels of satisfaction seems to be more effective (fewer claim errors) than having managers with different levels of satisfaction from their clerical employees. Thus, there is a manager-worker interaction on the basis of relative job satisfaction.

CONCLUSION

This appendix has illustrated the use of some of the major techniques for statistical analysis. In brief, two descriptive (frequency distributions and cross-tabulations) and four inferential methods (correlation, regression, analysis of variance, and *t*-tests and F-tests) have been presented. Since analysis of variance is used to test the significance of regression, it is difficult to completely separate the two techniques. An analysis of variance design without regression is customarily used in laboratory experiments and field experiments when the variables are under the control of the researcher. Readers are encouraged to consult one of the many statistics texts for further clarification and elaboration of these more sophisticated statistical techniques.

NOTES

1. The discussion of statistical analysis is adapted from J.L. Bowditch and A.F. Buono, *Quality of Work Life Assessment: A Survey Approach* (Boston: Auburn House, 1982), Appendix.

2. The section on sampling procedures is drawn from C. Moser and G. Kalton, *Survey Methods in Social Investigation* (New York: Basic Books, 1974), Chapters 5–7.

3. R.P. Runyon and A. Haber, *Fundamentals of Behavioral Statistics* (Reading, MA: Addison-Wesley, 1972), pp. 4–5, 163–166.

4. W.L. Hays, *Statistics for Psychologists* (New York: Holt, Rinehart & Winston, 1963), pp. 323–335.

5. W.F. Cascio, *Costing Human Resources: The Financial Impact of Behavior in Organizations* (Boston: Kent, 1982).

6. B. Turney and G. Robb, *Research in Education* (Hinsdale, IL: Dryden Press, 1971), pp. 99–100.

How to Read a Research-Oriented Journal Article

*T*his appendix is designed to help the reader apply the basic knowledge about OB discussed in this text in reading and understanding research-oriented journal articles. While many journal articles are conceptual in nature (with no direct empirical data gathering) or rely on qualitative analysis (as in case studies), others are based on relatively sophisticated research designs and statistical analysis. The focus of this appendix is on the more quantitative articles. Thus, a basic understanding of statistics (see Appendix B) as well as organizational research methods (Appendix A) is necessary to get the most out of such empirically based research reports.

To facilitate the discussion, we will make general comments about the nature of such research reports as well as specific comments about an article written by Aaron J. Nurick, "Participation in Organizational Change: A Longitudinal Field Study," published in *Human Relations*, a scholarly journal that focuses on both the descriptive and the analytical aspects of research. (See the end of this appendix, pp. 440–452, for a reprint of the article.)

OVERVIEW

The exact format and structure of journal articles often vary depending on editorial policies, institutional specifications, and individual preferences. Most empirically oriented journal articles, however, conform to the following outline, with minor variations: (1) title and abstract; (2) introduction and literature review; (3) study design and methodology; (4) results; and (5) discussion and conclusions.

In most cases, the article is preceded by an *abstract* that briefly describes what the study is about, how it was conducted, and its major findings. The purpose of the abstract is to outline the central theme of the study. The *introductory section* describes the issue or problem involved and what earlier studies have found (supported by reference to these efforts). This section will often contain the hypotheses to be tested, stated in their working form. The *methods* section provides an overview of the research design and data collection methods. Psychology journals are noted for a preponderance of tightly controlled laboratory studies, while sociology journals lean more heavily toward field studies. Journals concerned with OB research use both approaches. The methods section also describes the nature of the subjects (organizations, groups, or individuals) being studied and the method of data analysis. Usually sufficient detail is provided to allow for repetition of the study. As a way of facilitating meta-analysis (see pp. 401–403), a growing number of journal articles now include a detailed methodological appendix.

The next section focuses on the study's *results*. The results section states the major findings of the study in as dispassionate, noneditorial terms as possible. It describes the outcome of the study and whether particular hypotheses are supported or not supported by the data analysis. Finally, the *discussion* and *conclusions* section concentrates on the implications of the research and its relationship to prior research efforts. The authors attempt to explain their results: why the data emerged as they did, the significance for the field, and suggestions for future research. In instances where there is partial support for a hypothesis, the discussion will indicate the conditions under which the hypothesis in question was either supported or not supported. Occasionally, the results and discussion are combined in a single section, often in shorter articles, but normally they are kept separate.

An effective way to begin is to read the abstract, and to briefly scan the hypotheses, results, and conclusions. Initially the reader should not be too concerned about the details of the methods used in gathering and analyzing the data. The important point is to have some sense of the study without being enmeshed in details. It is particularly helpful to have a general understanding of the research before undertaking a more critical, deeper reading of the article.

APPLICATION AND DISCUSSION

Reading and understanding empirically based journal articles is not a simple process. In fact, OB professionals often labor over such articles in order to grasp their full meanings. They read aloud, underline, and look up additional information to clarify and ensure that they understand the author's intentions. Sometimes, they will even try to rework or rewrite the article to underscore its main points.[1]

To facilitate this process, a number of questions should be considered for a complete assessment:

1. What background research is used to amplify the significance of the central issue?
2. How are prior research findings used in developing the study's hypotheses?
3. What are the expectations about the results of the study prior to the data analysis?
4. How were the data collected and analyzed?
5. What do the results say?
6. How do the results differ from what was predicted?
7. What kinds of further research would be useful to extend knowledge derived from the present study?
8. What are the limitations of the present study?
9. How might you change the study to make it a better test of the hypothesis?

These questions, though not exhaustive, set the tone for a close reading of the article.

As a way of illustrating how to approach research-oriented articles, we present an analysis of Nurick's *Human Relations* article, section by section, with suggestions about what readers can do to amplify their understanding of such research.[2]

Title and Abstract (refer to p. 440)

Since the title captures what the article is about, it should accurately and precisely identify the nature of the study in concise and descriptive terms. In this case, the title clearly points out the focus of the research and the study's research design. It is a longitudinal field study, which means that data were collected at least two (or more) times at various time intervals in a natural setting.

The abstract is a very concise description of the article. It is valuable because it provides the reader with a brief synopsis of the research. As indicated in the Nurick abstract, it should provide general information about the study: the overall aim or concern of the research, how it was done, its main findings, and conclusion. This particular study also notes that the study was part of a larger experiment in a utility company. The main objective was to examine the effect of formal participation in implementing change—on direct (membership on a task force or joint committee) and indirect (non-membership) bases—on organizational members. The abstract provides an indication of how this was examined, and the conclusion that direct participation was effective.

After reading the abstract, you should begin to think about the series of questions just outlined as you prepare to study the body of the article.

Introduction and Literature Review (refer to pp. 440–441)

The introductory section raises the questions to be addressed and places the study in the context of prior research findings. In a sense, it provides the jumping-off point for the research. In the Nurick article, the lead sentence raises questions concerning the effectiveness of organizations that place virtually all decision-making power with top management. The remainder of the initial discussion focuses the reader's attention more closely on a nontraditional, participatory approach to decision making as part of a larger Quality of Work Life program.

Theoretical Background (refer to pp. 440–441)

The next section in the Nurick article is a review of the relevant literature on participation in organizational change. Frequently such a review is part of the introduction, but in this case it is set up as a second section. Since the purpose of the literature review is to place the current study in the context of previous research efforts and to establish the significance of the study, ideally such reviews are thorough but selective. In other words, the focus should be on those previous conceptual and empirical contributions that directly relate to the issue being studied rather than any study that is remotely related to the present research. In addition to citing previous theory and research, good reviews should also point out significant theoretical or methodological questions that are suggested by these efforts.

Because of the abbreviated nature of journal articles, previous research efforts are often only briefly noted. In the Nurick article, for example, the earlier works by Lewin and his colleagues, and Coch and French are used to indicate the beginning of an important trend in research into participation by employees in organizational change decision making. The writer has to assume that the average reader knows enough about these studies to understand their importance. It is obvious, however, that the beginning student would not necessarily have this knowledge. Thus, it is often useful to review the studies referenced in such articles to develop a firmer foundation in the area.

The remainder of this section in the Nurick article serves to define what is meant by participation and how it relates to the organizational changes in the present study. A basic model of the change process and the foci of participation models are described, and the reasons why there is frequent resistance to change are offered. Since some of the references are summaries and not research articles as such (the Lewin and Huse references for example), they can provide a good overview of the change process for readers with little background or understanding in this area.

As mentioned earlier, reviews of the relevant literature also point out limitations and qualifications suggested by previous research. In the Nurick article, for example, the last paragraph notes that participation in the change process is not necessarily a guarantee that resistance to the change will end. Specific situations or conditions under which participation is and is not effective in reducing resistance to change are also briefly noted. Thus, based on this review, the reader is able to establish a theoretical basis or rationale on which the hypotheses and data analysis can be evaluated.

Study Design and Methodology

The purpose of the design and methodology section in a journal article is to explicitly outline where and when the data were collected, the number and relevant characteristics of the subjects involved, and the methods and materials used to gather the data. This section should contain sufficient information concerning how the research was conducted to allow the reader to both evaluate and replicate the findings. Thus, a clear description of the research process should be provided: decisions about the data required for the study, the devices used for their collection, how the data were collected, the researcher-subject relationship, time and length of the study, nature and number of settings and subjects, and checks on the data collection process.

In the Nurick article, this section is broken down into two main parts: *The Experiment* and *Method*. This was done because this particular study was part of a larger research project, and to gain an appropriate understanding of Nurick's study it is important to have a sense of the overall research program.

The Experiment (refer to pp. 442–443)

Although the research is referred to as an experiment, the Nurick study is actually a blend between a field study and a field experiment (see Appendix A). While there were three data measurement and collection periods spread out over a thirty-six-month time frame, a control group was not always available (e.g., "Where feasible, similar organizations are measured as comparison sites"). In this study, there was a prestudy measurement, an experimental manipulation, one postexperimental measurement eighteen months after the start of the study and another eighteen months later (thirty-six months after the start), with no additional interventions between eighteen and thirty-six months. Thus, because there was no true control group, the reader is not always sure of a rigorous control.

As discussed in Appendix A, true field experimental designs are infrequent due to circumstances beyond the researcher's control. In the Nurick study, this difficulty is acknowledged and the effort to ensure uniformity across research sites is underscored. Additionally, it should be emphasized that this research is longitudinal rather than cross-sectional in nature, which allows for the analysis of change and the dynamics of how the change occurs. Readers should carefully consider the scope of the research design and its limitations in making their own decisions about the applicability of the findings to other situations.

Nurick provides a clear description of this particular research effort: the nature of the setting, time, and length of the study, how the project was defined and oriented, and the research process. The overall guiding hypothesis of the larger research project is also given, which in substance states that workers who are given the opportunity to contribute to organizational change will experience a higher quality of work life *and* contribute to increased organizational effectiveness as well. The main parts of this hypothesis that should raise questions are: (1) What is meant by "contribution"? (2) How is effectiveness measured? and (3) How does one know that quality of work life (QWL) improved? The first point relates to the independent variable, and the last two concern the dependent variables. Readers should attempt to identify the key elements of contribution, effectiveness, and QWL as they are used in this study.

The Participatory Process (refer to pp. 443–444)

This brief section amplifies how participation was encouraged and developed through the Quality of Work Life Committee (QOWC). Although it is clearly written, for added clarity the reader might diagram the QOWC/task force relationships and outline the process of issue development and refinement (see Figure C-1). As mentioned earlier,

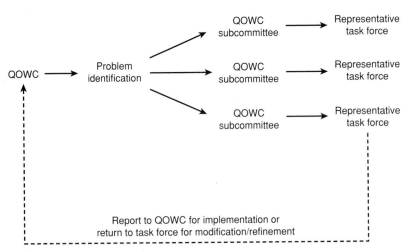

Figure C-1   QOWC Issue Development Process

this type of schematic representation can facilitate a more complete understanding of the intervention and research process. This section also describes the basis for *direct* and *indirect* participation. This is important since careful definitions should be stated for all essential variables, particularly if the variables are subject to a number of interpretations. As shown by Nurick's clear delineation of these variables, esoteric technical jargon should be avoided.

At this point the reader has a sense of the design of the study, and the main independent variable (participatory process) and one set of dependent measures (QWL survey). Additionally, we know that some participants were more directly involved in the change process than others.

Conceptual Model and Hypotheses   In this section, the author identifies an important aspect of the conceptualization and analysis plan of the research—the difference between objective (actual participation) and psychological (perceived influence) participation. By combining this conceptual distinction with the earlier definition of direct and indirect participation, the specific questions or hypotheses that guide this particular study are developed.

Part of the process of theory development is the creation of hypotheses. This is done through reviews of prior research and/or by pilot research that tentatively suggest a relationship between variables. Hypotheses are created in pairs, and taken together they are *mutually exclusive* and *exhaustive*. In other words, the pair of hypotheses exhaust all possible outcomes, as one hypothesis accounts for the outcomes that the other does not. As discussed in Appendix A, these mutually exclusive and exhaustive hypotheses are referred to as the *null* and *working* (sometimes termed the *alternative*) hypotheses.

In this study, the three hypotheses are stated in their *working* form. In all cases, direct participants are predicted to experience (1) greater perceived influence, (2) greater perceived acceptance of their influence, and (3) greater job satisfaction on a number of dimensions compared to the indirect participants. The *null* hypotheses would state that direct participants would perceive equal or less influence over these different variables than the indirect participants. The Nurick study employs what is referred to as a *one-tailed* hypothesis that predicts (1) a difference in the perceptions of direct and indirect participants and (2) the direction of that difference (that direct participants will perceive greater influence and satisfaction than indirect participants). In this study, a *two-tailed* hypothesis would predict a difference between direct and indirect participation, but would not specify what the difference (or direction of the difference) will be. Two-tailed hypotheses are weaker than one-tailed hypotheses, and they are more frequently used for pilot studies or exploratory research. In the Nurick article, the effects of direct participation are amply documented through his use of prior research and the rationale is clearly stated, so that he is able to construct the one-tailed, directional hypothesis.

At this point, the reader should have a good understanding of the background and questions raised by the research. Direct participation in bringing about organizational change is predicted to elicit more favorable attitudes and feelings than indirect participation. The next step is to examine the methodology that will be used to test this prediction.

Method (refer to pp. 445–446)

The main purpose of the methods section is to explain in complete detail how the data were gathered and how they will be analyzed. As pointed out earlier, readers should be able to replicate the study based on the information provided in the design and methods section. Although questionnaires or other data-gathering devices (especially those that have been copyrighted) have not been customarily included, journals are beginning to require detailed methodological appendixes to facilitate subsequent meta-analysis research.

The methods section typically details the process of data collection. In the Nurick study, we can see that data collection was done at three different times (longitudinal study), through surveys, interviews, company records, and observations. The ways in which data are collected are important to consider. It is generally accepted that using several types of data-gathering methods to explore a particular problem (or hypothesis) is preferable to using only one method in order to minimize the danger of having the methodology determine the results.[3] The Nurick study uses five different approaches to gathering the data, an appropriately large number of data collection techniques (see Appendix A).

Sample   In this paragraph, the relevant characteristics of the sample are provided. As discussed in Appendix B, in many studies respondents will be randomly sampled, although this was not the case in this research. The Nurick sample is based on those organizational members who were part of the entire data collection process. At this point, a question should be raised concerning how many employees were omitted because they did not respond to the three surveys over the thirty-six-month period. In many instances, there are underlying reasons why people do not respond to organizational surveys that are *not* part of a random process. Thus, a significant nonresponse rate can bias or raise questions about the representativeness of the data. In the Nurick study, however, we are informed in the next section that the response rate for the three different questionnaires was over 85 percent. This is a very high response rate, especially for a longitudinal study, since respondents are often lost through attrition (e.g., turnover; intraorganizational mobility).

Nurick also mentions that the respondents were "matched cases." This means that the direct and indirect participants were matched according to important sociodemographic characteristics that could influence their responses. Thus, the effect of these characteristics (e.g., union status or education) on the dependent variables is minimized.

Measures   This subsection identifies the specific attitude survey used in the research and some of the broad areas it covers. Since the Michigan Organizational Assessment Questionnaire (MOAQ) has been used in a number of research projects and is relatively well known, no other explicit information is necessary. The MOAQ utilizes a Likert-type scale (see Appendix A), and Nurick indicates that he combined discrete items into different scales or indices for analysis.

Footnote number 4 indicates how this was done and where further information on the process and the questionnaire can be found. In many instances, readers with additional questions are encouraged to consult the author.

Analytic Procedures   The way in which the data are analyzed must be logical and objective. The reader should be able to assess how and why this was done, and if there are any limitations on weaknesses in the study's design and methodology.

Nurick restates the main purpose of the study and some of the limitations in its design (e.g., a nonrandom sample). If randomization between groups (e.g., direct versus indirect participation) has occurred, in most cases it would be appropriate to use either analysis of variance or t-tests to look for differences between groups (see Appendix B). However, because it was not possible to ensure random placement of respondents in the direct and indirect participant groups, the author had to statistically control (hold constant) any variables other than participation that might have influenced the results. In this case, Nurick argues that the respondent's job level and the initial pretest score on the survey could influence the dependent measures. Thus, it is necessary to control for these variables in making comparisons between the direct and indirect participant groups. Because t-tests cannot control for the unwanted variance introduced by nonrandom sources, a more complex analytic procedure, *analysis of covariance*, is required.[4] As indicated by the discussion in the article, when such sophisticated statistical techniques are necessary, the reader should be provided with the underlying reasons and references as to how the technique is applied in research. Because this particular research effort is longitudinal in nature, Nurick points out that the same procedure is used over the different time intervals.

Results (refer to pp. 446–448)

The purpose of the results section is to present the findings of the research in as clear and straightforward a manner as possible. The evidence that is relevant to each hypothesis should be examined, including any data that may contradict the predicted outcomes. Careful distinctions should be made between fact and opinion, since the opinions or interpretations of the author are not appropriate for this section. Although researchers are expected to relate their work to previous research findings, such generalizations and qualifications should be included in the discussion and conclusions section.

In the Nurick article, the results are broken down into three sections: the preliminary analysis of direct and indirect participants over Time 1 (T_1) and Time 2 (T_2), and T_2 and Time 3 (T_3) *without* controlling for job level and pretest scores, and the controlled analysis for T_1 and T_2, and T_2 and T_3. In many journal articles, researchers will begin with the findings that are relatively simple and straightforward before proceeding to the more complex and sophisticated analyses. Although this preliminary analysis does not control for job level and pretest scores, the findings are easy to understand and provide a general indication of what is to follow. It should be noted, however, that this analysis does not provide information *between* direct and indirect groups, only analysis *within* those groups over time.

These preliminary results indicate that there were positive changes for both the direct and indirect participant groups from T_1 to T_2. These changes, however, were more substantial for the direct participants on all the influence and satisfaction/attitudinal scales compared to the indirect participants. There were no significant changes from T_2 to T_3 for the direct participants, while there was one significant change for the indirect participants (trust) during this time period.

Based on the presentation of the initial findings, the reader may raise some questions: (1) Why are the comparisons made only between T_1 and T_2, and T_2 and T_3, and not between the baseline (T_1) and the final findings (T_3)? (2) Although an overall measure of effectiveness was mentioned as part of the guiding hypothesis of the larger research project (see "The Experiment"), why is it not included as part of this analysis? (3) Why are there different sample sizes between T_1 and T_2, and T_2 and T_3 (although these are relatively small differences for the most part)? Finally, it should be noted that there is a misprint in the presentation of the data in Table I (the significance levels are incorrectly labeled) and there is inconsistent use of subscript versus superscript across the time periods in Tables I and II. Although authors and editors are thorough and careful in proofing articles and research reports, typographical mistakes often seem inevitable (as you *may* have found in this book!). Because tables and figures are consistently more difficult to proofread than textual material, readers should carefully check such tables to ensure an accurate interpretation of their meaning.

The main analysis in this study is the analysis of covariance, which holds the pretest score (T_1) and job level constant. As pointed out earlier, this procedure was followed because of concern that job level and the initial survey results could be directly related to the treatment effect (direct participation versus indirect participation). Thus, with these two nonrandom effects under control, the researcher was able to get a clearer understanding of the effects of direct and indirect participation in the change process. As indicated by Table III, a number of statistically significant differences *between* the direct and indirect participants were observed during T_1 and T_2, while there were only two significant differences from T_2 to T_3. Obviously, this raises several questions concerning the *meaning* of these findings, which is amplified in the discussion section.

Discussion and Conclusions

Discussion (refer to pp. 448−450)

In a discussion section in a journal article, the authors elaborate on the support or nonsupport of their hypotheses, relate the results to prior research efforts, and expand on their findings (qualifications and generalizations). In this study, the hypotheses were generally supported, although the positive effects of participation seem to be most significant during the first time period $(T_1$ to $T_2)$. Because this favorable trend did not continue during T_2 to T_3, one interpretation is that beyond a certain point participation does not necessarily improve perceptions of influence and satisfaction. However, another interpretation (which Nurick proposes) is that the significant changes that occurred for the direct participants during T_1 to T_2 were *maintained* during the subsequent period $(T_2$ to $T_3)$. This indicates that participation can bring about long-term improvement in attitudes and satisfaction.

One way for the reader to fully grasp the results and implications of the research is to examine the hypotheses that were *not* supported. In the Nurick article, this refers to influence over resources (in the short term only), influence over work hours, job involvement, and intention to turnover. If some of the expected findings are not corroborated, readers should raise questions concerning the underlying reasons and the specific situations that may have contributed to the results.

In the discussion, Nurick notes the link between objective (observed) participation and psychological (perceived) participation—an important contribution of this work to knowledge in the field. He also is candid about the difference between direct and indirect participation, noting that there were structural barriers that kept the direct participants from interacting with their (indirect) constituencies. Thus, one of the practical, applied conclusions resulting from this research is an acknowledgment that better integrative devices are needed (between direct and indirect participants) to foster collaborative problem solving. Although the analysis section relies on the survey data, in discussing the results and explaining them Nurick draws on his other data collection techniques—especially observations.

Because the discussion section is the place where it is appropriate to editorialize, Nurick amplifies on the longitudinal nature of the study, and the changes from Time 2 to Time 3. Much behavioral science research focuses on results found immediately after the manipulation of a treatment variable (e.g., T_1 to T_2) without an assessment of longer-term changes (e.g., T_2 to T_3). Such longitudinal studies are much more expensive and difficult to administer in terms of money, personnel, effort, and control. This discussion suggests that a table indicating the changes from T_1 to T_3 would have been beneficial. While these data may have been part of the original study, journal articles, by their nature, have to be brief, thus for whatever reason, they may have been excluded from this writeup.

Conclusions (refer to pp. 450–451)

Although the conclusions drawn about the research are often included in the discussion section, in many journal articles this final comment is set off by itself. The conclusions summarize, in a general way, the study and its findings—a concise restatement of the body of the paper and the study's inferences. Qualifications, limitations, and generalizations of the findings are also briefly noted. In many instances, authors will choose to suggest further work that needs to be done, or the next step in the research process that is suggested by the findings. As indicated by the Nurick article, remarks are often made about the general areas of research that are editorial in nature. In this case, the study is again tied in to the larger quality-of-work-life project of which it is a part.

NOTES

1. K. Weick, "How to Use Academic Journals in the Classroom" (paper presented at the Organizational Behavior Teaching Conference, Cleveland, Ohio, June 16–19, 1982).

2. For those interested in the writing of research reports, B. Turney and G. Robb, *Research in Education: An Introduction* (Hinsdale, IL: Dryden Press, 1971) is recommended. The following discussion draws from this work.

3. E. Webb, D. Campbell, R. Schwartz, and L. Sechrest, *Unobtrusive Measures: Nonreactive Research in the Social Sciences* (Chicago: Rand McNally, 1966); and N.K. Denzin, ed., *Sociological Methods: A Sourcebook* (Chicago: Aldine-Atherton, 1970), Part 12 on triangulation in research.

4. For a clear discussion of these more complex statistical techniques, readers are encouraged to consult a multivariate statistics text.

PARTICIPATION IN ORGANIZATIONAL CHANGE: A LONGITUDINAL FIELD STUDY[1]

AARON J. NURICK[2]
Bentley College

This study was carried out as part of a long-term Quality of Work Life experiment in one division of a utility. The experiment is part of a national effort to examine collaborative union-management problem-solving and change implementation. The purpose of the study was to determine the impact of a formal participative process of implementing change established as part of the experiment. Participation occurred in two levels or intensities: (1) direct via membership on either a joint committee or on one of several task forces, and (2) indirect or nonmembership. Subjects were measured at three points in time on a variety of perceptual and attitudinal measures. An analysis of covariance revealed that when job level and pretest scores were held constant, direct participants increased in their perceptions of influence in decision making and in organizational attitudes in comparison to indirect participants. A second analysis indicated that the changes persisted during an additional time interval. It was concluded that the participative process was a major intervention in the experiment. Recommendations for enhancing formal modes of participation were provided.

INTRODUCTION

Since the rise of the Human Relations school of organization theory some forty years ago, there have been persistent questions concerning the efficacy of traditional organizational designs which place the bulk of decision-making power in the upper portions of the hierarchy. A particularly salient decision-making area concerns the planning and implementation of various changes in an organizational system or subsystem.

The value of employee involvement in change processes has been recognized recently in the movement in this country to improve the quality of working life. The purpose of the present study is to investigate the effects of the participatory process established in an experimental Quality of Work Life project.

THEORETICAL BACKGROUND: PARTICIPATION IN ORGANIZATIONAL CHANGE

Since the pioneering studies by Lewin, Lippitt, and White (1939) and Coch and French (1948), there has been a plethora of research studies and popular articles devoted to the theme "participation." However, a well-articulated and integrated theory

[1] This study is based upon the author's doctoral dissertation completed at the University of Tennessee. The author wishes to acknowledge the contributions of Michael E. Gordon, Barry A. Macy, John M. Larsen, H. Dudley Dewhirst, and William Calhoun. Also, thanks are due to Edward E. Lawler and Stanley E. Seashore of the Institute for Social Research for making this work possible.

[2] From *Human Relations*, Volume 35, No. 5, 1982. Reprinted by permission. Requests for reprints should be sent to Dr. A. Nurick, Bentley College, Waltham, MA 02154.

encompassing this area is yet to appear. A recent conceptual treatise by Dachler and Wilpert (1978) describes participation literature as lacking in definition and "explicitly stated theoretical frameworks" (p. 1). However, they quickly add that the fragmentary nature of participation research may be indicative of problems inherent in the examination of a multidimensional phenomenon from divergent points of view. Seashore (1977, p. 3) recently commented that the "blanket label of participation" applied indiscriminately with respect to its varying forms is not useful for conceptual argument or empirical analysis. Therefore, participation in the present study will be examined as it relates to changes occurring within an organization.

The advent of a major change such as a Quality of Working Life Program brings about new ideas, structures, and behaviors that may depart significantly from usual patterns of organizational functioning. Thus, new behaviors are required of organization members to cope effectively with the changes. Much of the literature on organizational change is based on Lewin's (1947) three-stage change process of *unfreezing* old attitudes, values, or behaviors, *changing* these phenomena, and *refreezing* the new patterns, creating a new state of equilibrium. Organizational change may encounter resistance for several reasons. If a given change is perceived as being imposed by management or is seen as posing a threat to employee job security, prestige, or authority, resistance may increase (Huse, 1975). These factors are especially prevalent in labor-management cooperative programs as managers may feel an infringement on their prerogatives. Also, an easing of traditional bargaining relationships may cause union leaders to fear a weakening of their position vis-á-vis management. Participation by all relevant parties in the change process has been theorized as means to reduce resistance to change (Coch & French, 1948; Lawrence, 1954; Lippit, 1969).

Participation models (e.g., Lawler, 1975; Mann & Neff, 1961) specify that participation increases feelings of personal control, knowledge about changes, and feelings of trust in management. It is assumed that participation reduces ambiguity and thus alleviates the fear that changes will result in negative consequences. Many of these theoretical predictions have been substantiated by research studies demonstrating positive relationships between participation and performance (Coch & French, 1948; Marrow, Bowers, & Seashore, 1967), employee attitudes (Morse & Reimer, 1956; Powell & Schlacter, 1971; Seigel & Ruh, 1973; Tosi; 1970), and employee attendance (Lawler & Hackman, 1969; Scheflen, Lawler, & Hackman, 1971).

While the findings have been consistent, they have not been completely unequivocal. French, Israel, and As (1960), for example, failed to replicate the earlier findings of Coch and French (1948), concluding that participation was effective only for those employees who felt that it was a legitimate process. Evidence suggesting personality differences in relation to participation has also been presented. Vroom (1960) found that individuals who were more equalitarian as opposed to authoritarian and who had strong needs for independence responded more positively to participation. Jenkins (1974) noted that in many of the European industrial democracy experiments which rely heavily on more distant representative forms of participation, problems arise when employees have little actual influence over decisions. Apparently, individuals participating more directly in designing new work systems or pay plans experience greater benefits from the process (e.g., Coch & French, 1948; Powell & Schlacter, 1971).

THE EXPERIMENT

The American Center for Quality of Work Life has initiated several experimental projects in ongoing organizations dealing with collaborative (i.e., union and management) modes or problem solving and change implementation. The Institute for Social Research, University of Michigan, serves as an independent research and assessment component at many of the sites, applying a standardized thirty-six-month measurement process. Each experimental site, with the aid of its own internal and/or external consultants, develops a unique change program consisting of two distinct phases: an eighteen-month action period in which actual changes are implemented, and an additional eighteen-month "distillation" period in which changes filter through the organization. Measurements are implemented before any work changes are implemented (Time 1), after the eighteen-month action period (Time 2), and at the end of the entire thirty-six-month experiment (Time 3). Where feasible, similar organizations are measured as comparison sites. Evaluations of the experimental projects are not published until after the thirty-six-month assessment period. Although the experimental programs and change strategies differ across sites, each project is designed according to a basic underlying hypothesis:

> ...that when employees in any kind of organization, public or private, are provided expertly-structured opportunity to contribute to designing and implementing activities for organizational change, the organization will become measurably more effective, and the quality of working life for all employees will improve. (National Quality of Work Center, 1975, p. 3.)

The Quality of Working Life experiment upon which this study was based occurred within one division of a utility located in the southeastern United States. The division consists of some 380 employees including about 50 management and supervisory personnel, 145 engineers and associated professionals, 145 technical support personnel, and 40 clerical and administrative employees. This distribution of division personnel has remained quite consistent during the last decade. The major responsibility of the division is the planning and designing of power transmission facilities for the utility's power system.

The Quality of Work experiment was a collaborative effort of the utility and two unions: a local white-collar engineer's association and an international office workers union affiliated with AFL-CIO. The utility provided a rather unique site for a Quality of Work Project because of its long history of labor-management cooperation.

A joint union–management Quality of Work Committee (QOWC) was established in the division in June 1974, as the primary vehicle for organizational change. This fourteen member committee provided equal representation of both employees and management. The management positions were appointed by top management while employee members were elected by fellow employees.[3] The first activity of the QOWC was the selection of a team of external consultants to aid in implementing changes in the division. The committee met weekly often devoting an entire work day to the Quality of Work Program. The change program implemented by the QOWC and the consultants

---

[3] Midway through the change program, three original management members (first-line supervisors) were replaced by managers of a higher rank.

extended roughly over eighteen months encompassing the period September 1974 through March 1976 although there were some longer term changes in progress.

The initial phase of activities (September–October, 1974) involved familiarization with the experimental division and the utility in general. This was accomplished mainly through a series of individual and group interviews conducted by the consultants with 228 employees selected by the Quality of Work Committee from the division, utility top management, and the two unions. During this time the Institute for Social Research (ISR) administered baseline measures in the form of a broad-based attitude survey (Time 1). The results of the interviews were combined with selected items from the ISR Time 1 survey and fed back to the QOWC and others by the consultants through a week-long workshop. In this workshop, the participants discussed the consultants' most salient observations and identified major issues for the 1975 change program agenda as well as possible barriers to implementation. The following list constitutes the major issues or themes identified by the QOWC for the change procedure.

1. Quality of Work decision-making procedure
2. Division mission and goals
3. Management style and practice
4. Organization structure (staffing, workflow, and communication)
5. Career development
6. Reward-recognition systems
7. Union–management relations
8. Problems involving field survey crews

The implementation phase of the experiment occurred mainly during the period of January 1975 through March 1976. Several special task forces were launched during this period and new programs were begun including a new procedure for evaluation of individual performance, a merit award for outstanding performance, and a program of flexible working hours.

In November 1975, the consultants conducted a second workshop dealing explicitly with organization structure and workflow. During this workshop, several new issues surfaced including better methods for workload predictions and developing cost accountability procedures. The external consultants completed their contracted work in early 1976 and ceased direct contact with the experimental site.

The Participatory Process

At the first workshop described earlier, the consultants and the QOWC established a formal procedure for problem identification and subsequent change implementation. After a problem was identified, the QOWC appointed a subcommittee of its own members to approach the particular problem area. The subcommittee would appoint a task force consisting of division employees and would provide them with a charge which defined the problem and possible strategies for programs. In selecting task force members, each QOWC subcommittee would strive to make the group as representative of the division as possible. Each task force worked separately, communicating with the QOWC when necessary. Task force members would serve until the task force completed its work and provided its final report to the QOWC. The QOWC would then decide whether to implement the program or return it to the task force for refinements. Each task force periodically reported on its progress during weekly QOWC meetings. At this time the entire task force (usually averaging about 6–8 people) could attend the meeting and have direct access to the QOWC. Task force employees had direct input and could receive immediate feedback from both management and employees through their participation in the change process.

The formal change procedure resulted in relatively clear-cut distinctions in the intensity of employee participation in the Quality of Work Program. Clearly, a substantial portion of the division (i.e., QOWC and task force members) was actively contributing to the planning and implementation of new ideas. The remaining organizational members relied on their representatives to inform them of change activities as they occurred. While they learned of the change effort through various media (a newsletter, informal communications, feedback sessions), they served more as recipients rather than initiators of changes. In the present study, QOWC and task force members (consisting of about one-third of the employees) will be referred to as *direct participants* while the remaining members of the division will be classified *indirect participants*.

Conceptual Model and Hypotheses

Following the theoretical definition of French et al. (1960), the present study distinguishes between *objective* and *psychological* participation. Objective participation is operationally defined according to the level of involvement in the change process, in this case, direct or indirect participation. Psychological participation is defined and measured as the amount of felt or perceived influence a given individual may exert within a particular decision domain. Four major domains are specified: (1) influence over resources (i.e., hiring, promotions, pay raises); (2) influence over work activities (i.e., changing work procedures, methods used, scheduling); (3) influence over coordination activities (i.e., settling disagreements, how tasks are divided, solving work related problems); and (4) influence over working hours. Additionally, the influence scales are averaged to form a total influence index scale.

> **Hypothesis 1:** Direct participants will experience greater increases in perceived influence over (a) resources, (b) work activities, (c) coordination activities, and (d) working hours than indirect participants. Direct participants will also experience greater increases on (e) the influence index than indirect participants.

French et al. (1960) specified that participation is a two-way process implying not only the exercise of influence, but also the acceptance of that influence by others. Thus it is anticipated that those who participate more directly will feel that their input is welcomed, especially by those higher in the organizational hierarchy.

> **Hypothesis 2:** Direct participants will experience a greater increase in perceived acceptance of influence than indirect participants.

Research has shown that participation improves individual attitudes by increasing personal rewards. Locke and Schweiger (1979) indicate that participation enhances employee attitudes by providing opportunities for value attainment (i.e., intrinsic rewards stemming from increased influence in decisions). Thus one would predict positive effects of participation on *job satisfaction* (Morse & Reimer, 1956; Powell & Schlacter, 1971) and its research counterpart, reduced *intention to turnover* (Porter & Steers, 1973).

Several models (e.g., Mann & Neff, 1961) specify that participation increases feelings of personal control over and ownership of decisions. Such feelings are likely to increase personal *involvement* with the job and organization (Patchen, 1965; Seigel & Ruh, 1973). Finally, since participation increases knowledge about changes, individuals are less likely to feel that management is hiding something from them (Lippitt, 1969). Therefore, degree of *trust* in the organization is expected to increase (Lawler, 1975).

> **Hypothesis 3:** Direct participants will experience greater increases in (a) job satisfaction, (b) job involvement, (c) organizational involvement, (d) trust, and decreases in (e) intention to turnover than indirect participants.

METHOD

The third party measurement process developed by ISR closely followed the pattern of change activities in the utility. Surveys were administered before the change program was underway (T_1—September 1974), at the end of the first phase of the program (T_2—June 1976), and at the end of the formal experimental period (T_3—January 1978). In addition to the surveys, data were collected at the site through structured and unstructured interviews, company records and observation.

Sample

The sample for the present study consisted of those employees responding to the three waves of measurement (i.e., T_1, T_2, and T_3) in the ISR evaluation of the Quality of Work Project ($N5246$, matched cases). Of this sample, 85 percent were male, over half had graduated from college, and 75 percent were union members.

Measures

The measures were ascertained by the Michigan Organizational Assessment Questionnaire (MOAQ). The MOAQ is a broad-based attitude questionnaire covering many aspects of organizational life such as task attributes, supervision, group relationships, etc. All items were measured on seven-point Likert scales and averaged to form the various scales for this study.[4] Response rates for the three administrations of the questionnaire exceeded 85 percent of the division.

Analytical Procedures

The purpose of this study is to compare direct and indirect participants in the change process on several outcome measures over three points in time. Since subjects in this

---

[4] A listing of scale items along with internal consistency reliability measures and correlations across time is available in Nurick (1978) Appendix C. Preliminary factor analyses were performed on the items in developing the scales. Comparison of factor structures across time indicated a high degree of factor congruency and hence, stability of the measures. The data are available upon request.

quasi-experimental study were not randomly assigned to the treatment (i.e., participation), it is necessary to control for unwanted sources of variation. The recommended procedure for such a task is the analysis of covariance or ACV (Lord, 1963). The model employed will control for two concomitant variables or covariates: (1) job level[5] and (2) pretest (T_1) score on the dependent variable. It is assumed that these variables reflect initial group differences which could have an effect on the dependent variables. The specific procedure utilized is the multiple regression approach to ACV of Cohen and Cohen (1975). The dummy-coded group variable is entered into the regression equation after partialling the effects of the two covariates. Assuming homogeneity of regression is found, one examines the amount of incremental variance accounted for by the treatment variable (in this case, direct versus indirect participation) which is tested by an F ratio. If the incremental F ratio is significant, then one may conclude that there are differences between the "equated" groups on the dependent variable (Cohen & Cohen, 1975). Examining post-test scores with the effects of the pretest removed has been recommended as a method for determining change (Linn & Slinde, 1977; Lord, 1963). Thus the hypotheses in this study are expressed in terms of increases in dependent variables over time. The procedure is applied to the data over both time intervals (i.e., T_1–T_2 and T_2–T_3).

RESULTS

Before being subjected to the analysis of covariance, the data were first examined by comparing the variables across time for each subgroup. The results appear in Tables I and II. Pairwise t tests comparing the variables between T_1 and T_2 in Table I indicate substantial increases for the direct participation group on all of the influence scales as well as job satisfaction, job involvement, and trust. While the indirect participants showed gains on five out of the six influence scales during this time interval, there were no significant attitudinal gains for this group. The same tests for the interval between T_2 and T_3 (Table II) indicate only one significant increase. Indirect participants gained in trust during this period. The pattern indicates that there was little significant change in either positive or negative direction during T_2–T_3. *It should be noted that the pairwise t test is a comparison of raw gain on a particular scale and does not control for extraneous sources of variation such as prior score on a variable.* The variables were then tested by the more stringent analysis of covariance.

Results of Analysis of Covariance:
Direct versus Indirect Participants (T_1–T_2)

Table III provides the results of the analysis of covariance for each dependent variable. The incremental F ratios test for differences between direct and indirect participants on dependent variables while equating these groups on job level and pretest score. The results indicate significant differences between direct and indirect participants on influence over work activities, coordination activities, and the influence index. Direct participants therefore experienced greater increases in these variables.

---

[5] Job level is dummy-coded as four discrete categories: management, engineering and technical engineering, associate and technical support, and administrative and clerical. The measure was obtained from company records.

TABLE I Means, Standard Deviations, and Pairwise *t* Tests (T_1 versus T_2)

Variable	Mean (T_1)	SD (T_1)	Mean (T_2)	SD (T_2)	N	$t(T_1$ versus $T_2)$
Direct participants						
Influence-resources	2.12	1.31	2.40	1.49	78	2.68[b]
Influence-work activities	3.43	1.50	4.12	1.36	78	4.96[c]
Influence-coordination	3.27	1.59	3.78	1.52	78	3.84[c]
Influence-hours	1.58	1.24	2.95	1.79	77	5.56[c]
Influence-index	2.62	1.12	3.32	1.10	77	6.54[c]
Acceptance of influence	3.85	1.43	4.50	1.27	79	5.06[c]
Job satisfaction	5.17	1.32	5.52	1.05	80	2.66[b]
Job involvement	3.69	1.12	3.93	1.08	80	2.71[b]
Organizational involvement	6.13	0.91	6.12	0.77	80	−0.14
Trust	4.32	1.44	4.55	1.33	78	2.09[a]
Intention of turnover	2.15	1.39	2.08	1.11	80	0.52
Indirect participants						
Influence-resources	2.34	1.15	2.37	1.20	138	0.27
Influence-work activities	2.51	1.25	3.05	1.32	144	5.11[c]
Influence-coordination	2.09	1.05	2.57	1.27	144	5.10[c]
Influence-hours	1.39	0.96	2.90	1.67	140	9.63[c]
Influence-index	1.81	0.77	2.47	0.99	139	8.39[c]
Acceptance of influence	3.20	1.37	3.50	1.21	145	3.37[c]
Job satisfaction	4.99	1.24	4.98	1.23	147	−0.11
Job involvement	3.58	1.06	3.50	1.10	146	−1.00
Organizational involvement	5.71	1.31	5.56	1.11	148	−1.69
Trust	3.65	1.35	3.62	1.30	144	−0.31
Intention of turnover	2.52	1.42	2.56	1.33	149	0.50

[a] $p < .01$
[b] $p < .001$
[c] $p < .05$

Significant differences were also found between direct and indirect participants on perceived acceptance of influence. According to the values in Table III, this was the largest effect found ($F = 13.82, p < .01$). Direct participants increased more over the time period in their perception than influence in decisions was accepted by those higher in the organization.

Table III also reveals the predicted positive effects of participation on attitudinal variables. Significant differences between direct and indirect participants were found for job satisfaction, organizational involvement, and trust once the effects of the two covariates were partialled. The greatest effect appears to be on organization trust ($F = 8.47, p < .01$). Anticipated differences in intention to turnover and job involvement were not found.

TABLE II **Means, Standard Deviations, and Pairwise *t* Tests (T_2 versus T_3)**

Variable	Mean (T_2)	SD (T_2)	Mean (T_3)	SD (T_3)	N	$t(T_2$ versus $T_3)$
Direct participants						
Influence-resources	2.35	1.47	2.52	1.65	82	1.54
Influence-work activities	4.10	1.34	3.96	1.29	82	−1.38
Influence-coordination	3.74	1.52	3.79	1.45	82	.51
Influence-hours	2.94	1.80	3.11	1.88	81	.82
Influence-index	3.29	1.10	3.36	1.22	81	.71
Acceptance of influence	4.50	1.25	4.53	1.27	82	.27
Job satisfaction	5.52	1.04	5.54	1.18	82	.20
Job involvement	3.93	1.07	3.89	1.08	82	−.53
Organizational involvement	6.09	.79	6.16	.85	82	.87
Trust	4.56	1.30	4.56	1.34	82	.00
Intention of turnover	2.06	1.11	2.07	1.27	82	.10
Indirect participants						
Influence-resources	1.36	.76	1.37	.80	156	.16
Influence-work activities	3.03	1.32	3.00	1.23	158	−.38
Influence-coordination	2.55	1.24	2.54	1.15	158	−.14
Influence-hours	2.80	1.63	2.93	1.68	155	.93
Influence-index	2.42	.94	2.44	.90	153	.33
Acceptance of influence	3.47	1.15	3.56	1.27	156	1.13
Job satisfaction	5.00	1.23	5.08	1.15	158	.92
Job involvement	3.50	1.07	3.54	.99	157	.62
Organizational involvement	5.56	1.11	5.59	1.10	159	.48
Trust	3.59	1.26	3.79	1.31	156	−.46[a]
Intention of turnover	2.58	1.34	2.47	1.38	159	−1.10

[a] $p < .05$

Results of Analysis of Covariance (T_2–T_3)

The ACV comparing direct and indirect participants was repeated for the data between T_2–T_3.[6] The results are shown in the second column of Table III. Significant differences between the two groups are shown for influence over resources ($F = 6.19$, $p < .05$) and influence over coordination activities ($F = 6.94$, $p = .01$). No other significant differences were found during this time interval.

DISCUSSION

The results presented in the previous section are indicative of generally positive effects of participation in organizational change processes during the first eighteen months of the program. Those employees who participated more directly in the organizational change program apparently derived greater benefits from the process. Direct participants perceived themselves as having more influence, especially over work activity decisions, felt that their inputs were accepted by those above them, and indicated more favorable attitudes toward their job and the organization than indirect participants. Analysis of the data during the second phase (T_2–T_3) indicates that the changes were

[6] For this analysis, T_2 scores were held constant as the pretest.

TABLE III Analysis of Covariance: Direct versus Indirect Participation Controlling for Job Level and Pretest Score

Variable	N	T_1–T_2 Incremental F^a	N	T_1–T_3 F
Influence-resources	220	2.05	238	6.19[c]
Influence-work activities	222	8.73[b]	240	0.98
Influence-coordination	222	5.03[b]	240	6.94[b]
Influence-work hours	217	0.10	236	0.21
Influence index	216	4.60[c]	234	2.84
Acceptance of influence	224	13.82[b]	238	1.93
Job satisfaction	227	5.37[c]	240	0.71
Job involvement	226	3.22	239	0.12
Organizational involvement	228	4.28[c]	241	1.83
Trust	222	8.47[b]	238	0.25
Intention of turnover	229	1.09	241	0.17

[a] For each dependent variable, tests for interaction between covariates and the treatment variable were not significant indicating homogeneity of regression coefficients. The ACV was therefore directly interpreted.
[b] $p < .01$
[c] $p < .05$

quite durable over time. Most variables maintained at T_3 the levels achieved at the T_2 time period. There is also evidence that direct participants increased more than their indirect counterparts during the second time period in influence over resources and coordination activities.

Of theoretical significance is the fact that the results establish a link between objective (i.e., observed) participation and psychological participation (i.e., perceived increases in influence). The major impact of participation seems to be on influence over work-related decisions. This is a likely outcome since most of the early change activities of the QOWC and the task forces were aimed at improving the planning, performing, and reviewing of work carried out by the division. Task forces worked in such areas as establishing engineering procedure guidelines and improving workload predictions. The focus of change activities shifted to more complex issues of structure, workflow, and pay equity. These developments provide some insight into the later increases in influence over resources (i.e., pay, promotion) and coordination activities for the directly participating members. Moreover, the results support earlier research findings (e.g., Patchen, 1970; Powell & Schlacter, 1971; Seigel & Ruh, 1973), that participation increases attitudinal variables such as satisfaction, involvement, and trust.

The findings become more salient when interpreted within the context of the structural attributes of the change process. While the direct participants comprised a considerable proportion of the division (about 33 percent), a sizable number of employees remained who were relatively isolated from the change process. The formal participatory process was plagued by structural deficiencies which created barriers between directly participating representatives (i.e., QOWC and task force members) and their constituents. The separation between direct and indirect participants resulted in a lack of communication engendering feelings of distrust and apathy among indirect participants about the change program. Dachler and Wilpert (1978) identified detachment and elitism as problematic consequences of formal modes of participation. While it was impractical for all organization members to directly participate, there was still a need for integrative devices to facilitate the interpersonal process essential for effective collaborative problem-solving. One possibility is the establishment of smaller committees or core groups at lower organizational levels which can be directly linked to the larger organizational group and special task forces by overlapping membership. Such a design, reminiscent of the linking-pin principle (Likert, 1961) would increase communication channels and provide more access to information concerning proposed changes. Several existing ACQWL/ISR sites utilize such a "multitier" committee structure (Lawler, 1977). Toward the end of the experimental period, the division recognized the need to institutionalize the experimental change process of the Quality of Work Program. To aid in this transition, another consultant was hired to work with the QOWC. A major feature of the new and permanent change structure was the development of smaller lower level committees to interact with the division level committee in hopes of reducing some of the communication problems.

The results of this study also demonstrate the usefulness of longitudinal measurement of organizational change. It has been recognized that behavioral and attitudinal change may require considerable time and that not all variables change at the same pace (Lawler, 1977). Repeated measurements reduce the appearance of short-lived changes that may be due to the initial euphoria of participating in a major experiment. The T_3 or "after" measures lend more insight into the permanence or "durability" of the changes (Seashore & Bowers, 1970).

From the results presented, it appears that the majority of changes occurred during the first eighteen months of the experiment, especially for the directly participating group. While little change occurred during the T_2–T_3 interval, it is apparent that the initial changes stabilized during this phase of the experiment. According to recent writings on the persistence of organizational change (Conlon, 1980; Goodman, Bazerman, & Conlon, 1980) organizational members make conscious decisions to continue new behavior or attitudes based on a reassessment of their original decision to adopt these new forms. Apparently the increases in influence and attitudes perceived by direct participants persisted since no significant reductions were shown as of the T_3 measurement. There were increases in two influence measures identified during the T_2–T_3 period that were not present during the initial T_1–T_3 measurement interval indicating a delayed effect. Therefore, there is some reason to conclude that the changes experienced were not due to artifacts of the experiment.

CONCLUSIONS

The present study has demonstrated that employees who were observed to participate more directly in a planned organizational change program experienced greater psychological benefits in the form of increased influence in work-related decisions and improved attitudes. These changes were shown to endure over a second eighteen-month time interval. The results presented here need to be complemented by additional research which addresses the relationship between participation and other criteria. For example, there is still uncertainty as to the effects of participation on productivity measures. It is apparent, however, that if formal modes of participation (i.e., committees) are utilized in a change program, appropriate structural arrangements that integrate the various parties are needed. While this study is not an evaluation of all organizational changes initiated at this particular site, it is evident that the change process itself was a major intervention. The findings of this study will be even more meaningful when considered as part of the entire assessment of this quality of work project.

REFERENCES

Coch, L., & French, J.R.P. Overcoming resistance to change. *Human Relations*, 1948, 1, 512–532.

Cohen, J., & Cohen, P. *Applied multiple regression/correlation analysis for the behavioral sciences*. Hillside, NJ: Lawrence Erlbaum Assoc., 1975.

Conlon, E.J. Feedback about personal and organizational outcomes and its effect on persistence of planned behavioral changes. *Academy of Management Journal*, 1980, 23, 267–286.

Dachler, H.P., & Wilpert, B. Conceptual dimensions and boundaries of participation in organizations: A critical evaluation. *Administrative Science Quarterly*, 1978, 23(1), 1–39.

Drexler, J., & Lawler, E.E. III. A union-management cooperative project, to improve the quality of work life. *Journal of Applied Behavioral Science*, 1977, 13(3), 373–387.

French, J.R.P., Israel, J., & As, D. An experiment on participation in a Norweigian factory. *Human Relations*, 1960, 13, 3–20.

Goodman, P.S., Bazerman, M., & Colon, E. Institutionalization of planned organizational change. In B.M. Shaw and L.L. Cummings, eds. *Research in organizational behavior*. (Vol. 2). Greenwich, CT: JAI Press, 1980.

Huse, E.F. *Organizational Development and Change*, St. Paul: West Publishing, 1975.

Jenkins, D. *Job power: Blue and White Collar Democracy*. New York: Penguin Books, 1974.

Lawler, E.E. III. Pay, participation, and organization change, In E.L. Cass, and F.G. Zimmer, eds., *Man and Work in Society*, New York: Van Nostrand Reinhold, 1975.

Lawler, E.E. III. Adaptive experiments: An approach to organizational behavior research. *Academy of Management Review*, 1977, 2(4), 576–585.

Lawler, E.E. III, & Hackman, J.R. The impact of employee participation in development of pay incentive plans: A field experiment. *Journal of Applied Psychology*, 1969, 53, 467–471.

Lawrence, P.R. How to deal with resistance to change. *Harvard Business Review*, 1954, 32, 49–57.

Lewin, K. Frontiers in group dynamics. *Human Relations*, 1947, 1, 5–41.

Lewin, K., Lippit, R., & White, R.K. Patterns of aggressive' behavior in experimentally created social climates. *Journal of Social Psychology*, 1939, 10, 271–299.

Likert, R. *New Patterns of Management*, New York: McGraw-Hill, 1961.

Linn, R.L., & Slinde, J.A. The determination of the significance of change between pre and posttesting periods. *Review of Educational Research*, 1977, 47, 121–150.

Lippit, G.L. *Organizational Renewal*, New York: Appleton-Century-Crofts, 1969.

Locke, E.A., & Schweiger, D.M. Participation in decision-making: One more look. In B.M. Staw, ed., *Research in Organizational Behavior* (Vol. 1). Greenwich, CT: JAI Press, 1979.

Lord, F.M. Elementary models for measuring change. In C.W. Harris, ed., *Problems in Measuring Change*. Madison: University of Wisconsin Press, 1963.

Mann, F.C., & Neft, F.W. *Managing major change in organizations*. Ann Arbor, MI: The Foundation for Research on Human Behavior, 1961.

Marrow A.J., Bowers, D.G., & Seashore, S.E. *Management by Participation*. New York: Harper & Row, 1967.

Morse, N.C., & Reimer, E. The experimental change of a major organization variable. *Journal of Abnormal and Social Psychology*, 1956, 52, 120–129.

National Quality of Work Center. *The Quality of Work Program: The First Eighteen Months*, Washington, D.C., 1975.

Nurick, A.J. *The effects of formal participation in organizational change on individual perceptions and attitudes: A longitudinal field study*. Unpublished doctoral dissertation, University of Tennessee, 1978.

Patchen, M. Labor-Management Consultation at TVA: Its Impact on Employees. *Administrative Science Quarterly*, 1965, 10, 149–174.

Patchen, M. *Participation, Achievement, and Involvement on the Job*, Englewood Cliffs, NJ: Prentice Hall, 1970.

Porter, L.M., & Steers, R.M. Organizational, work and personal factors in employee turnover and absenteeism. *Psychological Bulletin*, 1973, 80(2), 151–176.

Powell, R.M., & Schlacter, I. Participative management: A panacea? *Academy of Management Journal*, 1971, 14, 165–173.

Scheflen, K., Lawler, E.E. III, & Hackman, J.R. Long term impact of employee participation in the development of pay incentive plans: A field experiment revisited. *Journal of Applied Psychology*, 1971, 55, 182–186.

Seashore, S.E. *Participation in Decision Making: Some Issues of Conception, Measurement, and Interaction.* Paper presented at 37th Annual Meeting, Academy of Management, August, 1977.

Seashore, S., & Bowers, D. Durability of organizational change. *American Psychologist*, 1970, 25, 227–233.

Seigel, A.L., & Ruh, R.A. Job involvement, participation in decision making, personal background and job behavior, *Organizational Behavior and Human Performance*, 1973, 9, 318–327.

Tosi, H.A. A reexamination of personality as a determinant of the effects of participation. *Personnel Psychology*, 1970, 23, 91–99.

Vroom, V. *Some Personality Determinants of the Effects of Participation.* Englewood Cliffs, NJ: Prentice Hall, 1960.

Author Index

Subject Index